D0875963

WITHDRAWN

The Viennese Revolution of 1848

R. JOHN RATH

The Viennese Revolution of 1848

GREENWOOD PRESS, PUBLISHERS
NEW YORK

To Isabel

Preface

THE VIENNESE REVOLUTION OF 1848 can be written from two points of view. A historian can judge it either by the political standards of the mid-twentieth century or by those of 1848. If he does the former, he will be tempted to idealize the revolution as a glorious, though largely unfulfilled, struggle of an oppressed people to establish the same liberal, democratic form of government that the Western world cherishes today. If he lives in eastern Europe, he may focus his attention on the Utopian Socialist utterings of a handful of radicals and magnify them into clarion calls for a class struggle of the twentieth century Marxian Socialist variety. In either case he will very likely adjudge all revolutionaries as valiant fighters for freedom and condemn all conservatives, and even moderates, as reactionaries.

If the historian evaluates the revolution from the mid-nineteenth century point of view, he must constantly keep in mind that the political framework of 1848 was vastly different from that of 1957. In 1848, absolute monarchism was still the political ideology of most conservatives in central Europe. Constitutional monarchism was the ideal of the "enlightened," or "progressives." In the popular mind republicanism was associated with revolutionary anarchy, while socialism was abhorred as a diabolical scheme to overthrow organized society. Such a historian will make it his primary goal to assess the revolution from the point of view of such a standard of political values.

As a member of the mid-twentieth-century cultural community, I am, of course, deeply appreciative of the values of the democratic way of life; nevertheless, I have conscientiously attempted to evaluate the Viennese Revolution from the standpoint of the political ideologies of 1848, not those of 1957. I have tried to assume a neutral position and to point out the shortcomings of both the extreme left and the extreme right.

I have placed particular emphasis on Viennese public opinion immediately before and during the various phases of the revolution. In order to depict the passions and hatreds, idealism and naïveté of the revolutionaries and their almost childlike faith in the revolutionary shibboleths of the day, I have made extensive translations from the revolutionary literature. In these translations I have tried to preserve the flavor and spirit of the original as much as possible. Also even when copies of documents are included in such Austrian accounts as those of Reschauer and Smets and of Bach, I have used original contemporary records whenever they were available to me.

This book deals only with the revolution in Vienna. Revolutionary events elsewhere in the Habsburg monarchy or in other parts of Europe are mentioned only when necessary to bring the Viennese revolution into proper focus. A number of books in English dealing in a general way with the European revolutionary movement in 1848 are available to the reader who wishes to pursue his study beyond the limits of this book.

A biographical appendix, "Dramatis Personae of the Revolution," is included at the end of the book.

The most valuable source material for this volume is the 1848 Austrian Revolution Collection in the University of Colorado Library. I wish to express my appreciation to Eugene Wilson, the director of the library, for the kind and helpful manner in which he put this rich body of contemporary records at my disposal. Various librarians at the Widener Library of Harvard University and at the University of Texas Library went out of their way to make their resources available. I also wish to thank the directors of the Library of Congress and of the libraries of Princeton University, Western Reserve University, the University of Michigan, the University of Minnesota, the University of Chicago, the University of Illinois, the University of Iowa, the University of Missouri, and Ohio State University for making various volumes available to me through Inter-Library Loan. I wish to acknowledge my debt to the University of Colorado for a research grant and one-quarter faculty-research assignment to pursue this study, and to the Committee on Research and Creative Writing of the University of Texas for a substantial grant for the publication of the book.

I am indebted to Mrs. Therese Westermeier, of Fayetteville, Arkansas, for making approximately half of the longer translations from the revolutionary literature. Miss Jo Alys Downs made the two maps. Finally, to my wife must go my thanks for tedious hours of checking and proofreading and for the encouragement that was so valuable for the completion of the work.

Permission to quote excerpts from Thomas C. Mendenhall *et al., The*

Preface

Quest for a Principle of Authority in Europe 1715–Present (1948), has been granted by the publishers, Henry Holt and Company, Inc., New York. Excerpts from J. G. Legge, *Rhyme and Revolution in Germany: A Study in German History, Life, Literature, and Character, 1813–1850* (1918), are reproduced with the permission of the publishers, Constable & Co., Ltd., London.

R. J. R.

Contents

Maps

The Viennese
Revolution
of 1848

I. *The Prerevolutionary Empire*

N 1848 THE HABSBURG MONARCHY, like the rest of central Europe, was suddenly plunged into a maelstrom of revolution that epitomized the hopes and ideals, illusions and prejudices, strengths and weaknesses of early nineteenth-century liberalism and nationalism. The upheaval in the Austrian Empire was one phase of a larger middle-class revolutionary movement that engulfed most of Europe.

Those leaders—most of them members of the middle classes—who were responsible for the chain of events resulting in the overthrow of the absolutist regime hated the existing government. Believing that the prevailing political institutions of their country were hopelessly out of harmony with the real needs of society, they were convinced that the ruling classes had become exploiters of the large masses of the people. They were also possessed with an idea—the idea that certain liberal reforms would cure all the ills of mankind and help create a Utopia. They believed that the welfare of the whole nation lay in the well-being of every person. To assure the greatest possible freedom of the individual and the progress of mankind, they insisted, there must be a constitution that guaranteed to the "respectable" middle classes the privilege of cooperating in making laws and approving taxes and that restrained the sovereign from abusing the rights of individual citizens.

Those responsible for the revolution, however, had never had any real acquaintance with liberal institutions. A stern censorship and a ubiquitous police system had prevented more than a faint shadow of Western political ideas from entering the Austrian Empire. Herein lay one of the main weaknesses of the Revolution of 1848 in Austria. To the Austrian radicals, liberalism was only an ideal, a fantasy to dream about. It never was and never could have been a foundation for practical politics. It meant too many things to too many people.

As a consequence, after the initial wave of revolution, when the first concessions had been wrung from a helpless government, serious cleavages began to develop among the revolutionists themselves. The more moderate "liberals" felt that the revolution had fulfilled its mission. They now wanted peace and stability so that they could reconstruct society in accord with their interpretation of the revolutionary idea and, more important, so that they could take full advantage of the privileges they believed the revolution had assured them. Meanwhile, the inarticulate masses had come to believe that the revolution would bring them manna from heaven. When they discovered that they were just as hungry, miserable, and insignificant as before, they were confused, and resentful. They were easily incited by rabble-rousing demagogues to turn with savage fury upon the old regime and everything connected with it. The bitterness and total lack of restraint of the extremists inevitably aroused in the more wary, peace-loving "liberals" a fear that if the revolution was not immediately checked, their own political supremacy would be threatened. In turn, as the more moderate of the original revolutionary leaders tried to halt the revolution, the radicals became more determined than ever to push it further to the left. In doing so they drove all "respectable" groups into the ranks of the opposition. In the end, when the counterrevolutionaries succeeded in putting down the movement, they were greeted enthusiastically by a large majority of the populace.

The regime that was overthrown in 1848 still believed in the divine right of kings, with its premise that the monarch, responsible only to God, was to govern in accordance with God's divine laws and commandments.[1] The monarchy was the concern, not of the people, but of the high state officials. Such patriotism as existed in Austria was dynastic and personal. The main bond uniting the various peoples in the polyglot empire was devotion to the person of the monarch.[2]

Directly responsible to the Emperor were the various administrative offices that superintended the affairs of the empire. The United Court Chancellery supervised the administration of the hereditary Austrian provinces. The Hungarian Imperial Council and Chancellery and the Transylvanian Chancellery looked after the affairs of Hungary and Transylvania and directed judicial administration in their respective parts of the empire. There was a special imperial chamber for finances,

---

[1] See Alfred Kasamas, *Das Jahr 1848* (in *Politische Zeitprobleme*, No. 25), p. 2, for a brief but interesting discussion of this concept.

[2] See Hermann Meynert, *Kaiser Franz I. Zur Geschichte seiner Regierung und seiner Zeit. Nach Originalmittheilungen und ungedruckten Quellen*, pp. 40–41; Heinrich Ritter von Srbik, *Metternich, der Staatsmann und der Mensch*, Vol. I, p. 432; Franz Schnabel, *Deutsche Geschichte im neunzehnten Jahrhundert*, Vol. II, pp. 64–65; Otto Brunner, "The Political Ideas of the Hapsburg Monarchy," International Studies Conference, 10th Session (Paris, June 28–July 3, 1937), p. 4. (Mimeographed.)

rents, trade, industry, railroads, and the post office, and another chamber for minting and mining. There was a chief justiceship to overlook the judiciary in all non-Hungarian and non-Transylvanian lands. The Imperial War Council conducted military affairs. For the supervision of the police and censorship there was the Imperial Police and Censorship Office. The General Aulic Accounting Directory controlled public accounts. Finally, there was the Secret Aulic House, Court, and State Chancellery for foreign affairs.

The directors of these court offices were originally looked upon as counselors of the monarch and as real secretaries or ministers who acted in his name. They frequently served as an advisory council to deliberate upon affairs of state. Gradually this practice fell into disuse. Maria Theresa (who reigned 1740–80) and Joseph II (1780–90) relied mainly on the newly created Council of State, while Francis I (1792–1835) frequently bypassed both the Council of State and the State Conference, which he had established during the course of the Napoleonic wars, and more and more assumed personal responsibility for administration. When the practice of holding oral conferences ceased, the heads of the court offices submitted everything to the Emperor in writing. In time they sank to the level of mere administrators of their respective offices; the main function of the Council of State and State Conference came to be that of drafting elaborate and detailed reports on the host of matters referred to them by the monarch. In the end, Emperor Francis acted alone upon all matters, even the most trivial minutiae.[3]

Not only was every organ in the central government under the direct control of the Emperor, but also the provinces (except those having special prerogatives, such as Hungary and Lombardy-Venetia) were wholly dependent upon the central authorities in Vienna. The Emperor and his officials made all laws for them. Although in some provinces the historic estates still existed, they were not representative bodies in the real sense of the term but were merely privileged corporations composed of four

[3] Maximilian Bach, *Geschichte der Wiener Revolution im Jahre 1848*, pp. 95–102; Ignaz Beidtel, *Geschichte der österreichischen Staatsverwaltung 1740–1848*, Vol. II, pp. 213–36. See also [Franz Graf von Hartig], *Genesis der Revolution in Oesterreich im Jahre 1848* (hereafter cited throughout as *Genesis der Revolution*), pp. 26–37; also reprinted in full in English translation in William Coxe, *History of the House of Austria, from the Foundation of the Monarchy by Rhodolph of Hapsburgh to the Death of Leopold the Second: 1218 to 1792. With a Continuation by W. K. Kelly and Bound with Genesis; or, Details of the Late Austrian Revolution by Graf Franz von Hartig*, Vol. IV, *From the Accession of Francis I. to the Revolution of 1848. In Continuation of the History Written by Archdeacon Coxe. To Which Is Added, Genesis, or, Details of the Late Austrian Revolution. By an Officer of State;* for the section discussed above see pp. 19–28.

classes: the clergy, the nobility, the knights or inferior nobility, and the deputies from the royal towns. Usually they met once a year under the presidency of the governor of the province or a royal commissioner, but their rights were severely limited. They had no legislative powers, only administrative. They apportioned and assessed the taxes already fixed and dealt with such routine provincial matters as had been delegated to them. In addition, they had the right to send petitions for redress of grievances to the Emperor or to the provincial government. By the nineteenth century they were negligible as an active political force.[4]

Since all powers in the monarchy were concentrated in the hands of the sovereign, the task of governing the far-flung, heterogeneous Habsburg domains required a ruler with wisdom and strength. Unfortunately, Emperor Ferdinand (1835–48) was not endowed with such characteristics. Although he was kindly and well meaning, Ferdinand had suffered for years from epileptic fits that had seriously impaired his mind. Poorly educated and chronically ill, Ferdinand was incapable of ruling a vast empire.

At the beginning of his reign it became obvious that some kind of body had to be created to superintend the affairs of government on his behalf. For this purpose a special Council of State was formed under the presidency of the new ruler's uncle, Archduke Louis, with Prince Klemens Wenzel Metternich and Count Franz Anton Kolowrat as its other members[5]—an unfortunate combination. Although Archduke Louis was honorable and well intentioned, he was slow to act, untalented, and easily influenced. Metternich and Kolowrat were such bitter enemies that for years they had communicated with each other only in writing. In the Council of State Metternich was to be responsible chiefly for foreign affairs; Kolowrat, for domestic matters. Although Metternich maintained that he never intended to dam the flow of progress,[6] he

---

[4] Karl Hugelmann, "Die österreichischen Landtage im Jahre 1848," *Archiv für österreichische Geschichte,* Vol. CXI (1930), pp. 7–11; Hartig, *op. cit.,* pp. 37–40; P. E. Turnbull, *Oesterreichs sociale und Politische Zustände,* pp. 162–65; Rudolph Kiszling *et al., Die Revolution im Kaisertum Österreich 1848–1849,* Vol. I, pp. 21–23; William H. Stiles, *Austria in 1848–49: Being a History of the Late Political Movements in Vienna, Milan, Venice, and Prague; with Details of the Campaigns of Lombardy and Novara; a Full Account of the Revolution in Hungary; and Historical Sketches of the Austrian Government and the Provinces of the Empire* (hereafter cited throughout as *Austria in 1848–49*), Vol. I, pp. 69–71. Stiles was the United States chargé d'affaires in Vienna from April, 1845, to October, 1849.

[5] See Metternich's "Autobiographische Denkschrift," in *Aus Metternich's nachgelassenen Papieren,* published by Prince Richard Metternich-Winneburg, ed. and arr. Alfons von Klinkowström, Vol. VII, p. 618. Prince Richard Metternich was the son of the Chancellor.

[6] For Metternich's views on the shortcomings of the government from 1835 to

had an aversion for all revolutionary liberal and national ideas, whereas Kolowrat loved "to play the liberal opponent of the Metternich system."[7]

The two gladiators battled furiously. Only two days after the death of Emperor Francis they crossed verbal swords, and thereafter the highest council of the monarchy was the scene of constant quarrels and dissension. Personal rivalry, not the welfare of the monarchy, was all too frequently the determining factor in settling weighty affairs of state. As a consequence, the government drifted into a state of inertia that made any real accomplishments impossible. Although Kolowrat and other officials, including Metternich, saw the dangers of doing nothing, the central administration was so bogged down in confusion and apathy, so divided, and so concerned with maintaining the authority of the sovereign that it was unable to make long-overdue improvements.

Inevitably the weakness on top reflected itself in the lower divisions of the Austrian bureaucracy. There were over 140,000 government employees.[8] For the most part they were loyal and industrious, but they were usually too unimaginative to rise beyond the routine of their office,[9] and they were resentful of the slow promotions and poor salaries. One of the reasons for the low wages was the critical state of the country's finances. The deficit that existed at the beginning of Ferdinand's reign never disappeared while he was Emperor. Although taxes were increased, particularly those imposed upon the middle classes and the poor, the state revenues were not enough to cover expenditures. There was a yearly deficit of around 4,000,000 gulden ($1,920,000), and by 1847 the state debt had increased to 748,000,000 gulden ($359,400,000).[10]

All in all the Austrian governmental machine was at the point of breaking down. True, the picture was not entirely black. The lives and property of all subjects were secure. Justice was meted out impartially to everyone, no matter to what class or nationality he belonged. Persons of all nationalities and Christian faiths were employed by the government.

1848, see *ibid.*, pp. 617–22. For his political philosophy, see especially "Mein politisches Testament," in *ibid.*, pp. 633–42; Srbik, *op. cit.*, Vol. I, pp. 350–420. For a thoughtful contemporary defense of the Austrian Chancellor, see [Ludwig Guido von Usedom], *Politische Briefe und Charakteristiken aus der deutschen Gegenwart*, pp. 55–69; this is Usedom's only known work.

[7] Heinrich Friedjung, *Österreich von 1848 bis 1860*, Vol. I, p. 6. Translations from the German are the author's unless otherwise indicated.

[8] [Victor von Andrian-Werburg], *Oesterreich und dessen Zukunft*, Part I, p. 77.

[9] *Ibid.*, p. 55.

[10] An Austrian gulden or florin was worth about 48 cents in United States money. Andrian-Werburg observed that the state debt had doubled since 1815 and that the state budget had not been balanced for twenty-five years. *Ibid.*, pp. 106–107.

Most officials were personally incorruptible and preserved a sense of justice and fair play. The government was truly concerned with furthering the material welfare of the people. It was not the integrity and moral fiber of the monarchy that were on the brink of collapse, but the administrative machine. In the words of the highly conservative Alexander von Hübner: [11]

Administrative power was always falling more and more into the hands of little people, that is, into the hands of a bureaucracy that was still honorable and decent but without influence, without insight, without compass, and already more or less won over to the ideas that they were duty-bound to fight. Although distant thunder was heralding the approach of the storm, there was nobody who was able to direct the bewildered in the right direction or to calm the disheartened and get them to take courage. There was not a single word that spoke to the heart, to the noble instincts, to the higher feelings of the nation. There was nothing but silence and immobility.

The result of the confusion in government circles was that even so bitter an opponent of the Revolution of 1848 as Mathias Koch[12] saw in the regime a system that

was but pure negation. It was a brazen tablet with these indestructible words on it: "no concessions, no constitution, no innovations." In front of it there was a prostrate living organism called the state, with all its limbs benumbed by chains so that its mouth could not express the determined wish for one of those gifts [of freedom] or point its hand to them.

On the eve of the revolution the liberals reproved the Habsburg bureaucracy for its incompetence, sterility, and immobility. What particularly goaded them to the point of fury, however, was the government's attitude toward religion and education, the stifling press censorship, and the omnipresent police. Although the government generally held to the policy, begun in the eighteenth century by Joseph II, of strictly regulating all church affairs, it aided the Catholic clergy at every turn in strengthening their religious and moral influence over the Austrian people. The possession of strong religious convictions on the part of the Emperor's subjects was held to be indispensable to the molding of an upright, peaceful, and loyal citizen body. In 1820 the Jesuits were readmitted to the country, and in 1836 they were given permission to engage in educational activities. In 1816 the Congregation of the Liguorians, or

---

[11] As printed in Tim Klein (ed.), *1848. Der Vorkampf deutscher Einheit und Freiheit. Erinnerungen, Urkunden, Berichte, Briefe* (hereafter cited throughout as *1848. Der Vorkampf deutscher Einheit und Freiheit*), p. 123.

[12] M[athias] Koch, *Genesis der Wiener Revolution,* p. 10.

The Prerevolutionary Empire

Redemptorists, was established in Vienna as a place of refuge for men who wanted to live a life of deep inner piety. As the March, 1848, revolution drew near, some of the more liberal elements in the country began to express vehement opposition to the Jesuits, whom they turned into symbols of all they deemed abhorrent and evil in the religious and political life of the country. Their bitterness was also directed toward the Liguorians, whose ideals and practices were in many ways so similar to those of the Jesuits that the liberals considered them practically the same. Because of the privileges accorded the Roman church, many middle-class opponents of the Habsburgs began to look upon religion as a political force aimed at buttressing the old system and consequently to assume an attitude of indifference to religious life of any kind.

The adversaries of the regime denounced not only the religious policies of the Habsburgs but also their educational system. In the Austrian schools the chief objective was not to improve the minds of the pupils but to mold the children into upright, God-fearing, obedient subjects of the Emperor.[13] All schools in the empire were supervised by the Imperial School Commission, one of the bureaus of the united chancellery. Elementary education was under the direct superintendence of the clergy, with the local priest responsible for the conduct of the teachers and the morality of the students in his parish. In all schools, from the first grade to the universities, the teachers were forbidden to deviate from the officially prescribed textbooks and method books unless they first obtained permission to do so. Needless to say, there was no freedom of discussion or thought in the Austrian schools.[14]

On the censorship and the police system, headed by Count Josef Sedlnitzky, the liberals heaped their severest criticism. In the Habsburg monarchy all writings critical of religion, morals, the existing social and political order, or important personages, whether penned in Austria or in foreign countries, were prohibited. Expressions of nationalism, constitutionalism, liberalism, freedom, and other "dangerous" ideas were carefully expunged from printed works. In fact, nothing could be writ-

[13] In the 1840's the educational system was still much the same as it had been under Emperor Francis I. For a discussion of the use made of the Austrian schools to mold a desired citizen body during the reign of Francis I, see R. John Rath, "Training for Citizenship in the Austrian Elementary Schools during the Reign of Francis I," *Journal of Central European Affairs,* Vol. IV, No. 2 (July, 1944), pp. 147–64.

[14] Andrian-Werburg, *op. cit.,* Part I, pp. 56–57; Paul Molisch, "Die Wiener akademische Legion und ihr Anteil an den Verfassungskämpfen des Jahres 1848. Nebst einer Besprechung der übrigen 1848er Studentenlegionen (hereafter cited throughout as "Die Wiener akademische Legion"), *Archiv für österreichische Geschichte,* Vol. CX, Part I (1924), pp. 9–31.

ten about affairs of state, and, except for the official journals, there were no political newspapers in the country. Every book, article, and even advertisement printed in Austria, as well as foreign works circulated in the monarchy, had to be submitted to a censor, who exercised his own judgment in expurgating or changing passages of which he disapproved.[15] Since each censor was a sovereign authority over the manuscripts passing over his desk, confusion was inevitable. Articles proscribed in one place were permitted elsewhere. One newspaper published a report that was prohibited in another. One author fell into official disfavor for an idea he had expressed, while another printed the same thought with impunity.[16] Naturally the arbitrary excisions made by petty censors were a constant source of irritation to the opponents of the regime and had a depressing effect upon literary endeavors. As the Austrian writer Ludwig August Frankl, who had many difficulties with the censors, put it: "The self-assurance of those who wrote had fallen so low that they practiced a self-censorship of their own and destroyed every inborn thought, as Chronos[17] did his children."[18]

Nevertheless, stringent though the censorship regulations were, they were frequently evaded. Austria's most famous mid-century playwright, Franz Grillparzer, accurately described how often the censorship was circumvented when he wrote in his recollections of 1848:[19]

In principle the censorship still remained as severe as under Emperor Francis. But in practice it was infinitely milder, to be sure chiefly because of the impossibility of enforcing it. The reading and circulation of prohibited foreign writings was as general as anywhere in the world, and the most dangerous ones were the most widely circulated.[20] I myself saw a coachman reading *Oestreichs Zukunft*[21] on a coach box. The domestic press, of course, was supervised in every possible way. However, on the one hand, Prince Metternich from time to time took pleasure in giving proof

---

[15] See J. G. Legge, *Rhyme and Revolution in Germany: A Study in German History, Life, Literature and Character 1813–1850*, pp. 175–77, for interesting examples of the pettiness of the Austrian censorship.

[16] See especially Joseph Alexander Freiherrn von Helfert, *Die Wiener Journalistik im Jahre 1848*, pp. 5–9, for good examples of the inconsistent censorship.

[17] The personification of Time, who devoured his own children and destroyed everything that came into existence.

[18] Ludwig August Frankl, *Erinnerungen*, ed. Stefan Hock, p. 182.

[19] [Franz] Grillparzer, "Erinnerungen aus dem Jahre 1848," *Grillparzers sämtliche Werke*, ed. with introduction by August Sauer, Vol. XX, pp. 191–92.

[20] Eduard Bauernfeld maintained that at times the Austrian authorities themselves "connived at violations of the censorship and other transgressions and even helped to smuggle in prohibited books and journals, such as the *Grenzboten*." See his *Erinnerungen aus Alt-Wien*, ed. Josef Bindtner, p. 221.

[21] Andrian-Werburg, *op. cit.* See Chapter II.

of his liberal opinions, and men of a European-wide reputation, like Aulic Councilor Hammer,[22] or writers who had access to the Prince's company could pretty much have published what they wanted. On the other hand, one closed his eyes all too gladly when Austrians, supposedly writers of some reputation, let their works be published abroad. They needed only, in way of an open secret, to shorten their name a syllable or assume a false one to spare themselves nearly all questioning and ward off attack. Yes, the authorities were perhaps even secretly joyful because they believed that their necessary severity did not stand in the way of the development of the more distinguished literature. Actual political writers, of course, could count on less consideration.

But if the most outstanding literary men were cared for in the above manner, another class was in the most extreme distress, namely, the unimportant writers who could find no foreign publisher. In the same situation were the playwrights, who chiefly had the Viennese stage in view when they wrote their productions and who did not have the opportunity to compensate for their basic lack of talent by political allusions and vulgarities.

The police were also targets of criticism. Although the opponents of the regime did not look askance upon the main work performed by Sedlnitzky's organization, that of maintaining law and order, they abhorred the political police—the host of spies, informers, and *agents provocateurs* attached to the police director's office—whose task was to ferret out the innermost thoughts of the Emperor's subjects and to check the development of any revolutionary spirit. The police worked through fear and intimidation. Nevertheless, though Sedlnitzky's talebearers were offensive to most Austrians, the oppressiveness of the police system was tempered by the growing inefficiency and confusion that characterized Ferdinand's reign, as well as by those feelings of *Gemütlichkeit* and *Schlamperei* that so often softened the harshness of the regulations printed in the Habsburg lawbooks. Even though the police could and did intimidate malcontents and make them wary about openly attacking cherished officials and institutions, they could never extinguish the smoldering embers of discontent. They merely drove the opposition underground, thereby making "liberalism" all the more exciting and fascinating to many a bold spirit who might otherwise have remained unaroused.

Thus the shortcomings of the Habsburg political system were a powerful factor in producing the spirit of discontent and rebellion that was prevalent in Austria by the spring of 1848. Also, the prevailing eco-

[22] Here Grillparzer is apparently referring to Baron Joseph von Hammer-Purgstall, the president of the Royal Academy of Sciences.

nomic and social conditions gave real cause for dissatisfaction, although the living standards of the lower classes were substantially better than they had been during the eighteenth century and earlier.[23]

The large majority of the population made their living from agricultural pursuits. Even after Joseph II freed the peasants from personal bondage, they still had to pay dues to the owner of the land they farmed. Furthermore, the landlord usually had various political, economic, and judicial powers over the peasants living on his estates. The condition of the peasantry varied greatly in different parts of the monarchy, but in general the kinds of obligations they paid were the same everywhere. The most important was compulsory labor service (the *Robot*), the amount of which differed considerably from province to province and from peasant to peasant within a single province. Of the numerous payments in kind, the most onerous was the tithe (*Zehnt*), which included sundry taxes and varied from place to place according to custom or the various agreements that had been made. Sometimes the *Zehnt* actually amounted to approximately one-tenth of the crops; sometimes it was as little as one-twentieth. Other payments in kind included cattle, animal products, poultry, and honey. If the peasant had a vineyard, he nearly always had to pay the landlord for the use of the land for grape-growing, even when no grape crop was raised and even in cases where the land had not been used as a vineyard for many years. Furthermore, he was usually assessed fairly substantial sums when a holding changed hands.

Over and above these payments to the landlord were other taxes, the chief of which was the land tax, which usually amounted to 17 to 24 per cent of the net proceeds of the land. The peasant also had to give money for the support of the church and of various state employees. He had to provide horses and a conveyance for any person with an official order for such service, he had to quarter soldiers in his home, and he had to help build and maintain local roads and bridges.[24] As 1848 approached, not only did more and more peasants become dissatisfied with the dues exacted from them but also unhappy landlords in many parts of the em-

[23] Rudolph Stadelmann points this out in his *Soziale und politische Geschichte der Revolution von 1848*, pp. 5–8.

[24] See especially the excellent study by Jerome Blum, *Noble Landowners and Agriculture in Austria, 1815–1848: A Study in the Origins of the Peasant Emancipation of 1848*, Johns Hopkins University Studies in Historical and Political Science, Ser. LXV, No. 2, pp. 68–90. For older accounts see Ernst Victor Zenker, *Die Wiener Revolution 1848 in ihren socialen Voraussetzungen und Beziehungen* (hereafter cited throughout as *Die Wiener Revolution*), pp. 1–28; Beidtel, *op. cit.*, Vol. II, pp. 377–81.

ire began to agitate for the commutation of all peasant dues and serv-
ces into money payments.[25]

The lot of the peasants was comparatively fortunate when contrasted
with that of the urban workers. In the 1840's the industrial revolution
had made rapid progress in the Austrian textile industry, particularly in
the cotton-goods industries, centered chiefly in Bohemia and Lower
Austria. By 1847 there were 209 cotton-spinning mills in the monarchy
with a total number of 1,356,180 spindles. Although many woolen goods
were still made by the old hand methods, mechanization was also mak-
ng significant progress in the woolen industry and in silk-manufacturing
and paper-making. Water power was still generally used in the new fac-
ories, but steam engines were gradually coming into use; and by 1847
there were 469 steam engines operating in Austria, in addition to the
278 locomotive engines and 76 steamboat engines.[26] In many ways the
government tried to encourage the industrialization of the empire. It
ostered the building of railroads, abolished various prohibitive tariffs,
ncreased the number of schools for technical instruction, and helped
put more capital at the disposal of private industries.[27] The government
did nothing, however, to abolish the old system of monopolies, and the
privileged guilds that had come into existence in earlier centuries under
ntirely different economic conditions were still allowed to wield con-
iderable power.

The industrial revolution in Austria had brought in its train the usual
miserable working conditions that accompanied the establishment of the
actory system in other countries. Into the new industrial areas, particu-
arly Vienna, in quest of jobs streamed sons and daughters of impov-
rished peasants and destitute handicraft workers. The competition for
all available positions was keen. Since women and children would work
or a pittance, they were hired in large numbers by the factories (in
845, for example, approximately 60 per cent of the employees in the
otton and paper industries in Lower Austria were women and children).[28] The working day was usually twelve to fourteen hours for men,
women, and children.[29] Wages were wretched. It has been estimated

[25] Blum, *op. cit.*, especially points this out. See also Hugo Hantsch, *Die Ge-
chichte Österreichs,* Vol. II, pp. 330–32.
[26] Jerome Blum, "Transportation and Industry in Austria, 1815–1848," *The
ournal of Modern History,* Vol. XV, No. 1 (March, 1943), pp. 32–36.
[27] Beidtel, *op. cit.,* Vol. II, pp. 358–62; Srbik, *op. cit.,* Vol. II, p. 213.
[28] See Zenker, *op. cit.,* p. 61, table. See also Blum, "Transportation and Industry
n Austria, 1815–1848," p. 37, for other estimates.
[29] See especially Albrecht Tebeldi (pseud. Karl Beidtel), *Die Geldangelegen-
eiten Oestreichs,* pp. 142–43.

that in 1847 the weekly wage of children ranged between 20 kreutzer (16 cents) and 3 florins ($1.44), whereas the average weekly wage of male workers was only 5.22 florins ($2.51) and that of women 2.58 florins ($1.24). This was somewhat less than the average weekly wages in England (11 shillings, or $2.67) and in France (16.68 francs, or $3.32).[30] Meanwhile, during the thirties and forties there was a steady increase in the cost of living, which skyrocketed after the bad harvests of 1846 and 1847. Potatoes, for instance, a staple of the lower-class diet, cost 2.08 florins ($1.02) a metze (1.74 bushels). By 1847 the wages of the common laborer were insufficient to provide for the necessities of life.[31]

Economic dislocations and increasing unemployment furthered unrest. By 1847, 10,000 factory workers had been dismissed from their jobs in Vienna alone.[32] The suburbs of Vienna, where the factories were concentrated, were filled with unemployed proletarians who were rapidly growing destitute. In their idleness and misery some turned to drunkenness, prostitution, and even robbery and murder. Food stores, butcher shops, and bakeries were plundered.[33] In the winter of 1847–48 a private soup kitchen was organized to take care of the thousands upon thousands of hungry poor who came for a piece of bread and a bowl of "Rumford soup."[34]

Although the workers were desperate and ready to join any movement that might bring them bread, they had no feeling of class consciousness, in the Marxist sense of the term. There is no evidence that the Austrian workers had more than a very slight knowledge of the writings of the early nineteenth-century French Utopian Socialists. "They had no leaders, no program, no theories. They had only, to incite them,

[30] Zenker, *op. cit.*, pp. 63, 66–67.

[31] *Ibid.*, pp. 68, 75–76; Viktor Bibl, *Die Niederösterreichischen Stände im Vormärz. Ein Beitrag zur Vorgeschichte der Revolution des Jahres 1848* (hereafter cited throughout as *Die Niederösterreichischen Stände*), ed. Society for Modern Austrian History, p. 301.

[32] Joseph Alexander Freiherrn von Helfert, *Geschichte der österreichischen Revolution im Zusammenhange mit der mitteleuropäischen Bewegung der Jahre 1848–1849* (hereafter cited throughout as *Geschichte der österreichischen Revolution*), Vol. I, *Bis zur österreichischen Verfassung vom 25. April 1848*, p. 72.

[33] Heinrich Reschauer and Moritz Smets, *Das Jahr 1848. Geschichte der Wiener Revolution*, Vol. I, pp. 52–54; Otto Hartmann, *Die Volkserhebung der Jahre 1848 und 1849 in Deutschland*, p. 19.

[34] Ernst Violand, *Die sociale Geschichte der Revolution in Oesterreich*, pp. 54–55. Rumford soup was a cheap but very nourishing soup "invented" by Count Rumford (Benjamin Thompson), who, after leaving the American colonies and sojourning for a time in England, eventually entered the services of the King of Bavaria.

their suffering and despair."[35] The workers were not the revolutionary leaders of 1848. They fought on the streets of Vienna and on the barricades, but not to defend a proletarian program. The cause they championed was that of the lower middle classes, who were the radical extremists of 1848 in Austria.

The coming of the factory system brought to the verge of utter ruin the handicraftsmen and the workers in the domestic system of industry. The small masters in the trades that were becoming industrialized could not afford to install the expensive machinery required to modernize their shops, and their wares could not compete with machine-made products. Gradually but inexorably they found themselves pushed to the wall. Many were forced to seek employment in various capitalistic enterprises. Even more had to beg for work in the factories that had been the cause of their adversity. The less fortunate sank to the level of journeymen or day laborers. Some became beggars; others, objects of charity.[36] Especially piteous was the lot of the journeymen. Even before the coming of the industrial revolution to Austria the journeymen had had enough reasons for grumbling. The time when they could easily become master-craftsmen had long ago passed. Those fortunate enough to attain the envied rank of master were nearly always sons or sons-in-law of the privileged upper group. The rest had to be satisfied with the small incomes of wage-earners. Now even this meager livelihood was being taken away from them by the machines. Naturally, the journeymen were angry about their growing impoverishment and lashed out against those who they thought were responsible for their misery. Of all social

---

[35] Josephine Goldmark, *Pilgrims of '48: One Man's Part in the Austrian Revolution of 1848 and a Family Migration to America* (hereafter cited throughout as *Pilgrims of '48*), p. 19. See also Zenker, *op. cit.*, pp. 102–105; Stadelmann, *op. cit.*, p. 10; Robert Endres, *Revolution in Österreich 1848*, p. 45. Marx and Engels had the same opinion about the absence of a class consciousness among the Viennese workers of 1848. As late as September, 1848, they wrote about the Viennese workers: "The working classes, distrusted, disarmed, disorganized, hardly emerging from the intellectual bondage of the old regime, hardly awaking, not to a knowledge, but to a mere instinct of their social position and proper political line of action, could only make themselves heard by loud demonstrations, and could not be expected to be up to the difficulties of the moment." Frederick Engels, *Germany: Revolution and Counter-Revolution,* Vol. XIII of *Marxist Library: Works of Marxism-Leninism,* p. 70 (this work, which consists of the articles written on the Revolution of 1848 in Germany by Engels and edited and forwarded to the *New York Daily Tribune* by Marx, has been published in several editions, sometimes under Marx's name and sometimes under Engels').

[36] Zenker, *op. cit.*, pp. 50–55; Ernst Fischer, *Österreich 1848. Probleme der demokratischen Revolution in Oesterreich* (hereafter cited throughout as *Österreich 1848*), pp. 32–34. It should be noted that Ernst Fischer has been the most vocal of the handful of Communist deputies in the Austrian Nationalrat since 1945.

groups in Austria, the journeymen were the most bitter. It is no wonder that they formed the nucleus of the ultraradicals of 1848.[37]

The Jews were also among the prominent figures in the radical camp. In all parts of the empire they constituted a special second-class citizenry. They were treated worst in Bohemia and Moravia, and were scorned and abused in other parts of the monarchy. In such places as the Tyrol, Carthinia, and Carniola they were not tolerated at all. In Vienna only resident Jews had the right to engage in business, trade, or industry. Without the permission of the authorities nonindigenous Jews could remain in the capital only three days. Everywhere in the monarchy the Jews had no legal rights, could hold no landed property, and were forced to pay a special tax. They were excluded from state office and were not allowed to become judges, lawyers, teachers, or army officers. The Jews were the most oppressed "political pariahs" in the monarchy.[38]

Many of the more prosperous members of the middle class were also discontented. Although some of them had accumulated large fortunes, they found themselves ostracized by the social circles of the court and the high nobility and their role in the political life of the state was comparatively small. Only the big financiers, from whom the state required loans, had any real political influence. As the bourgeoisie felt that they had the brains, the know-how, and the money, they resented being excluded from privileges which they felt were due them. They yearned to replace the absolutist state with a liberal constitutional monarchy over which they could exercise considerable control.

Some of the more liberal nobility joined the middle classes in their demands for reforms. Because many of the lesser nobility were relatively poor, there was a deep cleavage between them and the grand seigniors. Moreover, a sizable number of the less affluent noblemen were state employees, whose positions were those of middle rank. Many of this group, still strongly under the influence of Josephinist ideas, were very unhappy about the trend of Austrian political life since the eighteenth century,[39] and a substantial number joined the middle-class opponents of the Habsburg regime in March, 1848.

In spite of the fact that a witches' caldron was bubbling in the capi-

[37] Endres, *op. cit.*, p. 32; Fischer, *op. cit.*, p. 34; Stadelmann, *op. cit.*, p. 13; Zenker, *op. cit.*, pp. 44–54.

[38] Reschauer and Smets, *op. cit.*, Vol. I, pp. 59–60.

[39] Endres, *op. cit.*, pp. 42–44; Hantsch, *op. cit.*, Vol. II, pp. 327–28; Engels *op. cit.*, p. 37.

The Prerevolutionary Empire

tal in the 1840's, most Viennese were as gay and lighthearted as always. As one contemporary witness observed:[40]

> The population of Vienna seems to a serious observer to be reveling in an everlasting state of intoxication. Eat, drink, and be merry are the three cardinal virtues and pleasures of the Viennese. For them it is always Sunday, always carnival time. Music comes from everywhere. The countless inns are full of revelers day and night. Everywhere there are crowds of idle fops and fashion dolls. Everywhere, in daily life, in art, and in literature, there prevails that delicate and witty jesting. For the Viennese the most important world events have happened only so that they can make a joke about them.

Vienna was still full of charm and the pleasures of living.

Nevertheless, under the surface there was a change. As 1848 approached there was a new seriousness of purpose, intermingled with a skeptical attitude toward the old values, an attitude reported by one of the liberal opponents of the Habsburgs, Franz Schuselka:[41]

> While not so many years ago in Vienna it often happened that an empty court carriage was greeted reverently as it passed by, now very many refuse to pay the respect due even those in the highest ranks. This can, indeed, be considered as a significant indication that the people are no longer the same as they used to be.

This change came about partly as a result of the spirit of opposition which certain national and liberal writers deliberately instilled in the populace for more than a decade before the outbreak of the 1848 Revolution.

[40] [Franz Schuselka], *Deutsche Worte eines Oesterreichers,* p. 24.
[41] Franz Schuselka, *Oesterreichische Vor- und Rückschritte,* pp. 197–98.

II. The Development of a Spirit of Opposition

Y THE 1840's enough incendiary material was on hand in the Habsburg monarchy to start a revolutionary conflagration. As early as the last years of the reign of Francis I some dissatisfaction with the *status quo* had been manifested. Much of this early opposition was "Josephinistic,"[1] and not liberal in nature, but it was the spirit of Josephinism that prepared the way for the liberal current that began to succeed it in the decade preceding 1848.[2]

With the wars of liberation against Napoleon and the spread of the ideas of the French Revolution to central Europe came a feeling of nationalism among certain peoples. Considerable hostility had resulted from Joseph II's attempts to make German the official language of the monarchy,[3] thus identifying Habsburg interests with those of the Germans. In the non-German groups, scholars, writers, and political leaders struggled to instill a pride of national accomplishments. In Hungary, Count István Széchenyi and Lajos Kossuth agitated for national reform and demanded the substitution of the Magyar tongue for Latin. In northern Italy, a number of writers busied themselves with stirring up hatred against the Austrians. In Bohemia, scholars like Josef Dobrovský and Josef Jungmann stimulated a revival of the Czech language and literature, while František Palacký aroused among his fellow-countrymen a feeling of pride in the great accomplishments of the Bohemian

[1] A collective term referring to the fusion of Austrian traditional ideas with the eighteenth-century philosophy of the Enlightenment that characterized the reforming era of Emperor Joseph II. Much of this spirit lingered on into the nineteenth century, particularly among some members of the bureaucracy. For an excellent work on Josephinism, see Fritz Valjavic, *Der Josephinismus. Zur geistigen Entwicklung Österreichs im 18. und 19. Jahrhundert.*

[2] See especially *ibid.*, pp. 97–98; Rudolph Kiszling *et al., Die Revolution im Kaisertum Österreich 1848–1849,* Vol. I, p. 9.

[3] Robert A. Kann, *The Multinational Empire: Nationalism and National Reform in the Habsburg Monarchy 1848–1918* (hereafter cited throughout as *The Multinational Empire*), Vol. I, p. 53.

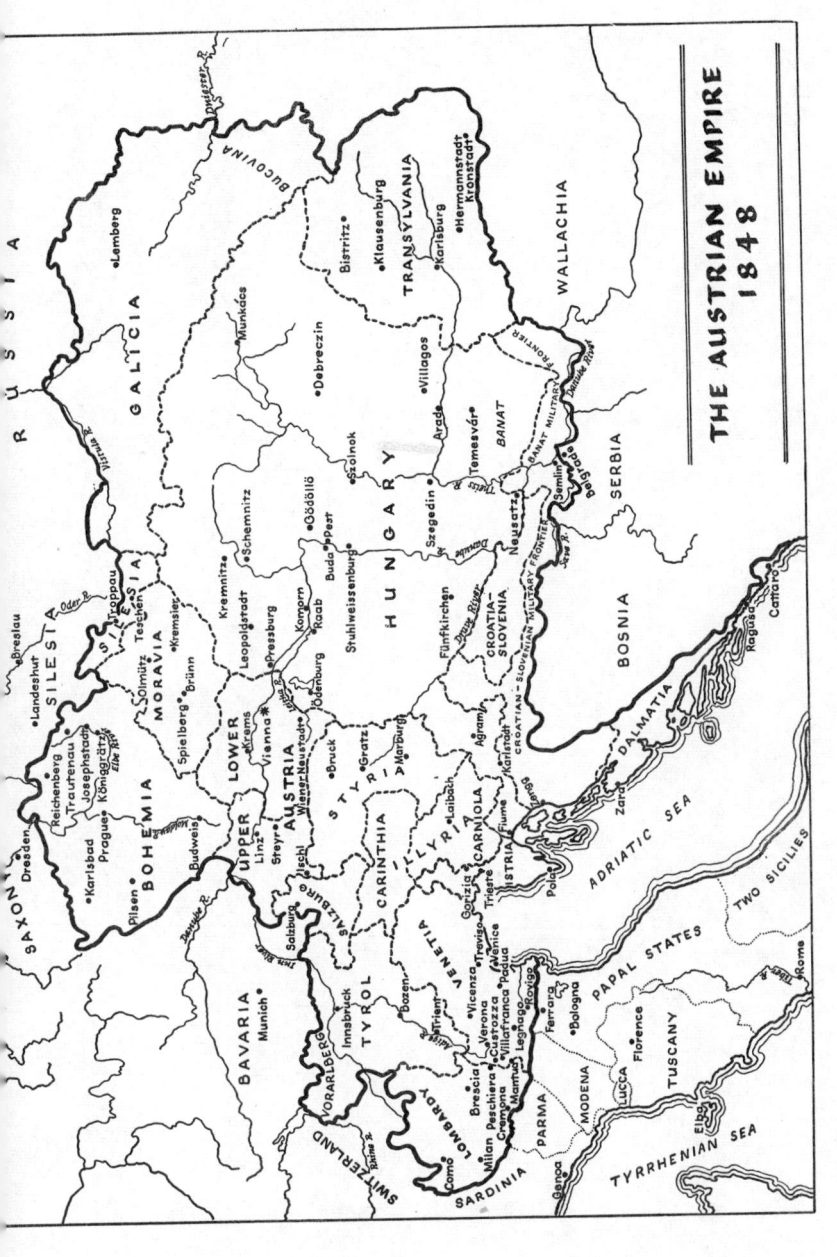

THE AUSTRIAN EMPIRE 1848

The Development of a Spirit of Opposition

people. Among the Slovaks, Antonín Bernolák, Jan Kollár, Ludevît Štúr, Michal Hodža, and Josef Hurban labored to create a Slovak literary language; and among the Ruthenians, scholars like Markijan Shashkevych and Jakov Holovatzki occupied themselves with collecting folklore and restoring ancient literary monuments. In Galicia, the upper-class Poles were loudly asserting themselves against the Germans; while in Transylvania, the Romanians were struggling to preserve their individuality in face of the Hungarian attempts to Magyarize them. The South Slavs were also stirring. Almost singlehandedly, Jernej Kopitar lifted the Slovenian tongue from a peasant vernacular to the status of a literary language, while the poet Valentin Vodnik helped to forward the Illyrian patriotic ideal among the Slovenes. In Croatia, Ljudevit Gaj exerted his efforts to create a feeling of South Slav solidarity in his fellow-countrymen, and among the Austro-Serbs, Vuk Stefanović Karadžić contributed much to arousing a feeling of Serbian nationalism.[4]

At first, the national movement was chiefly a cultural one, but it soon took on a liberal political color. Gradually some of the nationalist leaders began to make political demands: the Bohemians, for more privileges for the provincial estates; the Hungarians, for greater independence from Vienna; the Poles, for the restoration of an ancient kingdom that had been destroyed; the extreme Italian nationalists, for outright separation from the empire.

In Vienna during the early 1830's various literary men, such as Grillparzer, Bauernfeld, Count Anton von Auersperg, and Ignaz Castelli, were reading to each other satirical skits about the censorship and other unpopular government institutions. The censors, however, were too watchful to make it possible for any real opposition literature to be published in Austria. Auersperg got into difficulties with the censorship authorities,[5] and it was only Bauernfeld's friendship with Count Kolowrat that kept him out of trouble.[6] The sole outlet available to the Austrian liberals was the German press. During the late thirties some of the writers turned to it. Under the guise of anonymity, they sent articles for publication to such journals as the *Hamburger Nachrichten* and the *Nürnberger Korrespondenten.*

[4] Georges Weill, *L'éveil des nationalités et le mouvement libéral (1815–1848)*, Vol. XV of *Peuples et civilisations*, ed. Louis Halphen and Philippe Sagnac, pp. 370–86, 405–20; Kann, *op. cit.*, Vol. I, *passim;* Hans Kohn, *Pan-Slavism, Its History and Ideology*, pp. 11–65; Anton Springer, *Geschichte Oesterreichs seit dem Wiener Frieden 1809*, Vol. II, pp. 1–35.

[5] Franz Gräffer, *Kleine Wiener Memoiren und Wiener Dosenstücke*, ed. and annotated by Anton Schlossar and Gustav Gugitz, Vol. I, p. lxx.

[6] [Franz] Grillparzer, "Erinnerungen aus dem Jahre 1848," *Grillparzers sämtliche Werke*, ed. with introduction by August Sauer, Vol. XX, p. 195.

Until the early 1840's the criticisms of the prevailing regime were relatively ineffectual. Only a few isolated voices occasionally spoke out against the existing political immobility or expressed a faint yearning for liberty. Then came a sudden change. The pace of opposition quickened. Witty attacks on the government circulated through the salons and the coffeehouses. The number of political poems assailing the regime increased. Liberal passages were inserted into plays produced on the Viennese stage and were "acclaimed with great applause."[7]

Some writers, like Heinrich Landesmann (who wrote under the pseudonym Hieronymus Lorm), Albert Rimmer, Uffo Horn, Ludwig August Frankl, and Eduard von Bauernfeld, remained in Austria to attack social, administrative, and literary conditions in the country,[8] largely through political letters to various German newspapers. Other writers, like Ignaz Kuranda and Franz Schuselka, exiled themselves from their native land, either to escape the censors or to try to make a literary position for themselves in Germany.[9]

Some of the expatriates wrote for such papers as the *Allgemeine deutsche Zeitung* and the *Leipziger Zeitung*. But their most important organ was Kuranda's *Grenzboten*,[10] to which a host of patriotic Austrians still living in the empire, including such liberals as Julius Alexander Schindler, Prince Gustav Lamberg, Baron Anton von Doblhoff, Adolph Maria Pinkas, Cavalier Karl von Kleyle, Count Friedrich Deym, and Count Franz Anton Thun, were regular contributors.[11] The *Grenzboten* was founded by Ignaz Kuranda in 1841 in Brussels, and in 1842 its office was transferred to Leipzig,[12] where it began to devote itself largely to Austrian matters and to common German interests.[13] Soon it became the rallying point for the various opposition groups in the Habsburg monarchy, and its influence in Austria was tremendous.

---

[7] Franz Schuselka, *Oesterreichische Vor- und Rückschritte*, p. 201.

[8] Ludwig August Frankl, *Erinnerungen*, ed. Stefan Hock, p. 260.

[9] Eduard Bauernfeld, *Erinnerungen aus Alt-Wien*, ed. Josef Bindtner, p. 222.

[10] Ignaz Beidtel, *Geschichte der österreichischen Staatsverwaltung 1740–1848*, Vol. II, pp. 392–93.

[11] Frankl, *op. cit.*, p. 261.

[12] Constant von Wurzbach, *Biographisches Lexicon des Kaiserthums Oesterreich, enthaltend die Lebensskizzen derjenigen Personen, welche seit 1750 in den österreichischen Kronländern gelebt und gewirkt haben* (hereafter cited throughout as *Biographisches Lexicon des Kaiserthums Oesterreich*), Vol. XIII, p. 409.

[13] Otto Wittner, *Moritz Hartmanns Leben und Werke. Ein Beitrag zur politischen und literarischen Geschichte Deutschlands im XIX. Jahrhundert* (hereafter cited throughout as *Moritz Hartmanns Leben und Werke*), Vol. I, pp. 125–26; Heinrich Reschauer and Moritz Smets, *Das Jahr 1848. Geschichte der Wiener Revolution*, Vol. I, p. 24.

"Count Sedlnitzky put a price of 300 florins[14] on each copy. Baron von' Cotta was warned that if he continued to insert advertisements of the *Grenzboten* in his paper, the *Allgemeine Zeitung* would be prohibited in Austria."[15] In spite of the concerted efforts of the Austrian police to prevent the *Grenzboten* from being circulated in the monarchy, copies were smuggled in by the thousands and were read regularly by most Viennese intellectuals.

Even more influential than the liberal newspapers in stirring up public opinion against the regime were the anonymous books and pamphlets written by Austrian malcontents, published in Germany, and, in spite of the efforts of the government to keep them out, widely sold in the Habsburg monarchy. The first and most influential of these was *Austria and Its Future,* the first part of which was published by Hoffmann und Campe in Hamburg in 1842.[16] The author, as the government was later to discover to its horror and amazement, was none other than Baron Victor von Andrian-Werburg, a well-educated state official who was believed to embody the aristocratic viewpoint in Austria.[17]

In his book, Andrian-Werburg examined the reasons for the tremendous weakening of his country's strength and prestige between 1815 and the early 1840's. During this period, he observed, there was no cohesive force to hold the monarchy together, and no feeling of Austrian patriotism, since the government dared not arouse it. If this failure were not remedied, he warned, in Austria "four full-grown and fully armed nationalities will stand opposed to each other as enemies," with their only common bond that of hatred of and resistance to the regime. The responsibility for the growing disintegration, he insisted, lay "in the wretched paper regiment, in the too-much governing of the bureaucracy, and in the destruction of all other powers in the state." Although the faulty tax system had helped to bring on disaster, he emphasized repeatedly that the chief evil rested with the bureaucracy, an inexcusably haughty and irresponsible bureaucracy that had "no interest except itself." If Austria was to be saved, an end had to be put to the "paper rule" and to the excessive centralization suffocating the monarchy. The police and censorship system, which had turned Austria into a Euro-

---

[14] At that time 300 florins amounted to $144 in United States money and was equivalent to 720 days' wages for the average common laborer in Austria.

[15] Frankl, *op. cit.,* p. 261.

[16] [Victor von Andrian-Werburg], *Oesterreich und dessen Zukunft.* The third edition of Part I, published in 1843, is cited in this book.

[17] Viktor Bibl, *Der Zerfall Österreichs,* Vol. II, *Von Revolution zu Revolution* (hereafter cited as *Von Revolution zu Revolution*), p. 40.

pean China, alienated all classes from the government, impaired the material welfare of the people, and ruined intellectual progress, should also be abolished. The people must again be given the right to regulate their private affairs.

Having diagnosed the malady, Andrian-Werburg prescribed the remedy for his country's ills. According to him, the salvation of Austria lay in inaugurating a system of responsible government. Each local commune should be given the right to administer its own affairs, to levy the local taxes, and to select its own officials. The provincial diets also had to be strengthened and enlarged to include representatives from the peasants and the middle classes. They were to be given power to choose their own officials, to vote provincial taxes, to apportion the taxes levied on the provinces by the imperial diet among the various communes in the province, to supervise all provincial undertakings, and to send petitions to the monarch. Thus the central government was to have little control over provincial and local affairs.

The powers of the Habsburg government in Vienna were to be sharply curbed by an imperial diet, which was to serve as the supreme representative body in the empire. Composed of deputies chosen by each of the estates in the various provincial diets, it was to meet once each year in the capital city, supervise the imperial budget, vote and apportion taxes among the provinces in the empire, debate and decide upon the proposals for laws submitted to it by the government, and send petitions to the Emperor.[18]

Although Andrian-Werburg undoubtedly exaggerated the shortcomings of the Habsburg regime,[19] the influence of his book was enormous. He put down in writing what many malcontents had been thinking privately. In spite of attempts to keep the book out of the country, thousands of copies were smuggled in. They were avidly read not only by the middle-class opponents of the government but also by many of the more liberal nobility, who saw in Andrian-Werburg's ideas a lever to raise their own influence in the administration of the country.[20]

Encouraged by the stir his book had made, Andrian-Werburg pub-

[18] Andrian-Werburg, *op. cit.,* Part I, pp. 23–24, 71, 140, 143–44, 152, 164, 189, 190–95, 200–202.

[19] Grillparzer wrote about Andrian-Werburg's book: "I have read the book *Austria's Future.* It contains much that is true, along with many untruths. In such writings it is impossible to avoid the latter." "Historische und politische Studien," *op. cit.,* Vol. XIV, p. 166.

[20] Viktor Bibl, *Die Niederösterreichischen Stände,* pp. 39–40. See also Reschauer and Smets, *op. cit.,* Vol. I, p. 22.

lished the second part of *Austria and Its Future* in 1847.[21] In it he presented his views on the developments that had taken place in the monarchy since the publication of the first volume. He admitted that much material progress had been made since 1842, but he deplored the fact that not a single urgently needed political reform had been inaugurated. The old system of half-measures, the insecurity, the stagnation and immobility were still present. The financial structure of the monarchy was precarious.[22]

Nevertheless, Austria could be saved if a few important reforms were made immediately. For one thing, Andrian-Werburg maintained, efforts must be exerted to strengthen the nobility who had recently thrown their weight in support of progress and reform in the provincial diets. This group must be given more rights and privileges. More power must be given to the provincial diets, the only bodies representing the common interests of the country. Not to be overlooked were the schools, which had to be released from the prevailing stifling intellectual bondage, and the establishment of a free press. The *Robot* and all other special taxes and services bearing on the peasants must be abolished, a much fairer system of taxes should be put into operation, and the financial structure of the monarchy had to be improved. Above all, if Austria was to be rescued from ruin, a system of local self-government must be inaugurated. Giving the people the right to determine their own affairs was the most important single reform needed.[23]

Because Andrian-Werburg's book was a clarion call to the liberal nobility to agitate for more rights for the privileged provincial estates, his ideas found little acceptance among the middle classes, who had long been suspicious of the nobility. The bourgeoisie found their champion, not in Baron Victor von Andrian-Werburg, but in Franz Schuselka. Of Schuselka's numerous attacks on the Austrian regime, the most important were his *German Words of an Austrian, Austria's Forward and Backward Steps,* and *Austria Rules Supreme If It Only Wills It.*[24]

Schuselka saw no hope in the aristocracy. He insisted that the nobles were concerned "with preserving, not the crown, but their own privileges." They would forsake the monarch as soon as he ceased serving their own selfish purposes. The Emperor, therefore, must never rely ex-

---

[21] Andrian-Werburg, *op. cit.,* Part II. The first edition of Part II, published in 1847, is cited in this book.

[22] *Ibid.,* pp. 9–13.

[23] *Ibid.,* pp. 66–67, 102, 105, 146–49, 168–70, 105–106, 123.

[24] Franz Schuselka, *Deutsche Worte eines Oesterreichers; Oesterreichische Vor- und Rückschritte; Oesterreich über Alles wenn es nur will.*

clusively on the privileged classes for support.[25] Neither must the Emperor rely on the clergy for aid. One of the greatest curses of the regime lay precisely in the fact that the Church had become all-powerful in Austria. "Rome is again giving laws to the Emperor. Bishops and monks are superior to the power of the state. Blindness and superstition are fettering the people."[26] The clergy was working hand in hand with the bureaucracy to support the moldering, iniquitous regime. "Indeed," Schuselka insisted, "the old church is the main prop of the corrupting and disgraceful old Austrian system," and the "bad religious situation is the source of all other evils in Austria."[27]

Unlike Andrian-Werburg, Schuselka did not advocate extending the powers and privileges of the estates. With derisive words he asserted that[28]

whoever hopes for real salvation from the estates, as they now are, is either politically blind or servile to prelates and aristocrats at the same time that he is engaging in opposition against the throne. The system of government of all Austrian lands, with the exception of the Italian kingdom and the Tyrol, is purely hierarchical and aristocratic. The peasants are not at all represented. The middle classes only seem to be represented. . . . At the side of hundreds of prelates and nobles there sit a few deputies from a few cities, and even they are by no means freely elected citizens but officials appointed by the government. In most cases they have all together but one vote, or they are not permitted to be present at all at the deliberations, as is the case in Lower Austria. Although they have all the rights and duties of seignorial authorities, even middle-class property holders are not allowed to have a voice in the diet, merely because they are not of noble birth.

The actions of these estates, which the newspapermen are making such a fuss about, are their asking for an increase in their privileges and the right to take part in the government. They are not thinking about the middle classes and the peasants.

To whom, then, was the Emperor to turn to save the empire from ruin? To the people. The people alone would "defend their throne as their own life."[29] The people alone would help him ward off the threatening disaster. In order to get their support, the Emperor must establish democratic institutions in the country. By doing so he would strengthen, not weaken, the empire. Schuselka insisted that it[30]

[25] Schuselka, *Deutsche Worte eines Oesterreichers*, pp. 136, 139.
[26] Schuselka, *Oesterreichische Vor- und Rückschritte*, p. 168.
[27] *Ibid.*, pp. 170, 171.
[28] *Ibid.*, pp. 248–49.
[29] Schuselka, *Deutsche Worte eines Oesterreichers*, p. 136.
[30] *Ibid.*, pp. 138–39.

is an error and a lie that monarchical and democratic principles are incompatible. How can a monarch be greater and more powerful than by being the first democrat? If he is this, he is the head and heart of the people. Then he stands among them and over them at the same time. Then he is one with the people. No people are striving for anarchy, least of all democratically free and equal people. Such people see everything great, mighty, noble, and sacred in their power united in the throne. They honor themselves by honoring their monarch. The two live mutually in and by one another; and just as a man controls himself by means of his nobler consciousness, free people control themselves through their monarch, who is the bearer, proclaimer, and executor of the mighty, the righteous, and the divine in the minds and the will of the people.

Thus Schuselka saw the road to salvation in a "citizen king." His program, which was supported by the more radical middle-class opponents of the government, made a profound impression upon a large number of malcontents.[31]

Even further to the left than Schuselka was the unidentified author of *Austria's Internal Politics with Reference to the Constitutional Question,*[32] which was printed in Stuttgart in 1847. Like Schuselka and Andrian-Werburg, the author of this treatise deplored the state of immobility and ossification into which the Austrian state machine had fallen. He lamented the stagnation of the economic and intellectual life of the country and the crass materialism, superficiality, and selfishness of the Austrian populace, and he severely criticized the censorship, police, and church. Like Schuselka, he attacked Andrian-Werburg for his adulation of the nobility.[33] Not the sovereignty of the aristocracy but the elevation of the people, he maintained, was necessary to prevent ruin; hence the whole citizenry, and not just the middle classes, must be strengthened. Instead of favoring the nobility and the middle classes, the government must begin looking after the interests of the proletariat. By founding agricultural colonies in Hungary, setting up industrial establishments to provide more jobs for the people, strengthening the existing guilds, and limiting the great powers of the industrial bourgeoisie over the artisans and workers, the Habsburgs must strive to improve the miserable lot of the poor.

The peasants, too, should receive more local self-government. All

---

[31] Frankl says that "Schuselka's pamphlets, Andrian's *Austria and Its Future,* and the *Grenzboten* were the three most significant publications of the forties in the publishing field." *Op. cit.,* p. 261.

[32] *Oesterreichs innere Politik mit Beziehung auf die Verfassungsfrage.*

[33] See especially *ibid.,* pp. 20–21.

hindrances to agriculture should be removed, the *Robot* and other peasant dues and services should be abolished, and the peasants should be given a more suitable political education. In short, if Austria was to be saved, the author of *Austria's Internal Politics* insisted, its government must follow the motto: "With the people and for the people."[34]

Similar views were expressed in the book *The Financial Affairs of Austria*[35] published in Leipzig in 1847 under the pseudonym Albrecht Tebeldi. The author was Karl Beidtel, a young lawyer in Brünn and the son of Ignaz Beidtel, a well-known Austrian jurist and historian. Painting a gloomy picture of the misery of the lower classes and the unhealthy state of Austrian agriculture, Beidtel discussed the crippling effect of the *Robot* and private indebtedness on both peasants and landowners and showed how taxes absorbed a wholly disproportionate amount of the income of every peasant. He also wrote at length about the miserable conditions of the industrial workers, particularly the artisans, whose work was being replaced by machines. Bitterly he lashed out against the selfishness, haughtiness, and irresponsibility of the nobility and insisted that the aristocrats were wholly incapable of giving decent leadership to the empire.[36]

In his exposé of the financial evils of the monarchy lay Beidtel's main contribution. He pointed out that the amount of gold and silver on hand was wholly inadequate to cover the large number of bank notes in circulation and that the chronic inability to balance the budget was bound to undermine the financial structure of the country. The only remedy was to declare a partial bankruptcy and refund without interest only a portion of the sums due the state's creditors. Although such a policy would hurt a few people, it was the only way to prevent disastrous inflation. Furthermore, it was imperative that a responsible legislative body be set up as soon as possible. Having lost all claims to respect, the existing estates should be replaced by a national assembly empowered to advise the monarch on legislative and financial matters.[37]

Even more outspoken in his denunciations of the Habsburg regime than the preceding four writers was the fifth and, chronologically speaking, the last of the major liberal publicists, Karl Moering, the mathematics and military-tactics teacher of Archduke Rainer's children and an officer in the imperial army, whose *Sibylline Books from Austria*[38]

[34] *Ibid.*, pp. 118, 105–12, 118, 80, 80–91, 104.
[35] Albrecht Tebeldi (pseud. Karl Beidtel), *Die Geldangelegenheiten Oestreichs.*
[36] *Ibid.*, pp. 142–77, 219–55, 275–83, 373–74.
[37] *Ibid.*, pp. 384–88, 380.
[38] [Karl Moering], *Sibyllinischen Bücher aus Oesterreich.*

The Development of a Spirit of Opposition

was published in Hamburg early in January, 1848. In eloquent prose Moering attacked the "Metternich system" for its immobility, stupidity, and alleged crimes. Bitterly did he upbraid the regime for its exclusive reliance on the privileged nobility and clergy and its assumption that the masses were lowly beasts useful only for paying taxes and performing menial tasks. He deplored the fact that the Austrian army was so wretchedly led by its officer caste and so devoid of patriotism that it was incapable of defending the country against foreign enemies.

Worst of all, Moering asserted, because of its inability to comprehend the spirit of the times and its contempt for public opinion, the regime had completely alienated all nationalities in the empire and had made it impossible for a feeling of Austrian patriotism to develop. Of the 38 million subjects in the empire, not a single citizen could be proud of being an Austrian. Instead of molding loyal, patriotic, Austrian citizens, the narrow, intolerant policies of the government had turned the Bohemians into Czechs, the Hungarians into Magyars, and the Lombards and Venetians into Italians. A continuation of such shortsighted policies must end in the total collapse of the monarchy. Only if the Emperor became a democratic ruler of and for his people could Austria be preserved.[39]

Bitter as were their criticisms of the prevailing institutions and practices in the Habsburg monarchy, not one of these five authors and none of the other "liberal" writers before 1848 expressed a desire for a constitution, a bill of rights, popular sovereignty, or a genuine "liberal" parliament. Except for Archduke Louis, no member of the imperial family was attacked. Emperor Ferdinand was mentioned only in terms of the most flattering and obsequious adulation. In all the opposition literature not once was a demand made for revolution.[40] Yet in spite of these omissions, the opposition literature helped to create an atmosphere of discontent and a desire for change.

The attacks on the Metternich regime by the liberal polemicists were partly responsible for arousing some of the provincial estates to demand more rights and privileges. As stated earlier, by the early part of the nineteenth century, the estates, dominated by the provincial nobility, had everywhere except in Hungary sunk to the status of advisory

[39] *Ibid., passim.* For a detailed summary of Moering's views, see Reschauer and Smets, *op. cit.,* Vol. I, pp. 78–82.

[40] Friedrich Engel-Jánosi, "Zur Genesis der Revolution von 1848. Die Verfassungsfrage im deutschen Österreich 1815–48," *Zeitschrift für öffentliches Recht,* ed. Hans Kelsen *et al.,* Vol. III (1922–23), pp. 579–81; Heinrich Ritter von Srbik, *Metternich, der Staatsmann und der Mensch,* Vol. II, pp. 215–21; Beidtel, *Geschichte der österreichischen Staatsverwaltung, 1740–1848,* Vol. II, pp. 393–95.

and administrative bodies.[41] During the reign of Francis I the Tyrolese, Carinthian, and Upper Austrian Estates had raised a few hesitant protests against certain administrative abuses but accomplished nothing.[42]

In the thirties and forties, however, the spirit of lethargy that had previously characterized the estates changed to one of intrepid, energetic activity; and in certain provinces the estates became organs for spirited opposition to the Habsburgs. The changed attitude came first in Hungary, where Joseph II's reforms brought the country just short of open rebellion. Later on, the Hungarian Diet voiced so many objections to the practices of the government in Vienna that its meetings were entirely suspended from 1812 to 1826. When the diet was again allowed to convene, it passed resolution after resolution intended to cripple the monarch's power and to establish Magyar supremacy over all other nationalities in the Hungarian part of the empire. As early as 1830 the Hungarian Diet had decreed that all officials except those in Croatia must be familiar with the Magyar tongue. In 1840 the diet established Magyar as the only language for official business and birth and death registers, and in 1844 it declared Magyar, with a few exceptions, to be the exclusive state language.[43]

During the 1840's the Bohemian Estates also began to assert themselves. In Bohemia the estates had always had more rights than those in any other part of the empire except Hungary. For a long time they did little to assert their authority, but in the early forties they began to investigate the conduct of the government authorities and to oppose them at every turn. They attacked the government's disposal of Bohemian domestic funds, quarreled over the distribution and allotment of the direct taxes, and claimed the right to approve or reject taxes. They demanded the right to initiate legislation, freedom of the press and speech, public court procedures, and the restoration of the old Bohemian constitution. Some members even said that the estates should become a national legislature in which all classes of citizens in the Czech nation should be represented. The Moravian Estates allied themselves with the Czech Estates to make similar demands.

[41] See especially [Gotthard Freiherrn von Buschmann and Ritter Anton von Schmerling], *Die niederösterreichischen Landstände und die Genesis der Revolution in Oesterreich im Jahre 1848* (hereafter cited throughout as *Die niederösterreichischen Landstände*), pp. 10–11.

[42] Engel-Jánosi, *op. cit.*, p. 576; Karl Hugelmann, "Die österreichischen Landtage im Jahre 1848," *Archiv für österreichische Geschichte,* Vol. CXI (1930), p. 12.

[43] [Franz Graf von Hartig], *Genesis der Revolution,* pp. 88–97; Srbik, *op. cit.,* Vol. II, pp. 192–207; Dominic G. Kosáry, *A History of Hungary,* pp. 185–218; A. J. P. Taylor, *The Habsburg Monarchy 1815–1918,* pp. 54–58.

The Development of a Spirit of Opposition

In several of the German provinces, however, the estates were comparatively quiescent. In Styria individual members of the estates were disposed to struggle against the government, but the majority did not permit them to make the estates a center of political opposition. For five years the Carinthian Estates refused to approve certain tax increases imposed on the provinces; otherwise they did little to break away from the old habit of accepting the government requests with quiet resignation. In the Tyrol, Upper Austria, Vorarlberg, and Carniola the estates slumbered on.[44]

Exactly the opposite was the case in Lower Austria. There the liberal movement in the estates grew to such proportions that it became a real danger to the government. As early as 1835 the session of the Lower Austrian Estates was a stormy one. In the early 1840's the opposition increased. In 1843 the estates asked for the abolition of all dues and services paid by the peasants and requested a reduction of taxes. In 1845 they sent a memorandum to the government condemning censorship. In 1846 they drew up plans for an agricultural credit bank, made proposals for municipal reform, pleaded for the reduction of the consumption and stamp taxes, asked for the introduction of an income tax and the right to approve taxes, and called the government's attention to the deplorable conditions of the wage-earners in Lower Austria. In 1847 they repeated their demands for reduction of taxes and petitioned the Emperor to improve elementary education in their province. Early in 1848 they presented a memorial to the Emperor for the abolition of military conscription. Furthermore, on several occasions during the forties the Lower Austrian Estates demanded that the state budget be made public, that the estates be consulted on all important matters concerning the province, and that the nonprivileged classes be adequately represented at their meetings.[45]

The more progressive members of the Lower Austrian Estates worked closely with the liberal middle classes, who supported them wholeheartedly. Some estates members, among them Baron von Doblhoff, Baron Andreas von Stifft, Cavalier von Kleyle, Count Albert Montecuccoli, Cavalier Anton von Schmerling, and Count Ferdinand Colloredo-Mannsfeld, played prominent roles in the opposition movement in Vienna. Anti-Habsburg papers in Germany, particularly the *Grenz-*

[44] Hartig, *op. cit.*, pp. 98–112; Srbik, *op. cit.*, Vol. II, pp. 185–87; Beidtel, *Geschichte der österreichischen Staatsverwaltung*, Vol. II, pp. 415–29; Engel-Jánosi, *op. cit.*, p. 576.
[45] See especially [Buschmann and Schmerling], *op. cit.*, pp. 14–21; Hanns Schlitter, *Aus Österreichs Vormärz*, Vol. IV, *Niederösterreich*, pp. 1–35; Bibl, *Die Niederösterreichischen Stände, passim;* Hartig, *op. cit.*, pp. 113–114.

boten, displayed a lively interest in the meetings of the estates and reminded the members to champion the interests of the people. The liberal elements of the Viennese intelligentsia were in constant touch with
the liberals in the Lower Austrian Estates and were coming to believe
that the estates, with all their faults, were the best available tools for
expressing their dissatisfaction with the *status quo,* if only because the
opposition in the estates could be cloaked with the mantle of legality.[46]

The most important of the liberal Viennese societies in which the
more radical estates members participated was the Legal-Political
Reading Club *(Juridisch-politischer Leseverein).* Modeled after the
Shakespeare Club and composed of such liberals as Grillparzer, Doblhoff, and Bauernfeld, it met regularly at the home of State Counselor
von Kleyle.[47] As early as 1840 a group of prominent jurists and other
intellectuals, among them Karl Eugen von Mühlfeld, Baron Franz von
Sommaruga, Alexander Bach, Joseph von Würth, Wildner von Maithstein, Moriz von Stubenrauch, and Anton Hye, met together and drew
up "a project for a club, the purpose of which was 'to give to the educated, and especially to the judicial public, an opportunity to become
familiar with the progress of literature in its widest sense by providing
them with the most important and most interesting periodicals and the
most significant artistic and scientific works.' "[48] The statutes of the
organization were approved by the Emperor in June, 1841,[49] and the
club opened its doors on January 2, 1842.[50]

At first, the Legal-Political Reading Club had 60 full-fledged members. In addition, there were a number of participants who paid
monthly dues and were permitted to use the club library and participate
in various club activities but were excluded from the administration and
direction of the association. Baron von Sommaruga was president of the
organization; Wildner von Maithstein was treasurer; and Hye was
the most influential member. Gradually the membership of the society
increased until by the end of 1847 it reached 211. The members were
"mainly from the judicial world, the high officials, and the military,"
but they also included "writers of all kinds, doctors, and theologians."[51]

---

[46] Reschauer and Smets, *op. cit.,* Vol. I, pp. 28–29; Hartig, *op. cit.,* pp. 114–15.
[47] Srbik, *op. cit.,* Vol. II, p. 237.
[48] Frankl, *op. cit.,* p. 276.
[49] *Ibid.,* pp. 276–77; Friedrich Engel-Jánosi, "Der Wiener juridisch-politische
Leseverein. Seine Geschichte bis zur Märzrevolution," *Mitteilungen des Vereines
für Geschichte der Stadt Wien,* Vol. IV (1923), p. 60. Hereafter cited as "Der
Wiener juridisch-politische Leseverein."
[50] Frankl, *op. cit.,* p. 278.
[51] *Ibid.,* p. 279. See also Engel-Jánosi, "Der Wiener juridisch-politische Leseverein," pp. 60–61.

Originally lawyers and state officials predominated, but as 1848 approached, the much more radical doctors of medicine and littérateurs like Ludwig Frankl, Karl Tausenau, and Ludwig von Löhner became the controlling group.

Although according to its charter the Reading Club was to concern itself mainly with providing reading material for its members, from the outset the club members engaged in much more lively activities. They held frequent banquets, discussed the burning questions of the day, and drafted proposals for reform. Members often wrote articles for the *Grenzboten* and other liberal German papers and helped smuggle copies of them into Austria. The Reading Club was "visited by all important foreigners from almost every nation of Europe, who made known more vividly than books and journals what was happening in Germany, England, and France, and who did not cease to stir up the native minds."[52]

Inevitably the Legal-Political Reading Club got into frequent conflicts with the police and censors. Although at first the censors were rather tolerant about the books and journals they permitted the club to have,[53] they banned many publications the members wanted to read, and every now and then seized prohibited volumes that had found their way into the library.[54] Numerous requests for permission to hold lectures on timely subjects were turned down. The more the club fell under the influence of its liberal elements and the more it began to concern itself with contemporary issues, the more the police began to harass it in petty ways. Nevertheless, since many significant men of state were members and since the club stood under the protection of high officials, the police never dared to close it or even to put it under effective surveillance. In spite of Police Chief Sedlnitzky's fears that the Reading Club was a cradle of revolution, throughout the forties it continued to be an assembling place for caustic critics of the regime who wielded considerable influence over the Viennese middle classes.[55]

Although of less importance than the Legal-Political Reading Club, the Concordia Society, founded in the fall of 1840 by a group of writers, musicians, actors, and artists, was also a rallying point for prominent

[52] Frankl, *op. cit.*, p. 280.

[53] In 1843, for instance, the Austrian censors allowed the club to subscribe to the *Leipziger Zeitung*, the leading newspaper in eastern Germany; and in 1844 two of the prominent liberal French newspapers, the *Constitutionnel* and *Le Siècle*, and even the *Grenzboten* were permitted to the club. Later the *Grenzboten* was prohibited. Engel-Jánosi, "Der Wiener juridisch-politische Leseverein," pp. 63, 65.

[54] *Ibid.*, pp. 65–66.

[55] Frankl, *op. cit.*, p. 283; Minna R. Falk, "Alexander Bach and the Leseverein in the Viennese Revolution of 1848," *Journal of Central European Affairs*, Vol. VIII, No. 2 (July, 1948), p. 140.

opponents of the government. Composers were to bring new songs to the meetings of the group. Painters were to exhibit paintings. Poets were to read new verses. Among the members were some of the most exciting figures in the Viennese cultural world: Grillparzer, Castelli, Johann Nestroy, Ferdinand Georg Waldmüller, A. M. Storch, Joseph Staudigl, Ludwig Löwe, Stephan Endlicher, Anton Schrötter, and Baron Andreas von Baumgartner. Even though solely political expressions were strictly forbidden, many of the meetings were given over to poems, witty epigrams, and plays of a definitely radical tone.[56]

A third organization gradually became a popular center of bourgeois opposition in the later 1840's, the Lower Austrian Manufacturers' Association (*Gewerbeverein*). On December 30, 1838, a group of about a hundred people, most of them engaged in industry and trade, met together to form the society, which was finally approved by the government and allowed to open its doors in January, 1840. Among its members were Count Colloredo-Mannsfeld, Mayor Ignaz Czapka, Baron Doblhoff, Endlicher, Baron von Baumgartner, Friedrich von Hornbostel, Baron Philipp von Krauss, Baron Louis von Pereira, and Count Moritz von Dietrichstein, all of whom were later to play important roles in the Viennese Revolution. The association soon made its influence felt. Not only did it occupy itself with promoting the introduction of new industrial methods, but also it exerted a decided influence on current affairs. The government came to look upon it as a kind of advisory body for "almost all matters dealing with industry. Its opinions were asked for, its criticisms listened to, and its suggestions often accepted."[57]

The association was also a favorite with the liberal intelligentsia of Vienna. The progressive opposition in the Lower Austrian Estates soon came into intimate contact with it, as well as with the Concordia Society and the Legal-Political Reading Club. By 1847 many joint meetings were being held by the liberal estates members and the more radical elements in the three organizations. These gatherings, many of which were held in the salon of Baron von Doblhoff and Eduard von Bauernfeld (who shared living quarters at the time) turned into a kind of extralegal parliament. The participants became the general staff of the political opposition and, as Grillparzer put it, "a powder mill for a coming explosion."[58]

Thus by late 1847 various liberal writers had imbued a large number

[56] Frankl, *op. cit.*, pp. 265–70; Wittner, *op. cit.*, Vol. I, pp. 81–82.
[57] Frankl, *op. cit.*, pp. 294–97.
[58] Quoted in Bibl, *Von Revolution zu Revolution,* p. 67. See also Srbik, *op. cit.*, Vol. II, p. 238; Falk, *op. cit.,* p. 143.

The Development of a Spirit of Opposition

of the intelligentsia with the feeling that radical changes must be made in the structure of the monarchy. In Lombardy and Venetia the populace was rioting. In Hungary the radical Lajos Kossuth was getting the upper hand over the more moderate reformers led by Count István Széchenyi. Galicia was seething with discontent after the suppression of the rebellion of 1846 and the liquidation of the independent republic of Cracow. The South Slavs were becoming increasingly bitter over the attempts of the Hungarians to dominate them. The Czechs were making bolder demands for autonomy, while the German parts of the empire contained many agitators. The stuff out of which revolutions are made was certainly at hand, but as late as February, 1848, no one in Vienna had the faintest inkling of the exciting events to come. As Eduard Bauernfeld observed:[59]

No one is less of a revolutionary than the Viennese. He is a kind of good-natured malcontent, who is ready to oppose anything and everything that is called "government" or "law." "Things must be different and better!" people called out to each other, but no one asked how. People saw that the surrounding nations had pulled off their chains—so they thought something must come out of it for them too! With this, the delight in opposition calmed down, and our Vienna went on pleasantly in its old accustomed life and ways. People listened with delight to the virtuoso Franz Liszt, who at that time was still not wearing a hood and who made music for a "Peter's pence." Banquets were held for Meyerbeer and his "Vielka," and triumphal processions were being planned for Jenny Lind.

[59] *Op. cit.*, p. 272.

III. *The Drift toward Revolution*

On February 29 the first news of the Paris revolution was published in Vienna.[1] Later accounts reported that riots and demonstrations had broken out on the streets of Paris on February 22 and that on February 24 Louis Philippe had been overthrown, a republic proclaimed, and a provisional government set up.

The news electrified the Viennese and unleashed the tensions and hatreds that had been building up. Everywhere there was great excitement and turmoil. At every possible meeting point the educated and well to do gathered to talk politics and give vent to their bitterness against the government, and particularly against Archduke Louis and Metternich,[2] who received anonymous letters full of threats and imprecations.[3] On the morning of February 29 a placard was posted on a pillar of the Kärtner Gate reading: "Within a month Prince Metternich will be overthrown! Long live constitutional Austria!"[4]

Wild rumors spread rapidly from mouth to mouth. Eager to hear the

[1] Princess Melanie Metternich's diary, Vienna, January 1–March 12, 1848, *Aus Metternich's nachgelassenen Papieren,* published by Prince Richard Metternich-Winneburg, ed. and arr. Alfons von Klinkowström, Vol. VII, p. 532; Hübner diary, February 29, 1848, Alexander Grafen von Hübner, *Ein Jahr meines Lebens. 1848–1849,* pp. 10–11; Vitzthum von Eckstädt to his mother, Vienna, February 29, 1848, Carl Friedrich Grafen von Vitzthum von Eckstädt, *Berlin und Wien in den Jahren 1845–1852. Politische Privatbriefe* (hereafter cited throughout as *Berlin und Wien in den Jahren 1845–1852*), p. 73. On February 29 the official *Oesterreichisch-kaiserlich-privilegirte Wiener Zeitung* (hereafter referred to as *Wiener Zeitung*) carried the news about the outbreak of the revolt on the 22d. On March 1 it reported the happenings of February 22 and 23, Guizot's resignation, and Molé's appointment to form a new ministry. On March 2 the *Wiener Zeitung* announced that a republic had been proclaimed in Paris and that a provisional government had been established. No. 60 (February 29, 1848), p. 270; No. 61 (March 1, 1848), p. 274; No. 62 (March 2, 1848), p. 280.

[2] Ernst Violand, *Die sociale Geschichte der Revolution in Oesterreich,* p. 62.

[3] Princess Melanie Metternich's diary, Vienna, January 1–March 12, 1848, *op. cit.,* Vol. VII, p. 537.

[4] Heinrich Reschauer and Moritz Smets, *Das Jahr 1848. Geschichte der Wiener Revolution,* Vol. I, p. 106.

news from Paris, large throngs crowded the coffeehouses to read the latest reports. The excitement soon became widespread. The workers were very much aroused; the petty bourgeoisie were in a state of ferment. Quickly the public bonds fell in value, and large crowds of people began hurrying to the banks to exchange their bank notes for gold and silver coin or to withdraw their savings. Within a few days the price of meat went up 2 kreutzer.[5]

Tidings of the demonstrations in Germany and Hungary increased the excitement to fever heat. On February 29 the government of Baden, terrified by mass demonstrations that had suddenly broken out in Mannheim and Karlsruhe, promised to institute trial by jury, create a national guard, and guarantee freedom of the press. At Stuttgart on March 2 a petition was presented to the King demanding that he convene a German assembly, unfetter the press, establish trial by jury, grant freedom of assembly, guarantee religious freedom, and equalize taxation. Similar demands were made in Hessen-Nassau. On March 5 a group of fifty-one well-known German liberals met at Heidelberg to make preliminary arrangements for a national assembly to draw up a constitution for a free and united Germany. On March 6 in Saxony the King was forced to call the estates into session and dismiss the hated minister, Falkenstein. On the same day the King of Bavaria convoked a meeting of the estates for the 16th to enact the reforms for which the crowds were clamoring.

Three days earlier, on March 3, Lajos Kossuth had made a fiery speech in the Magyar Diet at Pressburg, denouncing the policies of the Habsburg regime. He demanded that a constitutional government be immediately inaugurated in Hungary and that far-reaching changes be made in the government in Vienna, since it would be impossible for Hungary to maintain a constitutional government as long as the rulers of the rest of the monarchy strongly opposed all constitutional principles and a state council that worshiped the principles of absolutism directed the common affairs of the country. As long as "a corrupting puff of wind that benumbs our senses and paralyzes the flight of our spirit comes to us from the charnel house of the cabinet at Vienna," the Fatherland would be afflicted with the "curse of a suffocating breath." The bureaucracy in the capital was inexorably leading the empire to dissolution. An unnatural political system could be maintained for a while, for "between the patience of the people and their despair there

---

[5] Vitzthum von Eckstädt to his mother, Vienna, March 5, 1848, Vitzthum von Eckstädt, *op. cit.*, pp. 75–76; William H. Stiles, *Austria in 1848–49*, Vol. I, p. 102.

lies a long way," but in time there would come a moment of supreme danger. Recent events had shown that this moment had arrived.[6]

For three hundred years the people had been unable to extend constitutional government in Hungary because imperial absolutism had kept them in a state of subservience. But now they must substitute a free constitution for bayonet rule. In Hungary the people must hasten to establish a national government, independent of all foreign influence and entrusted with carrying out the reforms necessary to put the country on a constitutional basis.[7]

After receiving the full text of Kossuth's speech in Vienna on the evening of March 4, the Hungarian journalist Franz Pulszky immediately translated it into German and informed his acquaintances about it. They in turn took translated copies of the speech to the Legal-Political Reading Club, and from there the news of Kossuth's speech spread throughout Vienna.[8] Soon crowds of people were shouting their jubilation over Kossuth's ringing denunciation of the Habsburg regime.[9]

The reports of Kossuth's speech and the revolutionary rumblings in south Germany brought a new flood of rumors of impending bankruptcy that terrified commercial and business groups. Kossuth was rumored to have said that state bankruptcy was unavoidable and that the Hungarian Diet had prohibited the circulation of Austrian bank notes in Hungary. The crowds rushing to the banks to exchange paper money now increased to a great throng.[10] In many inns and shops proprietors refused to accept bank notes.

As the populace became more and more agitated by the ever increasing reports of revolutionary disturbances, various liberal elements in Vienna summoned courage to demand reforms from the government, and many individuals and groups hastened to draft petitions, obtain signatures for them, and send them to the authorities.

---

[6] Franz Pulszky, *Mein Zeit, mein Leben,* Vol. II, pp. 38–39, 42.

[7] *Ibid.,* pp. 43–47; Ludwig von Wirkner, *Meine Erlebnisse. Blätter aus dem Tagebuche meines öffentlichen Wirkens vom Jahre 1825–1852* (hereafter cited as *Meine Erlebnisse*), pp. 210–11.

[8] Pulszky, *op. cit.,* Vol. II, pp. 50–51.

[9] Hans Blum, *Die deutsche Revolution 1848–49. Eine Jubiläumsgabe für das deutsche Volk,* p. 149.

[10] Princess Melanie Metternich's diary, Vienna, January 1–March 12, 1848, *op. cit.,* Vol. VII, p. 534. A study of the official international exchange rates in the February and March issues of the *Wiener Zeitung* shows that the rush on the banks had no great effect on the value of the florin in the international money market. Before February 29 the value of £1 varied between 10 and 10.3 florins; on March 3, £1 was valued at 9.58 florins; on March 8, 10 florins; on March 12, 10.5 florins; and on March 17, 10.7 florins. The fluctuating relationship between the value of the French franc and the florin was about the same during this period.

On March 7 the Lower Austrian Secretary and Book Examiner, J. B. Freiberger, entreated Count Kolowrat to use his influence to restore "the confidence, love, and gratitude of the great masses of people in the monarchy" by persuading the government immediately to announce the abolition of the stamp tax and the sales tax on the "necessities of life." In addition, the Emperor must forthwith proclaim the freedom of the press and issue orders that henceforth all appointments and promotions in the civil service would be made only on a merit and seniority basis.[11]

The Book Dealers' Association of Vienna bestirred itself to demand the immediate abolition of censorship. As early as 1845 a group of Austrian writers, scholars, and artists had petitioned for a substantial relaxation of the censorship system,[12] but Metternich had refused even to receive the petition. In 1847 the Bohemian Estates had also unsuccessfully appealed to the Emperor for the same concession. Now the Book Dealers' Association, taking advantage of the general excitement, brought pressure on the government to grant freedom of publication. On March 8 representatives of the organization were granted a private audience with the Emperor at which they voiced their complaints about the intolerable oppressiveness of the censorship. On March 11 they sent a petition to the Lower Austrian Estates urging them to use their influence with the Emperor to induce him as quickly as possible to issue orders that all published works except "political or incendiary pamphlets" might be freely sold in Austria and that no foreign or domestic books would be confiscated.[13]

On March 4, under the leadership of Löhner and Bach, a group of doctors, writers, merchants, state officials, and other liberals, most of whom were members of the Legal-Political Reading Club, drafted a proclamation castigating the Habsburg rule and setting forth the radical

[11] The full text of this memorandum appears in Reschauer and Smets, *op. cit.,* Vol. I, pp. 128–29.

[12] The list of signers of this memorial, as printed in the German newspapers, was headed by Franz Grillparzer. Grillparzer insisted, however, that his was the third, and not the first, signature on the memorial and that Aulic Councilor Hammer and Endlicher had signed the petition before he did. He maintained that after Metternich expressed his disapproval of the petition Hammer and Endlicher erased their names from the top of the petition and inserted them in an inconspicuous place in the middle of the list, thus leaving Grillparzer's name at the head of the list. It was the altered list, Grillparzer insisted, that was sent to the foreign press. See Franz Grillparzer, "Erinnerungen aus dem Jahre 1848," *Grillparzers sämtliche Werke,* ed. with introduction by August Sauer, Vol. XX, pp. 192–94.

[13] "Petition of the Book Dealers' Association to the Lower Austrian Estates," Vienna, March 11, 1848, Reschauer and Smets, *op. cit.,* Vol. I, p. 149 n.

program of the self-styled "party of progress." The opening sentence of the proclamation reads:[14] "For sixty years we have suffered the oppression of an absolute government! For sixty years the 'paternal solicitude' of absolutism has consumed our property and our very lifeblood. For sixty years we have been under the yoke of despotic officials, the power of the bayonet, and the public and secret tools of the police!" The proclamation went on to say that during this period the spirits of the Viennese had been "enslaved" and every demand for justice "punished with imprisonment or death." All classes had suffered from the economic malpractices of the government and thousands had been condemned to starvation, while the credit of the state had been totally undermined, bankruptcy was threatening, and the Austrian people were standing "on the very brink of a deep, immeasurable abyss!"[15]

Responsibility for this catastrophe lay with the malicious enemies of the people who must be destroyed, not with the sword but "with the force of truth." The people must "drive the Louis Philippes of the Austrian state out of the ministries and from the councils charged with our welfare and with our most sacred interests." They must "charge the traitors of the Fatherland with high treason against the Emperor and the empire and submit them to the righteous judgment of our monarch and the contempt of the Austrian people." Above all, the proclamation continues,[16] it

is our most sacred duty, as good, honorable subjects of our Emperor, to free him from his and our enemies: his present counselors. Fellow Austrians! It is our most sacred duty to remove the barriers that until now have prevented an understanding between us, the loyal citizens, and our noble, beloved monarch—those inflexible paper barriers which until now have kept the heart of our Emperor sealed against the entreaties and complaints of the people.

Fellow Austrians! It is our finest and greatest task to restore confidence between the sovereign and his people and love and fidelity between the Emperor and us after they, to our deepest regret, have so long been shattered by the pernicious statesmanship of a regime hostile to the people.

Fellow Austrians! The time is now past when we can tranquilly fold our hands. The present time demands all our energy and all the courage and prudence of the citizens. Let us once and for all throw off the insult which our German brothers beyond our borders have so often hurled at us: that

[14] Published during the second week in March by the Leipzig bookdealer Ernst Keil, in an extra supplement of his *Leuchtthurm*. The complete text appears in Reschauer and Smets, *op. cit.*, Vol. I, pp. 123–27.

[15] *Ibid.*, p. 123.

[16] *Ibid.*, pp. 125–26.

we are not serious people but jolly revelers, not thinking people but good-natured subjects, not brave citizens but slaves parading in chains. Let us once and for all show that the welfare of our country means more to us than our daily bread, that not only our stomachs but our hearts and minds are in the right place, and that we are just as strong in freedom, justice, and the intellect as we are in love, wine, and song. Let us show our German brothers that the unabated efforts of our previous government to break the strength and the sound character of the Austrians were all in vain, and that we will, with enthusiasm and with unrelenting courage, carry to a victorious end the fight for the rights and liberties of the people which was begun by the Germans along the Rhine. Let us be worthy of ourselves, of a free citizenry, of independence of thought and will. Let us be men—men in every sense of the word!

But the people must act immediately. One "single moment of indecision and timorousness will lead us to ruin," to "sure political death." All Austrians must stand together in this great moment of danger, "unconquerable against all obstacles." To ward off inevitable ruin in this supreme hour of history, the people must immediately inaugurate the following reforms: [17]

1. *Ministries with definite portfolios.* Change and reduce the number of court offices and give them definitely prescribed spheres of action.
2. *A thorough reform of the entire administrative system.* Self-government in the communes and districts through free election of communal councils and district authorities. Just and equal distribution of the taxes on all classes of citizens. The right for everyone to acquire any kind of landed property. Abolition of the lottery and monopolies (on tobacco, salt, etc.). Freedom of trade. Credit institutions for agriculture and industry. Reduction of the number of officials.
3. *Provincial estates.* (*a*) Enlargement of the estates system by bringing in the middle classes and the peasants to represent their interest. (*b*) Restoration and expansion of the rights of the estates: consultation and advice on proposed legislation; a statement of annual income and expenditures. The right to approve and refuse taxes. (*c*) The transactions of the estates to be public.
4. *A united diet* to be called into session annually to give advice on laws and decrees that concern the whole state.
5. *Public court procedures.* Abolition of the present secret, inquisitorial courts. Defense of the parties concerned by attorneys of their own choosing. Delivery of the accused person to the competent judicial authorities within twenty-four hours.
6. *Abolition of censorship.* Granting of a press law. By freedom of the

[17] *Ibid.,* pp. 126–27.

press is understood the hereditary right of man to be able to impart his thoughts in a nonmutilated form. Freedom of the press is the only way to disseminate intellectual and moral information to all classes of citizens by means of good periodicals and books, to clarify the concepts of each individual concerning his position in the state, to watch over the activities of the authorities, to call the attention of the government to abuses in the administration, and thereby to bring about complete confidence and harmony between the authorities and the citizens. The criminal law or an appropriate press law offers protection against attacks on religion or against the head of the state, as well as against calumny and scandal.

7. *Religious toleration.* The abolition of all decrees suppressing individual creeds.

8. *Limitation of police despotism.* Personal liberty for the citizens. Written orders for arrest. Abolition of the political spy system. Preservation of privacy of correspondence.

9. *Improvements in education and in public instruction.* Abolition of the stultifying methods of instruction in the normal and elementary schools. Complete revision of the present plan of study. Abolition of denominational schools. Academic freedom and removal of prescribed courses of study in the universities.

10. *Universal arming of the people.* Actual use of the existing Civic Guard for guard service and to maintain order and security. Every citizen capable of bearing arms is to be enrolled and trained in the citizens' militia to protect the state against domestic unrest and insurrections and against foreign enemies. Changing the standing army to universal military service and the militia.

11. *Universal right to petition.* Every citizen is to have the right to bring his wishes and requests through his estates representative to the knowledge of the provincial diet or the united diet or to the imperial throne itself.

The program of the "party of progress" contained the most radical demands made by any group in the period immediately preceding the March revolution. However, the views expressed in it represented the opinions of one group of private citizens, not those of any official body or organized club. Of an entirely different nature was the memorandum inspired by Karl von Kleyle and signed by thirty-three liberal members of the Lower Austrian Estates on March 3. This memorandum was the profession of faith of the liberal estates members—a group to which the malcontents in the Austrian capital were turning in ever increasing numbers. The estates were a legal body supposedly reflecting public opinion in Lower Austria. Any memoir drawn up by members of that group was bound to have great influence on the populace of Vienna.

In this memorandum the estates members asserted that conditions

The Drift toward Revolution

in the monarchy were so serious that they would lead to ruin if they were not immediately corrected. The peasants were still burdened with onerous services and duties. The cities and local communities were still completely dependent on the bureaucracy, and the provincial estates had become mere pawns. The education of the people had come to a standstill, and the press was as muzzled as it had been for half a century. Taxes still bore heavily on the poor, customs barriers still separated the parts of the monarchy, and the deficit in the state finances was increasing alarmingly. The pressure of the cost of living weighed "heavily upon all classes of the population and in all parts of the monarchy. Distrust in commercial and industrial circles" was "ruining private credit" and had "already created great losses in capital everywhere." The Galicians had been filled with hatred ever since their rebellion was crushed in 1846, and in "the Italian provinces a burning hatred [was] flaring up against the Austrian government." The memorandum continued:[18]

Under these circumstances the estates must stand at the monarch's side to advise him. They must not waver on account of the disquieting doubt whether or not there may still be a way of warding off the approaching ruin or the petty apprehension of seeing their honorable aims misinterpreted. As loyal subjects of their Emperor and as good citizens of their Fatherland they must deliberate over the means to help and must express their opinions.

The undersigned members of the estates can see salvation only in the return of confidence in the government on the part of the whole populace. Distrust between individual classes and nationalities and between the people and the government appears to be the perennial source of ruin. If, in the place of fear of arrogance and suppression, we know that there is a legal code that assures true worth in the state to all persons, whether high or low, poor or rich, and to all nations in the empire, then all classes of people, strengthened in their love for the common Fatherland, will be ready to risk life and property for its preservation. Then, with their magnificent aid, the financial distress can give no cause for worry, and all endeavors to separate from a politically sound and great state will be folly.

Because of the immeasurable difficulties of the situation, only a patriotic and enlightened assembly can be expected, after calm and thorough deliberation, to give salutary advice about what political reforms are necessary to create that bond of confidence which will unite the parts of the empire now striving to separate from each other into a strong entity.

The undersigned members of the estates, therefore, request the most honorable Rules Committee in a constitutional manner to bring this im-

---

[18] The complete text appears in *ibid.*, pp. 131–32; and in Maximilian Bach, *Geschichte der Wiener Revolution im Jahre 1848,* pp. 165–69.

portant and urgent matter before the next meeting of the Lower Austrian Estates for consideration and ratification.

The liberal members of the estates did not limit their activities to formulating a memorandum but also persuaded other groups to draft petitions. One of the most liberal of their group, Count Colloredo-Mannsfeld, was president of the Lower Austrian Manufacturers' Association; other liberal estates members also had close connections with prominent members of the association, such as Rudolph Arthaber and Friedrich Hornbostel. After consulting with several members of the estates and with Colloredo-Mannsfeld, Arthaber drafted a petition to the Emperor to be proposed to the Manufacturers' Association at its regular meeting on March 6. Count Kolowrat and Archduke Francis Charles, the latter the patron of the organization, were present at the meeting, at which Arthaber read the petition aloud: [19]

Your Majesty!

Frightful events have taken place in Western Europe. All credit has reached its lowest level, all trade is paralyzed, and the greatest danger is imminent. Only a close, intimate union of the government with the estates and citizens, only a close, intimate union of Austria with the interests of the common German Fatherland, and only candor can again win the old, so often proven, confidence.

In this time of distress the most obedient Manufacturers' Association of Lower Austria ventures to assure Your Majesty that all its members are ready to sacrifice life and property for the hereditary imperial house, because they are convinced that Your Majesty will choose only the wisest and most expedient means to ward off this threatening evil.

Your Majesty's
most loyal and obedient Lower Austrian Manufacturers'
Association

Graciously accepting the petition, Archduke Francis Charles promised to deliver it to the Emperor. Since no one had expected that the address would be so favorably received by the Emperor's own brother, the applause that greeted his words of acceptance was tremendous. Many members all but wept for joy because the Archduke had promised to be their champion.[20]

In the Lower Austrian Estates the opponents of the government drafted still another petition. Again it was Karl von Kleyle who induced

---

[19] As printed in *Wiener Zeitung*, No. 78 (March 18, 1848), p. 351.

[20] Joseph Alexander Freiherrn von Helfert, *Geschichte der österreichischen Revolution*, pp. 233–34; [Franz Graf von Hartig], *Genesis der Revolution*, pp. 134–36; Reschauer and Smets, *op. cit.*, Vol. I, pp. 134–37; Bach, *op. cit.*, pp. 171–72.

The Drift toward Revolution

Eduard Bauernfeld and Alexander Bach to draw up a petition to be signed by as many inhabitants of Vienna as could be persuaded to add their names to it on short notice. The petition was then to be sent to the estates in the hope that it would be useful in persuading the more conservative members to join the reform movement. Bauernfeld wrote the first draft of the petition. Bach revised it and showed it to several friends and invited them to meet at his home to decide whether or not it should be circulated for signatures. On the evening of March 8, after objections were raised to various parts of the petition, Bach and Bauernfeld agreed to revise it and to present the changed copy to the group for consideration the next evening. The revised petition read as follows:[21]

To the most honorable Estates of the Archduchy of Austria below the Enns, to be delivered to the Honorable Rules Committee of the Estates.

For a number of years every true friend of the Fatherland has ardently desired, and the necessity therefor has been loudly expressed by many in speech and writing, that our beautiful and powerful Austria should enter upon the path of peaceful and real progress.

The recent events in western Europe make this demand appear all the more urgent and pressing, because they might become dangerous to world peace, as well as to the credit of the state, and the security of property, order, and justice in every realm. What is happening in Germany at this moment to protect the country from possible misfortune and to defend and strengthen it against the outside and the inside is known to everyone. Everybody is at the same time convinced that Austria, whose ruling family has worn the German imperial crown for centuries, can win true salvation only by close adherence to German interests and German policies. If the citizens of Austria feel themselves forced above everything else to declare their eternal love and loyalty to the illustrious imperial house, they at the same time consider it their sacred duty to suggest openly and freely the measures which in their opinion alone are suitable under such threatening circumstances to give new strength and new support to the dynasty, as well as to the whole Fatherland.

These measures are: the immediate publication of the state budget; the periodical convocation of a united assembly of the estates, representing all lands of the monarchy, as well as all classes and interests of the people, with the right to approve taxes and to control the financial administration, as well as to take part in legislation; the establishment of a legal status for the press through the introduction of libel laws; the establishment of the principle of publicity in the administration of justice and in the whole government; the granting of a municipal and communal charter suited to the times, and on the basis of it the representation of the agricultural, in-

---

[21] As published in the *Wiener Zeitung,* No. 78 (March 18, 1848), p. 351.

dustrial, commercial, and intellectual elements which are imperfectly or not at all represented in the existing estates.

The estates—even if in their present form they do not completely represent the whole country—have been convened, as the constitutional organ for the needs of the people, to carry our requests to our good monarch.

The undersigned request that the honorable estates of Lower Austria will consider the proposed measures in their next session and will send the appropriate proposals to the all-highest throne.

Vienna, March 9, 1848.

Everyone present at Bach's home approved and signed the petition and promised to obtain as many signatures as possible the next day from friends and acquaintances. Copies were left in the rooms of the Legal-Political Reading Club, the Manufacturers' Association, the Concordia Society, and elsewhere, and a large number of people signed them. Other copies were taken to bookshops, factories, and other places of business. In defiance of the police, Bach himself took a copy and rode from street to street, soliciting signatures. In this way a few thousand signatures were obtained, including those of some of the most important personages in the city. On March 11 the signed petition was taken to the Rules Committee, which was meeting in the Landhaus, with the request that the committee pass it on to the estates.

Considered from a present-day perspective, the demands of the Viennese radicals expressed in these petitions were surprisingly moderate. The petition for the abolition of monopolies and for freedom of trade is mild in comparison with the position then held by laissez faire theorists in western Europe. Included are the usual entreaties for freedom of the press, speech, and religion; but such typical "liberal" demands as freedom from search and the right of public assembly are missing. The hesitant appeals for provincial assemblies and a united diet, with members chosen by traditional Austrian, not modern democratic, methods and with the limited prerogatives of approving taxes and the budget and sharing in the legislation, are certainly a far cry from the demands of modern liberals. Also, it must be remembered that in the Austria of 1848 the person of the Emperor was still considered sacred. Even the most radical Viennese were unswerving in their loyalty to the Habsburg ruler. Not the Emperor but the bureaucracy was held responsible for the malfeasances of the government. To the liberals, Emperor Ferdinand remained the good-hearted, beloved father of the Austrian people whose every command was to be obeyed. Moreover, while the political reforms requested by the Viennese liberals were numerous, they could doubtless have been granted without disrupting the traditional monarchist rule of the Habsburg government.

The same can be said of the demands of the students—the most turbulent and revolutionary group in the capital on the eve of the March revolution. The students had been discontented for a long time. Many of them were living in wretched poverty, unable to afford warm food for weeks at a time and subsisting mainly on bread and water. Many lived in dark, damp, unheated basement rooms while they starved their way through the university with such funds as they could pick up from private tutoring. The Jewish students, whose lot was the worst of all, could usually not depend on even this meager income because the prevailing religious prejudices barred them from such employment. In Vienna in the forties the students formed a true intellectual proletariat.[22]

Want and misery were only one of the problems. Often the students were roughly treated by their professors, some of whom were gruff and coarse and totally ignorant of existing political and economic conditions.[23] Since only too frequently their instructors were uninformed or afraid to speak freely, it was inevitable that many a curious student turned to the few secret political societies[24] or to the subversive literature of the day. According to Anton Füster,[25] the radical professor of theology at the University of Vienna and later the chaplain of the Viennese Academic Legion, the Viennese students

read with indescribable pleasure the prohibited writings of men permeated with a spirit of freedom. There were clubs among the students of the University of Vienna that had the acquisition of prohibited books as their aim. The students were assessed according to their means so that these writings, most of which were very costly, could be purchased and circulated among the members. The academic laws were Draconian in regard to prohibited books. Whoever circulated such writings among his fellow-students or even read them by himself without telling others about them was punished

[22] Anton Füster, *Memoiren vom März 1848 bis Juli 1849. Beitrag zur Geschichte der Wiener Revolution* (hereafter cited throughout as *Memoiren vom März 1848 bis Juli 1849*), Vol. I, pp. 45–46.

[23] *Ibid.*, pp. 10–15.

[24] Max Doblinger, "Der burschenschaftliche Gedanke auf Österreichs Hochschulen vor 1859," *Quellen und Darstellungen zur Geschichte der Burschenschaft und der deutschen Einheitsbewegung*, ed. Herman Haupt, Vol. VIII, pp. 94–95.

[25] Füster, *op. cit.*, Vol. I, pp. 9–10. See also Paul Molisch, "Die Wiener akademische Legion," *Archiv für österreichische Geschichte*, Vol. CX, Part I (1924), pp. 32–36; Priscilla Robertson, *Revolutions of 1848: A Social History*, p. 201.

by being excluded from all educational institutions in the monarchy. In spite of this, they were generally read. In the University of Vienna they even circulated from bench to bench in the lecture rooms. The liberal *Gränzboten* especially was read for entertainment during the tedious lecture hours. Many students stinted themselves to save the money to join the above-named clubs. This explains the longing for freedom fully enough.

Especially active in voicing their discontent were the students and faculty members of the medical division, which provided several of the prominent leaders of the March revolution. Believing that medicine had no direct relation to politics, the government had relaxed its restrictions on medical instruction and its supervision of student life to a degree unknown to the other faculties of the university. Precisely on account of this comparative freedom, many of the professors had unique opportunities to make caustic comments on political and social conditions. Furthermore, the influence of the medical professors over their students was greater than elsewhere because in the Viennese General Hospital the faculty and students were in constant association.[26]

The students in the medical school took the first steps to draft a petition in behalf of all university students. On the evening of March 7 a group of medical students belonging to the Arminia and Liberalia societies, who were gathered at the "Blue Star" inn drinking wine and beer, suddenly decided to take the incentive in drafting a student petition. The next morning one of them spoke to some of his friends among the law students and learned that they had had a similar idea. Later that day, after the medical students had drafted a petition, they invited the technology and law students to a special meeting on Thursday evening, March 9, to decide which petition to accept. On the 9th the medical students' petition and two others were read at a meeting of about forty students. The first was turned down because it was too bold. The second was considered too humble and too vague. The third, "composed in an official style" and "peremptory and manly in tone," was chosen.[27]

All the participants in the meeting promised to persuade trustworthy members of the various student organizations to sign the petition. On the evening of March 11 another meeting was held to settle the last details of the final draft, which was to be presented to the assembled

---

[26] Füster, *op. cit.*, Vol. I, pp. 16–17; Josephine Goldmark, *Pilgrims of '48*, pp. 23–24.

[27] Ludwig August Frankl, *Erinnerungen*, ed. Stefan Hock, pp. 320–21; Doblinger, *op. cit.*, pp. 101–102.

The Drift toward Revolution

student body at the religious services the next day.[28] After a long discussion, the following was adopted by the group:[29]

Imperial Majesty!

A great event has shaken France and Europe and is endangering the general peace.

In such stormy times the students of Vienna are confidently approaching the throne of Your Majesty to express their willingness at every moment cheerfully to follow the call of Your Majesty to protect our common Fatherland against every enemy, whether from the West or the East.

Imperial Majesty!

Possessed of the conviction that freedom is the strongest bond between a prince and the people and that it makes the latter capable of and willing to do great deeds and to undergo hard trials with courage and persistence, the undersigned students of Vienna believe they are fulfilling the sacred duty of loyal citizens by respectfully expressing their opinion to Your Majesty that the realization of this freedom is a pressing necessity in such a critical state of world affairs. They therefore beseech Your Majesty to accord to Your people:

Freedom of the press and of speech in order to establish mutual understanding and confidence between the prince and the people; improvement of public instruction and especially the introduction of freedom in teaching and learning; equality of the various religious confessions in regard to civil rights; public procedures; universal representation of the people and, over and above, [universal representation] of the German parts of the country in the Confederation.

Imperial Majesty!

We have always been accustomed to look upon you as the friend and protector of the people, and now we look forward with confidence to your resolutions and await them loyally and respectfully. Your Majesty's most obedient students of Vienna.

On the night of March 11 the air was full of foreboding. The projected mass petition was no longer a secret. Both the secret police and the university authorities had learned about it. Furthermore, the professors had been ordered to be present at the religious services the next morning to use their influence in subduing the students.[30]

The next morning great excitement prevailed at the university. At

---

[28] Frankl, *op. cit.*, pp. 321–22; Molisch, *op. cit.*, pp. 38–40; Doblinger, *op. cit.*, p. 102; Adolf Pichler, *Das Sturmjahr. Erinnerungen aus den März- und Oktobertagen 1848* (hereafter cited throughout as *Das Sturmjahr*), pp. 2–3.
[29] As published in the *Wiener Zeitung*, No. 80 (March 20, 1848), p. 361.
[30] Pichler, *op. cit.*, p. 3; Füster, *op. cit.*, Vol. I, pp. 21–22; Molisch, *op. cit.*, p. 46.

an early hour students from all the institutions of higher learning in the city, including the Polytechnical Institute, gathered in the Aula, the great hall of the university.[31] The events were described by August Silberstein, one of the active student participants in the revolution, as follows:[32]

The meeting place was the university; the time, morning—March 12— 8:00 A.M.

What goings-on on March 12! The most motley groups, the liveliest discourses, the boisterousness, and otherwise a mixture of restless activity and trepidation—a dress rehearsal for the great movement. In the hall were tables and writing material; the signatures grew from minute to minute.

The dreadful news of the petition had already come from "good sources" to the fine ears of the highly praised police, who had not lost their spying noses. Through the hallowed hand of His Excellency the Chief Chancellor, Count von Inzaghi (once alive), [the police] decreed that the professors were to assemble in the consistory building (vis-à-vis the university) at nine o'clock in the morning of the said March 12 to restrain the godless youth and warn them against the criminal undertaking of beseeching for something new and putting their signatures on it. The professors did what they were told to do. They sat down around the green table around which they had so often sat in order just to sit there.

The professorial dignity in Vienna now had something of the holiness of a "mummified faculty." Conscious of their glorious sanctimoniousness, they sat here and waited patiently with festive countenances for the moment when they needed only to show their lofty faces to the criminal youth in order to make them fly away like chaff in front of a mighty hurricane, like light quicksand before the violent sirocco.

However, the number of criminal youth grew and grew. They filled the hall. They filled the university square. They filled the neighboring streets. Dreadful! Several servants who had been sent out came back with the sad news that they were in danger of being beaten. The professors stared at each other. Not even the school service uniforms gave protection. Something important had happened. It was a frightful moment!

Entrance into the big hall was refused the youth. So they pushed against the doors, and the doors to the hall burst open!

The doors to the hall burst open. The doors flew wide open. The doors

[31] *Oestreich's Befreiungstage! oder der 13. 14. und 15. März 1848 in Wien. Geschildert von Augenzungen. Mit allen bezüglichen Proklamationen und den wichtigsten Flugschriften. Erste censurfreie Broschüre* (hereafter cited throughout as *Oestreich's Befreiungstage*), p. 7.
[32] August Silberstein, *Geschichte der Aula. Die Wiener Universität und die akademische Legion vom März bis Ende October 1848* (hereafter cited throughout as *Geschichte der Aula*), pp. 14–18.

to the hall of light were open! Broken was the fortress which shut up the holy of holies, and the youth came in, inspired with freedom, shining with freedom. Their home was here. This was thenceforth the soil of their Fatherland, their new homeland, their rebirth!

> We enter it drunken with joy,
> The sanctuary of the heavenly!

And for the first time enthusiastic speeches resounded from the platform whose privilege was pedantry and "peace is the first duty of citizens."

The halls were henceforth dedicated and hallowed. A new god had taken up his abode. The first divine service was festive and noisy enough! The professors heard this. By all means we do not wish to damn them all together. Old liberalism also had its coryphaei here. At that time Hye and Endlicher, the former a professor of natural law and the latter of botany, enjoyed the respect and love of the students. They were sent as mediators, commanders, and messengers of peace. They were to pour oil on the troubled waters.

And Hye summoned all his eloquence. His lungs exerted themselves a hundred times with the word "legality," and the "legal ground" was tread so flat by him that without fail it would have become a new sixth continent if the youth had let him get away with it. But all the ranting and all the entreaties and fatherly warnings were in vain. First [let's talk] about signing in general; then about signing the names. A petition signed by "the students of the university" was needed. The signatures grew rapidly, like the rising clouds. The stormy air permeated everybody. The old soil of legitimacy was covered with the glowing lava of enthusiasm, and rich new seeds sprouted quickly out of soil that had doubled its strength.

The professors accomplished only one thing. The petition was not to be taken directly to the Emperor's living quarters by the youth but was first to be directed to the sewer of the government through the channel of professorial hands.

This mediation was accepted with the stormy, loud calls: "But still today! And to the Emperor!" The students gave orders to the professors for the first time. A topsy-turvy world was beginning. Pedants tore their hair and thought that the world was going to pieces or that the whole youth must receive a "2" in the next examination. Those most informed about the times were very happy and celebrated the occasion. Had the light or reflection of dawn finally broken through the dismal sky? Will morning actually come? This question made many a heart uneasy. It was soon to be decided!—

And at eleven o'clock in the forenoon the professors stood in the chambers of Councilor of State Kollowrat [*sic*], next to Metternich the most powerful man, to solicit an audience with the Emperor. They were sent to Archduke Louis, the archenemy of everything new, Metternich's ideological twin, Francis's dear brother, and the third of the holy trinity, "Metternich,

Francis, and Lewis!"—He was the chief leader of the Council of State. In fact, he was himself the Council of State, for if the other gentlemen did not propose worse measures than he already used, they needed only to nod (if they were really asked) and the state was advised, their 30,000 florins (convention money) yearly salary was earned, and their life's task was fulfilled.

This piece of furniture and indestructible heirloom from olden times was naturally highly displeased with the proposal and gave no hope of an audience. Carried along by the vortex of the times, Hye felt his heart warmed by his contact with the youth. He was liberal enough so he might still think honorably. He thawed out and argued for the necessity of reform and the urgency of an audience with various arguments and with all manner of eloquence.

Endlicher, who was often in close contact with the Emperor, who at times occupied himself with botany and through this became attached to the professor, called attention to his love and devotion to the imperial house and then openly declared that Metternich and his system were hated. Metternich's intimate friend was very indignant and dismissed the deputation very coldly and ungraciously in an imperial and royal archducal humor. Unlike all previous deputations, the deputies did not please his councilor-of-state-like heart through abject, shameless fawning.

We do not know whether "Emperor" Louis wanted to inflict torture, fire, or the sword for these unpleasant utterances about "Emperor" Metternich. We also do not know what secret powers influenced the "actual" Emperor at that time. (We can only suspect what these powers were and will point them out later on.) At 4:00 P.M. the deputation received the news in their homes that the Emperor would give them an audience at six o'clock in the evening and that he was ready to receive the emissaries of the university.

The audience was given. The usual court phrases, which made one neither cold nor warm, were rattled off, and the deputation departed in possession of a "deliberation" and with the knowledge that they had stepped on the imperial carpets. That was all!

The more cynical students had anticipated that the deputation would be turned away with nice but vague and meaningless phrases. When the deputies returned to the university to report the results of their mission, the students broke into derisive laughter. The failure of their first move made them all the more determined not to give up. On the same evening at another assembly in the great hall, it was decided that the next morning the students would march en masse to the Landhaus, where the Lower Austrian Estates were to begin their session. By their presence there they hoped to encourage the estates to bring pressure on the government to grant the concessions the liberals wanted. This time the students were determined not to allow the professors or any other group to talk them out of staging a mass demonstration.[33]

The Austrian police did not fail to report to the higher authorities all that was happening. There was no doubt in Police Chief Sedlnitzky's mind that public dissatisfaction was reaching a critical point. His admonitions were not without effect. Greatly alarmed by the thought that the revolution might spread to Austria, several government officials and members of the imperial family sought to influence the Emperor to make concessions. On March 4 Kolowrat's friend Archduke John went so far as to advise the monarch to make far-reaching constitutional changes and dismiss Metternich immediately.

Archduke John was not the only member of the imperial family who was clamoring for Metternich's removal from the government. Archduchess Sophie, who had long before fallen under the spell of Metternich's archrival, Kolowrat, also used her influence to stir up resentment against the Chancellor. After the Paris revolution and Kossuth's inflammatory speech in Pressburg, she became more convinced than ever that Metternich's highly conservative policies alone were responsible for the bad state of public opinion and loudly urged his dismissal. In Archduke John and also in her husband, Archduke Francis Charles, who had long been accustomed to defer to her will, she found ready confederates. The Palatine of Hungary, Archduke Stephen, also joined her camp and exerted his influence in Vienna to have Metternich removed.[34]

Metternich was fully aware of the shortcomings in the government, but foreign, not domestic, affairs had been his main sphere of activity, and, contrary to public belief, his influence over internal affairs was somewhat limited.[35] They were the domain of his rival, Count Kolowrat—the favorite of the Austrian liberals. Moreover, even on the eve of 1848 Metternich remained adamant in his conviction that the *status quo* must not be disrupted overnight. As he told Baron von Hübner when the news of the Paris revolution reached Vienna: "Everyone tells me that something must happen. That is entirely right. But what? Our monarchy is an old house. We cannot break through the walls,

---

[33] *Oestreich's Befreiungstage*, p. 8; Pichler, *op. cit.*, p. 4.

[34] Heinrich Ritter von Srbik, *Metternich, der Staatsman und der Mensch*, Vol. II, pp. 261–65; Grillparzer, *op. cit.*, p. 199; Bach, *op. cit.*, pp. 188–89.

[35] Note, for instance, Metternich's conversation with Baron Alexander von Hübner on February 29, 1848, as reported in Hübner's diary, Vienna, February 29, 1848, Hübner, *op. cit.*, pp. 11–14. See also Metternich's "Autobiographische Denkschrift," in *Aus Metternich's nachgelassenen Papieren*, Vol. VII, pp. 619–20.

open new windows and doors, and undertake great internal changes without danger."[36] Though Metternich was not unalterably opposed to change, he insisted that reforms must be gradual and well ordered. He saw salvation neither in immobility nor in upheaval but recommended that popular agitation be quieted by granting more rights to the provincial estates and convening a united diet in Vienna, composed of representatives from all the estates except those in Hungary. At the same time, he insisted that the state must proceed energetically against any popular uprising.[37]

The President of the Council of State, Archduke Louis, was far more obdurate. He emphatically refused to bend before the storm and insisted that the agitation must be dealt with firmly by putting Vienna under a state of siege and arresting the leaders of the reform party.[38] Others in the court joined him in arguing that reforms were dangerous, while the Emperor, ill and irresolute, vacillated and proved incapable of making decisions. So, in spite of the imminent danger, the government did very little to calm the storm and merely deluded itself into believing that Sedlnitzky's powerful police force could easily suppress any popular disturbances that might break out.[39]

The few moves the government made only added fuel to the flames of popular discontent. On March 9, after much delay, a special committee was appointed to examine the petitions being sent to the government and to make recommendations about the action to be taken on them. With considerable lack of imagination, the committee advised the government to disregard them and to punish the instigators of all petitions advocating changes in the political and social structure of the monarchy.[40]

Equally inept was the article printed in the official *Wiener Zeitung* on March 10.[41] The statement, authorized by Archduke Louis, informed the populace that the Emperor considered the change of government that had taken place in France an "internal matter" concerning only the French people. Nevertheless, if the German Confederation or any of the states constituting it were threatened by any enemy, "His

---

[36] Hübner diary, Vienna, February 29, 1848, Hübner, *op. cit.*, p. 11.

[37] Srbik, *op. cit.*, Vol. II, p. 267. See also Metternich's "Autobiographische Denkschrift," *op. cit.*, Vol. VII, pp. 619–22; and his "Mein politisches Testament," *ibid.*, pp. 636–39.

[38] Srbik, *op. cit.*, Vol. II, p. 268.

[39] Hartig, *op. cit.*, pp. 153–54.

[40] Srbik, *op. cit.*, Vol. II, p. 269.

[41] No. 70, p. 317. This manifesto was sent abroad to all Austrian embassies on March 10. See *Aus Metternich's nachgelassenen Papieren*, Vol. VII, pp. 599–600.

Majesty, the Emperor, will repulse such a breach of peace with all the means which Divine Providence has given him." The Emperor would take measures to ensure that Austria "is strong within and secure and respected outside her borders" so that

> no efforts will be made to overthrow the legal order, which could put his empire, consecrated by God, in a state of disorder which would make it easy prey for the attacks of every enemy. With this end in view, which is dedicated only to the welfare of his subjects, His Majesty counts on the trust and vigorous co-operation of the loyal estates of his empire, as well as on that of all classes of his subjects who have the preservation of legal order at heart and who have during these very agitated times preserved the faculty to measure the consequences to which the opposite road will inevitably lead.

After making this strong declaration of its intention to hold firm to the old order, the government took steps to ensure the prompt suppression of disturbances. The Viennese garrison was strengthened with troops from the neighboring districts, and on the night of March 11 the commanders of the troops in Vienna were ordered to keep their soldiers in the barracks and ready for immediate action during the next three days. The guard was increased at the Hofburg, the Ministry of War Building, the National Bank, and elsewhere. On the 12th the President of the Lower Austrian government, Baron John Talatzko von Gestieticz, was asked to confer with the officials of Vienna and the surrounding suburbs about emergency measures; on the same day this group drew up detailed plans to maintain order and security in the city.[42]

Until the very last moment the government was capable of thinking only in terms of force and repression. Not until the afternoon of March 12 did the Council of State, considerably disquieted by the turbulent scenes at the university earlier in the day, make a concession to appease the liberals. Even then, it merely inaugurated a plan that Metternich had championed for thirty years. The council agreed to call estates members from "all provinces whose estates are based on old, unchanged constitutional rights" to meet with a special committee in Vienna and report on "the conditions of their estates." The Emperor was to have the right to indicate what subjects were to be discussed at the meeting, and all proposals made by the assembled estates' delegates were to be submitted to the Emperor for final action.[43] If this concession had been

---

[42] President of the Lower Austrian government to Sedlnitzky, Vienna, March 12, 1848, Reschauer and Smets, *op. cit.,* Vol. I, pp. 163–65.

[43] Emperor Ferdinand to Count Inzaghi, Vienna, March 12, 1848 [Gotthard Freiherrn von Buschmann and Ritter Anton von Schmerling], *Die niederöster-*

made a month earlier, it might have received a joyous ovation and delayed or altered the course of the revolution. But it came too late. Few of the estates members heard about it until the next morning, and by then no such feeble gesture could halt the rebellion.

Yet the government was fully cognizant that a serious revolutionary movement was afoot. It was an open secret that the liberal members of the Lower Austrian Estates, leading figures in the Legal-Political Reading Club, radical writers,[44] disgruntled students, and other malcontents were plotting against the regime and that the liberals were enthusiastically supported by many of the Italians, Hungarians, and Poles in the capital.[45] From every quarter reports came to the government of the revolutionaries' plans to stage a demonstration on March 13, when the Lower Austrian Estates were to begin their session. In fact, there was a widespread belief among the more conservative Habsburg officials that the Viennese revolt was only part of a vast plot encompassing much of Europe.[46] No doubt the conservative supporters of the regime greatly exaggerated the extensiveness of the conspiracy, but there is some evidence that the plot was known outside Vienna. Baron von Wirkner wrote that as early as March 6 he had been told by the Pressburg police chief that the editor of the *Pressburger Zeitung,* Adolph Neustadt, had been invited to Vienna for a meeting on March 10, at which the final plans were to be made for the March 13 demonstration.[47] Undoubtedly other non-Viennese were also consulted by the plotters.

At first, the radical leaders apparently intended only to bring pressure on the government to grant a few of their demands. They would doubtless have been satisfied with such a slight concession as the convocation of a united diet, made up of representatives of the existing estates, to advise the Emperor on legislative and financial matters. Above all, the conspirators wanted to refrain from any show of force. However, the

---

reichischen Landstände, Appendix I, pp. 55–56. See also Metternich's "Autobiographische Denkschrift," *op. cit.,* Vol. VII, pp. 620–21.

[44] Grillparzer, *op. cit.,* p. 198; M[athias] Koch, *Genesis der Wiener Revolution,* p. 19.

[45] Count Hartig charged that "Hungarian agents, who were joined by Italians, Poles, and Germans, inflamed the heads of the Viennese by speeches and the distribution of money, and excited them to action on the appointed day." Hartig, *op. cit.,* p. 152.

[46] Count Ficquelmont went so far as to assert: "The similarity between the events in France, in Italy, in Berlin, and in Frankfurt, however, proves that the outbreak in Vienna was not an isolated one, and that there was in existence a widespread conspiracy that was prepared in and led from a central point." [Karl] L[udwig] Grafen Ficquelmont, *Aufklärungen über die Zeit vom 20. März bis zum 4. Mai 1848* (hereafter cited throughout as *Aufklärungen*), p. 48.

[47] Wirkner, *op. cit.,* p. 213.

The Drift toward Revolution

announcement by the government on March 10 that, come what may, the regime intended to hold fast to the old system made it clear to everyone that the Habsburgs would not voluntarily yield even a modicum of their absolute powers.[48] The radicals then decided that the government might be intimidated by a mass demonstration. If not, the estates members might at least be persuaded to head the reform movement. Accordingly, the opposition leaders made plans to organize a large popular demonstration. On March 10 and 11 various agitators went into the suburbs to get the help of the workers. On the evening of the 12th they were joined by students, who went to the industrial workers and the peasants to seek reinforcements for their own demonstration the next morning.[49]

Thus the plot was hatched. As Grillparzer, who was anything but friendly to the revolutionists, later wrote in his memoirs:[50]

A street demonstration was plotted on the occasion of the coming meeting of the Lower Austrian Estates, and the students were put at the head of it, because, being foolish youth, they alone were ready to pull the hot chestnuts out of the fire. The matter was discussed in the streets. Everybody knew it. The day and the hour were fixed. I remember laughing in the faces of several of the conspirators, all of whom I more or less knew. "Do you think that the authorities will let your demonstration be carried out?" I asked them. They had only to postpone the meeting of the estates or advise the fathers of the most hot-blooded students to send their boys into the country for a time and in the meantime show a little willingness for reforms (which actually happened in the imperial rescript on March 12, although it was too late) in order to bring about the miscarriage of all the preparations. But the unexpected actually happened. No hindrances were put in the way and the March 13 riot took place.

There is no doubt that up to the very last minute the government could have appeased the malcontents and probably spared the bloodshed the next day. Until the evening of March 12, when the students' petition was rejected, they had not definitely decided to march to the Landhaus. If the Emperor had graciously acceded to their demands, the students would not have staged their demonstration the next morning. But the regime had rebuffed the students, and the Emperor's decision

[48] For a good description of the impression the *Wiener Zeitung* announcement made on the Viennese liberals, see the report sent to the *Grenzboten* on March 11, Reschauer and Smets, *op. cit.*, Vol. I, pp. 151–52. See also Grillparzer, *op. cit.*, p. 191.
[49] Reschauer and Smets, *op. cit.*, Vol. I, pp. 154–55; Ernst Fischer, *Österreich 1848*, pp. 55–56.
[50] *Op. cit.*, pp. 198–99.

to call a meeting of representatives of all the estates was still unknown to all but a few estates members. Fate—and the obtuseness of high government officials—seemed to be conspiring to bring to the doorsteps of the proud and mighty Habsburgs the revolutionary tempest that was uprooting traditions and striking down cherished institutions all over Europe.

IV. *The March Revolution*

ONDAY, MARCH 13, was a mild, cloudy day in Vienna. In the early morning hours the markets were operating as usual, and shopkeepers and their helpers were getting ready to open their stores for business. Otherwise the streets were almost deserted. Only a large poster on St. Stephen's Cathedral reminded the passers-by of the intense excitement reigning in the city. It read: "Viennese! Liberate your good Emperor Ferdinand from the bonds of his enemies! Whoever wants Austria to prosper must want the overthrow of its governors!"[1]

In only a few places was there any activity that might have warned the early morning pedestrians of something unusual brewing. By 7:00 A.M. a large number of students had assembled at the Polytechnical Institute to march to the university in a body. There was also an unaccustomed stir at the medical school in the Alser suburb, where students were hurrying from house to house to collect their colleagues for the impressive demonstration that had been planned. From 7:30 on, there was a great commotion at the university and in the surrounding streets. Following the orders they had received, the professors unsuccessfully tried to deliver their customary lectures. Although most of their students appeared in the classrooms, there was so much noise and confusion that the ordinary routine of teaching became almost impossible. The university had assumed a new physiognomy. The halls were no longer filled with servile, expectant note-takers but were jammed with noisy, ebullient young revolutionists.

In vain the professors sought to dampen the ardor of the students and restrain them from overt action. Professor Anton Hye in particular tried to calm them in a speech in which he reported the results of his mission to the Emperor on the previous day. To quote the bombastic words of one of the student participants[2] in the revolution, in Hye's talk the

[1] Heinrich Reschauer and Moritz Smets, *Das Jahr 1848. Geschichte der Wiener Revolution,* Vol. I, p. 173.

[2] August Silberstein, *Geschichte der Aula,* pp. 18–19. In the last sentence of the

grain of gold, called "consideration," which had been thrown out to the
deputation, this grain of gold the professor exerted himself to beat as
broad as possible in order to cover the future and the past in a shining
manner with this little gold plate. A futile act! Different blood ran in the
veins of the youth from that which had been for years held in check by a
professor's diploma and diluted by an imperial appointment! One felt that
it was "now or never!" The approval of the people and the quiet hand-
clasps of the right-thinking that had been received during the past twenty-
four hours encouraged everyone, and people insisted upon an immediate
answer. That fury which alone makes revolutions, that holy rapture of
enthusiasm which overthrows in a moment what centuries of evil have
built up and which all at once tears away and washes away the rocks of the
old like a cloudburst—they had made their appearance!

And the professors still could not feel the spirit of the times. They believed that the time for haggling, the time for "grace" and dispensations
was still at hand. Their revolutionary spirit would have raised itself to the
maximum in most humbly submitting still another "memoir" to the most
high feet of His Majesty.

And it was Professor Hye who again and again exerted all his efforts to
conjure up the spirit of "law and order" in every possible form. One
should stick to the tried path and not depart from it. But the tighter the
bow becomes the more one pulls it back. The more the pen swells the
stronger one presses down on it. Just as powerful was this pressure from
above the professor's desk in causing the stream from the fountain of
enthusiasm to gush upwards, and it rose high to the sunny heaven of
freedom.

The loud fury soon drowned out the weak voice of legitimacy, and the
waves of revolution struck and raged over the head of the professor, who
did not, however, wish to drown and therefore hurriedly changed himself
and swam along and pretended at least to have a destination. He did so
until the wave carried him to the bank of the ministerial bureau, where he
then stepped out and took up his abode.

In spite of Hye's exhortations, the cry "To the Landhaus! To the
Landhaus!" re-echoed through the halls. The moment Hye left the lecture platform the students began streaming out of the building. Only a
few, fearing that their names might be inscribed in the black book, remained behind. In closed ranks the excited mass began their procession
to the Landhaus, where the Estates of Lower Austria were beginning
their session. On the way they were joined by other students and mal-

---

quotation Silberstein is referring to Hye's subsequent actions during the revolution. At the end of March, Hye became an unofficial adviser to the government
and on May 1 was made general secretary of the Ministry of Justice.

contents and by a host of the curious. Approximately four thousand people approached the Landhaus "in tightly closed columns, serious and quiet as a grave, without weapons, without sticks, but in the best of order." Calls of "They are here! The students are coming!" were heard on all sides, and the crowd that in the meantime had gathered in front of the building opened its ranks to enable the marchers to pass through.[3]

As early as 8:30, while Hye was still haranguing the students at the university, a throng of people had begun collecting in front of the Landhaus. They consisted almost wholly of well-dressed, prosperous-looking people, among them writers, artists, lawyers, doctors, and prominent businessmen. They were quiet and peaceful[4] and seemed merely to be waiting for someone to tell them what to do.

After the students appeared there was an awkward moment of hesitation. The crowd expected the students to lead them, but apparently the students had made no plans beyond the actual march on the Landhaus. Originally they had intended merely to embolden the estates, but the doors to the meeting hall were closed and no one knew what was going on within.

At this decisive moment, when the popular movement might well have failed for lack of a clear-cut program of action, a young doctor from the General Hospital, Adolph Fischhof, grew restive and, fearing that the golden moment might slip away, cried out in a loud voice, "Gentlemen! Listen!" Everyone turned to him, and four young men raised him to their shoulders so that he was in full view of the crowd. Others cried, "Quiet! Be Still!" Then Fischhof began speaking:[5]

It is a great, significant day on which we find ourselves assembled here. It is a day when, after a long, long time, the Austrian Estates are meeting up above to express the wishes of the people and to lay the ideas of the times before the throne. But if this day is to fulfill what it seems to promise, we must be equal to it.

Therefore, let us encourage the men who are meeting up above by our cheers, strengthen them by expressing our approval, and lead them to the desired goal by our assistance.

Today we have a serious mission to fulfill. What matters is that we muster up courage, that we are resolute, and that we hold out with stout hearts. Whoever has no courage on this day belongs in the nursery.

Time is pressing. Perhaps only this moment belongs to us. So we are rapidly and vigorously, briefly and sincerely, telling what we need, what

[3] *Oestreich's Befreiungstage,* p. 8.
[4] *Ibid.,* pp. 8–9; Franz Pulszky, *Mein Zeit, mein Leben,* Vol. II, p. 58.
[5] Manuscript of the speech given to Reschauer by Fischhof and printed in Reschauer and Smets, *op. cit.,* Vol. I, p. 183.

we demand, and what we stand for. We leave it to the men up above to make the detailed statements.

Above all, we demand freedom of the press! The wishes of individuals remain unnoticed so long as they are only spoken out singly. They are like drops of water which, if they fall down singly, are drunk up by the ground, vanish in the sand, evaporate in the air. But if the individual wishes flow together in the thousand channels, rivulets, and brooks of the press, they will gradually become mighty, irresistible streams of public opinion, and woe to the statesman who would have the impudence to steer the ship of state against the stream.

One of the most celebrated English parliamentary speakers, Sheridan,[6] in speaking of the power of the press, said: "Give me a servile upper house. Give me a venal lower house. But leave me a free press, and I will dare them to touch even one of the liberties of old England."

Therefore, let us, above all, lay greatest stress on a free press!

But this freedom alone is insufficient. The people have a right not only to express their wishes through the mouth of the press but also to assert their sense of justice through the mouths of jurors and give expression to their will through the mouths of their representatives whenever decisions are made about their destiny, their well-being, and their misfortunes. In addition, the minds must be unfettered. Learning must become free in Austria. Ill-advised statesmanship has kept the peoples of Austria apart. They must now meet together as brothers and increase their strength through union.

With this, the weaknesses of one nationality will be balanced by the good qualities of the others, and the merits of all will be increased through their union, which, if used for the good of the state, will raise Austria to a pinnacle of well-being and power hitherto undreamed of.

Let us, the ambitious Germans, possessed by ideas as we are, the tenacious, industrious, patient Slavs, the chivalrous and spirited Magyars, the adroit and sharp-sighted Italians, think of the common problems of the state and work with united and therefore greater power, and no doubt can rise among us that Austria's position among the states of Europe must become an imposing one.

So that this beautiful prospect for the future will not become clouded for us, during this festive hour we want to co-operate most energetically with high-throbbing hearts, swelled with courage and hope!

Hail to Austria and its glorious future!

Hail to the united peoples of Austria!

Hail to freedom! !

---

[6] Richard Brinsley Sheridan, some of whose most eloquent speeches in the House of Commons were delivered in opposition to the war against the American Colonies and in defense of revolutionary France.

Fischhof's speech was frequently interrupted by tremendous applause. It kindled a fire in all who heard it, not because the speaker had made particularly radical demands, but because he had dared to say anything at all critical before a large public gathering. His speech ended the crowd's indecision and encouraged others to speak out. One orator after another rose up to harangue the assemblage:[7]

People climbed on top of the well house, scrambled up the balcony, and spoke from the windows. Speakers got up from tightly packed groups and spoke in front of the diet building, in Herren Street, in Strauch Street, on the Freiung and on the Hof, on Ball Square, and elsewhere. Amid jubilant applause, they spoke with special enthusiasm for the imperial house; freedom of the press; a constitution; a responsible ministry; a national guard; freedom of religion, conscience, and teaching; public administrative procedures, the abolition of the secret police, the dismissal of Metternich, and so on.

The impromptu speakers were constantly interrupted by loud denunciations of Metternich and enthusiastic cheers for Emperor Ferdinand and Archduchess Sophie and Archduke Francis Charles, who were at the moment looked upon as champions of the popular cause. Thunderous calls resounded for Metternich's resignation. The crowd was filled with a desire for action. Another young doctor from the medical school, Joseph Goldmark, jumped up to urge the people to hurry to the estates and force them to go to the Emperor and demand the immediate dismissal of Metternich. "To stay in this court making speeches will not help us or our fellow-citizens. We have had enough talk among ourselves. Now is the time to get the estates to act!"[8] His daring proposal was greeted with a storm of approval. The crowd turned to the Landhaus and made for the doorway leading to the assembly room. The few guards barring the doors were shoved aside, and the mob pressed forward to the entrance to the room.[9]

At this moment the Marshal of the estates, Count Montecuccoli, stepped out of the room and asked the crowd what they wanted. Fischhof came forward and called Montecuccoli's attention to the citizens' and students' petitions, saying that the desires of the crowd were expressed in them. "These wishes," the Marshal responded, "are also those of the estates." He continued with the "happy news that His Majesty

---

[7] *Oestreich's Befreiungstage*, pp. 9–10.

[8] Josephine Goldmark, *Pilgrims of '48*, p. 42.

[9] *Ibid.*, pp. 42–43; Reschauer and Smets, *op. cit.*, Vol. I, pp. 186–90; Maximilian Bach, *Geschichte der Wiener Revolution im Jahre 1848*, pp. 8–10.

has resolved to convene the estates of all the provinces for advice on reforms." Someone in the crowd broke in with "No half measures!" Others cried out, "No delay!"

"Gentlemen," Montecuccoli said, "we estates are all for progress and have fought for it for years." Then he added a word of caution: "I warn you, don't leave thé paths of legality. Give us the necessary peace to deliberate over your wishes. In this noise and confusion any deliberation is impossible. Clear the room."[10]

Montecuccoli's words made an impression. Nevertheless, the crowd was still suspicious, and the prevailing uncertainty about what was happening in the estates increased the tension. Outside, the rumor spread that Fischhof and other leaders had been put under arrest. Suddenly the cry, "Treason! Treason!" rent the air. Only Fischhof's timely appearance at a window of the Landhaus prevented a riot. Montecuccoli again assured the populace that the estates were upholding the interests of the people and would send a deputation to the Emperor urging him to champion the popular cause. To dismiss all doubt about the good intentions of the estates, the Marshal asked the crowd to choose a dozen persons in whom they had confidence to attend the deliberations of the estates.[11]

While Dr. Fischhof and others were selecting the twelve deputies, Maximilian Goldner, a Jewish medical student from Hungary, began reading Kossuth's speech to the Hungarian Diet. His voice was not penetrating enough, and the Tyrolese jurist Franz Putz continued the reading. The speech inflamed the crowd, and during the reading there were constant interruptions with shouts of "Constitution! Constitution!" "Down with Metternich! Down with Archduke Louis!" "Curses on our oppressors!"[12]

While Putz was reading Kossuth's speech, a piece of paper was thrown into the street from one of the upper-story windows of the Landhaus. It contained the information that the estates were sending a petition to the Emperor asking him to summon an estates committee from all the provinces to advise him about reforms that should be made and to co-operate with him in making new laws. This news came at an unfortunate time. The contrast between the almost cringing obsequiousness of the petition and Kossuth's savage denunciations of the Habsburg

[10] Reschauer and Smets, *op. cit.*, Vol. I, p. 190.

[11] Joseph Alexander Freiherrn von Helfert, *Geschichte der österreichischen Revolution,* pp. 243–44; Reschauer and Smets, *op. cit.,* Vol. I, pp. 190–91; Bach, *op. cit.,* pp. 11–12.

[12] Adolph Pichler, *Das Sturmjahr,* pp. 4–5; Hans Kudlich, *Rückblicke und Erinnerungen,* Vol. I, p. 179.

system was too great. Shouts of anger resounded from all sides. Someone screamed, "That is a mere scrap of paper!" Another yelled, "That is nothing! Nothing! Tear it up!" Still others roared, "The estates are traitors. Down with the estates! Let's go to the Hofburg without the estates!" A young medical student named Hermann grabbed the offending sheet of paper and tore it to shreds. The unheard-of had happened. A writing addressed to the Emperor had been destroyed in the presence of thousands, and enraged rioters were shouting defiance against "legal" reforms proposed by the traditional estates. It was an outright revolt against authority.[13]

At this time a medley of confused and angry cries echoed through the streets. Among them could be heard shouts of "Down with Metternich!" "Drive out the Jesuits!" "Put the Civic Guard under arms immediately!" "Constitution! Constitution!" Clearly something had to be done, and quickly. The estates made another attempt to quiet the furious throng. Count Colloredo stepped out to a balcony to assure the crowd that their wishes would be laid before the Emperor. "But today," some agitator interrupted. "We have remained peaceful long enough!" The angry people resumed their shouting. Colloredo could not make himself heard and finally withdrew.

At this tense moment an insignificant incident occurred that turned the excited crowd into an unruly gang of plunderers. It had long been the duty of the porters of the Landhaus to close the side door to the building every day at noon. That custom was again followed today. Simultaneously gunfire was heard from the neighboring National Bank. To the crowds outside, this meant that the estates must be locking up the people's deputies and trying to break up the demonstration. Rumors flew that the deputies were under arrest and were being mistreated.[14] In a fury the crowd now rushed into the Landhaus, forced their way into the room where the estates were assembled, tore up seats and benches, broke down doors, and knocked out windows.

It was obvious that the disorder had assumed proportions which made it impossible for the estates to continue their meeting. Count Montecuccoli closed the session with the words, "The movement has taken on a character which makes it urgent immediately to send a deputation to His Majesty." Then, with Montecuccoli at their head, the estates left the Landhaus and went as a body through Herren Street to the Hofburg to present the demands of the people to the Emperor. The

---

[13] Reschauer and Smets, *op. cit.*, Vol. I, pp. 196–99; Bach, *op. cit.*, pp. 19–23; Robert Endres, *Revolution in Österreich 1848*, p. 12.

[14] Pichler, *op. cit.*, p. 6; *Oestreich's Befreiungstage*, p. 10.

riot now took a new turn. Up to this point the movement had been merely a street demonstration. Now it assumed real political importance. Instead of handling just a brawling crowd, the Emperor's officials had to negotiate with the legally established Lower Austrian Estates, who had made the popular cause their own.[15]

By the time the estates left the Landhaus, the multitude filled not only the streets and squares surrounding the Landhaus but also the Ball Square, in front of the Chancellor's office, the Michael Square, beyond the main entrance to the Hofburg, and the streets running into them. Those who suggested that the crowd patiently await the Emperor's decision were shouted down. Although the rioters still respected their beloved Emperor Ferdinand, and although they broke into loud *vivas* when Archduke Francis Charles and his wife Sophie showed themselves, they repeatedly shouted violent imprecations against the despotic police, the tyrannical government, and Metternich, who had become the symbol of everything abhorrent in the regime. They were determined not to leave the streets until the whole system was overturned. Many of the agitators had become desperate men. As Hans Kudlich, who was himself a participant in the revolution, said:[16]

[It was] clear to all of us that if we were unsuccessful and did not win, it would mean the same as marching to the Spielberg![17] Even the less compromised feared suppression by the military. For all of us there was, therefore, no choice! We had to proceed energetically. All the fury of the revolution had to be unleashed to make those in power afraid.

It was precisely for the purpose of terrifying the government into submission that the more radical revolutionists redoubled their efforts to bring a large mass of suburban workers into the city to join the well-dressed multitude that had originally gathered in front of the Landhaus. Only a relatively small number of suburban workingmen had responded to the call of the students the previous night. Not until after the demonstrations had already started did most of them learn what was happening in the city. Toward noon other agitators hurried out to the suburbs again to beseech the workers for support. This time their efforts were successful. In response to the entreaties, more and more

[15] See especially [Franz Graf von Hartig], *Genesis der Revolution*, pp. 162–63; [Gotthard Freiherrn von Buschmann and Ritter Anton von Schmerling], *Die niederösterreichischen Landstände*, pp. 29–31; Rudolph Kiszling *et al., Die Revolution im Kaisertum Osterreich 1848–1849*, Vol. I, p. 40; *Oestreich's Befreiungstage*, p. 10.

[16] Kudlich, *op. cit.*, Vol. I, pp. 193–94.

[17] The Spielberg was a prison in Moravia in which political prisoners were frequently held.

laborers left their work, picked up iron forks, sticks, stones, and other improvised weapons, and hurried toward the inner city.[18]

Panic seized the more prosperous inhabitants of Vienna when they saw the "factory rabble" surging into the city. The city gates were hurriedly locked and cannon were put on the walls to defend the capital against possible attack. Only a few of the workers found their way to Herren Street, in front of the Landhaus, before the gates were closed, but the presence of even this handful was enough to encourage the demonstrators to become all the more vehement in their demands. The workers who were left outside the city stormed the gates, first the Schotten then the Franzen; but the military and the Civic Guard forced them to withdraw. The most bitter fighting took place at the imperial stables, where the workers tore down lampposts and used them for battering rams. The gunfire of the guards finally drove them off.[19]

Meanwhile, nothing had been done to break up the demonstration in front of the Landhaus. The guard at the Hofburg and a few other public buildings was strengthened, but the Emperor was very reluctant to use force against the Viennese, and the commander of the imperial troops in Vienna, Archduke Albert, was admonished at all costs to prevent a collision between the military and the populace. The troops were strictly enjoined to use their weapons only in case of extreme necessity.

Not until around 1:00 P.M. did Archduke Albert receive orders to quell the disturbance. If force became necessary, he was to make every effort to spare lives. Troops were immediately sent to occupy the squares and streets around the Hofburg, to secure the thoroughfare between the Rothenthurm Gate and the Kärtner Gate, and to patrol the streets leading into that passageway. After the Hofburg and the main streets of the inner city were placed under guard, the troops proceeded to clear the Landhaus and the streets surrounding it. Two companies were sent to Herren Street to drive out the crowd but were turned back by the howling mob, who showered them with rocks, pieces of furniture, and other heavy objects. Several troopers were wounded.

At this juncture Archduke Albert, accompanied by several officers, came forward to urge the mob to return peacefully to their homes. An impudent ruffian hurled a piece of wood at him and hit him on the head, whereupon he quickly remounted his horse and rode away. The commandant of Vienna also tried to pacify the throng, but the rabble

---

[18] Kudlich, *op. cit.*, Vol. I, p. 194; Ernst Victor Zenker, *Die Wiener Revolution*, p. 112.

[19] Zenker, *op. cit.*, p. 113; Endres, *op. cit.*, p. 16.

threatened to tear him off his horse and lynch him. After these vain efforts to disperse the multitude, the Pioneer Regiment was ordered to take energetic measures to clear the streets. When the regiment arrived at the Landhaus, the crowd flung rocks and wounded one of the soldiers, a captain. Suddenly the command "Move forward with fixed bayonets and fire!" cracked through the air. A salvo of shots was fired, and the first victims of the revolution fell to the street, four of them hit by bullets and the fifth, a woman, trampled to death. The crowd, now terrified, rapidly scattered, and the Pioneers pursued them with fixed bayonets to the Michael Square.[20]

This unexpected attack on the crowd, unarmed except for sticks, rocks, and other crude weapons, shocked the mob and intensified their anger. The revolutionary leaders saw to it that the wounded were led through the city on horses as warning examples.[21] The news that the army had shot at the people spread throughout the city and the surrounding suburbs. In all streets there were now cries of "To arms! To arms!" "We must get arms!" "Let's attack the arsenal!" "Ring the tocsin!" Bulletin boards, guard huts, and paving stones were fashioned into crude weapons. At various points in the city barricades sprang up. Vienna was in full rebellion. As someone cried out, "God be praised! Now freedom has had its blood bath. Now things can be accomplished!"[22] The author of *Oestreich's Befreiungstage* later waxed rapturous over the "blood bath." He wrote: "Certainly this was so resolved in the councils of eternal fate! Out of this greatly damned command, out of this bloody seed, the directing hand of the Almighty ripened a glorious harvest, not too dearly bought, which, without this, would not have matured so rapidly and perhaps not in years."[23]

In a few moments bitter fighting broke out in various parts of the city. Some of the crowd[24]

got into a fight with the cavalry on the Freiung, who pounced upon them. Others went to the Schotten Gate, which was broken down by force. Several hundred, mostly proletariat, broke through the detachment of soldiers who

---

[20] Helfert, *op. cit.*, pp. 246–47; Bach, *op. cit.*, pp. 31–39, 189–91; *Oestreich's Befreiungstage*, pp. 11–12; Vitzthum von Eckstädt to his mother, Vienna, March 16, 1848, Carl Friedrich Grafen von Vitzthum von Eckstädt, *Berlin und Wien in den Jahren 1845–1852*, pp. 79–80; Kiszling *et al.*, *op. cit.*, Vol. I, pp. 40–41; Princess Melanie Metternich's diary, Feldsberg, March 12–16, 1848. *Aus Metternich's nachgelassenen Papieren*, published by Prince Richard Metternich-Winneburg, ed. and arr. Alfons von Klinkowström, Vol. VII, p. 540.

[21] *Oestreich's Befreiungstage*, pp. 12–13.

[22] Pichler, *op. cit.*, p. 7.

[23] *Oestreich's Befreiungstage*, p. 12.

[24] *Ibid.*, p. 13.

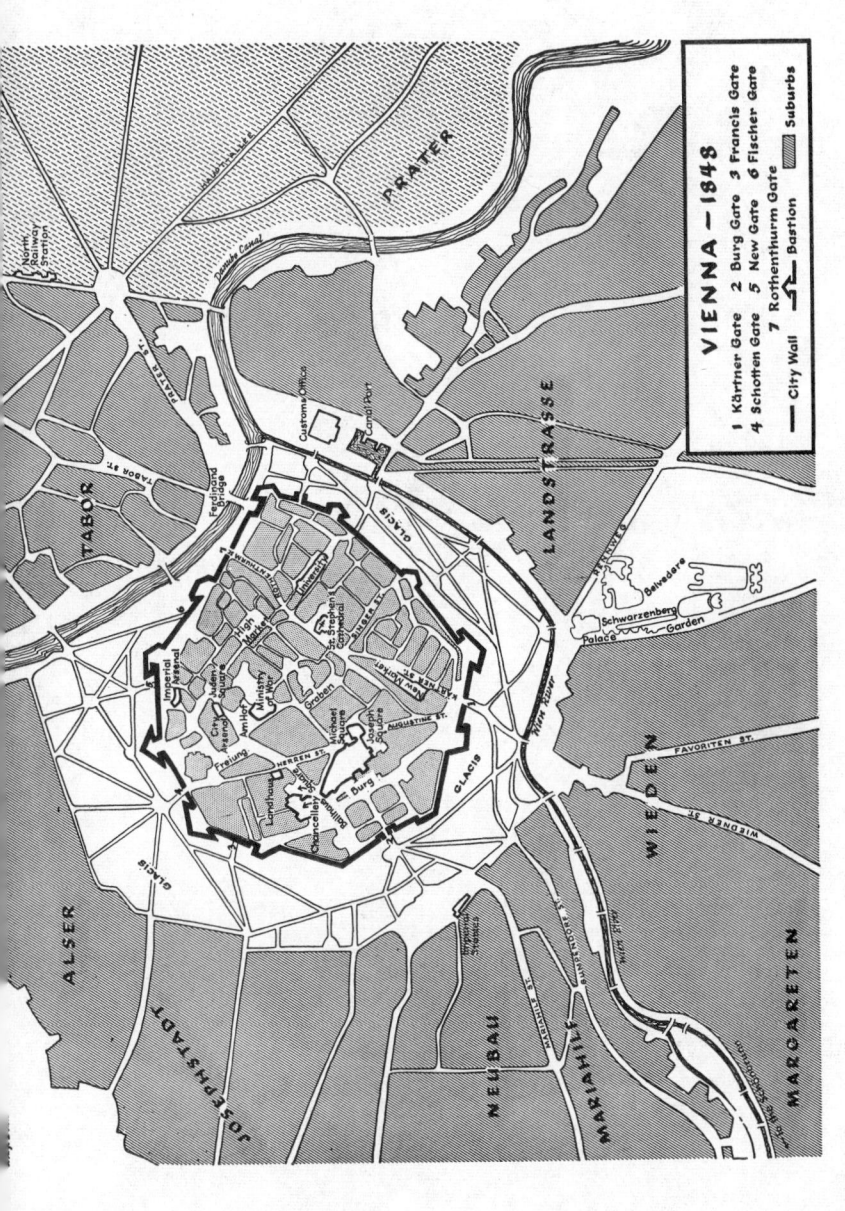

VIENNA — 1848

1 Kärtner Gate   2 Burg Gate   3 Francis Gate
4 Schotten Gate   5 New Gate   6 Fischer Gate
7 Rothenthurm Gate
— City Wall   ⌐ Bastion   ▨ Suburbs

shut off the entrance to the palace at the Haidenschuss and threatened to seize the civic arsenal. Cavalry had been stationed here, and their leader immediately sprang forward and commanded them to charge. With this a deplorable fight began! Soon the Hof[25] was cleared out and the fugitives were forced into the neighboring side streets, where the battle still continued. Blood flowed at Juden Square and in Färber, Jordan, Current, and Paris streets, the last two of which were closed off by barricades. Several corpses remained on the ground. But the greatest bitterness was aroused by the shooting coming from the basement of the police building in Spengler Street, as a result of which, it is said, four citizens were killed.

Gradually the military forced back the crowd and cleared the streets. By 5:00 P.M. the rebellious mobs were scattered, though here and there small groups still stayed together. About this time the following placard was posted, apparently for the purpose of trying to placate the Viennese populace:[26]

Proclamation.

An unfortunate disturbance occurred today at the meeting of the Lower Austrian Estates. A crowd of people forced the estates to interrupt their deliberations to submit their demands to His Majesty. They were ready to do this in the praiseworthy belief that it would pacify them. His Majesty received the estates members graciously and assured them most benevolently that everything which appertains to present conditions would be examined at once by a committee appointed for that purpose and would be submitted to His Majesty for decision, and that he would as quickly as possible make decisions for the general welfare of all his beloved subjects. Accordingly, His Majesty looks confidently on the ever constant loyalty and attachment of the inhabitants of this capital, expecting that peace will be restored and will not again be interrupted.

Vienna, March 13, 1848.

Johann Talatzko Baron von Gestieticz,
President of the Royal Lower Austrian Government.

Too much blood had been shed for the populace to be appeased by such vague, meaningless promises. The people demanded immediate concessions and threatened dire outrages if their demands were not granted at once.[27] Nevertheless, a temporary truce was arranged. The

[25] The Am Hof Square, where the civic arsenal was located.

[26] Translated from one of the 18- by 24-inch placards printed on March 13, 1848, in the University of Colorado 1848 Austrian Revolution Collection (hereafter cited throughout as Univ. Colo. 1848 Coll.), No. II/113. See also *Oestreich's Befreiungstage*, pp. 13–14.

[27] See especially Vitzthum von Eckstädt to his mother, Vienna, March 13, 1848, Vitzthum von Eckstädt, *op. cit.*, p. 78.

Civic Guardsmen, who had already been ordered out, were greeted everywhere with jubilation.[28] Ten of the guard officers now went to the Hofburg to demand that the military be ordered out of the city, that the students be armed, and that Metternich be dismissed before nine o'clock that evening. In return they promised that the Civic Guard would maintain peace and order in the city but added that if the above stipulations were not met by 9:00 P.M., the Civic Guard would itself take over the leadership of the revolutionary movement.[29]

When they arrived at the Hofburg the Civic Guard deputation found a government without a leader and in a state of utter confusion. The Emperor was suffering from another of his attacks. The court was divided,[30] as was the State Conference, composed of Archduke Louis, Archduke Francis Charles, Prince Metternich, and Count Kolowrat, among others. Earlier in the afternoon the State Conference had met with the deputies from the Lower Austrian Estates, who had come "more in the character of mediators" between the populace and the throne "than as petitioners on their own account," hoping that by assuming such a position they would absolve themselves from any charge of complicity in the revolution in case it should end in failure.[31] After a long wait they were finally told that the Emperor had granted the estates permission to deliberate on the popular demands. When Montecuccoli told Archduke Louis that the estates could not deliberate because they had been driven out of their meeting place, the State Conference approved the drafting of the lukewarm, noncommittal proclamation quoted above. That was as far as the conference would go toward appeasing the people. When the Lower Austrian Marshal implored Archduke Louis to make further concessions to quiet the people, the Archduke refused to do so and dismissed the deputation.[32]

In the meantime, other delegations were arriving at the palace. Shortly after 5:00, representatives of the Civic Guard came to seek an audience with the Emperor. The estates members who were still at the palace now aligned themselves with the Civic Guard deputation. Both groups warned the State Conference of the urgent need to appease the mob,[33] but their efforts were fruitless.

At this critical moment a third deputation reached the Hofburg, from

[28] *Oestreich's Befreiungstage,* p. 14.

[29] Vitzthum von Eckstädt to his mother, Vienna, March 16, 1848, Vitzthum von Eckstädt, *op. cit.,* p. 80.

[30] Kudlich, *op. cit.,* Vol. I, p. 194.

[31] Hartig, *op. cit.,* p. 167.

[32] Viktor Bibl, *Die Niederösterreichischen Stände,* pp. 326–27.

[33] Hartig, *op. cit.,* pp. 170–72.

the University of Vienna and the medical faculty, led by the *Rector Magnificus*. The deputies went to the court "to inform them about the distressing condition of the capital and to ask for an immediate concession—the arming of students and citizens—in order to prevent further misfortune."[34] Long and ardently the rector argued for the arming of the students, insisting that this was the only way to ward off further disaster. The request was finally granted, and the Academic Legion was authorized.[35]

On the same evening the court made another concession to propitiate the angry throng that still jammed the streets near the Hofburg. It yielded to the urgent demands of the Civic Guard deputation, backed by the furious clamor of the raging mobs in the streets outside, for the dismissal of Chancellor Metternich. This painful decision was arrived at only after a heated argument between the various court factions. Throughout the afternoon Archduchess Sophie and her husband, Archduke Francis Charles, as well as Archduke John, bent all their efforts to convince Archduke Louis that getting rid of Metternich was the only way to ward off an attack on the Hofburg. They were strongly opposed by Archduke Albert and Archduke Maximilian, and, of course, by Metternich, who argued that bending before the storm could lead to unspeakable disaster and urged that Prince Alfred Windischgrätz be put in charge of all military and civil affairs in the capital and given full powers to restore order. Thus the "Hofburg battle" over Metternich raged vehemently until around 7:00, when the cries for Metternich's scalp became so furious that they could no longer be denied. By then even the highly conservative Archduke Louis believed that the palace itself might immediately be invaded if Metternich was not dismissed.[36]

Nevertheless, for a time Metternich remained obdurate in face of all the clamor. At 8:30 Archduke John reminded him that only a half-hour remained before the truce guaranteed by the Civic Guard would expire. Various deputies hastened to give their assurances that peace would immediately be restored if the chancellor would resign. Finally, shortly before 9:00 Metternich surrendered.[37] Turning to those around him,

[34] *Oestreich's Befreiungstage,* p. 15. See also *Wiener Zeitung,* No. 75 (March 15, 1848), p. 339.

[35] Hartig, *op. cit.,* pp. 172–74; Helfert, *op. cit.,* p. 251.

[36] Princess Melanie Metternich's diary, Feldsberg, March 12–16, 1848, *op. cit.,* Vol. VII, pp. 541–42; Heinrich Ritter von Srbik, *Metternich, der Staatsman und der Mensch,* Vol. II, pp. 280–82; Hartig, *op. cit.,* pp. 175–76.

[37] Princess Melanie Metternich records that she heard the news of Metternich's resignation around ten o'clock. Diary, Feldsberg, March 12–16, 1848, *op. cit.,* Vol. VII, p. 541. All evidence the present author has found indicates that Metter-

he declared that "he did not want to take the responsibility for the blood that had been shed in Vienna and would not stand in the way of the government. He was resigning with the feeling that he had served the state according to his duty."[38] When Archduke John and Archduke Francis Charles came up to express their gratitude for the sacrifice he was making, Metternich rejoined that "it had been his duty throughout his life to work for the well-being of the monarchy as he saw it. If it is thought that his services endangered its welfare, it was no sacrifice for him to resign."[39] Then he sat down and wrote out his resignation:[40]

Your Most Gracious Majesty! I see myself forced to take a step, the reasons for which I feel it my bounden duty to render to Your Majesty in way of fullest confession.

My feelings, views, and resolutions have been the same during my whole life, and they will never be extinguished in me. I have expressed them in the motto which I am leaving to my successor as a constant reminder and guide. My motto is: Strength in justice!

My conscience convinces me that I have always been true to it in my private life as well as in my public endeavors, and I say it boldly—the facts prove it.

I am resigning in face of a higher force than even that of regents themselves.

My innermost desires are and will remain dedicated to the sacred person of Your Majesty, to the throne as the most secure prop of the empire, and to the happiness of the latter.

May His Majesty graciously accept this expression of my feelings as proof of my deepest respect in this moment of my resignation.

Vienna, March 13, 1848.   Metternich.—

The next night Metternich secretly left Vienna. He first went to Prince Liechtenstein's castle at Feldsberg, on the Lower Austrian-Moravian border, and thence by way of Olmütz, Prague, Dresden, and Hanover to England.

The crowds in the streets were told that the Emperor had authorized the arming of the students and citizens and that Metternich had re-

---

nich resigned, as stated above, shortly before the expiration of the Civic Guard truce at 9:00 P.M.

[38] *Ibid.*, p. 542. See also Srbik, *op. cit.*, Vol. II, pp. 282–85; Helfert, *op. cit.*, pp. 252–54; Vitzthum von Eckstädt to his mother, Vienna, March 16, 1848, Vitzthum von Eckstädt, *op. cit.*, p. 81.

[39] Hartig, *op. cit.*, p. 17.

[40] *Aus Metternich's nachgelassenen Papieren*, Vol. VII, pp. 603–604. See also Maria Theresia Wanderer, *Revolutionsstürme Achtundvierzig. Ereignisse, Urkunden, Briefe, Dichtungen*, p. 30.

signed around 9:00[41]—at the very moment when the Civic Guard truce was to expire. The news spread rapidly through the city. The cry "Metternich is gone!" resounded through Vienna, while happy, jubilant masses surged through the capital joyfully giving thanks to Ferdinand the Benevolent for having liberated them from the tyranny of the odious chancellor.[42]

Tempering the spirit of jubilant celebration on the evening of March 13 was the fear of an imminent proletarian uprising. The middle-class liberals, who had been the foremost champions of the revolution, were afraid that the movement might end not only with the overthrow of the hated "Metternich system" but with the destruction of all property rights as well. Although everyone was now peaceful within the city gates, unruly mobs were looting and burning the suburbs at will. They destroyed the lighting system and set fire to the gas escaping from the broken pipes. Outside the main city gates they burned the tax-office buildings. Metternich's villa and many tobacco shops were sacked. At 9:30 mobs set fire to the Mariahilf Street wall and broke many windows in buildings along the street, while other gangs demolished houses in the industrial suburbs of Fünfhaus and Sechshaus. Bakeries, butcher shops, and food shops were plundered. But the greatest damage was to the suburban factories. Like naïve children, angry workmen, enraged by the simple-minded belief that the machines were responsible for their poor wages, went from factory to factory destroying the machinery and setting fire to the buildings.[43] Arson, pillage, and plunder reigned in the suburbs on the night of March 13.

As disquieting reports of these excesses came into the inner city, fear seized the property-holding middle classes and the court circle. Their apprehension increased to near-panic when some of the workers poured

---

[41] *Oestreich's Befreiungstage*, p. 16; Vitzthum von Eckstädt to his mother, Vienna, March 16, 1848, Vitzthum von Eckstädt, *op. cit.*, p. 81; *Wiener Zeitung*, No. 71 (March 14, 1848), p. 335.

[42] Hans Kudlich wrote about the concessions made by the court on the 13th: "Metternich resigned. The supporters of Archduchess Sophie shed no tears for him. The arming of the people was granted. The first victory was won. The whole group in control of the government had proved to be impotent scarecrows, without ideas, without any sound human understanding, wavering back and forth, and, above all, not honest! As soon as they had to rule by other means and had to speak other than through the mouths of cannon they were at wits' end. Because of a lack of grapeshot they lost their absolute, untouchable position in March, and they won it back in October, not on account of their understanding and not for convincing reasons, but because of the power of their cannon." *Op. cit.*, Vol. I, p. 195.

[43] *Ereignisse in Wien am 13., 14., 15. März 1848* (four-page pamphlet published in Vienna during the March revolution), p. 2, Univ. Colo. 1848 Coll., No. II/67; *Oestreich's Befreiungstage*, pp. 17–18; Zenker, *op. cit.*, pp. 113–15.

into Vienna, and residents hurried to Civic Guard headquarters to enroll in the militia and then to the arsenal to get weapons. The students, equally disturbed by the happenings in the suburbs, also thronged to the arsenal to pick up arms and volunteer for service in the Academic Legion, which the Emperor had just authorized. Immediately after receiving their weapons, the students divided themselves into patrols and marched through the streets of the city to quell any further disturbances. Wherever they appeared they received an enthusiastic welcome from the populace. The reinforced Civic Guardsmen also moved about, calming the overexuberance of the citizens. Other members of the two groups proceeded outside the city walls to protect the capital against any attack by the turbulent workers, and still others went to the suburbs to try to halt the destruction and looting. Although they were too few in number to bring order in the suburbs during the night, they did succeed in restoring a measure of peace and order within the city walls and in reassuring many a terrified Viennese property-owner that the world was not coming to an end.[44]

Early on the morning of the 14th the Viennese found two placards posted on the street corners in the city. One, printed in the *Wiener Zeitung,* announced the arming of the students and Metternich's dismissal.[45] The other urged all Viennese to co-operate with the government in its efforts to restore peace, order, and security. For this purpose "all heads of homes and families" and "all factory and shop-owners" were urged "to keep at home all those entrusted to their care, in so far as they do not belong to the regular armed citizenry, so that the crowds of people on the streets are not increased."[46]

These proclamations did little to quiet the people, who resented the implication that the government was interested only in restoring tranquillity. Students or Civic Guardsmen were on guard everywhere in the city except the Hofburg, the Chancellery Building, and the National Bank, but cannon were still mounted on the city walls,[47] and many suspicious Viennese believed that the troops were merely being held in readiness to march against the people at a propitious moment. Men

[44] Pulszky, *op. cit.,* Vol. II, pp. 60–61; Pichler, *op. cit.,* pp. 9–14; *Oestreich's Befreiungstage,* pp. 17–18; *Wiener Zeitung,* No. 75 (March 15, 1848), p. 339; Helfert, *op. cit.,* p. 258.

[45] No. 71 (March 14, 1848), p. 335.

[46] Baron Talatzko von Gestieticz, "Proclamation," Vienna, March 14, 1848, Univ. Colo. 1848 Coll., No.II/25.

[47] *Wiener Zeitung,* No. 77 (March 17, 1848), p. 347; Vitzthum von Eckstädt to his mother, Vienna, March 16, 1848, Vitzthum von Eckstädt, *op. cit.,* p. 81; William H. Stiles, *Austria in 1848–49,* Vol. I, p. 108.

kept hurrying to the civic arsenal to get arms, and by 11:00 the arsenal was empty. At that time it was estimated that around 40,000 weapons had been handed out.[48]

Meanwhile, the suburban workers resumed the previous night's vandalism with unabated violence. A group of about fifty attacked the parsonage of the Mariahilfer Church and tore up documents and papers. Factory buildings were burned at Fünfhaus, Sechshaus, Meidling, Mödling, Himberg, Liesing, and elsewhere, and the machines in them were destroyed. Before the day was over many factory-owners and tradespeople who had been overlooked the previous night were ruined.[49]

Reports that the attacks on middle-class property were being renewed struck terror in the hearts of the bourgeois property-holders, who had already been deeply shaken by the ravages in the suburbs the previous night. To consider what steps should be taken to meet this threat, the Manufacturers' Association hurriedly called a meeting. A deputation was sent to the military to implore them to put down the disturbances, and concerted efforts were made to persuade the students and Civic Guard to take energetic measures against the rioters. In addition, a proclamation, signed by Colloredo-Mannsfeld, Arthaber, Bach, and Bauernfeld, was circularized advising the Viennese to wait peacefully and patiently for the legal changes that had to be made to consolidate the gains already acquired by the revolution:[50]

. . . this work—the task of enlightened, genuine representatives of the people—is possible only if there is order and peace. What has been neglected for thirty years cannot be thoroughly corrected in a few hours or days. Therefore, let us wait patiently for this consolidation of what has been won through order, peace, and trust in ourselves and our true friends. Let us not be influenced by the actions of foreign countries, and let us remember that we are first of all sons of a glorious Fatherland, which we must preserve. Let us remember that we are Austrians and that as such we have been called upon to put our affairs in order by ourselves. Agreement and unity for order and law! Austria above everything!

Composed as it was of wealthier middle-class citizens, the Manufacturers' Association thus threw its influence squarely behind the forces of law and order. Obviously the government sorely needed the support of this influential organization, for a flood of rumors was increasing the general excitement. It was said (correctly, as it later developed) that Prince Windischgrätz had been given dictatorial powers to suppress the

---

[48] *Oestreich's Befreiungstage,* p. 20.
[49] *Ibid.,* pp. 20–21; Zenker, *op. cit.,* pp. 116–17.
[50] Reschauer and Smets, *op. cit.,* Vol. I, p. 356.

rebellion, that Vienna was on the point of being put in a state of siege, and that all persons who had taken a prominent part in the previous day's disturbances were to be arrested. It was even whispered that the Emperor had been forced to abdicate because he had refused to approve these arbitrary measures.

Naturally, the distrust engendered by such rumors incited the revolutionaries to make new demands. No longer were the previous day's concessions sufficient, for they could too easily be taken away by the same hand that gave them. Further safeguards against despotism were necessary. A national guard had to be created so the people could protect their liberties. Reactionary officials, such as Archduke Louis, Count Sedlnitzky, and Archduke Albert, must be removed from the government. Freedom of the press must be granted, a liberal municipal administration established, public court and administrative procedures inaugurated, and a united diet immediately convened. Here and there were cries for a constitution.[51] Deputation after deputation marched to the Hofburg to voice the new demands of the people, while radical students urged the crowd to back up their exhortations by storming the imperial palace.[52]

Meanwhile, the court was coming to the conclusion that military force must be used if the agitated rabble made any further demonstrations. With Metternich's resignation, the liberal clique in the court had obtained what they wanted, and they now united with the conservative archdukes to try to preserve the *status quo*. All the members of the imperial family realized that Archduke Albert must be dismissed, for in the eyes of the people he was responsible for the bloodshed of the previous day. He was to be replaced as commander of the military forces in Vienna by the redoubtable Prince Windischgrätz, who was to have full powers to restore order, even to placing the capital in a state of siege if the situation required it. In the absence of the Emperor, who was again ill, the court drafted a proclamation announcing that Windischgrätz had been given full powers "to restore and maintain peace and order" in Vienna.[53]

Around 3:00 the proclamation was posted on the street corners. Crowds of demonstrators tore down the placards wherever they saw

---

[51] *Wiener Zeitung*, No. 75 (March 15, 1848), p. 339; *ibid.*, No. 77 (March 17, 1848), p. 347; Vitzthum von Eckstädt to his mother, Vienna, March 16, 1848, Vitzthum von Eckstädt, *op. cit.*, p. 82; Helfert, *op. cit.*, pp. 258–59; Reschauer and Smets, *op. cit.*, Vol. I, pp. 347–48, 350–51.
[52] Bach, *op. cit.*, pp. 68–69.
[53] Talatzko von Gestieticz, "Proclamation," Vienna, March 14, 1848, Univ. Colo. 1848 Coll., No. II/114.

The March Revolution

them. To the revolutionaries it was now clear that the court was planning a counterrevolution, and they hastened to ward off such a stroke. More radical students drew up plans to storm the Hofburg that night.[54] A large crowd of people who had gathered in the imperial riding school, next to the palace, selected twelve men to go to the Emperor and demand the immediate dismissal of Windischgrätz, the establishment of a national guard, and the abolition of censorship.[55] Others collected in the street in front of the Legal-Political Reading Club, to which many people had been coming all day to look for leadership and direction.[56] Some fanatics ran around the city like wild beasts, screaming out imprecations against Windischgrätz and adjuring the Viennese to teach the reactionaries a lesson.

Only because the government gave in to the clamors was another violent mob demonstration averted. Sometime after midafternoon[57] it was announced that the Emperor had approved "the establishment of a national guard for the maintenance of lawful peace and order and for the protection of persons and property in the capital."[58] Around 5:00 another placard was posted to inform the populace that censorship of the press was to be abolished and that a press law would be published as soon as possible.[59]

When these concessions became known, there was considerable rejoicing. A large group of celebrators streamed to Joseph Square, not far from the main entrance to the Hofburg, to decorate the statute of Joseph II with garlands of flowers and a flag on which were written the words "Freedom of the Press."[60] Yet enthusiasm was mingled with misgivings. Since the arsenal had been opened to the populace the previous

[54] Bach, *op. cit.*, p. 72; Vitzthum von Eckstädt to his mother, March 16, 1848, Vitzthum von Eckstädt, *op. cit.*, p. 82.

[55] *Oestreich's Befreiungstage,* pp. 23–24; Heinrich Friedjung, *Österreich von 1848 bis 1860,* Vol. I, p. 21.

[56] "Der juridisch-politische Leseverein," *Die Constitution. Tagblatt für constitutionelles Volksleben und Belehrung* (hereafter cited throughout as *Constitution*), No. 1 (March 20, 1848), p. 6. The *Constitution* was founded and edited by Leopold Häfner. The newspaper was last issued on October 25, 1848.

[57] The *Wiener Zeitung* reported that the imperial order announcing the establishment of the National Guard was generally known by 4:00 P.M. No. 77 (March 17, 1848), p. 347. Vitzthum von Eckstädt wrote his mother on March 16 that the news about this concession was made public around 3:00 P.M. Vitzthum von Eckstädt, *op. cit.*, p. 82.

[58] Copy of the Talatzko von Gestieticz, "Proclamation," Vienna, March 14, 1848, placard Univ. Colo. 1848 Coll., No. II/30.

[59] *Ibid.* See also Univ. Colo. 1848 Coll., No. II/136; Vitzthum von Eckstädt to his mother, Vienna, March 16, 1848, Vitzthum von Eckstädt, *op. cit.*, p. 82.

[60] *Oestreich's Befreiungstage,* pp. 26–27; *Wiener Zeitung,* No. 77 (March 17, 1848), p. 347; Hartig, *op. cit.,* p. 183.

night and large numbers of students and citizens had already received weapons and ammunition, many people wondered what the authorization of the National Guard signified. The wording of the announcement of freedom of the press also aroused fear in many of the uneducated that the court was trying to deceive them. Not until thirty writers of Vienna posted a notice explaining that abolition of censorship meant the same as freedom of the press were suspicions quieted.[61]

But even these concessions had come too late. If they had been accorded by a generous government on the previous day, together with a promise that the court would draft a comprehensive program of reforms, freedom of the press and a national guard might have satisfied the population. By the afternoon of the 14th the revolutionaries were no longer content with the relatively mild demands made the previous day. They were beginning to rally around the program outlined in a four-page pamphlet widely distributed among the Viennese on the evening of the 14th. The pamphlet read as follows:[62]

Citizens of Vienna!

Yesterday the people raised their voices in behalf of desires that have long been suppressed, and you all know what kind of an answer was given! Citizens and friends! Beginning *today* we no longer need to fear *such* an answer. Our wishes are all the closer to the point of fulfillment! Let us not leave them there! No matter what hindrances may still stand in the way, justice and the times are for us! We need only to *want* and we shall *have!* But we must know *what* we want! Listen to the reason for this! It is said that above all there must be order and security, but I ask, "How do you wish to restore them? Again through *force of arms,* as was attempted yesterday!? We have seen the consequences! Therefore, how?" Answer: "Only through unity!" But I ask further: "On what basis do you wish to found this unity?" Answer: "Only in all *agreeing* on what they want." But if we are to agree about this, we must *know* what we want! Also *everybody* must know the points on which everyone agrees. They must be the banner around which all true friends of the people and of public well-being can group themselves!

Fellow-citizens! There can be no doubt about these points! For so many years we have experienced what is *lacking* and what *oppresses* us. That is enough for us to know what is now *necessary!* Above all, *"freedom of the press"* is necessary, so that the good citizens can openly express their com-

---

[61] *Wiener Zeitung,* No. 77 (March 17, 1848), p. 347; *Oestreich's Befreiungstage,* p. 28. A copy of the Viennese writers' manifesto appears in Reschauer and Smets, *op. cit.,* Vol. I, p. 379.
[62] *Bürger von Wien!* Translated from an original copy printed on March 14, 1848, Univ. Colo. 1848 Coll., No. II/43.

plaints and desires and need no revolutions to do this! You know that not only this point, but also the very urgent and necessary universal arming of the people, has already been granted through the establishment of a national guard under the very highly respected Count *Hoyos!*

Since we accept this with the happiest gratitude, it can only be a challenge for us to go further to that which *is no less necessary* and is likewise a general wish: a fair and equal apportionment of taxes and the *main thing* in regard to this: *public accounting of the use made of the taxes,* and *also responsibility for the highest state officials!*

However, such responsibility of the officials to the people cannot exist when the people are not actually *represented* by men chosen from their midst who publicly protect and forward their general interests! Therefore, *genuine, universal representation of the people*—no secret Estates!

Citizens! With this the foundations are laid for the fulfillment of all other just wishes of the people. If we have genuine popular representatives, they will not fail immediately to urge the decrease of the standing army in time of peace, as well as a reduction of the excessive expenditures therefor! They will work vigorously for the improvement of the judiciary, for freedom of religion, for the improvement of public education, industry, and commerce, as well as for all other timely needs of the people!

Citizens! Let us be on guard *not* to ask for *too much* and for nothing that is *untimely!* But let us also not allow days of fulfillment to pass away which often do not return again in half a century! Let us only demand what our German brothers have long had and have again won for themselves! We are worth no *less* than they are, for we are no less *sincere* and *well-intentioned!* Out of these sincere and good convictions on the part of all let us first of all *establish our rights.* Let us search for *unity* in clear and universally recognized principles of justice. Let us seek for *unity* in genuine *order* and *security!* I repeat this in saying: Long live our good Emperor! Long live our good rights! Long live the good power of unity—the best and only one through which real order and security can be restored and secured forever! Away with all enemies of the people, of justice, of harmony, of order! Long live everyone who is loyal to the well-being of the Fatherland!

Thus the author of the pamphlet saw the road to peace and freedom mainly in the establishment of a national assembly chosen by all classes of Austrians. If only a true parliament were created, he believed that all the other reforms would be assured. On the evening of the 14th his program was the rallying point for all malcontents in the capital, together with another demand which was backed more and more vociferously—the demand for a consitution. In the morning hours of the 14th spasmodic cries for a constitution had been heard. By the evening of the same day many had come to regard a constitution as the cure for all the ills of the empire. Calls for a constitution echoed on the streets of

Vienna, and countless deputations went to the Hofburg reiterating the demand.[63]

Rumors of a coup planned by the government were spreading rapidly. The government was said to be sending the student legion to the suburbs, not to check the excesses of the proletariat but to get them out of the way so that the military could safely extinguish the embers of the revolution. This tale aroused great excitement at the university, and only with difficulty did the more responsible leaders convince the students that the rumor was groundless. Then a new question arose. Students asked why the Academic Legion should again be exposed to the raging workers when they still had no constitution. However, after considerable disagreement they finally resolved to send more patrols to the suburbs.[64] When the patrols arrived in the factory districts, they were told that the workers were planning to storm the Hofburg. Then came the disquieting information that a large body of ruffians were pushing their way along the Simmering heath to plunder the suburbs adjoining it and ravage the industrial districts. Students raced about investigating these reports, but nowhere did they encounter any serious disorders during the night.[65]

Just before midnight came another rumor, this time that the capital had been put under a state of siege. This particular report had some basis in fact, for around 11:00 the mayor of Vienna received a package of placards announcing the fact and was ordered to make arrangements for posting them at a time to be determined later. Some of the copies of the proclamation inadvertently fell into the hands of the students. Headed by Anton Hye, a deputation hastened to the Hofburg to protest against words in the poster referring to Vienna's being placed in a state of siege. As a consequence, at 2:00 A.M. on the 15th Windischgrätz was instructed to have new posters printed with the offensive phrase struck out. The revised placard was posted at 4:00 A.M.[66] It read:[67]

Having been vested with full authority by His Royal Apostolic Majesty

---

[63] Hartig, *op. cit.*, p. 184; Füster, *Memoiren vom März 1848 bis Juli 1849*, Vol. I, p. 40.

[64] Füster, *op. cit.*, pp. 39–40; Vitzthum von Eckstädt to his mother, Vienna, March 16, 1848, Vitzthum von Eckstädt, *op. cit.*, p. 83.

[65] See especially Pichler, *op. cit.*, pp. 17–18.

[66] Reschauer and Smets, *op. cit.*, Vol. I, pp. 388–92; Kiszling *et al.*, *op. cit.*, Vol. I, p. 46; Paul Müller, *Feldmarschall Fürst Windischgrätz. Revolution und Gegenrevolution in Österreich*, pp. 93–95.

[67] Windischgrätz, "Proclamation," Vienna, March 15, 1848, Univ. Colo. 1848 Coll., No. II/23.

to establish and maintain peace and order in the capital, I order all citizens of this city obediently to comply with the public measures which are necessary for the restoration and maintenance of peace and security and to support these measures with courage and active co-operation. I expect them to co-operate with me in this common cause in the interest of their own welfare and with the same honesty, devotion, and loyalty which they have at all times shown.

In addition, I add a strict warning that any insulting of the royal troops must be carefully avoided.

Vienna, March 15, 1848.

Alfred Prince Windischgrätz,

Royal Lieutenant Field Marshal.

Even though the ominous words about putting Vienna under a state of siege were omitted from the proclamation, the news that the court was planning to suppress the revolution had already spread among the Civic Guard and student patrols on the streets. Immediately the whole spirit of the revolution changed. Gone was the almost childlike trust in the court which had up to this moment characterized the Viennese. In its place there was now a deep mistrust of the government and a strong determination to fight to the bitter end to defend the concessions already won and to wrest new ones—especially the much-sought-after constitution—from the regime.

The Viennese were not placated by the following announcement by the government:[68]

In consideration of present political conditions, we have decided to bring together the estates of our German and Slavic realms, as well as the central congregations of our Lombardo-Venetian kingdom, by having them send delegates to our throne to make sure that their advice will be given on legislative and administrative matters. To this end we shall make the necessary arrangements so that this assembly can take place on the third of July, if not earlier.

Vienna, March 14, 1848.   Ferdinand.—

On the morning of the 15th, when the people read this placard, which was posted side by side with Windischgrätz' provocative proclamation, their reaction was bitter and disdainful. At the university, amid the derisive laughter of the students, a copy of the placard was burned and Windischgrätz' tactless proclamation was snatched from the bulletin boards and torn into shreds. Instead of cheering the news that Archduke Albert, Count Apponyi, and Count Sedlnitzky had resigned

[68] Original placard in the Univ. Colo. 1848 Coll., No. II/52.

from the government, the Viennese remained dejected over the niggard-liness of the court's act. One malcontent on the streets protested, "Metternich is away, but his spirit still rules us."[69]

The air was full of suspicion and charges of treason. The promise of a united diet was a far cry from the universal representation that was now being demanded. Still no word about a constitution had been uttered from above. Many still believed that the abolition of censorship was a trick and doubted the honesty of the government's intentions in authorizing a national guard. When the people learned that many student and citizen patrols had again been ordered to the suburbs and that the leaders of these patrols did not know why they had been sent, mistrust grew. Many a worried revolutionary asked, "Is it to get the citizens' militia out of the city so that the people will be helpless when Windischgrätz puts the city under a state of siege?"

Clearly something had to be done to prevent the angry, surging masses on the streets from getting out of hand. An anonymous member of the wealthy class made a serious effort to quiet the throng by writing a pamphlet entitled *Uncensored People's Paper,* which was widely distributed in Vienna late on the morning of the 15th. This interesting tract, full of naïve explanations and exhortations for the crowd to be peaceful, read as follows:[70]

The great work has been completed. Unfortunately it has been associated with deeds of which every citizen would be ashamed were it not known that only *robbers* are finding pleasure in destruction and burning. *We do not want to be robbers and arsonists!*

Many do not know how much we have won. The abolition of censorship now makes it possible for us to speak out, print, and circulate our wishes in thousands of sheets.

Do you know what a *press law* is?

A press law is a law to protect your children from being led into immorality, to prevent the spreading of lies, and to prevent the defamation of honorable citizens.

Is a scoundrel who has no religion himself to be allowed to abuse our religion? No. We want religion. We will not let ourselves be abused.

Do you know who can be punished according to the press law? *Only the writer can be punished.* Now we want to educate you through our newspapers. We will show you that we have the courage to express the wishes of the people. You do not need to shout out your wishes in the streets. You can have them printed.

[69] Reschauer and Smets, *op. cit.,* Vol. I, pp. 400–402; *Oestreich's Befreiungstage,* pp. 30–31; Helfert, *op. cit.,* p. 269.
[70] *Volksblatt ohne Censur,* Univ. Colo. 1848 Coll., No. II/207.

Only those of us who wish to write books or for newspapers can be punished, and we know what laws exist in the countries with the most freedom. We will be able to help ourselves, for we have been given the *legal* way to get help.

The estates of all the provinces are now to assemble together. The estates were the first to express the wishes of the people courageously and without a trace of hesitation. We want to give them our trust.

Who is to give us laws in the future?

Who is to deliberate on the press law?

The estates are to do this. They are men of the people. They know our needs. They will give us much better laws than we would have if we were to be given a new law in all haste—perhaps overnight.

Accordingly, let us trust the estates!

There are false friends among us who want to stir us up because they find pleasure in *scandals*.

Every respectable citizen must now wish to have peace again so that he can go about his own business.

Who gains from breaking windows and setting houses on fire? Nobody!

And we have to see who profits thereby.

There are thieves in every big city. Where is it easiest to steal? Where there is disorder.

Thieves wish to encourage the people to be disorderly so that they can steal.

Whoever has a good tool loves it. The machines are also tools.

Before the machines were discovered half the population had to go around in rags. Now every industrious person can have decent clothing because the machines help us do our work.

Does anyone want to eat raw grain? I don't. If there were no mills we would have to beat stones together the whole day long to get flour for bread.

Who goes about gladly in the dark? Only pickpockets. *Therefore, let us not break the street lamps to pieces.* Only the glass-blowers can gain therefrom. Every respectable citizen and every worker who intends to be honest is happy over what the Emperor has granted us and will not spoil the pleasure of others by destroying their property. The citizens have won their property through hard work. For this reason it is the basic principle of every sensible person to respect the *person* and *property* of our *fellow human beings. Be Christians!* The poor women and children, who are not accustomed to all the noise prevailing in our city for three days, are living in fear and terror.

Let them have peace.

The Emperor has approved the bearing of weapons by the citizens themselves. Do you comprehend the great trust implied in this?

Citizen soldiers are everywhere being greeted with jubilation. You can demonstrate the greatest respect for them if you restore order just as the citizen soldiers are doing it.

Many a person has now accepted the tokens and weapons of a good citizen who has the intention of stirring up others. Do not believe them. *Whoever is a partisan of freedom is already peaceful.*

Do not believe any rumors. Only believe what has been publicly proclaimed. The Emperor himself has spoken to us, for the convocation of the estates *was signed by the Emperor himself.*

Every good citizen belongs to the National Guard, but you must come there in person and enroll in it. We have received what we asked for. Now let us enjoy it.

We will now take care to educate the people. Then you will see that we have attained *three* great things:

National Guard, freedom from censorship, an imperial diet.

The imperial diet is to give its advice about new laws. Our good Emperor will get acquainted with all our wishes through the imperial diet.

The magistrate of the city of Vienna, in an effort to restore normal conditions, had the following proclamation posted on the streets:[71]

For the purpose of contributing to public tranquillity, all merchants and businessmen, as well as all shopkeepers, are requested immediately to reopen their offices, places of business, and stores to the public. The preservation of law and order and the disadvantages to trade in·general and to all those participating in it that will result from keeping them closed for a longer time make this urgent.

By the magistrate of the royal capital and residential city.

Vienna, March 15, 1848.

These attempts to calm the populace had little success. Not until the next day were the shops and businesses reopened, and the pamphlet failed to soothe the exasperated, impatient crowds. Fearing that further bloodshed was imminent, the Lower Austrian Estates created a provisional committee of twenty-four members, twelve of them chosen by the estates and the rest by a citizens' committee formed earlier in the day, to decide what should be done at this critical moment.[72] The citizens' committee had come into existence at a meeting of "respectable citizens" summoned at 7:30 A.M. by Mayor Czapka to consult with him on the measures that should be taken to restore peace and order. At the meeting a quarrel broke out between the Mayor and an opposition

[71] *Wiener Zeitung,* No. 77 (March 17, 1848), p. 347.

[72] Lower Austrian Estates, "Proclamation," Vienna, March 15, 1848, Univ. Colo. 1848 Coll., No. II/115. See also *Wiener Zeitung,* No. 77 (March 17, 1848), p. 347.

element, led by Alexander Bach, over the leadership of the committee and the extent of its powers. The result was that those present at the meeting rejected the Mayor's leadership and chose twenty-four persons to form the committee.[73]

While various legal bodies were working for the restoration of peace and order, other groups were presenting the latest demands for a constitution to the court. Archduchess Sophie's personal physician and Baron Sommaruga, her eldest son's tutor, implored the Archduchess to persuade the Emperor to ride through the streets of the city in the hope that his appearance would soothe the crowds long enough for the government to decide what to do about the new demands.

This advice proved invaluable. Toward noon Emperor Ferdinand made a short journey through the inner city, accompanied by Francis Charles and Francis Joseph. The crowds loudly protested their loyalty and affection for their beloved Ferdi the Benevolent. The Emperor was deeply moved. In tears he thanked the populace for their devotion and muttered over and over again, "I promise you everything." His simplicity and kindhearted demeanor so stirred the populace that they detached the horses from his carriage and pulled the royal equipage through the streets back to the Hofburg.[74]

However, as the day wore on and there was still no announcement of a constitution, the favorable impression made by the Emperor's journey wore off. From hour to hour the crowds grew larger around the Hofburg and in the nearby streets, and agitators harangued them to storm the Hofburg. Other orators bobbed up to preach strange new doctrines of social democracy that greatly alarmed the more responsible revolutionaries. Eduard Bauernfeld wrote about the speeches made on the forenoon of March 15:[75]

Ideas of social democracy which had never before been heard on the politically virgin soil of Vienna struck our ears. These ideas found credulous and even enraptured listeners among the naïve population. I do not deny that I was surprised and frightened. Who can judge how far a wildly excited and uneducated mob can be led by the Utopia of the abolition of property, of the common ownership of goods, and the like. In short, anarchy stood clearly before my eyes in Michael Square and I felt that it was the most terrible monstrosity imaginable!

[73] The announcement of the formation of this committee was made the next day in a proclamation by the magistrate of the city, a copy of which was printed in the *Wiener Zeitung,* No. 77 (March 17, 1848), p. 347.
[74] Reschauer and Smets, *op. cit.,* Vol. I, pp. 406–11; Stiles, *op. cit.,* Vol. I, p. 110; Helfert, *op. cit.,* pp. 269–70; *Oestreich's Befreiungstage,* p. 36.
[75] Eduard Bauernfeld, *Erinnerungen aus Alt-Wien,* ed. Josef Bindtner, p. 274.

It was obvious that another day of hesitation might bring far more violence than that of the 13th. By afternoon even the most unimaginative member of the State Conference realized that a dramatic gesture of appeasement was imperative.[76] An imperial proclamation—intended to be a sort of Magna Charta of the revolution—was hastily drafted. In it the concessions that had already been granted were listed and a constitution was promised. At 5:00 P.M. a herald left the Hofburg and read this proclamation to the crowds assembled at the Michael Square.[77] In a voice quivering with emotion he read:[78]

We, Ferdinand the First, by the grace of God, Emperor of Austria; King of Hungary and Bohemia, the fifth of this name; King of Lombardy and Venetia, of Dalmatia, Croatia, Slavonia, Galicia, Lodomeria and Illyria; Archduke of Austria; Duke of Lorraine, Salzburg, Styria, Carinthia, Carniola, Upper and Lower Silesia; Grandduke of Transylvania; Margrave of Moravia; Count of Habsburg and Tyrol, etc., etc., have adopted such measures as we have recognized as necessary to fulfill the wishes of our loyal people.

In our proclamation on the abolition of the censorship, freedom of the press is guaranteed like that in all the lands where it exists.

The National Guard, based on property and intelligence, is already performing most useful service.

The necessary provisions have been made to convene *as soon as possible* delegates from all the provincial estates and from the Central Congregation of the Lombardo-Venetian Kingdom, with an increased representation of the middle classes, and with due regard to the existing provincial constitutions, with a view of establishing the *Constitution of the Fatherland* which we have resolved to establish.

Therefore, with all confidence we expect the people to become tranquil, that studies will again proceed along their regular course, and that industry and trade will again revive.

We entertain this hope all the more because, having been in your midst

---

[76] Mathias Koch later maintained that it had been the vacillation of the government that had made the granting of a constitution unavoidable. He wrote: "Because of the fact that the government accepted petitions daily and hourly and because it was inveigled into giving unilateral promises, the government arrived at a point where it always had to change its decisions and never gained firm ground on which to establish a system. Thus it happened that it was at last forced to grant a constitution which neither the estates nor the people had proposed. The party that had expressly made such a constitution their goal did not come forward until a few days after March 13." *Genesis der Wiener Revolution,* p. 25.

[77] *Oestreich's Befreiungstage,* p. 37.

[78] As translated from one of the original placards in the Univ. Colo. 1848 Coll., No. II/198.

today, we have been deeply convinced that that same loyalty and attachment which you have uninterruptedly demonstrated toward our predecessors for centuries and also to us upon every occasion inspires you now the same as before.

Given in our Imperial Residence and Capital City of Vienna, this fifteenth of March, one thousand, eight hundred and forty-eight, in the fourteenth year of our reign.

Ferdinand.

LS

Count Carl Inzaghi,
   Chief Chancellor.

Baron Franz von Pillersdorff,
   Imperial Chancellor.

Baron Joseph von Weingarten,
   Imperial Chancellor.

   In accord with his Royal Apostolic
   Majesty's express command:
   Chevalier Peter von Salzgeber,
      Royal Counselor.

The general rejoicing that followed the proclamation completely destroyed the tension and gloom that had pervaded Vienna.[79] The author of *Oestreich's Befrieungstage* described the city's reaction to the news:[80]

Hardly had the word "constitution" been uttered when it was repeated everywhere. Heralds ran through the streets, towards the suburbs, and even beyond. They went both on foot and on horse, carrying a white flag in one hand and in the other the blessed paper held high above. Constantly they called out, "Freedom of the press! ! Constitution! ! !" The word "constitution" is giving a new movement to the waves of the time—a movement that will be felt over the whole globe and which will strike many a pillar of absolutism with thunder and lightning.

When the news arrived at the university, so says the *Wanderer*,[81] the

[79] Friedrich Hebbel described his reactions to the news of the granting of a constitution as follows:

"Now I am living in a different Austria: an Austria in which I am more secure, like Prince Metternich, an Austria in which freedom of the press has been proclaimed, the arming of the people has been introduced, and a constitution has been promised! Who has time to write down the details? But this much must be said here and now! I discovered an entirely new state immediately after I saw the last proclamation of the Emperor." *Tagebücher,* ed. Felix Bamberg, Vol. II, p. 297.

[80] Pp. 39–40.

[81] A Viennese daily newspaper, edited by Ferdinand Seyfried.

students assembled in University Square. The proclamation was read to them. The drums were sounded for prayer, and in a moment everyone fell down on his knees, raised his arms towards heaven, and the tears in the eyes of the people silently expressed their most eloquent gratitude. It was an indescribably beautiful sight! Yes, just enjoy it. Enjoy the joy of victory fully! Give up your whole soul to the happiness of the new freedom. Your part in winning it is none the lesser.

If I could only always preserve such a feeling, which I had never known before: to see a whole populace so happy as though enchanted by heaven! They all fell into each other's arms. Hands were shaken which had never touched each other before. Friends and enemies kissed each other. Italians and Hungarians embraced the Germans. And as if this was to be the first beautiful fruit of the young freedom, the formerly divided nationalities melted together into a single feeling—the happiness of their common Fatherland.

The journalist Ludwig August Frankl also described the atmosphere in Vienna during the moments immediately following the reading of the imperial proclamation: [82]

A fanatical storm of rejoicing is shaking the city. From the ground floors up to the highest stories the windows of all the houses are full of people. Handkerchiefs are waving. Flowers are flying. There is joy in every face. Cheers come from every mouth. The whole living generation is enjoying a moment which greatly surpasses every good fortune of human destiny, no matter how sweet and great it may be. The whole world and the thousand years of world history have had few festivals like this, and the people who are taking part in it feel like gods.

Numerous deputations went hurrying to the palace to thank the Emperor for the great gift he had bestowed upon the Austrian people. The citizens' armed forces marched in a body to the Hofburg to express their gratitude. When they arrived at Joseph Square, the Emperor and several members of his family appeared on the balcony of the imperial library. He was greeted enthusiastically by the immense crowds below, who joined in singing the national anthem. In the evening Vienna and all the suburbs were aglow with brilliant lights, and a magnificent torch-light parade was held in the inner city. Thousands of people—Germans, Hungarians, Italians, Bohemians, Poles, and Jews—jostled each other in brotherly harmony to celebrate the dawn of a new freedom. Total strangers embraced one another on the streets and joined in singing

[82] *Erinnerungen,* ed. Stefan Hock, pp. 330–31.

"Gott erhalte" and cheering Ferdinand. Others adorned the statue of Emperor Joseph with banners and flowers. The whole population of Vienna seemed to be participating in a festival of brotherly love and a demonstration of devotion to their Emperor.[83]

On the same evening the carnival spirit prevailing in the Habsburg capital was further stimulated by the arrival in the city of a deputation of about 150 Magyars, led by Kossuth, who had been sent by the Hungarian Diet at Pressburg to demand a separate Hungarian ministry. They were escorted through Vienna by National Guardsmen, amid loud *vivas* from the inhabitants. The next day Vienna was still under the spell of the Hungarian deputies, particularly Lajos Kossuth, who made such an impression on the Viennese that they carried him through the streets on their shoulders. The same night the government decided to comply with the demands of the Hungarian deputation for a separate ministry, and on the 17th the deputation returned to Pressburg.[84]

On the same day an imposing funeral service was held in Vienna for the victims of the March revolution. At noon the National Guard, the Academic Legion, and the Civic Guard assembled in the courtyard of the general hospital, where the funeral procession was to begin, to pay homage to those who had fallen. Thousands of Viennese gathered along the line of march from the hospital to the cemetery. Headed by the citizens' military forces and accompanied by clergymen representing all creeds in Vienna, the procession left the hospital at 2:30 P.M., escorted by students, National Guardsmen, and friends of the victims. At the cemetery the bodies were placed in a common grave.[85]

By the 17th life in Vienna was beginning to resume its normal course, with one significant exception. The large number of arrests that were begun on the night of March 13 continued unabated. More persons were being imprisoned than had been arrested during the "Metternich era." This time it was the revolutionaries, not the old regime, who were responsible for the arrests, and it was their own comrades-in-arms who were being imprisoned. The "members of the Legal-Political Reading

[83] *Ibid.*, p. 331; Eduard Bauernfeld, *op. cit.*, p. 280; Pichler, *op. cit.*, pp. 20–21; *Oestreich's Befreiungstage*, pp. 41–42.

[84] Pulszky, *op. cit.*, Vol. II, pp. 62–64; Pichler, *op. cit.*, pp. 21–22; Stiles, *op. cit.*, Vol. I, pp. 111–12.

[85] *Wiener Zeitung*, No. 79 (March 19, 1848), p. 358; *Ereignisse in Wien am 13., 14., 15. März 1848*, pp. 2–3; Friedrich Unterreiter, *Die Revolution in Wien vom März und Mai 1848. Mit allen ihren Ursachen und Wirkungen fortlaufend bis auf die nächsten Tage, auf das freisinnigste nach eigener Anschauung und den besten Quellen dargestellt* (hereafter cited throughout as *Die Revolution in Wien vom März und Mai 1848*), Vol. I, pp. 97–101.

Club and the Estates, young officials, and rich people,"[86] all of whom had stood in the forefront of the revolution, rounded up the proletarian leaders responsible for the destruction of machinery, the burning of the factories, and the damage to other property on the night of the 13th and the days immediately following. During the course of the March revolution so many lower-class rioters were led in chains to prison that the buildings were soon overflowing. As early as March 15 two hundred prisoners had to be taken to improvised jails, and still the arrests continued. Everywhere the police, encouraged by the wealthy, went out into the factory districts to search the houses of suspected arsonists and robbers. On March 23 large numbers of suspected malefactors were still being imprisoned, to be held until they could be tried in the regular criminal courts of the city.[87]

Thus, even before the March revolution was over, the moderate leaders were helping to arrest some of their former companions in sedition. Before the Emperor granted the constitution on the 15th, deep cleavages were seriously weakening the solid revolutionary phalanx that had wrung the first concessions from the monarchy. All classes of malcontents had worked together to bring on the revolution. A sprinkling of liberal nobles, the prosperous middle classes, the lower middle classes, and the students had all joined in the demonstrations in front of the Landhaus on the morning of the 13th. Responding to the appeals of the middle classes, the workers supported them later in the day by storming the city gates and rioting in the suburbs. Even the liberal court party had taken advantage of the demonstration to help bring about Metternich's dismissal. With the chancellor's resignation, the liberal clique within the Habsburg court attained its goal and began to throw its influence on the side of the regime. Of much more consequence, the riots in the suburbs made many of the liberal nobles and wealthier bourgeoisie extremely nervous and apprehensive. The liberal nobles in the Lower Austrian Estates feared that the reform movement might slip out of their hands, and the more affluent middle classes were terrified by the thought that the moderate political revolution they hoped to lead might end in a violent social revolution. They continued along with the revolution for a time, but not without serious misgivings about the future.

On the extreme left, the workers, leaderless, ignorant, starving, and seemingly impotent, had indulged in their first orgy of plunder. Sud-

[86] [Ernst Violand], *Enthüllungen aus Oesterreichs jüngster Vergangenheit* (hereafter cited throughout as *Enthüllungen*), pp. 16–17.
[87] Bach, *op. cit.*, pp. 60–62.

denly awakened to a feeling of power in a "free" society, they were a potentially powerful and savage army that could be led to ferocious acts by any rabble-rouser who could win them over to his purposes. Between them and the "respectable" bourgeoisie were the students, intelligentsia, petty artisans, and traders, who at this early stage constituted the radical vanguard of the revolution. It is true that, except for the "liberal" court faction, these groups continued to work together for a time, but the seeds of discord that inexorably led to further violence and finally to the overthrow of the revolution were sown before the March revolution had ended.

V. *The Literature of the Revolution*

URING THE DAYS of the March revolution and immediately thereafter, the Viennese were drunk with freedom. Austria had suddenly broken with her past, and the most cherished traditions had become objects of derision. The old temple of tyranny had been destroyed, or so they thought; the new edifice to replace it was still to be built. People were jubilant, expectant, and optimistic about the future.

In their intoxication, the inhabitants of the capital wined and dined, danced and sang, marched and paraded with a joy that had rarely been seen even in fun-loving Vienna. Above all, they wrote poems—or, rather, doggerel—songs, tracts, editorials. Free at last to write without fear of censor or police, the students and other intellectuals who had assumed leadership of the revolution turned out enormous quantities of literature. Between the night of March 14 and the early morning hours of the 16th, 45 poems were composed; on the 16th, 19 more were produced; and 45 others were penned on the 17th. From March 14 to April 1, the budding generation of revolutionary poets wrote no fewer than 436 poems,[1] if such they can be called.

In caricatures, epigrams, and pamphlets, Viennese wits praised the revolution, attempted to explain its cause, or attacked their former enemies, real and alleged. Rumors, scandals, and exposés were accepted by the credulous masses, who were eager to believe any evil about the ousted officials. Naïve, crude, inaccurate, and bombastic though many of these productions were, they represented the revolution in all its storm and fury, and they do give insight into the mood of the Viennese during the days of the March revolution.

Many writers sought to explain the causes and the significance of the revolution. Of such a nature was the brochure addressed to the *Wide-Awake Citizens of Our Great and Glorious Austria!*[2] printed on the

---

[1] Joseph Alexander Freiherrn von Helfert, *Der Wiener Parnass im Jahre 1848*, p. xxii. See also Carl Elbinger, *Witz und Satire Anno 1848* pp. 8–9.

[2] Ignaz Wildner von Maithstein, *Wackere Mitbürger des grossen herrlichen*

The Literature of the Revolution

evening of March 14, immediately after the news of the end of censorship became known. Because it is typical of the fierce attacks on the Metternich regime, the brochure is quoted below in full:

Alongside the banner of justice, always so sacred to the Austrian throne, a man who fortunately is not of Austrian origin[3] has only too long established a system that honors the promises solemnly and publicly made before all Europe as little as it did the promise it had made in private that we were to be burdened with a debt of 900 million gulden (at 5 per cent) to destroy the French Republic and the despotism that sprang from it. (These soldiers are now better prepared to fight us than they were at the time before we had the debts!!) It is a system, I say, that has harvested disgrace wherever it wanted to establish itself, a system which has reduced our prestige in foreign lands almost to zero, a system that misled Charles X into arbitrarily rescinding laws the whole nation had made and thereby prepared his own destruction,[4] and a system that supported Dom Miguel[5] and Don Carlos[6] until both, who were willing to give their very lives for the throne, fled from the Fatherland they had cherished from their infancy. It is a system that supported Holland against oppressed Belgium until the latter raised her head;[7] that destroyed the constitution in Southern Italy that had been so solemnly granted[8] and has only just now been restored; and that supported the Sonderbund in Switzerland[9]—that reprehensible breach in the Swiss Federation.

It is a system that fell to pieces because, instead of directing the mind into wholesome channels, it fettered the mind in all Austria, in all Italy, and in all Germany, where freedom of the press had so solemnly been promised thirty-three years ago in the Act of the Confederation.[10] These eternal lords of material things wanted to repress material things and acted in the

---

Oesterreich! Copy of the brochure in the Univ. Colo. 1848 Coll., No. II/227. In this and subsequent translations from brochures, proclamations, etc., paragraph divisions have been introduced for convenience in reading.

[3] Metternich was a native of the Rhineland.

[4] Doubtless an allusion to the July ordinances of Charles X, which precipitated the French revolution of 1830.

[5] Miguel Maria Evaristo de Bragança (1802–66).

[6] Carlos María Isidro de Borbón (1788–1855).

[7] In 1830 the Belgians successfully revolted against the Netherlands.

[8] The 1820 revolution forced Ferdinand IV, king of the Two Sicilies, to grant a constitution to his subjects. The constitution was abrogated the next year, when an Austrian army was sent to Naples to put down the revolution.

[9] The Sonderbund was a league formed in 1845 by seven Catholic cantons of Switzerland to oppose the Protestants and alter the federal constitution. The Sonderbund was dissolved by the Swiss Diet, but its members refused to disband, and the diet sent an army against the Sonderbund forces and defeated them in November, 1847. The victory prevented Austrian and French intervention and led to the adoption of a more centralized constitution in 1848.

[10] Signed at Vienna on June 8, 1815.

same way as the owner of a machine who, instead of using the steam in the boiler for useful purposes, shuts it up and shuts it up until it suddenly blows up and causes death and destruction on all sides.

It is a system that for years has suspended the same Hungarian constitution it so solemnly swore to protect and that even now has not allowed it to operate fully. Based as it is on false principles, it is a system that has engendered universal distrust and has almost completely destroyed state credit for the times of danger that lie ahead. It is a system that, because it—this can be said to our great honor!—can find no more public defenders within the country, has repeatedly entered into a bond with foreigners who have lent their pens to defend such breaches of promise. It is a system that nourishes national hatreds and does not permit that joyful spirit of brotherly love which is natural to us to come into being. In short, it is a system that has brought misfortune everywhere because it does not hesitate to break its promises and because it does not respect that which is cherished by strong men, namely, to be master of the first promise but slave to any promise once given.

Wide-awake fellow-citizens! This man coming from a foreign land has pushed the destructive system to such a point that he puts scions of the imperial house—which loves us and is badly advised only because of his authority—in a position where they directed their deadly weapons against us,[11] thereby seriously endangering those beautiful ties which for centuries kept us all cheerfully loyal to the imperial house, both in days of joy and in days of danger. "To this point and no further," said the Emperor, with his now enlightened eye and with his heart beating warmly for us, and down fell the foreigner and his system of broken promises and the enslavement of the minds and hearts (which, regardless of national differences, were all beating joyfully for the Fatherland and the throne and for justice, freedom, and order). The words of the Act of the Confederation stipulating that we are to have no censorship have already been put into effect. They will now always be a reality. There will be no more disillusionment. The banner of justice, which always flies beside the throne, will never again be torn to shreds.

Citizens, among whom I count with joy the brave sons of our old, venerated university, who have so valiantly preserved the fame of their alma mater, have been entrusted with arms and given the right to perform guard duty and to patrol the streets. Everybody's heart beats joyfully at the sight of the old flags that have been fetched from the university and the civic arsenal in order again to entrust to the spring air the old glory of the upright Viennese, so gallantly earned on the walls of Vienna against the Turks and the French.[12] In short, a National Guard has been granted us. Both of

[11] A reference to Archduke Albert, supreme commander of the troops who fired on the Viennese on March 13.

[12] The author is referring to the siege of Vienna by the Turks in 1529 and again in 1683, and to the Napoleonic Wars against Austria.

these institutions—freedom from the tyrannical censorship and the National Guard—are the true foundation upon which the structure of the new system will be built and upon which the constitution for the Fatherland, which the Emperor has also promised us, will be established in the same sense in which it has so long been interpreted in other German states. What has happened will now be told to the public! I can gladly say that much that is good will come out of it, but there will also be much that is absurd. This is the case everywhere under the sun, particularly under such a preposterous system as we have had. If we have the courage boldly and earnestly to face what is wrong, with calm and deliberation, we may be assured that that Divine Providence which has made this empire great and promises a glorious future for it will give us the strength to heal these unpleasant wounds.

Let us be united and strong in our dealings with foreign countries, as well as in facing domestic problems. Let us clasp the hands of all nationalities like brothers so that no single inch of land will be lost to our throne. Let us show the world that Austria can be strong if it *only will be*. Let us also maintain close relations with our German brothers and risk our lives and property for their and our independence so that no danger can threaten us from either East or West. We shall succeed admirably in all this if we strengthen the bond that up to now has held all of us together, namely, *"Loyal love to our hereditary throne,"* which has recognized the needs of the times and which will be ready to strive just as hard to satisfy them as previously it stalwartly pursued the course of justice and the political system given to it by a foreigner.

Freedom! Order! Justice! Love for our prince and our Fatherland! Let these be the watchwords of the Civic Guard and every fellow-citizen, and most assuredly the malaise that the perverted system of the man who has fled has brought upon us will be healed as soon as possible, which is what all of us most earnestly wish.

Vienna, March 14, 1848, immediately following the proclamation of the abolition of the censorship.

Dr. Wildner-Maithstein.

Also characteristic of the maledictions heaped upon the deposed government was the following *Volksfreund* article, entitled "What Happened in Vienna,"[13] a denunciation of the Habsburgs for ordering the soldiers to fire on the Viennese on March 13:

---

[13] "Was sich in Wien ereignet hat," *Der Volksfreund. Zeitschrift für Aufklärung und Erheiterung des Volkes,* No. 1 (March 28, 1848), pp. 1–3, copy in the Univ. Colo. 1848 Coll., No. II/209. The *Volksfreund,* edited by Joseph Rank, was one of the many revolutionary newspapers that appeared during the early days of the revolution. The first issue appeared on March 28, 1848; the last, on October 19. The paper came out three times a week until the middle of June, when it became a daily.

The *Volksfreund* takes you at once into the midst of history. Imagine that it is March 13, one o'clock sharp. All Vienna is astir. In all the streets there is nothing but soldiers and Viennese, Viennese and soldiers. The soldiers are standing all around the imperial residence with sabers drawn and fixed bayonets, helmet after helmet, shako after shako, gun after gun, cannon after cannon. Around Prince Metternich's palace there is cannon after cannon, grenadier after grenadier. In Herren Street there are gunners, grenadiers, and engineers. On the city walls there is one cannon after another. Military drums are at all street corners. All the city gates are closed and barricaded with soldiers. And in the midst of all these frightful things at least a hundred thousand unarmed Viennese are hurrying to and fro.

At one o'clock the soldiers were still quiet. So were the guns and cannon. Even the horses of the cuirassiers and hussars were not stamping and snorting as usual, but stood like silent fortifications and looked on in fear and amazement. But the Viennese were screaming and shouting all the more. You might ask, "But why are the Viennese shouting and screaming so madly?" The *Volksfreund* can only tell you briefly and with a smile: "The good Viennese wanted only to speak to their kind Emperor in a peaceful manner, for they had harbored worthy desires in their hearts for years. They finally put these desires into words and took them to their Emperor."

You might smile in amazement and ask, "Is that all? Does it take all this to tell our dear Ferdi that so and so is how we feel, dear father of our land? This and that are what your most loyal people and most loyal empire desire. Grant them to us and we shall enthrone you in our hearts and swear to you that our hearts will not waver unto eternity. Thousands and thousands of Viennese are rushing through the imperial palace every day and the Emperor lives but one flight up. Why didn't the loyal Viennese simply go there and present their wishes?" This is what you ask. However, the *Volksfreund* must unfortunately give you an answer you don't like to hear, namely: "The Viennese actually did go there and announce themselves to the Emperor and handed him a number of requests in writing, but then all of a sudden cannon were brought up, grenadiers approached, cuirassiers rode up, bayonets were sharpened, and guns were loaded. That pleasant going to and coming from the palace was all over now. The Emperor now no longer lived one flight above his Viennese. He lived in a frightfully guarded fortress a thousand miles away from his Viennese!"

You will become purple with rage and say: "There must be something more to this. Our Emperor did not answer in such a devilish manner. We also know our Ferdinand, and whoever wants to make him responsible for something when it is not true will have to deal with us, by God, may we live or die!" That's fine talk. The *Volksfreund*, however, is even more enraged than you are, for we know who gave that devilish answer in the Emperor's place. It was Prince Metternich and his good friends, for these people have for long, long years done nothing but try to turn the good heart of the Emperor, which is so full of love, against his people. It was these people who got hold of the entreaties of the loyal Viennese on the 13th of March and told the Emperor: "Your Majesty! The Viennese are rebels. They themselves don't know what they want. By their requests they want only to arm themselves so that they can kill Your Majesty." And even before the Emperor had said "yes" or "no" these malicious advisers ordered adjutants to fly hither and yon with the command: "Soldiers advance! Bring the cannon forward! Load and stand ready!"

Now was the time for the Viennese to flush with anger. They actually did become so enraged that they scarcely knew what they were doing. Thousands and thousands ran hither and yon. Thousands of others screamed with savage frenzy. Even the loudest peal of thunder would be a trifling thing compared to this. It seemed as if millions of angels were blowing the trumpets of the last judgment. One could not hear himself speak. However, instead of subsiding, the frightful tumult increased every minute. There was no longer any chance of recognizing the good Viennese. In their sullen vengeance, the people looked upon the cannon as if they were shooting forth flowers and candy. People had as little respect for the bayonets and feared them as if they were made of leather. The Viennese is usually touchy when some one tramples upon him, but this time he ran about under the horses of the cuirassiers and hussars as if his feet were made of steel and iron. Then all at once there was a command in Herren Street: "Fire!" And a number of guns were fired.—O Lord! Seven men waver, totter, and fall down on the pavement. They are dead, and their blood is flowing under the feet of the people. O Lord! Who gave the order to shoot? Did the Viennese have arms? Is that why the military came up so quickly to kill and murder? No! Only a few pieces of wood and a few stones had flown in the air. The commandant was slightly hit. That is why he gave the order to fire.

Our great general, Archduke Charles,[14] how your heart would have bled if you now saw the young commandant acting in this manner! You had to die so you would not live to see this! Charles, you were brave in battle and gallant in front of your soldiers. You commanded them to shoot and to spare no ammunition. Today, however, it was the bravery of facing a people who had nothing in their hands, who could not advance or retreat because of the crowd, and who could at the most only throw pieces of wood in the air. Did this bravery mean anything to the young impetuous commandant? Are the students and Viennese now to be dispersed like dirty trash? Have the Viennese lost all desire to carry out their wishes? That is a poor judgment! Now it means blood for blood. One can die only

[14] Archduke Charles Louis (1771–1847), the son of Emperor Leopold II and probably the outstanding Austrian general of the Napoleonic Wars. He was considered to be one of the most liberal of the early nineteenth-century Habsburg archdukes.

once. We have started. In God's name, let us continue. Whoever still fears death is a scoundrel!

The oversimplifications of the above article seem highly sophisticated when compared with the quaint views on the accomplishments of the March revolution expressed in the following essay, entitled "The Governmental Clockworks":[15]

You should become acquainted with every one of the great wheels—the ministers—down to the very tiniest ones—the practitioners. Good people, up to now these governmental clockworks have been hidden from you behind Chinese walls, and you could not see how many useless wheels hummed along, how many an important wheel always ran backwards instead of forwards, and how so many a big important wheel no longer had any cogs and yet was not thrown out. Poor people! Year after year you paid the state watchmaker. The wheels were oiled with the sweat of your brows. Nevertheless, this did not help. The Austrian governmental clockworks always cost more and more and always ran worse and worse. Then our beautiful, glorious Vienna finally rose up in anger, beat her fist on the governmental table, raged, and stormed, and shouted: "Good gracious, this can no longer go on. Out with the old wheels. Brand new ones must replace them. The best watchmakers must fashion them, and the whole Austrian people must be present when they are put into the clock so that the governmental clockworks will be improved."

The shouting became so loud that it reached the ears of the Emperor. Immediately he said: "What? Are my governmental clockworks that bad? And my ministerial wheels hummed to me day and night that everything is going along splendidly!" And the Emperor immediately took down the dial and with his own hands removed the bad ministerial wheels. In this way was the first and very worst wheel cast aside[16]—the one that blocked the progress of every other one that wanted to go forward. Along with this one big wheel, others were also cast out, and this will continue for some time. But the Emperor has decided: "In the future I will not govern with just one single adviser. I am the father of my people, and in the future I want to see my children around me, and I will ask them what they want, what they need, and what they lack. From every nook and corner of my realm the best and smartest men are to be selected and sent to my court. We will rule together, and together we will repair the governmental clock-

---

[15] "Das Staatsuhrwerk," *Ankündigung der in unserem Verlage neu zu erscheinenden Zeitschrift: Der Volksfreund,* pp. 2–3, Univ. Colo. 1848 Coll., No. II/233. In a short paragraph at the end of the article, which has been omitted here, the writer explains that regular readers of the *Volksfreund* would gain insight into political affairs that would help them instruct their representatives about what to do to foster the interests of the people.

[16] A reference to Metternich's dismissal.

works. Then you will see how fine it will be to study the governmental clockworks together."

The best Emperor, dear people, wants your advice; therefore, won't you also need the proper insight? Indeed, you will send your smartest men to the court, but won't you also need to know how you are to test them and what you should tell them to do? Must you not know definitely whether or not they will change the governmental clockworks to your best advantage and whether or not the clock actually strikes the hour it shows on the dial?

While some writers were content to "explain" the revolution, a much larger number penned verses praising the accomplishments of the revolution and its heroes. They wrote tributes to the beautiful women of Vienna, who had inspired the revolutionary fighters by showering them with ribbons, scarves, and roses,[17] and to the heroes who had freed their fatherland from the oppressor's chains.[18] Even the dead Joseph II was not spared the gush of words.[19] Especially numerous were poems in praise of freedom of the press, the National Guard, and the Viennese students. The following poem was written on March 15 by a native of Danzig who happened to be in Vienna during the revolution:[20]

> The press is free! The bells ring forth,
> And joy resounds from every hall;
> Proclaim it far to distant shores:
> The press is free! Scale freedom's wall!
> What long years of hard suppression,
> Humiliation and dismay,
> Are now erased through heroism,
> And the work of *one* great day.
>
> Speak freely now from inner soul,
> Bring cherished wishes to the light;
> Freedom's foe has now been killed,
> Victorious now are truth and right.
> Pour forth your hearts with passion filled,
> A bless'd age dawns clear and bright.
> Now your lips may speak unsealed,
> Let honor be your only guide.

[17] See especially Karl Appel, *Loblied der Damen Wiens,* Univ. Colo. 1848 Coll., No. II/5.

[18] See especially the *Volkslied* published by Carl Gerold, Univ. Colo. 1848 Coll., No. II/206.

[19] See especially J. P. Lyser, *Ein Frühlingstag vor dem Denkmale des Kaisers Joseph des Zweiten. Dem Volke, das Er liebte und schätzte, am 15. März gewidmet,* Univ. Colo. 1848 Coll., No. II/135.

[20] Friedrich Gerhard, *Die Presse frei! Wien, 15. März 1848. Erstes censurfreies Gedicht,* four-page pamphlet, Univ. Colo. 1848 Coll., No. II/89.

For many a victim should you mourn;
The dead deserve well many a tear,
For those who fell on freedom's morn,
Brave heroes of this day so dear.
Rest in peace! This we have sworn!
Inscribe these words upon their bier:
This dear blood of German born
Was shed because of censor's shear.

Let every prince in German district
Remember well the lesson here:
Have faith in each and every subject,
Let bold, free word find ready ear.
If people's welfare is your object,
Then never their free word do fear,
And never let your mind be subject
To a ready flatterer's sneer.

In Austria, with its banners gleaming,
Eagles rise to solar height;
Germans will be praises singing,
When *this* day's news is brought to light.
Shake hands, good people, just and daring,
As friends and brothers, let us fight.
A Prussian joins you, freedom praising,
What joyous feeling to have light.

Another young enthusiast was inspired to deliver the following note of gratitude on behalf of the free press:[21]

The Press to Its Deliverers!

A word! For every man is free,
  To sing and shout on every hand;
He may rejoice and shout with glee,
  And twine a leaf in freedom's band!

The free press gives its thanks to all
  Who bravely, boldly, smote its chains;
In all our glorious Austria,
  No word need perish, for freedom reigns!

Above all else, the press shouts *"Hail!"*
  To those who dared the first bold word,
Which so long quaked, afraid and frail,
  Guilty of crime if it were heard.

[21] *Die Presse an ihre Erlöser!*, one-page sheet, Univ. Colo. 1848 Coll., No. II/60.

> In loud unison now all unite:
> "Long live the *students,* hail! hail! hail!"
> Who did the people's tyrant smite,
> And gave us freedom without fail!
>
> The press shouts out: "Hail *Fatherland!*
> And hail, our paternal Emperor, too!"
> Who long enchained by tyrant's hand,
> Now stands before us, great and true!

The first poem written during the March revolution was the "Song for the National Guard." Composed by J. F. Castelli, a Viennese student, on the night of March 13, while he was performing guard duty at the university,[22] it went as follows:[23]

> Arise, brothers! Gun in hand,
> And cockade in your hat!
> We finally are a nation,
> And guard must thus be had.
> The watchword is: sweet liberty!
> The password is: security.
>
> In one short day we now have gained
> That which for years we prayed;
> The odious friends of darkness
> Have all at once been stayed.
> The press is free, the lights are bright,
> And Austria with Germany will unite.
>
> Long live the youthful heroes, brave,
> Who first the Hydra monster slew,
> Who, deeply touched by German spirit,
> With courage won our freedom true.
> And if there flowed some noble blood,
> We thank it for this freedom's flood.
>
> Long live our Emperor Ferdinand,
> Who all our wishes has fulfilled.
> O guards, take care of Austrian nation,
> So that the tumult will be stilled.
> But over now is that short war!
> Take care! And not our freedom mar.

The Viennese students, the gallant heroes of the revolution, inspired

[22] Helfert, *op. cit.,* pp. xx–xxi; Maria Theresia Wanderer, *Revolutionsstürme Achtundvierzig,* p. 32.
[23] *Oestreich's Befreiungstage,* pp. 77–78.

most of the hymns of praise. It was only natural that their valiant deeds should call forth a host of verses. Probably the first of the many songs and poems dedicated to the academic youth was the "Choral Song for the Viennese Student Legion," written by Siegfried Kapper on the evening of March 14 in the guard room of the university. Written to be sung to a sonorous tune composed simultaneously by Henry Litolff, the lyrics read:[24]

> Awake, awake, O brother!
> A great day is dawning!
> A second will not come again!
> Come march in rank, O brother,
> The victor is he who is daring!
>
> Raise high, raise high our rights,
> And guns, good and shining!
> All *Austria's* sacred rights,
> And freedom's bright, proud lights,
> In glorious battle uniting!
>
> Forward without falter!
> Let citizens' hearts beat out!
> Let ne'er our spirits waver.
> And thanks to bold March *warriors*
> Austria's people will loudly shout!

At about the same time Frankl composed "The University," the most popular of the many poems dedicated to the students. It was written during the night of March 14, while Frankl was on sentry duty before the criminal-court building at the Alser Glacis, and was printed the next day. At least 100,000 copies of the poem were sold, and nineteen musical settings were composed for it.[25] The poem read as follows:[26]

> Lo, who be these so proud in bearing?
> The bayonets flash, the flags fly free.
> They come with silver trumpets blaring,
> The University!

[24] Henry Litolff and Siegfried Kapper, *Chorgesang der Wiener Studenten Legion. Zur Feier der 4 Tage im März 1848! 12. 13. 14. 15. der heldenmüthigen Studirenden-Legion an der Wiener Hochschule brüderlich geweit,* four-page pamphlet, Univ. Colo. 1848 Coll., No. II/236.

[25] Helfert, *op. cit.,* pp. xix–xx.

[26] Translated by J. G. Legge in his *Rhyme and Revolution in Germany,* pp. 271–72. For a copy in German of the first printed edition, see Ludwig August Frankl, *Die Universität. Erstes censurfreies Blatt aus der Josef Stöckholzer von Hirschfeld'schen Buchdruckerei,* Univ. Colo. 1848 Coll., No. II/83.

> The daylight hour at last is breaking
> Our hopes and prayers have yearned to see;
> 'Tis your young hearts to light awaking,
> O University!
>
> When Kaiser Joseph came in thunder
> To bind the tongue's sweet liberty,
> Who dared to burst the bonds asunder?
> The University!
>
> Our tongues wake with the lark to singing;
> O hear their dithyrambic glee!
> Heart calls, and heart sends answer ringing,
> All hail, the University!
>
> Where spirits of the dead are beckoning,
> The dead who died for freedom, see—
> With the first victim paid her reckoning
> The University!
>
> And when our sons in reverence finger
> Each glorious page in history,
> On thy name, writ in gold, they'll linger,
> Our University!

Another poem dedicated to the university that appeared on March 15 was the "New Folk Hymn for Vienna Students." The poet, Ludwig Eckardt, a member of the National Guard, included the notation that it was written "on the night of March 15, the 'Ides of March,' for ignoramuses." It read:[27]

> May God save all us students
> In our struggle for the light,
> Bring an end to erring darkness
> With no ruthless lash in sight!
> In time of peace, the pen is mighty,
> In time of war it is the sword;
> He who is by both protected,
> Is doubly strong, we give our word.
>
> May God save all our peoples,
> Who without hatred, hand in hand,
> In the far zones of our country
> Fought as one to save our land!
> We are worthy of the freedom

[27] Ludwig Eckardt (National Guardsman), *Neue Volks-Himme der Wiener Studenten,* two-page sheet, Univ. Colo. 1848 Coll., No. II/64.

For which all worthy burghers fight;
May the tricolor of our banner
E'er stand for duty, love, and right!

May God save the press unshackled,
Securest bond of German free;
Let the cènsor's hand not limit
Flow of thought or liberty.
May thought be free as air we breathe,
And mighty as the Danube's flow.
May no student from our high schools
E'er lax in sacred duty grow.

May God save our Deliverer,
Emperor Ferdinand, now also free!
For many dangers hovered ever
Betwixt the prince and his country.
For our free learning blood was shed,
And for the weal of one and all;
Those who fell while this defending
Fame shall place in future hall.

May God save all Austria,
Which first among all others stands!
May our ardor never falter,
May always restless be our hands!
As in our poetry, so in living,
Let us create a new dawn for all,
Which, heavenward, to hearts uplifted
Rises proud o'er German wall!

No matter how wretchedly the works were written, most Viennese
greeted each new song or poem with loud praise. The newsboys who
hawked them at a kreutzer or two each could never keep enough copies
on hand, and the publishers who printed them made sizable profits.
Within a few days the new revolutionary songs were being sung in all
the streets.

Unfortunately, not all the Viennese could participate in this revelry
without a few misgivings. Although universally enthusiastic about the
outcome of the revolution, the Jews were perturbed by sudden outbursts
of anti-Semitism in several parts of the empire, including the capital.
On the eve of the March revolution a considerable amount of anti-
Semitism existed not only in the Habsburg monarchy but also in much
of central and eastern Europe. The sudden release of long-suppressed
emotions and energies served to bring it out into the open. As stated

earlier, in 1848 the Jews were subject to various discriminations and had to pay a special tax—a price for toleration. Even though most of them made their living from trade and commerce, quite a few had found their way into literature, medicine, and the arts and sciences.[28] Doubtless because they constituted a second-class citizenry, many Jews were among the foremost revolutionary leaders. Fischhof, Goldmark, and Goldner—the three men who did most to incite the crowd before the Landhaus to rebellion—were Jews, as was a student named Spitzer who fell as one of the first victims of the revolution. The Jews saw in the revolution not only the overthrow of an unpopular, oppressive regime but also a prelude to their emancipation.

Nevertheless, in spite of the fact that the liberals recognized the contributions of various Jews to the revolution, most of the citizens continued to regard them as a band of hagglers, petty traders, and usurers and remained indifferent or hostile to their pleas for emancipation. When petitions were circulated in favor of Jewish liberation, few non-Jews signed them. Their opponents drew up counterpetitions demanding that the Jews be kept subservient or wrote and circulated pamphlets reviling them.[29]

Many Viennese delighted in a malicious tract written by a certain Friedrich Steiner on "The New Jewish Citizens' Militia," in which the author described in an insulting manner the efforts of the Jews in the Leopoldstadt quarter to enroll in their new militia.[30] Though the Jews were reviled by a few such anti-Semitic pamphleteers, they suffered no physical violence in Vienna. At Pressburg, however, people openly insulted the Jews and spoke of running them out of the city. In Raab a bloody pogrom was averted only because students arrived and frightened away the rioters. At Stuhlweissenburg a popular assembly drew up a petition demanding that the Jews close down their businesses and leave the city immediately if they did not want to be chased out.[31]

Such anti-Semitic demonstrations inspired the writing of the following tract in defense of the Jews:[32]

[28] Josephine Goldmark, *Pilgrims of '48*, pp. 97–98.
[29] Dr. Hammerschmid, "Die Emancipation der Juden betreffend," *Wiener Zeitung*, No. 90 (March 30, 1848), p. 418.
[30] Friedrich Steiner, "Die neue Jüden-Bürger-Miliz," Friedrich Unterreiter, *Die Revolution in Wien vom März und Mai 1848*, Vol. II, pp. 17–20.
[31] Franz Pulszky, *Mein Zeit, mein Leben*, Vol. II, pp. 87–89.
[32] Abraham, "Bürger, stosst die Juden nicht zurück!" *Oesterreichische konstitutionelle deutsche Zeitung. Ein Blatt für Politik, Kunst und Wissenschaft aller Völker*, No. 2 (April 4, 1848), pp. 7–8, Univ. Colo. 1848 Coll., No. II/157. The *Oesterreichische konstitutionelle deutsche Zeitung*, edited by H. Löw, first appeared on April 1, 1848. The paper was published three times a week. On April

Citizens, don't reject the Jews!

Intermingled with the first rejoicing over the new freedom is the shrill tone of intolerance. But this is not the intolerance of the Middle Ages, which was based on a pious madness for burning heretics at the stake. It is the intolerance of egotism, of privilege, and of caste. It is not the Christian who is intolerant, but the shoemaker, or the tailor, or the glovemaker. This type of intolerance has produced scenes at the sight of which a constitutionally free citizen should hide his face in shame. The worst took place at Pressburg. Here a great number of citizens are Germans, who, with their patrician haughtiness and with their mercenary spirit, are putting their individual interests above the welfare of the city, the country, and the people. They could not bear to see a Jew carry a saber, become a master cobbler, open a shop, or even become a citizen. A silver-plater, who was formerly a butcher's helper, and a hotelkeeper, who was formerly a hotel servant, were the leaders of a riot against the Jews. Windows were broken and people were beaten. The rabble, lusting for plunder, were stirred up, and finally in a large assembly of citizens it was decided the Jews must leave the city! While this was happening, in the same city the imperial Estates of Hungary magnanimously gave up their feudal privileges and emancipated the formerly oppressed and scorned citizens outside their own city. But the tune is different in regard to the Jews. Thus especially in Vienna a couple of pamphleteers are stirring up the public against them. What they are writing is sheer madness, crass ignorance, and a clumsy abortion of the mind and heart. But the cry of the prostitutes—"Let's oppose the Jews! Let's have no more Jews! Leave the Jews as they are!"— has seduced the public. Selfishness—the handmaiden of intolerance—is easily brought into play. In the intelligent capital, where the intricate commercial intercourse and the existence of big industrial establishments had already wiped out social differences, suddenly, instead of the constitution, instead of the stability of the empire, instead of freedom, the Jew has become the subject of conversation day and night. His moral elevation, his place in the new political relationships, and his amalgamation in the new state are not at all discussed. The conversations concern themselves only with how the Jews should and could be suppressed, excluded, and isolated. That is an extremely sad state of affairs for every friend of the Fatherland and of humanity!

Citizens, don't reject the Jews! They have fine talents, and most of them lead temperate, orderly family lives. Since up to now they have been excluded from the common endeavors of others, their activity has been limited to their own families and community. Enslaved as they were by thousands of restraints on their civic relations, they were not *permitted*

---

14 the title was changed to *Oesterreichisch deutsche Zeitung*. After August 13 it ceased publication.

to be anything but hagglers. Their haggling comes from the sinful old laws and that accursed political system based upon robber knights and servile subjects, taxpaying citizens, and Jewish ghettos. The practice of usury arose from the easy movability of property. When almost every day one could expect to be driven out of his house or country, to be plundered or taxed in an arbitrary fashion (the Bohemian Jews paid a 22½ per cent property tax alone), which has been the case in the past, one *had* to possess property that could easily be transported and that was very profitable. Every human being wants to live. This instinct of self-preservation alone was responsible for corrupting Jews brought up in accord with the purest moral teachings, for they had to use underhanded methods to find their way around the laws of the land just to earn their bread, while being beaten, or through even harder blows upon human dignity and human rights.

The Jew is not bad. He is not arrogant. He is no haggler. Nor is he a usurer. A thousand times, no! It is not the Jew, but it is the Abraham, or the Moses, or the Itzig. And even these individual persons were made that way only because of the slavery which oppressed their fathers and ancestors for centuries.

Accept them among your midst, citizens! Then you will see what a high moral code, what a spirit of sacrifice, what high intellectual qualities, what a renunciation of private interests, and what love for prince, country, and people the Jew—the liberated Jew—is capable of.

All those who through blind prejudice vent their spleen upon the Austrian citizens of Jewish faith will then be ashamed, for perhaps even just a decáde will restore what a thousand years have spoiled. Freedom is a very warm hothouse.

Citizens, don't reject the Jews! They want to live *with* you and to fight *for* you. Without you they would have to live by and fight for themselves. They stand before you, not demanding, but imploring you to accept them in your midst. The children of the country are imploring you to accept them so that they can contribute to the country's welfare with all their strength.

Citizens, don't reject the Jews!

Abraham.

The attacks against the Jews were relatively mild compared with those against the censorship, the police, and those officials whom the revolutionary myth had transformed into villains. The more scurrilous the vilification of the "bureaucrats," the more avidly it was devoured by the newly liberated populace.

With delight the Viennese read this mock necrology of the censorship:[33]

[33] Heinrich Reschauer and Moritz Smets, *Das Jahr 1848. Geschichte der Wiener Revolution*, Vol. I, p. 382.

Authentic Report

Concerning the Death on March 14, 1848, and the Burial Services
of Mrs. Good-Woman Censor, born at Midnight.

On March 14, 1848, died the oldest matron of Vienna, who, like a
certain Count St. Germain,[34] unfortunately lived many years and sur-
vived the greatest phenomena of the times. Her name was Mrs. Good-
Woman Censor. She died after several hours of painful convulsions which
paralyzed her brain. The preliminary symptoms had been evident for a
long time. In spite of her venerable old age, she is mourned by nobody. The
deceased was a twin sister of Mrs. Torquata Torture, who was sentenced
to death by a decree of Maria Theresa on January 3, 1776. She thus sur-
vived her worthy sister by seventy-two years and two months.

The body, which was lifeless even while she lived, was buried on the 16th
in the midst of great gloom. The earth received it *erga schedam* for eternal
rest in its bosom. The funeral ceremonies were held, not with solemn expressions of sorrow, but rather with an ostentatious display of rejoicing.
Although a great number of people attended out of curiosity, there were
few mourners.

The corpse, embalmed with asafetida and with incense from the horns
of miserable creatures, was clothed in a robe made of snake skins. It was
in a coffin made of apastric wood, with the appropriate four-squared coat
of arms, on which there were painted, in brilliant colors, a blind worm, a
vampire, a crab, and an owl. It was carried by four jailers of the criminal
court. On top of the coffin was a copy of Llorente's *History of the Holy
Inquisition*,[35] bound in tiger skin.

Directly following the coffin, visible in deepest mourning, were her
closest relatives, Mrs. Damnatur and Mrs. Rejiciatur, who, moved by
deepest grief, left our city immediately afterwards. More composed was her
distant relative, Mr. Transeat.[36] Several brothers, who lived on the banks
of the Danube, closed the little procession, which was seen by everybody
but no one desired to accompany it. Instead of a song of mourning, one
could hear the melodies, "We Lead a Free Life" and "Things Cannot Go
On Like This Forever." Silently and quietly the small procession returned
from Klederling, where the burial took place, and in way of offering a

---

[34] The author is probably referring to the Comte de Saint Germain, a French
diplomat and adventurer who died about 1784. A student of the occult, he claimed
to possess the philosopher's stone and elixir of life.

[35] Juan Antonio Llorente, *History of the Inquisition of Spain, from Its Establishment to the Reign of Ferdinand VII.* In 1809 Joseph Bonaparte commissioned
Llorente to examine the archives of the Inquisition and write its history. With the
departure of the French from Spain, Llorente also found it prudent to go to Paris,
where the first edition was printed in 4 volumes in 1817. The first German edition
was published in Stuttgart in 1824.

[36] *Erga schedam, damnatur, rejiciatur,* and *transeat* were terms used by the
censors in examining written material before publication.

mourning feast to her memory they spent the night in the catacombs under St. Stephen's Square, because the city was illuminated with many lights, which her friends could not bear to see.

The Viennese also chuckled over the verses about the "Dead Censor," written by the renowned Saphir and first published in *Der Humorist* on March 16:[37]

> See he sits there on the mat,
>   Has the censor's pen with him;
> In a spirit which is mad
>   He condemns what's good with vim!
>
> Still where is the strength he wages,
>   Where the sharp discrimination?
> For most of what was on the pages
>   He consigns to condemnation.
>
> Where is the pen which if unshackled
>   Is the mind's best protégé?
> Like the bloodhound in the forest
>   It doth on noblest creature prey.
>
> The same finger that so quickly
>   Through the closely packed lines races,
> Like a stag with ten big antlers
>   Darts forth after cool spring's traces.
>
> This sweet note of questioning
>   With an ever open mind?
> Lo, its life's condemned to fading
>   And sure death has made it blind.
>
> Farewell to him! Home he withdraws
>   To where free press can never be,
> And sad death with censor's claws
>   Our dear speech will ne'er set free.
>
> Where the serpent "Delatur"
>   Eats up every corpse in sight,
> And Hell itself gives its "Damnatur"
>   To be used as a transit right!
>
> Bring to me the gift of pen,
>   Strike the tune for the death lament!

[37] Helfert, *op. cit.*, pp. 60–61. *Der Humorist* was founded in 1837 and was issued six times a week. It was published under the name *Der politische Horizont*, from September 24 to November 26, 1848, when its original name was restored.

All is buried there with him,
   Which his joy there can augment.

Lay beneath his head the columns
   Which he daily did devour,
Which surround him all so solemn,
   For his way is long and dour.

Also scissors deftly sharpened,
   Which with such a skillful grip
From fine heads to thought accustomed
   Scraped hair and skin without a slip.

Give him also ink to paint:
   "In suspense" for one long year,
So he can radiate his blackness
   Among white ghosts whom he'll pass near.

The secret police received their share of abuse. In a tract entitled *The Confidants,* written on March 28, a certain Severin von Schmitz attacked them thus: [38]

> *And have you long and always asked?*
> *Take heed, for you have been arraigned!*
> *You're locked in jail. And you ask why!*
> *But justice gives just one mute sigh!*
> —Maltitz.

A nice word was added to the German vocabulary when people began referring to police spies—those bloodhounds, those renowned hunters—as "the confidants."

"I would gladly live in Paris were it not for the fact that so many Parisians live there," wrote a great man. We have also cried out for just as long a time: "I would gladly live in Vienna were it not for the fact that so many confidants live there."

The confidant was the same to the spoken word as the censor was to the written one. At any rate, the writer fared better than the talker. The censor entertained himself with striking things out; the confidant locked us up. The censor wrote, "It is not permitted"; but the confidant said, "He will be let out no more." The censor damaged only intellectual freedom; but the confidant often took our personal freedom from us.

This enforced silence, so abhorrent to all human beings, has oppressed us long enough. The following anecdote will partly illustrate how afraid we were of these boorish muzzlers:

In an inn there were three guests all full of sweet wine. The one was cry-

[38] Severin von Schmitz, "Die Vertrauten," Unterreiter, *op. cit.,* Vol. II, pp. 10–16.

ing. He was a Pole. The other ranted and cursed. He was a Hungarian. The third slept. He was an Austrian. The Pole seemed to be weeping over hopes now entombed. The Hungarian seemed to be preparing for the next diet. The sleeping Austrian seemed to be having bad dreams. What was he dreaming about? When he woke up he asked in a frightened voice, "Did I snore, sir?" His companions said he had not and then laughed and asked for an explanation of his strange question. Whereupon the Austrian took a deep breath, like someone from whose heart a heavy burden had been lifted, and answered very gravely: "I am fortunate. Do you know, gentlemen, that snoring is a police offense?"

There is much bitter truth in this jest. Now we can, of course, laugh over it. In a warm room one can talk most cheerfully about snowstorms.

Those who engaged in the work must know what good the confidants accomplished. We don't know! We know only that they ruined every public amusement place for us, and that they frightened even the most pleasure-loving circles. We know only that they were the sad cause of all this. Foreigners do not feel at home with us. They originated the proverbial saying that in Vienna one cannot sneeze a single time without having a confidant asking him about it. So many of them know that there is no other city in the whole world so overflowing with these tramps as our dear friendly Vienna! These confidants have cost the state thousands of gulden. Even the most stupid among us can tell you whether all of them together are worth even the interest paid for all this money spent on them. I say: The worst possible opinion that people had about them is better than what they actually were. Their pay—to end with Börne—was without doubt the most valuable thing about them.

If you had remained where you belonged, our curses would not have reached you. You should have paid attention to and lain in wait for the thieves and swindlers. You would have earned your salaries if you had spied a lost wallet and questioned a pickpocket about it. Nobody will thank you for the chance word—often thoughtless and spoken in haste—which you snatched up with fanatical joy and reported to "higher places."

We had no representatives of the people; instead, we had persons who trampled upon the people! Not satisfied with the fact that they oppressed and aggrieved the good people, they pitilessly listened to the cries of anguish that came from the tormented hearts! Who does not understand that a worm that has been stepped upon turns? You have stepped on the whole people and have forbidden us to do even this. Such accursed work can bring happiness neither to the tormentors nor to the slaves.

I still remember vividly how I once grew angry when a foreigner called the confidants "imperial employees." In my opinion they never were employees of the Emperor. Certainly our good, beloved Emperor never intended to permit his loyal people to be spied upon. He, the good Emperor, thought much more of his subjects than to allow them to be watched in such a petty way. However, those who are not even worthy of the drop of ink which it takes to sign their names are the ones who thought up this wretched idea! Whoever helped to think it up must himself have had it in mind. Or at least his concept of "freedom of thought" must have been much worse even than his lack of good sense! What a poor, low opinion those who believed that such spies were necessary must have had of us. The disgrace falls on them, not on us, for the very fact that they felt that spies were necessary gives proof of the full measure of their guilt. An honest man is not afraid of public opinion. Whoever fears it and timorously listens to every word which an unknown person says about him is much worse, in my opinion, than the person who has freely spoken that free word. Can I call such good persons angels? Who can prevent me from calling a scoundrel a scoundrel?

Accordingly, let us have freedom of speech—wholly unlimited freedom of speech! God gave us the power of speech, and human beings cannot take this beautiful gift of God away from us! How loudly and how universally freedom of speech in these days has expressed its love and devotion to the Emperor and to the imperial house! But because we praise the sun which gives us light and lovingly warms us with its rays, the other stars have no right to force us to sing the same song of praise to them. The good Christian trusts only one God. Whoever bends down in worship of all gods worships none of them.

Accordingly, let us have freedom of speech—wholly unlimited freedom of speech! We who not long ago were the laughing stock of all nations have now won attention and respect and aroused astonishment. As oppressed and timid as we formerly were, we now proudly and boldly call ourselves Austrians! The word, formerly spied upon and imprisoned, has sprung its fetters. Freedom of speech will sprout forth where the weight of the secret police bore down for such a long time. We have been given the privilege of witnessing the death of that which has lived so long. We can have the fine hope that a new life will blossom forth as a consequence of its death.

I am very happy to have sung a funeral dirge to you. No one will allow you to be awakened to the new life. I will ring the bells of progress until you finally go on your last procession, and then I will erect a tombstone for you that will be better than you all expected!

Vienna, March 28.
Severin v. Schmitz.

The Vienna police force and the city-government officials were attacked in a brochure bearing the title *The Robbers' Nest of Administrative and Police Officials, or: The Bureaucracy of Administrative Officials in Vienna.*[39] At the top of the first page were pictures of four

---

[39] *Das magistratisch-politische Raubnest, oder: die Wiener magistratische Beamten-Bureaukratie,* copy in the Univ. Colo. 1848 Coll., No. II/279.

Viennese officials hanging on a scaffold. The text below read as follows:

The long desired time of freedom has finally come, but unfortunately the time of divine justice is still not here. As long as the bureaucratic mask is not torn off in Vienna, the administrative and police officials will boldly continue to carry on their deceitful political tricks against justice. Is it possible that your bureaucracy can still exist in Vienna? You bloodhounds! You who have morally and physically murdered more than 30,000 families through your bureaucracy and have made complete beggars of them! You blasphemers of justice and of the Emperor's name! You hangmen! And you still continue to enjoy the constitutional freedom which we citizens purchased with our blood? You bureaucrats who in broad daylight robbed and pilfered all our tradespeople and built prisons and slaughter houses and drank thousands of bottles of champagne with this blood money. You masked Christian hounds! Do you think you can get by with your trickery and hypocrisy? Do you believe that we will not discover your villainous tricks because of the courteous flattery in which you are now engaging? You scoundrels! You thieves! You moral and physical murderers of citizens and businessmen! Have you no sense of honor at all? Have you no human dignity in your black hearts which restrains you from awaiting your fate with such an absurd bearing? I can name you thousands of families besides myself whom you have most shamelessly pilfered and robbed. I can name several thousand individuals whose records you forged so that the government would be so deluded by your tyrannical verdicts that it would never mitigate the diabolical sentences you imposed upon His Majesty's subjects.

No one is in a position to count up the hours and days all the Viennese tradespeople spent in jail because their records were forged. I, the undersigned, have in a period of twenty-five years spent 1,008 hours in jail, not as a criminal, but merely for business reasons—because I sold a broom for 8 kreutzer[40] Viennese money, because I sold a pint of brandy, and because I brought your evil work to the attention of higher authorities. Sheer politics! On February 8, 1848, I finished the last eight days of my arrest—this time because I called a policeman who had insulted me first a snotty boy. None of my witnesses were listened to, and the spies forged my records. In 1843 I showed the government that the whole police bureau was a horde of thieves and robbers. I even had witnesses to prove it. However, the wretched blackguards sentenced me to a three-day arrest because my method of writing was too rude.

Indeed, my dear fellow-men and unfortunate tradespeople, let us clasp hands as friends so that we can destroy this monstrous nest of robbers in time, before this malicious brood of insects will destroy the good and honest officials whom we still have and whom we need so desperately. Let us not delay in destroying these rascals, for they neither deserve the name of of-

---

[40] About 6½ cents in United States money at that time.

ficials nor to live peacefully among us citizens in our free glorious Vienna. The Liguorians were the chief swindlers. They were wolves in sheep's clothing. But these scoundrels are ten times worse. These archscoundrels have already deserved the gallows because of their practices.

Therefore, friends and brothers, listen to the voice of an experienced and cruelly deceived man who for many years was bitten and tortured by these mangy dogs. Do not permit them to have the upper hand any longer, for remember that we are a free people and no longer slaves. Don't let Czapka —that murderous swindler who is the real leader of this robber brood— steal in among you. He has already published a letter of defense and apology,[41] but it is all a lie and a deception. However, all these malicious rascals will get their just reward for their evil deeds, not only here on earth, but also in the next world. This consoles me, but I get even more consolation from the fact that I know that these bad fellows can no longer publicly harm the citizens and the free Viennese. For we are a free, constitutional people, and we have sacrificed our blood for the just cause. So let us also enjoy our freedom and be free for all eternity. Let us grind the tyrants into dust.

Responsible for this:

Anton Ullmeyer,

Leopoldstadt, grosse Stadtgutgasse Nr. 376.

The choicest abuse was directed against Count Sedlnitzky and Chancellor Metternich. Sedlnitzky was charged with all kinds of heinous crimes. In a tone that strikingly foreshadows the spirit of Julius Streicher's *Der Stürmer,* the following tract accused him of adultery and rape:[42]

The Secrets of Vienna.

Sedlnitzky, the Seducer of Women.

The yoke of tyranny has fallen. The disgraceful, enslaving fetters have been broken. Our thoughts and minds will no longer be restricted and suppressed by arbitrary methods. By the will of the people and through the grace of our Emperor we are free. Speech is free and thought is free, and no villainous torturer is standing behind us to imprison us for a year for speaking the truth.

We have driven them off, those scoundrels who committed, and were not punished for committing, the most scandalous crimes and the most cruel acts of infamy, of which hell itself would be ashamed. While they

---

[41] Czapka had written a pamphlet defending himself against various charges that had been made about his conduct during the March revolution. See J. Czapka, Ritter von Winstetten, Former Mayor, *Öffentliche Erklärung,* Univ. Colo. 1848 Coll., No. II/274.

[42] Sch., *Die Geheimnisse von Wien. Sedlnitzky, der Mädchenverführer,* two-page sheet, Univ. Colo. 1848 Coll., No. II/259.

The Literature of the Revolution

trampled upon justice and upon the people, woe to anyone who dared complain about this treatment or utter the tiniest word of discontent.

The people have for a long time known who their torturers and tormentors were. Metternich, Sedlnitzky, and the Liguorians have been hated for a long time. Then came the 13th of March, and this fierce hatred was brought into the open. They are no longer with us, these demons in human form, who constantly played under cover and deceived the Emperor, the people, and the country, whose kindness they abused for the sake of their own scandalous, treacherous behavior.

Sedlnitzky was the worst of all. He was the most common, vulgar scoundrel. I could tell you tales about that wretch that would surprise you, but I will mention only this much here:

Among the many vices of this charming man was lasciviousness. Woe to the young girl who was unfortunate enough to have him become fond of her. With the help of his obliging secret police, he always succeeded in getting her into his clutches. And what could such an unfortunate girl do against such a high-ranking rascal who also was the minister of police? To which authorities was she to take her complaints?

If ever a woman dared to ask him to spare somebody who was in the hands of the police, she could gain the favor only through satisfying the lust of His Excellency. Anyone who resisted him fared badly, or if she had the courage to reproach him for his scandalous actions, she was assaulted by him. He did this more than just once, this despicable, godless sinner! I know several victims of his insatiable lust, and those who worked near his private room must have often heard the pleading and the screaming of those who were being abused.*

My readers will still remember a certain young woman who several years ago was found cruelly mutilated and dissected and whose murderer has up to now remained undiscovered. According to rumor Sedlnitzky was the cause of this affair. He is said to have seduced the girl and then handed her over to the Liguorians to abuse her. They in turn committed the crime because she repeatedly refused their advances and attempted to escape the clutches of the no less voluptuous clergy. Be that as it may, it is worthy of note that the well-known and highly praised police could not find the slightest trace of the criminal. This happened in Vienna, and it is said that no special attempt was made to investigate the matter.

The Liguorians were not too good to commit such a crime. We know that from their reputation among the people.

We should consider ourselves lucky to be rid of all those nice gentlemen.

Sch.

---

* "I vouch my life for the truth of this report about Sedlnitzky." (Footnote in the original.) It goes without saying that this footnote by the anonymous author does not prove the veracity of his charges. Sedlnitzky had many faults, but immorality was not one of them.

The hatred of Metternich that prevailed during the days immediately after his overthrow was well summed up in Grillparzer's bitter epitaph: [43]

> In this dark vault, too late for his renown,
> Autocracy's Don Quixote lays him down.
> Falsehood and truth he twisted to his will,
> Deceived first others, then himself, with skill;
> Into grey-headed fool from rogue he passed,
> For he believed his own fond lies at last.

Like Sedlnitzky, Metternich was charged with innumerable transgressions. He was even ridiculously charged with being[44]

Metternich,
the Murderer of the Young Napoleon.

Metternich, that wicked demon who, to the ruination of Austria, held the reigns of government in his hands for so many long years, whose chief political accomplishments lay in stupefying and crippling the minds of the people and in dividing the nationalities, who used his entire time of service to enrich himself at the cost of the state while at the same time imposing upon it a debt that will be difficult to wipe out, who believed that the enslavement of a nation was the foundation for the best government, and who, finally, betrayed the Emperor, the people, and the whole world, has also committed entirely different sins which are unknown to most of us. Metternich is also a poisoner—a murderer.

As is known, the young Napoleon[45] was brought up at our court. When it was discovered that he had a great affection for the land in which his father had played such a great role, it was resolved to get rid of him to prevent him from following in the footsteps of his father by eradicating him. Metternich talked so long and so convincingly to the now dead Emperor Francis that he finally convinced him, through his specious reasons, of the necessity for such an act, and he finally gave in and left it to the Prince to carry out his plan.

At first an attempt was made to destroy the young man in a natural way. Shameless pictures were used to inflame his fiery phantasies. He was put in the company of people who undermined his chastity. (A certain Henriette played the chief role in this.) In short, an attempt was made to bring about his death through debauchery. But since this took too long, it was decided

---

[43] Translated by J. G. Legge, *op. cit.*, p. 264. For a copy in German, see Tim Klein (ed.), *1848. Der Vorkampf deutscher Einheit und Freiheit*, p. 136.

[44] L. S., "Metternich, Mörder des jungen Napoleon," Unterreiter, *op. cit.*, Vol. III, pp. 16–18.

[45] François Charles Joseph Bonaparte (1811–32), Duke of Reichstadt and titular king of Rome, who lived at the court of Vienna from 1814 until his death in 1832 of tuberculosis.

to accomplish the goal by a faster method. Metternich had poison sent in from Italy. 10,000 florins were paid to prepare it. It was a poison that killed very slowly. A certain Doctor M——, who died several years ago, confessed on his deathbed that he had given the poison to the young Napoleon on Metternich's orders. He received 4,000 ducats to keep quiet about it. Everyone can easily see why the affair was hushed up and why all possible measures were taken to keep it secret. The young Napoleon was the sacrifice of the mad Metternich. His mother, the dead Maria Louisa, realized that her son had not died of natural causes, for when she arrived in Vienna, she threw herself into her father's room and wailed: "My son! My son! He has been murdered!"

Napoleon Bonaparte, who died on the Isle of Saint Helena, also died of poison. He did not die of cancer of the stomach, which is what one tried to make people believe. Metternich let him be poisoned by the English, for even the captured lion was feared.

And this grey-haired sinner is still alive. He has still not been crushed by the guilt that burdens his conscience. That such a man can still enjoy being alive! Nevertheless, we have a God who judges. He will have to give an account to Him for the crimes which he has committed against us, and Hell will be his reward.

L.S.

The above facts have been taken from a book entitled, *Letters from One Who Is Dead,* which was strongly proscribed during Sedlnitzky's times because it contained the truth.

In a lighter vein, someone composed a mock passport for the former Minister:[46]

Metternich's Passport.

Chief Landstrasse (March 15) Recruiting District of Vienna. 1848.

The Great Empire of Stupidity, Devil's Mountain

Passport

for

Prince Clemens Wenzel Lothar von Metternich-Winneburg, of Johannisberg of Devil's Mountain; Secret House, Court, State, and World Betrayer; Ruling Prince for the Suppression of Healthy Human Reason; Knight of the Secret Order of Spies in Ducats; the Only Possessor of the Un-Christian Order of the Only Christian Nicholas; Allied Chief Blood-Sucker of all the Blood-Sucking Ministers; Possessor of the Grand-Cross and about sixty-four more undeserved Orders in Diamonds, all of which, on account

---

[46] "Metternichs Reisepass," Unterreiter, *op. cit.,* Vol. II, pp. 108–11.

of the heavy pains in his chest and heart, he wears on his back so that everybody can see them, etc., etc., etc.

Place of Birth:	At Unclean-Devil's Johannisberg.
Domicile:	Sat like a leech on the moneybags of the Austrians.
Address:	Lived at Ballplatz; now Landstrasse No. Wandering and Fugitive.
Religion:	None at all; now and then Russian.
Class:	Formerly landed nobility; now misery.
Occupation:	Fatherland's, king's, state's, citizens', and people's money-squeezer.
Skills:	A seventy-five-year-old actor.
Specialties:	Bad character roles, chiefly intriguers. Plays the last role very naturally.
Other Occupations:	Money-swallowing, drinking the blood of the people, and scoffing at the world.
Age:	See skills. It would have been better if he had never been born.
Stature:	Lame, like the Devil.
Face:	Not to be looked at.
Eyes:	Those of a Liguorian.
Mouth and Tongue:	Pointed.
Nose:	Repulsive, long.
Hair:	Not a single good one.
Other Characteristics:	Has the heart of a raven-like minister. Cowardly. Always ready to run away.
Original Signature:	No longer has any name; hence, only an +.

He is traveling from here via England to Russia and Knoutland Siberia. This passport is valid forever.

All well-intentioned and honorable civil and military officials are asked in the name of the good cause to permit the holder of this pass freely to go to his destination but not to return. They are requested to give him all due assistance.

Executed by the former mayor and by a discouraged police spy of the Capital of Unclean-Devil's-Johannisberg in March, 1848.

I. G. Czapkerl,
Displaced Mayor.

O. W. All Spies.

I. A. Soul Bearer,
Minister of the Secret Spies.

In way of warning it is added that any falsification of this passport, regardless of place or intention, will be punished as a major crime in accord with the laws of reason and the true religion and in consequence of a firm resolution made on March 13, 14, and 15, 1848.

The Literature of the Revolution

Of all the satires written about Metternich none was repeated with more pleasure than this parody on the Lord's Prayer, which first appeared in the capital on March 14:[47]

Father Metternich, who art in Vienna, give us a better regime. The will of the subjects be done, in Austria as it is in Hungary. Forgive us our justified insults and screams, as we forgive you the new un-Christian loan. Lead us not into temptation through nonforgeable bank notes, but deliver us from all evil by means of real silver. Amen!

During the days that followed the overthrow of the old regime, while unpopular officials were the object of vicious and mocking attacks, Emperor Ferdinand was spared from all criticism. At no time during the March revolution was there an unfriendly word against him. In no way was he held responsible for the evils of the Habsburgs. He was regarded as a man who "had as little evil and falseness in him as a new-born child."[48] He was believed to have been the innocent pawn behind whom the culprits operated. The Viennese wholeheartedly agreed with their Citizens' Committee when it drafted the[49]

Address of Thanks
delivered by the Undersigned.

Long live our Constitutional Emperor!
Hail! Hail! Hail!

May our rejoicing reach the heavens, and may the Almighty God, who directs the destiny of nations, hear our fervent prayers: that He long protect our good father and that He bless the government, supported by the love of a loyal people who will defy all storms of the times and who will give their life and blood for their magnanimous Emperor and for their freedom.

Your Majesty! We Austrians shall prove that we are worthy of freedom. We shall prove this in a firm alliance with all our comrades, regardless of race or tongue. We shall prove it in the face of all Europe, which will now recognize in us a rock of strength against every enemy of intelligence and independence.

[47] As printed in the *Constitution,* No. 2 (March 22, 1848), p. 13.
[48] Hans Kudlich, *Rückblicke und Erinnerungen,* Vol. I, p. 196. See also Adolph Pichler, *Das Sturmjahr,* pp. 20–21; Vitzthum von Eckstädt to his mother, Vienna, March 16, 1848, Carl Friedrich Grafen von Vitzthum von Eckstädt, *Berlin und Wien in den Jahren 1845–1852,* p. 83.
[49] Univ. Colo. 1848 Coll., No. II/68. Also printed in the *Wiener Zeitung,* No. 76 (March 16, 1848), p. 343.

Your Majesty! We loyal citizens bend our knees before our Emperor *Ferdinand* who now reigns in new glory.

*The Magistrates and Citizens' Committee
of the City of Vienna.*

The citizens of the capital joined in singing the new version of "Gott erhalte," which was written during the course of the March revolution:[50]

*Ferdinand,
the First Constitutional Emperor.*

May God preserve our Emperor,
Our dear Emperor Ferdinand,
Who hath his temple, full of splendor,
Adorned with palm leaf's verdant band,
Who'll ne'er his people's wishes ignore,
Will fulfill them all throughout the land;
May God preserve our Emperor,
Our dear Emperor Ferdinand!

Freedom of the Press and National Guard.

May our spirits now strive upward
And only *freedom* build our house;
Free speech has now at last come forward,
Guns we have to protect our house.
For constitution all united
Are the people of the land,
And dawn brings forth, as new created,
Our good Emperor Ferdinand.

Constitution for all Lands of Austria.

May God bless the happy moment
Which his royal word has brought;
Prince and people ever confident,
Austria's power is newly wrought.
To our German fellow-men
We extend a brotherly hand,
So they'll sing for what we yen;
May God keep Emperor Ferdinand!

Thus the March revolutionaries enshrined Emperor Ferdinand among the heroes of their revolution. In the myth that sprang into existence, "Ferdinand the Good" was exalted as the liberal monarch who

[50] "Ferdinand der erste constitutionelle Kaiser," Univ. Colo. 1848 Coll., No. II/74.

would lead the Austrian people out of the wilderness of despair into a constitutional Utopia. For a short time at least, he was the Sir Galahad of the new era—a naïve attitude without question, but one to be expected of a people who had suddenly gained their freedom after centuries of censorship and police regimentation.

VI. The First Days of Freedom

HE NEWS of the March revolution in Vienna had an electrifying effect on all parts of the Habsburg Empire. In the larger cities of the German provinces, such as Linz, Graz, and Innsbruck, hastily improvised citizens' committees took over the local governments. In several towns noisy food riots broke out, butcher shops and bakeries were plundered, and here and there a sales tax office was set on fire. But the newly formed citizens' military forces, patterned after those in Vienna, quickly succeeded in suppressing disorder. Everywhere in the provinces there was great enthusiasm for the revolution, and the Viennese received many messages of gratitude for their contribution to the cause of freedom. Only in the Tyrol was there a faint note of disapprobation, and this was limited chiefly to peasant circles.

Meanwhile, peace had been restored in Vienna. By the morning of March 16 the capital had resumed its normal appearance, and most shops and offices were open for business as usual. National Guardsmen and soldiers of the regular army were performing guard duty together at the city gates, which were again open to traffic. An order was posted on the streets asking the Viennese to return to work as soon as possible so that trade and industry would not suffer.[1] Another proclamation invited the citizens to enroll in the National Guard.[2]

The people on the streets were jubilant over the victories that had been won and at every opportunity expressed their devotion to the students. Even the Emperor joined in paying homage to them. At 11:00 A.M. on the 16th he drove in an open carriage to the university, where he showered the students with words of praise and affection. The professors and students responded with thundering hurrahs and shouts of "Long live the Emperor!" In the evening there was another

[1] Magistrate and Provisional Citizens' Committee of the City of Vienna, "Proclamation," March 16, 1848, Friedrich Unterreiter, *Die Revolution in Wien vom März und Mai 1848*, Vol. I, pp. 94–95.

[2] Commander-in-Chief of the National Guard, "Proclamation," Vienna, March 16, 1848, Univ. Colo. 1848 Coll., No. II/27.

torchlight parade, led by the students and faculty of the university and the Polytechnical Institute, the Legal-Political Reading Club, the Men's Glee Club, and all the National Guardsmen not on duty. The procession began at 7:00 and ended around 9:30 with the singing of the German anthem and a new anthem especially written to commemorate the new freedom.[3]

Only one incident marred the quiet of Vienna on the 16th. In the afternoon a National Guard detachment and a crowd of friends commanded by a butcher named Wöss marched to Mayor Czapka's home to express their dissatisfaction over his "antirevolutionary behavior" and to demand his resignation. When Czapka failed to appear at the window of his house, the crowd grew angry and threatened to force its way in. A certain Wiedermann, a singer at the Breslau Theater and an officer in the National Guard, succeeded in quieting the tumult by suggesting that the demonstrators choose a six-man deputation to speak to the Mayor. When they returned to the house, they found it deserted.[4]

Meantime, at the city hall the citizens' committee was trying to convince Czapka that his conduct during the revolution had made him so unpopular that he could no longer serve as mayor. When word came of the demonstration in front of his house, Czapka fled from the capital with his wife and children.[5] Soon thereafter placards were posted announcing that Vice-Mayor Bergmüller had been provisionally appointed to the office of mayor.[6]

With Czapka's precipitous departure from Vienna the last prop of the regime was gone from the city administration, and Vienna was wholly in the hands of middle-class liberals. On March 18, to emphasize that a new era had been ushered in, the government formally proclaimed the end of the state of siege,[7] which had, in fact, never been instituted but had been considered a threat to freedom.[8]

Early in April the popular Lieutenant Field Marshal Count Auersperg was named commanding general of Lower Austria.[9] With his appointment, the liberals no longer needed to fear, for a while at least, that Habsburg troops would be used against them.

---

[3] *Oestreich's Befreiungstage*, pp. 45, 49–50.
[4] *Ibid.*, pp. 48–49; Unterreiter, *op. cit.*, Vol. I, pp. 92–93.
[5] J. Czapka, *Öffentliche Erklärung*, pp. 1–2, Univ. Colo. 1848 Coll., No. II/274.
[6] Baron Johann Talatzko von Gestieticz, "Proclamation," Vienna, March 16, 1848, Univ. Colo. 1848 Coll., No. II/26.
[7] Windischgrätz, "Proclamation," March 18, 1848, Univ. Colo. 1848 Coll., No. II/128. Also printed in *Wiener Zeitung*, No. 80 (March 20, 1848), p. 361.
[8] *Wiener Zeitung*, No. 82 (March 22, 1848), p. 374.
[9] *Ibid.*, No. 96 (April 5, 1848), p. 453.

At the same time the government took steps to organize the National Guard as a working unit. The creation of the guard, with Count Hoyos as its commander, had been approved by the Emperor on March 14. Three days later the Civic Guard was also put under Hoyos' command.[10] The Academic Legion was set up within the National Guard. The professors at the university "imagined the students could, in this manner, reconcile the duties of the scholar with those of a man in arms, be kept away from the influence of bad morals, and thus not loosen the tie of respectful intimacy between themselves and their preceptors."[11] Count Colloredo-Mannsfeld was appointed commander of the legion, and Anton Füster, the popular professor of theology at the university who had appointed himself field chaplain, was confirmed in this position by the students. Originally it was planned to divide the legion into four corps, the juridical, the medical, the philosophical, and the technical, each with its own commander. In this way all the main branches of the university and the Technological Institute except theology were to be represented. The students at the Art Academy also insisted on having their own corps within the legion, and the number of corps was increased to five.[12]

In a very short time the Academic Legion numbered about 5,000 men, divided into 32 companies, each with an average membership of 150 to 200 men. The legionnaires wore a uniform consisting of gray trousers without braid, a loosely fitted blue German tunic with padded arms and a row of black buttons, and a German hat with a black feather and a German cockade. On the front of the cockade was inscribed the first letter of the corps to which the legionnaire belonged: J for juridical, M for medical, P for philosophical, T for technical, and A for the artists. Under the letter was the number of the company to which the legionnaire belonged. While on duty the officers wore a scarf around their waists. When off duty officers and enlisted men dressed alike.[13]

The original intention had been that membership in the legion should be restricted to students, candidates for advanced degrees, doctors of

[10] "Order of the Civil and Military Governor, Prince Alfred Windischgrätz, to the Commander of the National Guard, Count Hoyos," Vienna, March 17, 1848, Univ. Colo. 1848 Coll., No. II/17.

[11] Baron [Franz Xaver] Pillersdorf, *Austria in 1848 and 1849. The Political Movement in Austria. During the Years 1848 & 1849* (hereafter cited throughout as *Austria in 1848 and 1849*), tr. George Gaskell, p. 86.

[12] Friedrich Kaiser, *1848: Ein Wiener Volksdichter erlebt die Revolution. Die Memoiren Friedrich Kaisers* (hereafter cited throughout as *Memoiren*), ed. Franz Hadamowsky, pp. 27–29.

[13] Heinrich Reschauer and Moritz Smets, *Das Jahr 1848. Geschichte der Wiener Revolution*, Vol. II, pp. 24–25.

philosophy, medical doctors, and teachers.[14] But many people who had no connection with the university found their way into the legion and soon wielded no small amount of influence over the impressionable young soldiers. Some of them were demagogues who took advantage of membership in the organization to enlist the students' support for their own ends.[15]

With all its faults, the Academic Legion at least resembled a military unit within a few weeks of its creation. It was otherwise with the National Guard. At the outset guardsmen had no special uniforms but wore civilian clothes distinguished by a white band around the upper left arm.[16] The guard was divided into semiautonomous companies, which were to choose their own commanders.[17] Each of the four platoons in a company was to have one commissioned and three noncommissioned officers, over whose appointment the company commander had considerable influence.[18]

The provisions for the organization of the National Guard were issued on March 16. Unfortunately more than a set of rules was required to establish an efficient unit, and the guard was an undisciplined, confused, untrained body. Part of the difficulty lay with the leadership. Although the Emperor had honored Count Hoyos with the title Lieutenant Field Marshal, Hoyos was not a military man. He was a Habsburg court official and chief master of the hunt; he knew little or nothing about military organization. He was a kind, good-natured cavalier who was willing to do almost anything to make himself popular with the Viennese, but he was completely lacking in administrative talent. Too, at the age of seventy he was too old to take the decisive, forceful steps necessary to whip an undisciplined, self-willed band of democrats into an effective militia. For the most part, he limited his duties to writing a large number of confusing daily orders in the style and form of a regimental commander.[19]

Much of the source of the guard's difficulties lay in the companies themselves. Whenever a hundred or more men wanted to form a com-

[14] Outline of the organization of the Academic Legion, *ibid.*, p. 24.

[15] Pillersdorf, *op. cit.*, pp. 86–87.

[16] Commander-in-Chief of the National Guard, "Proclamation," Vienna, March 16, 1848, Univ. Colo. 1848 Coll., No. II/27.

[17] Count Hoyos, "Daily Order to the National Guard," March 16, 1848, Univ. Colo. 1848 Coll., No. II/184.

[18] Count Hoyos, "Daily Order to the National Guard," March 16, 1848, *Constitution*, No. 1 (March 20, 1848), pp. 7–8.

[19] Kaiser, *op. cit.*, p. 27; Maximilian Ehnl, *Wenzel Cäsar Messenhauser, Nationalgarde-Oberkommandant von Wien 1848* (hereafter cited throughout as *Messenhauser*), p. 53.

pany, they met in a local inn and elected their officers. Since many of them ardently desired to become officers, it frequently happened that after the elections only thirty or forty enlisted men were left in the company. Furthermore, company captains were often selected whose only qualification was that they had the means to do something for the men in their charge. Their military ability or their political views were seldom taken into consideration. Captains who dipped heavily into their personal funds to do favors for their troops often found themselves deposed when the company found another captain who would be still more generous.[20]

It is not surprising that the Viennese saw no attraction in enlisting in the National Guard. Although a large number of people had enrolled in its ranks during the first few days after its creation, by the first week in April the guard had a total strength of only 7,200 men.[21] Plainly something had to be done if the citizens were to have an effective armed force.

In the hope of augmenting the guard, on April 8, the Minister of Interior announced provisional regulations that would be in effect until the united diet enacted a definitive statute for the guard. According to the regulations, the duty of the National Guard was to protect the monarch, the constitution, and the laws of the country; preserve domestic peace and order; and defend the independence and integrity of the state against enemy attack. All Austrian citizens between nineteen and fifty years of age except journeymen, servants, or daily or weekly wage-earners were obligated to serve in the guard. The clergy, active members of the regular army or the militia, all finance and security guards, and the physically unfit were also exempted. Persons between fifty and sixty could volunteer for guard duty if they could meet the physical qualifications.

Every city, village, or market with a population of more than one thousand was entitled to organize a National Guard unit, with a local National Guard Administrative Council to take care of such matters as providing uniforms, arms, and ammunition for the unit. The chairman of the council was to be the National Guard commandant.[22]

Despite the regulations many problems remained unsolved. The question of how much authority the commander-in-chief was to have,

---

[20] Kaiser, *op. cit.*, pp. 29–32.

[21] Reschauer and Smets, *op. cit.*, Vol. II, pp. 70–71; "Was haben wir errungen? Was haben wir zu hoffen?" *Constitution*, No. 22 (April 15, 1848), p. 331.

[22] Pillersdorf, "Proclamation," Vienna, April 8, 1848, Univ. Colo. 1848 Coll., No. II/111.

which was already causing dissension in the guard, had not been decided. How far and in what way the guardsmen could exercise their political rights as citizens had not been settled.[23] Moreover, the radicals opposed the exclusion of the working classes from guard service and loudly declaimed against an army of the middle classes. Moreover, the regulations did not settle the question of uniform. The Viennese began a noisy battle of words over how their armed forces were to be dressed. When the fashion debate finally ended, a highly impractical uniform had been agreed upon. It consisted of a most unmilitary-looking blue tunic with two rows of white metal buttons, shoulder pads, and red piping. The trousers were gray with red braid on the sides. The headdress was a black-lacquered leather shako with a red and white cockade.[24]

The Viennese also followed with avid interest the measures taken to turn the absolutist government into a responsible, "liberal" democracy. The first constitutional ministry in Austrian history was appointed on March 17 with the following members: Count Franz Kolowrat, minister-president; Count Karl Ficquelmont, minister of foreign affairs; Baron Franz von Pillersdorf, minister of interior; Count Ludwig Taaffe, minister of justice; and Baron Karl von Kübeck, minister of finance.[25] On March 27 Baron Franz von Sommaruga was made minister of education,[26] and on April 3 Lieutenant Field Marshal Peter Zanini joined the cabinet as minister of war.[27]

These men were familiar with the work of the particular departments to which they were assigned. Although all the ministers had the trust of the Emperor, the Viennese disliked and suspected two of them—Taaffe and Ficquelmont. Taaffe, a competent jurist, had been head of the Austrian judicial administration for many years, but the fact that he was an aristocrat and a "stiffnecked bureaucrat" did not add to his charm or popularity. Ficquelmont was well versed in foreign affairs but was suspect because he had married the granddaughter of the Russian General Kutuzov. He was dubbed a protégé of Metternich and, worse, a hireling of the Russian Czar.

Most of the other ministers met with the favor of the populace. Among them was the Minister-President. Although Kolowrat had been in charge of domestic affairs since 1825 and had been a member of the

---

[23] Ehnl, *op. cit.*, p. 53. [24] Reschauer and Smets, *op. cit.*, Vol. II, p. 72.
[25] *Wiener Zeitung,* No. 78 (March 18, 1848), p. 351; *ibid.,* No. 81 (March 21, 1848), p. 365.
[26] *Ibid.,* No. 84 (March 24, 1848), p. 385; *ibid.,* No. 88 (March 28, 1848), p. 405.
[27] Rudolph Kiszling *et al., Die Revolution im Kaisertum Österreich 1848–1849,* Vol. I, p. 49.

Council of State from 1835 to 1848, he had always had the reputation of being a bitter enemy of Metternich, and that alone was sufficient to make him popular with the liberals. Kübeck had been president of the Imperial Exchequer, but he was a friend of Kolowrat and was respected for his competence in financial matters. Because Zanini, who had been a member of the Imperial War Council, was of middle-class birth, the revolutionaries looked upon him as one of them. Sommaruga, the second president of the Lower Austrian Court of Appeals just before the revolution, was one of the most active members of the Legal-Political Reading Club.

The most popular of all the ministers was the one who held the most important portfolio—Baron von Pillersdorf, the minister of interior. A statesman with many years of service, Pillersdorf had long been a dauntless opponent of the Metternich government and had joined in many of the pre-1848 liberal movements in Vienna. Of more importance, he had a reputation as a champion of liberal reform. This, plus his unmistakable talent for elocution, made him the man of the hour. He was the Moses who was to lead the children of Austria out of the desert of absolutism into the promised land of freedom.

Whatever reservations the populace had about the new ministry were partly offset by some of the changes made in the structure of the government. On March 29 the imperial police were completely reorganized and put directly under the control of the Minister of Interior. At the same time the espionage system was formally abolished. This action was followed by the abolition of the Council of State on April 4 and of the Emperor's private cabinet, the State Conference, on the next day.[28] With the elimination of these highly unpopular bodies, the most bitterly hated of the Emperor's advisers left the imperial service. Archduke Louis and Count von Hartig were gone. Metternich had left for England on the night of the 14th, and Sedlnitzky had been dismissed soon thereafter. Archduke Albert was relieved of his command, and General Windischgrätz returned to Prague. In spite of the fact that a few persons rather closely allied with the old system had been appointed to the new constitutional Ministry, the way was open for reform.

The changes made by the new ministry during the first weeks of its existence met with enthusiastic approval. After declaring, on March 19, that all existing laws and regulations would be maintained in force until such time as they were legally declared null and void,[29] the government

---

[28] *Wiener Zeitung*, No. 89 (March 29, 1848), p. 411; Unterreiter, *op. cit.*, Vol. II, pp. 45–46.

[29] Emperor Ferdinand, "Proclamation," Vienna, March 19, 1848, *Wiener*

the next day decreed a substantial lowering of the sales tax on food, which had been a particularly heavy burden on the lower classes. The tax on milk, potatoes, artichokes, cabbage, beets, and other common vegetables was abolished, and substantial reductions were made in the tax on other foodstuffs like fruit, flour, bread, grain, and wine. Furthermore, no tax was to be paid on small purchases when the tax amounted to less than 3 kreutzer (2 2/5 cents).[30] Also on March 20 an amnesty was declared for all persons who had been imprisoned for political crimes.[31] Five days later came the order that private letters would no longer be opened by the censors.[32]

Climaxing the reform program of the Ministry was the imperial manifesto of April 11 promising to free the peasants from all services and dues incumbent on the land on January 1, 1849. In the intervening time the estates were to propose suitable laws to make this promise a reality. Even before the abolition of the peasant dues was legally effected, arrangements could be made between individual peasants and landowners to settle the dues incumbent on the land by satisfactory compensation to the proprietor.[33] This decree pacified the peasants in the crown lands and filled them with gratitude for the Emperor and his government. Most of them now lost all interest in continuing the revolution and threw their support behind the re-establishment of law and order. The promise to abolish the *Robot* was one of the shrewdest moves made by the government during the course of the revolution.

The Viennese, though elated by these reforms, clamored for still more. Some radicals expected the Ministry to abolish all remnants of the absolutist system and to redress real and imagined grievances without delay. Almost every day deputations appeared before the Ministry with special demands.[34] Here and there agitators talked about bringing mob pressure to bear upon the Ministry, and since the government had ordered the police to allow the free expression of complaints, not much could be

---

Zeitung, No. 82 (March 22, 1848), p. 373; Karl Schneider, *Der Reichstag von Kremsier,* No. 2 in *Aus Österreichs Vergangenheit. Quellenbücher zur österreichischen Geschichte,* ed. Karl Schneider, p. 9.

[30] Baron Johann Talatzko von Gestieticz, "Proclamation," Vienna, March 20, 1848, *Wiener Zeitung,* No. 81 (March 21, 1848), p. 365.

[31] Emperor Ferdinand, "Imperial Decree," Vienna, March 20, 1848, *Wiener Zeitung,* No. 83 (March 23, 1848), p. 379.

[32] William H. Stiles, *Austria in 1848–49,* Vol. I, p. 115.

[33] Emperor Ferdinand, "Proclamation," Vienna, April 11, 1848, *Wiener Zeitung,* No. 105 (April 14, 1848), p. 497; *ibid.,* No. 109 (April 18, 1848), p. 517; Emperor Ferdinand, "Proclamation," Vienna, April 25, 1848, *ibid.,* No. 118 (April 28, 1848), p. 565; Stiles, *op. cit.,* Vol. I, p. 115.

[34] *Wiener Zeitung,* No. 106 (April 15, 1848), p. 502.

done to curb demonstrations.[35] Within the course of a few weeks demagogues and rabble-rousers were to take advantage of the new freedom. At times they were able to arrogate to themselves the power behind the government largely because of the great influence they wielded upon the two groups, the workers and the students, who had been raised to a strategic position by the March revolution and who had had no opportunity to learn that freedom implies responsibility as well as privilege.

If the workers were to lash out against their poverty and deprivation, they would constitute a potentially dangerous revolutionary army. It was mainly from despair over their miserable living conditions that they had burned factories and plundered food stores on the night of March 13. The disturbances of the March revolution only made conditions worse. Until the damaged factories could be put back into operation the workers were without jobs or income. Too, for some weeks after the revolution many Viennese were too busy celebrating the victory to settle down, and others were occupied with their activities in the National Guard. The general instability produced by the revolution had damaging effects on trade and industry. State bonds fell 40 per cent in value on the stock exchange. Many shopkeepers did little business for weeks after the revolution.[36] On March 28 a large number of manufacturers and tradespeople sent a deputation to the Ministry to beg for an appropriation of 3 million florins ($1,440,000) to help get the factories and various businesses back in operation.[37] The government did not grant this sum but did persuade the National Bank to advance a loan of 2 million florins ($960,000) to needy manufacturers and merchants.[38]

With trade and industry crippled, the number of unemployed workers rapidly increased. So did their discontent. In the days of the old regime the workers had usually accepted their lot with mute resignation, and the police had always been at hand to repress any open expression of dissatisfaction. Now the workers had gained a new self-respect and sense of power. Since freedom of speech and assembly was guaranteed to them, they could hold assemblies and present their requests to their employers. They could and did demand higher wages, a ten-hour working day, the strict limitation of the number of apprentices assigned to any employer, the reduction of the number of women employees in industry,

[35] "Pillersdorf to Police Directors in All the Provinces," Vienna, March 28, 1848, *Wiener Zeitung,* No. 89 (March 29, 1848), p. 411.
[36] Vitzthum von Eckstädt to his mother, Vienna, April 7, 1848, Carl Friedrich Grafen von Vitzthum von Eckstädt, *Berlin und Wien in den Jahren 1845–1852,* p. 89; Unterreiter, *op. cit.,* Vol. III, p. 36.
[37] *Wiener Zeitung,* No. 90 (March 30, 1848), p. 418.
[38] *Ibid.,* No. 93 (April 2, 1848), p. 437.

the establishment of a definite ratio between handwork and machine work, care for the sick and invalids, the administration of the funds for needy workers by the workers themselves, and more humane treatment of the workers by the employers and their foremen.[39]

Some employers were induced to grant some of the demands. On March 18 the Vienna-Gloggnitz Railway Company reduced the working day to ten hours in the factories and workshops, and the other railway lines and several factories soon followed this example.[40] Employers who did not voluntarily adopt the ten-hour day found themselves besieged with petitions and demonstrations. Some factory-owners also increased wages by 10 per cent,[41] thus putting pressure on others to do likewise. As a result, wages and working conditions gradually improved in a number of trades.

Concerted efforts were made to halt the alarming increase in unemployment. Some of the idle workers were put to work repairing the factories and machines. Others were given jobs on new public works projects begun in the Prater (the park), on the Danube Canal, along the Wien River, and on various buildings.[42] Unfortunately, although they were started with the best of intentions, the government projects merely served to increase the workers' discontent. They were poorly run, and no special attempt was made to keep the workers busy. Many were paid for loafing, and, being idle, they had plenty of time to grumble. Soon the projects became a gathering place for malcontents, who were easily led by any demagogue who wanted to use them for his own purposes.

For the students, the heroes of the revolt, the Viennese workers had a respect and admiration akin to worship. The students were the learned priests of the holy gospel of liberalism, which would turn the earth into a paradise. Lacking a political philosophy or leaders of their own, the great proletarian masses looked to the students for help and guidance and at every turn supported their efforts to establish a more democratic society.

The peasants also had an almost childlike faith in the omniscience of the academic youth. Country people from far and near made pilgrimages to the university to complain about injustices long suffered or to entreat the students to punish hated landlords or petty officials.

In fact, persons from all the underprivileged classes turned to the

[39] Ernst Victor Zenker, *Die Wiener Revolution,* pp. 128–29.
[40] *Wiener Zeitung,* No. 80 (March 20, 1848), pp. 61–62.
[41] Zenker, *op. cit.,* p. 125.
[42] Ernst Violand, *Die sociale Geschichte der Revolution in Oesterreich,* p. 75; Zenker, *op. cit.,* pp. 123–24; Minister of Interior, "Proclamation," Vienna, April 22, 1848, Unterreiter, *op. cit.,* Vol. III, pp. 36–38.

students for aid. Discontented workers fetched the students to expostulate with a stubborn employer. The matron whose only son was commandeered for the army asked the Vienna students to secure his release. If a father deserted his wife and children, the students intervened to patch up the quarrel and induce him to return home. Even fights between neighbors were brought to the university for adjudication. The students collected money, food, and clothing for those in dire need. When there were complaints about long-drawn-out legal procedures, they threatened the lawyers and even the judges and demanded quick action. If an official failed in his duty, they enjoined him to mend his ways. Before long, even a hint by someone with a grievance that he would take his complaints to the university served as a very successful means of intimidation.[43]

Much of the work of the students in behalf of the downtrodden and oppressed was centered in the Student Committee, originally established at the request of the Ministry to advise the government on university matters. At first the members of the committee were chosen by the various schools and classes of all the institutes of higher learning in Vienna. When this type of representation proved unsatisfactory, the members were elected by the various companies of the Academic Legion. The students exerted considerable political influence through the Student Committee, which sent petitions to the Ministry on behalf of the needy or reported on the machinations of suspected reactionaries. It became the representative of the Viennese workers and the mediator between them and the government. The Aula, the large assembly hall at the university, remained open night and day and was nearly always jammed with people who came to enlist the students' help or to listen to political debates.[44] The Ministry soon learned that the students constituted a political force to which they must listen with respect and consideration.

In reward for their services the students gained the love of the people. Hardly a deputation appeared at the capital without coming to the university to address eulogies to the valiant scholars; and, as related earlier, the Viennese press joined the chorus of praise, with countless poems, pamphlets, and newspaper articles.[45] The poor came to the uni-

---

[43] Violand, *op. cit.*, pp. 78–80; August Silberstein, *Geschichte der Aula*, pp. 51–52.

[44] Paul Molisch, "Die Wiener akademische Legion," *Archiv für österreichische Geschichte*, Vol. CX, Part I (1924), pp. 72, 75; Silberstein, *op. cit.*, p. 50; Reschauer and Smets, *op. cit.*, Vol. II, pp. 36–38; Violand, *op. cit.*, p. 80.

[45] Joseph Alexander Freiherrn von Helfert, *Geschichte der österreichischen Revolution*, p. 314; Molisch, *op. cit.*, p. 68.

versity to donate a few kreutzer to them. The well to do became "student fathers" and volunteered to lodge poor students and take care of their personal needs. They defrayed the costs of parties at various hotels and taverns, paid for the expenses of the Academic Legion and other student organizations, and took up collections for various student causes. The student fathers wore calabash-shaped hats to advertise the fact that they were public-spirited citizens' to whom needy students could turn for help.[46]

The students were too busy at politics and soldiering to pay much attention to their studies. Lectures were poorly attended. Students boycotted the classes of the unpopular professors, who were in the majority. Some of the faculty members themselves were now more interested in intriguing to become officers in the legion than in lecturing to their classes.[47]

Intoxicated with their new political role and flattered by the attention suddenly showered upon them, many students began to feel that they were the architects of the new democratic state.[48] The first time they directly interfered with the government was when the Ministry announced the new press law. At the same time that the government ended censorship of the press on March 14, it had promised that a new press law would be drafted as quickly as possible. Following instructions given on the 17th, the Imperial Chancellery drafted the law, with the advice and co-operation of such liberals as Hye, Stubenrauch, Bach, and the publisher Gerold.[49] The model was the Baden law, which was considered to be the most liberal press law in Germany.[50]

The provisions of the law, which was proclaimed by the Minister of Interior on March 31 and made effective as of April 1, gave unqualified amnesty to all persons charged with transgressions against the censorship up to April 1. Thereafter the name of the publisher and the editor responsible for the publication was to be clearly indicated. The publisher of any newspaper appearing up to three times a week had to give a bond of 1,000 florins ($480) guaranteeing that he would discharge his responsibilities in accordance with the new law. For newspapers appearing more often than three times a week, the bond was 2,000 florins ($960). Copies of all publications except scientific, artistic, or technical writings were to be given to the appropriate officials. Defa-

---

[46] Kaiser, *op. cit.*, pp. 37–42.
[47] Anton Füster, *Memoiren vom März 1848 bis Juli 1849*, Vol. I, pp. 75, 36–37.
[48] Stiles, *op. cit.*, Vol. I, pp. 116–17.
[49] Joseph Alexander Freiherrn von Helfert, *Die Wiener Journalistik im Jahre 1848*, pp. 45–46; [Franz Graf von Hartig], *Genesis der Revolution*, pp. 208–209.
[50] G. Wolf, *Aus der Revolutionszeit in Österreich-Ungarn (1848–49)*, p. 5.

mation of the monarch was punishable by a prison term of one to five years; defamation of a member of the royal house, by six months to one year; and attacks on a member of the upper class, by fourteen days to six months. For an attack on the constitution of the realm the sentence was three months to one year, and those who penned obscene writings or drew indecent pictures were to be imprisoned for a period of one day to three months, depending on the nature of the offense. The writer, publisher, editor, printer, and in some instances even the seller were held liable for punishment.[51]

When a copy of this new law was brought to the university on April 1, there was a loud protest. The students saw it as an attempt by the Emperor's advisers to curb the liberties that had been won. When Hye attempted to defend the law by explaining that it was even more liberal than the Baden law, he was shouted down. A certain Dr. Giskra jumped on the rostrum to criticize the law point by point and to warn his colleagues about its inherent dangers. Kuranda, who had just returned to Vienna from Germany, cried out that the liberals in Baden had recently demonstrated against their own law. In an impassioned speech Schuselka denounced "this April fool joke." After a stormy session, the students chose a deputation to go to the Minister of Interior and demand that the press law be rescinded immediately. Finally the deputation returned and assured the students that Pillersdorf had promised to nullify the law.[52]

In compelling the Ministry to bend before their will the students had won a resounding victory. The Ministry's inability to enforce its own decrees when an agitated throng demonstrated against it was a lesson not lost on the Viennese students in the ensuing months of the revolution.

Like the students, members of the National Guard began to look upon themselves as an important political force. It was to be expected that the National Guard and the Academic Legion would frequently pull in opposite directions and send conflicting petitions to the government. In order to reconcile differences of opinion between the guard and the students two liaison committees were created: the Administrative Committee and the Central Committee of Citizens, Students, and National Guards. The Administrative Committee dealt with uniforms, munitions, and other supply matters. The Central Committee was to

---

[51] See the text of the law as printed in the *Oesterreichische konstitutionelle deutsche Zeitung*, No. 2 (April 4, 1848), p. 5, Univ. Colo. 1848 Coll., No. II/157.
[52] Adolph Pichler, *Das Sturmjahr*, pp. 25–26; Silberstein, *op. cit.*, pp. 50–51; Molisch, *op. cit.*, pp. 75–76; Reschauer and Smets, *op. cit.*, Vol. II, pp. 39–43.

The First Days of Freedom

unite and represent the political opinions of all the citizens' armed forces. Although it had no executive power, no legal voice, and no position of legitimate authority, it expressed the opinions of the people's army and wielded a tremendous influence. It came to be looked upon as the real organ of public opinion in Vienna, and in due time it grew to be something of a state within a state with power to paralyze the Ministry when it chose.[53] In many ways it was comparable to the Jacobin Club of the French Revolution.

The revolutionary groups represented by the Central Committee, and particularly the students, were ardent proponents of union with Germany. They wanted Austria to merge with the other German lands to form a single democratic state comprising all the German-speaking peoples in central Europe. The members of the Academic Legion decorated themselves not with Habsburg but with German colors and wore German hats and the German national cockade—decorations that most Viennese had never seen before. At the Aula impassioned pro-German speeches were made such as had never before been heard.[54] The students saw the road to democracy in a united Germany.

The students were not alone in this belief. The vast majority of Viennese considered that the concessions won in Germany were their own victories and that the steps taken in Frankfurt to create the German National Assembly would lead to the creation of their own Parliament. To many Germans in the Habsburg monarchy the liberal reforms to be made in Austria were of secondary importance to those to be made in Germany. In this sense the Viennese Revolution of 1848 was as much a German as an Austrian revolution.[55] What element of specifically Austrian patriotism that was in evidence on the eve of the revolution was rapidly transformed into a tremendous enthusiasm for union with Germany.[56]

The strong undercurrent of German national feeling permeating the Habsburg capital from the beginning of the revolution burst forth in a noisy display on April 2. On the night of April 1 a band of twelve legionnaires had unfurled a large red, black, and gold German flag on top of the tower of St. Stephen's Cathedral, one of Vienna's most venerated shrines. The next morning the students went in a body to St. Stephen's Square to stand below the flag and sing praises to the German

[53] Violand, *op. cit.*, pp. 80–81; Unterreiter, *op. cit.*, Vol. III, pp. 31–32.
[54] Füster, *op. cit.*, Vol. I, pp. 100–101; Silberstein, *op. cit.*, pp. 49–50.
[55] See especially [Karl] L[udwig] Grafen Ficquelmont, *Aufklärungen*, pp. 48–49.
[56] Hartig, *op. cit.*, p. 227.

fatherland. From there they marched to the statue of Joseph II, the much-loved "German Emperor," to demonstrate their devotion to the German nationalist cult. Then the students, together with a sprinkling of professors, members of the Vienna Male Glee Club, and a host of onlookers, proceeded to the Hofburg and demanded entrance so that they could deliver a German flag to the Emperor. When the crowd had sung the German national anthem, the Emperor appeared on a balcony, asked the students to hand him a German flag, and had it mounted in front of his window.[57]

After this token of the Emperor's blessing, thousands of German flags suddenly appeared in windows along the streets and alleys of the city and the suburbs.[58] The Habsburg colors quickly became a bitter reminder of Austrian absolutism, and the German flag the symbol of freedom. As an "assembly of Viennese citizens" wrote to the *Constitution:*[59]

Brothers! The German flag is flying on the dome of St. Stephen's! Now we all know only *one* Germany. One for all and all for one! Only in this way can we find glory and salvation in the face of both internal and external enemies. Therefore, this flag is sacred to us, for whoever does not follow it is lost. In our loyal, noble-minded Vienna we want to see no other colors and banners than the one flying on St. Stephen's. Long live our constitutional Emperor Ferdinand! Long live Germany!

Soon, wearing or flying the black and yellow banner invited reproach and even threats. To the excitable Viennese, black and yellow were the colors of a reactionary.[60]

Imbued with nationalist fervor, the Austro-Germans quite naturally took great interest in what was happening in Frankfurt. On March 5 fifty German liberals, most of them from the southwestern states, had gathered at Heidelberg to make plans for convoking the German National Assembly. This group appointed a committee of seven to invite to a preliminary parliament at Frankfurt all persons in Germany who were or had been members of the various state diets, together with prominent liberal intellectuals. Nearly six hundred persons, the great majority of them from south Germany, responded to this invitation and

[57] Pichler, *op. cit.*, pp. 26–28; *Oesterreichische konstitutionelle deutsche Zeitung,* No. 2 (April 4, 1848), p. 7, Univ. Colo. 1848 Coll., No. II/157. See also *Wiener Zeitung,* No. 94 (April 3, 1848), p. 443; Ficquelmont, *op. cit.*, p. 65.
[58] Ficquelmont, *op. cit.*, p. 65; Stiles, *op. cit.*, Vol. I, p. 119.
[59] No. 15 (April 7, 1848), p. 200.
[60] Stiles, *op. cit.*, Vol. I, p. 119; Hartig, *op. cit.*, p. 226.

met at Frankfurt on March 31. Since there were only two Austrians in Frankfurt at the time, the Viennese felt that they should also send representatives to the Preliminary Parliament. The deputies were chosen by various groups. The students elected their representatives on April 3: Schuselka, Kuranda, Giskra, and Schneider. The faculty selected Endlicher, Mühlfeld, and Schilling. The Lower Austrian Estates, the Writers' Club, and the citizens of Vienna also sent deputies.[61] Before the delegates left for Frankfurt on April 5, they assembled in the square under the dome of St. Stephen's, on which the red, black, and gold flag was proudly waving, while a large throng of Viennese jammed the streets leading into the square. Everyone joined in singing Arndt's "What Is the German's Fatherland?"[62]

> What is the German's Fatherland?
> The Prussian, or the Swabian kind?
> Where Rhenish grapes bloom ripe and full?
> Where curves his flight the Baltic gull?
> Ah, no! no! no!
> His Fatherland must greater grow!
>
> What is the German's Fatherland?
> Point out to me its farthest bound!
> Wherever rings the German tongue
> And praises God the German song,
> There shall it be!
> There, German, make your Germany!
>
> There shall the German's country lie,
> Where scorn meets Gallic frippery,
> Where France reaps hatred from the land,
> And German clasps a German hand!
> There shall it be!
> There is the whole of Germany!
>
> There is the whole of Germany!
> O God, regard it from on high;
> Grant German courage to us all
> That we may love it true and well.
> There shall it be!
> There is the whole of Germany!

[61] Reschauer and Smets, *op. cit.*, pp. 50–51; Ficquelmont, *op. cit.*, p. 65.
[62] Translated from the German by Thomas Riggs, Jr., in Thomas C. Mendenhall *et al.* (eds.), *The Quest for a Principle of Authority in Europe 1715–Present: Select Problems in Historical Interpretation,* pp. 207–208.

The singing of the anthem was followed by various eulogies of the German people. When the impressive ceremony was over, the deputies, wearing German ribbons and bearing German swords, marched in pairs through the ranks of the Academic Legion to the railway station and proceeded to Frankfurt, only to learn upon their arrival that the Preliminary Parliament had been dissolved on April 4.[63]

Before leaving Frankfurt the members of the Preliminary Parliament had provided for the election of members for the German National Assembly by universal suffrage on the basis of one representative for every 50,000 inhabitants. The assembly was to convene on May 1. Until then, a committee of fifty was to watch over the proceedings of the old diet of the Germanic Confederation.[64] Six Austrians—Andrian-Werburg, Schuselka, Schwarzer, Schüler, Bach, and Palacký—were selected to serve on this committee, but Palacký, a native of Bohemia, refused the appointment.[65]

On April 16 the Austrian Ministry ordered all provincial officials to draw up plans for the elections to the Frankfurt Assembly.[66] The electoral districts were to be so divided that there would be one for approximately every 2,500 inhabitants. Five electors chosen in each such electoral district were, in turn, to select the actual deputies to go to Frankfurt.[67] In Vienna and its suburbs the electors were named on April 29 and 30, and on May 3 they met to nominate the deputies for the National Assembly.[68]

The hoisting of the German flag on the tower of St. Stephen's Cathedral and the selection of deputies, first for the Preliminary Parliament and then for the Frankfurt National Assembly, brought a new flood of literature glorifying the German national state the liberals wanted to create. Arndt's anthem was printed in dozens of editions. Austrian writers like Karl Moering, J. P. Lyser,[69] and Anastasius Grün penned praises to the German colors, German unity, freedom, and the National

---

[63] Reschauer and Smets, *op. cit.*, Vol. II, pp. 51–52.

[64] Heinrich Laube, *Das erste deutsche Parlament*, Vol. I, pp. 73–91.

[65] Rudolf Stadelmann, *Soziale und politische Geschichte der Revolution von 1848*, p. 51.

[66] *Wiener Zeitung*, No. 107 (April 16, 1848), p. 507.

[67] Magistrate and Provisional Citizens' Committee, "Proclamation," Vienna, April 22, 1848, Univ. Colo. 1848 Coll., No. II/272.

[68] Magistrate and Provisional Citizens' Committee, "Proclamation," Vienna, April 25, 1848, *Wiener Zeitung*, No. 117 (April 27, 1848), p. 559.

[69] J. P. Lyser wrote a number of poems glorifying the 1848 Revolution. He was also editor of the biweekly Viennese paper *Oesterreichs Parole. Schutz für Wahrheit, Recht und Pressfreiheit*, which was published from April 1 to April 29, 1848

The First Days of Freedom

Assembly.[70] Most of the compositions were of the same eulogistic tone as Jurende's "Song about the German Emperor":[71]

> Who can the German Emperor be?
> A Prince who is himself a slave,
> And sheds the blood of people brave,
> Who does not think and feel with them,
> And only toys with their love for him:
> This prince, with German wine I swear,
> Can ne'er the German Emperor be.
>
> Who can the German Emperor be?
> A prince who with his hard knout rules,
> As slaves his folk abjectly schools,
> Who is not subject to the mind,
> Can ne'er set free but only bind:
> This prince, by German oak I swear,
> Can ne'er the German Emperor be.
>
> Who can the German Emperor be?
> A prince who's free in brave, free land,
> Who shelters it with iron hand,
> Who gives his people equal rights,
> Who e'er his subjects' love requites:
> This prince, by German Rhine I swear,
> The German Emperor must always be.
>
> Who can the German Emperor be?
> A prince who to his word is true,
> And ne'er breaks Teuton faith, true blue,
> Who's strong and brave on every hand,
> To wage strong fight for German land:
> This prince, by our sunshine I swear,
> The German Emperor must always be.

At first the Viennese liberals gave little thought to the kind of union that would be most practical or to the fact that union with Germany might be dangerous for the preservation of the Habsburg monarchy.[72] The *Constitution* went so far as to demand the immediate creation of a

[70] Joseph Alexander Freiherrn von Helfert, *Der Wiener Parnass im Jahre 1848*, pp. xl–xli.
[71] *Constitution*, No. 8 (March 30, 1848), pp. 84–85; reprinted in Helfert, *Der Wiener Parnass im Jahre 1848*, p. 99. J. Jurende was either the son or the nephew of the editor of the *Vaterländische Pilger*. He wrote many articles and verses during the 1848 Revolution, chiefly for the *Constitution*.
[72] Ficquelmont, *op. cit.*, p. 48.

German republic, with the Austrian Emperor as its president.[73] As the time approached for the election of deputies to the Frankfurt Assembly, much of the discussion about German unity crystallized into a dispute over federation versus confederation. Those in favor of a federal Germany, primarily the radicals and the progressives, argued that Germany could be strong only if all its components were closely knit. If Germany was to be only a confederation, the many kingdoms, principalities, duchies, and counties would always be a source of weakness and confusion, for they would follow their own particular interests without regard to the welfare of Germany as a whole. In a confederation the German people would remain weak and unable to protect their liberties. Honor and strength could be attained only in a federal state.[74]

The more conservative members of the population looked with reservation upon union with Germany. They feared that if a German federal state was created, Austria would become merely an insignificant border province in a large empire. More important, union of the German sections of Austria would alienate all non-German nations in the Austrian monarchy,[75] with the result that only German Austria would "be left to sit in the deliberations at Frankfurt, like a cripple among healthy men."[76] Furthermore, they believed that a close internal union with Germany might bring severe economic hardships to the Austrian people. Austrian industry would be unable to compete with German manufactures; and Vienna, with its palaces and luxury goods, would lose all economic significance.[77]

Thus the conservatives felt that Austrian interests could be preserved only in a confederation. They argued that in a confederation "the sovereignty of every component part would not only be preserved but mutually protected"; every component state could develop "in a natural way that makes allowance for all its nationalities." Every member state would fight with all the resources at its command to protect Germany against foreign enemies and at the same time "profit internally

[73] E[rnst] V[ictor] Zenker, *Geschichte der Wiener Journalistik während des Jahres 1848* (hereafter cited throughout as *Wiener Journalistik 1848*), p. 43.
[74] See especially Herrman Cohn, "Ein- oder Zwei- Kammer-System; Bundesstaat oder Staaten-Bund!" *Constitution,* No. 29 (April 25, 1848), pp. 447–49; *Der deutsche Adler an die deutschen Bewohner aller Provinzen Oesterreichs,* Univ. Colo. 1848 Coll., No. II/85.
[75] Zenker, *Wiener Journalistik 1848,* p. 43.
[76] Gotthard Freiherrn von Buschmann, "Aufruf an alle wahren Oesterreicher in der Frankfurter Sache," *Wiener Zeitung,* No. 111 (April 20, 1848), p. 530.
[77] August Zang, *Flugschrift 1848 für das allgemeine gleiche Wahlrecht: Lebensfrage für die österreichische Monarchie,* p. 6. Pamphlet originally published in Vienna, April 8, 1848.

through intellectual and material union." Moreover, the road would be open for Austrians to make a constitution of their own, "which would hold together all the nationalities with equal love." Only in this way could Austria become a strong state in the German union. The program of the Viennese conservatives was expressed by Baron Gotthard von Buschmann when he wrote in the *Wiener Zeitung*: [78]

Austrians, be free Germans! However, in order to remain free, above all be free Austrians! Again I call out to you: No German federation but a German confederation! Be great and proud Germans but also proud Austrians! Let the Austrian flag wave by the German one on St. Stephen's tower! Elect prudent men, not enthusiastic, intoxicated youths, for Frankfurt! Wear the Austrian colors at the side of the German ones, and the Slavs, Hungarians, and Galicians will wear them with joy along with the colors of their land. Long live Austria! Long live every nationality in Austria! Long live Germany through a strong Austria!

It might be said that what the more conservative Viennese really wanted was unification with Germany without surrendering sovereignty. As the dramatist Friedrich Hebbel described it in his diary: [79]

The dear Austrians! Now they are thinking about how they can unite themselves with Germany without uniting themselves with Germany! This will be difficult to carry out—just as difficult as two people who want to kiss each other but at the same time want to turn their backs to one another.

At first the Ministry maintained a neutral attitude about the kind of union that was to be effected with Germany. However, when the liberal German politician Friedrich Christoph Dahlmann made an open pronouncement advocating the exclusion of Hungary from the new German federation, the Ministry finally made a flat declaration in favor of confederation: [80]

Although the Ministry wants under no circumstances to influence in any way the elections for the German people's parliament, the question of whether Germany will in the future be a federation or a confederation, which has already come up, has moved the Ministry to express its views.

Filled with the desire to have a close union with Germany, Austria will gladly seize any opportunity to prove its loyalty to the common German cause.

However, it can never completely renounce the special interests of the

[78] Buschmann, *op. cit.*, p. 530.
[79] Friedrich Hebbel, *Tagebücher*, ed. Felix Bamberg, Vol. II, p. 299, entry dated April 18, 1848.
[80] Printed in the official section of the *Wiener Zeitung*, No. 112 (April 21, 1848), p. 535. See also Ficquelmont, *op. cit.*, p. 58.

different parts of its territory belonging to the German confederation. It cannot approve any unqualified submission to the assembly of the confederation or give up its independence in internal administration. At the same time, it reserves for itself the unqualified right to pass on each of the resolutions of the assembly of the confederation.

In so far as this is not reconcilable with the nature of a confederation, Austria is not in a position to join one.

Although the Viennese were sharply divided over the issue of whether Germany should become a federation or a confederation, all factions were united in their antipathy toward Prussia. The Austrians had long been suspicious of the ambitions of the Hohenzollern family. Their distaste for the Prussian ruling house was greatly increased by the news that King Frederick William IV had ordered his soldiers to fire on the Berlin populace on March 18. When the King proclaimed to "the German nation" on March 21 that he was taking over the leadership of the German people on that day "of great danger to the German nation,"[81] their enmity turned to fury.

This ill-timed and presumptuous declaration of the Prussian sovereign was greeted with scorn and derision by the German populace in Austria. The *Volksfreund* took the King to task for attempting to become emperor of Germany after murdering 2,000 of his own subjects. "Whoever shoots down *2,000* brave citizens with grapeshot because they pleaded with him has never been a German emperor, and the Germans will always protect themselves against such a sovereign in the future."[82] In a lead article the more conservative *Wiener Zeitung* passed bitter judgment on the Prussian King for his misdeeds and concluded:[83]

Austria's arms have up to now protected the German colors on all its battlefields at all times, no matter how stormy. An Austrian prince brought glory to all Germany on the Rhine even while being persecuted by the Prussians. The House of Habsburg has on its side centuries of history and the love of the people when it asserts its old position of presidency in the German Empire.

The Austrian Emperor, however, recognizes that now only the representatives of the German people will make the choice and that this choice must be a free one.

The German nation is not taking sides in favor of or against any par-

---

[81] Frederick William, "Proclamation to My People and to the German Nation," Berlin, March 21, 1848, Reschauer and Smets, *op. cit.*, Vol. II, pp. 27–28.

[82] *Volksfreund*, No. 1 (March 28, 1848), p. 4, Univ. Colo. 1848 Coll., No. II/206.

[83] "Antwort der Deutschen Nation an den König von Preussen," *Wiener Zeitung*, No. 85 (March 25, 1848), p. 387.

ticular dynasty, but only in favor of the independence of the new German Diet. It protests against the usurpation of the place of honor by a German leader.

The German nation implores Your Majesty not to sow new seeds of discord and not to dishonor the hour in which Berlin is burying its dead who fell for German freedom and for German unity!

From the ultraradical *Constitution* came the most violent expression of ill will, in an article entitled "Do We Want to Become Prussians?"[84]

The tragic consequences of the high treason of the Metternichian politics to the Fatherland and to the Imperial House are only now becoming apparent. At the moment of the political rebirth of the German people the most brilliant branch in German history—we Austrians—is standing almost completely paralyzed, suffering from the deep wounds that Jesuit politics have inflicted upon us. May that accursed high traitor avoid the German soil! May he hide the shame of the short life still left to him in a far-off corner, like a despised old man, like a tumor cut out from the Fatherland! We have sunk so low in the respect and trust of our German colleagues that that Christian-Prussian king—the greatest of all Prussian heroes—who explained that the slaughtering and shooting down of his Berlin subjects was only a misunderstanding and who has wanted to join Germany and Russia together can dare to proclaim himself the German King. Look at Berlin! There people ride through the streets only with white flags, and the King plays with the constitution—for it is only a game—and hopes to put a second crown on his not always disinterested head to replace the one that is halfway lost. However, he who is slow and steady wins the race! As ill-treated as we Austrians were by the immeasurably depraved man and his minions and as dishonored as we were in foreign countries, we still have vigor and strength in us. Spring has been called into being in our lands by the Emperor's own words. Now, fellow-citizens of Germany, we are again equal, and we again have the luster of the Austrian name and the glory of history before us!—Now we are worthy of being trusted! And who deserves the most trust? Our Emperor, who in a paternal manner fulfilled our wishes and gave himself to us the moment when the first ray of truth penetrated to where he was; or that king who scornfully answered his people with cannon and then, once he was conquered, took refuge in entreaties?—Austria is putting herself at the head of the German movement by not letting herself be surpassed by anyone in love of genuine freedom. Austria is the freest state in Germany; therefore, she is the first state in Germany. We have still not lost the sympathies of all the German tribes. The beautiful memories of the Austrian Emperor are still a bond. One word, or one deed, and he is the German Emperor, and Germany's future is saved!

[84] "Wollen wir Preussen werden?" *Constitution*, No. 5 (March 27, 1848), pp. 33–34.

Great times require resolute, rapid steps. If our Emperor should appear at Frankfurt, surrounded by all the representatives of the German nation, such a step would be taken. The princes would follow. Then a jubilation that would reach to Heaven itself would resound through all the German countries, and the hundreds upon hundreds of barriers which separate us German brothers would fall away in a moment. At the same time we would be the strongest and mightiest people in Europe and the masters of European politics. If we do not do this, Prussian intrigues will destroy German unity and harmony, the Fatherland will fall into the abyss, and the ignominy of Jena[85] will be repeated. A strong, energetic, liberal Austria will and must now save Germany from Prussian usurpation. But if we are to become strong, our constitution must become a reality as soon as possible. We can delay no longer. The greatest danger is in delay. We must have a liberal ministry that has the trust of the people and that will openly and honestly proclaim the principles according to which it intends to govern. We need actions. We must call representatives from all Austrian lands together as soon as possible. We must have a constitution, in actual fact, for we do not want to become Prussians!

Although the Viennese despised and scorned the Prussians, they never distrusted them or hated them as vehemently as they did the Russians. The Prussians were suspected of desiring to usurp leadership in Germany. The Russians were feared because it appeared that they wanted to rob the people everywhere of their newly acquired freedom. In 1848 "Russophobia" became almost a mania with the revolutionaries. A proclamation of Czar Nicholas on March 26, printed in the *Wiener Zeitung* on April 6, in which he attacked the whole liberal revolutionary movement,[86] very nearly frightened the Viennese out of their wits. In reply a pamphlet entitled *400,000 Russians* was hastily circulated in Vienna. The dire warnings contained in it filled the populace "with anxiety, dread, and terror."[87] An unknown correspondent to the *Constitution*[88] declared that

[85] In the battle of Jena (October 14, 1806), Napoleon annihilated the Prussian army and forced the Prussians to sign an ignominious truce, thereby destroying the last barrier to complete domination of Germany.

[86] *Constitution*, No. 17 (April 10, 1848), pp. 237–38.

[87] *Der freie Wiener. Wochenschrift für Scherz und Ernst, Novelle und Erzählung, Ironie und Satyre, Kunst und Literatur, Politik und Volks-Interessen*, No. 6 (April 17, 1848), p. 24, Univ. Colo. 1848 Coll., No. II/56. *Der freie Wiener*, edited by Alexander Medis, was first issued on April 1, 1848, and thereafter twice a week until July 10, when it came out four times in one week. After that it appeared irregularly until it ceased publication on August 9.

[88] "Antwort auf das jüngste Manifest des russischen Czaars," *Constitution*, No. 17 (April 10, 1848), p. 238.

just as the Czar threatens to continue his tyranny for a long time and wishes to assemble all his Russians under his long knout, we who are imbued with the love of freedom can call upon the living God for help in rallying all the people under the banner of freedom to oppose the Czar and his soldiers. Poland, Germany, Hungary, in fact, the whole civilized world, will form an unbreakable union of all free peoples and will shrink from no sacrifice to protect the honor and security of the free and civilized world.

The editors of *Der freie Wiener* sought to reassure the Viennese: [89]

To be sure, Russia is a power that must be watched and kept in check. Russia, however, is also a power that if it makes a general attack against the West, will be the symbol for an uprising of all nations. Then the Russians must either conquer or be destroyed forever. And do not believe that they and their enslaved hordes will be victorious in this battle with all the rest of free Europe.

The furor caused by the Czar's pronouncement inspired the famous Viennese wit Saphir to write his humorous "Europe's National Rhyming Song to 'My Beloved Russians' ": [90]

> They're coming! They're coming! The sweet and dear Russians,
> Which with nothing will rhyme except in crude Russian!
> Hardly once does he sneeze, their all-mighty ruler!
> They come from the Urals, the Don, and the Dniester,
> From Novgorod, Kazan, from Kiev and Turkestan,
> The serfs and the slaves. A horrible caravan!
> They want to enchain us, and then to enslave us,
> These butchers of freedom, in servitude's omnibus!
> But how do lands civilized accept these crude plunderers,
> These filthy barbarians, these heartless despoilers?
>
> The people of Europe, in these raging times,
> Will greet the Russians with the following rhymes:
>
> What then will say the German?
> "The Russians we'll unman!"
> What then will say the Magyars?
> "We'll rout these damned hussars!"
> What then will say the Czech?
> "Their blood will flow unchecked!"
> What then will say the Croat?
> "We'll not their race promote!"
> What then will say the Wallachians?
> "We'll choke the bloody dragons!"

[89] No. 6 (April 17, 1848), p. 24.
[90] Helfert, *Der Wiener Parnass im Jahre 1848*, pp. 142–43.

What then will say the French?
"We'll take their pants and they'll blench!"
What then will say the British?
"Goddam! For our mercy they'll wish!"
What then will say the Italians?
"And we still need these Satans?"
What then will say the Scandinavian?
"Down with the *Samojeden!*"
What then will say the Jew?
"Let's roast them all for stew!"

By and large, the Viennese were inclined to look with favor upon any people who openly showed their contempt for the czarist government. They showed a great interest in the Poles, among whom the news of the March revolution had created considerable excitement. There was a mass demonstration at Lemberg, where a petition was drafted demanding amnesty for political prisoners, exclusion of non-Poles from state offices, use of the Polish language as the official tongue, and assumption of the title King of Poland by the Habsburg Emperor. The Governor of Galicia, Count Stadion, freed all political prisoners and promised to send the petition to the Emperor.

In Vienna the strivings of the Poles for more autonomy caused some consternation among the conservatives, for they feared that the nationalist movement in Galicia might eventually lead to independence. In 1848 the Viennese conservatives, like most of their fellow-citizens, had great admiration for the Poles. Yet they insisted that Austria should never give them complete independence, arguing that the Polish peasants, who comprised the vast majority of the population and were very loyal to the Habsburg Emperor, bitterly opposed independence, since they feared that freedom would place them at the mercy of their own nobility.[91] Furthermore, the Viennese conservatives believed that an independent Poland would be an easy target for Russian invasion.

The progressives insisted that only an independent Poland could protect Germany against a Russian invasion. Carl Dolde, in an article on "A Free Poland,"[92] spoke for the left on this issue:

The Russian Goliath is looking at us with disdain. The rising self-consciousness among the nationalities and the fact that we are celebrating the tabernacle feast of freedom are distasteful to him. He is already holding

[91] *Wiener Zeitung,* No. 102 (April 11, 1848), pp. 483–84; *ibid.,* No. 125 (May 5, 1848), p. 602.
[92] Carl Dolde, "Ein freies Polen," *Constitution,* No. 21 (April 14, 1848), pp. 308–309.

his weapons ready in his clumsy hand, and his tongue wants to shout out the call for battle. We need a David, and we have one. Everyone knows the new David who will hurl his rock at the Russian giant. His foot is rooted in the north and his head is in Paris. The David of the nineteenth century is a free Poland. . . .

Only through Poland can we ward off the danger hovering over us, at least for the present. Germany must be united before we can be a match for the barbarian in the northeast; but Poland can successfully open the glorious prelude for the big battle, for she will fight for her highest treasure— for her freedom. What I am saying is the desire of all the good people of our German Fatherland. We have seen the jubilation over Austria's and Prussia's amnesty to the captured Poles. We can win only if what has been begun so gloriously will be consistently carried further. Poland is difficult. She will rise up. If she wins her freedom through revolt, we will have lost a future friend. If our part of Poland falls into the hands of the Russians, slavery and barbarism will exist in the very heart of Europe. Austria's Italy opened the eyes of all Europe when she called out: "Too late! Too late!" Let us take care that Poland will not do the same. Let us not rashly play the same game!

The various political factions in Vienna were in accord in their attitude toward the Czechs. In this case, however, the Austro-German position was one of hostility, even though the Czechs were struggling to attain the same liberties the Viennese had gained during the March revolution.

As early as March 11 a large assembly meeting at the Wenzelsbad in Prague had chosen a committee of twenty-eight members to draft a petition to the Emperor demanding considerable increase in the powers of the Bohemian Diet and such concessions as freedom of speech, assembly, religion, and the press; abolition of the standing army; abrogation of feudalism; establishment of a public budget; use of the Czech language in the schools and courts; trial by jury; and exclusion of non-Czechs from public offices. On March 20 a large deputation brought this petition to Vienna. Three days later the Habsburg government approved some of the requests but reserved the most important demands for consideration by the united estates. On March 29 the Czechs sent a new petition to Vienna, most of which was agreed to by the Emperor on April 8. The Emperor approved the equality of the Czech and German languages in the schools and all branches of the government, promised to establish a common administration for Bohemia, Moravia, and Silesia—the three lands of the Bohemian crown—and agreed to convoke a Bohemian diet, the members of which were to be elected on the basis of a democratic franchise. Furthermore, it was stipulated that henceforth only persons who knew both Czech and German could be appointed to state offices in Bohemia.

Despite the fact that one of the basic tenets of the early nineteenth-century liberal credo in which the Viennese revolutionaries had grown up was the freedom and self-determination of all nationalities, the newly liberated Austro-Germans were deeply angered by the concessions their Emperor had made to the Czechs. For the future the Austro-Germans visualized not a Habsburg but a German empire that was to embrace all the lands of the historic Holy Roman Empire. They could not see how any sensible people could voluntarily decline to share the future in store for the German race. Yet not only did the Czechs refuse to participate in the proceedings of the Frankfurt Assembly, but also they demanded self-rule and complete equality with the Germans. That alone sufficed to arouse the antipathy of the Germans.

Typical of their attitude on the language question was the following strongly worded article, "The Czechs and Their Language," which was published about a week after the Czech demands for language equality first became known in the Habsburg capital: [93]

The cry for the supremacy of the Czech language is again resounding through all regions of Bohemia, Moravia, and Silesia. The German language is to have the same relationship to it which the Slavic languages in Hungary have to the Hungarian. In a word, the Czechs want to have the German language subordinated to the Czech. There is no quarrel over whether this demand is legitimate. The rabid hotheads are shouting that they want this and that they will get it even if it costs them their lives. They should, however, realize that every passion destroys itself. Whoever drives anything to extremes will himself be injured by it. Whoever sows hatred will harvest dragon's teeth. They seek to base their claim on the fact that Bohemia, Moravia, and Silesia are Slavic lands. This assertion, however, is only half true. Half of the population of these provinces, without quarreling about a man here or there, is good German. There are approximately 6,140,000 inhabitants, and certainly half of these are German-born. They love their mother tongue as much as the Czechs do theirs. In addition, the Czechs claim that these lands were originally Slavic lands. Whoever knows history knows that until the time of the migrations of peoples, or up to the fifth century after the birth of Christ, these lands were inhabited by Germans. It was only then, when a large number of them hunted for other places to live, that the Slavs pushed their way into these regions. It is indisputable that a large number of Germans remained in the Riesen, Erz, and Fichtel Mountains. The German names of the valleys, rivers, fields, brooks,

---

[93] "Die Czechen und ihre Sprache," *Constitution*, No. 5 (March 27, 1848), pp. 43–45.

mountains, and hills in these regions prove this. In the places into which the Germans wandered later on the Slavic names were kept. The fact that the Czechs, after having been independent for several centuries, later became tributary to the Germans and then even became united with the German imperial crown was a consequence of the world conditions of the time. But the Germans were the tyrants of the Slavs in Bohemia. If the Czechs were oppressed and robbed of their freedom, this happened both to them and to the Germans living beside and among them. To assert that the Germans tried to destroy their nationality is nothing but unjustified hatred and petty slander. If the German language was introduced in the army and in the higher educational institutions, the very nature of the army made it necessary, and in the case of the latter this introduction brought with it the higher culture the German people had attained in the course of time after hard battles. No German wants to rob the Czechs of their nationality. That would be unjust and tyrannical. Since both nations are in common possession of these provinces, they have to get along with each other. They can progress along the beautiful paths of freedom only if they have friendly relations with each other. Woe to those who are conjuring up the bitter language battle just at a time when so much legislation of all kinds needs to be passed in these provinces, particularly in behalf of the peasant, who is groaning under the heavy yoke of manorial burdens. Through this untimely battle they are making all other good things impossible. . . .

The Austro-Germans were even angrier when they learned that on April 8 the Emperor had agreed to the equality of the Czech and German languages in the schools and the government and that he had made other far-reaching concessions to the Czechs. A petition was drafted reaffirming the status of Bohemia as part of the territories of the German Confederation.[94] The Austro-Germans protested that the Emperor's promise to establish a common administration for Bohemia, Moravia, and Silesia was tantamount to creating a state within a state.[95] Officials who did not speak the Czech language might now be subject to dismissal in Bohemia, and the Viennese held that the public offices should never be allowed to become a monopoly of the inferior Czechs. Many objections were voiced to the introduction of the Czech language in the schools. The Austro-Germans maintained that the superior German culture must be preserved intact in Bohemia, especially in the universities.[96]

The refusal of the Czechs to participate in the election of representatives to the Frankfurt Assembly greatly embittered the Austro-Germans.

---

[94] Robert A. Kann, *The Multinational Empire,* Vol. I, p. 172.
[95] See especially *Wiener Zeitung,* No. 100 (April 9, 1848), p. 476.
[96] See especially *ibid.,* No. 103 (April 12, 1848), p. 490.

When Palacký learned of his appointment to the Frankfurt Committee of Fifty, he sent an open letter declining the honor, proclaiming instead the independence of the Bohemian nations from Germany, and insisting that the establishment of a strong Germany was incompatible with the existence of the Habsburg Empire, which was so necessary to the Czech nation and to the whole of Europe.[97] Then, when elections for deputies to the Frankfurt Assembly were announced in Bohemia, the Czech nationalists did all they could to obstruct them. As a consequence (from the German point of view), the elections were a dismal failure. Of the sixty-two electoral districts in Bohemia, elections were actually held in only twenty, and in these only a minority of the electorate voted. In Prague, with a German population of 66,000, only three ballots were cast.[98]

During the elections the Austro-Germans accused the Czechs of inflicting a reign of terror against the Germans, of being in league with the Russians, and of seeking to "slavify" the Austrian Empire. They charged them with being the leaders of the reprehensible Pan-Slav movement, designed to overrun the German nation with the aid of Russia.[99]

Among the Viennese there was no unity of attitude in regard to the Italians. In Milan the report of the Vienna insurrection produced bloody fighting on March 18 between the Milanese and Marshal Radetzky's troops. After five days the Austrians were compelled to retreat through Lombardy to the fortresses of the Quadrilateral (Mantua, Verona, Peschiera, and Legnago).[100] On March 22 the Venetian liberals occupied the arsenal without encountering any resistance and proclaimed a republic. From Milan and Venice the revolt spread to all Lombardy-Venetia. By late March the Austrians held nothing in Italy but the Quadrilateral.

In general, the more radical groups in Vienna argued from the first

[97] For an English translation of this letter, see "Letter sent by František Palacký to Frankfurt," *The Slavonic and East European Review*, Vol. XXVI (April, 1948), pp. 303–308.

[98] Otto Wittner, *Moritz Hartmanns Leben und Werke,* Vol. I, pp. 195–96; Reschauer and Smets, *op. cit.*, Vol. II, p. 163.

[99] For a good example of the way the Germans denounced the Czechs for refusing to participate in the Frankfurt Assembly, see Franck, "Panslavismus vor der Thür," *Constitution*, No. 41 (May 8, 1848), pp. 616–17.

[100] An interesting and revealing account of Radetzky's actions during these days may be found in his reports to Count Ficquelmont from March 18 to March 30, in Joseph Alexander Freiherrn von Helfert, "Radetzky in den Tagen seiner ärgsten Bedrängniss. Amtlicher Bericht der Feldmarschalls vom 18. bis zum 30. März 1848," *Archiv für österreichische Geschichte*, Vol. XCV (1906), pp. 145–62.

that the Lombards and Venetians had just as much right as the Viennese to rebel against the Habsburgs to gain their independence.[101] The war the Habsburg army was fighting in Italy was wholly unjustified and could be supported only by such arguments as the romantic notion that the honor of Austrian weapons demanded its continuance.[102] After all, it was the Austrians who were responsible for the revolts in Italy, for the malodorous policies of the old regime had "prepared the way for this sad event."[103] Now that the Lombards and Venetians had an ardent longing for freedom, largely as a result of Austria's past mistakes, what could the Austrians do against "the rebellious Italians, who will mark every one of the Austrians' steps with death before it will be possible for [them] to meet the danger?"[104] And why fight against a people who were merely struggling for the same freedom? Such a war could be only a war of subjugation and would be a thousand times more damaging than the loss of the Italian provinces.[105] No, the radicals insisted,[106]

> We do not want to have it,
> That free Italian land,
> We'll ne'er let them transmit
> Us there like puppet band.
>
> We will not stain our honor,
> Nor Italian blood pollute.
> Our hands will ne'er be vendor
> Of soiled and bloody loot.
>
> The honest folk on the Po
> Are all their freedom worth.
> Their lives with happiness aglow
> In their homes so full of mirth.
>
> What matter quarrels of princes
> To our free German land?

101 See [Ernst Violand], *Enthüllungen aus Oesterreichs jüngster Vergangenheit*, p. 62.

102 Adolph Lugano, *Der Fortbestand Oesterreichs bedingt durch eines innigen Anschluss an Deutschland als Herz eines central-europäischen Völkerbund*, pp. 18–19.

103 "Oesterreich und Italien," *Constitution*, No. 11 (April 3, 1848), p. 130.

104 Carl Elmar, "Schwärmer—oder——?!" *Constitution*, No. 11 (April 3, 1848), p. 133.

105 Franz Schuselka, "Das Vaterland in Gefahr," *Wiener Zeitung*, No. 93 (April 2, 1848), p. 437.

106 "Lied eines Deserteurs aus dem Corps der Freiwilligen nach Italien," *Constitution*, No. 27 (April 21, 1848), pp. 422–23.

Must we commit outrages
Upon noble Italian band?

Why care about the structure
Which princely knowledge built,
To oppress with tyrant's rigor
Free people to the hilt?

In ruin their work has fallen;
It can no longer be.
And people will never again
Be divided in unity.

We do not want to step upon
The free Italian lands.
We cannot with strong weapon
Fetter the people's hands.

So long as the Alpen snows
Look on this beautiful land,
So long as swift Po flows
To sea from Italian sand.

So long as German blood
Is astir in all our breasts,
So long as such hot flood
Is pulsing in Italian chests:

That long shall Alpen gate
All enemy troops deter,
Even if human hate
For war the fires stir.

Although the radical democrats argued loudly in favor of abandoning the attempts to suppress the revolt in Lombardy-Venetia, a large number of Viennese supported Marshal Radetzky's efforts. They cursed the Lombards and Venetians for their lack of gratitude and treachery in rebelling against an Austria that had made them more prosperous than any other Italian state except Tuscany.[107] They reviewed Austria's historic rights to Lombardy and insisted that without those lands Austria could not form a defensive bulwark for Germany in the south.[108] Plaintively they discussed the disgrace that would come upon Austria if she had to give up her Italian kingdom, which had been bought "with Austria's richest province, Belgium; paid for with our noblest blood;

---

[107] Lugano, *op. cit.*, p. 18; *Wiener Zeitung*, No. 94 (April 3, 1848), p. 444.
[108] "Zur Verständigung," *Wiener Zeitung*, No. 125 (May 5, 1848), p. 602.

and belonging to us as a consequence of the most sacred treaties, part of them going back for one and a half centuries."[109]

On March 23 the King of Sardinia declared war on Austria, deeming the moment auspicious to assume leadership in the Italian national movement to expel the Habsburgs from the Apennine peninsula. No longer was it a matter of suppressing the more or less understandable revolt of provincials. Now it was a matter of defending German soil against a foreign enemy. Volunteer corps were immediately organized and sent to Italy to Radetzky's assistance. Viennese citizens gave clothing, weapons, munitions, and money to help defend the empire.[110] A few days after the corps were organized, approximately four thousand men had enlisted.[111]

As time went on, the Viennese became just as divided in their opinions about the Hungarians as they were about the Italians. When the Hungarian deputation came to the capital on the last day of the March revolution, the Viennese welcomed them enthusiastically. No word of dissension was voiced when on March 16 the Emperor promised the Hungarians a separate ministry or when on April 3 a constitutional government was formed in Hungary under Lajos Batthyány.

In early April the Hungarian nationalists were regarded as front-rank fighters for freedom. Their activities in Pest were eagerly followed by the Viennese, and the newspapers reported in full the latest news from Hungary.[112] Believing that the Hungarians and Germans must work together for the common cause of freedom,[113] most Viennese were more than willing to further amicable relations with them. Their sentiments were expressed in these verses:[114]

> Land of Hungary! Bound so closely
> To our Austria, now so free,
> Tell us where thy wounds do bleed,
> Do you not some balsam need?
>
> Have we not to you now shown
> What a firm will can enthrone?

[109] *Wiener Zeitung,* No. 87 (March 27, 1848), p. 399.
[110] See especially *ibid.,* No. 89 (March 29, 1848), p. 412; *ibid.,* No. 94 (April 3, 1848), p. 444; and *Constitution,* No. 11 (April 3, 1848), p. 132.
[111] Reschauer and Smets, *op. cit.,* Vol. II, p. 56.
[112] Zenker, *Wiener Journalistik 1848,* p. 44.
[113] "Ungarns Stellung im Oesterreichischen Staatsverbande," *Wiener Zeitung,* No. 100 (April 9, 1848), p. 476.
[114] W. Belzar, "Aufruf an Ungarn," in Helfert, *Der Wiener Parnass im Jahre 1848,* p. 130.

Has wax not turned to iron today,
And has not night changed into day?

We want of you our brothers to make;
We curse whoe'er this bond will break!
Hail to you! We greet each other;
Austria's heart won't desert a brother!

Why should not the German free
In free land of Hungary be?
Why should not the Hungarian free
In Vienna a brother see?

He who for us so much has done
Will not the noble Hungarian shun.
You love not one bit less than we
Ferdinand, King of Hungary!

Break down all the deep abysses,
Throw away all prejudices!
Free are only word and thought,
Which God to all his people brought.

Hold ye not to old prescriptions,
Aged through hoary generations.
In the era of reform
Every chain will break ere morn.

Compromise over trivia, therefore,
Then of big things we'll have more.
Where such people do unite,
They hold high our freedom's light.

When the Hungarians showed that they were not satisfied with a separate ministry but wanted to make Hungary an independent country in all but name, the Viennese became more critical and reproached the Magyars for taking advantage of the weakness of the monarchy to push through a separatist program. The refusal of the Hungarians to send troops to help Marshal Radetzky in Italy aroused suspicion. Some even feared that the Hungarians were keeping their troops at home in order to subject the Germans and Slavs living in Hungary.[115] In the spring of 1848 the cleavage between the Austrians and Hungarians, which was to end in the terrible war against the Magyars in 1848–49, was already beginning.

---

[115] See especially Zang, *op. cit.*, pp. 4–5.

The First Days of Freedom

In summary, it may be said that in the first days of freedom were foreshadowed the troubles that were to come to the Viennese. The constitutional Ministry, some of whose members had risen through the ranks under the old regime, was timid and vacillating and slow in granting reforms, thereby encouraging the radicals to use direct action to accomplish their aims. The wretched conditions of trade and industry and the concomitant unemployment helped engender a smoldering hatred in the proletariat that made them responsive to any agitator. Suddenly catapulted into a position of great influence and unchecked by a sobering sense of responsibility, the politically inexperienced students and workers became the prey of demagogues who were ready to use the victims for their own purposes.

Viennese public opinion during the first few weeks of the revolution revealed the growth of national differences that were to contribute powerfully to the final suppression of the 1848 Revolution in the Habsburg Empire. A large group insisted on preserving Austria's special interests in any German empire that might be created, a conviction that made it almost impossible for the Frankfurt Assembly to devise a really effective union of all German-speaking people in central Europe. In March and April arose the bitter enmity between the Czechs and the Germans that was to be climaxed by the bombardment of Prague in June, 1848, as well as the division of opinion over Austria's Italian policy that was to handicap Radetzky's army throughout the course of the revolution. There also arose the feeling of distrust toward the Hungarians that was to end in a civil war. The Viennese Revolution was beginning to fail, in part at least because it served to intensify rather than to reconcile the nationalist loyalties in the sprawling monarchy.

VII. *The Kindling of Flames of Hatred*

WELVE DAYS after the end of the March revolution, in an article entitled "What Is Necessary," the *Wiener Zeitung* counseled the Viennese toward moderation and self-restraint in their efforts to establish a constitutional democracy:[1]

Above all, peace is necessary so that trade and business will again flourish, so that everyone can attend to his own affairs, so that studies will be resumed and assiduously pursued, and so that the fearful and pessimistic can be reassured.

Patience is necessary. Many people think that all their wishes and all their private interests should immediately be complied with. Many expect to see new laws every day: important and unimportant tax or press laws, education or trade laws, or even a completely finished constitution. An old structure has been destroyed, and a new one is to be constructed. One cannot hew the individual stones or build the doors and windows before the plan for the whole edifice is ready. We want to build a solid, habitable, sound edifice, in accord with our needs, open to the sun and light, and protected against all attacks and all storms.

Unqualified trust in our good constitutional Emperor is necessary. The wall which stood between him and his loyal people has fallen. Our voice has reached him and his heart. He knows that what we want is best not only for us but for him and for his house. He wants to and will fulfill our wishes. From now on Austria's banner bears the inscription: the greatest possible progress in education, welfare, and freedom; a popular, free, strong constitution; a free press; better education for the people; freedom of teaching and learning; the National Guard to protect us against internal dangers; and the military to protect us against foreign ones.

An *esprit de corps* is necessary. There must be no division according to classes or nationalities, but every citizen must cherish as his highest aim the promotion of everything that contributes to the happiness of his Fatherland and his fellow-citizens.

Unselfish patriotism is necessary. Everybody must work at his own job intelligently and industriously and must make sacrifices for the common welfare without trying to advance himself or make himself noticed! Special

---

[1] "Was uns Noth thut," *Wiener Zeitung*, No. 89 (March 29, 1848), p. 411.

The Kindling of Flames of Hatred

talents or merits, as well as actions, will speak for themselves. Eminence or position is not just a reward. It carries with it the obligation to be all the more energetic and active in working for the common good. The true reward is the consciousness of having of one's own accord been of use to one's free Fatherland.

It is necessary that not everyone desire to rule. Proposals for general improvements—and we need them—can be made by the press, and genuine representatives of the people will gladly make reforms and give us new laws. But not everyone should feel that he is himself entitled to give or dictate new laws. If everybody puts his hands on the wheels of a wagon, some holding back, some pushing forward slowly, and some pushing forward with too strong a shove, the wagon will either stop or upset.

Energetic, good use of the free press is necessary. Praise be to God and eternal praise to Austria that it has not yet been abused! But be careful! Do not be too hasty in discovering every old injury that has no likelihood or possibility of speedy remedy. A well-intentioned but thoughtless printed word can often become a spark in a barrel of powder. The free press remains a sun which sheds its rays, warms, and spreads blessings. It is the sun of freedom and justice. It never becomes a meteor fraught with misfortune.

God's almighty blessing and mercy are necessary! May He shed His plentiful blessings upon the whole empire so that the seeds of freedom and goodness that have been sown will prosper and bear rich fruit; so that our constitutional Austria will always become stronger and more prosperous and will become and remain our joy, pride, and love; and so that our good Emperor, whom God preserves and blesses, can call out, joyfully and most happily: "My pious, loyal, beloved people are happy, great, and mighty! Ruler of all, I thank Thee! Amen."

If the Viennese had taken to heart the exhortations of the *Wiener Zeitung,* they might have been spared much of the turbulence and bloodshed that were to plague them in the months to come. Yet even in peaceful times not all citizens could be expected to show the restraint and selfless devotion the *Wiener Zeitung* program required of them; and in a time of revolution, led by a people suddenly free to write, think, speak, and act with little or no restraint after centuries of censorship and police rule, counsel such as this was certain to go unheeded.

As the radicals began to look with distrust upon the more conservative members of the Ministry, the character of the revolutionary literature underwent a change.[2] In March the printing presses of the capital were occupied with turning out tributes to the accomplishments of the revolution and its heroes and denunciations of officials of the old regime.

[2] Ottocar Weber, *1848. Sechs Vorträge,* p. 30.

Late in March and early in April, radical agitators took advantage of the freedom of the press to found journals that sought to outdo each other in irresponsibility and sensationalism. The first of the new journals was the *Constitution,* a daily newspaper launched on March 20 under the editorship of Leopold Häfner, "a malcontent of the lower middle class, who envied and hated everyone who wore a better coat or had better manners than he had."[3] From the beginning Häfner used his paper to attack priests and monks, men of wealth, aristocrats, bureaucrats, the Emperor's personal advisers, and other prominent personages who aroused his enmity. The *Constitution* was a great financial success. By its attacks on respectable citizens it pandered to those who were embittered with their lot. By midsummer its circulation reached 40,000.[4]

The success of Häfner's *Constitution* brought many imitators. Ten days after the appearance of the *Constitution* the first issue of the daily *Freimüthige*[5] was printed. This new paper for "thinkers and laughers . . . yielded nothing in maliciousness" to the *Constitution* and "surpassed it in cheapness and cynical coarseness."[6] It was edited by Moriz Mahler, a former theatrical critic. Because of Mahler's unsavory reputation, at first no honest journalist would write for his paper, and most of the articles that were not reprinted from other sheets were written by Mahler himself.[7] His own contributions were unrestrained in their insolence and political ignorance. They were, in fact, in complete accord with the aims of the newspaper as announced by Mahler in the first issue: "Elegance, classical haughtiness, and philistine knowledge are not suited to the rapidly moving times or to journalism. We must live from day to day like beggars. What we gain today must be squandered tomorrow. 'Long live rascality!' said Borne."[8]

The *Freimüthige* devoted itself primarily to political satires. On April 11, Joseph Tuvora joined forces with Mahler and became the political

---

[3] Joseph Alexander Freiherrn von Helfert, *Der Wiener Journalistik im Jahre 1848,* p. 28; Friedrich Kaiser, *Memoiren,* ed. Franz Hadamowsky, p. 46.

[4] Constant von Wurzbach, *Biographisches Lexikon des Kaiserthums Oesterreich,* Vol. VII, p. 173.

[5] The first issue appeared on April 1; the last, on October 25, 1848. See especially *Verzeichniss der im Jahre 1848 in Wien erschienenen Zeitungen und periodischen Schriften (Als Manuscript gedruckt).*

[6] Joseph Alexander Freiherrn von Helfert, *Geschichte der österreichischen Revolution,* p. 318.

[7] Kaiser, *op. cit.,* pp. 47–48.

[8] As quoted in Helfert, *Die Wiener Journalistik im Jahre 1848,* p. 35. Ludwig Börne (1786–1837) was a liberal political writer and satirist who had great influence on early nineteenth-century German liberals.

editor. Tuvora was as bitter as Häfner and as cynical as Mahler, and he had long been known to be responsive to bribery.[9] Mahler and Tuvora were a successful team, and their journal represented the antithesis of integrity and decency; but the Viennese enjoyed it, and especially the radicals.

The third of the radical newspapers that came into existence in the early days of the revolution, and one that exerted a powerful influence in pushing the revolution further to the left, was Ernst Schwarzer's *Oesterreichische Zeitung,* or *Allgemeine Oesterreichische Zeitung,* as it was renamed two weeks after its first appearance.[10] Its editor had been a soldier, poet, secretary, painter, commercial agent, baker, brewer, financial manager, economist, and editor before coming to Vienna in March to begin his journalistic career. In contrast to the *Constitution* and the *Freimüthige,* Schwarzer's paper was refined, dignified, and free from personal vilification and invective. It was designed to be an organ of moderate progress that opposed all efforts to destroy "constitutional-monarchical freedom," to stir up "disorders and lawlessness," and to establish a "rule of the fist or of the lungs."[11]

In its way, the *Allgemeine Oesterreichische Zeitung* was just as radical as its competitors; moreover, it had a real political program. It worked unfalteringly for a close union of Austria with Germany, the abolition of all special privileges of the nobility, the freeing of the peasants from all personal services and dues, the legal and social equality of the proletariat, and the recognition of the right of everyone to work. The paper opposed the policies of the Ministry and fought it constantly.[12]

The *Constitution* and the *Freimüthige* set the tone for the venomous literature that was beginning to appear in larger and larger quantities. Dozens of new journals appeared in print, some to discontinue publication with the second or third issue, others to continue in some form or other throughout most of the revolution. Innumerable satirical pamphlets and scandal sheets attacking unpopular persons or groups were sold on the streets. No one was safe from vilification. Intimate details

---

[9] Ernst Victor Zenker, *Wiener Journalistik 1848,* p. 34; Helfert, *Die Wiener Journalistik im Jahre 1848,* pp. 36–37.

[10] A new and radically different edition of the old *Oesterreichischer Beobachter* under new management. The first issue came out on March 31; the last, on October 16, 1848. It became a daily after April 2. On April 13 its name was changed to *Allgemeine Oesterreichische Zeitung.*

[11] Printed advertisement, Univ. Colo. 1848 Coll., No. II/255.

[12] Helfert, *Die Wiener Journalistik im Jahre 1848,* pp. 38–39; Zenker, *op. cit.,* pp. 36–37.

of family life were exposed to the public. Private differences were aired in public. Persecution and even death were loudly advocated for persons who incurred the hatred of the radicals.[13]

Particularly savage were the attacks on the aristocracy and the bureaucracy. The *Constitution* held that aristocrats could no longer be set apart from ordinary folk but must grow up and be educated in the midst of the whole populace.[14] They were no longer to look upon themselves as a ruling caste. If they still felt that it was their God-given mission to represent stability in the monarchy, they must do so in Parliament or by championing their theories in the free press. If they were ever foolish enough to attempt to regain their former influence by trying to restore the overturned system, not only they but the Habsburg monarchy would be destroyed.[15]

Naturally the radicals' definition of "aristocrat" was loose enough to include anyone they chose. Alexander Medis defined the word as follows:[16]

Not only he who is proud of his patent of nobility and who adheres to the noble belief that only the nobleman is born while the common man is just dropped in a litter, but everyone who wishes to go backward instead of forward, who shrugs his shoulders and fears "anarchy" whenever anyone speaks to him about freedom, who sits in his office with his pen behind his ear to abuse the accursed rabble—the people. We must also include every priest who, clothed in the mask of holiness, preaches in a holy nasal tone from the pulpit against reform or sends books to the people in which the fall of religion, the ruination of the church, and the doom of the world are set forth. All these people together form the aristocracy on the basis of nobility and property! For only the property-owner—the Philistine, endowed with property, who believes that he was created just to enjoy the luxuries of life—fears "anarchy." But he fears anarchy only because he is trembling over his sacks of gold and the comforts which he enjoys in his silken dressing robe! And only the most cowardly priest, who has attached himself like a vampire to the veins of the throbbing industrial life of the

[13] M[athias] Koch, *Genesis der Wiener Revolution,* pp. 30–31; William H. Stiles, *Austria in 1848–49,* Vol. I, pp. 117–18; Friedrich Unterreiter, *Die Revolution in Wien vom März und Mai 1848,* Vol. II, pp. 106–107.

[14] *Constitution,* No. 11 (April 3, 1848), pp. 129–30.

[15] Dr. St., "Aristokratie, Bureaukratie und Constitution," *Constitution,* No. 8 (March 30, 1848), pp. 80–83.

[16] [Alexander] M[edis], "Offener Markt für politische Standreden. Freiheit und Aristokratie?" *Der freie Wiener,* No. 6 (April 17, 1848), p. 23, Univ. Colo. 1848 Coll., No. AII/56. Medis was a penniless Tyrolese medical student. He wrote several articles and poems during the revolution and was editor of the radical newspaper *Der freie Wiener.* He died shortly after the revolution after spending some time in a mental institution.

common people and has sucked one drop of blood after another from it until he now stands in the midst of his possessions and estates, preaches against reform because he knows that in accordance with the spirit of reform the clergyman—the true preacher of salvation—should not be a usurer and should not own more than he needs for a respectable living!

The aristocracy, Medis continued, had formed a "prison wall" to enslave the good. The people

can and will never be free, never independent, and never fully constitutional until the prison wall of the aristocracy is torn down so that not one single stone remains upon another.

Oh, this aristocracy! These tame beasts of their princes, these blood-thirsty bulldogs opposing the people! But take heed, my friends, that you are not treated like mad dogs! Mad dogs are killed. History has proved this, and if you do not believe my words—for I belong to the rabble—then send a deputation to Paris and ask the lampposts and water pipes about this!

According to the radicals, the aristocrats were not the only ones who had failed to change their contemptuous attitude toward the people and their freedom. The bureaucrats too were incapable of understanding that in a constitutional state they were the servants of the people. Instead of devoting themselves to the welfare of the country, the bureaucrats were still using it as a tool to serve their selfish interests. Before Austria could be a free country in fact as well as in name, the servants of despotism must be replaced by men of the people with a reputation for decency, integrity, and kindness, men of intelligence permeated with a love of freedom and a burning desire to do well by their fellow-men.[17]

The members of the extreme left had a bitter aversion for all government officials and did not confine their denunciations to the lesser bureaucrats but attacked the Emperor's personal advisers and the members of his Ministry as well. The Emperor was enjoined to dismiss all those advisers who had served in the Metternich government, for no "honorable man in his sixties or seventies will change his convictions overnight and love what he hated only yesterday." The bureaucrats themselves were warned:[18]

Resign! That is what thousands of people are calling out to you. *Resign!*

[17] "Welchen Einfluss werden die Ergebnisse der grossen Märzwoche auf die österreichische Bureaukratie üben?" *Constitution*, No. 7 (March 29, 1848), pp. 64–66.

[18] *Offene und ehrliche Bitte der getreuen Oestreicher an ihren geliebten Kaiser*, Univ. Colo. 1848 Coll., No. II/36.

You are old, infirm, and inactive. You can be nothing but a hindrance. *Resign!* This is a critical time for the monarchy. In Italy, Poland, Hungary, Bohemia—in fact, everywhere—there are uprisings and revolts. At least perform this one genuine patriotic act and *resign!*

The members of the Ministry, particularly Pillersdorf and Ficquelmont, were not spared from attack: Pillersdorf, the former darling of the liberals, had infuriated the radical journalists when he issued the March 31 press law, which very act branded him as a coward and a willing tool of the reactionaries. He was warned that the people "want men who have learned to look boldly into the eyes of everybody and not men who begin to tremble when a breeze blows from somewhere for fear that the breeze might possibly turn into a storm." He was told:[19]

Baron von Pillersdorf, minister of the interior, to whom were entrusted the welfare, the well-being, the happiness, and the unhappiness of the state and the nation, and its rights, you are not such a man! All your actions in favor of the people and their rights can be told in few words: a few pacifying posters on the street corners admonishing the people to lead a peaceful philistine existence, and an edict to the police. All your other actions were against the people and their rights! Actions? But they cannot be called actions. They represent only a quiet, helpless watching of all things that come to pass and now and then a hasty signature!

Ficquelmont was reprehended even more bitterly. It was said of him that, since he had been trained in the Metternich school of diplomacy, he had no intention of conducting the affairs of his office in a democratic manner but merely continued the old system of secret diplomacy. He was accused of sharing Metternich's ignorance of the German people and of being a decided opponent of German unification.[20] The main charge leveled against the Foreign Minister was that he was much too friendly with the Russians. In Vienna it was rumored that when the Czar learned of Ficquelmont's appointment as minister of foreign affairs, he was so happy that he gave Ficquelmont's sister-in-law a share in a Siberian gold mine—so valuable a gift that a group of speculators immediately offered her 7 million rubles for it.[21] There were loud cries that Austria had been sold to the Czar, that the Austrian government was making a huge loan to the Russians, that Ficquelmont

---

[19] Alexander Medis, "Offenes Schreiben an die Herrn Minister des Innern und Aeussern," *Der freie Wiener*, No. 6 (April 17, 1848), p. 22, Univ. Colo. 1848 Coll., No. II/56.

[20] Franz Schuselka, *Beleuchtung der Aufklärungen des Herrn L. Grafen Ficquelmont*, pp. 3–4, 29–30, 45.

[21] [Karl] L[udwig] Grafen Ficquelmont, *Aufklärungen*, pp. 101–102.

was handing Poland over to Russia. He was even accused of making an agreement with the Czar that "if a new movement breathing freedom should be formed in our midst, an army of Russian locusts will engulf our land."[22]

So bold did the opponents of the government become in attacking Ficquelmont that they circulated the following[23]

Notice

of the sovereign Austrian people to its responsible
Minister of Foreign Affairs.

Dear Count Ficquelmont!

In consideration of the fact that your services are too costly for us to be able to pay you for them any longer,

In consideration of the fact that up to now we have waited in vain for an answer to the questions we have directed to you in the press,

In consideration of the fact that you are inflexibly and unfeelingly holding firm to a system of mysteriousness, in spite of every public warning,

In consideration of the fact that on account of your lack of popularity, in the broadest sense of the word, you have lost all trust,

In consideration of the fact that it would be as impossible for you (a loyal executor of Metternich's ukases for so many years) to become a liberal (without committing godless apostasy) and to declare that your whole life has been a lie since that time as it would be for a *deus ex machina*—we have resolved that we would be fully satisfied if you would finally resign from your office, for which you would be given a suitable pension for your work from that time on.

Looking forward to such a declaration from you at the earliest possible moment, we remain—affectionately, with good will to you as a private person.

Written in our capital and residential city of Vienna.

On April 11, 1848.

The sovereign people of Austria! ! !

Although Ficquelmont and Pillersdorf, the ministers under heaviest attack, resolved to continue in office for the time being, other members of the government grew tired of the irresponsible attacks and resigned. On April 3 Kübeck left the post of minister of finance and was replaced by Baron Philipp von Krauss. The next day Minister-President Kolowrat, already under attack, resigned pleading ill health, and Ficquelmont was asked to assume the presidency of the council in addition to his duties as minister of foreign affairs. On April 20 Taaffe left the

[22] Medis, "Offenes Schreiben," p. 22. See also Schuselka, *op. cit.*, p. 4.
[23] Unterreiter, *op. cit.*, Vol. III, pp. 19–20.

government. He was replaced as minister of justice by Sommaruga. Ten days later Zanini, the minister of war, came under fire and withdrew, and Count Latour took his place.[24] The lesson was not lost on the Viennese; they were to use the same tactics many times in the future.

The leftist journals did not concern themselves solely with politics. The *Constitution* and the *Allgemeine Oesterreichische Zeitung* in particular printed articles on how to improve the economic conditions of the country and especially of the proletariat.[25] They advanced schemes to make more raw materials available to manufacturers so that they could employ more workers[26] and suggested that trade and industry could be stimulated if the government would make peace with Italy, free the country from British influence (that is, take steps to meet the competition of low-priced British manufactured goods), abolish the customs line between Austria and Hungary, establish unrestricted free trade within the monarchy, rescind the tariff on all raw materials imported for manufacture into finished products, and establish good commercial relations with Poland.[27] None of the radicals mentioned the primary reasons for the sudden depression: the confusion, lack of order, and insecurity that had resulted from the March revolution and the continual turmoil that followed it.

The radical journalists were much more interested in improving the lot of the suburban working class than in strengthening the Austrian economy. Loud were their cries for shorter hours and higher wages for the workers. Insistent were they that employers treat their employees like human beings,[28] that the rich give work to the proletariat so they could earn their bread and would not have to beg for it,[29] and that the government provide work for the unemployed. The following appeal to

[24] Ficquelmont, *op. cit.*, pp. 104–108; *Wiener Zeitung*, No. 95 (April 4, 1848), p. 447; *ibid.*, No. 111 (April 20, 1848), p. 529; *ibid.*, No. 113 (April 22, 1848), p. 541; *ibid.*, No. 120 (April 30, 1848), p. 577; Rudolph Kiszling *et al.*, *Die Revolution im Kaisertum Österreich 1848–1849*, Vol. I, pp. 53–57.

[25] Zenker, *op. cit.*, pp. 44–45.

[26] "Was haben wir errungen?" *Constitution*, No. 22 (April 15, 1848), p. 335.

[27] See especially "Politische Handelsverhältnisse," *Commercieller Völkerbund. Zeitschrift für Politik, Industrie, Handel und Arbeit*, No. 1 (April 22, 1848), pp. 4–5, Univ. Colo. 1848 Coll., No. II/208. Only eight issues of *Commercieller Völkerbund*, a biweekly edited by J. Sandrini, were published, the first on April 22, the last on May 24, 1848.

[28] An example of this kind of denunciation of the managerial class was the article "Ein freies Wort für gedrückte Arbeiter, an den Herrn Direktor der k. k. Staatsdruckerei," signed by "several Viennese typographers," *Constitution*, No. 13 (April 5, 1848), pp. 153–57.

[29] See especially "Gebt Arbeit! Arbeit!" *Constitution*, No. 14 (April 6, 1848), pp. 183–84.

the government to set up public works projects for the unemployed is typical:[30]

Give Work.

With this entreaty, which is not to be refused, I turn to the Minister of Interior, for I hope for little from a similar urgent entreaty to our magistrate. "Give work!" I cry out in the name of all those who are searching for work and are not finding it. "Give work!" I cry out in the name of all who know how the reaction is manipulating to increase the public distress in order to be able to scare the partisans of freedom through proletarian uprisings.

Not only do we have an extremely large number of destitute workers here, but large numbers of masons and day laborers are coming here from Bohemia and Moravia and are increasing the confusion and the danger. For God's sake, let no one raise the objection that Italy has first claim to our finances, for unemployment in Vienna is a much more threatening reality than the declaration of the republic in Venice. The provisional government of France has had the courage to shoulder the onerous question of the "Organization of Work" and has made it the main point of its program. Also the King of Prussia ordered the building of a church within a few days after the massacre in the streets of Berlin. It is unbelievable that our Minister of Interior will do less to create work. I urge him immediately to begin with those building projects which have long been planned, namely, the insane asylum, the church in Altlerschenfeld, and the extension of the canals in Fünfhaus and Sechshaus. I earnestly beseech you for this. With this entreaty I am fulfilling a promise which I made to some workers who came to me.

I shall introduce a regular series of articles dealing with the results of my request and the progress of the public works projects which have been undertaken.

Therefore, give work!

Now and then, intermingled with the pleas for more jobs and better working conditions were veiled suggestions and outright appeals to the workers to rise up and attain their rights by force of arms. For instance, the self-appointed spokesman of the proletariat, the journalist and editor Friedrich Sander, wrote:[31]

So listen for once, you rich people who look with disdain at our worn-out coats and at our rough, hard hands and who have never experienced sorrow and need, and only know how to reduce the wages earned with such

---

[30] *Constitution*, No. 8 (March 30, 1848), pp. 73–74. The appeal was unsigned but was doubtless written by Häfner.

[31] *Ibid.*, No. 25 (April 19, 1848), pp. 386–87.

wearisome toil. Listen, you who yawn in the coffee houses and ponder over whether the Russians, the Turks, or the devil will get us, and who quarrel over whether the German flag must be black, red, and gold, or black, gold, and red! We and we alone are unjustly bearing all the burdens of the times for you. Look at us. Because of your carousing many of us are suffering bitter distress, and many a father of a family is worried about where he shall get his bread the next day since all businesses are closed up. What is to happen to us? "Go with the volunteers to Italy!" Is this not so you can re- main sitting with your gold and your chocolate tarts! Those who have no other choice but hunger should go with the volunteers. Oh these volunteers! One hears all Hell laughing when he sees the faces of these courageous persons, so full of love for freedom and for the Fatherland. Who among you has given strength and inspiration to these troops by supporting them? And if we are only lucky enough to come home as victors? "Again work from four o'clock to eight o'clock!" And those whose arms and legs have been shot off? (Death would be most desirable!) "They will be organ- grinders!" Are you not ashamed of yourselves to disgrace the species to which you yourselves belong in such a way! Do you think that doing this makes you free? You are slaves yourselves, and you are also making us slaves! The more the one side works, the more it encourages laziness on the other. But those who want to be lazy should at least pay for the work in a decent way! It is inhuman to carouse while the poor people weep! Now is the time to console and to help, or the future will teach us what despair and bitterness can lead to, just as history has already shown this clearly enough!

Sander then appealed to the workers to band together and fight for their rights:[32]

You brothers, you workers and poor people, wake up! Do you not see that a great bell is being cast? Bring up your material for it while there is still time. Bring it before the work is completed and before the oven again cools off so that people will later know who made the bell ring and for whom it rings! Let us hold firmly together and stand up for our rights, which shameless despotism has kept and could keep from us for so long a time. Then we will know why we are fighting, and the sound of our weapons will resound throughout all Europe!

Let me repeat: Wake up! You are all worthy of the rank of princes. Freedom gives proof that all of you are descendants of the gods!

The denunciations of aristocrats, bureaucrats, employers, and men of wealth and the occasional appeals to the proletariat to unite had a powerful influence on the Viennese populace.[33] The incendiary articles

[32] *Ibid.,* p. 387.

[33] Vitzthum von Eckstädt to his mother, Vienna, April 21, 1848, Carl Friedrich

in the radical newspapers, the growing influence of the students and the liberal intelligentsia, and the proven inability of the government to hold troublemakers in check all helped produce an atmosphere of "good-natured anarchy" in the streets of the capital.[34]

The good-natured anarchy soon found its outlet in mock serenades inspired by Robert Bendix' comedy, "The Old Student," which opened on April 1 at the Theater an der Wien. The play, depicting German student life, had nothing particular to recommend it. The plot was thin and the acting mediocre. Nevertheless, overnight it became the most popular theatrical piece in all Vienna. The director had announced that students would be admitted at a very nominal price. When the first actor appeared on the stage, wearing German colors and long hair, there was a burst of applause. When a group of students came on the stage and sang various songs, including the popular song "What's Coming There from Above," wild cheers broke out, and the students in the audience joined in singing with the students on the stage. In other scenes the actors spoke from the stage to the students in the audience, who replied in turn. When the hero of the play shouted, "Long live freedom!" and another actor added, "And he who has given us freedom!" the students in the audience cheered the Emperor. However, the most popular scene in the whole performance was a short one in which an old maid was given a mock serenade.[35]

The play caught the imagination of the Viennese and particularly of the students. Night after night a noisy, lively throng jammed the theater. Soon mock serenades were carried from the theater to the streets and rapidly became a revolutionary institution. Bands of demonstrators would assemble at an agreed-upon hour in front of someone's home or office. A few musicians would accompany the songs, which were often interrupted by catcalls and threats.

Mock serenades were given unpopular political figures, for the radicals soon found that these noisy musicales were a simpler method of putting pressure on the government than organizing mob demonstrations. It was after such a serenade in his honor that Count Taaffe resigned as minister of justice on April 20. Another serenade was held for Pillersdorf, but when the quick-thinking Minister opened the doors of

Grafen von Vitzthum von Eckstädt, *Berlin und Wien in den Jahren 1845–1852,* p. 91.
[34] "Vor hundert Jahren. Vorboten der Zweiten Revolution," *Wiener Zeitung,* 241; *Jahrgang,* No. 106 (May 6, 1948), p. 2.
[35] Kaiser, *op. cit.,* p. 99; Joseph Alexander Freiherrn von Helfert, *Der Wiener Parnass im Jahre 1848,* pp. xxxvi–xxxvii; Carl Elbinger, *Witz und Satire Anno 1848,* pp. 12–13.

his house and invited the demonstrators to come in, the mockery and insults changed to cheers.

Agitators soon discovered that the serenades were an entertaining and effective means of frightening anyone who had incurred their anger. Night after night mock serenades were held for bakers and butchers who overcharged for their wares or refused to extend sufficient credit, for tavern-keepers who did not dispense enough free drinks, or for employers about whom there had been complaints. Bands of singers frightened strict landlords into forgoing their rents. Sometimes agitators organized serenades just to work off private grudges. The streets of Vienna were soon scenes of terrorism, and many revolutionaries began to look upon mock serenades as a kind of people's court of justice.[36]

The mock serenades were also directed against the Catholic clergy. On the night of April 5 a musicale was staged for the special benefit of Vincenz Eduard Milde, the archbishop of Vienna. The radicals regarded the Archbishop as an opponent of church reform,[37] a supporter of the old system, and a stubborn adversary of enlightenment.[38] According to rumor, he had opposed the hoisting of the German flag on the tower of St. Stephen's Cathedral and had ordered it taken down and torn in shreds. It was indignantly related that he had objected to holding a funeral celebration for the victims of the March revolution, that he had refused to consecrate the insignia of the former German Empire, that he had refused to declare himself in favor of the revolution, and that he had withheld his signature from a petition requesting the extending of political rights to the Jews.[39]

Although the Archbishop was later able to prove that there was no evidence to support any of these allegations, enough damaging charges were circulated about him to make him an object of hatred. On April 4 a student in the Archbishop's seminary received permission to remain in the company of Tyrolese compatriots until eight o'clock. His companions persuaded him to stay out late, and the seminarian did not return to his quarters until ten. The student was immediately expelled from the seminary. When his friends interceded with the Archbishop, he

[36] Kaiser, *op. cit.*, pp. 100–101; "Vor hundert Jahren," p. 2; Unterreiter, *op. cit.*, Vol. III, pp. 21–23; Hans Kudlich, *Rückblicke und Erinnerungen*, Vol. I, p. 226.

[37] Anton Füster, *Memoiren vom März 1848 bis Juli 1849*, Vol. I, pp. 92–95.

[38] A Voice in the Name of Many Seminarians, *Ein offener Brief an den Fürst-Erzbischof von Wien*, Univ. Colo. 1848 Coll., No. II/257.

[39] "Eine Katzenmusik sammt daran geknüpften Reflexionen," *Constitution*, No. 16 (April 8, 1848), p. 213; Archbishop of Vienna, "Proclamation to the Citizens and Inhabitants of Vienna," Heinrich Reschauer and Moritz Smets, *Das Jahr 1848. Geschichte der Wiener Revolution*, Vol. II, pp. 59–60.

refused to rescind the dismissal. In revenge, a band of impetuous students organized a mock serenade for the Archbishop's benefit on the night of the 5th. Milde was defamed and insulted and threatened with such dire calamities that he decided to leave his palace for residence in the country for an extended period of time.[40]

From the Archbishop's palace the serenaders proceeded to the Liguorian monastery. The Ligourians had long been an object of suspicion, and in late March and early April a number of tracts were circulated about them. In these writings the Liguorians were accused of having long been in league with the Jesuits. It was charged that their library contained diabolical books advocating adultery, murder, and treason. They were accused of stealing inheritances and were said to have established an order for fallen girls, the Penitent Sisters, solely for the pleasure of the brethren. It was even alleged that they had murdered Pope Clement XIV and that Cesare Borgia had once been the director of the order.[41]

A pamphlet entitled *A Little Light for Poor Souls about Jesuits, Liguorians, and Redemptorists,* by Friedrich Unterreiter, was widely circulated (10,800 copies were sold in three days) and succeeded in rousing the Viennese to a fever of hatred. The pamphlet was a masterpiece of unfounded charges and hysterical accusations:[42]

Is it really possible for you still to exist in Vienna and in Austria? Have you men of secrets and darkness not been blinded by the first ray of light that appeared on March 13?

You who are despised and feared, disgraced, condemned, and, unfortunately, protected—you who have been driven away and then have clung tenaciously to the human race as pitch does to the trunks of trees! You who barter away the word of God as Jews barter away rubbish! You who do good to a few in order to corrupt many? You whose secret institute for novitiates still contains those dangerous, shameful books which, in violation of the commands of both God and human beings, justify regicide, adultery, and treason, and who knows what else! In short, you who read, circulate, and formerly even taught much that was rejected as bad by natural moral sense! You who outside of a small disciplinary order recognize none of the existing statutes! You dare to wait for our new constitution! You who have never done anything good for your fellow-brothers

[40] Reschauer and Smets, *op. cit.,* Vol. II, pp. 59–62; Stiles, *op. cit.,* Vol. I, p. 120.

[41] See Friedrich Unterreiter, "Löschhörndl für das Armenseelenlichtl der Jesuiten, Liguorianer und Redemptoristen," Unterreiter, *op. cit.,* Vol. II, pp. 30–34; Peter Parth, "Worte eines Bürgers an seine Mitbürger, in Betriff des geschmähten Liguorianer," *ibid.,* pp. 35–40.

[42] Friedrich Unterreiter, "Armenseelenlichtl für Jesuiten, Liguorianer und Redemptoristen," Unterreiter, *op. cit.,* Vol. II, pp. 26–29.

now want to share something good with us? You whose wealth has been used only for political machinations, to the detriment of those who inherited it!

You are still in Vienna?

You whose words were supposed to give consolation but which not even once gave comfort to delinquents on their last journey? You who mainly exist for the purpose of swindling close relatives by means of your habitual, base legacy-hunting tactics?

You who, whether called Jesuit, Liguorian, or Redemptorist, hide the same atrocious system behind each of these names! You who under these names have been stamped with the pariah stamp of ignominy by the better public opinion!

You must really possess no feeling of honor. You must have no human and manly dignity in that lump of flesh under your left ribs, since you are shamelessly standing here, despised and scorned, and still want to stand here.

You who have sacrificed the lives of thousands of people and of several kings on the altar of your dark God, Ignatius Loyola!

You who slowly slaughtered one of the best popes [Clement XIV] with aqua tofana because he dissolved your disgraceful order!

And you can still exist?

You are still here, when the human soul stands still at the thought: "How is it possible that such an institute can exist since its horrible principles have long been known?" Do you believe that we do not know how many weaklings are in insane asylums because of your frightful teachings? Do you think the fact is unknown that you accept fathers of families (naturally only rich ones) in your order so you can inherit their property? Is it possible that you are still in Vienna, since, except for a few old praying sisters, nobody has any respect for you any more? Do you believe, pious fathers, that you can slip by under the principles of the constitution in order to undermine them, as it has happened in other states? No! No! It is not possible. You will certainly follow the pious examples of your Bavarian and Roman brethren and go far away to a place like China, Japan, or Greenland to accomplish your pious missionary activities there, for the Viennese are no longer cringing before your scourges, since they have 50,000 bayonets.

But when you leave—which we hope will happen soon and in a peaceful way—do not forget to read all those millions of Masses for us for which you have already been paid in cash!

It was such writings as this that incited the Viennese to descend on the Liguorian monastery. There they shamefully insulted the monks and ordered them out of the city. National Guardsmen in the neighborhood refused to interfere with the rioters, who finally dispersed late at night.

Early the next morning the news spread around Vienna that most of the Liguorians had fled from the city before dawn and that those who remained were busy removing the treasures of the order. Upon hearing this, large masses of people again collected at the monastery to force the Liguorians to leave their treasures behind. Detachments of the Academic Legion and the National Guard appeared on the scene, immediately ordered the inhabitants of the monastery into wagons, and drove them out of the capital. At the same time the possessions of the Liguorian order in Vienna were declared national property.

On the same day, the Convent of the Penitent Sisters, sponsored by the Liguorian order, was attacked by a large mob and its members insulted and threatened. The National Guard put the thirty-three women in the convent under their protection, escorted them to the city gates, and took over the property of the order in the name of the state. The government made no effort to defend the Liguorians or the Penitent Sisters from these attacks. On May 5 it passed a resolution sanctioning what the rioters had already done and abolishing the Liguorian congregation.[43]

There were still other demonstrations against the clergy. On April 8 mobs gathered in front of the mansion of the papal nuncio and the Scottish monastery.[44] The same night the Mekhitarist congregation was visited by mock serenaders.[45] After these manifestations the extremists limited their attacks on the clergy to writing tracts against them.

The radicals took advantage of the demonstrations against the Liguorians to urge the government "to prevent such illegal deeds of violence" by "abolishing by law all monasteries that still exist and converting them, together with all the very rich endowed lands belonging to them, into national property."[46] This wealth was to be used to bolster the finances of the state, to encourage trade and industry, to give jobs to the unemployed and destitute, and to promote other worthy causes.[47]

---

[43] "Eine Katzenmusik sammt daran geknüpften Reflexionen," pp. 213–14; Unterreiter, *op. cit.,* Vol. II, pp. 40–43; Füster, *op. cit.,* Vol. I, pp. 86–87, 91–92; Reschauer and Smets, *op. cit.,* Vol. II, pp. 63–67; Hermann Meynert, *Geschichte der Ereignisse in der österreichischen Monarchie während der Jahre 1848 und 1849 in ihren Ursachen und Folgen,* pp. 289–90.

[44] Stiles, *op. cit.,* Vol. I, p. 120.

[45] Mechitaristen-Congregation, *An die Bürger und Bewohner Wiens!* Univ. Colo. 1848 Coll., No. II/44.

[46] "Die Klöster," *Commercieller Völkerbund,* No. 1 (April 22, 1848), p. 8, Univ. Colo. 1848 Coll., No. II/208.

[47] *Ibid.;* "Die Aufhebung der Klöster oder die dicken und dünnen Pfaffen. Nebst einer gründlichen Darstellung von der Entstehung und Fortpflanzung der Klöster," Unterreiter, *op. cit.,* Vol. III, p. 6; *Constitution,* No. 33 (April 29, 1848), p. 516.

Only cloisters whose members were actually serving the interests of the country through teaching, caring for the sick, or ministering to souls were to be exempted from this confiscation.[48] Before the people seized their property, the monks and other clergy were requested to sacrifice it voluntarily to the state and return to the simple style of living of Jesus and his apostles.[49]

Not even the pope was immune from criticism. He was denounced in a pamphlet early in April:[50]

The dependence of Austria and Germany on the Roman See has always been a curse and misfortune for their people and princes. With their boundless mania to rule, their avariciousness and their fanaticism, the popes ruined these lands, dethroned the most worthy and the most illustrious German emperors, and slaughtered more than a million people. Their thunder of excommunication was more effective than the sword of the executioner and turned the most loyal citizens into traitors and murderers of their regents.

Oh! the delusions of the times! Yes, even the child fled from his father like a mangy animal and denied him food and shelter when the curse of the pope rested on his head. Gold was extracted from the poorest German under the guise of religious piety and flowed into the bottomless moneybag of his papal Holiness.

No sin was too great, no crime too bloody or horrible to prevent a person from being able to buy an indulgence for it in Rome. Popes have been accused of all kinds of infamous actions, of assassination, of incest, of lewdness, of poisoning. But woe to anyone who ever cast doubt on their holiness. They atoned for it with the most excruciating deaths. The reign of terror of the Roman church princes was an offspring of the darker centuries.

Now we have light. The human spirit has shaken off the chains unworthy of it. In the sunlight of truth we give thanks to the great God of the world, who has taken pity on our deep, servile ignominy, who has made of us a free, happy people, and who has opened up a Heaven for us which consists of the consciousness that one has performed His duty and that His sentiments are noble.

[48] "Aufruf an den katholischen Clerus der gesammten österreichischen Provinzen!" *Constitution,* No. 10 (April 1, 1848), p. 108.
[49] Dr. S——, "Offenes Schreiben. Hochwürdige, Ehrwürdige und löbliche Stifter, Klöster und Konvente der österreichischen Monarchie!" *Constitution,* No. 30 (April 26, 1848), pp. 464–65; *ibid.,* No. 33 (April 29, 1848), pp. 516–17.
[50] "Wider Seine Schein-Heiligkeit Papst Pius den IX. und für das Verheirathen der katholischen Geistlichen," Unterreiter, *op. cit.,* Vol. II, pp. 114–18. See also Vitzthum von Eckstädt to his mother, Vienna, April 7, 1848, Vitzthum von Eckstädt, *op. cit.,* pp. 88–89.

The Kindling of Flames of Hatred

I am a Christian—a genuine Catholic Christian. I do not want to belong to any other sect, and I want to go fearlessly on the dark road to death in the paths of our divine belief, but I want to know the flame of pure truth and not the foul, poisonous air of the cellar, which suppresses its clear rays and even threatens to smother them.

Among the Catholic clergy I have known very fine men, who have been as enthusiastic about the welfare of the state—the holy concern of the Fatherland—as about God, and who, without any foreign influence, have waved the banner of necessary reform and are ready to fight for victory with the proud courage of intelligence. The words of faith, of love, of the Fatherland, and of enlightenment will resound from the pulpit to Heaven itself.

One of the first reforms necessary at this moment is the renunciation of papal domination by Austria and the naming of one of its own bishops as minister of religion, whom the constitutional government will entrust with the supreme direction and administration of church matters.

The structure of the state rests on the pillar of religion, which gives it an indestructible stability. Therefore, how can we let the popes, living in a foreign land, assert their sovereign rule in Austria, to the pernicious destruction of the state edifice?

Pope Pius IX's amicable—yes, even crafty—disposition makes it necessary to declare our independence from him at this very moment.

It was Pius who brought into being the ruinous civil war in Italy! What he could not openly do against powerful Austria he did by means of wicked intrigues.

His speeches inflamed the hot-blooded Italians. He kindled the passions of the Lombards over and over again until they renounced their loyalty to Austria and took up arms against her. Would it not have been much more his concern to demand and implore the Upper Italians not to break their loyalty to their good monarch, who will maintain order and justice among them and who will grant their entreaties. "Revolt" was the word of the papal emissaries in Milan and Venice. "War! War!" was the word which was so often whispered to the cabinet at Turin from Rome that they declared it. The papal states are supporting the rebels with volunteers, money, and blessed weapons. While all kinds of prayers for the Pope are being intonated in the churches in Austria, thousands of Austrians are cursing him, for on account of the rallying cry, "Long live Pope Pius IX!" they are being assassinated with daggers, attacked on the public roads, torn to pieces, mutilated, and massacred without pity. According to the latest news from Rome, the Austrian flag has been torn down from the house of our Minister with scorn and insults, and the lives of all Austrians there are being threatened. And we are to refrain from calling him a pseudoholy, deceitful enemy of Austria! All Austrians look upon the rule of such a pope over our church with indignation. Their most ardent wish is that the constitutional government will strengthen the foundations of the state by naming a minister of religion for Austria who is independent of Rome.

The loss of Italy will be no disgrace for Austria, for it is unworthy of our mild rule, so full of blessings, and incapable of entering into a fraternal union with honorable nations. But it would be an outrage for Austria if she would herself become enslaved by a papal ruler who is under Italian influence.

As the month of April progressed, another issue temporarily drove the attacks on the Catholic church from the front pages of the radical newspapers: the delay of the Ministry in preparing a constitution.[51] There was a general feeling that the gains made on March 14 and 15 were worth very little unless they were guaranteed in writing.[52] Consequently, there were imperious demands for a constitution, accompanied by bitter denunciations of the Ministry for not having made public the basic principles that were to be incorporated in it. The radicals expressed their suspicions that the reason for the delay was that reactionary intriguers were working behind the scenes "to paralyze our benevolent monarch's best intentions" in hopes of winning him over to their purposes.[53] According to the agitators:[54]

Those persons from the high nobility who tremble for their privileges and immunities, those high civil and military officials who are concerned about their property and their high rank, certain doctors of law and of medicine who fear that their former privileges will be curtailed, and certain citizens who are afraid about their houses and their wealth—these enemies of ours and of our Fatherland are afraid of a good constitution, and even if our good Emperor wants to grant us one, they will fight it with all their might.

Accordingly, the Austrian people must frustrate such intrigues by joining the National Guard to protect the liberties already won and fight for the constitution if necessary. They must insist on a national constituent assembly to draft the constitution that had been solemnly promised on March 15. Representatives to the Assembly must be elected who had had no connection with the ousted government and who deserved the full confidence of the people "because of their knowledge and es-

---

[51] Ficquelmont, *op. cit.*, p. 73.
[52] *Der deutsche Adler an die Deutschen Bewohner aller Provinzen Oesterreichs.*
[53] See especially F. S. v. M., "Warum noch immer kein Programm?" *Constitution*, No. 17 (April 10, 1848), pp. 230–33.
[54] *Der deutsche Adler an die deutschen Bewohner aller Provinzen Oesterreichs.*

pecially because of their steadfast character."[55] Finally, the Ministry must hasten to write the constitution before the rabble again threatened the people with arson and destruction.[56]

Aiding the various leftist journalists in their efforts to obtain a constitution and other democratic goals were various revolutionary clubs. These clubs soon became the rendezvous of the extremists. "Here the masses received the first beams of the enlightenment and heard for the first time such words as liberty and sovereignty of the people."[57] One of these organizations was the Democratic Club, whose most active members were Häfner, Mahler, Tausenau, and Fenner von Fenneberg, all of them agitators who hoped to gain positions of power by their activities. The Democratic Club soon wielded tremendous influence, not only on the workers of the city and its suburbs, but also on the students of the Academic Legion.[58]

Even more important than the Democratic Club was the Association of the Friends of the People, in which Anton Schütte was most influential. Schütte was a rabble-rouser with a great gift for oratory.[59] Ever since March he had harangued audiences and club gatherings and had occasionally spoken in the Aula.[60] He had also addressed the Association of the Friends of the People at several meetings, at which the members "ate and drank and called each other by their first names" and listened to "speeches one and a half hours long," which consisted "of nothing but trivial phrases."[61]

On April 14 the association joined with the Academic Legion in staging a mass demonstration in the Odeon Hall—an auditorium about five hundred feet long and two hundred feet wide, reputed to be the largest in the world.[62] The purpose of the meeting was to protest the Ministry's delay in proclaiming a constitution. About six thousand people attended. At first everything was comparatively quiet and orderly, but the peaceful atmosphere of the assemblage changed when Schütte got up, demanded that the crowd present a petition to the Emperor, and pulled out of his pocket a proposed petition which had already been drafted and printed by the association. He read:[63]

Your Majesty:
On March 15 of this year you promised us a constitution for the Father-

[55] *Ibid.* [56] F. S. v. M., *op. cit.,* p. 232.
[57] Stiles, *op. cit.,* Vol. I, p. 122. [58] Kaiser, *op. cit.,* pp. 45–54.
[59] *Ibid.,* p. 44. [60] August Silberstein, *Geschichte der Aula,* p. 54.
[61] Friedrich Hebbel, *Tagebücher,* ed. Felix Bamberg, Vol. II, p. 298, entry dated March 29, 1848. [62] Stiles, *op. cit.,* Vol. I, p 123.
[63] Unterreiter, *op. cit.,* Vol. III, pp. 27–28.

land. This promise is holy to us! Up to the present moment this promise has not become a reality. Because of this, distrust is increasing daily, as a direct consequence of which all trade is hampered; there is lack of food, and the demagogic parties agitating for the overthrow of everything that exists are becoming more influential. All this, along with the dangers threatening from without the country, has induced us to submit to Your Majesty, in a most respectful manner, this petition so full of patriotic feeling for the throne and the Fatherland:

May Your Majesty:

1. Order the immediate convocation of the Constitutional National Assembly.

2. Bypass all institutions pertaining to the provincial estates, which have outlived their time, as well as all property, religious, and class restrictions on the suffrage, and issue calls for the election of the Constitutional National Assembly in accord with the election laws adopted by the Committee of Fifty at Frankfurt a. M. for the German National Parliament.

Your Majesty—the descendant of a ruling family whose power has been unlimited for almost six hundred years—has voluntarily given up his absolute power for the benefit of all nationalities belonging to his scepter in order to share the legislative power with his loyal people. The situation is dangerous because a constitutional oligarchy is thrusting itself between the people and the throne. The most recent happenings in western Europe, however, have taught us, with the warning voice of thunder, that only a constitution made by representatives elected on the broadest popular basis is a secure prop for the throne.

Vienna, April 13, 1848.   The Committee.

Schütte suggested that a public assembly of 100,000 be held at the Josephstadt Glacis to sign the petition, after which it was to be taken directly to the Emperor. During the heated debate that followed Schütte's proposal, the more levelheaded participants finally induced him to give up his idea of a monster petition and agree to have it sent, not to the Emperor, but to Pillersdorf by eight or twelve representatives of the people.[64]

Schütte's proposals alarmed the conservative and moderate groups in Vienna, who already looked upon him as a foreign agitator, a dangerous terrorist, and worst of all, a "republican." They accused him of inciting anarchy, hoping thereby to inflict a reign of terror upon the country.[65] He was also denounced as an emissary of dangerous south German republicans and as a secret agent of either the Czar or the

[64] Stiles, *op. cit.*, Vol. I, p. 123; Unterreiter, *op. cit.*, Vol. III, pp. 26–30; Kiszling *et al.*, *op. cit.*, Vol. I, p. 55.
[65] See especially Josef Neumann, *Anruf an einer sogenannten Herrn Dr. Schütte*, Univ. Colo. 1848 Coll., No. II/149.

Jesuits. The Legal-Political Reading Club recommended his expulsion from Austria, while the National Guard demanded that the government take strong steps to prevent him from disturbing the public peace.[66]

Seizing advantage of this surge of public opinion against Schütte, on April 18 the Ministry ordered the police to arrest him. He was escorted to police headquarters for investigation and then ordered to leave the monarchy. The conservatives applauded these energetic measures; the radicals professed to be horrified by this example of police despotism. Many who had formerly laughed at Schütte and called him a crackpot now considered him a martyr to the cause of freedom. In Schütte's deportation the radical press found new proof that the reactionaries were hard at work to suppress the revolution.[67] In the *Constitution*[68] appeared an article enclosed by a mourning border announcing Schütte's arrest and expulsion and declaring that this act of tyrannical despotism gave proof that

our freedom has been an illusion and a lie. What struck Schütte yesterday can strike all of us today. The scepter is again in the hands of the police!

Viennese, tear off the German colors from your breasts. You are not German. You never will be! Hardly a month has passed since our revolution, and we have already sunk so low that we are peaceful spectators when a German brother is called a "foreigner," is robbed of his personal freedom, and is chased away because he freely expressed his opinions in a so-called free land!

The Academic Legion also protested:[69]

Fellow-Citizens!

An important event has taken place. Personal freedom, without which the constitutional state is a lie, has been damaged. A member of the Association of the Friends of the People, Dr. Schütte, who willingly accepted an invitation to go to the Supreme Police Direction, was arrested on the Ferdinand Bridge by the police and escorted from Vienna under police protection. His present residence is unknown. In the name of the new order sanctioned by His Majesty, in the name of our acquisitions sealed with blood, in the name of the universal rights of man, and in the name of the newly guaranteed inviolability of every free citizen, we strongly protest against this and every similar highly illegal act which, in a brutal and high-handed manner, robs a German, no matter what his political colors may be, of his political freedom. This threatens the whole monarchy with the

[66] Reschauer and Smets, *op. cit.,* Vol. II, pp. 78–80.
[67] Stiles, *op. cit.,* Vol. I, p. 124; Zenker, *op. cit.,* p. 51.
[68] No. 26 (April 20, 1848), pp. 393–94.
[69] As printed in Reschauer and Smets, *op. cit.,* Vol. II, pp. 82–83.

old police servitude, puts the holy word of the Emperor in question, increases the distrust of the responsible Ministry, and gives people the most just reasons for suspicion.

Vienna, April 19, 1848. *The Whole Academic Legion.*

The attacks of the democratic journalists, the spirit of anarchy, the mock serenades, the agitation of sidewalk orators and the democratic clubs, and Schütte's rabble-rousing all helped to bring to a head another movement, which sent many Viennese property-holders into the anti-revolutionary camp. This was the demand for a sharp reduction or complete abolition of rents.

For several years there had been a housing shortage in Vienna and the suburbs, and rents had climbed steadily. Renters had long complained about the avarice of the landlords. Now the stagnation of trade and industry and the increase in unemployment had brought such misery to the lower classes that it was difficult or even impossible for many of them to pay their rents. To make matters worse, the time to make the customary quarterly advance payment was approaching.

To many an impoverished or unemployed worker the new freedom everyone was preaching meant economic betterment for himself and his family. How could a poor man be free if he was forced to pay in advance an outrageously high rent? Particularly in times of distress the landlords should voluntarily forgo the customary payment of rents in advance and collect them at the end of the quarter.[70] A sample formula was circulated for tenants to use in making this demand of their landlords. It read:[71]

Declaration

of the parties at house No. ——— in the suburb (or city) to their landlords.

We, the undersigned parties in your house, on account of the present distress, declare that we are not now in a position to pay in advance the rent from Georgi to Jakobi 1848 (or if the payments are semiannual, until Michaeli). We therefore request our landlord to take our declaration into consideration and to meet our wishes, which are expressed only because of the universally poor business conditions, by proposing a reduction in rents in line with present conditions and by voluntarily giving up rent payments in advance.

Furthermore, since the honorable government of the land will undoubtedly abolish the payment of rents in advance if the rent-paying populace of Vienna goes to it with the request, the Viennese landlords

[70] E. W. Pertteseilheim, "Vorschlag zur momentanen Abhilfe der nahenden und mit Grund zu befürchtenden Zinsnoth," *Constitution,* No. 24 (April 18, 1848), pp. 372–73.

[71] Reschauer and Smets, *op. cit.,* Vol. II, p. 88.

would demonstrate their noble behavior if they would anticipate this step by voluntarily giving up their previous rights to the same, and they would thereby assure themselves of a permanent place in the annals of the history of Vienna.

Therefore, the following are signing this with confidence that their wishes will be fulfilled. . . .

Extremists wanted to pay nothing at all. They reasoned that the property-owners had already collected enough rent to get back the capital they had spent in building the houses. This novel idea spread throughout the city, and many a tenant began to look upon a landlord trying to collect his rent as a usurer and even as a traitor to the new constitutional government. Landlords who insisted on the payments due them were frequently threatened.[72]

On April 17 a large assembly met at the Odeon Hall to discuss ways and means of bringing pressure on the government to support the anti-rent group. After a heated debate a committee was chosen to go to the Minister of Interior and to the Citizens' Committee of Vienna to present the demands of the assembly that all rents be reduced 25 per cent and that the payments be made, not in advance, but after the three-month rent period. This attack on property rights held sacred by middle-class liberals put fear in the hearts of the more prosperous bourgeois. As one of their spokesmen said in the debates at the Odeon Hall, "Today it is a matter of rent. Tomorrow it will be the coat, and then finally the shirt!"[73]

The anxiety of the Viennese bourgeoisie also permeated the National Guard. Since members of the guard were largely from the intelligentsia or propertied classes, they reflected the interests of the middle-class officials, bankers, industrialists, and merchants.[74] The National Guardsmen were content to let the rabble stage a mock serenade for the benefit of the clergy or some other unpopular group, but they looked askance at any movement that endangered their own interests. Some of the more conservative students also began to show their disgust at the "wanton abuses" of the radicals in the Academic Legion and elsewhere, "who were always ready for all kinds of madness, mock serenades, and even for the proclamation of a republic."[75]

In order to protect property and security against further attack, the

---

[72] Ernst Violand, *Die sociale Geschichte der Revolution in Oesterreich,* pp. 89–90.

[73] Reschauer and Smets, *op. cit.,* Vol. II, p. 89.

[74] Füster, *op. cit.,* Vol. I, pp. 102–103.

[75] Kudlich, *op. cit.,* Vol. I, p. 280.

Viennese Magistrate and Citizens' Committee formed the Security Committee to "maintain the existing laws, to safeguard public security, peace, and order, and to guard the personal and property rights of all inhabitants" against those who were working for "the overthrow of the whole legal order and for the dissolution of all civil society."[76] The committee was approved by the Ministry on April 20, and the government promised to back it with civil and military forces. The National Guard also assured the committee of its full support.

The Viennese were informed that the Security Committee would use all the powers at its command to repress further disturbances and that all persons who threatened their fellow-citizens would be turned over to the criminal courts for punishment. The property-holders were also assured that all persons who used illegal means to avoid payment of rents would be punished.[77]

Thus before the end of April some of the more prosperous groups who had engaged in the March revolution were beginning to look with apprehension at the doings of erstwhile revolutionary colleagues. Alarmed by the threat to their rights and wearied by the constant lawlessness and disorders on the streets, many Viennese were joining forces with the government to hold the revolution in check.

[76] "Magistrate and Provisional Citizens' Committee of the City of Vienna to Their Fellow-Citizens," Vienna, April 20, 1848, *Wiener Zeitung,* No. 113 (April 22, 1848), p. 541.
[77] *Ibid.*

VIII. *The Student Revolt and the Flight of the Emperor*

N APRIL 25 the Austrian people were granted their long-awaited Constitution, one bestowed on them by the Emperor, not drafted by a representative assembly. In his patent of March 15 the Emperor had promised as quickly as possible to convene representatives from the provincial estates to aid him in making a constitution. So long did Minister-President Kolowrat delay convoking these representatives that nothing had been done when he left the Ministry on April 4. By that time news had reached Vienna of the decision of the Frankfurt Preliminary Parliament to call elections for the German National Assembly on the basis of universal suffrage.

Obviously it was now too late to assemble a united estates committee patterned on the Prussian Diet of 1847. In order to appease the radicals, the government decided to draft the Constitution itself, with the understanding that the Parliament to be provided for in the Constitution could amend it later. Thus, under the pressure of the moment, a hastily drafted, poorly articulated document, copied from the Belgian and Baden constitutions but modified so as to give more power to the Ministry, was presented to the people as a gift from the Emperor.[1] The Constitution was to be in force only in Austria and Bohemia, not in Hungary or Italy.[2]

Under the provisions of the Constitution, the person of the Emperor was declared sacred and inviolable. All executive powers were vested in

[1] [Karl] L[udwig] Grafen Ficquelmont, *Aufklärungen*, pp. 74–77; Franz Schuselka, *Beleuchtung der Aufklärungen des Herrn L. Grafen Ficquelmont*, pp. 47–50; Franz Pulszky, *Mein Zeit, mein Leben*, Vol. II, p. 118; [Franz Graf von Hartig], *Genesis der Revolution*, pp. 266–69.

[2] Constitution, paragraph 2. Complete text of the Constitution may be found in Joseph Alexander Freiherrn von Helfert, *Geschichte der Oesterreichischen Revolution*, pp. 499–504; and in Heinrich Reschauer and Moritz Smets, *Das Jahr 1848. Geschichte der Wiener Revolution*, Vol. II, pp. 104–106.

him, although, to be valid, his orders had to be signed by a responsible cabinet member. Justice was to be administered in his name. He was to have the right to appoint all public officials, including the members of the Ministry; to confer all decorations of distinction and titles of nobility; to reward meritorious services; and to grant pardons and reprieves. He was to be supreme commander of the army and navy and was to have the right to declare war, make peace, and negotiate treaties with foreign governments, subject to the approval of Parliament.[3]

Parliament, which was to meet annually, was to be composed of two houses. The upper house, the Senate, was to be made up of all princes of the imperial house who were at least twenty-four years old, other persons appointed for life by the Emperor, and 150 members elected by the chief landowners in the country. The lower house, the Chamber of Deputies, was to have 383 members. A provisional election law was to be issued by the government prescribing how the members of the first Chamber of Deputies were to be elected. The final election law was to be drawn up by Parliament. The Emperor, who was to convene both houses of Parliament, had the right to dissolve them at any time. If he did so, however, a new Parliament had to be convened within ninety days. The sessions of Parliament were to be open to the public. No member of either house could be arrested while Parliament was in session without the special consent of the house of which he was a member.[4] The Emperor, as well as members of both houses of Parliament, had the right to make legislative proposals, and both houses were empowered to accept petitions and present them for discussion. To become law, bills must be passed by a majority vote in both houses and be approved by the Emperor. However, bills to improve or alter the constitution required approval by two-thirds of the members present in each house.[5]

The Constitution contained the usual provisions of a liberal bill of rights. Freedom of religion, speech, press, and assembly was guaranteed; the right of petition was granted to every citizen; and secrecy of correspondence was declared inviolable. No person was to be arrested or imprisoned in any other manner than that prescribed by law, and the reasons for his arrest had to be given to him in open hearing within twenty-four hours after he was taken into custody. All persons were declared equal before the law and were entitled to a public trial. Trial by jury was to be instituted in the criminal courts. Everyone was given the

---

[3] Constitution, paragraphs 8–14.
[4] *Ibid.*, paragraphs 16, 34–44.
[5] *Ibid.*, paragraphs 15, 45, 48–51.

right to own land, to engage in any lawful business he desired, and to "hold any office and honor."[6]

Although the Constitution was one of the most liberal in Europe, it was faulty in many respects. Drafted in haste to appease the radical element in Vienna, it had serious gaps and defects that made it virtually unusable as a basis for governing the country. Whether the Ministry was to be responsible to the Emperor or to the legislature remained unclear. There was no definite provision for séparation of powers. Nothing was said about the exact relationship of the provinces to the central government and the division of power between them. The total membership of the Senate was not specified, nor was the number of senators to be appointed by the Emperor.[7]

In spite of these and other defects, the Constitution was at first received enthusiastically. When it was published on April 25, thousands of Viennese gathered in the streets to cheer the Emperor. Many of the newspapers expressed their pleasure over the liberality of the Constitution, though they found points of which they disapproved.[8] The liberal nobility and the more prosperous bourgeoisie—who had directed the movement that had culminated in the March outburst—were well satisfied with it and remained so.[9]

After the first few days of enthusiasm, complaints about the Constitution were made by those political groups who had emerged in the vanguard of the revolution: the students, the lower middle classes, and the workers. The Democratic Club and the Association of the Friends of the People—the self-styled champions of the downtrodden—began to attack it, as did the Academic Legion, the Student Committee, and the Central Committee of Citizens, Students, and National Guardsmen. They were soon joined by the left-wing papers, particularly the *Constitution* and the *Allgemeine Oesterreichische Zeitung*.[10]

The radicals were especially critical because the Constitution had not been drafted by representatives of the people. They argued that a constitution given by an emperor violated the fundamental basis of a free

---

[6] *Ibid.*, paragraphs 17–31.

[7] See Anton Springer (ed.), *Protokolle des Verfassungs-Ausschusses im Oesterreichischen Reichstage 1848–1849*, pp. vi–vii, for a good critique of the Constitution.

[8] *Die Constitution und der Adel*, by the author of the pamphlet *Die österreichische Aristokratie*, pp. 4–5.

[9] Ernst Victor Zenker, *Die Wiener Revolution*, p. 133.

[10] *Ibid.*; Ernst Violand, *Die sociale Geschichte der Revolution in Oesterreich*, pp. 95–96; Friedrich Kaiser, *Memoiren*, p. 54; Ernst Victor Zenker, *Wiener Journalistik 1848*, pp. 53–55.

society: that every citizen had a right to participate in deciding all important political matters either directly or through representatives freely elected by him and his fellow-citizens.[11]

The absolute veto given to the Emperor also disturbed the spokesmen of the lower classes. They insisted that Parliament must exercise all rights of sovereignty. Furthermore, they disliked the provision that gave the Senate as much influence over financial matters as the Chamber of Deputies. They argued that matters affecting finances should be the exclusive prerogative of the lower house. Some even maintained that there should be no upper house at all.[12]

Late in April the radicals inaugurated a violent assault on the government that made their previous attacks pale by comparison. The Ministry was censured for its lack of energy and secretive methods. It was accused of filling government offices with adherents of the old system in order to undermine the freedom of the people—a crime that was no less grave than treason.[13] The members of the Ministerial Council were attacked with unfounded charges of having driven their "liberal" colleague Zanini out of the cabinet because he was not of noble birth and because he refused to second Minister-President Ficquelmont's diabolical scheme to call on the Russian army to march on Vienna and suppress the revolution.[14]

Inevitably, these and other attacks on the government had their intended effect on the people and heightened their fear of reactionaries. Under such circumstances, the good-natured anarchy that had prevailed a few weeks earlier began "to lose much of its good-naturedness,"[15] despite the fact that the special Security Committee had been created to keep revolutionary excesses in check. Early in May the number of mock serenades increased and took on a much more threatening aspect. Furthermore, legionnaires and guardsmen began to participate in them to a greater extent than before.

On the night of May 2 the mock serenades were especially noisy. According to the newspapers, Pillersdorf had instituted proceedings against the mobs who had assaulted the Liguorians in April. This news caused

[11] *Die Constitution und der Adel*, p. 5; Ficquelmont, *op. cit.*, p. 78; "Vorläufige Beurtheilung der neuen Constitution," *Constitution*, No. 31 (April 27, 1848), pp. 471–72.

[12] "Vorläufige Beurtheilung der neuen Constitution," pp. 472–73; Violand, *op. cit.*, p. 96; Zenker, *Die Wiener Revolution*, p. 135; "Seit acht Tagen," *Constitution*, No. 32 (April 28, 1848), pp. 490–91.

[13] *Constitution*, No. 39 (May 6, 1848), p. 599.

[14] R., "Zanini's Abdankung," *Constitution*, No. 36 (May 3, 1848), pp. 551–52; Ficquelmont, *op. cit.*, pp. 109–10.

[15] Hans Kudlich, *Rückblicke und Erinnerungen*, Vol. I, p. 254.

great excitement at the university, as did the report that the Archbishop of Vienna (who had returned to the capital) and various citizens had signed a petition requesting that the Liguorians be allowed to return to Vienna.[16] By way of answer the radicals decided to serenade the Archbishop again, and on the same evening a large crowd "of about 50,000 people, among them many students and members of the National Guard, took part in this innocent pleasure."[17] The huge gathering insulted the Archbishop and broke the windows in his house.[18]

From St. Stephen's Square the mob went across the Graben to Herren Street, where Minister-President Ficquelmont lived, to demand his immediate resignation and departure for St. Petersburg "for his health."[19] Shortly after eleven o'clock the mob arrived in front of Ficquelmont's home. Immediately they began a noisy serenade, punctuated by loud denunciations. Finally a spokesman of the crowd shouted: "Since the Minister does not seem to want to listen to us, we shall go home. Tomorrow more of us will come and more every day until he leaves." Then the demonstrators departed.[20]

The next night came the second installment of the serenade. Another huge throng of music-makers, most of them legionnaires, guardsmen, and workers, surged through the streets. When they passed the Emperor's palace, they were silent so as not to disturb his slumbers.[21] But when they reached Ficquelmont's home, they burst out in song and abuse and loudly demanded that he show himself at a window. Someone informed the serenaders that the Count was still at his office. Since nobody believed him, a deputation of twelve was chosen to go in and investigate. Smoking cigars, the deputies searched the house, jesting, sporting, and ruining rugs and furniture.[22] Failing to find the Minister-President, some of the throng proceeded to his office, leaving a detachment behind to watch his home. At the chancellery they sent a deputation to Ficquelmont to demand his resignation. After a tumultuous scene, Ficquelmont promised to submit his resignation to the Emperor within twenty-four hours, whereupon the rioters departed.[23]

---

[16] Hartig, *op. cit.*, p. 271; L. H. K., "Bericht des Abend-Concertes vom 2. Mai 1848," *Constitution*, No. 37 (May 4, 1848), p. 587.

[17] Vitzthum von Eckstädt to his mother, Vienna, May 8, 1848, Carl Friedrich Grafen von Vitzthum von Eckstädt, *Berlin und Wien in den Jahren 1845–1852*, p. 96 .

[18] Hartig, *op. cit.*, p. 271.

[19] L. H. K., *op. cit.*, p. 588.

[20] Ficquelmont, *op. cit.*, p. 113.

[21] *Constitution*, No. 38 (May 5, 1848), p. 592.

[22] Kudlich, *op. cit.*, Vol. I, p. 255.

[23] Ficquelmont, *op. cit.*, pp. 113–16; Reschauer and Smets, *op. cit.*, Vol. II, pp.

The next day Ficquelmont, true to his promise, handed in his resignation. Not one of his fellow-ministers protested his departure; they had considered his case hopeless since the evening of May 2.[24] The Minister of Interior, Pillersdorf, who had done nothing to suppress the demonstrations against Ficquelmont, succeeded him as head of the cabinet. Even after he became premier, Pillersdorf took no energetic action against the lawless mobs. He merely advised the Emperor, after everything was quiet again, to issue a proclamation under his countersignature,[25] mildly lecturing the Viennese on the necessity of keeping order and warning them that if they continued to take the law in their own hands their constitutional freedom would be impaired.[26] Thus from the first it was apparent to all that Pillersdorf was even more powerless than his predecessor in face of the extremists.[27]

The seventy-five-year-old Baron Johann von Wessenberg took over the Ministry of Foreign Affairs.[28] In order to bring into the government two liberals who were momentarily in the good graces of the democrats, new cabinet positions were created: the Ministry of Trade, Agriculture, and Industry, with Baron Anton von Doblhoff as its minister, and the Ministry of Public Works, headed by Imperial Councilor Andreas von Baumgartner. At the same time Baron Talatzko von Gestieticz was succeeded by Count Montecuccoli as president of the Lower Austrian government.[29] Meanwhile, Count Hoyos grew so tired of the radicals' ceaseless clamors that on May 2 he resigned as commander-in-chief of the National Guard. However, the guard now insisted so loudly that they wanted only Hoyos to command them that on the 7th he was reinstalled.[30]

By May most of the leading reins of the radical movement were in the hands of the Central Committee of Citizens, Students, and National

---

146–50; Vitzthum von Eckstädt to his mother, Vienna, May 8, 1848, Vitzthum von Eckstädt, *op. cit.*, p. 97.

[24] Ficquelmont, *op. cit.*, p. 117.

[25] Hartig, *op. cit.*, p. 272.

[26] Emperor Ferdinand, "Proclamation," Vienna, May 4, 1848, *Wiener Zeitung*, No. 125 (May 5, 1848), p. 601.

[27] Kudlich, *op. cit.*, Vol. I, p. 254.

[28] Rudolph Kiszling *et al.*, *Die Revolution im Kaisertum Österreich 1848–1849*, Vol. I, p. 61.

[29] *Wiener Zeitung*, No. 131 (May 11, 1848), p. 623; *ibid.*, No. 128 (May 8, 1848), p. 615; Friedrich Unterreiter, *Die Revolution in Wien vom März und Mai 1848*, Vol. III, p. 53.

[30] *Wiener Zeitung*, No. 124 (May 4, 1848), p. 595; *ibid.*, No. 129 (May 9, 1848), p. 619; *Constitution*, No. 38 (May 5, 1848), p. 591; Maximilian Ehnl, *Messenhauser*, pp. 53–54; William H. Stiles, *Austria in 1848–49*, Vol. I, p. 125.

The Student Revolt and the Flight of the Emperor

Guardsmen. Although the committee had been formed to act as a liaison between the Academic Legion and the National Guard and "to establish a power that would be capable of maintaining order and of checking excesses on the part of guardsmen and students,"[31] by May it had become the chief directing force of the popular democratic movement.[32] It was loudly championing universal suffrage, popular government, immediate convocation of Parliament, and the creation of more public works projects to give work to the unemployed. The committee was immensely popular with the students, the radical intelligentsia, and the lower classes, and by May the government was bending before its will. Pillersdorf created a special bureau to keep in constant touch with the committee.[33]

The Student Committee was also championing the democratic principles advocated by the Central Committee. On May 5 it drafted the following petition to the Minister of Interior:[34]

Petition
of the
Students of Vienna
to the
Minister of Interior.

Your Excellency!

The students of Vienna have always recognized that their first duty is to live up to the confidence which their monarch has placed in them, and which he has again expressed in his most recent proclamation, by working with all the forces at their command for the maintenance of order and security, both of which are necessary for the preservation of both the throne and freedom. Since they are firmly convinced that Your Excellency will give full consideration to their requests, which, if granted, will remove the distrust now prevailing among the people and calm their troubled minds, they are submitting a petition to Your Excellency from which they expect the best results if it is granted as soon as possible.

We are all convinced that confidence—mutual confidence—alone will make the government strong and powerful and the people happy and contented. A constitutional people especially must have such confidence in its representatives and in its legislative body. But the people will *not* have this confidence if the first Parliament—the one that has the most important

---

[31] Kudlich to a correspondent in Upper Austria, May 16, 1848, Kudlich, *op. cit.*, Vol. I, p. 263.
[32] Ernst Fischer, *Österreich 1848*, p. 66.
[33] Kudlich to a correspondent in Upper Austria, May 16, 1848, Kudlich, *op. cit.*, Vol. I, p. 263; Hartig, *op. cit.*, pp. 276–77, 279–82.
[34] Univ. Colo. 1848 Coll., No. II/161.

questions to decide and is so important to the whole future of Austria—is not composed of members elected in such a manner that the real will of the people—the genuine, total will—is clearly and genuinely represented in it.

In order that this first Parliament can create and consolidate such confidence by giving the necessary guarantees that all the people's interests will be sufficiently and suitably represented in it, that no class will have a preferred position or will be neglected, that the development of our constitutional freedom will be rapidly and energetically encouraged, and that all its resolutions, so important for the whole future, will express the character and true will of the people, the students are submitting to Your Excellency the following *recommendations for the provisional election law that is to be made:*

1. That *no kind of property qualifications* be required for persons elected to the second chamber; for the people can no longer trust a second chamber chosen on the basis of property qualifications, since they selected their representatives to the Frankfurt Parliament through universal suffrage.

2. That the qualifications established in the Constitution for the election of the members of the first chamber be changed in such a manner that ownership of *a not entirely insignificant landholding* will be substituted for the most important landowners as the requirement for voting. If this is not done, the people will be highly suspicious of the first chamber, for they will rightly fear that its members are nothing but representatives of the most dangerous of all aristocrats—the money aristocracy—and men who will never satisfy the true needs of the people.

3. That the members of the first chamber shall be elected *by the people themselves;* otherwise the people will rightly look upon the members thereof as a foreign and hostile caste, who, not being elected by the people, will represent only their own selfish interests.

4. That the Ministerial Council use its influence with His Majesty *to refrain from appointing members of the First Chamber.*

Only the full granting of *all these points* can arouse and establish that confidence which is so necessary and so indispensable. Only in this way will it be possible to mitigate the effects of the painful wound inflicted on the people through merely granting them a constitution when their universal wish was for the constitution to be given to them by the Emperor conjointly with a constituent assembly composed of representatives of the people. Only in this way will the people have a guarantee that all their interests are properly represented and forwarded. Only in this way will it be possible to modify the manifold defects of the constitution in a suitable manner and thus to fulfill the wish expressed by Your Excellency in your last proclamation,[35] for in this way the real opinions of the people in regard to the

---

[35] Pillersdorf's proclamation issued in the Emperor's name on May 4, in which

constitutional charter will be effectively expressed. At the same time the students request that the Ministerial Council persuade His Majesty to *convene Parliament as soon as possible,* for this alone can give the government that stability which is so necessary. Furthermore, the students request that *a Ministry of Labor be established* as soon as possible in the interest of both the working class and the property-owners.

The Committee of the Students of Vienna.

Vienna, May 5, 1848.

    2nd secretary: *Chairman:*

    Joseph Unger.   *Dr. Goldmark.*

Although Pillersdorf had always made every effort to be agreeable to both the students and the Central Committee, his ire was roused when he received the student petition, and he declared that the Student Committee was not entitled to speak for the whole populace. Piqued by this unexpected reaction, the students turned to the Central Committee for support. The committee backed the students by sending a similar petition to the Ministry on May 6.[36]

The Ministry's refusal to accept the student petition also angered the radicals, and the suffrage law proclaimed by the government on May 9 and published on the 11th aroused them still further. In this decree Parliament was convened for June 26. The provision was restated that 150 members of the Senate were to be elected by the most important landowners, among whom were included the administrators of wealthy church properties. Since the total membership of the Senate was now fixed at 200, the number of members the Emperor could freely select was limited to 50. The suffrage law provided that there were to be no religious or property qualifications for the members of the Chamber of Deputies. But it also stipulated that the elections would be indirect rather than direct; that the voters must be citizens; and that servants, daily or weekly wage-earners, or persons living on charity were not entitled to vote. In other words, while the whole of the middle class was enfranchised, the workers were not. In this way the government hoped to drive a wedge between the lower middle classes and the proletariat.[37]

The radicals violently opposed the new suffrage law because a bicameral Parliament was retained and because Parliament was to con-

---

the Viennese were urged not to endanger their freedom by engaging in constant disturbances.

[36] Paul Molisch, "Die Wiener akademische Legion," *Archiv für österreichische Geschichte,* Vol. CX, Part I (1924), p. 87; Maximilian Bach, *Geschichte der Wiener Revolution im Jahre 1848,* p. 371.

[37] Zenker, *Die Wiener Revolution,* p. 134; Fischer, *op. cit.,* p. 65; Kiszling *et al., op. cit.,* Vol. I, pp. 61–62.

vene on June 26, before the Frankfurt National Assembly could draft a constitution for all of Germany. They also objected to the provision for indirect elections, which, they maintained, prevented candidates from appealing directly to the people. The exclusion of the workers and proletariat from all voting privileges was the most strongly opposed provision of the law, for it meant that the foremost champions of democracy, the front-rank fighters for freedom, were being deprived of their right to vote. According to the left-wing journalists, if the workers were deprived of this right, a new revolution, more horrible than any the world had ever seen, would ensue. As in France, an Austrian government of, by, and for the well to do would be overthrown by a justly enraged proletariat.[38]

In a meeting on May 11, the Central Committee resolved to make a strong protest against the law and on the next day drafted a petition and circulated it for signature among the various companies of the National Guard and the Academic Legion. In addition, some hotheaded guardsmen and legionnaires demanded the removal of all regular army troops from the city and the creation of a genuine security committee to protect the people's liberties.[39]

The bold moves of the Central Committee and the students became wearisome and annoying not only to the ministers, many of whom were at the point of resigning, but to the inhabitants of the capital as well. By May most of the more conservative Viennese were convinced that peace and security would only be restored if the university was closed and the students sent home.[40] Toward the middle of May the Ministry resolved to get rid of the troublesome committee. However, it did not dare do so openly because of the support the committee received from the lower classes. Many property-holders in the National Guard were also concerned by the growing radicalism of the committee and were openly demonstrating their antagonism. It occurred to the Ministry to use this conservative faction to force the committee to disband.[41]

---

[38] *Constitution,* No. 44 (May 12, 1848), p. 639; Friedrich Sander, "Das Wahlgesetz. Stimme eines Arbeiters," *ibid.,* No. 46 (May 15, 1848), pp. 655–56.

[39] Anton Füster, *Memoiren vom März 1848 bis Juli 1849,* Vol. I, p. 109.

[40] Jakob Ehrlich, "Die Universität geschlossen, oder die Verschwörung der 105 schwarzgelben Manichäer gegen die Studenten," *Constitution,* No. 44 (May 12, 1848), pp. 640–41; *Wanderer,* No. 115 (May 13, 1848), p. 3, Univ. Colo. 1848 Coll., No. II/216. The *Wanderer* had been in circulation for thirty-five years. In 1848 it was issued daily and edited by Ferdinand Seyfried. In June, August Silberstein joined the staff as coeditor. On June 24 the name was changed to *Der Demokrat,* but on November 21 the old name was resumed.

[41] Violand, *op. cit.,* p. 97; Josephine Goldmark, *Pilgrims of '48,* p. 54; Zenker, *Die Wiener Revolution,* pp. 135–36.

The Ministry was highly successful in persuading the right-wing members of the guard to help, and the committee might have abolished itself had not the Ministry made a mistake that nullified all its endeavors. Fearing to take the initiative in carrying out the scheme, Minister-President Pillersdorf asked Hoyos to issue an order of the day warning the National Guard against participating in political activities. On May 13 Hoyos drafted the order, declaring that political activities were irreconcilable with the duties of the guard, since the only function of the guard and the legion was to maintain peace and security. If the guard turned itself into a political club, it could not fulfill its obligations. Accordingly, guardsmen were to stop participating in the unconstitutional Central Committee.[42]

When the committee learned that Count Hoyos had drafted this order, a delegation went to Pillersdorf to protest against its publication. Pillersdorf again assumed a conciliatory air and asked Hoyos to withdraw his decree. Hoyos agreed to do so if the Central Committee would dissolve itself voluntarily. The deputation agreed to this, and everything would have gone well had not Hoyos, for some unknown reason, had the mandate posted on the streets on the 14th. The proclamation caused a tremendous stir. The Central Committee resolved to declare itself in permanent session. When news came that the regular army had been ordered out to occupy various strategic points in the city, the general alarm was sounded for the National Guard to hurry to arms. Quickly the radicals in the guard, particularly those in the suburbs, and the students and workers formed a phalanx to protect the committee. The Ministry's inept move had given the democrats an opportunity to reunite all friends of freedom against the government. Everywhere there was a common feeling that the people would again have to resort to arms and organize a demonstration to prevent the Ministry from following a "reactionary course." Various democratic groups spent the night of May 14 getting their muskets ready and providing themselves with ammunition.[43]

At the university a meeting was called for 8:00 A.M. on the 15th. Long before that hour, legionnaires, guardsmen, students, and other citizens were milling around in the square before the building. When

[42] Hoyos, "Order of the Day" [May 13, 1848], Reschauer and Smets, *op. cit.*, Vol. II, p. 174.

[43] Ehnl, *op. cit.*, p. 54; Reschauer and Smets, *op. cit.*, Vol. II, pp. 173–76; Zenker, *Die Wiener Revolution*, pp. 135–36; Molisch, *op. cit.*, pp. 89–95; Füster, *op. cit.*, Vol. I, pp. 111–12; Vitzthum von Eckstädt to his mother, Vienna, May 15, 1848, Vitzthum von Eckstädt, *op. cit.*, pp. 99–100; Unterreiter, *op. cit.*, Vol. III, pp. 61–62.

the meeting opened, more than three thousand armed men, in addition to many other Viennese, were in the building. Tension was in the air. There was such a hubbub of talk that the speakers could scarcely make themselves heard. Goldmark arose to harangue the assembly on the reasons for the meeting. He raised many objections to the Constitution[44] and attempted at length to prove that the Central Committee was entirely legal and constitutional, since the members of the National Guard had the same rights as all other citizens to participate in political affairs. Then Legionnaire Hrzka jumped up to remind his audience that if the Central Committee was unconstitutional everything that had taken place since March was also illegal. If there was anything unconstitutional in all Vienna, he shouted, it was the Ministry, which insisted on staying in power when the majority of the populace opposed it. A tremendous ovation greeted these words.

Finally, after a long and noisy discussion, the assembly at the university voted that the Central Committee was constitutional. The crowd was still debating the tactics to follow to protect the committee when news came that troops had marched out of the barracks to occupy the city walls and gates. Immediately there was wild confusion. It was decided that the guard and all the other participants in the assembly should arm themselves and meet again at the university at three o'clock in the afternoon.[45] In the interim, a deputation from the Aula made the rounds of the city, warning the commanding officers of the regular army not to close the gates.[46]

In the afternoon, the members of the Central Committee also met to deliberate on the action they should take to defend themselves. Finally they agreed on a feeble statement to the Minister-President that the Central Committee was constitutional because the Constitution granted every citizen freedom of assembly and the right to petition the government.[47]

At the mass meeting at the Aula at three o'clock, the students resolved to send a deputation to Pillersdorf with three demands. The government was to (1) rescind Hoyos' order of the day, (2) order the most important guard posts in the city to be taken over by both the National Guard and the military, and (3) give adequate guarantees that henceforth the

[44] Kaiser, *op. cit.*, pp. 55–56.
[45] Josef Hrczka, "Der 15. Mai," *Constitution*, No. 49 (May 18, 1848), pp. 680–82; Bach, *op. cit.*, pp. 382–83; Reschauer and Smets, *op. cit.*, Vol. II, pp. 176–78.
[46] Kaiser, *op. cit.*, p. 56.
[47] "Declaration of the Political Central Committee," Vienna, May 15, 1848, *Wiener Zeitung*, No. 136 (May 16, 1848), p. 652.

The Student Revolt and the Flight of the Emperor

army would be called out only in cases of extreme urgency, and then only if the National Guard first requested help.

When the deputies reached the Hofburg, they found the Ministerial Council in session. After waiting a while in the antechambers, the deputies were finally given an audience with the Minister-President. When they told Pillersdorf of the demands of the group at the university, he asked that they be put in writing so that the Ministry could consider them properly. All this negotiating took time, and when by 5:30 no word had come to the Aula, the impatient assemblage sent a second deputation to the Ministry. While these deputations were joining forces to persuade the government to comply with the wishes of the people, still a third delegation appeared to warn the Ministry that the crowd in the Aula and in the streets was becoming more and more threatening. In spite of their threats, Pillersdorf surprisingly refused to yield. The most he would promise was that he and the rest of the council would gladly submit their resignations to the Emperor. At this the student representatives were overwhelmed with despair. They begged Pillersdorf at least to draft a proclamation to the people promising to deliberate further on their wishes. To this the council finally agreed.[48]

It was now about 7:30 in the evening, too late to satisfy the crowds with a proclamation. During the three and one-half hours the university deputies had been negotiating with the Ministry, the throngs had thought of still further demands, this time for far-reaching changes in the Constitution. They were demanding a unicameral assembly empowered to draft an entirely new constitution for Austria, universal suffrage, and union with Germany. Demagogues were urging the crowd to use their weapons against the government—and still another petition was drafted. When evening came there were more and more calls to march on the Hofburg.[49] Suburban workers, armed with shovels, spades, and forks, filled the streets. All day the Democratic Club had been sending emissaries to the factories to summon the workers into the inner city,[50] and the workers had been assuring the students of their support. As one worker expressed it: "The students are doing everything for us. . . . Shouldn't we sacrifice our goods and blood for our beloved students?"[51] By evening 10,000 workers were armed and ready.[52]

[48] *Wiener Zeitung*, No. 137 (May 17, 1848), p. 655; Reschauer and Smets, *op. cit.*, Vol. II, pp. 181–82; Bach, *op. cit.*, pp. 384–86; Kiszling *et al.*, *op. cit.*, Vol. I, pp. 129–30.

[49] Reschauer and Smets, *op. cit.*, Vol. II, p. 183.

[50] Kaiser, *op. cit.*, p. 58.

[51] *Constitution*, No. 48 (May 17, 1848), p. 671.

[52] August Silberstein, *Geschichte der Aula*, p. 55.

Between seven and eight o'clock in the evening the Student Committee finally ordered the revolutionaries to march to the Hofburg. Led by the Student Committee, the Academic Legion and the rest of the crowd around the university began the procession to the imperial palace. While huge crowds of sympathizers jammed the streets, the workers fell in line. As the demonstrators approached Ferdinand's residence, the cries "Down with the Constitution!" "A constituent assembly!" grew louder. When the representatives of the students came out of the Hofburg to announce that the Ministry was beginning to weaken and that concessions would be made tomorrow, calls of "Today!" rang through the crowd. When word came that the government had conceded a uni-cameral legislature, the crowd demanded to see it in writing.[53] Reports came that the government was yielding on other points, too. Around eleven o'clock the Ministry capitulated[54] and drew up the following proclamation:[55]

In consideration of its obligations to the throne and in order to pacify the aroused temper of the people as soon as possible, the Ministry has resolved to withdraw the Order of the Day of the National Guard on May 13, 1848, and to grant the two remaining points of the petition that was submitted to it.

Likewise, the National Guard has been promised that the Constitution of April 25, 1848, will provisionally be submitted to the Imperial Estates for deliberation and that the points in the election law which have given cause for concern will be re-examined. Since, as a consequence of these concessions, the Constitution will be first examined by the Imperial Estates, only one chamber will be elected for the first Parliament, and there will be no property qualifications at all for the elections. With this all doubts about an incomplete representation of the people should disappear.

Vienna, May 15, 1848.   The Minister of Interior
                                                          Pillersdorff.

Mingled with the shouts of approval greeting the news of the proclamation were doubts because the Emperor's name was not on the proclamation. The rioters were not quieted until Pillersdorf assured them on his word of honor that the Emperor would sign the proclamation the next day.

At five o'clock the next afternoon the imperial proclamation appeared on the streets. It was even more precise and definite than Pillers-

---

[53] Füster, *op. cit.*, Vol. I, pp. 115–19.
[54] Stiles, *op. cit.*, Vol. I, p. 129; Vitzthum von Eckstädt to his mother, Vienna, May, 15, 1848, Vitzthum von Eckstädt, *op. cit.*, p. 100; Silberstein, *op. cit.*, p. 56.
[55] Univ. Colo. 1848 Coll., No. II/123.

dorf's statement in acquiescing to the demands made by the democrats. It read:[56]

Proclamation.

For the purpose of quieting the disturbances in our residential city of Vienna on May 15, 1848, and to prevent violent disturbances of the peace, it has been resolved, on the advice of our Ministerial Council, to withdraw the Order of the Day given to our National Guard on May 13 in regard to the proceedings of the Political Central Committee. At the same time it has granted the two requests of the National Guard that the guarding of the city gates and the Hofburg is to be performed in common by the military and the National Guard, including all its divisions, and that the military is to be called in for assistance only in cases when their aid is necessary and only after the National Guard itself requests it.

In order to remove all other reasons for discontent and excitement, in accord with the advice of our Ministerial Council, we add the further stipulation that the Constitution of April 25, 1848, will be submitted to Parliament for deliberation and that the provisions of the election law which have given cause for apprehension will be re-examined.

So that the best possible constitution can be drafted by the constituent imperial assembly, we have resolved that only one chamber shall be elected for the first Parliament and that no property qualifications are to exist for the election of its members. In this way all doubts about insufficient representation of the people should be set at rest.

We cherish the conviction that all classes of citizens will look forward with peace and confidence to the early opening of Parliament.

Vienna, May 16, 1848.

(L. S.) *Ferdinand.*

Pillersdorff,
Minister of Interior and
Provisional President.

Latour,
Minister of War.

Sommaruga,
Minister of Finances.

Baumgartner,
Minister of Public Works.

Somaruga,
Minister of Justice and Education.
Doblhoff,
Minister of Commerce.

May 15 thus brought a resounding victory to the extreme left. When the Ministry finally mustered up courage to try to suppress a revolutionary committee that seriously threatened to usurp its authority, it

[56] Unterreiter, *op. cit.*, Vol. III, pp. 75–76.

failed to provide itself with adequate means to enforce its orders. The few available troops might have discouraged the extremists if it had not been an open secret that the government shrank from taking any measures that might result in bloodshed. As a consequence of the May 15 demonstration the whole cabinet resigned.[57] Even though it was obvious that the government merited little respect, the Emperor asked the men to remain in office on a provisional basis until such time as he could appoint a new ministry. The Emperor, too, lost a great deal of authority and prestige on May 15. Although even the radicals still referred to him affectionately, the very concessions they had wrung from him almost nullified his powers.

Just as the revolution of March 13 to 15 had been a "liberal" one, in the nineteenth-century sense of the term, the revolt of May 15 was a genuinely "democratic" one. On May 15 the radical democrats, who believed in popular sovereignty, were victorious over the moderate liberals of the March revolution, who merely wanted a Parliament of property-holders to check the Emperor's absolute powers and advise him on legislation. From the government the radicals won recognition of the principle of universal suffrage and also of popular sovereignty, in that the Emperor had been forced to agree to submit the Constitution he himself had granted to a democratically chosen Parliament. The new Parliament was to have the right to revise the "Emperor's constitution" in any way it saw fit. The people, not the monarch, now wielded all sovereign powers. Henceforth, in theory and in the eyes of the law, all classes of people were to be equal.[58] Popular sovereignty seemed to have triumphed over middle-class liberalism.

The conservative and moderate elements in Vienna were badly frightened by the May 15 revolution. They well knew that if the government had not capitulated to the radicals barricades would have been built throughout Vienna and the Hofburg would have been stormed. Immediately after May 15 many aristocrats and some of the wealthy bankers, industrialists, and merchants began to leave the capital for homes in the country or elsewhere in the monarchy.[59] Only rarely did a courageous opponent of the radicals like Julius von Zerboni exhort his fellow-

[57] *Wiener Zeitung,* No. 137 (May 17, 1848), p. 655.

[58] *Das Wiener allgemeine Arbeiter-Blatt,* No. 1 (May 22, 1848), pp. 1–2, contains an interesting discussion of this thesis from the workers' point of view. This newspaper was edited by M. Gritzner and Friedrich Sander. It began as a daily, but only seven numbers actually appeared, the first on May 22 and the last on June 2.

[59] Vitzthum von Eckstädt to his mother, Vienna, May 18, 1848, Vitzthum von Eckstädt, *op. cit.,* pp. 101–102.

citizens to protest tactics designed to overthrow the government and sow the seeds of dissension within the country.[60] Zerboni was almost alone in championing the cause of law and order. With the exception of the *Wiener Zuschauer*, the press supported the program of the extremists,[61] attacked the ministers, and clamored for their dismissal. Even the *Wiener Zeitung* joined in abusing the Ministry,[62] agreeing with other Viennese newspapers that the present ministers must be replaced by "strong and honest men of and from the people," not aristocrats or middle-class liberals "who came up under the old system."[63]

A few days after the May revolt, the tenor of the radical press abruptly changed, when an unexpected event brought consternation to both conservative and radical Viennese. Alarmed by the events of May 15, the imperial family had decided that the Emperor was no longer safe in Vienna and made plans to move him to another city.[64] Late on the afternoon of May 17 the Emperor and Empress took their customary drive to the summer palace at Schönbrunn in a light court carriage. Soon afterward, the family of Archduke Francis Charles and the few others selected to accompany the imperial family left the Hofburg unnoticed. When the royal family arrived at Schönbrunn, a servant there was entrusted with informing the Minister of War that the Emperor had decided to take a trip to the Tyrolese Mountains for his health and that his family were accompanying him. Not until the imperial carriage arrived at Sieghartskirchen, where they changed horses, did the Empress tell the Emperor that they were going on to Innsbruck. When the carriage arrived at Salzburg, the group stopped for an hour or so because the Emperor was ill and tired. The next day they reached Innsbruck, where the Emperor was greeted enthusiastically by the populace.[65]

The following day, May 20, the Emperor sent a letter to Minister-

[60] Julius von Zerboni di Sposetti, *Zuruf an alle Völker des freien Oesterreichs*, Univ. Colo. 1848 Coll., No. II/234.

[61] Zenker, *Wiener Journalistik 1848*, p. 56. *Der Wiener Zuschauer. Zeitschrift für Gebildete*, edited by J. S. Ebersberg, came out four times a week, and 196 numbers were printed, from January 3 to December 30, 1848.

[62] See especially No. 136 (May 16, 1848), p. 651, No. 138 (May 18, 1848), p. 661.

[63] Wintersberg, "Was noch geschehen muss," *Constitution*, No. 48 (May 17, 1848), p. 672.

[64] The teacher of Archduke Francis Charles's sons, Count Henry Bombelles, was entrusted with carrying out the details of the plan.

[65] Kiszling *et al.*, *op. cit.*, Vol. I, pp. 131–32; Hartig, *op. cit.*, pp. 297–99; "Tirol mit Vorarlberg in seinen socialen und politischen Zuständen," *Die Gegenwart. Ein encyklopädische Darstellung der neuesten Zeitgeschichte für alle Stände*, Vol. IV, pp. 97–98.

President Pillersdorf asking the Ministerial Council "to undertake those measures which the situation of the monarchy and the safety of the throne require so that the regular course of business will not be interrupted by my temporary change of residence."[66] At the same time he issued the following[67]

Manifesto to My People.

The happenings in Vienna on May 15 have convinced me that an anarchical faction, supported by the Academic Legion, which has been led astray by foreigners, and various sections of the Civic and National Guards who have swerved from their accustomed loyalty, has desired to deprive me of all freedom of action in order to enslave the loyal inhabitants of my capital and the provinces, who are universally angered by such individual presumption. My only choice was to liberate myself by force with the aid of the loyal garrison or to withdraw quietly for a time to one of the provinces, which, thanks to God, have still remained loyal.

There was never any doubt about the choice. I chose the peaceful and bloodless alternative and went to that mountainous land which has always been loyal, where at the same time I would be close to the news from the army which is fighting so bravely for the Fatherland.

The idea has not crossed my mind of withdrawing or curtailing the gifts, and what naturally follows them, which I made to my people during the March days. On the contrary, I shall always feel disposed to listen to the just complaints of my people, if they are made in a legal manner, and to take national and provincial interests into account; but these must be genuine popular desires, presented in a legal manner, deliberated upon by Parliament, and then submitted to me for approval, and must not be extorted by arms by a few unauthorized individuals.

I wanted to say this much for the general pacification of my people, who have been thoroughly frightened by my departure from Vienna, and to remind them at the same time that I have always been ready, with paternal love, to receive my returning children, even though they be considered lost.

Innsbruck, May 20, 1848.   Ferdinand

The Emperor's flight to Innsbruck made a deep impression on the Viennese. Even before the news of his departure was rumored, the *Wiener Zeitung*, whose editors surmised that some of the monarch's intimate advisers were suggesting this course to him, warned that if

---

[66] Ferdinand to Pillersdorf, Innsbruck, May 20, 1848, Hartig, *op. cit.*, Appendix III, p. 398.

[67] Hartig, *op. cit.*, Appendix III, pp. 396–98.

The Student Revolt and the Flight of the Emperor

the Emperor left Vienna "it would be the flight of Louis XVI. The last day of his sojourn here would be the first day of the republic. The Emperor not only can remain in Vienna. He must remain here."[68] The first official report of the Emperor's departure was brought to Vienna around nine o'clock on the evening of May 17, when the servant from Schönbrunn arrived at Latour's residence. Latour at once called his colleagues into session, and together they drafted the following proclamation:[69]

This evening, at nine o'clock, the unexpected information came by word of mouth to the Ministry that, on account of his health, His Majesty, accompanied by the Empress and His Highness, Archduke Francis Charles, his illustrious wife, and three princes, left the imperial residence and started on the road to Innsbruck.

The undersigned ministers, although not knowing the reasons for or the details about this journey, consider themselves obligated to inform the inhabitants of the capital about it.

They have considered it their first duty on the very same night to dispatch a trustworthy person, the Supreme Commander of the National Guard, Count Hoyos, to His Majesty to state that the population will be pacified only by the return of the Emperor or by a public statement giving the reasons why this is impossible. The same urgent request will be delivered to the Archduke by Count Wilczek.

The Ministerial Council likewise recognizes that at this important moment it is its sacred duty to dedicate its undivided concern and attention to the interests of the Fatherland, and, in accord with its responsibility, to act as circumstances demand. The co-operation of our fellow-citizens and of all well-disposed persons will enable it to maintain peace and order and to contribute to the pacification of the people. All further information the ministers may receive on this subject will always be truthfully and fully communicated to the public. Likewise, as soon as the Ministry receives orders or information from the Monarch, the same will be made public.

Vienna, May 17, 1848.

The Provisional Ministers:

Pillersdorf. Sommaruga. Krauss. Latour. Doblhoff. Baumgartner.

To avoid disturbing the populace during the night, the proclamation was made public early on the morning of the 18th. However, the students learned of the Emperor's departure during the night of the 17th,

---

[68] The article was written before the flight of the Emperor became known but was published on May 18. See No. 138 (May 18, 1848), p. 661.

[69] Univ. Colo. 1848 Coll., No. II/110. Count Wilczek was Pillersdorf's brother-in-law.

and Academic Legion patrols spread the news throughout the city.[70] Incredulous at first, the Viennese were reluctantly convinced when they saw the proclamation.

A few hardened democrats laughed at the "childish revenge" of the Emperor;[71] the vast majority, however, cried out in consternation. They could not understand how their Emperor could leave his people in such a stormy period when he was so badly needed.[72] Hundreds of them "forced their way into the Hofburg, not to set it on fire or to plunder it, but, weeping and plaintive, to find out why their 'good Emperor' had forsaken them."[73] Some feared that "without the Emperor Vienna would immediately go to ruin."[74] To the Viennese "it was easier to imagine the heavens without a sun than Vienna without an Emperor";[75] many of the most ardent revolutionaries of March were beginning to see "the grass growing rank in Minoriten, Michaeler, and St. Stephen squares" and to realize that the Emperor's departure from the capital meant that "Vienna has become the capital of the province of Lower Austria instead of the capital of an empire for forty million people."[76] Since they felt that the turbulent scenes at the Hofburg were at least partly responsible for the Emperor's decision to leave the palace, the people grew ashamed of the mob demonstration of May 15. Those who had boasted about their part in it now remained quiet or explained that they were simply obeying the commands of their officers.[77]

What most alarmed the Viennese was the fear that the flight of the Emperor portended the establishment of a republic in Vienna. To them, the term "republic" meant everything that all but the most radical abhorred: anarchy, "communism," and the division of property. The fear that a republic was imminent caused the great majority of Viennese to turn on the democratic factions that had been primarily responsible for the May 15 victory. The same students, democrats, and workers who had been hailed as brothers just three days before were now shunned and called arsonists, agitators, and traitors. Invective poured forth against the Academic Legion, "the presumptuous students," and the

---

[70] Silberstein, *op. cit.*, p. 60.

[71] Füster, *op. cit.*, Vol. I, p. 124.

[72] Silberstein, *op. cit.*, p. 60; Unterreiter, *op. cit.*, Vol. III, p. 79.

[73] Vitzthum von Eckstädt to his mother, Vienna, May 18, 1848, Vitzthum von Eckstädt, *op. cit.*, p. 103.

[74] Füster, *op. cit.*, Vol. I, p. 124.

[75] Silberstein, *op. cit.*, p. 60.

[76] Vitzthum von Eckstädt to his mother, Vienna, May 18, 1848, Vitzthum von Eckstädt, *op. cit.*, p. 104.

[77] *Ibid.*; Füster, *op. cit.*, Vol. I, pp. 124–25.

"irresponsible agitators." Persons who tore down antidemocratic posters were dubbed "republicans" and occasionally arrested, and there was a clamor to banish all foreign agitators from the country.[78] Many an advocate of peace and order denounced the workers as robbers who wanted control of the government in order to destroy private property.[79]

Only the two radical leaders Häfner and Tuvora were foolhardy enough to attempt to establish a "republican dictatorship." On the morning of May 18, they rode into the factory suburbs to seek the help of the workers in overthrowing the Ministry. They hoped to incite 30,000 guardsmen and workers to take over the most important government offices, establish a provisional government with Tuvora as its president and minister of foreign affairs and Häfner as minister of interior, arrest their opponents, and then dispatch emissaries to Hungary, Prague, Milan, and Germany to invite deputies to a people's congress in Vienna.

Although Tuvora and Häfner later protested that "the word 'republic' never passed [our] lips,"[80] the workers they approached felt sure they were proclaiming a republic. Häfner drove to Sechshaus to try to goad the workers into marching on the city. Then he went on to Gumpendorf. Meanwhile, Tuvora was trying to win the workers at Mariahilf to the plot. Astonished and bewildered, the workers refused to further the cause of the two agitators until they could get advice from the students.

Informed of the actions of the two agitators, the Viennese Security Committee commanded Goldmark and the National Guard officer Wünsche to arrest them. With the help of the Gumpendorf National Guard they seized Häfner and Tuvora and led them under heavy guard to the Esterhazy Palace. Upon their arrival a large crowd of people gathered to urge the authorities to hang them for treason and attempted to tear them from the hands of their guards. With the greatest difficulty the guard detachment succeeded in taking them to the National Guard headquarters in the city. There they had to fight off another mob, who loudly demanded that the two be handed over to them. Only the timely

---

[78] Kudlich, *op. cit.*, Vol. I, p. 224; Zenker, *Wiener Journalistik 1848,* pp. 59, 61, 137; Füster, *op. cit.*, Vol. 1, pp. 124–25; *Constitution,* No. 50 (May 22, 1848), p. 687; [Franz] Grillparzer. "Historische und politische Studien," *Grillparzers sämtliche Werke,* ed. August Sauer, pp. 175–77.

[79] S., "Die Reaction," *Das Wiener allgemeine Arbeiter-Blatt,* No. 4 (May 25, 1848), p. 8.

[80] J. Tuvora and L. Häfner, "Erklärung," *Ankündigungsblatt. Beilage zur Constitution,* No. 60 (June 3, 1848), p. 37.

arrival of a member of the Security Committee with a ministerial decree ordering Häfner and Tuvora to the criminal court for trial saved them from certain death.[81]

Other radical journalists, who before the Emperor's flight had inveighed against any attempt to restrain even the wildest agitators, quickly changed tactics when Tuvora and Häfner were arrested. Even the *Freimüthige* and the *Constitution* hastened to defend themselves against charges of complicity in the plot. On May 19 Mahler wrote an article in the *Freimüthige* in which he tried to disassociate himself from Tuvora's scheme: "It is certainly not my fault that my history is current with that of Tuvora. How can I help it if he went to Gumpendorf and talked with the people there about new ministers? The inhabitants of Gumpendorf understood him as little as I understand his stupidity."[82] The *Constitution,* temporarily edited by Gritzner after Häfner's arrest, printed a front-page article on the same day energetically denying that the paper had republican tendencies and maintaining that Häfner's trial would prove that he was anything but prorepublican.[83]

The reaction against the democrats was even more pronounced in the provinces. The Emperor's assertion on May 20 that an anarchical faction in Vienna was attempting to deprive him of freedom of action made a deep impression, and rumors spread that the Viennese radicals "had attacked the Emperor and had forced him at the point of arms to concede" to their wishes. There was a widespread belief that Ferdinand had fled from his palace under cover of darkness because he was no longer safe.[84] In the provinces the revolutionaries were called "anarchists, adventurers, and political speculators" who would not stop their agitation until a dangerous republic, like that of the United States, was erected on the ruins of the Habsburg monarchy.[85] Countless petitions were dispatched to Innsbruck professing the loyalty of the inhabitants to the Emperor[86] and beseeching him to move his residence from Vienna and convene Parliament elsewhere.[87] Here and there large

---

[81] Joseph Alexander Freiherrn von Helfert, *Die Wiener Journalistik im Jahre 1848,* pp. 62–67; Zenker, *Wiener Journalistik 1848,* pp. 64–67; Unterreiter, *op. cit.,* Vol. III, p. 83; Constant von Wurzbach, *Biographisches Lexikon des Kaiserthums Oesterreich,* Vol. VII, p. 173; *ibid.,* Vol. XLVIII, pp. 164–65.

[82] As quoted in Zenker, *Wiener Journalistik 1848,* p. 69.

[83] *Ibid.; Constitution,* No. 50 (May 22, 1848), p. 688.

[84] Brühl, *Wer ist Schuld, dass der Kaiser fort ist?* p. 2, copy in the Univ. Colo. 1848 Coll., No. II/178.

[85] Füster, *op. cit.,* Vol. I, p. 126.

[86] Kudlich, *op. cit.,* Vol. I, p. 244; Vitzthum von Eckstädt to his mother, Vienna, May 23, 1848, Vitzthum von Eckstädt, *op. cit.,* pp. 106–107.

[87] *Wiener Zeitung,* No. 145 (May 25, 1848), p. 693; "Montecuccoli to All

groups of people demanded to be allowed to march against Vienna to put down the monstrous radicalism.[88]

A host of Viennese from all classes also directed petitions and deputations to Innsbruck.[89] In addition to Hoyos and Wilczek, who had been ordered by the Ministry to go to the Emperor on the night of the 17th, other official and semiofficial groups chose delegations. The Central Committee of Citizens, Students, and' National Guardsmen and the provisional Citizens' Committee sent deputies begging Ferdinand to return.[90] The Writers' Club drafted an address that was signed by over 80,000 people and conveyed to Innsbruck by an impressive delegation.[91] The National Guard and various other clubs and organizations also wrote humble entreaties to His Majesty.[92]

Although they were vitally interested in persuading their sovereign to return to the capital, the Viennese thought it even more important to restore tranquillity and security in the city. On all sides were impassioned appeals for unity and unanimous support of the same Ministry that had been so bitterly attacked as late as May 17 [93] The feeling was widespread that only "unity and moderation, the close co-operation of all well-intentioned people, and untiring work for the preservation of peace and order, the security of persons and property, and the preservation of the constitutional throne" could save Austria.[94]

Acting in accord with the almost universal cry for peace and order, the Ministry moved swiftly to protect the city from possible riots by the radicals. On May 18 it issued a protest against the article in the *Wiener Zeitung* comparing Ferdinand's departure with the flight of Louis XVI.[95] On the same day the President of the Lower Austrian government, Count Montecuccoli, induced the Central Committee to dissolve[96] and turn itself into the Central Club of the National Guard for the Preservation of Peace and Order, with Montecuccoli as its chair-

---

Members of the Academic Legion," Vienna, May 25, 1848, Unterreiter, *op. cit.,* Vol. III, pp. 100–101.

[88] G. Wolf, *Aus der Revolutionszeit in Österreich-Ungarn (1848–49),* p. 7.

[89] Stiles, *op. cit.,* Vol. I, pp. 132–33.

[90] Reschauer and Smets, *op. cit.,* Vol. II, p. 224.

[91] *Wiener Zeitung,* No. 145 (May 25, 1848), p. 694.

[92] *Constitution,* No. 54 (May 26, 1848), p. 719; Vitzthum von Eckstädt to his mother, Vienna, May 23, 1848, Vitzthum von Eckstädt, *op. cit.,* p. 107.

[93] See especially *Wiener Zeitung,* No. 139 (May 19, 1848), p. 665.

[94] Special supplement of *Wiener Zeitung,* May 18, 1848, Univ. Colo. 1848 Coll., No. II/18.

[95] Provisional Ministry, "Proclamation," Vienna, May 18, 1848, *Wiener Zeitung,* No. 139 (May 19, 1848), p. 665.

[96] Montecuccoli, "Proclamation," Vienna, May 21, 1848, *Wiener Zeitung,* No. 143 (May 23, 1848), p. 685; Violand, *op. cit.,* pp. 107–108.

man. Meanwhile, the dormant Viennese Citizens' Committee came to life and passed a resolution establishing a Security Committee, composed of members of the Citizens' Committee and other inhabitants of the capital, to act as the executive organ of the Viennese government. Simultaneously all the citizens' forces in the city—the National Guard, the Civic Guard, and the Academic Legion—agreed to act in concert with the military and obey the orders of the Commandant of Vienna, Count Auersperg.[97] Also on May 18 Montecuccoli issued a proclamation warning the populace that any foreigners in the city who violated their privileges as guests would immediately be expelled from the country.[98] The Ministry gave sharply worded orders to repress all riots and nightly assemblages and to punish those who participated in them in the regular criminal courts.[99]

None of these strong measures stopped the run on the banks that commenced immediately after the Emperor's departure became known. The events of May 15 had seriously disturbed the middle classes and made them uneasy over the financial situation of the monarchy; and on the 15th, 16th, and 17th much more had been withdrawn from the banks than had been deposited. The news of the Emperor's flight created a near panic in the financial market and a serious run on the banks. People hurried to the banks either to change bank notes into silver coin or to withdraw deposits and savings. The throng became so great that army troops and National Guardsmen occupied the entrances to the National Bank and the other credit institutions to handle the crowd. All who could make their way into the banks received payments in silver, but the crowd was so huge that branches had to be improvised in the suburbs to relieve the pressure.[100]

Soon people were refusing to accept anything but coin in payment for goods and services.[101] Placards appeared on the streets warning the people that banks were no longer stable.[102] However, fortunately for the

[97] Provisional Ministry, "Proclamation," Vienna, May 18, 1848, *Wiener Zeitung,* No. 140 (May 20, 1848), p. 672; Kaiser, *op. cit.,* p. 60; "Order of the Day of the Minister of War," *Wiener Zeitung,* No. 139 (May 19, 1848), p. 665; "Hruby to Fellow-Citizens," n.d., copy in the Univ. Colo. 1848 Coll., No. II/244.

[98] Montecuccoli, "Proclamation," Vienna, May 18, 1848, *Wiener Zeitung,* No. 140 (May 20, 1848), p. 672.

[99] Provisional Ministry, "Proclamation," Vienna, May 18, 1848, *Wiener Zeitung,* No. 140 (May 20, 1848), p. 672; Montecuccoli, "Proclamation," Vienna, May 19, 1848, Unterreiter, *op. cit.,* Vol. III, pp. 84–87.

[100] Specific figures were printed in *Wiener Zeitung,* No. 149 (May 29, 1848), p. 711.

[101] Zenker, *Die Wiener Revolution,* pp. 137–38; Reschauer and Smets, *op. cit.,* Vol. II, pp. 221–22.

[102] For example, the two-page placard by Moritz Sporn, *Guter Rath an meine*

finances of the monarchy, calmer citizens assured the inhabitants that the First Austrian Savings Bank and other credit institutions had attained such solidarity that they could easily pay back all the money the depositors had entrusted in their care and still have considerable capital left.[103] Then a group of patriots stated in a proclamation to the Viennese:[104]

Peace, order, and security were yesterday the watchword of the day. Today let it be confidence. Confidence is the foundation of credit. Credit is the soul of trade and the life breath of industry. Our great credit institutions, "the banks and savings banks," were stormed with claims yesterday. Let us be genuine patriots and give back to them what we took out. Confidence arouses confidence. The circulation of money is to the state what the circulation of blood is to the human body. Securities create work just as work creates securities. He who means well by the Fatherland, he who wants to rescue trade and industry from the burdens under which they are groaning, he who loves the workingman, let him hear our call. The silver seeds which he puts into the bank and the gold grains which he puts in his savings bank will bear golden fruit for him.

Vienna, May 19, 1848.

All the protestations about the financial solvency of the country were at the moment of no avail. Although merchants, traders, and industrialists of the Lower Austrian Manufacturers' Association published a proclamation announcing that they would accept bank notes in full value for all payments due them,[105] large crowds continued to press their way into the banks. The demand for coin remained so great that the government granted the National Bank the right to limit the exchange of notes for gold and silver to 25 florins per person. At the same time the Ministry issued orders that "everyone is obligated to accept the notes of the National Bank for all payments at their full value. If any particular kind of coin is stipulated for payment, the debtor is to be allowed to choose whether he will make payment in this kind of coin or in bank notes, according to their value at the time payment is made."[106] Still the run on the banks persisted, and it was not until the

lieben Mitbürger wegen der Sparcasse in Folge einer höchst unnöthigen Belehrung des Herrn J. F. Castelli, Univ. Colo. 1848 Coll., No. II/278.

[103] A Person Interested in the First Austrian Savings Bank, *Ein Wort zur Zeit an die Interessenten der ersten österreichischen Sparkasse,* Univ. Colo. 1848 Coll., No. II/65; J. F. Castelli, *Offener Brief an meine lieben Mitbürger über eine unnöthige Furcht,* Univ. Colo. 1848 Coll., No. II/45.

[104] Univ. Colo. 1848 Coll., No. II/13.

[105] Vienna, May 21, 1848, *Wiener Zeitung,* No. 141 (May 21, 1848), p. 677.

[106] Sommaruga and Kraus, "Proclamation," Vienna, May 21, 1848, *Wiener*

Hungarian government declared early in June that it would accept all Austrian bank notes for circulation in Hungary that the fear of imminent bankruptcy abated and conditions became more or less normal.[107]

Thus the resounding victory of the radicals on May 15 proved short-lived. Ferdinand's flight from Vienna turned most of the populace against them and created a state of panic that a clever ministry could have exploited to suppress them once and for all. But cleverness was not one of the virtues of the Pillersdorf ministry. Within one week the Ministry was to recklessly throw away every advantage gained.

Zeitung, No. 142 (May 22, 1848), p. 681; "Circular of the Lower Austrian Government Concerning the Exchange of the Notes of the Lower Austrian National Bank and the Use of the Same as Legal Tender," Vienna, May 22, 1848, Univ. Colo. 1848 Coll., No. II/50. The last provision immediately led to so many erroneous suppositions that later the same day it was announced: "The Ministerial Council has resolved that the stipulation providing that the debtor is to choose whether he will make payment in the stipulated kind of coin or in bank notes according to their value at the time payment is made is limited to those payments which are due in gold coins or in foreign silver coins. For all other payments the principle holds that was established concerning the acceptance of bank notes at their face value." "Circular of the Lower Austrian Government Concerning the Use of Bank Notes as Legal Tender," Vienna, May 22, 1848, Univ. Colo. 1848 Coll., No. II/57.

[107] Reschauer and Smets, *op. cit.,* Vol. II, pp. 223–24.

IX. *The May 26 Revolution*

HE CONSERVATIVE Saxon diplomat Vitzthum von Eckstädt described conditions in Vienna a week after the Emperor's flight as follows:[1]

> The reaction is in full swing. May 15 is even being disavowed by the most violent opposition sheets. A panic-like fear has overpowered the good Viennese. The artificiality of the movement here and the hollowness and emptiness of the ranters have been completely exposed. It was a severe rebuke that the Emperor gave his capital. For it cannot be forgotten that Vienna's whole existence is at stake, and the city is striding in Hamlet's cloak and softly sighing, "To be, or not to be."

The Viennese were suffering pangs of regret for their past deeds. For the present the radicals were comparatively quiet, as were the approximately 16,000 workers in the city.[2] The students were also subdued. Surprised and dismayed by the sudden coldness with which the Viennese received them, the students began to suspect that they had been used as pawns by intriguing demagogues.

The Pillersdorf ministry was in a much better position than any government since March to assert its authority and check the extremists. Taking advantage of its position, the government ejected dangerous agitators from the capital. Concerted efforts were made to enlarge the public works program. An order was issued to lock up the Aula and other university assembly rooms after the close of the school year to prevent their use for political meetings.[3] On May 18 a law was proclaimed restraining abuses by the press of freedom of speech.

The new press law, drafted with the co-operation of the students and various Viennese writers and publishers, was a very liberal one, and most of the objectionable provisions of the April 1 law were carefully

---

[1] Vitzthum von Eckstädt to his mother, Vienna, May 23, 1848, Carl Friedrich Grafen von Vitzthum von Eckstädt, *Berlin und Wien in den Jahren 1845–1852*, p. 105.

[2] *Ibid.*, p. 106.

[3] *Wiener Zeitung,* No. 145 (May 25, 1848), p. 693.

omitted. No bond was to be required of any editor or publisher. Editors need not be Austrian citizens, and copies of everything printed no longer had to be submitted to the appropriate authorities. The law merely provided that each publication must have a responsible editor who was at least twenty-four years old and resided in Austria. Press transgressions were to be punished in accord with the general penal code, a provision much desired by the liberals. Treason was punishable by a maximum of ten years' imprisonment. Verbal attacks on the person of the sovereign that encouraged disrespect were to be punished by five years in prison. Authors of blasphemous writings or those slandering a recognized religious faith were to be imprisoned from one month to one year, while those who defamed persons or groups were to be arrested for three days to three months. Writers or publishers of tracts undermining public morality were to be imprisoned from fourteen days to six months. Anyone who deliberately spread false rumors disturbing to public security was subject to eight days' to six months' arrest. Editors were held responsible for everything printed in their papers. A special court was set up to try press cases. This court was to have its own judges and its own jury, the members of which were to be selected by the people.[4] Liberal though the law was, at the same time it protected the government against the worst abuses of the radical journalists.

To keep the democrats from pushing the revolution further to the left, the Ministry had only to dissolve the Academic Legion and revoke the concessions granted on May 15. The Vienna Citizens' Committee had already expressed an opinion that the legion should be abolished. Many of the more prosperous members of the National Guard had publicly asserted that it was impossible to restore peace and order or expect the Emperor to return to Vienna as long as the legion was in existence.[5] Many legionnaires themselves were weary of soldiering. Now that they were no longer in favor, a few of them stopped wearing their uniforms on the streets to avoid the risk of being insulted. A number of professors, students, and legionnaires advocated abolishing the legion and closing down the university.[6]

---

[4] "Provisional Order Concerning Press Abuses," Vienna, May 18, 1848, Univ. Colo. 1848 Coll., No. II/201; "Provisional Order Concerning Procedures in Press Matters," Vienna, May 18, 1848, Univ. Colo. 1848 Coll., No. II/203.

[5] Friedrich Kaiser, *Memoiren,* pp. 66–67; Paul Molisch, "Die Wiener akademische Legion," *Archiv für österreichische Geschichte,* Vol. CX, Part I (1924), p. 104.

[6] W. G. Dunder, *Denkschrift über die Wiener October-Revolution . . .,* pp. 4–5; Anton Füster, *Memoiren vom März 1848 bis Juli 1849,* Vol. I, pp. 127–29; Vitz-

The May 26 Revolution

Some of the professors, like Hye and Endlicher, assured Pillersdorf that the moderate teachers and students could persuade the academic youth to dissolve the legion, and they worked hard to win the majority of students over to the idea. On the evening of May 21 an assembly was called at the university to debate the question. The meeting was continued the next morning. Even such March leaders as Goldmark and Fischhof spoke repeatedly and heatedly in favor of disbanding, maintaining that the legion had fulfilled its purpose. The poet Adolph Purtscher and the chaplain of the legion, Füster, spoke against the proposal. After three hours of debate, the students overwhelmingly voted against abolishing the legion; however, they agreed to close the university, to cease all political activities, and to discontinue all legion functions until the beginning of the new term on October 1—provided the Ministry would give adequate assurances that the concessions made on May 15 would not be rescinded. When the various companies of the Academic Legion voted on the matter, the majority voted against disbanding but admitted that the legion was not a political body and that its members should refrain from political agitation.[7]

Thus the Ministry almost achieved its goal. But instead of accepting the promises of the students in good faith, the government decided to close the university anyway, and on the morning of May 24 a proclamation signed by the Minister of Education appeared on the streets announcing that all lectures at the university, the Polytechnical Institute, and the Art Academy were to cease as of that day. Those students who did not live in Vienna or who were going on vacation outside the city were to turn in their weapons before leaving. The public was to be excluded from the rooms of the university until the fall term began.[8] The students would probably have been willing for the university to close until October. They were perplexed and angry about the order to abandon their weapons before leaving town, but even so they would probably not have revolted if the Ministry and the Academic Legion commander had not taken other actions that goaded them into rebelling.

On the morning of May 25 Count Colloredo-Mannsfeld, the legion commander, posted an open letter on the street corners asking the

---

thum von Eckstädt to his mother, Vienna, May 23, 1848, Vitzthum von Eckstädt, op. cit., pp. 105–106; Constitution, No. 52 (May 24, 1848), p. 703.

[7] Füster, op. cit., Vol. I, pp. 129–33; Molisch, op. cit., p. 106; Heinrich Reschauer and Moritz Smets, Das Jahr 1848. Geschichte der Wiener Revolution, Vol. II, pp. 240–43.

[8] Minister of Education, "Proclamation," Vienna, May 24, 1848, Maximilian Bach, Geschichte der Wiener Revolution im Jahre 1848, p. 428.

members of the Academic Legion to tell him frankly whether or not they trusted him. He demanded an unqualified "yes" or "no" within twenty-four hours. He promised that if they indicated a lack of confidence in him, he would immediately resign as their commander. If they answered in the affirmative, he would entreat them to dissolve their organization without delay.[9]

The students read Colloredo's letter with astonishment and some anger at Colloredo's manner of requesting this vote of confidence. Some of the legionnaires scrawled, "Goodbye, Colloredo!" on the posters, and the Student Committee drafted an ironic answer to the Commander's letter and posted it on the same day.[10] The letter began with a reminder to Colloredo that "street corners are not a suitable place for a father to discuss and arrange family affairs with his sons." He was assured that the students had complete trust in his patriotism, courage, and intelligence, but he was reminded that the legionnaires were also patriotic and did not need the Commander's advice about matters concerning their honor. The students had already seriously examined the question of whether or not the legion should disband and had come to the conclusion that "now more than ever before it is our duty in common with the National Guard to exert all our strength to protect and foster the salvation of the whole Fatherland." They had been glad to have Colloredo as their leader, and would look with regret on his departure from their midst.[11]

The Student Committee also drafted a short proclamation to the inhabitants of Vienna assuring them that, despite rumors to the contrary, the Academic Legion would "under no circumstances disband" but would continue to work "to protect the constitutional gains and to preserve peace and order."[12]

On the morning of the 25th the ministers drew up final plans to rid themselves of the Academic Legion. Count Montecuccoli was charged with drafting a proclamation announcing the government's intentions, which was to be posted early the next morning. At the same time, orders were issued that both students and the general public were to be excluded from the university at six o'clock the next morning. Count Hoyos

---

[9] *Wiener Zeitung,* No. 147 (May 27, 1848), p. 693; "Colloredo-Mannsfeld to All Members of the Academic Legion," Vienna, May 25, 1848, *ibid.,* No. 146 (May 26, 1848), p. 690.

[10] Füster, *op. cit.,* Vol. I, p. 135; William H. Stiles, *Austria in 1848–49,* Vol. I, p. 134.

[11] "Student Committee to Commander of the Academic Legion, Count Colloredo," Vienna, May 25, 1848, *Wiener Zeitung,* No. 149 (May 29, 1848), p. 711.

[12] "Student Committee to the Inhabitants of Vienna," Vienna, May 25, 1848, *Wiener Zeitung,* No. 149 (May 29, 1848), p. 711.

and Count Colloredo were charged with seeing that the university was closed.[13]

When he heard about these plans, Colloredo called a meeting of the officers and representatives of the Academic Legion for the evening of the 25th in the Aula. There he personally appealed to them to dissolve their organization. His entreaties were rejected with a determined "We don't want to!"[14]

Following instructions, Count Montecuccoli drafted two proclamations. In one he exhorted the Viennese to remain at home after 9:00 P.M. on the 26th. "All fathers of families" were asked to enforce this command in their households.[15]

The second proclamation was lengthy. It began with a reminder to the Viennese of the Emperor's announcement that "an anarchical faction, supported by the Academic Legion," had forced him to flee from his capital, and that he would not return to Vienna until he was assured of the citizens' loyalty to him. Only a small faction in the legion was inciting the citizens to disobey the law and disturb the peace, continued the proclamation, but the rest of the monarchy was blaming the student body and the populace as a whole for the excesses. For these reasons, as of May 26 the Academic Legion was abolished as a separate unit of the National Guard. Those members who were obligated to serve in the National Guard were instructed to enroll in the guard within eight days in the district in which they lived. However, as long as they regularly attended classes, students need not join the guard. Those who decided not to enlist were to deliver their weapons to the civic arsenal within twenty-four hours. Finally, Montecuccoli announced that the buildings of the university, the Polytechnical Institute, and the Art Academy were to be closed until further notice.[16]

Thus on the night of May 25 the government issued its challenge to the students. Obviously the resistance of the legionnaires, their many sympathizers among the suburban guardsmen, and their well-wishers among the population could be expected. Yet the Ministry took few steps to bolster its authority. The National Guard was charged with

[13] Montecuccoli, "Memoir to the Constituent Parliament," late July, 1848, Reschauer and Smets, *op. cit.*, Vol. II, p. 306; [Ernst Violand], *Enthüllungen*, p. 29; "Colloredo-Mannsfeld to Academic Legion," n.d., Reschauer and Smets, *op. cit.*, Vol. II, p. 305.

[14] Kaiser, *op. cit.*, p. 67.

[15] Montecuccoli, "Request" [Vienna, May 25, 1848], Friedrich Unterreiter, *Die Revolution in Wien vom März und Mai 1848*, Vol. III, p. 97.

[16] "Montecuccoli to All Members of the Academic Legion," Vienna, May 25, 1848, Unterreiter, *op. cit.*, Vol. III, pp. 99–106.

enforcing the decree. On paper the guard now had a strength of 37,689, but of this number only 3,986 guardsmen—the only ones whose loyalty to the government was assured—belonged to guard units within the walls of the city. The police were disorganized, and there was no gendarmerie. There were 11,310 troops in the Vienna garrison, but according to the promise made by the Emperor on May 16 they could be called upon for assistance only if the National Guard requested them. Even if the military were called out, the government could be certain of having only 15,296 men to face 38,368 legionnaires and suburban guardsmen, not counting the citizens who might support the legion.[17]

Around four o'clock on the morning of May 26 the decree dissolving the Academic Legion was discovered by a few legionnaires on night duty. Immediately they took it to the university, where it was heatedly discussed by the handful of legion members who happened to be in the guardroom. Shortly after 5:00 A.M. Count Colloredo, accompanied by Professors Hye and Endlicher, appeared at the university, showed the decree to the commander of the guard, and ordered him to remove his men from the university and lock the doors. The students protested and seized their arms to defend themselves. Their officer declared that he could not carry out an oral order from Colloredo, especially since Colloredo was no longer commander of the legion. Colloredo then wrote out the order, and, with the support of Hye and Endlicher, commanded the guard detail to follow him out of the building. But the students continued to resist his orders, and Colloredo finally hastened to Montecuccoli to report.

About the same time the Commandant of the city, General Sardagna, also appeared at Montecuccoli's residence to complain about the students' defiance and to ask Montecuccoli to accompany him to the university to see whether the two of them could induce the youth to obey. By the time Sardagna and Montecuccoli arrived at the university a sizable crowd of students had assembled. At first they listened to Montecuccoli quietly, but the hall began filling with students, and soon they were interrupting him with cries of "We won't listen to you!" "We won't dissolve!" "The workers won't let you!" Montecuccoli again warned the students of the consequences of defiance. Finally someone proposed sending a deputation to Pillersdorf to protest the order. At this juncture Füster appeared in the hall and passionately warned the students that any dealings with the Ministry were useless. He insisted

[17] Molisch, *op. cit.*, p. 109.

that their only salvation lay in taking up arms immediately. Tremendous applause greeted his words.[18]

Then came news that a battalion of the Nugent Infantry Regiment was marching toward the university. The angry students began screaming, "We are betrayed! We are betrayed!" Hurriedly locking the doors of the university, legionnaires hastened to take up positions at the windows of the building. When the troops reached the square in front of the university, the major in command ordered the legionnaires to evacuate the university without delay. The sight of two students pointing guns at his head caused him to waver. General Sardagna tried to mediate between the two forces and promised that the military would not use their weapons unless the students attacked first. The students were not satisfied. Speaking in behalf of those in the university, Füster indignantly told Sardagna: "If you do not order the military to leave at once, you will have to answer for any misfortune that may befall us. The students will not leave. Any bloodshed will be on your head."[19] Sardagna straightway ordered the troops to leave.[20]

The news of the events at the university spread rapidly through the city. Füster had sent to the suburbs for help, and a large number of workers promptly armed themselves with such tools as were at hand and prepared to come to the defense of the students. At the report that troops had been called out, pandemonium broke loose. Most of the National Guardsmen, angered because the military had been called out without their requesting it, went over to the side of the students, while thousands of workers, armed with shovels and spades, streamed toward the gates to force their way into the inner city. Others hurried to the Polytechnical Institute to join the youth. Headed by the technical students, the workers marched into the capital. In a short while, ten thousand workers and suburban guardsmen had entered the inner city.[21]

Meanwhile, the students and their sympathizers within the city had been frantically building barricades to protect themselves against attack by the military. At the university, stools and benches were piled up to

---

[18] Füster, *op. cit.*, Vol. I, pp. 136–37; Montecuccoli, "Memoir to the Constituent Parliament," late July, 1848, Reschauer and Smets, *op. cit.*, Vol. II, pp. 306–307; Violand, *op. cit.*, p. 30; *Wiener Zeitung*, No. 147 (May 27, 1848), p. 693; Bach, *op. cit.*, pp. 435–37.

[19] Füster, *op. cit.*, Vol. I, pp. 137–38.

[20] *Wiener Zeitung*, No. 147 (May 27, 1848), p. 693; Kaiser, *op. cit.*, p. 72; Stiles, *op. cit.*, Vol. I, p. 135; Bach, *op. cit.*, p. 438.

[21] Füster, *op. cit.*, Vol. I, pp. 144–46; Kaiser, *op. cit.*, pp. 72–79; Molisch, *op. cit.*, pp. 112–13; August Silberstein, *Geschichte der Aula*, p. 64.

form protective walls. In the surrounding streets, elderly men and women and young children tore up paving stones and carried chests, barrels, and furniture out of the houses to erect barricades. By 10 A.M. a network of barriers had been raised at strategic points in the city.[22]

The very people who had renounced the Academic Legion the day before now sided with the legionnaires. Women made bullets and collected stones. Landlords and monks brought barrels of wine and beer and baskets of bread and other food to the "academicians"; elegant homes were turned over to the legionnaires for fortifications.[23]

By now the government was forced to realize that its ill-conceived plan had failed. Still, though many student deputations arrived at the Ministry to plead for the withdrawal of the order, it was not until noon that the Ministry informed a delegation headed by Goldmark and Füster that it would rescind the decree, and the official order was not posted until 1:00 P.M.[24] The students laughed at this gesture. The same Ministry that in the morning had boldly announced it would never rescind its orders was now doing so. What would prevent the government from countermanding the countermand after the barricades had been removed? Nothing was said about guaranteeing the promises made by the Ministry on May 15. Understandably, the students were beginning to doubt whether they could ever deal honestly with such a government.

The cabinet characteristically submitted to the demands of the revolutionists one by one. At 2:00 P.M. it made the following concessions:[25]

The promises of the Emperor on May 15 and 16 of this year will be fully carried out.

[22] Silberstein, *op. cit.*, p. 64; Kaiser, *op. cit.*, pp. 80–83; Füster, *op. cit.*, Vol. I, p. 144; Vitzthum von Eckstädt to his mother, Vienna, May 27, 1848, Vitzthum von Eckstädt, *op. cit.*, p. 109.

[23] Kaiser, *op. cit.*, p. 83; Silberstein, *op. cit.*, p. 65.

[24] Füster, *op. cit.*, Vol. I, pp. 147–48. The proclamation, dated May 26 and signed by Pillersdorf, Sommaruga, Krauss, Latour, and Baumgartner, read as follows: "In compliance with the urgent desires of the populace to avert greater dangers and in accord with the demands of the Academic Legion, the Ministerial Council has resolved not to insist on the execution of the order to dissolve the Legion and merge it with the National Guard. It expects that the Academic Legion will of its own accord offer the guarantees that will make security and the return of the Emperor possible." "Ministerial Resolution," Vienna, May 26, 1848, *Die freie Presse, ein Volksblatt,* No. 10 (May 31, 1848), p. 37, copy in the Univ. Colo. 1848 Coll., No. II/165d. *Die freie Presse* was a daily newspaper edited by J. Neidl. The first issue came out on May 20, the last on June 23, 1848.

[25] "Ministerial Proclamation," Vienna, May 26, 1848, *Die freie Presse,* No. 10 (May 31, 1848), p. 37.

The Academic Legion remains unchanged.

The military will immediately return to the barracks, and the guard duty at the gates will be performed in common by equal contingents of the National Guard, the Academic Legion, and the military.

Vienna, May 26, 1848.

Pillersdorff,   Sommaruga,   Krauss,   Latour,   Baumgartner.

Shortly afterward two other brief proclamations were issued. One announced that the military were being given "orders immediately to retire" to the barracks and that labor would "immediately be provided for the workmen."[26] The other confirmed the retirement of the troops to their quarters and stated that henceforth they would "be called out only at the request of the National Guard."[27]

By 4:00 P.M. troops were no longer to be seen on the streets. Nevertheless, no move was made to take down the barricades. The revolutionaries were much too suspicious of the government to lay down their arms. By now they were demanding much more than guarantees that the Academic Legion would not be abolished and that the promises made on May 15 and 16 would not be withdrawn. Their minimum demands were expressed in this placard which was posted about 6 P.M.:[28]

What We Demand

The military is to leave Vienna within 24 hours and the environs of the same in 4 hours. The Civic and National Guards and the Academic Legion are responsible for the peace. The Ministry guarantees fully the gains of May 15, 1848. Hostages from the nobility are answerable for this with their heads.

The Emperor is to be ordered to return to his residence within 13 days or to name a deputy who is to take up his residence in Vienna, the capital of the empire.

No barricades will be removed and no muskets will be given up before then.

One for hundreds of thousands.

In another poster displayed around the same time, the extremists also called for the following:[29]

[26] Pillersdorf, Baumgartner, and Krauss, "Proclamation," *Die freie Presse,* No. 10 (May 31, 1848), p. 37. Also in *Wiener Zeitung,* No. 147 (May 27, 1848), p. 693.

[27] Pillersdorf and Latour, "Proclamation," Vienna, May 26, 1848 [Franz Graf von Hartig], *Genesis der Revolution,* Appendix II, p. 393.

[28] Unterreiter, *op. cit.,* Vol. III, pp. 115–16.

[29] *Ibid.,* pp. 116–17.

What We Want

Since we have discerned that the reactionary party intends to curtail the victory of the sovereign people, we want:

1. The whole military to leave Vienna to garrison the Russian and Italian borders.

2. All the gains of May 15 to be preserved intact, and the constituent assembly to be convened in Vienna as soon as possible.

3. The officials to send representatives to the provinces to let our brothers there know that all we have done was only in the common interest of the whole monarchy.

4. The dissolution of the monasteries.

5. The introduction of an income tax and a tax for the poor.

6. The military to take an oath to the constitution.

7. The equality of all nationalities.

8. The closest possible union with Germany.

9. The earliest possible return of the Emperor and the preservation of the victories of May 15.

10. All those who through false representations induced the Emperor to go away to be tried by a people's court.

In the name of the people.

As time went on, still further demands were voiced. The revolutionaries insisted that the military deliver thirty-six cannon to the National Guard for their use in safeguarding the liberties of the people. They also wanted permission for the students and citizens to create an independent committee to govern Vienna and protect the rights of all the people of the monarchy.[30] Fervent appeals such as the following were made to the Viennese:[31]

Vienna, Evening of the 26th. Viennese! Do not give up the barricades. Do not remove a single stone from them. Do not lay down your muskets until all the demands made today, and for so long before today, are approved, and do not trust them [the government] until we have full guarantee that they will be fulfilled.

Everything those in high places have done since March has been a web of lies and betrayal! The veil has been torn away, and the abominations of the Camarilla stand unmasked before us! Woe to them! We stand firm and courageous unto death, and we want to see if a heart burning for freedom does not scorn death better than a hired mercenary! So come, Windischgrätz, with your regiments: We well know how to preserve the victories of May 15. Your bayonets—the wretched black-yellow reaction!—will be too

---

[30] Violand, *op. cit.*, pp. 31–32.
[31] *Constitution,* No. 55 (May 27, 1848), p. 727.

few for you. For us there are hundreds of thousands and the invincible power of true morality! We stand on the legal basis of the godlike freedom. You are rebels!

As long as a single soldier still stands in Vienna, as long as the Emperor or his deputy is absent, and as long as the 15th of May is not guaranteed in the fullest measure, we can still be betrayed every hour. After such deceptions there is no longer any trust! We no longer trust anyone but ourselves!

Workers, students, guardsmen, citizens, Hungarians, Tyrolese—yes, soldiers, girls, women—fight in our ranks! We will and must win! We will crown Vienna with the laurel garland of freedom. The provinces will bow before us in shame.

Long live—three times long live—freedom! And now, away to the barricades!

Fully aware of its helplessness against such determined opposition, the Ministry advised a deputation headed by the Vice-Mayor of Vienna that a committee composed of students and members of the Citizens' Committee and National Guard was urgently needed. This proposal was accepted enthusiastically by members of the Citizens' Committee who were present, and some of them left immediately to bring deputies from the National Guard and the students to a meeting at the city hall at seven o'clock the same evening.[32]

For the most part, the representatives at the meeting consisted of members of the former Central Committee.[33] The question of a name for the committee came up, and finally after a lengthy debate it was agreed that the new organization should bear the impressive title of Committee of Citizens, National Guardsmen, and Students of Vienna for the Preservation of the Rights of the People.[34] However, the Viennese were to refer to it as the Security Committee.

The discussion then turned to the problem of clearing Vienna of barricades. The group decided that the following demands would have to be granted by the Ministry before the revolutionaries laid down their arms: (1) in the future the city gates were to be guarded only by the National Guard, (2) all unnecessary military forces were to be removed from Vienna, (3) Count Hoyos was to be turned over to the students as a hostage to guarantee that the promises made on May 15 and 16 would be carried out, and (4) the Ministry was urgently to entreat the

---

[32] "Protocol of the First Sitting of the Security Committee," May 26, 1848, *Wiener Zeitung*, No. 162 (June 12, 1848), p. 767.

[33] Hartig, *op. cit.*, p. 302.

[34] "Protocol of the First Sitting of the Security Committee," May 26, 1848, *Wiener Zeitung*, No. 162 (June 12, 1848), p. 767.

Emperor to return to Vienna as soon as possible or, if his health did not permit it, to send a prince as his deputy. The committee also decided to appoint a committee of ten of its members to remain in permanent session in the city hall.[35]

The first action of the Security Committee was to arrest those considered responsible for the betrayal of the legion, especially Montecuccoli, Hoyos, Colloredo, Endlicher, Hye, and the Imperial Chamberlain, Count Dietrichstein. Hoyos, Hye, and Dietrichstein were seized at their homes and submitted quietly to imprisonment in the university. Colloredo seized his sword to defend himself and fled through a rear door of his residence. After warnings from Pillersdorf and Latour, Montecuccoli spent the night of the 26th in the Alser barracks and the next night fled to Gastein with his wife and family. Endlicher also managed to escape.[36]

During the night of the 26th, students, workers, and guardsmen continued to man the barricades. "Fires were made in the middle of the streets; students with their Calabrian hat and feathers, National Guardsmen with their helmeted caps, *ouvriers* without coats, and peasant women without bonnets, seated on paving stones around the bright blaze, indulged in coarse jokes and laughter, or in songs."[37] Food and drink were brought to the "heroes of the barracks" by real or pretended friends among the populace. The city was gradually settling down when around midnight the rumor that Windischgrätz was coming spread through the capital. There was a frenzied outburst of activity. Bells began ringing, gunfire burst out, and the workers tore down more pillars, iron railings, and paving stones to reinforce the barricades.[38] It was soon learned that the rumor was false, but the turbulence continued until the early morning hours.

The next day only guardsmen, students, and armed workers could be seen in the streets.[39] The newly created Security Committee convened in the morning to make plans for electing a new commander for the National Guard.[40] At ten o'clock the Ministry met to consider—and at length approve—all the demands made by the Security Committee on

[35] *Ibid.*

[36] Kaiser, *op. cit.,* pp. 84–85; Montecuccoli, "Memoir to the Constituent Parliament," late July, 1848, Reschauer and Smets, *op. cit.,* Vol. II, pp. 308–309; Stiles, *op. cit.,* Vol. I, pp. 141–42.

[37] Stiles, *op. cit.,* Vol. I, pp. 138–39.

[38] *Ibid.,* p. 139; report in the *Allgemeine oesterreichische Zeitung,* May 27, 1848, quoted in Bach, *op. cit.,* pp. 455–56.

[39] *Wiener Zeitung,* No. 148 (May 28, 1848), p. 708.

[40] "Protocol of the Second Sitting of the Security Committee," May 27, 1848, *ibid.,* No. 162 (June 12, 1848), pp. 767–68.

the previous evening. In the afternoon the new concessions were announced to the populace:[41]

The Ministerial Council recognizes the extraordinary conditions that have made it necessary for a Committee of Citizens, National Guardsmen, and Students to be formed to look after the order and security of the city and the rights of the people, and approves the resolutions made by this committee on the 26th of this month as follows:

1. The posts at the city gates are to be occupied only by the National and Civic Guards and the Academic Legion. The other posts are to be occupied by the National and Civic Guards and the Academic Legion, together with the military. The posts in the buildings of the war department are to be occupied by the military alone.

2. Only such military forces as are necessary for this service are to remain here. The remainder will leave as soon as possible.

3. Count Hoyos remains subject to legal proceedings, under the supervision of the Citizens' Committee as a pledge for what has been promised and as surety for the gains won on the 15th and 16th of May.

4. Those responsible for the events of May 26 will be brought to public trial.

5. The Ministry urgently requests His Majesty to return to Vienna as soon as possible or, in case he is prevented from doing so by illness, to appoint an imperial prince as his deputy.

At the same time the Ministry is asking the new committee to inform it about the kind of guarantees that can be given to ensure the personal safety of His Majesty and the imperial family.

Furthermore, it places all state property, as well as that of the imperial court, and all public establishments, collections, institutions, and public corporations in the capital under the protection of the people of Vienna and of the newly formed committee, and hereby declares the same independent of any other authority. The Ministry immediately transfers to this committee full responsibility for public peace and order, as well as for the protection of person and property.

The same Ministry finally announces that it can continue to discharge the business of the state that has temporarily been confided to it only until such time as His Majesty dismisses it or until the Ministry is deprived of the means to make its decisions with complete safety and to carry them out under its own responsibility.

Vienna, May 27, 1848.

In the name of the Ministerial Council,
Pillersdorf.

Although the Ministry thus conceded every request of the Security

[41] Pillersdorf, "Proclamation," Vienna, May 27, 1848, Univ. Colo. 1848 Coll., No. II/24.

Committee, still no move was made to tear down the barricades. However, a severe thunderstorm drove the fighters from the barricades and made it possible for pedestrians to pass freely through the streets. Then the Security Committee's promise of a full week's wages to all laborers, including those who had participated in the revolution, persuaded most of the workers to withdraw to the suburbs. The rest gradually began to clear away the barricades. The streets of the city began to resume their normal appearance, despite the qualms of some of the extremists, who still doubted the Ministry's sincerity.[42]

The extremists also lost their hostages—Hoyos, Dietrichstein, and Hye. During their brief imprisonment they were treated with every courtesy by the students. Count Dietrichstein was told almost immediately after his arrest that he would soon be freed, and he was, in fact, released on the evening of the 27th, with profuse apologies for any discomforts he had suffered.[43] After a short investigation proved conclusively that Hoyos had played a wholly passive role on May 26, he was also set at liberty, on May 30.[44] Professor Hye was turned over to judicial authorities and was tried by the criminal court on June 8. The court could find no evidence at hand to justify his arrest. The Security Committee also declared that the charges against him could not be substantiated and that his demeanor throughout the period of his investigation was above reproach.[45]

Thus the radicals lost their prey. However, they had won a resounding victory. The government had overplayed its hand and had been forced into another ignominious surrender. The students and their allies among the lower middle classes and the proletariat were the recognized leaders of Vienna.[46] Their Security Committee watched over every move of the authorities and superintended the police and the military. Radicalism was the order of the day. Though lip service was still paid to the constitutional monarchy, in actual fact anarchy and republicanism were not far distant. Without doubt the events of May 26 represented the extreme left point reached by the Austrian Revolution of 1848.

The radicals were exultant. The following months were given up to

[42] The reactions of the extreme left to the clearing of the barricades are given in the *Constitution*, No. 56 (May 29, 1848); p. 729.

[43] Füster, *op. cit.*, Vol. I, pp. 157–58.

[44] Security Committee, "Proclamation," May 30, 1848, Reschauer and Smets, *op. cit.*, Vol. II, p. 295.

[45] Security Committee, "Proclamation," Vienna, June 10, 1848, *Wiener Zeitung*, No. 163 (June 13, 1848), p. 771.

[46] Vitzthum von Eckstädt to his mother, Vienna, June 2, 1848, Vitzthum von Eckstädt, *op. cit.*, p. 114.

festivals, assemblies, and triumphal processions. Not an evening passed without at least one demonstration of revolutionary enthusiasm.[47] The Ministry was regarded as merely a necessary provisional apparatus to hold together the administration of the monarchy until Parliament could establish a government better suited to the needs of a constitutional state.[48] Until the middle of August it was completely subordinate to the Security Committee. For its part, the committee, of which Dr. Adolf Fischhof was made chairman on June 1 and Karl Freund and Friedrich Hornbostel his deputies, was the "revolutionary tribunal in whose hands the fate of Austria had been laid." It was the only organ in which the masses had any confidence.[49]

The Security Committee chose Lieutenant Field Marshal Zanini to succeed Hoyos as commander of the guard; when Zanini refused to accept the post, Colonel Pannasch was chosen. Pannasch obtained the permission of the Minister of War to accept the appointment and was confirmed in his position by the Ministry. The Security Committee reorganized the police, hoping to make it a more popular institution, and placed it under the committee's surveillance. The committee then established jury trial and provided for the election of the members of the Parliament. The committee also strove to counter the wild rumors that were constantly exciting the populace and to quell the resistance to all law and order that was developing among certain elements of the population.[50]

One of the main objectives of the committee was to provide work for the unemployed. To this end it appointed a Labor Committee of sixteen members chosen from the Security Committee and the Citizens' Committee. The Labor Committee was charged with securing food and work for the idle, largely by organizing public works projects but also by taking steps to prevent non-Viennese workers from coming to the capital.[51]

[47] *Vorwärts! Politisches Volksblatt*, No. 3 (June 3, 1848), pp. 10–11, contains an interesting description of one of these fraternal festivals. Univ. Colo. 1848 Coll., No. II/212. *Vorwärts* was edited by Philip Stern. Twenty-one issues appeared, the first on June 1, the last on June 23, 1848.

[48] *Wiener Zeitung*, No. 153 (June 2, 1848), p. 727.

[49] Ernst Victor Zenker, *Die Wiener Revolution*, p. 140. See also Violand, *op. cit.*, p. 33.

[50] Kaiser, *op. cit.*, pp. 91–95; "Protocol of the Second Sitting of the Security Committee," May 27, 1848, *Wiener Zeitung*, No. 162 (June 12, 1848), p. 767; *Wiener Zeitung*, No. 153 (June 2, 1848), p. 727; Ernst Violand, *Die sociale Geschichte der Revolution in Oesterreich*, p. 120; Reschauer and Smets, *op. cit.*, Vol. II, pp. 355–56.

[51] *Wiener Zeitung*, No. 154 (June 3, 1848), p. 732; Violand, *Die sociale Geschichte der Revolution in Oesterreich*, p. 122; Zenker, *op. cit.*, p. 144.

The Labor Committee went to work with enthusiasm. It exhorted workers to respect the property rights of others,[52] put pressure on employers to hire as many workers as possible, and urged the government to expand the projects that had been inaugurated in March in the Prater and along the Danube and the Wien. These projects were enlarged and were vaguely similar to the National Workshops then in operation in France. Men employed on them were paid 25 kreutzer (20 cents) per day, and women and children over twelve were paid 18 kreutzer (14½ cents).[53] Children under twelve years of age could not work.

Unfortunately, the evils that had beset the program at the outset now multiplied. Much of the work, the cost of which was borne by the city, was useless. More and more workers were occupied with the pointless earthworks project in the Prater. They were poorly supervised and managed, and most of the workers were quick to learn that they could earn a day's wages by doing little more than reporting for work. Just as in Paris and in Berlin, where similar projects had been inaugurated, the "right to work" program was degenerating into "the right to laziness."[54]

Naturally the news that people were being paid for doing little or no work spread rapidly, and, as in Paris, a horde of vagabonds and idlers streamed into Vienna. The workers in the factories, many of whom were paid little if any more than the "Prater idlers," were naturally envious, and many of them left their jobs to work on the government projects, which by the end of May were employing over twenty thousand workers.[55]

Clearly something had to be done to prevent a mass exodus from the factories and workshops. Many factory-owners and master-craftsmen were overwhelming the Security Committee with complaints that their workmen were leaving them, and many small businessmen, who had formerly been among the staunchest defenders of democracy, were finding their businesses still further depressed by the May revolutions and began to turn against the radicals. To counteract the flow of work-

---

[52] "Proclamation of the Security Committee to the Workers," Vienna, May 31, 1848, *Wiener Zeitung,* No. 153 (June 2, 1848), p. 727.

[53] Violand, *Die sociale Geschichte der Revolution in Oesterreich,* p. 123; Zenker, *op. cit.,* p. 145.

[54] Violand, *Die sociale Geschichte der Revolution in Oesterreich,* pp. 125–26; Josephine Goldmark, *Pilgrims of '48,* pp. 62–63; Zenker, *op. cit.,* p. 145.

[55] Violand, *Die sociale Geschichte der Revolution in Oesterreich,* pp. 125–26; Zenker, *op. cit.,* pp. 145–46; Priscilla Robertson, *Revolutions of 1848: A Social History,* p. 229.

ers to the Prater, the Security Committee passed a resolution providing that anyone who was not an earthworker by trade would be hired on the public works projects only if he had a written certificate from his last employer stating that he was no longer able to give him work. On June 12, in order to check the influx of workers from the provinces, whose wages were weighing heavily on the city budget, the committee passed a resolution that workers from outside Vienna were no longer to be employed on the government projects.[56]

These measures irritated the idlers and made them ready prey to agitators. When on June 15 the Security Committee refused their pleas for better working conditions, the workers rioted at the Prater and in front of the building where the committee held its meetings. A workers' delegation went to the committee to insist that the wages on the public works projects be increased by 12 kreutzer and that, in addition, all workers be paid their regular wages on Sundays, holidays, and on rainy days when they could not work. They threatened to join the counter-revolution if their demands were not immediately granted. The committee chairman, Dr. Fischhof, who as an assistant doctor at the Vienna General Hospital received only 15 kreutzer more (a total wage of 40 kreutzer, or 32 cents a day) than the wage paid to the men employed at the Prater, tried to convince the deputation how impossible it was to fulfill such demands and berated them for threatening to join the reaction. The leader of the deputation replied in such insulting fashion that Fischhof ordered his arrest and had the other deputies ejected from the room. Also, he commanded the National Guard to clear the streets of all demonstrators.

Committee members and students went to the work sites to warn the people against listening to the agitators, but their efforts were in vain and the proletariat held stubbornly to their demands. The next day the committee began to compromise, decreeing that, although the workers were not to be paid when they were not actually at work, in any rainy period bread would be sold to them for 6 kreutzer on the first day and for 3 kreutzer on subsequent nonworking days. Then the National Guard was told to be ready to put down workers' disturbances, and the students returned to the workers to plead with them to be content with these concessions.

On the 17th the workers again came to the city to protest, but the National Guardsmen succeeded in breaking up the demonstrations.

[56] Security Committee, "Proclamation," Vienna, June 3, 1848, *Wiener Zeitung,* No. 156 (June 5, 1848), p. 739; *ibid.,* No. 155 (June 4, 1848), p. 726; Reschauer and Smets, *op. cit.,* Vol. II, p. 359.

Finding themselves deserted by the students and opposed by the guard, the people quietly returned to work. Some of the agitators who had stirred the workers to revolt were arrested; others fled. The public works supervisors received strict orders to bar all but workers from the projects. With this, peace was restored.[57] The Viennese revolution had reached its peak in the form of a political, democratic revolution.

[57] Füster, *op. cit.*, Vol. I, pp. 224–35; Rudolph Kiszling *et al.*, *Die Revolution im Kaisertum Österreich 1848–1849*, Vol. I, pp. 147–48; Reschauer and Smets, *op. cit.*, Vol. II, pp. 406–11.

X. *The High Tide of the Revolution*

N VIENNA radical journalism reached its height in vituperation during the period of the May 26 uprising. During this
time the editors and writers on the few moderate newspapers
had a rather precarious living and suffered unceasing attacks
from the radicals. Baron Karl von Hock, who had resigned as editor of the moderate *Constitutionelle Donau Zeitung*[1] a few days before May 26, quietly departed from the capital. Bäuerle, the editor of
the *Wiener allgemeine Theaterzeitung*,[2] left Vienna with his family for
a short visit to the country after his home was broken into by armed
demonstrators. Stubenrauch and Heyssler,[3] coeditors of the *Wiener
Zeitung*, were expelled from the Academic Legion.[4] On May 29 they
omitted the imperial eagle and the words *Oesterreichisch-kaiserlich-
privilegirte* from the title[5] in an attempt to remove the stigma of being
a privileged progovernment sheet.[6]

In the weeks following the May revolutions the only papers in Vienna
that were openly and unreservedly proconservative were John B. Weis's
Der constitutionelle Hansjörgel;[7] Sebastian Brunner's *Wiener Kirchenzeitung*,[8] which devoted its pages mainly to defending the church; and

[1] Published from April 1 to July 6, 1848.

[2] Established in 1820 and the most widely circulated paper in the monarchy
before 1848.

[3] Moriz Heyssler had been editor of the *Wiener Zeitung* since December, 1847.
Stubenrauch joined him as coeditor on March 19, 1848.

[4] Joseph Alexander Freiherrn von Helfert, *Die Wiener Journalistik im Jahre
1848,* p. 70.

[5] See No. 149 (May 29, 1848), p. 711.

[6] No. 150 (May 30, 1848), p. 715.

[7] This weekly came out under the name *Hans-Jörgel. Volksschrift im Wiener
Dialekte,* from March 27 to April 15, 1848. On April 15 its name was changed
to *Der constitutionelle Hansjörgel.* It suspended publication from October 5 to
November 12 and then ceased on December 28, 1848.

[8] *Wiener Kirchenzeitung für Glauben, Wissen, Freiheit und Gesetz in der
katholische Kirche.* The paper, which was founded on April 15, 1848, to defend
Catholic interests, came out three times a week. It ceased publication on December 30, 1848.

Joseph Ebersberg's *Wiener Zuschauer*,[9] which dared to publish articles submitted by such staunch conservatives as Mathias Koch, Georg Emanuel Haas, and Quirin Endlich criticizing the excesses of the radical journalists.

During this period a host of "democratic" papers were founded to join the *Constitution* and the *Freimüthige* in abusing so-called "reactionaries." Outstanding among these new papers was the *Wiener Katzenmusik*, or *Charivari*, edited by Sigmund Engländer,[10] the first issue of which appeared on June 9. The paper devoted itself to poking fun at the aristocrats, the Camarilla (the Emperor's supposed secret advisers), "Philistines," and Innsbruck society.[11]

Even more radical in content was A. J. Becker's *Radikale*,[12] which first appeared a week after the *Wiener Katzenmusik*. From the beginning it was the "real herald of the reddest democracy."[13] Articles were printed in it so savagely critical of the government that they were refused by other papers. Becker published wild charges about intrigues of the court party and agitated unceasingly to move the revolution further to the left.

Another paper that vied with the *Constitution* in irresponsibility and radicalism was the *Politischer Studenten-Courier*,[14] edited by Adolf Buchheim and Oskar Falke, which first appeared on June 24. It became the important organ for the most radical of the students and also exerted considerable influence on other extremists in Vienna.[15]

Vying with the *Wiener Katzenmusik*, the *Radikale*, and the *Po-*

[9] Originally a youth magazine, founded by Ebersberg and first called *Die Feierstunden* and then, after 1831, the *Oesterreichischer Zuschauer*. On January 19, 1848, Ebersberg changed the name to *Wiener Zuschauer. Zeitschrift für Gebildete* and turned the paper into a political journal devoted to championing conservative interests. It was published four times a week.

[10] *Wiener Katzenmusik. Politisch-literarisches Tagblatt für Spott und Ernst mit Karrikaturen.* At first the paper was published four times a week. Later the name was changed to *Wiener Charivari* and it was issued six times a week. The last number came out on October 27, 1848. Although during the first half of April Engländer was an editor of the *Constitutionelle Donau Zeitung*, he was one of the most radical of the revolutionary journalists. In *Wiener Katzenmusik* he heaped abuse upon everyone whom he judged a "reactionary," and he wrote articles for the *Radikale* preaching against the conservatives. After the capitulation of Vienna, he managed to escape to Leipzig.

[11] E[rnst] V[ictor] Zenker, *Wiener Journalistik 1848,* pp. 93–94; Helfert, *op. cit.,* pp. 80–81.

[12] *Der Radikale. Abendzeitung für das In- und Ausland,* a daily, published from June 16 to October 26, 1848.

[13] Zenker, *op. cit.,* p. 88.

[14] *Politischer Studenten-Courier* was a daily newspaper. On August 22 its name was changed to *Politischer Courier.* The last issue appeared on October 26, 1848.

[15] Helfert, *op. cit.,* pp. 81–84; Zenker, *op. cit.,* pp. 87–90.

The High Tide of the Revolution

litischer Studenten-Courier in unwarranted demagoguery and sometimes in obscenity were a number of other sheets, some of which lasted
only a short while. An example was the *Wiener Tageblatt für alle
Stände*,[16] edited by Adolph Ungár, which first appeared on June 5.
Others were the *Wiener Gassenzeitung*,[17] A. H. Ehrlich's *Bst! Bst!
Warum? Volksfragen*,[18] J. Neidl's *Die freie Presse*,[19] and F. B. Friedmann's *Gerad'aus*.[20] In the new papers, in the established journals, and
in countless placards and pamphlets, bitter accusations were levied on
the enemies of the democrats. The scathing attacks on the ministers
continued unabated.[21]

The Emperor was now referred to in a new tone. Instead of sub-
missively and humbly entreating Ferdinand to return to his loyal subjects, the radical newspapers began to imperiously "demand" his return.[22] There were predictions that the Emperor's continued absence
from Vienna would mean the destruction of the empire and that, if the
Emperor did not at once "break the fetters of the Camarilla," the Habsburg dynasty would fall.[23] There were hints that by remaining in Inns-

[16] A daily, of which only thirty issues appeared, the last dated July 12–13, 1848.
[17] *Wiener Gassenzeitung. Zur Belehrung des Volkes geschrieben von Terzky.*
The first issue of this daily scandal sheet appeared on June 3; the last, on October
26, 1848.
[18] This paper appeared four or five times a week and was edited by A. H.
Ehrlich. The first issue came out on June 14; the last, on August 5, 1848.
[19] *Die freie Presse. Ein Volksblatt* was a daily paper published from May 20 to
June 23, 1848. Julius Neidl also brought out two other papers during the course
of the revolution. On July 25 his *Reichstags-Kourier* was published for the first
and only time. From August 30 to October 25 he was owner and publisher of the
Neue politische Strassenzeitung.
[20] *Gerad'aus! Politisches Abendblatt für's Volk* was a small daily paper edited
by Fritz Bernhard Friedmann and distributed in Vienna from May 10 to October
26, 1848.
[21] A. Niederhuber, "Das Ministerium muss in Anklagestand versetzt werden,"
Constitution, No. 56 (May 29, 1848), pp. 729–30; Wilhelm Schlesinger, "Um's
Himmelswillen gebt uns Vertrauen, um's Himmelswillen seid liberal!" *Wiener
Zeitung*, No. 151 (May 31, 1848), p. 719.
[22] Note, for instance, the following article: "We still lack any official news
about the return of the Monarch. The danger for the state is becoming greater,
the unity of the monarchy is threatened, and the condition of all citizens is becoming more and more oppressive. On account of this situation, we therefore demand
that the Ministry issue an order to His Majesty either to return to Vienna within
ten days or appoint a regent until he does, or else make up his mind that the
Imperial Assembly will take the necessary steps to prevent the fall of the monarchy. The law and the welfare and preservation of the monarchy stand higher
than the Emperor." *Der Unpartheyische. Politischer Zeitblatt*, No. 7 (June 7,
1848), p. 28, Univ. Colo. 1848 Coll., No. II/195. The *Unpartheyische*, edited by
Mathias Emanuel Löbenstein, was first issued on June 1. On July 5 the name was
changed to *Wiener allgemeine Zeitung*. The last number came out on August 12.
[23] *Der Unpartheyische*, No. 7 (June 7, 1848), pp. 25–26; *Oesterreichisches*

bruck the Emperor was breaking that "personal relationship between the people and the chief of state" so essential in a monarchy.[24] The editor of the *Volksfreund* summoned the courage to publish a parody of the Lord's Prayer:[25]

Our Father, who art in Innsbruck, respected be thy name. Yet may our will be done, for we constitute the sovereign people. Give us this day our daily bread, freedom, and equality. Forgive all politically condemned their so-called "debts," but do not consider it evil if we do not forgive our debtors, Monticucoli [*sic*], Breuner,[26] etc. Lead us not into temptation and Russia's arms, but deliver us from the evil of reaction! Amen.

One of the radicals described the Emperor as "a Tiberius who with a friendly countenance gave his people freedom" when he was afraid to do otherwise, but then cunningly lay in wait like a fox for the moment when he could flee from Vienna, take away the concessions, and put his subjects in bondage again. Some again compared the flight to Innsbruck with Louis XVI's flight to Varennes[27] and predicted that, as in France, it could end only in the fall of the monarchy.

Although the democrats became remarkably daring in their references to the Emperor, they saved their more savage attacks for the real villains, the Camarilla, who had supposedly led the simple-minded Emperor astray. In a vein unlike the reputedly delicate wit of the Austrians was this satirical assault:[28]

Look Out!
Buy this Leaflet quickly before it is confiscated! ! !
Necrology for the Camarilla
[Picture of a tombstone]

Mephisto Bombellerl[29] and *Xantippe Cibirinni*,[30] in behalf of them-

---

Volksblatt, No. 9 (June 24, 1848), p. 36, Univ. Colo. 1848 Coll., No. II/155. The *Oesterreichisches Volksblatt*, a daily, was edited by Andreas Schumacher. Only nineteen issues appeared, the first on June 14 and the last on July 5. The motto of the paper was: "People will remain different in property, talent, and speech, but they must all become equal before the law and in their duty to work."

[24] "Rückkehr des Kaisers," *Die freie Presse*, No. 17 (June 7, 1848), pp. 65–66, Univ. Colo. 1848 Coll., No. II/165e.

[25] *Der Volksfreund*, No. 7 (June 7, 1848), p. 25, Univ. Colo. 1848 Coll., No. II/195.

[26] Montecuccoli and Breuner were blamed by the Viennese radicals for persuading the Emperor to flee from Vienna on May 17.

[27] Adolf Pichler, *Das Sturmjahr*, p. 167.

[28] Copy in the Univ. Colo. 1848 Coll., No. II/9.

[29] Count Heinrich Bombelles, who had supervised the plans for the Emperor's flight.

[30] Catharine Cibbini, the Empress's harp-player and later the Emperor's nurse,

selves and their beloved *brothers* and *sisters,* hereby announce the death of their *dearly beloved and well-reared adopted child,*

CAMARILLA,

which is most *tragic* for them but most *gratifying* to all other people and greeted with universal jubilation. Camarilla was the Ministerial Adviser of the *Secret* Conference, Head Protectress and Proprietress of Spy Infantry Regiment *Liguorian* No. 000, Ruler of the Empire for the Dulling of Human Understanding and the Elevation of the Aristocracy, Director and Protectress of the Bureaucratic Club, Mistress of the Domains of *Innsbruck, Ischl, Mudbath,* and *Error-Land,* Member of the Legal Faculty of Hell, Patroness of all *Czech* and *Hungarian-Croatian City* and *Country Military Affairs,* Founder and Active Member of Everything *Beautiful* for the Spread of *Natural* Products, of the Garden Society for the Propagation of *Exotic* Plants, and of the Pomological Society for the Growth of *Aristocratic Fruits,* Committee Member and Patroness of the Society of the Friends of Mock Serenades, Emissary of the Jesuit Creed and of the Women's Star and Cross Order of *Penitents,* Founder and Helper's Assistant of the *Historical Departure* and of the *Building of the Barricades,* Authoress of the Dictionary for Speaking and Writing Lies and Deception, Disperser of the *Aqua Fortis* of Peace, Member of the Committee for the *Unscrupulous* Fostering of Effrontery and Hypocritical Literature, etc.

The same died on August 8, 1848, as a result of a *reactionary relapse without atonement.*

With *silent contempt* the remains will be taken, on Saturday afternoon, August 12, at 2:00 P.M.,[31] from *Innsbruck* in the D——'s name to Hell and from there to her father Metternich's family vault in London.

The customary church services will be held by the Reverend Brunner'-schen, Veit,[32] and their associates in all enlightened Jesuit gatherings. Since the joyful expressions of condolence are *legion,* prayers will be said.

Can be procured in the Editorial Bureau of the *Omnibus,* in the City, Liliengasse No. 898.

The revolutionaries customarily used more direct language in dealing with the Camarilla, whose most nefarious members, according to the radicals, were the Jesuits. The placard entitled "Innsbruck, Ischl, the Camarilla, and the Aristocrats" was typical:[33]

---

who was suspected of having a sinister influence over him. See especially *Ursache und Geschichte der Octoberereignisse zu Wien,* by an eyewitness, pp. 28–29.

[31] On August 8 the Emperor finally decided to leave Innsbruck to return to Vienna. He arrived there on the afternoon of August 12.

[32] The two conservative clergymen, Sebastian Brunner and J. Emanuel Veit, whose pro-Catholic and antiliberal writings made them hated by the radicals.

[33] L. S., "Innsbruck, Ischl, Camarilla und Aristokraten," Friedrich Unterreiter, *Die Revolution in Wien vom Juni bis September 1848. Mit allen ihren Ursachen*

Whoever saw Ischl last year and visits it again today will hardly believe that it is the noisy, jovial Ischl that was the meeting place of the elegant and educated world. There is no life in the streets. There is no motley crowd. Everything is dead. The pedestrians are quietly whispering to each other. People are slinking about like ghosts. Yet this spa still has high and mighty guests. However, these guests are not here for the baths (they can wash themselves clean only with difficulty) but because they cannot endure the air of Vienna.

Here the aristocrats are sitting together at the home of one of Metternich's relatives and are advising each other, studying, and thinking about how they can take revenge on Vienna. Part of this highborn society is not far away in Innsbruck. Here also they do not have charitable opinions about the Viennese. Here they call students and National Guardsmen robbers and murderers and the workers beggars and bandits who should all be hanged, burned, and impaled.

The Jesuits—this race of marten, these loathsome worms—are crawling around everywhere and are seeking to increase the hatred wherever possible. They are always at hand whenever something infamous is to be carried out. These villainous souls are spreading the most diabolical rumors about the Viennese, and in their minds they are already seeing themselves entering our city victoriously, triumphantly, and disgracefully.

And what about our good Emperor? Our good Emperor is sitting in the midst of all this, surrounded by false advisers, rascally court pastors, and vile priests! His good, noble heart, which is certainly still full of love for his subjects, has been surrounded by an iron curtain. Hypocritical priests are singing a siren song near him so that he does not hear the just, sincere entreaties of his people. They are keeping him a prisoner. These despicable persons are filling him with hatred for his loyal subjects and are describing his capital as a den of assassins.

The plan of all these abject people is to keep the Emperor in their claws and away from his loyal people as long as possible. Through this they want to make the Viennese discontented. They hope that if all their entreaties for the return of the Emperor are fruitless the Viennese will undertake something that would be a crime against our Emperor. They want to turn the love and loyalty of the people into hatred and perfidy. They want to turn the malevolent and slanderous rumors they are telling the Emperor about us into a reality. Then, if their plans are successful, they want to attack us, destroy us through force of arms, rob us all of the rights and liberties which have been given to us, and lead us back to the old servitude and slavery. But these gentlemen made an error. We are and will remain loyal subjects of our Emperor.

---

und Wirkungen fortlaufend bis auf die nächsten Tage, auf das freisinnigste nach eigener Anchauung und den besten Quellen dargestellt (hereafter cited throughout as *Die Revolution in Wien vom Juni bis September 1848*), Vol. I, pp. 19–22.

The time will come when these scoundrels, these false advisers, will be destroyed. Ferdinand will find out who is surrounding him. He will return. He will realize that his people did not deserve having to dispense with the presence of the Emperor for such a long time.

However, with grief and sadness we note that the plan of the Camarilla to estrange the Viennese from their Emperor will not be at all difficult to carry out. During recent days we have seen how much has been written and spoken that must certainly be looked upon as injurious to the holy person of the Emperor, and we have seen with what little respect people have spoken about the person of the Emperor! How damaging many expressions sound! Citizens of Vienna, do not let yourselves be led astray through mutinous writings and speeches. The person of the Emperor is holy and inviolable to you. Watch over the press and punish those who dare to write or speak of His Majesty without the proper respect.

L. S.

Denunciations of the aristocrats and the clergy were even more violent than those following the March revolution. The nobility and clergy were looked upon (and rightly) as the leaders of the counter-revolution—and also of the Camarilla. Their domination had to be destroyed if the revolution was to be successful. As early as May 15, students and journalists were in full cry after the aristocrats, and by May 26 feeling in Vienna was high against them.[34] The few timid voices lifted in their defense[35] were drowned out by castigations of the "parasites" who lived off the "bloody sweat of the peasants."[36]

The whole institution of nobility was assailed as undemocratic and irreconcilable with every idea of freedom.[37] Although for some unexplained reason the radicals admitted that the "nobility—that toy of big children—might well be conceivable in a republican" state, it could never be tolerated "by a democratic constitution" because "the equality

[34] Vitzthum von Eckstädt to his mother, Vienna, May 15, 1848, Carl Friedrich Grafen von Vitzthum von Eckstädt, *Berlin und Wien in den Jahren 1845–1852,* p. 101; Hans Kudlich, *Rückblicke und Erinnerungen,* Vol. I, p. 273.

[35] See especially the placard by Johann Irsa, Univ. Colo. 1848 Coll., No. II/105; and the two-page brochure headed "Audiatur et altera pars!" and signed "Ein Aristokrat für Hunderte," *ibid.,* No. II/7. In the copy in the University of Colorado collection, the "rte" was scratched from the last word in the second brochure, making it read, "Ein Aristokrat für Hunde" ("An Aristocrat for Dogs," rather than "An Aristocrat in the Name of Hundreds").

[36] Bonifacius Mild, Duke of Angoulême, *Episteln an die Aristokratie, zu ihrem Troste und zu ihrer Erbauung,* p. iv. See also "Dem Adel betreffend." *Constitution,* No. 42 (May 10, 1848), pp. 627–28; *Die Constitution und der Adel,* pp. 17–18; *Die freie Presse,* No. 10 (May 31, 1848), pp. 38–39, Univ. Colo. 1848 Coll., No. II/165d.

[37] "Dem Adel betreffend," p. 628.

of all men" was the foundation of democracy. "The privileges of the nobility must perish before the rights of the people and the just claims of the whole nation."[38] The prerogatives of the aristocrats should be abolished so that in the future they would have no more prestige than that described in the following anonymous brochure:[39]

The Last of the Aristocrats

Motto: Now the sun in its course does rest,
Sets in the East and rises in the West!

It was the year of our Lord, 1948, on the 26th of May. An old man, supporting his weary head with his wrinkled hand, sat on the ruins of the famous imperial barricade. His threadbare clothing showed traces of filth and blood, and his torn shoes matched his hat, full of holes.

If someone had made a sketch of him, it would not have been necessary to explain the drawing by putting under it the title "proletarian."

He really was a proletarian—a proletarian of the new era, when the lack of earthly possessions no longer stamped a man as a proletarian, for this class counted among its members people who were looked upon by the good citizens as a group fallen into the ranks of the proletarians in spite of their extensive property or movable capital, partly because they were intellectuals incapable of fostering the interests of their fellow-citizens, and partly because of their evil intention to curtail or destroy the rights of the people.

Everyone refused to give such a proletarian a single article of clothing or to perform even the slightest service for him, even though very large sums were offered for them. Since this class was always work-shy, never learned a citizen's trade, and was never accustomed to or fit for any necessary work, it often happened that the clothing of the wealthiest princes could scarcely be differentiated from that of other beggars, and they actually wandered as beggars through the land, offering ten times its worth in gold for a piece of bread.

However, the gold was scorned, and the travels which they engaged in to earn a livelihood were only successful when they met English peasants, who in the last fifty years had settled in great numbers in Austria.

Even the Jews took no gold from these people, not even on days other than the Sabbath. At that time there were few Jews in Austria, because a pestilence called surplus of money was raging, and many of them died from it. Indeed, many left all their money in Austria and emigrated to seek a country where they could again acquire money by bartering and where

[38] "Wir brauchen keinen Adel mehr," *Der Volksfreund,* No. 70 (July 21, 1848), p. 282, Univ. Colo. 1848 Coll., No. II/210d.
[39] *Der letzte der Aristokraten,* Univ. Colo. 1848 Coll., No. II/6. Immediately under the title is the picture of a sad-looking aristocrat sitting on the ruins of a city; St. Stephen's tower is visible in the background.

The High Tide of the Revolution

money did not snow by the bushels down the chimneys upon them on every holiday, as was the case in Austria.

It is no wonder that under such circumstances the aristocracy soon disappeared in Austria. The nobles who were assimilated with the people were highly respected when they were not harping on their noble prerogatives and when they really protected the concerns of the people in the interest of good citizenship. Thus it came about that there was no more scandalous word than to call a noble an aristocrat.

For the past fifty years those people who were elected to Parliament three times in succession and received a certificate of citizenship at their fourth election have constituted the nobility.

Nobility was hereditary in so far as the sons of those who were already nobles could claim this certificate upon their second election as deputies.

The sun was already sinking, and he still sat motionless. He did not notice that he sat alone in the midst of destruction. There was not another living soul in the city, for the Hungarians, Bohemians, Italians, and others had gone with their families to their homelands. The Austrians had gone to Frankfurt with their adored regent, John IV,[40] and, indeed, in such haste that they left many valuables in the unfortunate city.

"I am now the sole ruler in this city. All these buildings belong to me. But of what use is my power? Of what use are all these treasures that are heaped up here in the city? All of my species have fled, and daily I saw thousands of brothers dying from wretchedness and worry, because they were despised by democracy—this archenemy of the nobility.

"My only living companions are now the black-yellow salamanders. Even the rats, who were my friends, are gone because on their own accord they left a deserted city.

"I feel that I am near my end. Who will perform the last rites for me? Or am I condemned to rot away on the barricade?

"But I will not lose courage: O setting sun, you will never again shed your mild rays upon the last aristocrat! Heed my farewell message, for you were kinder to our species than the people were. You have cast equal light and warmth upon each party. Yet we—and a dying man speaks the truth— we have jealously tried to withhold your might and warmth from those brave, loyal people whom we have led for many hundred years and who paid us taxes from their hard-earned money.

"The people have avenged themselves. Our fall was just. I feel it. My head is falling—!" And thus ended the last aristocrat!

Responsible editor: the *Studentenzeitung*.

[40] On June 29, 1848, the Frankfurt Assembly elected Archduke John to the position of imperial regent of Germany. Archduke John was extremely popular with the Viennese liberals.

The denunciations of the clergy were equally virulent. Although the radicals often tried to differentiate between the genuine men of God, to whom "respect and honor are due," and the clericals, whose chief aim was "to deprive the people of their money and soul,"[41] this distinction was usually lost. The clergy were attacked for not joining the National Guard, for not repudiating the practice of celibacy, and for not permitting the members of monastic orders to return to useful civilian life.[42] They were taken to task for using the pulpit to preach against the rights of the people, for failing to give up sinecures and pensions from the state, and for refusing to abolish monasteries and other benefices. They were chided for neglecting the teaching of the youth and for failing to comfort the despairing people.[43]

As in April, the main charge leveled against the clergy was the one expressed in the following article—that they refused to turn over church treasures to the state:[44]

Proclamation to All the Catholic Clergy in the Austrian Empire

"Do works of mercy and fulfill
the noble dictum of your divine
Lord and Master."

The financial resources of the state are almost exhausted. "Money and work" are the fearful watchwords of the working class, most of whom are unemployed in these stormy times.

Because of the complete standstill in commercial activities and trade, the Fatherland is in a most dangerous situation. Because of its crippled financial status and the loss of credit resulting from it, the state is in a crisis. Unemployment is increasing daily, and distress and misery have reached a climax. All this is the result of an accursed political system that has lasted for thirty-three years and has destroyed everything.

But how can this evil, which, like a cancer, consumes the very marrow of our once flourishing Austria, be remedied?

By offering sacrifices on the altar of the Fatherland. The well to do, the middle classes, and even the poorest class are all willingly making sacri-

---

[41] See especially "Der geopferte Altar," *Wahrheit*, No. 5 (June 8, 1848), pp. 18–19, Univ. Colo. 1848 Coll., No. II/217a. The *Wahrheit* was edited by K. Rosental. Only thirty issues appeared, the first on June 3, the last on July 13, 1848.

[42] Hirovssky, "Notizen. Frage an die Geistlichkeit," *Constitution*, No. 63 (June 7, 1848), p. 787; *Oesterreichisches Volksblatt*, No. 9 (June 24, 1848), p. 35, Univ. Colo. 1848 Coll., No. II/155.

[43] *Constitution*, No. 38 (May 5, 1848), p. 597; *ibid.*, No. 60 (June 3, 1848), p. 764.

[44] Joh. Nep. Brenner, "Aufruf an den gesammten katholischen Klerus des österr. Kaiserstaates," *Wanderer*, 35. Jahrgang, No. 115 (May 13, 1848), p. 1, copy in the Univ. Colo. 1848 Coll., No. II/215.

fices to save the Fatherland from complete ruin. Only the Catholic clergy, the richest group in the country, are hesitating to deliver up their monastic treasures. All others are giving as much as possible, but you who preach the word of God and talk about works of mercy are using the word of God only to accept or collect wealth, none of which you give away in turn. You alone are contributing nothing to the welfare of the state and the Fatherland. You are as unmoved by the universal misery as the pillars of Lot's wife, as cold as marble!

Because of the golden gift of freedom from our most gracious Emperor, we have had a new resurrection. Only you do not want to be aroused from your lethargy. You are just as comfortable now as you were before, leading your monotonous monastic life, resting on your eiderdown pillows and feasting at luxurious tables. You can sleep peacefully while the Fatherland, oppressed by misery, and its peace threatened on all sides, spends sleepless nights in anxiety, worry, and distress, and while need and misery make their nightly rounds.

Is this the way you carry out your divine mission? Is heartlessness your concept of religion? Are these the Christian works of mercy, which you are duty bound, in the eyes of God and the world, to perform for the state and the harassed nation? Can you not part from your mammon?

Open your chests of gold and silver! Spring the locks of your money boxes, and you will find millions of treasures heaped up to help the Fatherland! Give up your treasures, which you have so long amassed through usurious practices!

Why do we need altars, statues, chandeliers, chalices, incense vessels, and even silver trellises, golden and bejeweled monstrances, and vestments embroidered with gold and silver? Of what use are these valuable objects? For you they are dead treasures, locked up behind four walls, whereas if this church property were given to the state, it would provide an important new supply of funds for the state in the crisis confronting it.

The government has the sacred right to force you to give up your cloister treasures, which you heaped up by getting millions from pilgrimages, tithes, and other exactions, and for the most part from the peasant class. The people of a constitutional empire, who are ready to sacrifice their blood and property for their monarch, who is so benevolent, have the right to demand that you give up the treasures of your cloisters. These treasures, which presumably belong to you, are the hereditary property of the state. They are national property, the care of which has up to now been entrusted to you by the state. Why do you now hesitate so long, even though you have up to now not been called upon by our liberal government to give to its rightful owner property that does not belong to you? Do you not realize that if a serious popular demonstration ever broke out—by the people who have long enough endured trial by fire because of your stubbornness and hardheartedness—you would be treated without any consideration whatever? Do you want to wait for the moment when you will be compelled by force to deliver up this national property?

Therefore, do not hesitate any longer. Prove by deeds and not by words alone that you are patriots and worthy successors to the apostles. Give up your monastic property to the state. Through this noble act make yourselves worthy again of being Christians. Then you will again receive the respect due your position, which you have unfortunately lost almost entirely.

May the Catholic clergy in no way look upon this message as extortion. On the contrary, it is intended only to be a warning from an aroused mob. These words are spoken with the greatest sorrow about our oppressed Fatherland, which, although it has already had to mortgage its property for loans, does not wish to follow the example of France and Spain and dissolve the monasteries by force.

Vienna, May 10, 1848.   Jos. Nep. Brenner.

The bureaucracy, the Camarilla, the aristocracy, and the clergy were not the only victims of the radicals. Wealthy middle-class capitalists and moneylenders also came under attack, even though most of them had been ardent supporters of the March revolution. The Rothschilds were scolded for not contributing to the proletariat from their vast treasures and for not improving working conditions in the many factories under their control.[45] With increasing frequency notices about men of wealth, such as the following, were inserted in left-wing newspapers:[46]

Johann Hoffmann, middle-class owner of the domain of Altmannsdorf, owner of several houses, twice a millionaire, and a first-class miser, gladly places himself among the nobility and calls himself nothing but the "rich" Hoffmann.

On account of the prevailing distress this worthy gentleman has undertaken the following economies in his household:

The servant receives 8 florins monthly instead of 12 florins

The gardener	"	8	"	"	"	"	10	"
The coachman	"	8	"	"	"	"	11	"
The porter	"	6	"	"	"	"	8	"
The messenger	"	4	"	"	"	"	6	"

This "honorable man" seeks to use the savings won thereby to build a new house for his own use as soon as possible.

The major complaint against the wealthier middle classes was that they put the less fortunate in bonds of "interest slavery." It was charged

[45] See especially Emanuel Friedländer, "Das Haus Rothschild," *Constitution*, No. 51 (May 23, 1848), p. 698.

[46] *Wiener Tageblatt*, No. 2 (June 7, 1848), pp. 3–4, Univ. Colo. 1848 Coll., No. II/224. Following this provocative account, all Hoffmann's extensive property holdings are listed.

that, because of the usurious loans the poor had to secure from wealthy bourgeois "leeches" to keep themselves and their children alive, countless numbers "lost their personal freedom, and, torn from the side of their children, who are naked and hungry and who are grieving for their father, are languishing in arrest for their indebtedness." War was declared on "this foul sect and all their supporters."[47]

Incited by such attacks, many debtors refused to pay either interest or arrears on capital they had borrowed. From May until November moneylenders were fortunate indeed if they recovered even without interest money they had lent; they were usually reluctant to ask for the principal alone for fear of being denounced by the press or becoming victims of the mock serenades that continued unabated.[48]

The radical journalists occasionally sought to give positive advice. They paid special attention to the grave financial situation of the monarchy, which was appreciably worsened by the May disturbances. Some radicals expressed the opinion that, above everything else, confidence had to be restored if the danger of economic ruin was to be averted. To ensure that trust, businessmen must have confidence "that those guiding the helm of state [would] never undertake anything unpopular" and would always act legally and justly.[49]

Others argued that trust in itself was no longer enough. The state must have more money to take care of the poor and the unemployed as well as to assume its many other responsibilities. The only way the government could get the money quickly was through voluntary contributions from the people. "Austrian patriots" appealed to their fellow-citizens to give one florin (48 cents) each to the state treasury. They suggested that if twenty million inhabitants made this inconsequential sacrifice enough revenue would be obtained to provide for all the needs of the state.[50]

Still others insisted that the wealthy, "whose gold-decorated coats" were worth more than all the possessions of the poor, should give up their surplus gold and silver to atone for the way they had played falsely with Austria's finances for thirty years.[51] In addition, all persons with an annual income of 1,000 florins or more should voluntarily pay

---

[47] T. M. Jettel, *"Ad vocem* Blutigel," *Wanderer,* 35. Jahrgang, No. 115 (May 13, 1848), pp. 2–3, Univ. Colo. 1848 Coll., No. II/215.

[48] Ernst Violand, *Die sociale Geschichte der Revolution,* pp. 90–91.

[49] "Woher kommen die schlechten Zeiten?" *Bst! Bst! Warum? Volksfragen,* No. 25, p. 2, Univ. Colo. 1848 Coll., No. II/41.

[50] Austrian Patriots' Club, "Proclamation," Vienna, May 4, 1848, Univ. Colo. 1848 Coll., No. II/160.

[51] *Constitution,* No. 34 (May 1, 1848), pp. 527–28.

a reasonable percentage of their revenue in a special patriotic tax. Those who made more than 10,000 florins could well contribute one-fifth of their income, while those earning over 20,000 could easily pay one-third and still lead lives of luxury.[52]

The radicals considered it necessary for the government to take away the privileges of the powerful National Bank. When so many businessmen were suffering from financial insecurity and when so many proletarians were on the verge of starvation, why, the radicals asked, should the hard-pressed state provide huge sums for this immensely wealthy institution so that it could continue collecting 5 to 6 per cent interest?[53] The only way to end the exploitation of the poor by the National Bank was for the state to take over the bank. After assuming control, the state should issue enough paper money to liquidate the public debt, thereby relieving itself of the necessity of paying interest. All the property owned by Austrian citizens should be mortgaged as security for this paper money. If this were done, the financial troubles of the government would come to an end.[54]

Although the above suggestions indicate that the Viennese revolutionaries knew little or nothing about the class-struggle ideas of Karl Marx and his followers, these and other proposals clearly show that a small number of Viennese radicals were influenced by the "prescientific socialism" of such early-nineteenth-century French Utopian Socialists as Henri de Saint-Simon, Charles Fourier, and Louis Blanc and by the ideas of the anarchosocialist Pierre Proudhon. In an article in the *Constitution* on the distressing economic situation, a certain Eduard Eyring, writing in language at least vaguely reminiscent of Saint-Simon and Proudhon, recommended that, since "railroads, highways, canals, shipping, mining, and machine shops can truly flourish in the country only when such vast undertakings, which are used publicly and by everyone, become state property," the government should issue enough paper money, not only to buy up all outstanding public debts, but to take over such enterprises and presumably compensate the owners. The property thus nationalized could serve as adequate security for all paper money issued.[55]

[52] A. Niederhuber, "Wohlfeiles Brot! wohlfeile Presse!" *Constitution*, No. 37 (May 4, 1848), p. 585.

[53] "20. April. Ein grauer Tag. Finanzverwaltung und Nationalbank," *Constitution*, No. 41 (May 9, 1848), pp. 621–22.

[54] "Ideen über Finanzen," *Constitution*, No. 13 (April 5, 1848), p. 158.

[55] Eduard Eyring, "Das schnellste Mittel dem Staate, ohne Bedrückung der Unterthanen, von Schulden zu befreien, wie auch die grossartigsten Unterneh-

The insistence of the ultraradicals that it "is the duty of the government to give all citizens of the state the means to work in the kind of employment suited to them and to assure them of the necessities of life"[56] also suggests that French Utopian Socialist ideas were beginning to find their way to Vienna.

Various plans drawn up to put the "right to work" principle into effect also show a certain degree of similarity with proposals that had been made by French Utopian Socialists. One friend of the proletariat proposed that several hundred million florins in bank notes without gold or silver backing should be issued to provide money for public works projects.[57] Another expressed the opinion that a central bank and warehouse should be established to buy all unsold products of the factories so that the manufacturers would have the funds to buy new raw materials and thus keep their employees at work.[58] Still others advocated the establishment of public institutes for earth and construction workers similar to the French national workshops, superintended by the Ministry and assisted by technicians and businessmen. Enough capital was to be donated by the government to put them into operation. Every member of the institutes was to be provided with food, living quarters, heat, light, laundry, and bathing facilities and was to be paid a daily wage. He was to be free to join and leave the organization at will, and the institute could dismiss any member on grounds of immorality or laziness. Care was to be taken to ensure that the workshops would never gain an unfair advantage over private industry or force private concerns into bankruptcy.[59]

Although there is substantial evidence that socialist ideas were beginning to influence some Viennese radicals during the high tide of the revolution, the "literature" of the revolution clearly proves that this socialism was of the utopian variety of early-nineteenth-century bourgeois dreamers. There was no foreshadowing of present-day Marxian socialism, with its violent class-struggle ideology and its concept of a well-organized militant proletarian army. There were sentimental verses

---

mungen, welche dem Lande nothwendig sind, bewerkstelligen zu können," *Constitution*, No. 46 (May 15, 1848), p. 661.

[56] J. M. Glock, "Eine Zeitfrage," *Der Unpartheyische*, No. 7 (June 7, 1848), p. 27, Univ. Colo. 1848 Coll., No. II/195.

[57] N. F. P., "Ausserordentlicher Geldweg für die Arbeiter Wiens," *Constitution*, No. 63 (June 7, 1848), p. 786.

[58] *Constitution*, No. 65 (June 9, 1848), p. 803.

[59] Glock, *op. cit.*, p. 27; Wild, "Vorschlag in der Arbeiter-Angelegenheit," *Constitution*, No. 67 (June 13, 1848), pp. 818–19.

about the misery of the lower classes[60] and mawkish stories about the demoralization of working-class girls—"these pitiable creatures thrown into the arms of vice by the hard pressure of want."[61] There were loud protests because the workers were considered stupid rabble and were denied the right to vote on the grounds that they lacked the necessary education, were susceptible to bribery, and were by nature hostile to the middle classes.[62]

Proposals were made for a workers' club, which would serve as an educational and recreation center.[63] Common kitchens and associations of working-class families to buy food at wholesale prices were also suggested,[64] as well as special barracks for workers that would provide healthy, pleasant living quarters at nominal rents.[65] There was some support for a suggestion to establish colonies for the poor. Some workers even suggested the formation of construction workers' associations to erect buildings for rent; the profits from this enterprise were to be used to defray the living costs of the members of the association.[66]

The variety of proposals suggests that the radicals had no "party program," except perhaps for their united support of shorter working hours and higher wages. Furthermore, for the most part they admonished the workers to go slow in their efforts to improve their lot and never to attack the property rights of their "betters."[67] Above all, they were cautioned never to "desert the path of peace and order."[68] Even so radical a body as the Student Committee warned the workers that asking for unreasonable concessions or threatening the Viennese would bring severe punishment.[69] An article entitled "To the Workers" clearly expressed these views:[70]

[60] For a good example, see Julius Schwenda, "Proletarier," *Constitution*, No. 69 (June 15, 1848), p. 836.

[61] Glock, *op. cit.*, p. 27.

[62] W. Erhlich, "Die Emancipation der Arbeiter," *Die freie Presse*, No. 2 (May 22, 1848), pp. 5–7, Univ. Colo. 1848 Coll., No. II/165a.

[63] See especially Friedrich Sander, "Arbeiter-Verein," *Constitution*, No. 39 (May 6, 1848), p. 602.

[64] Ernst Victor Zenker, *Die Wiener Revolution*, pp. 159–60.

[65] Maximilian Bach, *Geschichte der Wiener Revolution*, p. 267.

[66] Zenker, *Die Wiener Revolution*, pp. 160–61.

[67] B. Brandstetter, "Wer ist denn Alles Arbeiter?" *Das Wiener allgemeine Arbeiter-Blatt*, No. 5 (May 29, 1848), p. 10.

[68] Ehrlich, *op. cit.*, p. 7.

[69] "Proclamation, Student Committee to the Workers," n.d., *Wiener Zeitung*, No. 168 (June 18, 1848), p. 798.

[70] E. Rarzoni, "An die Arbeiter!" *Oesterreichisches Volksblatt*, No. 7 (June 21, 1848), pp. 25–26, Univ. Colo. 1848 Coll., No. II/154.

You have distinguished yourselves in the eyes of all Europe through your orderly and honest behavior in the days of the barricades. You have defeated those aristocrats who were of the opinion that an honest heart could not beat under a work shirt and that no honorable blood could flow in sunburned, swollen hands. Preserve this well-earned praise. Do not give those refugees who from a distance have the courage to slander you and to mar the splendor of the throne an occasion to represent you as dangerous and unlawful people. Every person in the state is entitled to work from which he can make a living. The state has the obligation to give him work in some way or another.

The state, however, must have not only a heart but also a head, and if it gives work it must see to it that the product is in proportion to the pay and that it will thereby receive in return what it has expended in the production. In unusually bad times, such as the present, when the individual citizen can no longer employ all the workers he formerly could because there is less demand for his products, the state itself will undertake projects to give work, from which there will be no commercial gains, but which will create work for the poor and will ward off general hardship. Naturally, care must be taken that the workers who are still supported by private persons do not quit work. If they did, there would not be enough hands left for what industrial activity still existed and laziness would be encouraged. Capital would be expended that, by paying for laziness, would be partly lost.

A person can pay wages only as long as he has money, and if a person has money he can pay wages without incurring losses only if he receives something of value in return. If you want to be paid for rainy days, then you are asking that the state give you something for nothing—in short, that the state lose something. But who constitutes the state? Friends, it is your fellow-citizens! The citizen pays you. He is a taxpayer. If you weaken him, you are diminishing the amount of capital that can be taxed and are undermining the most important source of income for the state. The citizen also loses because he cannot get rid of his products and must live from his business capital. When that is used up, he will enter your ranks and will thereby make it more difficult for those who still have something to pay you. This will continue until credit completely disappears, general impoverishment sets in, and those among you who are not satisfied with what you now receive will have to be satisfied with nothing, because no one will have anything to give.

The distress in Austria is universal and calls upon each and every one to bear the inevitable with patience and sacrifice. Trust those who fought for freedom, with all and for all, in the foremost ranks. Let us remain united. Then we will be invincible. Workers, citizens, guardsmen, and students, be constantly of one mind and heart. Be a strong defensive wall for freedom and a bulwark against obsolete privileges and class distinctions, even if the black and black-yellow slaves are offering us a heartless and hypocritical system of politics. You make us weaker if you desert us, for whosoever works for what is unjust and unfair has deserted us and brings disunity to the cause of freedom. I turn to the majority—the better ones among you. I beg you not to listen to these propagandists but to contrast their actions with their words; and he who complains about his wages and does no work shall henceforth be cast out from the ranks of the men of the *26th*.

Auf Wiedersehen
E. Rarzoni, Jurist.

In the Vienna of 1848 there were few foreshadowings of a modern philosophy of the working class. There was no organization resembling a modern trade union; the first general workers' union, which was founded on June 24, was established solely to win for the workers the same rights and privileges of other citizens and to help them better themselves through self-education. The Radical Liberal Union, representing the factory workers, and the Concordia Club, whose leaders were genuine democrats, also worked within the Austrian legal framework.[71] Throughout the course of the revolution the students and other radical intelligentsia monopolized the leadership of whatever working-class movement existed.[72] Marx and Engels later wrote that the Viennese workers of 1848, "distrusted, disarmed, disorganized, hardly emerging from the intellectual bondage of the old regime, hardly awakening, not to a knowledge, but to a mere instinct of their social position and proper political line of action, could only make themselves heard by loud demonstrations, and could not be expected to be up to the difficulties of the moment."[73] The Viennese proletariat and their radical spokesmen were, in fact, almost as terrified of socialism as were the upper classes.

Almost the same can be said about the revolutionaries' attitude toward republicanism. Although some of the extremists were slowly moving toward free popular government, they were careful to reiterate their loyalty to the monarch.[74] They poked fun at those who feared the word "republican," but at the same time they gave assurances that "the democratic monarchy is the fulcrum of the whole German" and demo-

---

[71] Zenker, *Die Wiener Revolution*, pp. 175–79; Fischer, *Österreich 1848*, pp. 88–89.

[72] Ernst Violand, *Die sociale Geschichte der Revolution in Oesterreich*, pp. 91–92, 150–51; Zenker, *Die Wiener Revolution*, pp. 162–63.

[73] Frederick Engels [and Karl Marx], *Germany: Revolution and Counter-Revolution*, p. 70.

[74] William H. Stiles, *Austria in 1848–49*, Vol. I, p. 145.

cratic movement and that in 1848 Austria and Germany were far from ready for a republic.[75] "A good constitution with a liberal regent" was all the democrats wanted.[76]

Thus, even at its most radical extreme, the revolution remained a "liberal" middle-class movement. The major issues were not "monarchism versus republicanism," or "capitalism versus socialism," as was to be true a half-century later. There was no "class struggle," in the Marxian sense of the term, between the bourgeoisie and proletariat. The alignment was one between the nobility and the upper middle classes on the one hand and the radical students and left-wing intelligentsia, supported by the lower middle classes and the proletariat, on the other. The conservatives stood opposed to the radicals who wanted to turn the liberal revolution into a democratic one. For both groups, socialism and republicanism were anathema. Class warfare was still undreamed-of.

[75] *Constitution,* No. 52 (May 24, 1848), p. 703.
[76] S., "Die Republikaner," *Das Wiener allgemeine Arbeiter-Blatt,* No. 6 (May 30, 1848), p. 12.

XI. *The Beginning of the Way Back*

INEVITABLY, the violence and extremism of the democrats drove many Viennese out of the revolutionary camp. The desertions had begun immediately after Metternich's dismissal on March 13. With his fall, the liberal clique in the Habsburg court that had conspired with the revolutionaries attained their ends and had their fill of revolution. The liberal nobility, who had co-operated to the utmost in bringing on the events of March 13 to 15, were fearful that the reform movement might slip out of their hands, and also strongly favored curbing revolutionary activities even before the March revolution was over.

More important, the more conservative professionals of the middle classes, and also the business and financial leaders of the city who had spearheaded the revolutionary movement before March 13, were terrified by the working-class riots on March 13 and 14, the mock serenades, the violent outbursts of democratic journalists, and the clamor for the reduction of house rents. Very shortly after the revolution began, the property-holding middle classes, who had gained a substantial share of political power, became apprehensive that the moderate political revolution they hoped to lead might end in a more violent social revolution and began devoting their efforts to restoring peace and security. Many of the peasants, too, lost interest in the revolution after the Emperor's manifesto of April 11 promising the abolition of all peasant dues and services on January 1, 1849. The clergy, so violently abused by leftist agitators, naturally threw their influence behind the counterrevolution.

During the first two months of the revolution, radicalism was too popular a movement to be opposed openly. In April, although occasionally placards were posted denouncing the prevailing anarchy and the inability of the police to cope with agitators and foreign demagogues,[1] they were frequently written anonymously and posted secretly.

[1] Hans Kudlich, *Rückblicke und Erinnerungen*, Vol. I, p. 250; *Constitution,* No. 25 (April 19, 1848), pp. 377–80; No. 26 (April 20, 1848), pp. 401–403; No. 29 (April 25, 1848), pp. 452–53.

Such "moderate" papers as the *Wiener allgemeine Theaterzeitung,* the *Constitutionelle Donau Zeitung,* the *Wiener Kirchenzeitung,* and the *Wiener Zuschauer* were hesitant to attack the revolutionaries, and the semiofficial *Wiener Zeitung* was eager to support the new movement. Not until the Emperor's flight to Innsbruck did the more conservative middle classes venture to declare themselves openly against the extremists and to break their last ties with the revolution.

Emperor Ferdinand's humiliating departure and the May revolution not only terrified the upper middle classes of Vienna into joining forces against the democrats but also alienated millions of provincials. After Ferdinand's arrival in Innsbruck, the inhabitants of the country districts outdid each other in protesting their loyalty to the court and reviling the Viennese democrats as assassins, republicans, and anarchists. Even though the Vienna Security Committee sent stirring appeals to the provincials to be on guard against the efforts of "a stealthy, reactionary party" to arouse suspicions about "the efforts made for freedom in Vienna,"[2] by early June the non-Hungarian and non-Italian provinces were lost to the revolutionaries.

The strong revulsion of feeling against the extremists encouraged the ever increasing number of their enemies to strike back openly after May 26. One of the first to do so was Austria's renowned poet and dramatist and erstwhile liberal, Grillparzer. On June 8, after a long period of silence he published the following poem, "To Field Marshal Radetzky," in the *Donau Zeitung:*[3]

> Here's to my general! Now strike home;
>   Not only fame for thy fee!
> Thy camp encloses Austria,
>   Her separate members are we.
>
> By foolishness and vanity
>   Came our collapse and fall,
> But when thou leadest men to war
>   The old fire glows in all.
>
> Among them not a youth does fail
>   To know this better than you,

[2] "Proclamation, Security Committee to the Brave City Dwellers of the Provinces," Vienna, June 4, 1848, Univ. Colo. 1848 Coll., No. II/14. See also the "Proclamation, Security Committee to the Peasants," Vienna, June 4, 1848, *ibid.,* No. II/10; Protocol of the Second Sitting of the Security Committee, May 27, 1848, *Wiener Zeitung,* No. 162 (June 12, 1848), p. 768.

[3] Stanzas 1, 2, 7–9 translated by J. G. Legge in *Rhyme and Revolution in Germany,* p. 474; stanzas 3–6 translated from copy in Joseph Alexander Freiherrn von Helfert, *Der Wiener Parnass im Jahre 1848,* p. 226.

Who what he dreams and ne'er exists
  As wisdom dares to view.

Your force, so ever vigilant,
  Which always guards and shields;
Does not ask for safety when
  The drum beats in the fields.

And citizen of your roving city
  Knows that it's all he has,
And that if it's consumed with flames,
  He'll go down in ruin's crevasse.

And your ministers, the army chiefs,
  Who carry their sword on the saddle
To punish when'er there's need for it—
  Obedience means peace in battle.

Whom God as Slavs and Magyars made,
  They'll quarrel not for a word;
They'll follow a German battle-cry:
  "Vorwärts!" be the call, it is heard.

On help from all, at need of all,
  Are founded Kingdom and State,
For only in death man stands alone,
  In life and in strife finds a mate.

Shoulder to shoulder's the lesson
  Thy glorious victories teach;
In union of all comes victory,
  With happiness for each.

Grillparzer's poem, which was circulated throughout the empire, was greeted with stormy approval by the army and the partisans of law and order.[4] It encouraged the conservatives and moderates to voice their dissatisfaction with the constant disturbances and their longing for the return of peace and order. Almost immediately after the publication of Grillparzer's poem, the antirevolutionary group in the capital began to emerge from hiding.[5]

Their increasing boldness soon reflected itself in the journalism of the capital. As spring turned into summer the *Wiener Kirchenzeitung* became more audacious in championing the rights of the church, while

[4] Tim Klein (ed.), *Der Vorkampf deutscher Einheit und Freiheit*, p. 379.
[5] *Oesterreichisches Volksblatt*, No. 7 (June 21, 1848), p. 26, Univ. Colo. 1848 Coll., No. II/154.

the *Constitutionelle Hansjörgel* intensified its attacks on the democrats[6] and the *Wiener Zuschauer* devoted more space to onslaughts against "anarchists" and "republicans."[7]

In the summer of 1848 several new conservative newspapers came into being. By far the most effective of these papers was the *Geissel*,[8] owned and published by Adolph Bäuerle, which began publication on July 24 under the editorship of J. F. Böhringer.[9] Böhringer had been a chorus-singer and harpist before he decided to join the conservatives. His "daily of dailies" outdid even the radical scandal sheets in abuse and vilification and used the same weapons of vituperation, coarseness, exaggeration, and intimidation. Just as the rabid democratic sheets had slurred individual "reactionaries" for four months, the *Geissel* made a practice of singling out individual "radicals" for denunciation.[10] The *Geissel* was the reactionary counterpart of the radical *Freimüthige*.

Another influential conservative sheet founded in the summer of 1848 was August Zang's *Presse*,[11] which first appeared on July 3. It was the organ, not of reactionaries, but of the liberal middle classes who, after having led the revolutionary movement in March, had been frightened over to the opposition by the continuing trend leftward. In articles of rare objectivity, restraint, and learning, the paper examined the main issues of the day in a dignified and analytical tone. Selling for the incredibly low price of one kreutzer (less than one cent) per issue and delivered to homes, it was an instant success. In a short time it attained the unheard-of circulation of 15,000 copies.[12] More than any other journal, the *Presse* helped to harden bourgeois opposition to the extremists.

In the summer of 1848 the conservatives, heartened by the growing

[6] Kürnberger to Madame Betty Adam, Dresden, January 21, 1850, Ferdinand Kürnberger, *Briefe eines politischen Flüchtlings,* ed. Otto Erich Deutsch, pp. 63–64.

[7] E[rnst] V[ictor] Zenker, *Wiener Journalistik 1848,* p. 91.

[8] *Die Geissel. Tagblatt aller Tagblätter,* a daily published by Klopf and Eurich. It ceased publication in 1850.

[9] The writer of Adolph Bäuerle's biographical sketch in Constant von Wurzbach's *Biographisches Lexikon des Kaiserthums Oesterreich* (Vol. I, p. 119) maintains that Bäuerle was also the real editor of the paper and that Böhringer was the editor only in name.

[10] Alexander Freiherrn von Helfert, *Die Wiener Journalistik im Jahre 1848,* pp. 92–95; Zenker, *op. cit.,* pp. 91–92.

[11] The *Presse* was a daily newspaper published by August Zang and edited by Leopold Landsteiner. It continued in existence after the revolution and became one of the great Viennese dailies of the latter half of the nineteenth century.

[12] Helfert, *Die Wiener Journalistik im Jahre 1848,* pp. 97–111; Zenker, *op. cit.,* pp. 82–87.

opposition to the revolution, began to repay the radical newspapermen for the insults they had suffered from them. In an article entitled "A Few Words Concerning the Clandestine Press," published in *Gold und Larbe*,[13] the irresponsible left-wing journalists were rebuked in these words:[14]

When we obtained freedom of the press, the publishers declared that they wanted freedom of the press but that they would never tolerate its abuse. Yet, placards and pamphlets are appearing daily filled with nonsense, lies, and indecencies that offend the eyes and ears of every honest-minded person, and have a most deleterious influence upon the unenlightened masses. My good publishers, is this how to keep your word? Is this not an abuse of the press? Are you keeping in mind the welfare of the state and nation when you degrade the most sacred, the most powerful gift—the freedom of the press—into a most wretched means of money-making? Money-making. That is the right word, for these pamphlets have been printed for no other reason. Mere absurdities, lies, and indecencies are thrown together. Then a striking, piquant title is added, and a pamphlet is finished. After that they are carried out and hawked, and the kreutzers are collected. No one cares how dire the consequences may be, how the lofty mission of the press has been dishonored, or how much individual and national honor has been degraded. Shame on such mercenary spirits! This evil-doing must be checked. Herewith all honest-thinking men imbued with patriotism and honor who are connected with the publishing business are called upon to find the means to check this evil.

And are not you writers of such bungling pieces of work, you disgracers of the free, sacred word, ashamed of producing such vile works for the sake of a few miserable gulden? However, one appeals to you in vain in the name of honor, for whoever writes such stuff can have no honor. This plea is made to you—to all of you lords of the quill, you representatives of free, sacred speech—who are permeated with a feeling for justice and greatness. Do not let individuals who make their living in such a way disgrace our literary honor. Expose them publicly if you know who they are, and destroy them. They are the very people who have always disgraced the term "writer" and have dragged it in the mud of vulgarity. Show that you are armed with the destructive force of lightning. Rescue the honor of the worthy title of writer. Do not let this noble profession be dishonored by

[13] *Gold und Larbe. Politisch-literarisches Tagsblatt,* edited by E. Hell and A. Mailust. Only thirteen numbers of the paper were issued, the first on July 16, the last on August 2. The motto of the paper was "Woe to him who lies!"
[14] "Einige Worte über die Winkelpresse," *Gold und Larbe,* No. 4 (July 20, 1848), p. 14, Univ. Colo. 1848 Coll., No. II/92. Although the article was printed in *Gold und Larbe,* it should be noted that this paper attacked "reactionaries" more often than it did the radicals.

such monsters, for we do not want anyone to associate us by mistake with these scoundrels.

With ever increasing frequency the radicals were denounced as foreign emissaries, French hirelings, corrupters of the youth, republicans, and anarchists.[15] They were held responsible for the stagnation of business, for the misery stemming from the economic depression, and for the failure to make "people free and rich at the same time."[16] They were scolded for their unceasing disturbances and for their clamor against decent public officials.[17]

Warnings were sent to demagogues like Häfner, Tuvora, and Tausenau to mend their ways or suffer the just revenge of the people.[18] The unprincipled editor of the *Freimüthige*, Moritz Mahler, was especially maligned.[19]

Quite naturally the radical journalists greeted the bold attacks of the reactionaries with surprise, consternation, derision, and anger. Their monopoly on denunciation was at an end. They loudly claimed that the editors of the "reactionary press" were working feverishly "to bring the people back under their former yoke, to destroy the kernel of freedom, and to suppress democracy."[20] The conservative journalists were accused of inciting the Slavs to attack the Germans in order to destroy democracy and restore absolutism. They were called tools of the obscurantist Jesuits, working to rob the people of the victories won in the revolution under the pretext of protecting the monarchy against republicanism and anarchism.[21] They were charged with attempting to incite the people "to undertake a violent uprising," hoping thereby to win world sympathy when they used force to destroy them.[22]

---

[15] *Oesterreichisches Volksblatt*, No. 2 (June 15, 1848), p. 8, Univ. Colo. 1848 Coll., No. II/153.

[16] Heinrich Ehrlich, "Woher kommen die schlechten Zeiten?" *Bst! Bst! Warum? Volksfragen*, No. 25 (n.d.), p. 7, Univ. Colo. 1848 Coll., No. II/41.

[17] "Bitte um Gesunden Verstand und Menschlichkeit," *Gold und Larbe*, No. 3 (July 19, 1848), p. 11, Univ. Colo. 1848 Coll., No. AII/92.

[18] *Constitution*, No. 86 (July 7, 1848), pp. 970–71.

[19] For an example, see Sebastian Brunner, "What the Prophet Habakuk Prophesies about M. Mahler," published in the August 9 issue of the *Geissel* and quoted in part in Helfert, *Die Wiener Journalistik im Jahre 1848*, p. 96.

[20] Doppler, "Was versteht man unter Pressfreiheit?" *Nazional-Zeitung*, No. 30 (August 23, 1848), p. 118, Univ. Colo. 1848 Coll., No. II/146. The *Nazional-Zeitung. Politisches Volksblatt für demokratische Interessen* was owned and edited by Wilhelm Ehrlich. The notorious agitator Adolf Chaisés was coeditor. The first issue appeared on July 7, 1848; the last, on October 26.

[21] "Reaction und Jesuitismus," *Constitution*, No. 54 (May 26, 1848), p. 720.

[22] "Probates Mittel gegen die Reaction," *Gold und Larbe*, No. 4 (July 20, 1848), p. 13, Univ. Colo. 1848 Coll., No. II/92.

What particularly infuriated the radicals about the "reactionary" journalists was that so many of them were middle-class liberals who had deserted the revolution. They were despised as traitors to the cause of freedom. The anonymous author of the following article on "Philistine Life" voiced the sentiments of most democratic extremists:[23]

They are still with us, and will ever be, these precious Philistines, to whom nothing but their ego is sacred, and who yearn only for slavery. They wrap up their faces, yellowed with anger, in the mourning crepe of stupidity and go about with pompous gestures. They are truly fighting windmills against freedom, like Don Quixote. To be sure, they eat, drink, and sleep like other people, but they do not have a moment's peace, for their fury over this terrible freedom embitters their life. They are to be found everywhere in every class. Like ants, these dear, sweet Philistines wear themselves out trying to conquer these agitators, these Republicans, or whoever they may be. However, they fare no better than the bird who tried to carry away a mountain with his beak. They are so rightly a living proof of the almighty power of God, who, however, seems to have forgotten to supply them with a divine spark. Oh, you poor wretches! I would torment you to death if it were possible to joust with you in the intellectual field. Oh, you miserable creatures, you tormentors of freedom! Oh, you stable flies who torture the noble horse of freedom but are driven off by a switch of the animal's tail! You were kings in better times. Now you are an object of ridicule in the eyes of your fellow-men. Just keep on puffing yourselves up with your "moderate progress." You are still nothing but apostles of slavery. Your elders have reared you to be slaves, and that you really are. You are an unfortunate reactionary band, as indestructible and as intolerable as stupidity. Selfishness, hatred, and stupidity are written on the banner which you carry before you in your disreputable procession. Baseness is the air that prolongs your life. Keep up your agitation. Make yourselves important, you cowards, who will disappear like poltroons when it becomes clear that freedom is victorious and when your knout calls you. You are made of filth. You are without spirit or life. Odious and contemptible will be the lot of all of you. You are incapable of love and unworthy of the freedom you scoff at by your very existence. Farewell, Philistines. We'll see each other soon, for I love the sweet pleasure of heaping ridicule upon you, and you do become so angry about it in spite of the fact that you also shout at and insult the press.

Between the two extremes of reaction and radicalism an ever increasing number of moderates were veering away from the revolution

---

[23] "Das Philisterium," *Schwefeläther. Politisch-Satyrisches Abendblatt. Mit Original-Holzschnitten*, No. 2 (August 6, 1848), p. 5, Univ. Colo. 1848 Coll., No. II/181b. This paper was published by J. Nord and edited by Sitter. Only four issues were printed, the first on August 4, the last on August 9.

and drawing closer to the reactionaries. An article in *Der gerade Michel*, which bore the title "Big Parliament of Black-Yellow Reactionaries, Liberals, Constitutionalists, Democrats, and Republicans," described the warring factions in Austria:[24]

> The Camarilla, the high bureaucracy, and the aristocracy enter hand in hand, wavering and ghostlike. With trembling lips, murmuring softly, they implore the great Christopher to be with them in their dying hour, for the radicals, democrats, and republicans are inflamed with rage and are hissing at them. Bowing low to the left and to the right, they say: "Gentlemen! For centuries we were so happy most humbly and obediently to perform the most important services both for the Most Gracious Imperial House and for the state. (Great excitement.) Our high offices, our high rank, our high pay, our pensions and personal allowances speak for these distinguished services." (Great tumult. Someone shouts: "But who will speak for your services to the people?") Silently the three shadowy forms retire to the background and do not appear again.
>
> A liberal steps up jauntily and speaks: "The whole world knows that I have always been a liberal, for in my innermost mind I was never reconciled to the old form of government and now and then I spoke out a free word." (Voices are heard: "We know the liberals of olden times. They are nothing but hyenas who at first want everything, then not too much, then a little, and finally nothing at all.")
>
> A constitutionalist interrupts: "Gentlemen! We are nothing but lawyers. Our political club stood at the head of the constitution! We are the representatives of justice. We speak of justice for both sides, and without justice for both sides the lawyer cannot—"
>
> The radicals, democrats, and republicans jump up simultaneously and shout wildly: "We are the law! We'll make the law for the sovereign people! They have the right to make the laws! We are the true representatives of the people! We lead the sovereign people! There is no law and no sovereignty but ours! Blood! Blood must be shed! Blood is the cement of freedom—." (A terrible tumult breaks out. Suddenly three men—Order, Safety, and Peace—appear. Blood flows from many noses, and the bloody club is broken up and adjourned.)

The summer of 1848 found Viennese society sharply divided and—

---

[24] "Grosser Reichstag der Schwarzgelben Reactionäre, Liberalen, Constitutionellen, Demokraten, Republikaner," *Der gerade Michel! Für jeden Stand, für jedes Land! Ein periodisches Flugblatt von Michel Glaub*, No. 7 (n.d.), pp. 25–26, Univ. Colo. 1848 Coll., No. II/138. The first issue of this paper appeared sometime between July 17 and July 20 under the title *Der Wiener Michel gerad und glatt weg! oder: 96000erlei für jeden Stand für jedes Land! Ein periodisches Flugblatt von Michel Glaubrecht*. With number 2 (issued on July 20) the title was changed to *Der gerade Michel! . . .*, and the eight subsequent issues appeared under this title. The last issue appeared on August 9.

of more importance for the outcome of the revolution—national hatreds intensified to a degree hitherto unknown. Although the leaders of most of the non-German nationalities within the Habsburg Empire shared the German liberals' desire for freedom and constitutional government, they placed their national interests above their liberal aspirations. The Magyars wanted to be Magyars. The Bohemians and other Slavs desired a powerful Austria but one in which they would be as influential as the Germans. The Italians longed for a united Italy.[25] All these groups saw their national rights and claims threatened by the Germans.

At least some of the national difficulties within the empire stemmed from the fact that the Austro-Germans were unable to decide between their Germanism and a supranational Habsburg Empire. Only the ultra-radicals were willing to sacrifice nationalism for close union with Germany. Very few Austro-Germans clearly understood that they would have to renounce their citizenship in the Austrian monarchy if they were to become citizens of the German Empire.[26]

The Viennese watched with avid interest the happenings at Frankfurt. The German National Assembly held its first session, which was marked by festive celebrations, on May 18. On the following day Heinrich von Gagern was chosen president of the assembly. On June 3 a committee of fifteen was appointed to make proposals for a provisional central government. Later another committee, composed of thirty members, was set up to draft a constitution for a united Germany.

Each of the many factions in the assembly had a clear-cut political program. To the right were the conservatives, led by Joseph Maria von Radowitz and Georg von Vincke, both Prussians, who insisted that no fundamental constitutional changes could be made in Germany without the consent of the existing governments. The extreme democrats, led by Robert Blum, of Leipzig, desired a federal republic. Most of the deputies, including such men as President Von Gagern and the great constitutional expert Friedrich Christoph Dahlmann, were constitutional monarchists who wanted a liberal constitution for the united Germany that was to come into being but who felt that a monarch should be at the head of the new state.

During the weeks following the May revolutions the ultrademocratic faction at Frankfurt impressed the radicals in the Habsburg capital most favorably. The members of the Viennese left were ultranationalist,

---

[25] See Adolph Lugano, *Der Fortbestand Oesterreichs*, pp. 10–12, for an interesting contemporary evaluation of the basic differences among the nationalities.
[26] See Rudolf Stadelmann, *Soziale und politische Geschichte der Revolution von 1848*, pp. 125–28.

as well as ultrademocratic. To them the "black-red-gold" was not only the banner "of German unity" but also the emblem of German democracy and of "the German Republic."[27] They believed that "their nationalism, their material well-being, and, more important than all this, their very freedom" depended upon a close union with Germany at the earliest possible moment.[28] They concerned themselves little with the position the non-German nationalities were to have in the new Germany,[29] for they believed that the Habsburg monarchy was on the point of dissolution. Hungary seemed to be lost to the empire and the Italians were on the point of falling away. The Czechs were hatching a plot to tear themselves loose from the Germans, and the Poles were being held only at the point of a bayonet. The choice, therefore, lay in extinction, union with Germany, or a Slav-dominated empire that would inevitably fall under Russian domination and engage in a life-and-death struggle against the Germans.[30] This attitude helps explain why the Viennese extremists went to such ridiculous lengths in expressing their devotion to German unity and democracy. The radical papers even began to date "their news, not from Vienna, but from 'the United States of Germany.'"[31]

Nevertheless, though they were dedicated to the cause of German unification, the Viennese democrats were by no means satisfied with all the proceedings at Frankfurt. Many of them felt that the March revolution in Vienna had made the Frankfurt Assembly possible,[32] and they were impatient with the slow progress of the constitution-makers meeting at St. Paul's Church. They objected to the declaration of the National Assembly on May 27 that the constitutions of the individual states in Germany must conform with the national constitution.[33] The Austrian democrats especially opposed this resolution because, as one explained it:[34]

May 15th gives us the most precious right, all documented and sealed: the democratic monarchy has been assured. What if this Frankfurt declaration should take these precious gains from us? What if Frankfurt should

[27] Alexander Novotny, *1848: Österreichs Ringen um Freiheit und Völkerfrieden vor hundert Jahren* (hereafter cited throughout as *1848*), p. 74.

[28] Lugano, *op. cit.*, p. 28.

[29] Kudlich, *op. cit.*, Vol. I, p. 200.

[30] See especially Lugano, *op. cit.*, pp. 28–29; and K——l——u——t, a German in Vienna, "Schwarz, Roth, Gold!" *Constitution*, No. 37 (May 4, 1848), p. 583.

[31] William H. Stiles, *Austria in 1848–49*, Vol. I, p. 144.

[32] See, for example, Dr. B——, "Sturmschritt und Schneckengang," *Der Unpartheyische*, No. 7 (June 7, 1848), p. 27, Univ. Colo. 1848 Coll., No. II/195.

[33] Heinrich Laube, *Das erste deutsche Parlament*, Vol. I, pp. 220–21.

[34] Dr. B——, *op. cit.*, p. 27.

declare itself in favor of an aristocratic two-chamber system, and would, as a consequence of the above resolution, declare our constitution invalid? What if Bassermann and Welker [*sic*] and their supporters should force their liberalism on the assembly and want to experiment on us with their public welfare theories? Should we moderate our double-quick step in favor of their snail's pace and the slow gait of their basic historical development? Must we lose our gains and take our place on the tragic road to retrogression because they are so ossified in their out-of-date ideas that they are not able to understand and evaluate the present popular movement?

Ponder this, brave champions of freedom, and do not be hasty in making your decision!

Also, their profound distrust of Prussian and of Frederick William IV's efforts to take over leadership in Germany influenced the Viennese attitude toward the Frankfurt Assembly. Ever since Frederick William had signified his desire to rule Germany, a deep suspicion of Prussian motives had colored the atmosphere in Vienna. Violent anti-Prussian feeling again boiled up early in August when Frederick William (and, incidentally, the Austrian Emperor, too) ordered his troops not to swear allegiance to the head of the German government in Frankfurt. The following article in the *Nazional-Zeitung* is an example of the reaction this order had in Vienna: [35]

Address of the Democrats to the King of Prussia.

You king, who are always drunk and at the same time the greatest of liars, give up the throne which you are dishonoring and go to your brother-in-law in Russia. That is the land where misunderstandings flourish. Of course, Ireland would also be a nice region. There you and your fine brother could study new misunderstandings. However, Germany has understood you only too well—that is, all but Berlin, which you must still bring to an understanding with cannon and Cossacks before your departure.

But before you leave, still one more word to you, king of all actors. What do you mean in that part of your army order in which you say: "I have expressed myself in favor of the choice of His Imperial Highness, the Archduke John"? [36] As far as we know, you were not consulted when the choice was made. Therefore, you have no right to use these words. Furthermore, in this army order you call their commander-in-chief, the imperial vicar, "your personal friend." That is an insult to our beloved John that you must take back.

Further on in your army order we read: "Everywhere Prussian troops

---

[35] H., "Adresse der Demokraten an den König von Preussen," *Nazional-Zeitung*, No. 16 (August 7, 1848), pp. 63–64, Univ. Colo. 1848 Coll., No. II/145.

[36] Late in June Archduke John was chosen imperial vicar of Germany.

act for German interests." Are there any but German concerns for Prussian troops? Give us an answer, King.

Now, however, comes the most base of all: "And in accord with my orders are to be subordinated to His Imperial Royal Highness, the Imperial Vicar." That deserves chastisement, for here you are openly behaving like a rebel, and you must know what punishment is fitting for rebels. Such punishment cannot be dispensed with, for such language cannot be left unpunished by Germany. Or are we to believe that this army order was dictated by champagne? That would excuse you, King, but not your ministers, for they are duty-bound to give you such important documents to read again when you are sober so that such a disgraceful, bungling piece of work, manufactured while you were drunk, will not be sent out to the world to infuriate other people.

In conclusion, we beseech you, King, no longer to disturb the work of German unification that is to be completed; otherwise the crown might fall from your head, and when you bend over to pick it up you might find that you no longer have a head on which you can put it. In the name of all democrats.

H.

Fear of Prussian ambitions, coupled with the radicals' support of close union with Germany, greatly influenced the viewpoint of many Austro-Germans toward German unity. As the summer wore on, "radical" and "pro-German" came to have the same meaning for propertyholders.[37] Many conservatives feared that close union might mean not only the absorption of Austria by Germany but also the destruction of Habsburg traditions, the end of independent legislation in Austria, and a further thrust of the revolution to the left.[38]

The worst fears of the conservatives were assuaged by the decision of the Frankfurt Assembly on June 28 provisionally to appoint an imperial regent as head of the central government of Germany[39] and by the election of Archduke John of Austria as regent the following day, by a vote of 436 to 85.[40] Now that a universally popular Habsburg prince was at the head of Germany, it seemed assured that Austria's special interests would always be safeguarded in the united Germany to come.[41]

The attitude of the Viennese liberals toward the German question

[37] Vitzthum von Eckstädt to his uncle, Vienna, July 28, 1848, Carl Friedrich Grafen von Vitzthum von Eckstädt, *Berlin und Wien in den Jahren 1845–1852*, p. 128.

[38] Baron [Franz Xaver] Pillersdorf, *Austria in 1848 and 1849*, p. 42. See also L. B. Namier, *1848: The Revolution of the Intellectuals*, p. 99.

[39] See Laube, *op. cit.*, Vol. II, pp. 10–12, for the provisions of this law.

[40] *Ibid.*, pp. 12–13; Legge, *op. cit.*, p. 388.

[41] See especially F. Kürnberger, "Erzherzog Johann, Oesterreich und Deutschland," *Beilage zur Wiener Zeitung*, No. 195 (July 16, 1848), pp. 24–25.

was influenced, in part at least, by their almost psychopathic fear of the Russians. As stated previously, in March and April various Viennese newspapers had been full of dire warnings that the Czar was about to order his troops to put down the revolutions in central and western Europe. Throughout the course of the revolution there were recurrent rumors of troop movements on Russia's western borders and reports that a Russian army, 250,000 strong, was ready to march into central Europe at a moment's notice.[42] Excerpts from letters written by Austrians living on the eastern and northern borders were published to acquaint the Viennese with the terror that was seizing the inhabitants of the border regions and to put them on guard against suspicious-acting Russians and their Austrian sympathizers. According to rumor, some of the Emperor's advisers and nearly all the reactionaries were feverishly preparing the way for a Russian invasion when the auspicious moment arrived.[43] Loud were the demands of Viennese radicals for the creation of a strong, united Germany to form a powerful protective barrier against the despotic Russians.

This strong Russophobia must be kept in mind when one studies the attitude of the Austro-Germans toward the Slavs. The Austro-Germans lived in constant dread that if German domination of the monarchy was ever supplanted by Slav hegemony Russia would have an enormous influence on the affairs of the Habsburg Empire.[44] Even such a radical German as Karl Marx felt that behind the Pan-Slav theory "stood the terrible reality of the *Russian Empire.*"[45]

The fear that the Pan-Slav movement was Russian-inspired at least partly explains the violent hostility of the Germans to the Pan-Slav Congress. To the great consternation of the Austro-Germans, 350 delegates from all Slavic regions except Bulgaria met in Prague from June 2 to June 12 to make plans to create a united Slavic front.[46] On June 12 a

---

[42] See, for example, "Die Russen nach Wien," *Volksfreund,* No. 43 (June 24, 1848), p. 173, Univ. Colo. 1848 Coll., No. II/210b; and *Constitution,* No. 86 (July 7, 1848), pp. 965–66.

[43] See, for example, *Constitution,* No. 31 (April 27, 1848), pp. 481–82; *ibid.,* No. 86 (July 7, 1848), pp. 966–67; "Die Russen nach Wien," pp. 173–74.

[44] R. E. v. E., "Das Journal des Debats über die Oesterreichische Lebensfrage," *Wiener Zeitung,* No. 152 (June 1, 1848), p. 723.

[45] Frederick Engels [and Karl Marx], *Germany: Revolution and Counter-Revolution,* p. 58.

[46] Josef Macůrek, "The Achievements of the Slavonic Congress," *The Slavonic and East European Review,* Vol. XXVI, No. 67 (April, 1948), p. 330. See also Hans Kohn, *Pan-Slavism, Its History and Ideology,* pp. 70–74, for a brief but good discussion of the Pan-Slav Congress.

manifesto was issued to the nations of Europe offering "a brotherly hand to all neighbouring nations who are prepared to recognize and effectively champion with us the full equality of all nations, irrespective of their political power or size," and demanding the conversion of the Habsburg monarchy into "a federation of nations all enjoying equal rights, whereby regard would be paid not less to the different needs of these nations than to those of the united Monarchy."[47]

This manifesto of the Pan-Slav Congress awakened the Austro-Germans to the realization that the Slavs were a powerful, disintegrating force who would eventually destroy the monarchy.[48] They denounced the Slavs as traitors to a monarchy that had cherished and nourished them and by specious arguments tried to prove that history, customs, religion, common sense, and justice were against the claims of the Pan-Slavs for hegemony.[49] To a man they vowed that as long as a single German still lived the Slavs would never gain control of the monarchy.

The strong anti-Russian and anti–Pan-Slav feeling of the Viennese also affected their attitude toward the Poles, but not as much as the disorders that broke out in various parts of Poland during the spring of 1848. During the latter half of April the Prussian army became involved in a civil war with Polish nationalists in Poznań and forced them to surrender on May 9.[50] On April 25 a revolt also broke out in Cracow, this time against the Austrians, which was easily suppressed on the 26th. Anti-Austrian disturbances also took place in Lemberg on the same day.

The Viennese democrats were uncertain how to interpret these events. Some blamed the returning emigrants for inciting the Cracow revolt

---

[47] Translated for and printed in *The Slavonic and East European Review,* Vol. XXVI, No. 67 (April, 1948), pp. 309–13.

[48] "Deutsche Brüder in Oesterreich!" *Wiener Zeitung,* No. 174 (June 25, 1848), p. 827; "Der Slavismus im Reichstage," *Wiener Postillon. Verbunden mit dem Anzeigeblatt des Dienstfreundes,* No. 18 (July 22, 1848), p. 69, Univ. Colo. 1848 Coll., No. II/222. The *Wiener Postillon* was the name assumed on July 8 by the paper edited by C. A. Ritter and founded on July 1 under the name, *Der Dienstfreund. Wochenblatt zur Aufklärungen, Belehrung und Erheiterung für Alle mit besonderer Rücksicht für die dienende Klasse.* The motto of the *Wiener Postillon* was "Things must become better." After the name was changed to *Wiener Postillon* the paper came out six times weekly. It remained in existence until October 25, 1848.

[49] Freund, "Der Slavismus," *Constitution,* No. 69 (June 15, 1848), p. 832; "Das neue Slavenreich," *Wiener Zeitung,* No. 155 (June 4, 1848), pp. 735–36.

[50] C. E. Black, "Poznań and Europe in 1848," *Journal of Central European Affairs,* Vol. VIII, No. 2 (July, 1948), pp. 191–203; Namier, *op. cit.,* p. 77.

and tried to minimize the significance of the anti-Habsburg demonstrations at Lemberg.[51] There was a noticeable tendency to gloat over the way the Poles were embarrassing the Prussians and to describe the revolt against the hated Junkers in Poznań as a war "against barbarism and suppression"; but there was an almost universal feeling that the whole Polish question had to be handled with the utmost diplomacy.[52] The Viennese radicals still insisted, as they had in March, that the restoration of an independent Poland was a holy duty, but at the same time they now maintained that the Poles could gain their liberty only if they linked their cause with that of the German liberals.[53] If the Poles separated themselves from Germany, it was argued, they would inevitably fall prey to the Russians. Therefore, although the just demands of the Poles must be granted, all Germans, whether in Austria, Prussia, or the smaller states, must take a strong stand against Russian machinations in Poland, for not only the fate of Poland but also that of Germany and the whole civilized world depended on their doing so.[54]

The Russophobia and strong German nationalist predilections of the Austro-Germans also ran through their writings about the South Slavs. Under the leadership of Ljudevit Gaj, a Croatian national committee had been established in March to work for the union of all South Slavs. This committee convoked an assembly of the three united kingdoms of Dalmatia, Croatia, and Slavonia to meet at Agram on March 25 to consider what demands should be made of the Emperor. At the assembly the South Slavs expressed a wish to remain under the Hungarian crown but demanded a vast degree of autonomy. Three days later the Habsburgs appointed Baron Josip Jelačić ban of Croatia.

The new Ban immediately began touring the countryside shouting defiance at the Magyars. When the Hungarians tried to introduce their "Magyarization" program into Croatia, Jelačić announced that he would refuse to carry it out. When the Pest government issued instructions to the Ban that its orders must be explicitly obeyed and when the Archduke Palatine of Hungary announced that Jelačić's actions were unconstitutional, Jelačić called a diet to meet at Agram on June 5 to make laws in the name of the Croatian people. Thereupon the Habs-

[51] "Polen," *Wahrheit,* No. 13 (June 17, 1848), pp. 50–51, Univ. Colo. 1848 Coll., No. II/217b.
[52] K. Z., "Die Lösung der Polenfrage," *Die freie Presse,* No. 3 (May 23, 1848), p. 9, Univ. Colo. 1848 Coll., No. II/165b.
[53] Niederhuber, "Polen und seine Wiederherstellung," *Constitution,* No. 64 (June 8, 1848), p. 792.
[54] K. Z., *op. cit.,* pp. 9–10.

burg Emperor issued a manifesto prohibiting this assembly and ordered the Ban to come to Innsbruck to explain in person his unlawful actions. Jelačić refused to obey the order and on June 5 made a speech before the Croatian Diet in which he thundered against the Magyars. On the same day the Croatian Diet declared that all orders of the Hungarian government were illegal. On June 10 Emperor Ferdinand formally removed Jelačić from office, but on June 19, after the Ban appeared in person in Innsbruck with a formidable delegation, he was reinstated. When he returned to Agram, he received a tremendous ovation, and on June 29 the diet granted him unlimited powers in matters concerning the administration and defense of the country. In the meanwhile, the Serbs within the monarchy were won over to the Croatian cause and prepared to assist the Croats in open defiance of the Hungarian government.

The Viennese looked with growing concern upon the attempts of the South Slavs to assert their independence. At first some of the more conservative circles were inclined to blame the unreasonable and tyrannical nationalization policies of the Magyars for the troubles in Croatia. They regarded Jelačić as a savior who almost singlehandedly was rescuing the South Slav areas from anarchy.[55] However, when they learned that various South Slav nationalists were also calling the Germans their oppressors, and were complaining because the German language was given preference over the Slav tongues in their schools, some of them began to look askance at the South Slav national movement. Such impertinent assertions by an "inferior race" were too much for the conservatives, who protested that use of the German language in the secondary schools was a tremendous advantage to the Slavs because only a knowledge of German could make them part of the great cultural community of central Europe.[56]

The Viennese democrats, nearly all of whom were very sympathetic to the Hungarians, could see only evil in the anti-Hungarian movement in Croatia. They expressed the opinion that the Croatians were every bit as free as the Hungarians and charged the South Slavs with opposing the Hungarians and the Germans only because they were blind tools of reactionaries who had stirred them up to wreck the Hungarian constitution, put the South Slavs under Russian domination, and destroy

[55] *Wiener Zeitung*, No. 187 (July 8, 1848), pp. 72–73.
[56] "Antwort der Deutschen auf den Artikel: 'Der Slovenische Verein in Laibach, zur Verständigung an die Deutschen,'" *Beilage zur Wiener Zeitung*, No. 183 (July 4, 1848), pp. 5–6.

freedom everywhere in Europe. They warned the reactionaries that the nationalist volcano they had created in Croatia would in the end annihilate them as well as everyone else.[57]

The Viennese similarly denounced the Czechs for their separatist tendencies. It has already been noted that the Viennese were infuriated when Palacký refused to serve on the Frankfurt Committee of Fifty and when the Czech nationalists interfered with the elections to the Frankfurt Assembly. Early in May an effort to appoint Palacký minister of education in the Viennese cabinet added more fuel to the fire. The Austro-Germans violently protested this proposal:[58]

A Czech as head of the German University of Vienna! What a reward that would be for the students for their March victories. The whole proposal seems to be so Metternich-Sedlnitzky-like that it looks as if these gentlemen made it to increase the antipathy between the Austrians and Bohemians and to reward the Czechs for their "black-yellowness."

Palacký did not become minister of education, but other things fanned the flames of hatred and suspicion of the Czechs. As April turned into May, Czech extremists grew increasingly vocal about their distaste for the Germans.[59] When Count Ficquelmont was forced to resign as minister-president on May 4, the Czech nationalists proposed that the Emperor be invited to Prague, where the Viennese rabble could not rob him of his freedom. On May 20 the President of the Bohemian Government, Count Leo Thun, who had replaced Count Rudolf Stadion[60] during the preceding month, openly proclaimed that he would obey no orders from Vienna that were in opposition to the wishes of the Emperor. After the Emperor fled to Innsbruck, the Bohemians hastened to assure him that if he would move his residence to Prague they would guarantee him complete freedom of action. On May 29 Count Thun created a separate provisional government in Prague, with a governmental council which included some Czechs.[61] At the same time Czech demands for the conversion of the Habsburg monarchy into a federal state rang louder and louder.[62]

[57] *Constitution*, No. 36 (May 3, 1848), pp. 567–68; Adolf Eisenthal, "Proclamation," Vienna, April 27, 1848, *ibid.*, No. 35 (May 2, 1848), p. 536.
[58] *Wanderer*, No. 115 (May 13, 1848), p. 4; Univ. Colo. 1848 Coll., No. II/215.
[59] [Franz Graf von Hartig], *Genesis der Revolution*, pp. 309–10.
[60] For a brief time in the spring the Bohemians hoped that Archduke Francis Joseph would succeed Stadion as head of the Bohemian government.
[61] Maximilian Bach, *Geschichte der Wiener Revolution*, pp. 526–34; *Wiener Zeitung*, No. 154 (June 3, 1848), p. 731.
[62] *Wiener Zeitung*, No. 154 (June 3, 1848), p. 732.

The Viennese Ministry, which first learned from Czech newspapers of the creation of the new Prague government, vigorously asserted the unconstitutionality of this measure and ordered the President of the Bohemian Government not to comply with it.[63] For their part, the Austro-Germans berated the Czechs for their gross ingratitude[64] to the benevolent Germans. They charged the Czechs with attacking innocent Germans and with opposing the efforts made at Frankfurt to unite Germany merely to arouse the Germans to fight.[65] They also expressed the opinion that it was not the Czechs but diabolical reactionaries who were responsible for stirring up the nationalist agitation in Bohemia. This theme was elaborated by the democratic sheet the *Wahrheit*:[66]

The idea of your nationality did not originate with you. Years ago, when you began to play politics with your language in order to exalt your individuality—even then I do not believe that the impulse came from you. Foreign gardeners spread manure on your soil, not to grow flowers and roses for you, but to cultivate poisonous plants to destroy the national life germinating in Austria. You have gained advantages from it. You have developed your language and have adapted your culture to your native home. We express our thanks and gratitude to you for this. The sympathy you showed us at the beginning proves that you knew nothing about the evil intentions of those who have separated you from us. But those who lead you by the nose decided something entirely different. They undermined and agitated so long that you let yourselves be persuaded that Austria's liberation and Germanization are objectionable. The artifice was successful, and you deceived people allowed them to take away your happiness and are taking steps against your own well-being.

Do you know who these masters are? They wear long pigtails, have long noses, and are called aristocrats, or, to put it plainly, reactionaries.

And while you thought that you could use them as tools of the fanaticism with which you have inoculated and inculcated yourselves and while you fondly imagined that you could use them for your purposes, you were slyly being outwitted by them, since they are the original fanatics who are using your madness for their own self-preservation. They are using you as a tool to carry out their aristocratic aims by involving you (I shudder to say it) in a civil war. As a preliminary to this, they have already led you to denying

---

[63] *Ibid.*, p. 731.

[64] For a good example of the bitter hatred of the German democrats for the Czechs, see Anton Füster, *Memoiren vom März 1848 bis Juli 1849*, Vol. II, pp. 4–5.

[65] Lugano, *op. cit.*, p. 27.

[66] "An die Czechen," *Wahrheit*, No. 5 (June 8, 1848), pp. 17–18, Univ. Colo. 1848 Coll., No. II/217a.

your citizenship in a cowardly manner by inducing you to go to the Emperor in Innsbruck as persons who did not share in the battle for freedom in Vienna. Such callous degradation must make you ignominious to the whole world and also in the eyes of the Emperor himself.

These restless mentors will lead you still further astray. You will then curse in vain when the whole world around you, which is now still gladly sharing every good fortune with you, fully enjoys a secure freedom while you and your phantom of Pan-Slavism lie in ruins. Save yourselves while the game is still not lost, for you have only partly succumbed to the Jesuit poison of the aristocratic reactionaries.

The Czechs were also alluded to as the false Girondists of the Austrian revolution. Some Viennese Germans maintained that, just like the French Girondists, the Czech party was intriguing with the court to destroy the German people. The Czechs were stirring up the provinces to make war against revolutionary Vienna just as the Girondists incited the inhabitants of the Vendée against Paris. The French Girondists, said the Viennese, were at least honest. But the Czech Girondists were playing a false game. They were bowing to the aristocrats and intriguing with the Camarilla, while at the same time protesting their liberal convictions. They were trying to deceive the German provinces and exploit the aristocrats in order to win control of the rest of the monarchy and destroy Germanism. Was this honest? "Yes, Czech honesty!"[67]

When they learned that the Czechs had called the Pan-Slav Congress, the Germans were worried, and their disquietude increased as they followed the proceedings of the congress. Germans in Bohemia denounced the congress as high treason. After this display of Slavic unity they were more than ever convinced that only a close union with Germany could save them from Slav domination.[68]

A showdown was impending. For weeks Prague had been the scene of noisy demonstrations and rowdy brawls between Czechs and Germans. The Pan-Slav Congress inflamed the Czech extremists all the more. Serious disturbances of the peace seemed imminent, and the military commandant, General Windischgrätz, made preparations to deal with them.[69] The Prague garrison was put on an alarm basis, and reinforcements were summoned.

[67] Joseph Hrczka, "Unsere Girondisten," *Constitution*, No. 61 (June 5, 1848), pp. 766–67.

[68] *Constitution*, No. 52 (May 24, 1848), p. 703.

[69] Hermann Kriebel, *Ueber die Bezwingung innerer Unruhen, nach den Erfahrungen der Geschichte in der ersten Hälfte des XIX. Jahrhunderts,* in *Beiträgen für die Geschichte der Jahre 1848–49,* ed. Prince Franz zu Windisch-Grätz, p. 13.

The Beginning of the Way Back

When the news of Windischgrätz' defensive preparations spread through Prague, the Czech nationalists scurried around for arms and ammunition to protect themselves against the Germans and the hated general who had argued that the March revolution in Vienna should be put down by force. On June 11 the students demanded two thousand guns, with ammunition and a battery for the use of the student legion. Windischgrätz peremptorily rejected their request, saying that all munitions in the city were needed by the regular troops. Thereupon the students made a stirring appeal to the citizens of Prague for support, arguing that every caution needed to be taken against those who wanted again to put the Czechs in chains.

The next day a large crowd of people assembled in the city to participate in the celebration of a "Slavic mass." During the festivities a fight broke out between the radicals and the conservatives. Soon a guard detail was drawn in. During the fighting that ensued, a bullet fired at random through a window of Windischgrätz' house fatally wounded his wife. Meanwhile, barricades were rising up over Prague. The President of the government, Count Thun, tried to mediate between the students and the military, but in vain. The fighting had become too savage to be checked by an appeal to reason.

On the next day, after an uneasy truce was arranged, Windischgrätz began negotiating with the insurrectionists in the hope that he could induce them to capitulate without further bloodshed, but they demanded much more in the way of concessions than the commander would approve. Growing impatient at the refusal of the rebels to lay down their arms, Windischgrätz placed the city under a state of siege and demanded hostages. Infuriated by the general's demands, the Czech extremists broke the truce on the 16th. Immediately Windischgrätz ordered such a fierce day-and-night bombardment of the city that on the 17th the students surrendered unconditionally. The political clubs were closed at once, the National Guard was dissolved, and several hundred people were arrested.

The suppression of the Czech revolt was the first real victory of the Habsburgs against the revolution. It encouraged reactionaries to think that by biding their time they could eventually crush the revolution elsewhere in the monarchy. With the overthrow of the Prague extremists, the way lay open for the conservative groups in Bohemia to make an alliance with the Emperor against the Viennese.

Nevertheless, most Austro-Germans failed to appreciate the significance of this victory, which was, in fact, a turning point in the revolution. The Germans in Bohemia believed that Windischgrätz had bombarded Prague as a favor to them and showered him with gratitude. Many of the Viennese democrats felt that the Czechs had richly deserved their defeat.[70] A few Viennese democrats shuddered at the thought that if[71]

Windischgrätz had been with us on the 15th or 26th of May, the most earnest protests of the Aula would have been rejected, many a young heart now beating loudly for freedom would be covered with grass, and many a house, now a temple of freedom, would have been burned down by shells that spare nothing. A mercenary and a shameless aristocrat like Windischgrätz, to whom no one less than a baron is a person, spares nothing if he considers it too modern. His aim is absolutism. Despotism and rule by the aristocracy are his ideal.

Although the Viennese radicals still hated Windischgrätz as much as ever, the general feeling prevailed in Vienna that Prague was where he rightly belonged. As a certain A. Schumacher wrote in an article on "The Czech Conspiracy in Prague":[72]

Prince Windischgrätz is hardly the man to maintain peace in any part of our country. The mere mention of his name, the mere rumor that he is coming near, has been enough to turn the citizens of Vienna into fanatics. But in Prague he was in his place. He was not sent there by a constitutional Ministry. He did not represent the law or the people. He himself said that he was not dependent on the Ministry. He had come to cut ripe stalks of grain and to bind the sheaves of death. Windischgrätz was well fitted for that. As the absolute tool of an absolute will, he stood on the very soil where he throve. It was not a question of holding down a conspiracy. It was a question of hurrying it up. He was not to prevent the Czechs from having what they wanted. He was to urge them on. The revolt had to come. Windischgrätz was better qualified for it than anyone else.

In the same vein the radical *Volksfreund* commented:[73]

The events in Prague, on the whole, seem to have confused the public and the newspapers all the more since the battle has ended and there is no longer any possibility that fighting will again break out. The Czechs (when we say Czechs we mean the insane or corrupt Slav party of the Czechs,

[70] See especially Paul Müller, *Feldmarschall Fürst Windischgrätz. Revolution und Gegenrevolution in Österreich*, pp. 118–19.

[71] "Windischgrätz," *Wiener Tageblatt*, No. 15 (June 23, 1848), p. 1.

[72] A. Schumacher, "Die Czechenverschwörung in Prag," *Oesterreichisches Volksblatt*, No. 9 (June 24, 1848), p. 33, Univ. Colo. 1848 Coll., No. II/155.

[73] "Noch einmal Windischgrätz und die Prager Ereignisse," *Volksfreund*, No. 43 (June 24, 1848), pp. 174–75, Univ. Colo. 1848 Coll., No. II/210b.

which, in union with another insane or corrupt party, has designs on turn-ing and uses every conceivable means—even a barbaric union with Russia if it would be necessary—to turn Austria into a Slav empire, at the expense of the Germans and Hungarians) this Slav party has been defeated on the field of battle, and Windischgrätz has remained the victor. Because of the great and justified embitterment of all Germans over the Slavic association of lunatics in Prague, the prospects have become great since his victory that Windischgrätz may even become a popular and much-loved man, for peo-ple suspect the wild, hate-brewing, fear-inspiring doings of the Czech party, with all their armed Swornost League, too much not to be happy that a powerful fist has finally given this party a death blow.

We must not, therefore, be surprised over the satisfaction that was first expressed over Prince Windischgrätz's victory. This satisfaction was uni-versal, and the *Volksfreund* shared in it and still does. For this victory can be decisive, not only for the fate of the Germans in Prague and in all Bo-hemia, but for the fate of all Bohemia, if it is sensibly used in a spirit of freedom and if the corpses of the defeated Czech party have served to avert a civil war. Furthermore, the victory in Prague can have the best consequences, not only for Bohemia, but also for Hungary and Transyl-vania and for the whole monarchy, for we know only too well how a victory for the Czech party would have encouraged, intoxicated, and spurred on to the utmost degree all the Slavs in the monarchy. The victory over the Czech party in Prague is and remains a joyful event. A victory for German concerns in Bohemia and in the monarchy can never be a misfortune, for the Germans bring humanity and freedom to the conquered. A small, de-feated party like the Czechs, over against whom there will always be forty million Germans, can be well satisfied with this price. Whether Win-dischgrätz fought in the name of and for German matters is another ques-tion. It is a question over which the opinions of our newspapers are now divided. Unfortunately most of them have fallen into the error of assuming that Windischgrätz has all of a sudden become a hero and a front-rank fighter for the party of retrogression (reaction).

The Czech rebels had no sympathizers in Vienna. The Italian in-surgents, however, still had quite a few partisans among the Viennese democrats in the summer of 1848, even though the favorable progress of the war in Italy had made them less numerous and less vocal than in the spring. The Italians did not follow up their resounding victories in March with a strong drive to oust the Austrian troops from the penin-sula. Marshal Radetzky was left undisturbed long enough for him to re-group his troops and obtain reinforcements. By May the Habsburg forces were strong enough to begin a successful counteroffensive against the Italians. On May 29 Radetzky defeated them at Cartatone, and on June 10 at Vicenza.[74]

Meanwhile, the French Foreign Office was putting pressure on the Habsburgs to end the Italian war as soon as possible. The British were urging them to appease the Italians by giving up Lombardy. The Habsburgs would retain only Venetia. Since the Ministry in Vienna also cherished the hope of making an armistice with the Italian insurgents, it sent a trusted emissary, Karl von Schnitzer, to Casati, the head of the Milanese provisional government, to inform him that the Habsburgs would agree to the independence of Lombardy if the Lombards would assume a fair portion of the state debt, make appropriate commercial treaties, respect the private property of the imperial family, and indemnify the Austrian officers and officials who had suffered losses in the rebellion. However, when Casati demanded that the South Tyrol and Venetia also be given to Lombardy and insisted that the Italian question had to be settled by all the Italian people, the negotiations abruptly ended[75] and Radetzky resumed the campaign. Rapidly he captured Treviso, Padua, and Rovigo. On July 23 to 25 he inflicted a crushing defeat on the Piedmontese at Custozza, and on August 8 he reentered Milan in triumph. By now Charles Albert had had enough, and on August 9 the Sardinians signed an armistice in which Piedmont pledged herself no longer to support Lombardy-Venetia.[76]

When the Habsburg troops began to win victories in Italy, Field Marshal Radetzky and his men gained the admiration and respect of most Viennese.[77] Furthermore, after the Lombard provisional government rejected the peace proposals in June, many Viennese who had formerly advocated self-determination for the Italians joined those who had always favored the war in Italy. By the summer of 1848, a large number of Austro-Germans had come to the point of view that the

[74] Rudolf Kiszling, *Fürst Felix zu Schwarzenberg. Der politische Lehrmeister Kaiser Franz Josephs* (hereafter cited throughout as *Schwarzenberg*), pp. 31–32.

[75] Alfred Ritter von Arneth, *Johann Freiherr von Wessenberg. Ein österreichischer Staatsmann des neunzehnten Jahrhunderts* (hereafter cited throughout as *Wessenberg*), Vol. II, pp. 231–37; Ferdinand Strobl von Ravelsberg, *Feldmarschall Radetzky. Sein Leben und Wirken* (hereafter cited throughout as *Radetzky*), pp. 22–23; Kiszling, *op. cit.*, pp. 34–37.

[76] Arneth, *op. cit.*, Vol., II, p. 247; Kiszling, *op. cit.*, pp. 37–38.

[77] Note, for instance, the article "Italien," *Wahrheit*, No. 13 (June 17, 1848), p. 50, Univ. Colo. 1848 Coll., No. II/217b; and the flattering praise of Radetzky and his troops in the speech given by Folwarczny at Krems on August 19, 1848, Univ. Colo. 1848 Coll., No. II/172. The Viennese especially applauded Radetzky after the Emperor awarded him the Grand Cross of the Maria Theresia Order on July 28 for his victories in Italy. Emperor Ferdinand to Radetzky, Innsbruck, July 22, 1848, Ravelsberg, *op. cit.*, p. 56.

Italian insurgents must be crushed, not only for the sake of the Habsburg empire, but for the sake of all Germany as well.[78] In ever larger numbers they began to ask:[79]

How long will it be before people in Germany, in Vienna, and in the Viennese Ministry will understand that the Lombardo-Venetian region is the same for Austria, and through Austria for Germany, as Alsace is for France, that the Po is the same for us as the Upper Rhine is for the French, that Venice is the same here as Strassburg is there, and that the line of the Mincio and the Adige is the same for Germany as the French border fortresses on the Left Bank of the Rhine and on the Belgian frontier are for France?

The extreme left in Vienna refused to join in the general acclaim of Radetzky.[80] They feared that the successes in the Apennine peninsula would strengthen his influence over the affairs of the monarchy, a frightening prospect, for to them the General was an out-and-out reactionary, an enemy of freedom, and a Russian hireling.[81] Furthermore, many Viennese democrats still felt that as a matter of principle the Habsburgs should give their Italian subjects a right to determine their own affairs. Also, some believed that the German empire that was to come into being would be much stronger if Austria retained only the wholly German portions of her former possessions in Italy, like the South Tyrol and Istria.[82]

On August 14, after the signing of the truce in Italy, a Parliament deputy named Selinger moved that a rising vote of thanks be given to Radetzky's victorious army in Italy.[83] While the deputies of the center stood up and cheered, the deputies on the left (most of them Viennese) remained seated in ominous silence. The left and right (mostly Czechs and Galicians) then joined together to defeat the motion.[84]

---

[78] Dr. E. E. Sch——r, "Frankreich's Einrücken in Oesterreichisch-Italien sei ein *causus belli* für Deutschland," *Beilage zur Wiener Zeitung*, No. 221 (August 12, 1848), pp. 55–56.

[79] "Die Italienische Frage," *Wiener Zeitung*, No. 165 (June 15, 1848), p. 781.

[80] Vitzthum von Eckstädt to his mother, Vienna, August 11, 1848, Vitzthum von Eckstädt, *op. cit.*, p. 135; Hübner diary, Vienna, July 29, 1848, Alexander Grafen von Hübner, *Ein Jahr meines Lebens 1848–1849*, p. 183.

[81] Helfert, *Der Wiener Parnass im Jahr 1848*, p. lxi; *Constitution*, No. 52 (May 24, 1848), pp. 703–704.

[82] *Constitution*, No. 73 (June 20, 1848), p. 862.

[83] The Austrian Parliament began its session on July 22.

[84] Minutes of the 21st Session of Parliament, August 14, 1848, *Wiener Zeitung*, No. 223 (August 15, 1848), pp. 400–401; "Der Selinger'sche Antrag und die Armee," *Beilag zur Wiener Zeitung*, No. 225 (August 17, 1848), p. 59. The left objected to the proposal partly because their sympathies were still with the Italians but also because they looked upon it as a glorification of war and as an attempt

The division of public opinion in regard to the Hungarians was roughly along the same lines as that in regard to the Italians. In general, the conservative and moderate Viennese were inclined to criticize the Magyars, whereas the radicals, true to their liberal-national convictions, tended to favor them. But, as had been true in regard to the Italians, public opinion was considerably less favorable to the Magyars in the summer of 1848 than in April. In ever increasing numbers the Austro-Germans became bitter over the fact that the Hungarians had an independent ministry. They also grew fearful that the Hungarians were striving for complete separation from the Habsburg monarchy and were seeking to extend their own absolutist rule over most of the Habsburg lands in eastern and southeastern Europe. It seemed that no matter how conciliatory the Germans might be, the Hungarians would refuse to compromise either with them or with the other nationalities in the monarchy.[85]

The Magyars still had ardent defenders in the Habsburg capital, who felt their moves for independence were justified. The refusal to send troops to Italy, for which many Viennese criticized them, was defended on the ground that the Hungarians had to protect themselves against the Croatians, Slovenes, Slovaks, and other nationalities whom Russian agitators had stirred up against them.[86] The chief argument of the ultraradical champions of the Magyars in Vienna was that the Germans must always work hard to strengthen the Hungarians because only a strong, democratic Hungary united with a free, democratic German-Austria could thwart Slav aspirations to dominate the Habsburg monarchy.[87]

Obviously, by the summer of 1848 the nationality problem was becoming a serious threat not only to the Habsburg monarchy but also to the successful outcome of the whole revolution. On the one hand, the Czechs, Poles, Hungarians, and Italians were aspiring to destroy the dominant position the Germans held in the empire, and the Croats, Slovenes, Serbs, and Slovaks were struggling to throw off the yoke of the dominant Magyars. On the other hand, all but a small handful of Ger-

---

of the Ministry to get parliamentary approval for unlimited credit for the prosecution of the war. The right, constituted mainly of Czechs and Poles, looked upon the Italian war as a fight against nationalism.

[85] "Die Ungarischen Fragen," *Wiener Zeitung,* No. 179 (June 30, 1848), p. 856.

[86] M. Töletényi, "Ungarn," *Constitution,* No. 36 (May 3, 1848), p. 567–68; "Ungarn," *Wahrheit,* No. 5 (June 8, 1848), p. 19, Univ. Colo. 1848 Coll., No. II/217a.

[87] "Verhältniss zwischen Oesterreich und Ungarn," *Beilage zur Wiener Zeitung,* No. 193 (July 14, 1848), p. 19; Lugano, *op. cit.,* p. 23.

The Beginning of the Way Back

mans were determined to defend their hegemony throughout central Europe. Unless some way could be found to allay the bitter antagonisms the revolution had unleashed between Germans and non-Germans and to reconcile the fundamental differences between them, a violent struggle for supremacy was imminent.

At least a few Viennese appear to have realized that the nationality question was explosive and could end in a tragic civil war similar to the Wars of Religion or the Thirty Years' War. Those aware of the danger tried to ward it off by admonishing their fellow-citizens "not to be led astray by the cry for nationality."[88] By and large, however, the Austro-Germans were incapable of understanding that, to non-Germans, "freedom" meant freedom from age-old German domination as well as from absolutism. Their feelings of superiority prevented them from admitting that the aspirations of subject nationalities for freedom were as natural and honest as the longings of the Germans for political liberation. If it ever occurred to them that their Germanism was isolating them from the other nations in the monarchy, they were not in the least concerned. They looked to the German, not the Austrian, Empire for salvation and believed that it would protect them against any threat to their supremacy.

Thus, unwittingly and indifferently, the German radicals permitted the Habsburg court and the imperial army to exploit to their own advantage the acute national differences in the empire. After the bombardment of Prague and suppression of the democratic movement in Bohemia, General Windischgrätz, who had long been stirring up his troops against the Viennese "anarchists," did not conceal his hopes that the army could be turned against the radicals. During the summer of 1848 he made Prague a rallying point for an army with which he intended to subdue the revolutionaries in the Habsburg capital when the opportune moment was at hand. He was in constant touch with the court at Innsbruck and with other army leaders and sent emissaries to organize the necessary forces. Marshal Radetzky, who was also in close contact with Windischgrätz and the court, threw his influence against the government in Vienna. As the summer went on, General Jelačić too came into a more intimate relationship with the court. Thus the imperial court became the center of the intrigues to weaken and eventually to destroy the revolution.[89]

[88] "Nationalität," *Wiener Zeitung*, No. 160 (June 9, 1848), p. 758.
[89] Müller, *op. cit.*, pp. 127–30; Bach, *op. cit.*, pp. 566–74; Heinrich Reschauer and Moritz Smets, *Das Jahr 1848. Geschichte der Wiener Revolution*, Vol. II, pp. 387–89; Endres, *Revolution in Österreich*, 127–28.

In June, although the imperial court was beginning to make counter-revolutionary plans, it responded to the unceasing clamor of the Viennese for the Emperor's return to the capital by sending the popular Archduke John there to act as his deputy. This decision was announced in an imperial manifesto on June 16. The Emperor's subjects were told that his "personal health" did not permit him "to undertake the trip to Vienna now." However, in order not to delay the convocation of Parliament or hinder the necessary co-operation between the sovereign and his Ministry, His Majesty had decided to send his "dear uncle" to Vienna as his representative, with "full powers not only to open Parliament but also to look after all matters of government requiring the Emperor's decision" until he himself could return to Vienna.[90]

Although a few Viennese suspected that behind the Emperor's refusal to come to Vienna lay some kind of plot,[91] the great masses of people joyously greeted the news that the "great commoner" and his bourgeois wife were returning to act in the Emperor's name.[92] Extensive preparations were made to welcome him to the city on the 23rd—the day announced for his arrival. However, the Archduke deliberately delayed his arrival so that he could enter the Hofburg unnoticed on the evening of the 24th. On the next day he issued a proclamation promising that the rights and freedoms of the people would be protected and calling on them to co-operate in preserving peace and order.[93] Then followed a round of meetings with the National Guard officers, the City Council, the Security Council, and many other groups. On the 27th an impressive procession was organized in the Archduke's honor.[94]

Archduke John was so busy attending the various ceremonies given for him and receiving the numerous deputies sent to him by groups of admirers that he scarcely had time to tend to affairs of state. Then on July 2 word came to Vienna that on June 29 he had been appointed imperial regent of Germany.[95] The news created a great sensation.[96]

---

[90] Emperor Ferdinand, "Proclamation," Innsbruck, June 16, 1848, *Volksfreund,* No. 40 (June 21, 1848), p. 164, Univ. Colo. 1848 Coll., No. II/210.

[91] "Erzherzog Johann kommt," *ibid.,* p. 161.

[92] Friedrich Kaiser, *Memoiren,* p. 103.

[93] Reschauer and Smets, *op. cit.,* Vol. II, p. 416.

[94] *Zopf und Schwert. Volksblatt,* No. 1 [June 30, 1848], pp. 3–4, Univ. Colo. 1848 Coll., No. II/235. This paper, edited by "Götz and Vansen" and published by Klopf and Eurich, lasted only from June 30 to July 10.

[95] The official delegation notifying the Archduke of his appointment arrived in Vienna on July 4. Archduke John formally accepted the office the next day.

[96] Vitzthum von Eckstädt to his mother, Vienna, July 4, 1848, Vitzthum von Eckstädt, *op. cit.,* p. 120; Stiles, *op. cit.,* Vol. I, pp. 146–47.

The Beginning of the Way Back

The Archduke departed for Frankfurt on July 8, promising to return to Vienna on July 17 to officiate at the opening ceremonies of the Austrian Parliament.

On the same day he left for Frankfurt, Archduke John dismissed the Pillersdorf ministry. By early July Pillersdorf had become generally disliked,[97] especially by the Viennese democrats. There had been many complaints about his lack of energy and his Ministry's weakness and irresolution.[98] His failure to proceed more energetically in behalf of the Prague democrats in June was now bitterly denounced by the Viennese radicals, even though only the month before most of them had applauded Windischgrätz' bombardment of Prague.[99] The democrats were also angry because the Pillersdorf ministry had issued an order that the members of Parliament were to be elected by indirect rather than direct elections. When the government announced that it had taken over the task of drawing up a provisional order of business for Parliament, they were still more incensed. To the ultraradicals this was an act of betrayal[100] that could have been committed only by an "unscrupulous agent of the Camarilla" and a "shameless middleman and go-between of the aristocrats."[101]

The Democratic Club took the first overt steps that led to the overthrow of the Pillersdorf government. At a meeting on the evening of July 7 the club members resolved to send a deputation to Archduke John the next morning to demand the dismissal of the Ministry. The deputation received a surprisingly friendly reception and unexpected support. In fact, the Archduke went so far as to tell the deputation that he had long felt that Pillersdorf was unfit for the job of minister-president. Upon these assurances of the Archduke's sympathies, the deputies hurried to the Security Committee to report this conversation. The committee hastily voted 147 to 6 that it no longer had any trust in Pillersdorf. It then dispatched its own deputation to the Archduke to tell him of the vote and to urge him to name the still-popular Minister of Commerce, Baron Doblhoff, to the post of minister-president. The deputation returned soon afterward with the news that Archduke John had just ac-

---

[97] Eduard Bauernfeld, *Erinnerungen aus Alt-Wien*, p. 293.

[98] See especially "Das neue Ministerium Pillersdorf," *Volksfreund*, No. 40 (June 21, 1848), p. 162, Univ. Colo. 1848 Coll., No. II/210.

[99] "Das Ministerium hat abgedankt!" *Extrablatt zur Constitution*, 2:00 P.M., July 8, 1848.

[100] *Constitution*, No. 85 (July 6, 1848), pp. 957–59, gives an example of the hysterical denunciations heaped upon Pillersdorf by the extreme left.

[101] "Das Ministerium hat abgedankt!"

cepted Pillersdorf's resignation and had charged Baron Doblhoff with creating a new ministry.[102]

Baron Doblhoff sent to the Archduke at Frankfurt a list of the proposed new ministers,[103] which was published on July 19, two days after John returned to Vienna. Baron Doblhoff accepted the office of minister of interior and temporarily that of education, but upon his own request he was not made minister-president. That post was reserved for Baron Wessenberg, an old diplomat who had had long years of experience in the Habsburg diplomatic service and had been minister of foreign affairs in the previous cabinet. Wessenberg also retained the portfolio of foreign affairs. The opportunistic liberal lawyer Alexander von Bach joined the government as minister of justice, while the radical editor of the *Allgemeine österreichische Zeitung*, Ernst von Schwarzer, assumed the post of minister of public works. The silk-manufacturer and spokesman of the Manufacturers' Association, Theodor Hornbostel, succeeded Doblhoff as minister of commerce. Count Latour continued as minister of war, and Baron Krauss retained the position of minister of finance.[104]

Thus four of the old ministers—Doblhoff, Latour, Krauss, and Wessenberg—remained, whereas three—Pillersdorf, Sommaruga, and Baumgartner—left the Ministry. With the appointment of Bach, Hornbostel, and Schwarzer, the new government was considered appreciably more radical than the former one, and the democrats greeted it with loud applause. The moderate liberals looked upon it with reserve, and the conservatives were quite disturbed by it.[105]

In actual fact, the appointment of the new Ministry changed nothing. The new government was weak and incapable of halting the growing disintegration of the monarchy. Vitzthum von Eckstädt aptly described the state of affairs in the monarchy when he wrote:[106]

Here again we have a new ministry that promises just as little firmness as the previous ones. A motley colorless group has been thrown together. It is without power and unity. The imperial vicar's departure for Frankfurt is imminent. The Emperor is so feeble and in such pain that for the time being we cannot think of his coming here. Archduke Francis Charles is impossible. We are living in a monarchy without monarchs.

[102] Protocol of the Security Committee, morning session, July 8, 1848, *Wiener Zeitung*, No. 190 (July 11, 1848), p. 104; *Constitution*, No. 88 (July 10, 1848), p. 984; Hartig, *op. cit.*, pp. 329–30.

[103] *Wiener Zeitung*, No. 194 (July 15, 1848), p. 141.

[104] *Ibid.*, No. 198 (July 19, 1848), p. 177.

[105] Zenker, *op. cit.*, p. 100.

[106] Letter from Vienna, July 26, 1848, Vitzthum von Eckstädt, *op. cit.*, p. 124.

The Beginning of the Way Back

To make the situation even more appalling, by July there were actually[107]

seven governments within the Austrian monarchy: a provisional and loyal one in Vienna—a provisional one at Prague*—an independent royal one at Pesth—a rebel one at Agram—a provisional one at Milan—and a republican one at Venice. If one adds the fashionable Camarilla at Innsbruck there is a wicked seventh. Too many cooks spoil the broth! And still it seems that there is no governing at all in poor old Austria. Complete anarchy (political confusion) faces us at every turn.

Given this state of confusion, people were wondering, "Tomorrow will we live to see from Parliament a proclamation of the republic, the appointment of a regent, or the coronation of John I? Or will there be barricades?" To one observer who asked this question it already seemed clear that, "sooner or later, be it from Verona, Prague, or Agram, the savior in need will appear with bayonets and cannon to create order."[108] Even some of the radicals, who had been victorious on the barricades in May, were beginning to suspect in July "that every new gain brings us closer to destruction."[109] By midsummer an unhealthy cynicism like that reflected in the following article, "Are We Better Off?" was replacing the boundless enthusiasm prevailing during the early days of the revolution:[110]

I am a visionary—a fool and a dreamer, if you wish. Why shouldn't I tell you that first? Every morning when I stretch my legs out of bed after a good sleep and after I've said the Austrian Lord's Prayer, which, as you well know, begins with the words, "Our Father, who are in Innsbruck, come back to thine kingdom and do not lead thy people into temptation, etc.," then my first thought is: What kind of a face is our dear Fatherland making today? How are the dear striped petticoats of the two ladies Cibini and Sturmfeder? What are the doctors saying about the stomach-ache of our people? Have the Hungarians drunk a brotherly toast with their Croatian comrades? And apropos Windischgrätz! My dear faithful Bombardier Windischgrätz! How is he after that nicely executed game of bullets, which even Rappo couldn't have done better? And the Italian war? The shirt I am putting on is a horror to my eyes. I should give it to the

---

[107] "Sieben Regierungen in Oesterreich," *Volksfreund,* No. 40 (June 21, 1848), p. 162, Univ. Colo. 1848 Coll., No. II/210.
* No longer exists. (Footnote in the original.)
[108] Vitzthum von Eckstädt to his uncle, Vienna, July 28, 1848, Vitzthum von Eckstädt, *op. cit.,* p. 127.
[109] Hübner diary, Vienna, July 31, 1848, Hübner, *op. cit.,* pp. 184–85.
[110] "Steht es schon besser mit uns?" *Zopf und Schwert,* No. 1 (June 30, 1848), pp. 2–3; Univ. Colo. 1848 Coll., No. II/235.

Minister of War so it can wander to Italy to the "shirtless defenders of the Fatherland,"[111] for whose equipment the "man in London"[112] had millions on the books! And the state debt—that terrible ghost, that oppressive and worrying nightmare of our present time? And the first Parliament, which is flying the black-yellow banner at its door?

Are we already better off?

One would like to pull the covers up over the tip of his sleeping cap, sullenly and in ill-humor, and sleep and sleep. That's how well off we are! The air weighs upon us uncannily. In spite of freedom of the press, a constitutional imperial assembly, and a democratic monarchy, we breathe with difficulty. And why? Why must an unfortunate Fatherland, whose predicament cannot be compared with that of any other in history, suffer? We are not standing with pure souls in our holy struggle. Let us each of us admit whether he has not often been overcome with a despair as dark as hell itself over the future of Austria and whether the thought that the monarchy is out of step has not, momentarily at least, discouraged him and made him shudder. No one seems to have any real confidence in himself. I mean no one has a confidence strong as the rocks themselves that things must get better for us! Everyone is screaming, declaiming, parading, and trotting over the field of words. With us, true, genuine, sound radicalism is more of a phantom than a reality. The word, the genuine word of action, is nowhere basically understood. The old Austrian irresolution still haunts each of us. And truly, if you believe and fear that streams of blood are necessary for radicalism to attain its goal, then we shout out a thousand times, "No! You are mistaken!"

This much history has already taught us: Blood is not the cement that holds together the structure of progress. Radicalism does not need corpses; it conquers by its principles. Listen, therefore, you radicals of every color! We do not expect much from your work in the first Parliament! Many of you have unclean hearts! We are already seeing traitors, apostates, and deserters in your midst. Corruption, sociability, and persuasion will do the rest. But curses upon everyone who, when examining himself to see whether he is pure, backs away from himself and from the spirit of the times if he finds that he is not a radical! That group of real, sound, loyal, and ever loyal radicals will be small and very easy to break down in the first Parliament. For this reason we look forward to it with fear and say:

We are by no means better off.

Meanwhile, life went on in Vienna more or less in the groove described by the writer of the following article:[113]

---

[111] In the spring and summer of 1848 the Viennese were bombarded with appeals to send money, clothing, and equipment to the Habsburg soldiers in Italy.
[112] Metternich.
[113] "Unsere Zustände," *Schwefeläther,* No. 1 (August 4, 1848), pp. 1–2, Univ. Colo. 1848 Coll., No. II/187a.

The Beginning of the Way Back

Our Conditions

Anyone who doesn't live in Pannigl Street in Wieden must admit that conditions are not nearly as depressing here as they appear to be. Only if he looks at the windows of the different houses as he passes through the streets does he see what a gloomy fate is in store for Vienna. Otherwise everything still has the merry old physiognomy.

The customhouse, postal, and municipal officials are just as rude as ever before, and there are enough other people, too, who make the complete beautification of the city impossible.

The people in Vienna are now being divided in general into those who have already received a mock serenade and those who are about to get one. The former have a certain moral superiority over the latter, and thus there is continuous tension between the two parties, and often at various meeting places parliamentary method is violated. The parliamentary method is also one of our acquisitions. It means that no one may beat up another person, no matter what stupid stuff he chatters, but may merely call him an ass.

In conformity with this main division, the people fall into three classes: the radicals, the liberals, and the conservatives. The radicals everywhere make a point of their radicalism. That is why they tore out so many trees on the glacis and the bastions on May 26. They are doing the most proselytizing, for to them only the right of reason is valid. That is all well and good with many people who, if their tailors lay claim to certain articles of clothing, simply show their membership card for some radical club and say, "Sir, there is no historic right." The liberals are also called the moderate party. They are very much like crickets and grasshoppers, for with them one also always thinks that the chirping comes from their mouths, whereas it is really made merely by rubbing their wings together. In politics they are the same as in life, and in real life they never drink more than one mug of beer, and eat ten rolls with it. Finally, the conservatives are those who now prefer to hang their heads. But this is chiefly because they are being dragged along like calves on the wagon of time. They have another characteristic similar to that of another animal in that they can't stand the color red. Their chief talent lies in tearing down liberal posters. In addition, they write placards against the Jews and posters urging peace, order, and security; send deputations to Innsbruck; and make themselves a laughingstock in every possible way. They always stand still and hold on to their coattails so they won't accidentally take a step forward. They might be pictured as huge human stomachs held up by two legs. This division of mankind was brought about by the new order of things, just like the street corner debate between Mr. Haffner and Anton Langer, and just like the fraternization festivity in the Augarten, where the press was said to be unbridled and yet is continually being harassed.

These fraternization festivities are likewise a new invention of our times.

They may be defined in the following way: "Get intoxicated in the easiest possible way." Their aim is actually to make all men brothers. That is why the guests usually beat each other up toward the end of the festivities.

With regard to more remote internal affairs, like, for example, the finances, everything is going ahead at full speed. Almost no more finances are left.

The tax system is also subject to regulation. In addition to the tax, a supplementary tax has been introduced, for people live more pleasantly in social groups. The consumption tax will probably be canceled entirely and an income tax will be introduced in its place. Because of this many people are already beginning to complain that they have no income.

The organization of labor is to be expected next, and for this reason the National Guard is already busily practicing how to shoot.

Likewise, provision has been made for a good system of universal education, for the construction of a new criminal building has already been approved. With regard to our foreign affairs, we can speak as satisfactorily about them as Kossuth did about those in Hungary, since our razors come from England and we have the most friendly understanding with the inhabitants of the Cordelleras Islands.

In Italy the honor of our weapons will soon be saved. Only a couple more thousand people need to be shot down, and this will also serve to reform our army.

From Russia we have nothing to fear. There cholera is at present the minister of internal affairs. The minister knows us and will see to it that everything will be peaceful.

The French Republic means well by us. From time to time it sends us emissaries and allows very good speeches in favor of the bicameral system to be made in the National Assembly. Our relations with England are the best of all. There everything is gold. So we may be consoled and look toward an undisturbed future.

But only the next Parliament will be able to decide whether the Heumarkt bridge over the Wien will soon be completed.

By the middle of July the revolutionary front that had seemed impregnable in March had developed dangerous weak points. Czechs and Germans were eyeing each other with suspicion and hostility. The Poles and Italians were resentful of the Germans, the South Slavs were struggling against the Magyars, the Magyars were striving to loosen the ties that bound them to the Germans, and the Austro-Germans stood ready to forsake the international Habsburg monarchy for a national German empire. In Vienna large numbers of moderates were deserting the revolution for the ranks of the ultraconservatives. Thus even before the first Austrian Parliament held its opening session, the Austrians had traveled far on the road leading back from revolution to reaction.

XII. The Opening of Parliament and the Defeat of the Proletariat

T NOON ON JULY 22 the thunder of cannon announced the departure of the Emperor's deputy, Archduke John, for the opening session of Parliament.

Ever since the Emperor's promise of May 16 to convene Parliament and the decree of June 1 establishing the election procedures,[1] Viennese "democrats" had waged a lively campaign to induce the voters to elect only "liberal" deputies—"men of the people." The Security Committee had appointed a special committee to win voters for its own slate of deputies.[2] The City Council had also set up an electoral

---

[1] According to this decree, there was to be one representative for every 50,000 inhabitants. The members were to be chosen through a rather complicated system of indirect elections. Each province was to be divided into as many electoral districts as the number of representatives it was entitled to send to Parliament. These districts were to be subdivided into subdistricts of about 2,500 inhabitants, in each of which the voters were to select an elector to help choose the Parliamentary representative for the whole district. All citizens at least twenty-four years old who had lived in their voting precinct at least six months and who were not servants, daily or weekly wage-earners, or persons living on charity were entitled to vote for the electors. "Ministerial Proclamation," Vienna, June 1, 1848, *Wiener Zeitung*, No. 155 (June 4, 1848), p. 735; *ibid.*, No. 152 (June 1, 1848), p. 723. On June 10, after the radicals protested against the exclusion of the lower classes from the polls, the government passed a resolution giving the workers equal voting rights. See especially "Kein Wahlcensus!" *Oesterreichisches Volksblatt*, No. 2 (June 15, 1848), pp. 5–6, Univ. Colo. 1848 Coll., No. II/153; "Das Wahlgesetz," *Constitution*, No. 63 (June 7, 1848), p. 784; *Constitution*, No. 66 (June 10, 1848), p. 805; President of the Lower Austrian Government, "Proclamation," Vienna, June 11, 1848, *Wiener Zeitung*, No. 162 (June 12, 1848), p. 767; "Proclamation of the Viennese Security Committee to the Workers," June 11, 1848, *Wiener Zeitung*, No. 165 (June 15, 1848), p. 782. However, the government turned down the radicals' demands to substitute direct for indirect elections. See especially *Constitution*, No. 69 (June 15, 1848), p. 829; "Protest gegen die indirekten (mittelbaren) Wahlen," *Volksfreund*, No. 42 (June 23, 1848), p. 171, Univ. Colo. 1848 Coll., No. II/210a; "Direkte Wahlen," *Volksfreund*, No. 42 (June 21, 1848), p. 163, Univ. Colo. 1848 Coll., No. II/210.

[2] Protocol of the Evening Sitting of the Security Committee, June 9, 1848, *Wiener Tageblatt*, No. 6 (June 11, 1848), Univ. Colo. 1848 Coll., No. II/224.

committee. The radical newspapers had exhorted the populace to turn out en masse to ensure that "no officials, no officers, no professors, no capitalists, no clergy," no one who had prospered under the old regime would be elected.[3]

In spite of these strenuous efforts, three of the fifteen deputies chosen from Vienna[4] were members of the government (Wessenberg, Pillersdorf, and Doblhoff). Only four of the fifteen candidates recommended by the Security Committee were actually elected: Füster, Fischhof, Goldmark, and Schwarzer. The rest of the deputies were moderate or conservative in their political beliefs.[5] Thus less than one-third of the deputies chosen by the Viennese belonged to the extreme left. Of those elected in the provinces, the radicals won even a smaller minority. There were only a few "leftist" German deputies, a small sprinkling of "democratic" Poles, a handful of Italians, and at the beginning, one or two South Slav representatives.

Of all the deputies in Parliament the extreme left were the only genuine revolutionaries. They alone denied all historic rights and privileges. They alone wanted to erect a wholly new edifice constructed on democratic principles. Although they were willing to retain the monarchy, they insisted that it must be a thoroughly democratic monarchy. They also desired a highly decentralized federal state in which equal rights would be assured to all nationalities in the empire.[6]

In the center of Parliament was the largest group—the "law and order" party—which championed the program of the Ministry; most of the members were liberals, who represented a middle-of-the-road liberalism somewhere between the extremes of the left and the right. They favored a united, constitutional monarchy with the greatest possible individual freedom consonant with a strong, orderly state. Although they were first of all Austrians—not Germans, Slavs, Italians, or Poles—they demanded equal rights and duties for all citizens and for all nationalities. They believed that the legislative power should be vested in the crown and a bicameral legislature and that the monarch should have a limited veto power over all legislation. The executive power was

[3] "Guter Rath für die Wahlmänner in der Stadt und auf dem Lande," *Volksfreund*, No. 43 (June 24, 1848), p. 175, Univ. Colo. 1848 Coll., No. II/210b.
[4] The elections were held in the capital between June 13 and June 19.
[5] Maximilian Bach, *Geschichte der Wiener Revolution*, pp. 584–88; Rudolf Kiszling *et al.*, *Die Revolution im Kaisertum Österreich 1848–1849*, Vol. I, p. 158; Heinrich Reschauer and Moritz Smets, *Das Jahr 1848. Geschichte der Wiener Revolution*, Vol. II, pp. 430–34.
[6] [Ernst Violand], *Enthüllungen*, pp. 54–55; Hermann Meynert, *Geschichte der Ereignisse in der österreichischen Monarchie*, pp. 518–19.

to be exercised by the Emperor and a responsible ministry, and the judicial administration was to be conducted in the name of the Emperor.[7] On the whole, the program of the center was pretty much that of the April 25 constitution.

To the right of the center was a group of about thirty Galician peasant deputies, who "understood no single word of German." Before voting, they waited for a signal from Stadion, the governor of Galicia. In their midst were a few Hungarian peasants from Bucovina,[8] who were enemies of both the educated Poles and the more radical Germans.[9]

Also on the right were the Czech deputies. Like the other conservative members, they demanded a decentralized federal empire in which the Slavs and other nationalities would have room to develop an autonomous government. They were extremely suspicious, not only of any projected union with Germany, but of the dominant German element within the Habsburg monarchy.[10]

The middle classes were clearly ascendant in Parliament. Of all the deputies, 60 per cent belonged to the bourgeoisie; 25 per cent were peasants; and a mere handful represented the clergy and nobility. By nationality, 190 of the 383 deputies were Slavs.

It was to this highly diversified and sharply divided group that Archduke John spoke on July 22. In his opening address he emphasized the necessity for all the deputies to work together to draft a constitution. He assured them that all nationalities in the empire were considered equal by the Emperor and implied that a close union would be effected with Germany. He expressed the hope that all outstanding differences with Hungary could be mediated in an amicable manner and added that the war in Italy was being fought only "to maintain the honor of Austrian arms and to protect the legitimate interests of the state." He explained that the financial crisis of the monarchy required extraordinary measures, which the Ministry would soon propose to Parliament. At the same time, he stated his conviction that "the surest guarantee for the spiritual and material development of Austria lay in the calling together of representatives of the people" to deliberate on all matters of general interest. In conclusion, in behalf of the Emperor he wished the deputies well and declared the constituent Parliament formally open for business.[11]

[7] Meynert, *op. cit.*, pp. 516–18.

[8] Franz Pulszky, *Mein Zeit, mein Leben,* Vol. II, p. 124.

[9] Violand, *op. cit.*, p. 54.

[10] *Ibid.*, pp. 52–54; Alexander Novotny, *1848,* p. 93.

[11] Minutes of the Parliamentary Session of July 22, 1848, in Karl Schneider, *Der Reichstag von Kremsier,* pp. 25–28.

Immediately following the Archduke's speech came a reply from the President, Franz Schmitt, which had been prepared in advance. In the name of the people he thanked Ferdinand the Good for convening Parliament to work for the rebirth of the Fatherland and promised him that the opening of Parliament marked "the marriage of the illustrious constitutional throne with free, and therefore honorable, people."[12] After the President finished, the Archduke left the hall. Then Parliament adjourned until July 24.

In the summer of 1848 Parliament did not live up to the high hopes aroused by the President's opening speech. The deputies' inability to proceed in an orderly, businesslike manner was demonstrated from the first. They lacked experience in parliamentary tactics,[13] and their "entire ignorance of all parliamentary proceedings" bordered on the ridiculous.[14]

The fault did not lie altogether in the caliber of the men elected to Parliament. Such deputies as Rieger, Palacký, Stadion, Bach, Helfert, Schmerling, Lasser Havlíček, Löhner, Kudlich, and Schuselka were among the most illustrious men in the empire. However, the old regime had prevented men of talent from participating in public political discussions.[15] Part of the trouble stemmed from the Viennese democrats, who incessantly tried to force Parliament to move left.[16] The language

---

[12] *Ibid.*, pp. 28–29.

[13] Vitzthum von Eckstädt to his uncle, Vienna, August 2, 1848, Carl Friedrich Grafen von Vitzthum von Eckstädt, *Berlin und Wien in den Jahren 1845–1852*, pp. 129–30.

[14] William H. Stiles, *Austria in 1848–49*, Vol. I, p. 151. See also Auerbach diary, September 12, 1848, Berthold Auerbach, *Tagebuch aus Wien. Von Latour bis auf Windischgrätz. (September bis November 1848)*, p. 9. Auerbach was a liberal German novelist and story-writer of Jewish extraction. He is particularly known for his pictures of life in the Black Forest. Among his best works are his edition of Spinoza's collected works, *Schwarzwälder Dorfgeschichte, Barfüssele, Edelweiss*, and *Walfried*.

[15] See Bach, *op. cit.*, pp. 602–604.

[16] Dunder, *Denkschrift über die Wiener October-Revolution*, pp. 22–26. Typical of this pressure on the deputies was the article "To the Representatives of the People": "Arise, you men of the people! Your day's work is beginning! You must show whether you are worthy of our trust and whether you are a match for the great task for which you declared your capability when you accepted the office.

"Consider well that the welfare of a whole nation depends on your honest, earnest, and unshakable will and efforts. Don't forget that this is a nation that has for a long number of years languished under the inexorable pressure of a horrible despotism, that was abandoned to the scorn and ridicule of other free nations, but that has sprung its fetters, become conscious of its rights, and will never again permit anyone to forge new fetters for it. Therefore, you select among the people, have an honest, firm, unshakable will! Your task is great, and your work will be difficult. However, the reward awaiting you is no less great. For you

question also produced continual friction. Slav delegates, who knew no German, insisted that it should not be spoken exclusively in Parliament. After long and acrimonious debate, it was finally agreed that German was to be the official tongue but that the proceedings were to be translated into all the languages spoken by the delegates. The constant use of interpreters naturally slowed the work of Parliament.

The sessions were too short and too infrequent for much business to be transacted. They seldom began before ten or eleven o'clock and usually ended three or four hours later. Afternoon and evening meetings were rarely held. Often there were only two such brief sessions in a whole week, which meant that a single subject might be discussed for weeks before it was finally disposed of.[17] The result was that during the first few weeks not much was accomplished in Parliament other than agreement on the order of business and the appointment of committees to draft a constitution and draw up a declaration of basic rights.[18] The first significant act of Parliament, the freeing of the peasants, did not take place until early in September.

Meantime, the streets of Vienna continued to be the scenes of noisy demonstrations and riotous activities. Although everyone grumbled about the hard times, there had rarely been so many elaborate festivities in Vienna as early in August:[19]

In one place there is an announcement about some good cause, and in the end the public is ridiculed. In another there is a fraternization festival with

---

will not only be rewarded by being able to carry with you the glorious, proud conviction that you have co-operated in making the people happy, and by being thanked by millions of your contemporaries, but later generations will honor your memory, and history will devote its most beautiful pages to your fame and praise. However, if you deceive the people by not fulfilling their justified expectations, then woe—three times woe—to you! Then, branded with the scorn and curses of your fellow-citizens, you will see the betrayed people trample upon your product. You will see that they will not let their acquisitions be torn away from them through cunning or even with bayonets or bullets. Then history will forever pillory your doings as high treason.

"Therefore, remember that two ways are open to you. The one leads to honor and immortal fame; the other, to disgrace and shame. Your actions will soon teach us which of the two you are taking." "An die Vertreter des Volkes," *Wiener Postillon,* No. 18 (July 22, 1848), p. 70, copy in the Univ. Colo. 1848 Coll., No. II/222.

[17] Reschauer and Smets, *op. cit.,* Vol. II, p. 465.

[18] Schneider, *op. cit.,* p. 15; Anton Springer (ed.), *Protokolle des Verfassungs-Ausschusses im Oesterreichischen Reichstage 1848–1849,* pp. 3–6.

[19] "Die politische Damenwelt," *Der Stadttrompeter. Volksthümliche Zeitschrift für Humor und Satyre,* No. 1 (August 7, 1848), p. 1, Univ. Colo. 1848 Coll., No. II/15. The *Stadttrompeter* was edited and published by Schweickhardt. Only three issues appeared in print.

a torchlight parade, and yet the same old darkness remains. Here a female group fraternizing (!) with the whole National Guard; there a performance for the creation of a German fleet, in which no one is taking part, thereby indicating that the Viennese absolutely do not want to be afloat now. Here a gathering in some local tavern where wine is the only spiritual element that is to be seen and where the group is gradually dissolved in a fog. Here, there, and everywhere are clubs, all of which have been formed for the sole purpose of disorganization. Of all these societies the funeral society alone has a humane purpose, namely that of getting the people out of the world in a sensible manner!

Except when their services were needed to put down disturbances of the peace, National Guardsmen and Academic Legionnaires swarmed about, their long swords awkwardly clanking on the paving stones, "while a great many of the creatures to whom they were attached seemed themselves rather appendages to the unmanageable sabre."[20] Mingled with the uniformed militiamen were sad-faced "intellectuals," with their long mustaches and "most earnest, dour countenances,"[21] trying to prove that the Viennese could also devote themselves to serious purposes.

At night more enthusiastic champions of democracy used highly undemocratic methods to vent their spleen upon "black-yellows" and other supposed enemies. In July and August the number of mock serenades increased. On the evening of August 3 an unpopular vegetable-dealer on the Fischhof received a mock serenade. On the 7th a similar demonstration was held for a house-owner in Schottenfeld who had seized the property of a factory-worker for nonpayment of rent.[22] Another "concert" was held for a master carpenter who had aroused the ire of the mob. On the night of August 9 catcalls were showered upon a landlady on Mariahilfer Street. Still another crowd staged a mock serenade before the home of a landlady on New Street, in Leopoldstadt, who had confiscated the possessions of tenants who failed to pay their rent.[23] Three nights later there was a mock serenade in Reinprechtsdorf. On the 18th a hated house-owner and an unpopular master-locksmith were honored by the noisy, impromptu musicians. The next night a landlady in Alser Suburb was serenaded for three hours because she had allegedly

[20] Stiles, *op. cit.*, Vol. I, p. 154.
[21] "Die Gemüthsseite unseres politischen Lebens," *Schwefeläther,* No. 2 (August 6, 1848), p. 5, Univ. Colo. 1848 Coll., No. II/181b.
[22] *Wiener Zeitung,* No. 217 (August 8, 1848), p. 351.
[23] *Ibid.,* No. 219 (August 10, 1848), p. 367.

insulted a soldier.[24] Obviously popular sovereignty was degenerating into anarchy. As Baron von Hübner described it:[25]

We are in a state of complete revolution. The streets of Vienna show this clearly enough. One sees almost only unwashed students in questionable dress, National Guardsmen who do not know how to handle their sabers, and proletariat and prostitutes of the lowest kind. The "well-intentioned," as they call themselves, or the "black-yellows," are either locking themselves up in their houses or have fled to Baden, Hietzing, Döbling, or other places in the neighborhood, and are sighing for the Emperor and trembling in their family circles. As has always been the case at this time of the year, the aristocrats are living in their castles in the country. The young lords are fighting in the Italian army or are streaming to Prague to serve under Prince Windischgrätz. Many young people from the middle classes are following this example. Between noon and three o'clock the inns in the inner city, as well as the taverns and beers halls in the suburbs, are filled. The streets are empty. Only at the stations of the carriages for hire there stand the idle coachmen—the aristocrats of the lower classes—who make fun of those in power for the day.

For the excitable, emotional, oftentimes illogical Viennese there was only one person whose magical presence could rescue the city. Ferdinand the Good had to return to the capital. The deputations to Innsbruck had never ended, although briefly the feeling had prevailed that Archduke John might prove a suitable temporary deputy. However, after the Archduke's departure for Frankfurt, Ferdinand's absence was felt more acutely than ever before.[26] By August the Viennese were redoubling their efforts to induce the Emperor to return. In an open letter published in *Gold und Larbe,* Emperor Ferdinand was warned:[27]

Nothing on earth is imperishable; therefore, no one must play with or joke about the most sacred feelings of human beings. "Confidence in return for confidence!" In these words we were addressed in your name by a man whom Your Majesty sent to us as his representative and who is now called upon to guide the fate of Germany. Let this great word become a truth! We have done our part. Now you do yours also. Austria, Europe, and the

---

[24] *Ibid.,* No. 228 (August 20, 1848), p. 447.

[25] Hübner diary, Vienna, July 24, 1848, Alexander Grafen von Hübner, *Ein Jahr meines Lebens. 1848–1849,* pp. 181–82.

[26] Stiles, *op. cit.,* Vol. I, pp. 151–52; Hübner diary, August 3, 1848, Hübner, *op. cit.,* p. 188.

[27] "Offenes Sendschreiben an den Kaiser von Oesterreich," by "a man of the people," written during the fifth month of the liberation, *Gold und Larbe,* No. 3 (July 19, 1848), pp. 9–10, Univ. Colo. 1848 Coll., No. II/92.

whole world are eagerly watching your next step, and future generations will hold strict judgment on it. You have acquired the name of "benevolent." Now earn for yourself the more worthy term of the "just."

Your Majesty! It is not possible for you to be indifferent to the happiness of your people and to the honor of your dynasty. Now let your immediate return save both of these in a regular way.

Your Majesty! Return in all haste to the castle of your forefathers. There is still time. In another minute it might be "too late."

The Emperor was informed that he had no choice in the matter. He could not do without his people, even though they could readily dispense with him.[28]

For the first time the Emperor was ridiculed. The *Charivari* made fun of him in the following dialogue between "two illustrious individuals":[29]

Kratzelberger. So he really doesn't want to come.
Maier. No, he just doesn't want to come.
K. Well, if he absolutely doesn't want to come?
M. Well, we will then fetch him.
K. And when we have fetched him?
M. Then we will keep him.
K. Yes, but what will we have if we keep him?
M. Yes, that's true. If we keep him we have nothing.

In a more serious and imperious vein, Julius Krenn, a member of the Academic Legion, wrote:[30]

If our imperial house believes that it can ensure its further existence by open insolence, which is already degenerating into disrespect and scorn for the nation, this is just as wretched an error as it is a disastrous one. If the imperial house continues to do this a while longer, the people will find in the incipient anarchy a rising republic that is more endurable than our present desperate conditions. Only the return of the Emperor can improve the situation. We must not beseech it. We must demand it. We have a right to demand it. For I ask, openly and honestly, what is the Emperor? What is every regent? The first servant of the state and nothing more. He is there for our sake; but we are not here for his sake. Therefore, he must not turn a deaf ear to the voice of the people when it calls out to him; for such

[28] *Constitution*, No. 106 (July 30, 1848), p. 1125.
[29] As given in Friedrich Unterreiter, *Die Revolution in Wien vom Juni bis September 1848*, Vol. II, p. 60.
[30] Julius Krenn, "Was müssen wir thun, wenn der Kaiser nicht kommen will? Eine höchst wichtige Zeitfrage," *ibid.*, Vol. I, pp. 25–26.

a call warns him of his duty, and his duty is to fulfill the total will of the nation. If he neglects this duty, he has voluntarily ceased to be what he was—a majesty—for the majesty—the supreme power—has been conferred on him by the people, who honor him as the executor of their will, as expressed in freely given laws. Therefore, no more monarchs by the grace of God. We need monarchs who have the trust of the people.

Realizing that if he did not immediately return to his capital the respect of the Viennese for the throne might be seriously undermined, on August 5 the Emperor told a committee of Parliament, which had come to Innsbruck with a resolution demanding his return,[31] that he would gladly fulfill their wishes. He assured them that, in spite of the fact that he was still in bad health, he would begin his journey to Vienna on the 8th, accompanied by the Empress, Archduke Francis Charles, and the Archduke's son, Francis Joseph, and arrive in Vienna on the 12th. The other members of the Habsburg family would leave Innsbruck on August 9 and would reach Vienna on the 13th.[32]

Although many Viennese were overjoyed at the prospect of having their Emperor with them again, some of the radicals circulated this ironic announcement of his return:[33]

People's and National Comedy of Vienna
Under the Personal Direction of the Honorable Ladies:
Freedom, Order, and Equality!
Today, Saturday, August 12, 1848
For the Enjoyment of the Austrian People
First Performance:
The Return of the Emperor,
or
The Triumph of Democracy

A good drama and comedy, with military and civil scenes, without fighting and skirmishes. Singing and shouting, natural stage setting. Translated into German from the Innsbruck dialect and prepared for all Germany by all the members of the honorable Parliament. Scenes prepared by Minister Hornbostel. Music by Arndt ("What Is the German's Fatherland?") and by Hayden ("National Anthem").

[31] Vitzthum von Eckstädt to his uncle, Vienna, July 29, 1848, Vitzthum von Eckstädt, *op. cit.*, pp. 128–29.

[32] Doblhoff, "Proclamation," Vienna, August 8, 1848, Univ. Colo. 1848 Coll., No. II/20. See also the report of the deputation to Parliament, Innsbruck, 2:00 P.M., August 5, 1848, *Wiener Zeitung*, No. 218 (August 9, 1848), p. 355.

[33] Univ. Colo. 1848 Coll., No. II/76.

The Viennese Revolution of 1848

Cast:

The Constitutional Emperor (named the Good)	Mr. *Ferdinand*
The Empress (called the Pious)	Mrs. *M. Anna*
The Brother of the Emperor	Mr. *F. Carl*
His Son (an Expectant Prince)	" *F. Joseph*
The Minister-President	" *Dobblhof*
The President of the Imperial Parliament	" *Schmitt*
The Minister of War	" *Latour*
The Minister of Justice	" *Alex. Bach*
The Minister of Culture	" *Schwarzer*
The Minister of Finance	" *Kraus*
The Minister of Commerce	" *Hornbostl*
Peter Sebastian, Father Confessor	" *Brunnerl*
A Jesuit	" *Bombellerl*
His Intimate Friend	Mrs. *Cibinni*

German soldiers, guards, and various students; members of the black-gold-red and black-yellow parties; parliamentary deputies; Galician peasants; brave citizens and honest men; knights without fear and reproach; court sycophants and mercenaries, and court tale-bearers; cripples of the times; clergy; and committee members of the order of the double-tongued.

The Setting is partly in Nussdorf and partly in the Capital City of Vienna.

The Action takes place A.D. *1848, in the First Year of Salvation, August 12, 1848.*

Note

1. Whoever wishes a *free* seat must prove that he has the proper merits and that he is himself *worthy* of having one.

2. The number of *acts* is undetermined.

3. Since the drama—the *only one* in the history of Austria— *will be performed only once,* and since only the *worthy acting of all* participants can contribute to the *welfare* of the Austrian people, we hope that each and every one will act according to his ability in such a way that this drama will occupy an honorable place in the world.

4. Everyone may express his *approval loudly,* but we urgently beg of you, in the interest of the *good cause,* to refrain from any manifestations of *disfavor,* and *thus* thwart all intermezzos leading to disorders and to disturbances of the peace.

5. Free tickets and free entrance are prohibited to all secret spies and confidants, and every *free*-minded person is justified in using the strongest measures to throw out such unwholesome persons in case they try to sneak in.

6. The beginning of the drama will be announced by cannon shots,

which, however, are not to be fired at the command of Prince *Windisch-grätz*, and therefore no one need fear anything *hostile*.

On Leave: Counts Hoyos, Montecuccoli, Brandis, and Leo Thun.[34]

Because the news of the return of the Emperor made the reactionary Messrs. Ebersberg, Endlich, Neumann, and Stadion[35] ill, these same gentlemen have announced that they are unable to take part in today's activities.

Curtain Time: 3:00 P.M. Closing Time: Toward Evening.

You are invited in a most friendly and brotherly manner by

The Free Inhabitants of the Capital

On the day the monarch returned to Vienna, the changed attitude of the Viennese toward him was painfully noticeable. At Stein the imperial party was met by the ministers, by twenty members each of the City Council, the Security Committee, and the administrative council of the National Guard, and by twenty officers of the Vienna garrison, who accompanied the Emperor and his entourage on the steamboat from Stein to Nussdorf. When the ship arrived at Nussdorf at three o'clock in the afternoon, salvos were fired to welcome the royal couple, and various National Guard and military detachments saluted the returning sovereign.[36]

Along streets lined on both sides by National Guardsmen in uniform, the imperial party was driven through Vienna to the Schönbrunn Palace. The Emperor's carriage and those of the more important retainers of the monarch were followed by generals of the imperial army, the commander of the National Guard, and a National Guard cavalry squadron. The Emperor, the Empress, Archduke Francis Charles, and Archduchess Sophie sat together in an open carriage. The "Emperor looked pale, stared at his knees, and greeted the people in a mechanical manner. The Empress had evidently been weeping" and "seemed to be adorned with a martyr's palm. The Archduchess wept behind her lorgnette, and her husband seemed very upset." Some of the Viennese "thought these were tears of joy, and they waved their hats and handkerchiefs, shouted *viva*'s, behaved themselves, and were overjoyed."[37] On the whole, however, the shouts of welcome were extremely weak and

---

[34] Hoyos, Montecuccoli, and Brandis had aroused the ill will of the radicals by their conduct during the May revolutions. Thun was hated for his actions in Prague in June.

[35] Ebersberg, Endlich, and Neumann were conservative Viennese journalists. Stadion was governor of Bohemia and leader of the conservative Galician deputies in Parliament.

[36] Unterreiter, *op. cit.*, Vol. II, pp. 67–68.

[37] Hübner diary, Vienna, August 12, 1848, Hübner, *op. cit.*, p. 189.

absent in some places as the Emperor drove past. At other points in the city there were actually loud hisses mingled with shouts of praise. The band of the Academic Legion played Arndt's "What Is the German's Fatherland?" rather than the Austrian national anthem when the imperial couple approached, and some of the National Guard companies stood rigid in stony silence when the procession passed them.[38]

The next day the Emperor issued a proclamation to his "loyal Viennese" in which, ironically enough, he thanked them for the proof of their "old, unchangeable love" for him on the preceding day. He expressed the hope that August 12 would "eternally shine in the history of the Fatherland as a day of solemn commemoration of the new union between the free people and a constitutional Emperor," and that henceforth "peace, unity, order, and lawfulness [would] prevail" so that the "building up of our new constitutional state" would prosper and succeed. Then he concluded: "In collaboration with the self-elected representatives" of all the peoples of Austria, "and supported by my responsible advisers, I hope that I can carry to a glorious end the difficult task of constructing a new Fatherland, which has been assigned to me by Providence."[39]

The Emperor's statement of his sincere desire to co-operate with Parliament made little impression on the extremists. On August 19, when a huge parade was given in honor of the Emperor by the Vienna garrison and the citizens' militia, the radicals demonstrated their contempt for the monarch. About 50,000 armed men participated in the review. To the tune of the national anthem the imperial troops marched by the Emperor, in accord with the regulations, without any cheers of any kind. Part of the National Guard companies passed by in silence; others heartily shouted, "Long live the Emperor!" Instead of looking toward the Emperor, as stipulated by military rules, the Academic Legionnaires turned their faces away from him and filed by in utter silence. Worse still, instead of the national anthem, the bands of various companies played the derisive revolutionary "Fuchslied" and "What's Leather-Pants Papa Doing?"[40]

The conservatives were infuriated by the students' deliberate in-

---

[38] Anton Füster, *Memoiren vom März 1848 bis Juli 1849,* Vol. II, pp. 69–71; Unterreiter, *op. cit.,* Vol. II, pp. 68–69.

[39] Emperor Ferdinand, "Proclamation to His Loyal Viennese," Vienna, August 13, 1848, Unterreiter, *op. cit.,* Vol. II, pp. 70–71.

[40] Hübner diary, Vienna, August 20, 1848, Hübner, *op. cit.,* p. 192; Füster, *op. cit.,* Vol. II, pp. 87–88; Meynert, *op. cit.,* pp. 526–27; Ottocar Weber, *1848. Sechs Vorträge,* p. 41; Legion Commander Koller's memoir, in Reschauer and Smets, *op. cit.,* Vol. II, pp. 486–87.

sults of the monarch. As a consequence, several students lost the free lodgings given to them by wealthier citizens.[41] Court and government circles were also enraged by the conduct of the Academic Legion, even though on the 20th the Legion commander personally apologized to Archduke Francis Charles, Doblhoff, and Latour for the misconduct of the men under his command.[42]

Most Viennese had hoped that the Emperor's presence in Vienna would bring peace, order, and security. On the contrary, the effects were just the opposite. As long as Ferdinand was in Innsbruck the radical extremists had some interest in maintaining order, if only to prove that the Viennese could get along without a monarch. Now the extremists found it to their advantage to encourage brawls and disorders to show that the Emperor could not preserve the peace.[43] More than ever before Vienna was now a scene of constant tumults and disturbances.[44] There was no force able to check the growing anarchy. The government seemed helpless in face of the constant turbulence. Although the Security Committee was looked up to by the radicals,[45] its repeated exhortations to preserve peace were to no avail.[46]

Behind most of the antimonarchic disturbances were the radical democratic clubs. To them especially Anton Schütte addressed himself when he returned in the middle of August to the same Vienna from which he had been expelled in April. Under his direction an assembly of 10,000 people was held in Odeon Hall to draft a communication to the extreme left in the Frankfurt Assembly. Schütte's appeals proved irresistible, and the crowd expressed in a strong republican vein their belief that national salvation lay only in the program of the extreme left at Frankfurt. Schütte also induced the Security Committee to draw up a similar address, which was signed by the members of the committee, 100 members of Parliament, and various radical clubs.

Schütte also spoke to a large crowd in the assembly hall of the university. There he warned his hearers, very few of whom were students, that the reaction was getting ready to strike back. He told them Friedrich Hecker, a radical German revolutionist, would soon be sent to Vienna and asked the assembly to sign the Odeon Hall address as a reward to

[41] Füster, *op. cit.*, Vol. II, p. 88.
[42] Legion Commander Koller's memoir, in Reschauer and Smets, *op. cit.*, Vol. II, p. 487.
[43] Meynert, *op. cit.*, p. 526.
[44] Stiles, *op. cit.*, Vol. I, p. 153; Dunder, *op. cit.*, p. 14.
[45] See, for instance, the letter of the Democratic Club to the Security Committee, Vienna, August 7, 1848, *Wiener Zeitung*, No. 219 (August 10, 1848), p. 367.
[46] Meynert, *op. cit.*, p. 525.

Hecker for promising to come. After stormy applause, Schütte asked for a show of hands, declared that the majority had voted in favor of subscribing to the address, and announced that it would be dispatched to Frankfurt in the name of the Viennese students.[47]

Although the more conservative Viennese were willing to tolerate the actions of the Democratic Club, they were angry with the Security Committee, the students, and the Academic Legion for supporting Schütte. The Security Committee, they argued, was not just a political organization but a committee charged with preserving order, peace, and security. As such it was not entitled "to express sympathies which the people of Vienna do not share."[48] The participation in the proceedings by the students and the Academic Legion aroused such hostility that the Civic Guard and National Guard denounced them to the Ministry for their dangerous "republican" tendencies and demanded that the government take strong measures to suppress them.[49]

The furor aroused by these demonstrations brought into the open conflicts that for some time had been threatening to split apart the citizens' armed forces. The large majority of National Guardsmen bitterly resented the radicalism of the Academic Legion,[50] and by August the citizens' militia was sharply divided into right and left wings. The fact that the National Guard was operating under the wholly inadequate organization decree of April 10 also made petty conflicts unavoidable. As the duties of the guardsmen had not yet been prescribed, many of them shirked their obligations and quarreled over their right to carry weapons and the necessity of providing protection. Because discipline was only a matter of good will, enlisted men often defiantly refused to carry out their officers' commands. The National Guard was woefully demoralized. The Viennese lost interest in the organization to such an

---

[47] Minutes of the Sitting of the Democratic Club, August 21, 1848, *Der Volksfreund*, No. 102 (August 26, 1848), p. 411, Univ. Colo. 1848 Coll., No. II/211; *Beilage zur Wiener Zeitung*, No. 230 (August 23, 1848), p. 67; Meynert, *op. cit.*, p. 526.

[48] *Beilage zur Wiener Zeitung*, No. 230 (August 23, 1848), p. 67.

[49] Minutes of the Sitting of the Democratic Club, August 21, 1848, *Volksfreund*, No. 102 (August 26, 1848), p. 411, Univ. Colo. 1848 Coll., No. II/211. Upon receiving this remonstrance the Ministry dispatched a pointed letter to the Student Committee asking whether the resolutions recently passed by the crowd in the Aula represented the views of the whole student body. "Doblhoff to Student Committee," Vienna, August 19, 1848, *Wiener Zeitung*, No. 230 (August 23, 1848), p. 463. In reply, the Student Committee assured the government that few students were present in the Aula assembly that had approved Schütte's address and promised that in the future the Aula would no longer be used for popular meetings. "Student Committee to Minister of Interior," Vienna, August 19, 1848, *ibid*.

[50] Dunder, *op. cit.*, p. 7; Unterreiter, *op. cit.*, Vol. II, p. 72.

extent that between May and August its membership decreased from 40,000 to 18,000. By August the National Guard was on the point of dissolving.[51]

The government, too, was weak and ineffectual. Although Minister-President Wessenberg was an experienced bureaucrat, he lacked the energy and resolution necessary to guide the country in turbulent times. With the exception of Latour and Bach, who were hated by the democrats, the rest of the members of the cabinet were unimaginative, mediocre officials. The Ministry thus lacked the necessary strength to gain the respect of either the conservatives or "the men of progress."[52] As a consequence, the only body in Vienna that had any appreciable influence on the revolutionists was the Security Committee,[53] which was nothing more than an extralegal stepchild of the revolution.

Meanwhile business conditions grew still worse in Vienna. By August the nobility had left the city, thereby dealing a serious blow to the many luxury industries. The constant agitation, the ever present disturbances of peace and security, the attacks on unpopular personages, and the uncertainty about the future had a devastating effect upon business activity. Government securities sank lower and lower. As raw materials became more difficult to obtain and everyone reduced his spending as much as possible, many manufacturers and master-craftsmen had to curtail their operations or even go out of business. Because of the continuing fear that paper money would soon become worthless, gold and silver disappeared from the banks and all but vanished from sight.[54]

By far the hardest hit were the proletarian masses in the city. When people lost their jobs in private industry, they swelled the ranks of the idlers in the Prater and other public works projects. The earthworkers were a constant threat to the security of the city; moreover, the public works projects were very costly for the impoverished government. By the middle of June between 36,000 and 44,000 florins per week were distributed in wages to the workers on hastily devised jobs for the destitute.[55] These sums had to be considerably increased to pay for the grow-

[51] "Administrative Council of the Viennese National Guard to Parliament," n.d., copy in the Univ. Colo. 1848 Coll., No. II/90; Dunder, *op. cit.,* pp. 17–18.

[52] Hübner diary, August 14, 1848, Hübner, *op. cit.,* pp. 190–91.

[53] Hübner diary, August 3, 1848, *ibid.,* p. 188.

[54] Dunder, *op. cit.,* p. 15; Doppler, "Warum werden die Zwanziger so selten?" *Nazional-Zeitung,* No. 16 (August 7, 1848), p. 61, Univ. Colo. 1848 Coll., No. II/145.

[55] Baumgartner, "Proclamation," Vienna, June 18, 1848, *Wiener Welt-Courier. Rundschau der politischen Welt-Ereignisse, für Jene, welche das mühsame Durchlesen der Zeitungen und Journale ersparen wollen; nebst einem Anhange: zur Besprechung der wichtigsten Tagesfragen,* No. 8 (June 20, 1848), p. 29, Univ.

ing number of workers who flocked to the projects from private jobs or from the surrounding districts[56] in spite of the Security Committee's efforts early in June to prevent such an influx.

In order to exert some kind of control over the workers, Minister of Public Works Schwarzer created the Provisional Central Committee for Workers' Affairs under his direct supervision. Its duties were to promote better working conditions, supervise the employment given to needy laborers, provide the money for the public projects, oversee the work performed, and devise effective methods to restore normal working conditions as quickly as possible.[57] The committee again ordered the dismissal of all "foreign workers" from the public works projects and instructed the Viennese earthworkers to register with the committee and accept such jobs in private industry as it could find for them.[58] On its part, the Security Committee commanded the police and Civic Guard to prevent begging on the streets.[59]

These measures proved wholly ineffectual. The radicals maintained that there were no foreign workers in Vienna. Furthermore, since practically no earthworkers registered with the committee, no other jobs could be procured for them. It was obvious to the Ministry that the earthworks had to be closed up sooner or later, and the workers on them absorbed by private industry. Yet if the projects were abolished all at once, the persons employed on them would suffer indescribable hardship. Therefore, the committee decided not to do away with them overnight but to pass a measure that would spur some of the earthworkers to hunt for other jobs. To accomplish this the Minister of Public Works ordered that on August 18 the daily wages on the public works projects were to be reduced by 5 kreutzer for women and children under fifteen. Later on the Ministry intended to follow this reduction with a similar decrease in the pay of adult male workers. The earthworkers were notified of the decree when they came on Saturday, August 19, to receive their weekly pay.[60]

Colo. 1848 Coll., No. II/226. The *Wiener Welt-Courier* was a daily newspaper edited by Erwin. The first issue came out on June 13; the last, on July 3.

[56] See especially *Ursache und Geschichte der Octoberereignisse zu Wien*, by an eyewitness, p. 17.

[57] Ernst Victor Zenker, *Die Wiener Revolution*, p. 203.

[58] *Ibid.*, p. 204.

[59] Protocol of the Sitting of the Security Committee, forenoon, July 17, 1848, *Wiener Zeitung*, No. 199 (July 20, 1848), p. 191; Protocol of the Sitting of the Security Committee, July 20, 1848, *Gold und Larbe*, No. 4 (July 20, 1848), p. 15, Univ. Colo. 1848 Coll., No. AII/92.

[60] *Wiener Zeitung*, No. 231 (August 24, 1848), pp. 471–72; "Rückblicke,"

The Opening of Parliament and the Defeat of the Proletariat

Although the government unquestionably had to take steps to cut the ever increasing number of idlers on the projects, the way in which the wage reductions were announced was unfortunate. Before he issued the fiat, Minister Schwarzer did not bother to consult the Security Committee, even though that committee was also deeply concerned over the fact that the earthworks projects were rapidly destroying the morale of the Viennese workers. Furthermore, the timing of the announcement not only infuriated the workers but also aroused the fears of the radicals that the government was deliberately provoking the proletariat to revolt so that it could destroy them as a revolutionary force.[61]

At first the earthworkers merely grumbled when they read the proclamation. The next day they decided to send deputations to all legal and revolutionary authorities in the city to entreat them to rescind it. In case these efforts were fruitless, they planned to declare a general strike.

On Monday morning a large number of workers from the suburbs entered the city. Most of them went to the Tuchlauben, where the Security Committee held its meetings, to implore the committee's assistance in persuading Schwarzer to cancel the decree. The committee dispatched deputies to the Minister of Interior, where they met a workers' delegation on the same errand. Schwarzer told both groups that he would not back down, even though the workers came with shovels and axes to intimidate him.[62] Another group of workers proceeded to the university to enlist the students' aid. Füster promised the angry crowd that he personally would go to the ministers. But his efforts were equally fruitless.[63]

The largest groups of workers had gathered in front of the former Liguorian monastery, where the Labor Committee had its office, and in front of the offices of the city magistracy. When the authorities refused to yield to the demands of the demonstrators, many of whom were women, the tumult became uproarious. At this moment the City Council called upon the Civic Guard and several National Guard companies to disperse them. The workers taunted and insulted the guardsmen when

Beilage zur Wiener Zeitung, No. 236 (August 30, 1848), p. 75; Schwarzer's explanation to Parliament on August 22, 1848, Minutes of the 27th Sitting of Parliament, August 22, 1848, *Wiener Zeitung,* No. 230 (August 23, 1848), p. 460.

[61] Ernst Violand, *Die sociale Geschichte der Revolution in Oesterreich,* pp. 140–41; Zenker, *op. cit.,* pp. 208–10. This is, of course, Karl Marx's contention. See Frederick Engels [and Karl Marx], *Germany: Revolution and Counter-Revolution,* p. 68.

[62] Unterreiter, *op. cit.,* Vol. II, p. 77.

[63] Füster, *op. cit.,* Vol. II, pp. 99–100.

they arrived, and some of the guardsmen paid the workers back in kind. In a short time the citizens' armed forces managed to clear the place. Other guard companies were also successful in scattering the mobs jammed at the Hohen Markt and in the Tuchlauben.[64]

The situation still seemed dangerous. The workmen had repeatedly threatened to fetch their tools and return to the city to enforce their rights. As a consequence, the City Council called out the entire National Guard and ordered all the city gates locked and cannon placed on the walls. But these preparations proved unnecessary. By evening the crowds had been dispersed and driven out into the suburbs.[65]

On the next day, August 22, there were no disturbances, although great excitement prevailed in the suburbs and the workers were sullen and bitter. In Parliament the same day Minister Schwarzer was enthusiastically applauded when he described the strong measures the Ministry had taken to restore order and declared that this was the first time in months that the government had not weakly retreated when confronted by an imposing popular demonstration. The Minister of Justice, Alexander Bach, was even more blunt. He stated that the Ministry would never waver in fulfilling its obligations to maintain order and security. Although the government would respect the constitutional freedom of association and of assembly, it would energetically prosecute any abuses of this right. Under no circumstances would it tolerate "anarchical and republican movements."[66]

On the morning of August 23, instead of turning to their regular work, the earthworkers at the Prater molded a statue of Minister Schwarzer out of clay and straw. They set the figure on a donkey and then stuck a kreutzer piece in his mouth and a placard on his chest bearing the inscription "The Kreutzer Minister." To the people gathered around the statue, who were assuming the role of "mourners," they announced: "He swallowed four kreutzers, but he choked on the fifth!" Around two o'clock the workers started a mock funeral procession. They intended to march throughout the city in hopes that they could win Viennese public opinion to their side.

With women and children at the head of the procession and the effigy of the unpopular Minister on a donkey behind them, the "mourners"

---

[64] *Wiener Zeitung*, No. 231 (August 24, 1848), p. 472; Füster, *op. cit.*, Vol. II, pp. 101–104; Unterreiter, *op. cit.*, Vol. II, p. 77; Stiles, *op. cit.*, Vol. I, pp. 160–61.
[65] *Wiener Zeitung*, No. 231 (August 24, 1848), p. 472; Stiles, *op. cit.*, Vol. I, p. 161.
[66] Minutes of the 27th Sitting of Parliament, August 22, 1848, *Wiener Zeitung*, No. 230 (August 23, 1848), pp. 460–61.

The Opening of Parliament and the Defeat of the Proletariat

made their way through the Prater to the Stern-Allee. As the workers marched they became more and more excited. On the way they mauled a couple of Civic Guardsmen who warned them to turn back. Meanwhile, the government had summoned the Leopoldstadt National Guard, and a large number hurried up. At the Praterstern the demonstrators encountered a detachment of about 150 Civic Guardsmen, along with a sizable National Guard contingent from the Leopoldstadt and Landstrasse areas, who ordered them to go no farther. A quarrel ensued that ended in a bloody fight. The Civic Guard advanced with drawn sabers, and the National Guard columns charged into the crowd. In the battle several persons were killed and many were wounded among both the demonstrators and guardsmen. The rioters, pursued by the Civic Guard, fled to the Tabor to seek the help of the workers there.[67]

In the meantime a general alarm had been sounded in the inner city, and the inhabitants, panic-stricken, rushed to lock up their houses and shops. In a moment the streets were deserted. The City Council declared itself in permanent session for the duration of the emergency.[68]

All National and Civic Guard companies in the city were called out. A few radical National Guard companies refused to join forces with the government, and the members of the Academic Legion emphatically stated that they would not move against their friends the workers. However, the large majority of the National Guard companies were composed of solid, middle-class citizens who trembled at the very thought of a proletarian uprising and were determined to teach the rabble a lesson.[69] In large numbers they hurried to their posts and ran through the Rothenthurm Gate to meet the proletarian "thieves" and "murderers."

Together with the Civic Guard, the National Guard attacked the workers. They beat them with their sabers, stabbed them with their bayonets, and shot them down mercilessly. When they returned to the city, the women of Vienna waved handkerchiefs and crowned their bloody bayonets with garlands of flowers. Thus the Viennese bourgeoisie revenged themselves upon the lower-class radicals.

Within a few hours all opposition had ended. By evening a few

[67] Füster, *op. cit.*, Vol. II, pp. 106–108; Unterreiter, *op. cit.*, Vol. II, pp. 78–80; Friedrich Hebbel's account in *Augsburgische allgemeine Zeitung*, as printed in Tim Klein (ed.), *Der Vorkampf deutscher Einheit und Freiheit*, pp. 380–81; Stiles, *op. cit.*, Vol. I, p. 161.
[68] "Proclamation," City Council, Vienna, August 23, 1848, *Wiener Zeitung*, No. 231 (August 24, 1848), p. 472.
[69] Friedrich Kaiser, *Memoiren*, pp. 108–109.

curiosity-seekers still roamed the streets, while here and there an occasional agitator still sought vainly to stir up the public against the National Guard.[70]

According to a placard printed by the democrats, 18 workers were killed, 152 were seriously wounded, and 130 received slight wounds. Among the Civic Guard there were 1 dead, 3 missing, 4 seriously wounded, and 18 slightly wounded; while the National Guard suffered 1 dead, 5 seriously wounded, and 1 slightly wounded.[71] The city government of Vienna published a proclamation on August 27 maintaining that only 6 workers were killed, 36 seriously wounded, and 80 slightly wounded, whereas among the Civic Guard only 13 were wounded, two critically. No casualty report was given for the National Guard.[72]

The government took advantage of the victory against the proletariat to assume complete control of Vienna. On August 24 it issued two orders designed to anticipate and prevent future excesses. In one it declared that, in accord with paragraphs 70 and 71 of the Austrian Criminal Code, all persons who threatened or resisted the National Guard were to be imprisoned from six months to five years.[73] The second proclamation announced that henceforth the Ministry alone was to give all orders dealing with public peace and security, and all executive branches located in the capital were instructed to disregard orders from any other source. The National Guard was placed under the direct supervision of the Minister of Interior. Furthermore, all work was to be temporarily discontinued on the public works projects where there had been disturbances the previous day. All persons employed on them had to submit proof of their good conduct and competence before they would be permitted to resume their jobs.[74]

This surprising and unusual boldness of the Ministry spelled the doom of the revolutionary Security Committee. Ever since the members of Parliament had begun to assemble in the capital, there had been heated debates about whether this extraordinary body should continue to exist.[75] As early as July 16 the Vienna City Council had refused to send

---

[70] *Ibid.,* p. 109; Füster, *op. cit.,* Vol. II, pp. 107–109; Hübner diary, Vienna, August 23, 1848, Hübner, *op. cit.,* pp. 193–94.

[71] Univ. Colo. 1848 Coll., No. II/142.

[72] Captain of the Civic Guard, "Proclamation," Vienna, August 27, 1848, Univ. Colo. 1848 Coll., No. II/127.

[73] Ministerial Council, "Proclamation," Vienna, August 24, 1848, *Wiener Zeitung,* No. 232 (August 25, 1848), p. 477.

[74] Ministerial Council, "Proclamation," Vienna, August 24, 1848, *ibid.*

[75] "Rückblicke," *Beilage zur Wiener Zeitung,* No. 236 (August 30, 1848), p. 75; *Zopf und Schwert,* No. 1 (June 30, 1848), p. 4, Univ. Colo. 1848 Coll., No. II/235.

any more representatives to attend the committee's meetings.[76] During the workers' disturbances from August 19 to August 23, the Security Committee had stood by helplessly, aiding neither the government nor the demonstrators. Now, after the government's proclamations on the 24th, the moderates on the committee proposed abolishing it.[77] In order to make the dissolution more palatable, the Ministry sent a memorandum to the committee thanking its members profusely for their fine work in preserving freedom and order.[78] Thereupon, on August 25 the committee, after ceremoniously depositing in the civic arsenal and the university the flags the various nations of Austria had dedicated to it, declared itself dissolved.[79]

The government also took steps to place the earthworkers in private industry as soon as possible. A special Committee for the Assistance of Destitute Tradesmen in Vienna was appointed to help impoverished small businessmen and master-craftsmen provide employment for the earthworkers. The National Bank promised to advance money to the new committee to further this project.[80]

The committee immediately asked each trade guild in the city to suggest how business conditions could be improved and workers re-employed.[81] After preliminary inquiries, the committee applied itself energetically to its task. In a relatively short space of time the number of public project workers was substantially reduced.[82] By early September, for example, 212 of the earthworkers employed at the Brundfelde project had been given boat or train fare and sent back to their homes outside Vienna; jobs had been procured for 268; 16 had been handed over to the authorities for expulsion from the project, and 19 elderly or infirm persons incapable of working had been sent to charitable institutions.[83] Similar reductions took place on the other public projects.

The rapid liquidation of the public works projects brought no great protest from the Viennese proletariat. When Karl Marx came to Vienna

[76] "City Council of the City of Vienna to the Security Committee," July 17, 1848, *Wiener Zeitung,* No. 201 (July 22, 1848), p. 208.
[77] Füster, *op. cit.,* Vol. II, p. 121; Ernst Violand, *Enthüllungen,* pp. 59–60.
[78] Doblhoff to the Security Committee, Vienna, August 23, 1848, in Unterreiter, *op. cit.,* Vol. II, pp. 84–85.
[79] Unterreiter, *op. cit.,* Vol. II, p. 85; Violand, *Enthüllungen,* pp. 59–60.
[80] Committee for the Assistance of the Destitute Tradesmen in Vienna, "Proclamation," Vienna, August 24, 1848, *Wiener Zeitung,* No. 233 (August 26, 1848), p. 490.
[81] *Ibid.*
[82] Zenker, *op. cit.,* p. 211, says they were reduced by half.
[83] *Wiener Zeitung,* No. 241 (September 5, 1848), p. 574.

hoping to find the capital fertile soil for agitation, he was bitterly disappointed. When he told the Democratic Club on August 28 that the events of August 21 to 23 were merely a class struggle between the bourgeoisie and the proletariat, he was loudly criticized. Even so radical a democrat as Hermann Jellinek arose to argue with him. Marx was no more successful in his talks to various workers' groups early in September. Everywhere he encountered opposition to his ideas. He was "appalled" by the close relationship between the workers and certain members of the middle class and the workers' inability to understand the need to wage class warfare against the bourgeoisie. On September 7 Marx left the inhospitable Austrian capital a disillusioned man, muttering about the immaturity of the Viennese revolutionary leaders.[84]

Nevertheless, although the workers failed to realize it, the conflict on August 21 to 23 was a kind of limited class struggle that served to make the proletariat conscious of the fact that they had formed a class of their own. Class opposed class in the fighting on August 23. The proletariat battled with the Civic and National Guards, which were composed of men of property and other "respectable" bourgeoisie and supported by the more prosperous and moderate bourgeoisie. It is true that the radical lower middle classes—the suburban guardsmen (mainly master-craftsmen, small-scale traders, and artisans), the Academic Legion, and the radical intelligentsia—did not join with the National Guard, but they did not assist the workers, either. The contest was between the more prosperous bourgeoisie and the proletariat, with most of the radical lower middle classes standing on the sidelines.

Seeing themselves deserted by all the middle-class groups in Vienna, the workers realized that they were cut off from other classes. As a consequence, they were forced to develop a feeling of class-consciousness. As the relatively conservative editors of the *Wiener Zeitung* described it:[85]

[August 23] has separated the workers, as such, from the other classes. It has given them an idea—that of their own misfortune. It has bequeathed them a historical tradition. It has turned them into a state within a state. The workers have seen the contrast between their defenseless poverty and armed property. And at this moment there came into being a proletariat that formerly did not exist.

The defeat of the proletariat on August 23 was to have a decisive

[84] Zenker, *op. cit.*, pp. 213–14; Franz Mehring, *Karl Marx: The Story of His Life*, p. 205.
[85] "Rückblicke," *Beilage zur Wiener Zeitung*, No. 236 (August 30, 1848), p. 75.

effect on the course of the revolution. By early August the students, the lower middle classes, and the proletariat alone constituted the active revolutionary front in Vienna. All the other classes who had co-operated in bringing on the March rebellion had been frightened away long since. Yet until August 23 the revolution still represented a very powerful force, largely because the radical democratic leaders could always count on rallying the dissatisfied workers in the suburbs to intimidate the government and the conservative bourgeoisie into doing their bidding. On August 23 this union was irreparably shattered. The students and the lower middle classes stood by in silent neutrality. Consequently, the democrats not only lost their army, they also lost their political directing body, the Security Committee. The committee did not move to defend the workers and meekly dissolved at the first show of courage and determination on the part of the Ministry.

At the same time, the Ministry was now able to test its own strength. August 23 was the first time during the whole revolution that the government firmly refused to submit to the mob.

The Ministry suddenly realized that it could remain master of the situation in a critical emergency if it only held firm and did not let itself be intimidated. It discovered that it could count on more than a handful of army troops garrisoned in the city to support its efforts to preserve peace and order and obey its commands.

The first turn of the tide had come on June 17, when Windischgrätz destroyed the Czech democrats, with the approval of the Viennese democrats. Then followed the victory over the Italians at Custozza on July 25, again with the support of the Viennese radicals, who praised the conquest of Marshal Radetzky's Italian army. Now on August 23, while the lower-middle-class revolutionaries stood on the sidelines, their allies, the workers, were soundly defeated. The next step in the forward march of the counterrevolution was to be taken on September 11 to 13. This time the lower-middle-class radicals themselves were to be dealt a shattering blow.

XIII. The Defeat
of the Lower Middle Class

HE DEFEAT of the proletariat on August 23 delighted the champions of law and order in the Habsburg capital. For them, the time for revolution was long past. They had long been terrified by the antics of the lower-class radicals, who they feared were bent on subverting law and morality in order to establish socialist and republican institutions in the monarchy or to "turn Austria over to the Jews."[1] They wanted political differences to be resolved on the floors of Parliament in an orderly fashion, not on the streets by an agitated, anarchistic rabble.[2] They loudly applauded the Ministry for at last successfully asserting its authority.

The hearty support the "more respectable" bourgeoisie gave the government at first surprised and consternated the democrats.[3] Although they themselves had failed to support the workers, the consequence of their inaction did not at first seem to dawn upon them. When it did, the radicals let out a howl of rage against the "slaughterers" of the workingmen. They were particularly incensed with the Civic and National Guardsmen for firing upon the defenseless workers.[4] Although, according to the official casualty report, no one younger than fifteen had been killed or wounded on August 23, the radicals wrote mawkish accounts of the guardsmen's mowing down scores of defenseless children. Though the women at the Prater were armed with rocks, clubs, and other weapons, and though only ten of them had been wounded,[5] the dem-

---

[1] Joseph Alexander Freiherrn von Helfert, *Die Wiener Journalistik im Jahre 1848,* pp. 127–28; "Radikale und antiministerielle Presse," *Wiener Zeitung,* No. 240 (September 3, 1848), pp. 562–63; "Der 23. und 24. August als Folge des 15. Mai," *Das Portefeuil,* No. 4 (August 26, 1848), p. 26, Univ. Colo. 1848 Coll., No. II/163. The *Portefeuil* was published by J. Ludwig and edited by A. Julius. Only four issues appeared; the first on August 22, the last on August 26.

[2] *Beilage zur Wiener Zeitung,* No. 230 (August 23, 1848), p. 67.

[3] Anton Füster, *Memoiren vom März 1848 bis Juli 1849,* Vol. II, pp. 19–20.

[4] Hermann Meynert, *Ereignisse in der österreichischen Monarchie,* pp. 529–30.

[5] Captain of the Civic Guard, "Proclamation," Vienna, August 27, 1848, Univ. Colo. 1848 Coll., No. II/127.

299

The Defeat of the Lower Middle Class

ocrats reported the Civic Guard's murder of "seventy-year-old wives" and "nursing mothers who knelt down before the Municipal Guard and beseeched them to spare their lives since they were innocent."[6]

The democrats also denounced the City Council and the Ministry as responsible for the whole bloody affair. The City Council was said to have ordered out the Guards illegally and to have tried to incite students against workers and citizens against citizens.[7] However, their greatest fury was directed against the Ministry, and especially against the Minister of Public Works, who was accused of setting off the bloody carnage with his "5-kreutzer decree." In their eyes Schwarzer was a turncoat. No longer the great "commoner," whose appointment to the Ministry had been welcomed by the radicals in July, Minister Schwarzer was now an ingrate. If the government wanted to heal the grievous scars left by the events of August 23, Schwarzer must be removed. Shortly after the workers' revolt,[8] the Minister submitted his resignation, which was finally accepted on September 23.[9]

With the radicals so very bitter, there could be no peace and tranquillity in Vienna. Inflammatory speeches, spectacular processions, unending mock serenades, and elaborate celebrations honoring prominent democrats kept the populace in a continual state of excitement. As August turned into September the number of women participating in these "revolutionary exercises" increased steadily. In spite of masculine protests about the indecent conduct of the newly liberated Viennese "ladies," women from all walks of life appeared at public pleasure resorts or came as spectators to the meetings of the radical clubs, the National Guard, and the students.[10] "Carrying their lorgnettes," many members of the fair sex besieged the deputies in Parliament "in a manner which even our brave Radetzky did not use in attacking a fortress."[11]

The National Guard was constantly checking noisy demonstrators. Here the people's armed forces had to arrest a worker who wildly urged his listeners to storm the prisons and free the occupants.[12] There they

[6] Quoted in Helfert, *op. cit.*, p. 128.
[7] Ehrlich, "Lebendiger Tod des Gemeinde-Ausschusses, und die Grabrede für denselben," *Nazional-Zeitung*, No. 30 (August 23, 1848), p. 117, Univ. Colo. 1848 Coll., No. II/146.
[8] Wessenberg to Archduke John, Vienna, September 3, 1848, Alfred Ritter von Arneth, *Wessenberg*, Vol. II, p. 259
[9] *Wiener Zeitung*, No. 259 (September 26, 1848), p. 761.
[10] See especially F. B., *Die weibliche Nationalgarde in Wien. Buchstäblich wahr*, Univ. Colo. 1848 Coll., No. II/273.
[11] "Die politische Damenwelt," *Der Stadttrompeter*, No. 1 (August 7, 1848), p. 1, Univ. Colo. 1848 Coll., No. II/15.
[12] *Wiener Zeitung*, No. 234 (August 27, 1848), p. 501.

had to intervene to protect an unpopular landlady[13] from some disgruntled tenant who had gone out "to fetch the democrats." Now and then they had to rescue an overenthusiastic conservative like Herr Böhringer, the editor of the *Geissel,* from an infuriated mob after he displayed a black-yellow flag at his office.[14]

To add to the excitement and confusion, a new religion was introduced in Vienna in August, the German-Catholic faith, which was founded in Prussian Silesia in 1845 by Johannes Ronge. Ronge was immediately excommunicated by the Catholic church, whereupon he demanded that the Germans sever all ties with Rome and establish a German national church. Ronge's bold course of action immediately made him a hero to the German liberals, who saw in his movement a new form of opposition to the highly unpopular Catholic hierarchy and the autocratic German governments. When he attempted to spread his new faith in Prussia, Ronge was forced to flee and was also expelled from other parts of Germany.

No attempt was made to win converts to the new faith in the Habsburg monarchy until late July, 1848, when the German-Catholic religion was introduced in Vienna by the curate of the suburban parish of Erdberg, Hermann Pauli.[15] To win converts to his creed, Pauli posted a public announcement inviting the public to the salon of the Vogel Inn on Sunday, July 30, to listen to the first lecture in Vienna on the German-Catholic teachings. About two hundred persons attended the meeting. The next Sunday a second meeting was held, this time in the Straussen Inn, in Josefstadt, where Pauli received considerable applause from his listeners.[16] Thus encouraged, Pauli arranged for a large public meeting in the Odeon Hall on August 15, to which about 8,000 persons came. Pauli, clothed in a black cassock, exhorted his audience to become disciples of the new cult, whose main tenets, as described in the public invitation to the Viennese to attend the meeting, were as follows:[17]

[13] For example, *ibid.,* No. 246 (September 10, 1848), p. 626.

[14] *Ibid.;* Auerbach diary, September 14, 1848, Berthold Auerbach, *Tagebuch aus Wien,* p. 22; Friedrich Unterreiter, *Die Revolution in Wien vom Juni bis September 1848,* Vol. II, p. 87.

[15] Pauli said that once when he was ill he withdrew from pastoral work to search for a new religion that was both humane and rational. He maintained that he found both these attributes in the German-Catholic movement.

[16] Heinrich Reschauer and Moritz Smets, *Das Jahr 1848. Geschichte der Wiener Revolution,* Vol. II, p. 478.

[17] Scheibe, *Eine neue Religion in Wien! und entdeckte Verruchtheit Metternichs,* Univ. Colo. 1848 Coll., No. II/176.

The Defeat of the Lower Middle Class

A New Religion in Vienna! and Discovered Wickedness of Metternich

Church reforms are following our political revolts.

The Roman Catholic religion, the same as the Lutheran, is undeniably facing great formal changes, and there is no doubt that the German-Catholic religion, which is halfway between the two, will find very many adherents. Following the example of other German cities, a German-Catholic society has already been formed in Vienna, and it has approached the Ministry to grant it a house of prayer.

Since it will definitely be to the interest of the Viennese populace to learn to know the nature of the German-Catholic religion, we shall make a statement of its principles here.

The German-Catholic religion teaches everything to its adherents that the Roman Catholic religion teaches, with the following exceptions:

1. It does not recognize the ecclesiastical power and supreme authority of the Roman pope.

2. The Holy Mass is not held in Latin, which none of the auditors understand, but in the German language.

3. The German-Catholic clergy are permitted to marry, because no unmarried priest can fulfill his calling as a beloved educator of the people and as a giver of happiness and comfort.

4. They reject auricular confession, and in its place have a general confession similar to that of the Protestants, and thereafter they partake of the Lord's Supper.

5. They reject indulgences.

6. They do not consider it meritorious to live in cloisters and lead a contemplative monastic life.

The founder of the German-Catholic religion is the Catholic priest Ronge, from Prussian Silesia, who has declaimed passionately against the abuses of the Roman Catholic religion from the pulpit. At the very beginning he found many adherents, even though a bull of excommunication was thundered out against him.

Finally he had to flee from Prussia, since no worldly laws could protect him against the persecution of the clergy. Ronge visited Saxony, Bavaria, Baden, and Württemberg, where he established German-Catholic communities everywhere.

But he could also not maintain himself there. The police were always at his heels. However, Ronge had to endure the greatest persecution from Metternich. He not only prohibited him from stepping across the Austrian borders, on pain of death, but *he also put a price of 100 ducats* [about $225] *on his head* in order forever to close the mouth of this reformer of the Christian Church, whose successful gift of eloquence and strong morality were everywhere praised by his followers.

Through this, Metternich, this old sinner, encouraged the most outrageous assassination. But there was no single person in all Germany so depraved that he would have drawn his murderous dagger against Ronge.

In order to escape Metternich's bloodhounds, Ronge sought asylum in France, but after the hour of freedom struck in Germany and Austria, Ronge hurried again to his Fatherland.

It is said that Ronge is already on his way to Vienna, where he will give his sermons.

Since in a short time the number of German-Catholics in Germany has risen to several hundred thousand, among whom there are distinguished intellectuals, it should at least be worth while to listen to Ronge's sermons in order to decide whether his reforms are actually timely and sensible, whether they are contrary to the teachings of the Divine Redeemer of the world, and whether they have the strength and inspiration to give real comfort and peace to the adherents and to ennoble their souls. Through our free institutions we have complete freedom of religion, and Ronge will not have to await imprisonment and death within the walls of Vienna, from which Metternich has fled.

Since their number has already reached more than 800, on Tuesday, August 15, the German-Catholics of Vienna will meet in the great Odeon Hall.

The rumor is being circulated that Ronge arrived in Vienna today.

Scheibe

Alarmed that a heretic like Pauli could attract a crowd of 8,000 Viennese, the Catholic clergy feared that if something was not done immediately to stop him, Austria might be plunged into another terrible religious war. They began "to inveigh against the German-Catholics in placards,"[18] while Sebastian Brunner denounced them in the pages of his *Kirchenzeitung.* Soon posters appeared on the city walls, warning the people against dangerous religious innovators who were seeking to rob the people of their faith.[19]

Considerable opposition was thus stirred up against the German-Catholics. On the evening of August 17 a heated argument between German-Catholics and their opponents led to fist fights in St. Stephen's Square.[20] The next evening, when 4,000 people gathered in Odeon Hall to attend another German-Catholic meeting,[21] a band of hecklers, crying out that the workers were coming to break up the assembly, ended the service just as Pauli began speaking.[22] From that moment on the

[18] *Nazional-Zeitung,* No. 30 (August 23, 1848), p. 120, Univ. Colo. 1848 Coll., No. II/146.

[19] Hübner diary, Vienna, August 20, 1848, Alexander Grafen von Hübner, *Ein Jahr meines Lebens. 1848–1849,* p. 192.

[20] *Wiener Zeitung,* No. 230 (August 23, 1848), p. 463.

[21] *Ibid.,* No. 227 (August 19, 1848), p. 436.

[22] Reschauer and Smets, *op. cit.,* Vol. II, p. 479.

German-Catholic movement began to wane. When the group met again in Odeon Hall on August 29, there were barely 300 people on hand. When Pauli appealed for money, most of his hearers melted away.[23] Even Ronge's personal appearance in the Odeon Hall on September 17 did little to reverse the steady decline of the movement. Although the German-Catholics did finally organize a congregation on September 24, they continued to be a small group until the revolution ended, when the movement was suppressed.[24]

The opposition of the conservatives to the German-Catholics gave ample testimony that the "partisans of law and order" had been greatly strengthened by the return of the Emperor and the defeat of the proletariat. As has been pointed out before, for a long time many people in Vienna had been extremely tired of the revolution.[25] After the overthrow of the proletariat the numbers of antirevolutionaries were increased by the return of many families to Vienna.[26] By the first of September, in spite of the fact that the wearers of the Habsburg colors were still openly insulted and serenaded, an ever increasing number of Viennese appeared on the streets with black-yellow armbands to show their hostility to radicalism.[27] Here and there the "black-yellows" even dared to repay the insults they had suffered from the democrats during the previous months. According to the assistant editor of the *Constitution*, by the end of August the reaction had progressed "so far that a free democratic word" could not "be spoken without one's being turned over to the city captaincy as a republican, that everyone" who had "expressed opinions in the radical papers differing from those of the black-yellows" did not "dare to go on the streets without saber and pistol," and that every day there was "a new placard against the radical press," "against the Jews," and "against the republicans, in which category" were "included all who did not toot with reactionary horns."[28]

In all parts of Vienna, opponents of the "black-red-golds" were hold-

[23] "Die Deutschkatoliken in Wien," *Die goldene Mittelstrasse. Populäres Organ der gemässigten Partei,* No. 1 (September 5, 1848), p. 3, copy in the Univ. Colo. 1848 Coll., No. II/59. *Die goldene Mittelstrasse* was edited by F. A. Rosental and appeared from September 5 to December 16, 1848.
[24] Reschauer and Smets, *op. cit.,* Vol. II, pp. 479–80.
[25] Füster, *op. cit.,* Vol. II, p. 97.
[26] *Die goldene Mittelstrasse,* No. 1 (September 5, 1848), p. 2, Univ. Colo. 1848 Coll., No. II/59.
[27] Füster, *op. cit.,* Vol. II, p. 120; *Der Kampf um die schwarzgelben Bänder oder: Wer ist eigentlich ein Schwarzgelber?* Univ. Colo. 1848 Coll., No. II/105; *Die goldene Mittelstrasse,* No. 1 (September 5, 1848), p. 2, Univ. Colo. 1848 Coll., No. II/59.
[28] Gritzner, in the name of the whole editorial staff of the *Constitution, An Wien!* (Vienna, August 30, 1848), Univ. Colo. 1848 Coll., No. II/93.

ing secret meetings and making plans to strike back at the revolutionaries.[29] At first, lack of organization impeded the conservatives. However, at a large meeting on September 5 they decided to form a patriotic organization named the Constitutional Club as a rallying point for all those who wanted to preserve the constitutional monarchy and ward off republicanism and anarchy. The program of the club, as announced by its provisional directing committee on September 8, read as follows:[30]

Permeated with the conviction that the unceasing agitation of the party working for the overthrow of the constitutional-monarchical principle in Austria, and, along with it, for the ruination of our great, glorious, common Fatherland, *must finally, in all earnestness, be kept within limits,* on September 5, in a large assembly held in the hall of the Roman Empire, the creation of a club was resolved, the aim of which is to be, in connection with *filial clubs to be founded in all provinces, to preserve the constitutional-monarchical principle, in the true sense of the word, for the best welfare of the whole imperial state and to extend it further in a legal way.* Therefore the most sacred aim of the *"Constitutional Club"* will be *to declare that every retrogression to absolutism, which threatens our freedom that has been won, as well as every bold encroachment in the direction of republicanism, is treason to the Fatherland and to constitutional freedom, and that it will oppose both with all its strength.*

The time for revolution and uprooting is *and must be* over! ! ! Now it is a matter of *building up*—of *building up* on the basis of *genuine constitutional freedom! !*

All well-intentioned persons must now come together. They have long enough remained silent in face of the terrorism of certain anarchists. They must come together so that *freedom* will become a beautiful *reality* that will bring to all of us the blessings that we are justified in expecting. A long period of irresolution and mere quiet watching, while the republican party is working for the realization of its plans with restless activity and energy, would be *treason* to the Fatherland and *treason* to our freedom and to our constitutional Emperor! !

The voice of our oppressed Fatherland is earnestly calling to us in way of warning! Therefore, everyone whose heart is beating for genuine constitutional freedom and whose love for the hereditary constitutional imperial house has not been extinguished, and whoever is working for the true welfare of the *whole great, free Austria* give us now your hand as brothers for this holy union.

---

[29] Füster, *op. cit.,* Vol. II, pp. 93–95.
[30] Provisional Committee of the Constitutional Club, *Programm des constitutionellen Vereines* (Vienna, September 8, 1848), Univ. Colo. 1848 Coll., No. II/169.

A person will become a member of the Constitutional Club by writing his name in the club register.

Thus the program of the club was broad enough to bring a large number of people together. Its members did not have to adhere to any definite aim except opposition to republicanism and anarchy. That in itself was enough to make the club extremely popular. Seeing that the club was "something against the radicals,"[31] the partisans of law and order hurried in large numbers to join. By the middle of September, according to report, between 22,000[32] and 30,000 persons had gone to the Landhaus to get their membership cards.[33] By September 27 the club was well enough advanced to enable it to insert a large, paid proclamation "to All Provinces in Regard to the Creation of Affiliated Clubs" in the *Wiener Zeitung*[34] urging

all well-intentioned persons, not only in the provincial and district capitals but in all other cities in the provinces and in the larger communities, to get together without delay and pledge themselves to work together in fraternal harmony and in close connection with the Viennese Constitutional Club for the deliverance of our threatened Fatherland and for the preservation of the freedom won in March.

Whenever a group of patriots formed such a club, they were to notify the Viennese club of this fact so that the parent organization could "immediately send them its statutes and work with them in fraternal reciprocity for the great goal which must be common to all clubs"—turning the club's motto, "Freedom, Legality, and Order," into a "beautiful reality for the whole, great, free Austria!"[35]

The government, encouraged by the growing strength of the conservative movement, grew more determined than ever to preserve its power. It did not have long to wait before it was put to another test of strength, this time against the group that constituted the core of the revolution: the lower middle class.

By September the situation of the master-craftsmen, artisans, and petty shopkeepers of Vienna and the suburbs was becoming desperate. Although the Committee for the Assistance of Destitute Tradesmen,

---

[31] Auerbach diary, September 14, 1848, Auerbach, *op. cit.*, pp. 22–23.

[32] Hübner diary, Vienna, September 17, 1848, Hübner, *op. cit.*, p. 205.

[33] Auerbach diary, September 14, 1848, Auerbach, *op. cit.*, p. 23.

[34] Provisional Committee of the Constitutional Club in Vienna, "Aufruf des Wiener constitutionellen Vereines an sämmtliche Provinzen, in Bezug auf die Bildung von Filial-Vereinen," Vienna, September 22, 1848, *Wiener Zeitung*, No. 260 (September 27, 1848), p. 782.

[35] *Ibid.*

which had been created on August 24, utilized what resources were available to aid manufacturers and craftsmen, partly with money, partly with raw materials, and partly with advances for their manufactured wares, and the Minister of Finance used his influence with the National Bank[36] to persuade it to put 500,000 florins ($240,000) at the disposal of the committee, this help was totally inadequate—a fact the spokesmen of the hard-pressed traders, manufacturers, and craftsmen well realized. A group of them turned to the City Council to ask for the establishment of a commercial bank, which would be supported by a loan of 500,000,000 florins from the National Bank, but the proposal was turned down on the ground that the National Bank could not possibly supply the money. Another group suggested that people's banks be created to provide cheap, easy credit for the poorer classes, but this proposal was also rejected.[37]

Among the most ardent champions of a people's bank was the unemployed Viennese clock-maker August Swoboda,[38] who for months had been agitating for the establishment of such a bank to make loans at low interest to master-craftsmen and owners of small manufacturing enterprises.[39] The capital for the institution was to be obtained by forcing all house-owners in Vienna to lend a fixed sum of money to it. Although the spectators in the galleries loudly applauded Swoboda when he presented his plan to Parliament, it was rejected as impractical.[40]

In the summer Swoboda came forward with another project that would accomplish the same objective but did not require approval by the government. He founded a "Private Loan Institute without Collateral" to lend money to needy small manufacturers and craftsmen. For this purpose 200,000 shares of stock at 20 florins ($9.60) each were to be sold to the public to obtain a capital of 4,000,000 florins ($1,920,000) for the institute. An interest of 5 per cent was to be paid to the holder of each share. In addition, nonshareholders were invited to take out membership in the institute by paying a low membership fee of 10 kreutzer (8 cents). Then, without putting up any collateral, a member could borrow from the institute a sum of money proportionate

---

[36] Protocol of the 32nd Sitting of Parliament, August 29, 1848, *Wiener Zeitung,* No. 236 (August 30, 1848), p. 518.

[37] Ernst Victor Zenker, *Die Wiener Revolution,* pp. 215–17.

[38] Practically nothing is known about Swoboda except that he was about fifty years old at this time and had been a clock-maker and perhaps also a second-hand dealer and a piano-tuner.

[39] Franz Pulszky, *Mein Zeit, mein Leben,* Vol. II, pp. 200–201.

[40] Ernst Violand, *Die sociale Geschichte der Revolution in Oesterreich,* p. 151; Zenker, *op. cit.,* pp. 150–53.

to the property he owned. The money was to be paid back at the rate of 2 florins (96 cents) a month for every 50 florins ($24) borrowed. Swoboda hoped that the shares of the institute would be accepted as legal tender by the public, just like National Bank notes, and anticipated that 30,000 Viennese would take out membership cards. All the members together were to guarantee the solvency of the enterprise.[41]

The financial interests immediately recognized that Swoboda's enterprise was basically unsound—if for no other reason than that it rested solely upon mutual trust at a time when trust was so singularly lacking[42]—and refused to participate in the scheme.[43] The general public thought otherwise. Thousands of Viennese hastened to take out membership in the organization. When they learned that in their private capacity Ministers Doblhoff and Hornbostel had purchased a substantial number of shares, the public flocked to buy shares.[44] It was soon reported that the institute had 40,000 members.[45] But before long the enterprise was recognized for what it was—a grandiose swindle— and the shares stopped selling. The stockholders, furious at seeing their investments in the enterprise vanish overnight, demanded that the government return their money, insisting that the state was responsible for the whole affair.[46]

Around seven o'clock on the evening of September 11 a group of angry shareholders appealed to the Vienna City Council to underwrite the securities of the Swoboda Institute. The City Council maintained that it could do nothing to guarantee the solvency of a private institution but promised to submit the whole matter to a special committee for investigation. The refusal of the City Council immediately to comply with their petition infuriated the lower-middle-class visitors who had jammed the galleries. They unceremoniously sprang from their seats and chased the members of the council out of the hall.[47]

The crowd then hurried to the Ministry of Interior building at Juden Square where they were joined by a mob of artisans, students, shopkeepers, and small manufacturers who were trying to compel Minister Doblhoff to underwrite the Swoboda enterprise. In the square in front of his headquarters the demonstrators threatened to find means to re-

---

[41] *Wiener Zeitung*, No. 248 (September 13, 1848), pp. 646–47; Violand, *op. cit.*, p. 152; Unterreiter, *op. cit.*, Vol. II, pp. 93–94.

[42] *Wiener Zeitung*, No. 248 (September 13, 1848), p. 647.

[43] Pulszky, *op. cit.*, Vol. II, p. 201.

[44] Füster, *op. cit.*, Vol. II, p. 125.

[45] Zenker, *op. cit.*, p. 219.

[46] Violand, *op. cit.*, p. 155.

[47] Füster, *op. cit.*, Vol. II, p. 127.

imburse themselves by force if the ministers refused to guarantee the stock. A deputation representing the crowd pushed its way into Doblhoff's apartment. The Minister explained that Swoboda's undertaking was a purely private one and that the state was under no circumstances obligated to guarantee it. However, alarmed by the increase of the tumult outside, he added that he would give them a definite answer the next morning. The demonstrators were not content with this equivocal response. Crowds of ruffians tried to shove their way into the building and fought with those who attempted to stop them. Serious rioting was prevented only because at this moment National Guardsmen rushed up, occupied the ministerial building, and persuaded the crowd to go home.[48]

Early on the morning of September 12 the square in front of the Ministry of Interior building again filled with people anxiously awaiting the Ministry's statement. At 8:30 it came. The Ministry repeated Doblhoff's assertion that the Swoboda Institute was a private enterprise and that the Ministry could under no circumstances guarantee its solvency. However, to protect the tradesmen against serious loss, it was appointing a commission to make a careful examination of the matter in order to prevent further frauds on the part of the institute.[49]

This language exasperated a people who had grown accustomed to seeing the government yield to their demands at the slightest show of disorder. The presence of the National Guard merely augmented the tension and made the danger of a serious uprising all the more imminent, since many guardsmen immediately broke ranks and joined the tumultuous throng in the square. At this moment the crowd, apparently acting upon orders, stormed the Ministry building to search for Doblhoff and force him to comply with their demands. The mob broke down the main door, chased away the few loyal National Guardsmen who were defending it, surged into the building, and shattered furniture, doors, and windows. Doblhoff was rescued at the last moment by some members of the Academic Legion, who succeeded in smuggling him out of the building through a side door.[50]

The National Guard commander, alarmed because some of his men

[48] Hübner diary, Vienna, September 11, 1848, Hübner, *op. cit.*, pp. 200–203; William H. Stiles, *Austria in 1848–49*, Vol. I, p. 168; Reschauer and Smets, *op. cit.*, Vol. II, pp. 506–507.

[49] Stiles, *op. cit.*, Vol. I, p. 168; Zenker, *op. cit.*, pp. 220–21.

[50] *Wiener Zeitung*, No. 248 (September 13, 1848), p. 647; Hübner diary, September 12, 1848, Hübner, *op. cit.*, pp. 203–204; Füster, *op. cit.*, Vol. II, p. 126; "Report of Legion Commander Koller," Reschauer and Smets, *op. cit.*, Vol. II, pp. 508–10.

had assisted the rioters, appealed to the army commandant for help, and at one o'clock two grenadier battalions marched to Juden Square to reinforce the loyal National Guardsmen. Guard detachments were also sent to the city gates to strengthen the regular guard details. At the same time, the government posted proclamations reassuring the Viennese and urging them to return to their homes and support the legal officers of the state in their efforts to maintain order.[51] Fathers and businessmen were instructed to keep their families, apprentices, and workers at home or at their places of work. The Viennese were warned that anyone disobeying the commands of the legal authorities would be punished with up to six months' imprisonment.[52]

The mustering of the regular army and the posting of these announcements still further angered the mob, who were quieted only by the news that the Ministry had ordered the troops to return to their barracks.

The disturbances on the 12th were merely a prelude to further riots the next day. On the morning of the 13th the streets of the inner city were filled with artisans, tradesmen, and workers from the suburbs, apparently summoned by the radicals in revenge for their defeat in August. At the university it was debated whether the Ministry should be overthrown or whether the students should insist that the Security Committee be straightway re-established. Oskar Falke, the editor of the *Studenten-Courier*, delivered a speech denouncing the conduct of the Ministry as inimical to the rights of the people and urged the re-creation of the Security Committee to safeguard the rights of the people. Others jumped up to second his proposals and, for good measure, to clamor for the arraignment and trial of various unpopular government officials. Falke's arguments were accepted by the audience in the Aula, who also resolved that everyone in favor of the reinstallation of the Security Committee should wear a placard upon his hat bearing the words "Citizens of Vienna! Only the re-establishment of the Security Committee can save us!" Twelve thousand copies of the poster were printed forthwith and handed out to the crowd. The assemblage sent a deputation to the Ministry to demand the reinstallation of the popular committee.[53] The deputation met with little success. The Minister of War, Count Latour, heatedly accused the students of proclaiming a republic during the

[51] Doblhoff, "Proclamation," Vienna, September 12, 1848, *Wiener Zeitung*, No. 219 (September 14, 1848), p. 653.

[52] Ministerial Council, "Proclamation," September 12, 1848, *ibid.*

[53] Dunder, *Denkschrift über die Wiener October-Revolution*, pp. 13–14; Füster, *op. cit.*, Vol. II, p. 139; Protocol of the 41st Sitting of Parliament, September 13, 1848, *Wiener Zeitung*, No. 250 (September 15, 1848), p. 663; Unterreiter, *op. cit.*, Vol. II, pp. 95–96.

morning, while Doblhoff, in the presence of Ministers Krauss and Schwarzer, excitedly told Füster, the leader of the delegation, that he would oppose to the death reviving the Security Committee, for he would never again tolerate two supreme executive authorities in the capital.[54]

The atmosphere was explosive. The students and petty bourgeoisie were bent on coercing the government to do their bidding, while the Ministry was determined under no circumstances to submit to them. Alarming rumors were spreading around the city: the rabble was preparing to storm the city hall to seize the funds deposited in the city treasury; the insurgents were planning to destroy the Ministry of Interior building; the students were getting ready to overthrow the government and dissolve Parliament in order to establish a republic in Vienna.[55]

The authorities took quick measures to defend the city against what seemed to be an imminent revolt. The entire National Guard was ordered out and stationed at the city hall, Joseph Square, the city gates, and other strategic points in the city. When the rumor reached Count Latour that the students intended to overthrow the Ministry, he instructed the military to leave the barracks and proceed immediately into the inner city. Three infantry battalions, with six cannon, quickly set out toward the university. Others were dispatched to the Ministry of War building and elsewhere. The loyal National Guard companies fraternized with the troops, and both were greeted enthusiastically when they arrived in the city.[56] But many of the suburban guardsmen and Academic Legionnaires openly sympathized with the revolutionaries. Two armed, determined groups now faced each other. Plainly the moment was critical. A single rash move could set Vienna aflame.

The Austrian Parliament must be given credit for averting warfare. At the beginning of the September 13 session a proposal was made and accepted that Parliament immediately put 2,000,000 florins ($960,000) at the disposal of the Ministry to make advance payments without interest to the hard-pressed business and manufacturing groups in Vienna. The Finance Committee was given instructions to act upon the plan within twenty-four hours. When Latour rushed into the hall to inform

---

[54] Füster, *op. cit.*, Vol. II, pp. 140–43.

[55] Unterreiter, *op. cit.*, Vol. II, p. 97; Vitzthum von Eckstädt to his mother, Vienna, September 16, 1848, Carl Friedrich Grafen von Vitzthum von Eckstädt, *Berlin und Wien in den Jahren 1845–1852*, p. 138; Violand, *op. cit.*, p. 202.

[56] Auerbach diary, September 13, 1848, Auerbach, *op. cit.*, p. 13; Hübner diary, Vienna, September 13, 1848, Hübner, *op. cit.*, p. 205; Unterreiter, *op. cit.*, Vol. II, p. 97; Füster, *op. cit.*, Vol. II, pp. 145–50.

Parliament that he had called out the military because a plot was afoot to overthrow the government and abolish Parliament, the assembly at once declared itself in session for the duration of the emergency and sent a committee to the university to investigate reports that the students were planning a rebellion. Then, in spite of the strenuous protests of the Minister of War, Parliament ordered the troops to return to their garrison.[57] On its part, the government issued a proclamation assuring the Viennese that a rumor that the Ministry intended to dissolve the Academic Legion was groundless.[58]

All these measures had their effect. The withdrawal of the military convinced the students that the Ministry was not plotting against the Academic Legion, and the students declared their support of Parliament. Gradually the crowd of demonstrators left the city, and by midnight the streets of Vienna were almost deserted. On the next day Parliament accepted the advice of its Finance Committee and voted a credit of 2,000,000 florins in non-interest-bearing loans to master-craftsmen and small manufacturers, and the government used part of this sum to redeem shares in the Swoboda Institute, up to 20 per cent of their value. Thereafter the lower middle classes lost interest in demonstrating against the government.[59]

The actions of Parliament in this crisis resulted in a great victory for the forces of law and order. Lower-middle-class malcontents had tried to frighten the Ministry into guaranteeing the solvency of the Swoboda Institute and then into reinstating the Security Committee, and the government had proved resolute and strong in both instances. For the second time in less than a month the Ministry had emerged triumphant over the revolutionaries, and this was an even greater victory than the one in August, when the leaderless, unorganized proletariat had been defeated. In September the "petty bourgeoisie" found themselves abandoned. Not only had the upper middle classes loudly applauded the Ministry, but also the proletariat, remembering the desertion of the lower middle classes on August 23, had refused to come to their assistance.

The events of September 11 to 13 also widened the breaches that had

---

[57] Protocol of the 41st Sitting of Parliament, September 13, 1848, *Wiener Zeitung*, No. 219 (September 14, 1848), pp. 653–54; Auerbach diary, September 13, 1848, Auerbach, *op. cit.*, p. 13.

[58] Ministry, "Proclamation," Vienna, September 13, 1848, *Wiener Zeitung*, No. 250 (September 15, 1848), p. 663.

[59] Protocol of the 42nd Sitting of Parliament, September 14, 1848, *Wiener Zeitung*, No. 250 (September 15, 1848), p. 663; Josephine Goldmark, *Pilgrims of '48*, p. 85.

plagued the National Guard since the May revolutions. The conservative guard companies were infuriated with the guardsmen who had broken ranks to join the demonstrators and with the Academic Legion for having sided with the revolutionaries.

The strength and unity of the Academic Legion, too, were profoundly affected by the events of September 13. On that afternoon Matthias Koller,[60] deeply shaken because so many men in his organization refused to obey his orders, resigned as commander. Then the Student Committee quickly appointed the ambitious portrait-painter Josef Aigner,[61] the only one of the five corps commanders who happened to be present, as the temporary commander until a permanent one could be elected. On September 15, Aigner managed to pack the polling place with his own supporters and get himself elected as commander of the legion.[62] Many of the more responsible elements in the legion were indignant over these maneuvers, and Aigner's election made the cleavages in the Academic Legion greater. By the end of September the Academic Legion had degenerated into a divided, undisciplined, incompetently led mob.[63]

Emboldened by its victories, the Ministry took steps to bridle the radical press, which was still as factious as ever and was becoming increasingly republican in sentiment.[64] After the issuance of the press law on May 18, the radical editors knew that they were liable for trial and prosecution if they went too far in their attacks on the government and

---

[60] When Colonel Pannasch was appointed supreme commander of the National Guard on June 2, with the consent of the students he appointed his friend Matthias Koller, a retired army captain, *de facto* commander of the Academic Legion. When the Security Committee ousted Pannasch from his position in July and replaced him with Adjutant General Valentin von Streffleur, Koller continued in his post as legion commander.

[61] On November 23, 1848, the Habsburg military court condemned Aigner to death for the part he had played in the revolution, but Windischgrätz pardoned him unconditionally.

[62] Kaiser, *op. cit.*, pp. 115–18.

[63] Ehnl, *Messenhauser*, pp. 57–58.

[64] Note, for instance, Hans Kudlich, *Rückblicke und Erinnerungen*, Vol. II, p. 137; "Kleine Experimente. Anton Langer und die Republik in Österreich," *Schwefeläther*, No. 2 (August 6, 1848), p. 8, Univ. Colo. 1848 Coll., No. II/181b; Füster, *op. cit.*, Vol. II, pp. 117–19; and [Emanuel Kopetzky], *Ergebnisse der von dem kaiserlich-königlichen Militär-Gerichte geführten Untersuchung wider die Mörder des k. k. Kriegsministers, General-Feldzeugmeisters Theodor Grafen Baillet von Latour* (hereafter cited throughout as *Ergebnisse*), p. 120. An English translation of Kopetzky is included in William Coxe, *History of the House of Austria*, Vol. IV, pp. 333–463, under the title *Results of the Investigation instituted by the Imperial-Royal Court-Martial, respecting the Murderers of the Minister of War, General Field-Marshal Theodor Count Baillet von Latour*. The above citation is on p. 426.

venerated persons and institutions; but they believed that the government would not dare move against them, and that, if it did, no jury would convict them. In the beginning they were right. In June and July almost two hundred complaints of press abuses were placed in the hands of the state's attorney, who at first felt unable to initiate prosecution.[65]

In August, heartened by the steady swing of public opinion to the right, the government finally took action against the radical press. On August 16 the editors of the *Studenten-Courier,* Oskar Falke and Adolf Buchheim, were arrested, along with their collaborator, Heinrich Blumberg,[66] for having published articles praising republicanism in the July 11 and 12 issues. Although Buchheim and Falke were released after Anton Füster put up the required bail and Blumberg was freed after an angry mob threatened to storm the jail,[67] all three were formally tried on August 24, as well as the editor of the *Freie Wiener,* J. M. Schleichert, who had reprinted one of the offending articles in a special supplement of his paper. A large crowd jammed the courtroom to show their sympathy for the defendants, and the prosecuting attorney bent over backward not to offend them. The jury deliberated scarcely half an hour and found all the defendants not guilty. The crowd of well-wishers in the courtroom broke out in an ovation and jubilantly escorted the editors to their newspaper offices.[68]

Other editors were not so lucky. The next press case resulted in a conviction. On August 31 Adolf Ungár, the editor of the *Wiener Tageblatt,* was tried for having falsely accused a landlady of perjury and, amid the applause of the spectators present, was sentenced to three weeks in prison.[69] On September 7 Ungár was again tried for other press offenses, this time on three different charges of injuring the honor of three Viennese citizens. He was sentenced to eight days' arrest for the first misdemeanor, twenty-four hours' arrest for the second, and three days' arrest for the third.[70]

Sigmund Engländer, the editor of the *Wiener Katzenmusik,* was a bit more fortunate than Ungár. On September 3 he was declared not guilty when tried for having injured the Schloissnigg family by falsely

---

[65] Helfert, *op. cit.,* p. 159.

[66] Besides assisting with the *Politischer Studenten-Courier,* Blumberg was editor of the *Ohnehose,* founded on July 7. The name of the latter was changed to *Der Proletarier* on July 18, when the police objected to the title, and then on July 24 to *Der Volksmann.*

[67] *Wiener Zeitung,* No. 228 (August 20, 1848), p. 447.

[68] *Ibid.,* No. 234 (August 27, 1848), pp. 500–501; E[rnst] V[ictor] Zenker, *Wiener Journalistik 1848,* pp. 90–91; Helfert, *op. cit.,* pp. 166–75.

[69] *Wiener Zeitung,* No. 239 (September 2, 1848), p. 554.

[70] *Ibid.,* No. 245 (September 9, 1848), pp. 615–16.

calling them usurers, money-suckers, and stubborn landlords in the pages of his paper.[71] However, eight days later, when he was tried for having impugned the honor of Prince Windischgrätz and slandered officers of the Austrian army, the jurors found him innocent of the first charge but guilty of the second and sentenced him to three days' arrest.[72]

Next came the turn of the *Wanderer* and the *Radikale*. On September 18 a certain Miguel Étiènne was sentenced to three weeks' arrest for having referred to the National Guard of the Third Vienna District as "miserable scoundrels" in an article published in the June 6 issue of the *Wanderer*.[73] Three days later a Sigmund Kolisch received three weeks' arrest for having insulted the honor of the military in an article published in the *Radikale* on July 11.[74]

These trials enraged the radical press but did not persuade them to moderate their sensational, irresponsible, and vituperative tone. On September 19 Auerbach could still record in his diary about the Viennese press:[75]

"Traitor," "scoundrel," "slut," "Mephistopheles" are common expressions used against unpopular public personalities. How can a place be found, along with all this, for a sensible discussion based on clear proof? Such are the sheets written for a people who just a few months ago were surrounded with spies and who still have a most abominable military system, a rotten bureaucracy, a decayed educational system—in short, everything is still as it was in the old times.

Much more effective than the press trials in dampening the enthusiasm of the Austrian revolutionaries were the steps taken to free the Austrian peasants from the *Robot* and other services. The idea did not originate with Parliament. For a long time before 1848, many landowners had agitated for the substitution of cash payments for peasant services,[76] and, as will be remembered, Emperor Ferdinand had issued a manifesto on April 11 promising to free the peasants from the *Robot* and all other dues and services on January 1, 1849. However, the belief prevailed that the sanction of Parliament was needed to make the Emperor's promises binding and effective in all parts of the empire. Since a large number of deputies in Parliament were peasants, they set

[71] *Ibid.*, No. 241 (September 5, 1848), pp. 574–75.
[72] Helfert, *op. cit.*, p. 177.
[73] *Wiener Zeitung*, No. 254 (September 20, 1848), pp. 712–13.
[74] *Ibid.*, No. 258 (September 24, 1848), pp. 753–54.
[75] Auerbach, *op. cit.*, pp. 27–28.
[76] Jerome Blum has particularly emphasized this point in his *Noble Landowners and Agriculture in Austria*.

The Defeat of the Lower Middle Class

about taking steps to ensure the carrying out of the Emperor's earlier promises.

On July 24 Hans Kudlich, the youngest deputy in Parliament and an ardent champion of peasant interests, submitted a written proposal for Parliament to declare that "from now on all servile relationships, together with all rights and obligations coming therefrom, are abolished." The question of "whether and how any indemnification is to be provided" was to be reserved for future discussion.[77] The debates on the measure began on August 8. Kudlich argued that all popular constituent assemblies must end any infractions or limitations of human rights.[78] The main quarrel, however, centered on whether or not the landlords should be indemnified for the substantial losses they would suffer through the abolition of the dues and services. The radical left, including Kudlich, spoke ardently against indemnification in any form, while the center and right, as well as the government, insisted that fair compensation must be made. During the course of the debates seventy-three amendments to Kudlich's original proposal were offered.

The Viennese public followed the discussions with great interest, and numerous articles appeared in the newspapers expressing the views of various Viennese groups about Kudlich's scheme. Many radicals were skeptical of the proposal, and some "considered the installation of a republic as much more practical and nearer than the abolition of manorial burdens." On the other hand, many conservatives "suddenly discovered a socialistic, and others even a communistic, measure" in Kudlich's plan and "shook their heads and regretted to see that the property rights that had been declared sacred by the Viennese workers might be attacked in Parliament itself."[79]

Not until August 31 and September 1 was the issue finally decided in favor of a proposal to pay a fair indemnity only for dues and services originating in the ownership of property. No compensation was to be given for services or dues that came from any bonds of personal dependency.[80]

The main difficulty that had held up the passage of the bill was now overcome, but still another obstacle had to be surmounted before the bill became law. A question arose over the proclamation of the law. The

[77] Hans Kudlich to Parliament, Vienna, July 24, 1848, Karl Schneider, *Der Reichstag von Kremsier*, pp. 29–30. Kudlich also made a brief speech in favor of the motion on July 26.

[78] Minutes of the Sitting of Parliament on August 8, 1848, in *ibid.*, pp. 30–43.

[79] Kudlich, *op. cit.*, Vol. II, pp. 137–38.

[80] Parliamentary Resolution in the Sittings of August 31 and September 1, 1848, Schneider, *op. cit.*, pp. 43–46.

radicals insisted that, even before the law received the sanction of the Emperor, Parliament should announce that it had passed. Minister of Justice Bach, supported by the conservative deputies, argued that the monarch must approve every bill passed by Parliament before it could become law. Thus the passage of this very first bill by the Austrian Parliament brought to a head the important question whether sovereignty was vested in the Emperor or in Parliament.[81] Finally on September 7 the large majority of deputies voted in favor of the government. On the same day the law received the Emperor's official approval and was officially proclaimed.[82]

On Sunday evening, September 24, a tremendous demonstration was staged in Vienna to honor Kudlich for his efforts in getting the "emancipation bill" through Parliament. A large number of peasants who had come to Vienna from the surrounding regions were joined by students and National Guardsmen. All told, about 20,000 people participated in paying homage to their young champion.[83]

The students and other Viennese radicals who joined the peasants in celebrating the abolition of feudalism did so mainly because of their conviction that, since they had helped to give the peasants their freedom, the peasants would steadfastly back them in their radical demands. They were thoroughly mistaken. Instead of making radicals out of the peasantry, the abolition of manorial services turned them into supporters of law and order. They had now obtained everything they wanted from the revolution, and they were as grateful to the Emperor as they were to Parliament.

Thus, by the end of September the large peasant masses in Austria were either indifferent to the outcome of the revolution or—as was especially true of the religious country folk—hostile to the radicals. With the exception of Hungary, the revolution was now limited to the radical lower middle classes and proletariat in Vienna. Nearly everyone else was showing antagonism to it. Finally cognizant of the seriousness of the situation, the radicals became more closely united than ever before.[84] There was no real party of moderation between these two extremes.[85] The atmosphere was heavy and oppressive. Vienna was on the brink of a new revolution.

[81] Hübner diary, Vienna, September 4, 1848, Hübner, *op. cit.*, p. 198.
[82] Hübner diary, Vienna, September 7, 1848, *ibid.*, pp. 200–201.
[83] Füster, *op. cit.*, Vol. II, pp. 160–61; Unterreiter, *op. cit.*, Vol. II, p. 102.
[84] Ernst Fischer, *Österreich 1848*, p. 97.
[85] [Daniel] Fenner von Fenneberg, *Geschichte der Wiener Oktobertage. Geschildert und mit allen Aktenstücken belegt,* Part I, p. 84.

XIV. *The October Revolution*

N September the Habsburg court decided that the revolutionaries had discredited themselves sufficiently and that the counterrevolutionary forces were strong enough to proceed against them. The Viennese radicals had suffered two bitter defeats in the August and September uprisings. With Marshal Radetzky's entry into Milan on August 6 and the successful end of the Italian war, Radetzky was beseeching the court for permission to march to Vienna to put down the revolution. In Croatia, Jelačić was collecting a formidable army to move against the Hungarians. Count Latour was secretly sending him money and arms for this purpose. Meanwhile, the Habsburg consul at Belgrade was recruiting men for an army of Hungarian Serbs to attack the Magyars, assisted by Marshal Radetzky, who sent a Croatian border regiment home to be at Jelačić's disposal.[1] By the first of September everything seemed ready for a successful counterattack.

Acting upon the advice of Windischgrätz and others, the court decided to move against Hungary first. Trouble had long been brewing between Austria and Hungary. As has been noted earlier, for some time the "Magyarization" policies of the dominant Hungarians had deeply troubled the Slavs, and a large number of Austrians were becoming increasingly anxious over the growing separatist tendencies of the Hungarian nationalists. An attack on the Magyars would be welcomed, not only by several million Croatians, Slovenians, Serbs, and Slovaks, but by hundreds of thousands of Czechs, Poles, and Germans as well. Furthermore, if Jelačić's effort to crush the Magyar revolution was successful, the counterrevolutionaries could easily suppress the revolution in Vienna at a later date.

Up to this time the Habsburg court, although seriously disturbed about developments in Hungary, had feigned a neutral role between the Magyars and the Croats. On the one hand, it had simulated a non-existent hostility to Jelačić and had commanded the imperial troops in

[1] Franz Pulszky, *Mein Zeit, mein Leben,* Vol. II, p. 141; Heinrich Friedjung, *Österreich von 1848 bis 1860,* Vol. I, pp. 68–69.

Hungary to obey the orders of the Batthyány ministry; on the other hand, it had refused to allow the Hungarian government to organize a national army to subjugate Croatia-Slavonia. Now the court's policy of supposed neutrality abruptly changed. On August 31 Archduke Stephen, the palatine of Hungary, was informed that steps must immediately be taken to restore Hungary to the dependent relationship to the crown that had been stipulated by the Pragmatic Sanction. The Hungarian Ministry was asked to come to Vienna to confer with the Austrian government and Jelačić about the best way to accomplish this. Meanwhile, the defense of the military borders was placed directly under the supervision of the Imperial Ministry of War.

Infuriated by this sudden change in attitude, on September 4 the Hungarians dispatched 120 members from Parliament to the Emperor to point out the dangers of his actions. The deputies were admitted to the Schönbrunn Palace on the 9th. They urged Ferdinand to send all Hungarian troops home to defend their own land, to order the regiments in Hungary to move against all rebels, to free the Croatians from military despotism, to punish all reactionary conspirators, and, finally, to take up his residence in Hungary. The Emperor replied that he was firmly resolved to preserve the empire but that he could under no circumstances come to Hungary. On September 11 Jelačić and his troops crossed the Drau River to attack the Magyars. On the following day the Batthyány ministry resigned.[2]

In desperation, the Magyars, goaded by the indomitable Kossuth (who became the commanding figure in Pest after the resignation of the Batthyány cabinet), resolved to bypass the Emperor and make a direct appeal to the Austrian Parliament to bring the Austrian people into a common defense against their rulers.[3] This deputation, which came to Vienna on the 19th, was no more successful than the earlier one to the Emperor. In accord with the wishes of the Austrian Ministry, the deputies of the right and center simply voted not to receive the Hungarian emissaries.[4] The Hungarian radicals were little comforted by the cheers and torchlight parade held in their honor by the Viennese. They

---

[2] Alfred Ritter von Arneth, *Wessenberg,* Vol. II, pp. 260–63; Friedjung, *op. cit.,* Vol. I, pp. 70–72; Rudolf Kiszling *et al., Die Revolution im Kaisertum Österreich 1848–1849,* Vol. I, pp. 214–17. Széchényi had committed suicide on September 5, and Deák, Esterházy, and Eötvös had resigned from the cabinet a few days before the 12th.

[3] Paul Müller, *Windischgrätz,* p. 135.

[4] Protocol of the 44th Sitting of Parliament, September 19, 1848, *Wiener Zeitung,* No. 254 (September 20, 1848), p. 709; "Die Deputation der Ungarn an den Reichstag in Wien," *Beilage zur Wiener Zeitung,* No. 255 (September 21, 1848), p. 97; Pulszky, *op. cit.,* Vol. II, pp. 199–200.

could not help realizing that both government and Parliament in Vienna had broken completely with the Magyar regime.[5] Making the best of a bad situation, on September 21, the Hungarian Parliament handed over the government to a home-defense committee, under the chairmanship of Kossuth,[6] which exerted almost superhuman efforts to muster as large a defense force as possible against the Croatian invaders. Four days later Archduke Stephen resigned from his position as palatine.[7]

Meanwhile, on September 11 Jelačić had crossed the Drau, anticipating a quick victory over the enemy. Fifteen days later his troops reached Stuhlweissenburg without having met any resistance. This represented the farthest point of their advance. The insufficient training of Jelačić's troops and the inadequate officer corps handicapped him from the outset, and only a few of the imperial troops stationed in Hungary deserted the Magyars. When Jelačić first met the enemy in open conflict on September 29, the weaknesses of his position were evident. Although he was not defeated, he won no real victories either. Then, hearing reports that strong Hungarian militia contingents were pressing forward and that the Hungarian General Moga had received reinforcements, on September 30 Jelačić abandoned his drive toward Pest. The next day his troops began a rapid march in the direction of the Austro-Hungarian frontier on the Leitha.[8]

While the Ban of Croatia was waging his short, ineffective campaign in Hungary, the imperial court sent Lieutenant Field Marshal Francis Lamberg, who was reputed to be a staunch friend of the Hungarians, to Pest as imperial commissioner to Hungary and appointed him commander-in-chief of all Hungarian and Croatian troops. Almost as soon as he arrived on September 28, a fanatical mob murdered him on the bridge between Ofen and Pest.[9]

Up to this time many in the Habsburg court and the Viennese Ministry still hoped to avoid an outright break with Hungary; however, after the report of Lamberg's assassination, it was unanimously decided that every effort must be made to crush the Hungarian revolution. In an imperial manifesto of October 3 war was declared on the Magyars. The Hungarian Parliament was abolished, and the country was placed under

---

[5] Hübner diary, Vienna, September 19, 1848, Alexander Grafen von Hübner, *Ein Jahr meines Lebens 1848–1849*, p. 207; Otto Wittner, *Moritz Hartmanns Leben und Werke*, Vol. I, p. 259.

[6] Dominic G. Kosáry, *A History of Hungary*, p. 234.

[7] Friedjung, *op. cit.*, Vol. I, p. 75.

[8] Kiszling *et al.*, *op. cit.*, pp. 220–26; Müller, *op. cit.*, p. 143.

[9] [Emanuel Kopetzky], *Ergebnisse*, p. 128.

martial law. Jelačić, who was appointed commander-in-chief of all troops in Hungary, Transylvania, and Croatia and was named imperial commissioner for Hungary, was provided with extensive powers to restore order and apprehend and punish Count Lamberg's murderers.[10] In a burst of indignation, the Magyar home-defense committee declared the October 3 manifesto null and void, denounced Jelačić as a traitor, and announced that all persons supporting him would be considered traitors.

The Viennese democrats also reacted violently to the manifesto. For weeks the radicals in the capital had been increasingly alarmed over the rapid growth of "black-yellow" sentiments and had raged against the reactionaries who were threatening to destroy constitutional freedom.[11] Embittered by their defeat on September 13, the extremists were preparing for an assault on the Ministry that had refused to bow before their demands on September 11 to 13.[12] Though the plight of the lower middle classes and workers was bad before September 13, their misery and suffering were even worse toward the end of September.[13] They were practically on the verge of starvation. By late September the situation in Vienna seemed so alarming that the enthusiastic March revolutionist Adolf Pichler, who had just returned to the capital after several months on the Italian front, sadly noted that in Vienna he saw "here and there the colors of the red Republic" and "a confused state of disorder that must only too soon arouse a presentiment that something must happen very quickly."[14]

For these reasons the government's declaration of war against Hungary could not have been more poorly timed. The Viennese democrats, believing that the Magyar cause was interwoven with their own, had looked upon the Hungarian independence movement as a fight for the same aims and against the same enemy.[15] Naturally the Hungarians in Vienna worked hard to convert the Austrians to this idea. Early in August, Pulszky, the Hungarian undersecretary of state in Vienna, was

[10] Imperial Manifesto, Schönbrunn, October 3, 1848, *Wiener Zeitung*, No. 275 (October 5, 1848), p. 857; *Das Tagebuch des Polizeiministers Kempen von Fichtenstamm, 1848 bis 1859* (hereafter cited throughout as *Tagebuch*), ed. Karl Mayr, p. 109.

[11] W. G. Dunder, *Denkschrift über die Wiener October Revolution*, p. 24; *Die Schwarzgelben sollen leben! Vivat Hoch*, Univ. Colo. 1848 Coll., No. II/180.

[12] William H. Stiles, *Austria in 1848–49*, Vol. II, pp. 170–71; Kopetzky, *op. cit.*, p. 125.

[13] Friedrich Unterreiter, *Die Revolution in Wien vom Juni bis September 1848*, Vol. II, pp. 108–109.

[14] Adolf Pichler, *Das Sturmjahr*, p. 133.

[15] E[rnst] V[ictor] Zenker, *Wiener Journalistik 1848*, p. 108.

authorized to pay various journalists to represent Magyar interests in the Viennese press. The next month Kossuth empowered him to spend additional sums to propagandize for Hungary in the Austrian capital. Although the total amount thus spent was not great, it was of some help in stirring up pro-Magyar feeling in Vienna[16] and in convincing the Viennese democrats that the war against Hungary was a prelude to the destruction of the constitutional system in Austria.[17]

To add more fuel to the fire, on September 29, the Pest journals published some papers taken from one of Jelačić's couriers proving that the Viennese government had given money to the Croatian Ban and had promised him men and munitions for his army. The next day the papers were also printed in Vienna. When Latour was questioned on October 1 about these compromising documents, he freely admitted that Jelačić had repeatedly asked him for support, which he had provided. Although the majority in Parliament approved Latour's course of action, the apprehensive Viennese radicals were almost uncontrollably angry.

Up to this time the radical journalists had reserved their virulence for Jelačić, of whom they spoke only in such terms as "robber captain," "most eminent traitor," one who had "trampled upon constitutional laws over a hundred times," and an evil man who was preparing for a bloody civil war.[18] Now the Minister of War became the chief object of their fury. On October 3 the *Allgemeine Oesterreichische Zeitung* denounced Latour as a notorious liar whose most cherished ambition had always been to suppress the liberties of the people, and demanded his arrest and trial for his misdeeds.[19] The next day the *Constitution* asked how it was possible for Parliament and the people to allow such a traitor to walk on the streets a free man.[20] Also on the 4th the *Wiener Krakeh-*

---

[16] See especially Auerbach diary, October 8, 1848, Berthold Auerbach, *Tagebuch*, p. 61; Dunder, *op. cit.*, p. 24; Vitzthum von Eckstädt to his mother, October 6, 1848, Carl Friedrich Grafen von Vitzthum von Eckstädt, *Berlin und Wien in den Jahren 1845–1852*, p. 143; Daniel Fenner von Fenneberg, *Geschichte der Wiener Oktobertage*, Part I, pp. 120–21; Zenker, *op. cit.*, pp. 109–10; Kopetzky, *op. cit.*, pp. 130–31.

[17] Stiles, *op. cit.*, Vol. II, p. 92; Anton Füster, *Memoiren vom März 1848 bis Juli 1849*, Vol. II, p. 175.

[18] For instance, the two-page placard headed by the words "Jellachich ist verwundet, seine Armee gänzlich geschlagen und zum Rückzuge gezwungen worden," Univ. Colo. 1848 Coll., No. II/102.

[19] Zenker, *op. cit.*, pp. 114–15; Heinrich Reschauer and Moritz Smets, *Das Jahr 1848. Geschichte der Wiener Revolution*, Vol. II, p. 554.

[20] Zenker, *op. cit.*, p. 116; Friedrich Unterreiter, *Die Revolution in Wien vom Oktober bis zu Ende 1848. Mit allen ihren Ursachen und Wirkungen fortlaufend bis auf die nächsten Tage auf das freisinnigste nach eigener Anschauung und den besten Quellen dargestellt* (hereafter cited throughout as *Die Revolution in Wien vom Oktober bis zu Ende 1848*), Vol. I, pp. 5–6; Kopetzky, *op. cit.*, p. 123.

ler printed a picture of three ministers, clearly meant to be Latour, Bach, and Wessenberg, hanged in effigy, while in the *Studenten-Courier* there was the inflammatory five-stanza poem "To the Lamppost!"[21] which began:[22]

> They will not learn, they nothing learn,
> These courtly high-born peers!
> In vain the clanging trump of doom
> Assails their stubborn ears.
> > That only after bloody throes
> > Doth Freedom's dawn expand
> > To golden light, dispelling night,
> > They cannot understand.
> So, since the high-born will not learn
> A fresh, new age is nigh,
> Then hang the high-born gentlemen
> High on the lampposts, high!

The poem closed with a repetition of the appeal to the Viennese:

> My German people, would you learn
> The road to your salvation?
> Then let not Freedom, stifled, die
> 'Neath indolent stagnation.
> > At dark, on guard, they challenge "Blood!"
> > The watch-word of the foe;
> > They forge new chains, inflict fresh pains—
> > Their blood, their blood must flow!
> Though checked and crossed, with dauntless will
> Your purpose glorify,
> And hang them, tyrants, priests and slaves
> High on the lampposts, high!

Ably seconding the efforts of the journalists were the radical clubs of the capital. Most prominent among these were the Democratic Club, presided over by the irrepressible Tausenau; the Association for the Preservation of the Rights of the People;[23] the Liberal Club on the

---

[21] Unterreiter, *Die Revolution in Wien vom Oktober bis zu Ende 1848,* Vol. I, p. 6; Dunder, *op. cit.,* p. 36; Zenker, *op. cit.,* p. 116; Kopetzky, *op. cit.,* pp. 123–24.

[22] As translated by J. G. Legge in his *Rhyme and Revolution in Germany,* p. 478. Copies of the complete poem in German can be found in Dunder, *op. cit.,* pp. 34–36, and in Joseph Alexander Freiherrn von Helfert, *Der Wiener Parnass im Jahre 1848,* pp. 380–81. The second and third stanzas are omitted in the Legge translation.

[23] *Ursache und Geschichte der Octoberereignisse,* p. 32.

Wien, led by the notorious Adolf Chaisés; the Landstrasse Liberal Club; the Josephstadt Workers' Society; the Concordia Workers' Society; the Handicraft Workers' Club; the Gundersdorf Democratic Club; the Union of Guards Sympathizing with the Legion; and the German Women's Club.[24] Fearful that the Ministry's opposition to the Hungarian revolution would be a deadly blow to them and to everything they stood for,[25] on October 3 these organizations created the Central Committee of Democratic Clubs to co-ordinate their efforts.[26] The Central Committee, and particularly Tausenau, the leader of its political section, worked feverishly to inflame the masses against the Ministry and goad them to take desperate measures to prevent the government from carrying out its plans against the Hungarian democrats.[27]

At this tense moment Latour unwisely issued orders for some of the troops garrisoned in Vienna to proceed to Hungary to strengthen Jelačić's forces. The Ceccopieri battalion, composed of several companies from Italian regiments, departed on October 5. Although many of the enlisted men resented the orders, no revolt broke out when the troops left.[28] The Richter battalion, which was to start early the next morning, was not so well disciplined. This battalion was made up of German troops, some of whom had been stationed in Vienna for fourteen years and had many intimate ties with the Viennese, including members of the various democratic clubs.[29] Most of the soldiers in the battalion insisted that they would remain in Vienna. Their mutinous sentiments were encouraged by their friends in the clubs, who plied them with money, drink, women, and propaganda to influence them to rebel against their commanding officers.[30]

---

[24] Fenner von Fenneberg, *op. cit.,* Part I, pp. 89–90.

[25] Ernst Violand, *Die sociale Geschichte der Revolution in Oesterreich,* pp. 204–205.

[26] Fenner von Fenneberg, *op. cit.,* p. 90.

[27] Violand, *op. cit.,* p. 205; Dunder, *op. cit.,* p. 33.

[28] [Johann Peter Theodor Lyser], *Die Wiener-Ereignisse vom 6. Oktober bis 12. November 1848. Geschildert von einem Augenzeugen. Mit allen während dieses Zeitraums erschienenen Kundmachungen und Proclamationen* (hereafter cited throughout as *Wiener-Ereignisse*), p. 9; Schütte diary, October 6, 1848, *Die Wiener Oktober-Revolution. Aus dem Tagebuch des Dr. Schütte* (hereafter cited throughout as *Tagebuch*), p. 1.

[29] Stiles, *op. cit.,* Vol. II, p. 92; Dunder, *op. cit.,* p. 77.

[30] Friedrich Kaiser, *Memoiren,* p. 118; Dunder, *op. cit.,* p. 33; Vitzthum von Eckstädt to his mother, Vienna, October 7, 1848, Vitzthum von Eckstädt, *op. cit.,* p. 146; Stiles, *op. cit.,* Vol. II, p. 92; *Ursache und Geschichte der Octoberereignisse,* pp. 44–45; Carl Stavenhagen, *Wiens furchtbarer Oktober 1848. Die Belagerung, Vertheidigung und Einnahme der österreichischen Kaiserstadt, nach*

The working-class inhabitants of the suburb of Gumpendorf, where the barracks of the departing troops were located, were particularly aroused by the news that the "democratic" soldiers of the Richter battalion had been ordered to fight their Hungarian compatriots. By late afternoon the excitement there had reached great heights. In spite of the efforts of the National Guard commander of the district to quiet them, all evening huge crowds of workers, suburban guards, and women milled around the barracks and the inns and coffeehouses in the neighborhood, imploring the soldiers not to desert them.[31]

The same evening several hundred people attended a joint meeting of the democratic clubs. Tausenau incited the group to draft a storm petition to the commander of the Gumpendorf barracks, which a group of about two hundred persons were to take there.[32] Accompanied by a number of Hungarians, the deputation arrived in Gumpendorf around midnight.[33]

In the meantime, a delegation of suburban guardsmen appeared before the Minister of War with a written request that the Richter battalion be kept in Vienna. Count Latour sent the deputation to the military commandant of Vienna, Count Auersperg, who turned down their request. On the same night the commander of the Academic Legion, Joseph Aigner, warned Latour that troops of the Richter battalion and the Wieden and Gumpendorf National Guards were plotting an insurrection and had asked for and received the support of most of the students. In spite of Aigner's admonition, Latour took no precautions to avert a rebellion other than calling out two cavalry divisions to enforce the order to the Richter battalion and instructing the Minister of Interior to summon the National Guard.[34]

At 4:00 A.M. the Richter battalion was ordered to begin its march. The troops immediately asked the radical Gumpendorf National Guard and other fellow-citizens for help. From Gumpendorf the alarm went from suburb to suburb. In a very short time suburban guardsmen were hurrying up from Wieden, Gumpendorf, Mariahilf, and Neubau to cut off the streets surrounding the barracks.[35]

---

zuverlässigen Beobachtungen und Quellen. Mit vielen bildlichen Darstellungen nach der Natur, p. 8.

[31] Dunder, *op. cit.,* pp. 78–81; Stiles, *op. cit.,* Vol. II, pp. 92–93.

[32] Unterreiter, *Die Revolution in Wien vom Oktober bis zu Ende 1848,* Vol. I, pp. 7–11.

[33] Dunder, *op. cit.,* p. 81.

[34] Kopetzky, *op. cit.,* pp. 5–7.

[35] Schütte diary, October 6, 1848, Schütte, *op. cit.,* p. 1.

The October Revolution

At 5:30 the arrival of the two cavalry divisions to escort the obstinant battalion to the railway station caused the soldiers to alter their tactics. The insurgents now decided to stop the march with force at the North Railway Station instead of at the Gumpendorf barracks. Most of the throng proceeded to the station to make last-minute plans to resist the military there. A small number remained behind to delay the grenadiers as long as possible.

The Richter battalion set out about 6:00 A.M. On the way, repeated attempts were made to stop the march of the troops. From all parts of the city and the suburbs Viennese rushed to the railway station or to the marching column to give what help they could.[36]

When the troops arrived at the North Railway Station, they found it and the nearby railroad bridge occupied by a large number of angry workers, National Guardsmen, and members of the Academic Legion, who had hurried there in spite of Aigner's determined efforts to prevent the students from mixing in the affair.[37] Discovering the station in the hands of the mob, the rails already torn up, and part of the railroad bridge destroyed, the troop commander ordered the soldiers to march across the Tabor Bridge and board the train at Floridsdorf. At the Tabor Bridge several arches had been ripped out and a barricade built across it. The first detachment of the Richter battalion, the Hess company, passed through the barricade to the Danube Bridge. However, amid the cheers of the mob, the rest of the soldiers refused to cross it. In the meantime, when the Hess company came to the Danube Bridge and saw it defended by a crowd of defiant people, most of them decided not to pass over and insisted on returning to the Tabor Bridge to rejoin their comrades.[38]

Meantime the Ministry and most of the higher military officers in Vienna were assembled in the Ministry of War building.[39] When this group learned that most of the National Guardsmen could not be relied upon, Latour ordered General Hugo von Bredy to go to the Tabor

---

[36] Dunder, *op. cit.*, pp. 92–95; Fenner von Fenneberg, *op. cit.*, Part I, p. 122; Stiles, *op. cit.*, Vol. II, pp. 93–94; Maximilian Bach, *Geschichte der Wiener Revolution*, p. 699.

[37] Kaiser, *op. cit.*, pp. 121–23; Paul Molisch, "Die Wiener akademische Legion," *Archiv für österreichische Geschichte*, Vol. CX, Part I (1924), pp. 130–31; Stavenhagen, *op. cit.*, p. 9.

[38] Unterreiter, *Die Revolution in Wien vom Oktober bis Ende 1848*, Vol. I, pp. 13–15; Fenner von Fenneberg, *op. cit.*, Part I, pp. 122–23; Stiles, *op. cit.*, Vol. II, p. 94; Dunder, *op. cit.*, pp. 95–99; *Revolution, Belagerung und Erstürmung von Wien im October 1848...*, pp. 6–7.

[39] Kopetzky, *op. cit.*, p. 7.

Bridge with the Nassau infantry regiment, several detachments of sappers and cuirassiers, and three cannon, to force the soldiers to obey.[40]

Around eleven o'clock these troops arrived at the bridge. A tremendous crowd had gathered there, most of them angry citizens who were determined to "protect the liberties of the people" in case the rebellious soldiers were attacked. When General Bredy pleaded with the people not to incite the troops, the crowd tried to pull him from his horse and would have attacked him personally if he had not promised to return to the Ministry of War for new orders.

Immediately after he returned from Latour with instructions that the rebellious troops must march, a group of workmen captured one of the cannon and a powder wagon without meeting any resistance. Then, just as they seized a second cannon, General Bredy commanded the Nassau regiment to fire. The Academic Legion and the disaffected National Guardsmen immediately returned the attack, and the rebellious Richter grenadiers also joined the battle. After a brief period of furious fighting, during the course of which General Bredy was mortally wounded, the mutineers gained control of the bridge and soon forced the imperial troops to retire. By twelve o'clock the battle of the Tabor was over.[41]

A half-hour later the victors entered the inner city with their booty: two cannon and Bredy's hat and saber. Shortly afterward a group of students and guardsmen went to St. Stephen's Square to ring the cathedral bell. The conservative guards of the Kärntner quarter stationed there had orders to prevent anyone from ringing the bell and fought them off. A fierce combat ensued, during which guns were fired. At that moment the radical Wieden guardsmen were walking down Kärntner Street toward St. Stephen's Square. As soon as they saw what was happening, they ran to support the attackers. The Kärntner guards were soon forced to take refuge in the cathedral.

When word of the conflict within the city came to the war office, Latour ordered the commander of the cuirassiers to go to St. Stephen's with his men and two cannon to free the guards. When they arrived, another skirmish took place, this time between the military and the

---

[40] Schütte diary, October 6, 1848, Schütte, *op. cit.*, p. 1; Reschauer and Smets, *op. cit.*, Vol. II, pp. 565–66.

[41] Schütte diary, October 6, 1848, Schütte, *op. cit.*, pp. 1–2; Unterreiter, *Die Revolution vom Oktober bis zu Ende 1848*, Vol. I, pp. 15–27; Lyser, *op. cit.*, p. 10; Fenner von Fenneberg, *op. cit.*, Part I, pp. 123–24; Dunder, *op. cit.*, pp. 99–106; C. Grüner, *Die Geschichte der October-Revolution in Wien, ihre Ursachen und nächsten Folgen* (hereafter cited throughout as *October-Revolution*), pp. 5–6; *Revolution, Belagerung und Erstürmung von Wien*, p. 7.

citizens. Immediately placed at a disadvantage, the cuirassiers had to withdraw to the Graben and then fight their way out of the city as best they could. By the middle of the afternoon, with the exception of the relatively small number of troops stationed around the Ministry of War building, scarcely a soldier was to be seen in Vienna.[42]

While these outbreaks were taking place in the city, left-wing deputies repeatedly urged the President of the Austrian Parliament, Anton Strobach, to summon Parliament for an extraordinary session,[43] but he steadfastly refused to do so on the ground that the Ministry should deal with street disturbances.[44] Only after learning about the fighting on St. Stephen's Square and after bitter exchanges between the radical deputies and the conservative Czechs did Strobach consent to call an extraordinary session for four-thirty in the afternoon.

Shortly after four o'clock several deputies gathered in the meeting hall. Indignant at the delay in convoking a formal session, they immediately decided to open an informal one. Pillersdorf was elected temporary chairman and Goldmark secretary. On hearing that plans were afoot to murder Latour, Wessenberg, and Bach, the deputies present at the meeting commissioned Borrosch, Smolka, and Goldmark to make every effort to rescue them.[45] A little later, when Parliament began its formal session, the deputies chose Vice-President Smolka as their president in place of Strobach, declared Parliament in permanent session,[46] and created a permanent committee to act in the name of Parliament when it was not meeting.[47]

For some time before the opening of Parliament, a raging mob at Am Hof in front of the Ministry of War building had been crying for Minister Latour's head and threatening at any minute to break down the main gate to the building. Apparently hoping to quiet the throng by a show of confidence, Latour ordered the gate opened and instructed the soldiers guarding the building not to fire upon the people. This

[42] Kopetzky, *op. cit.*, pp. 8–10; Grüner, *op. cit.*, pp. 7–8; Fenner von Fenneberg, *op. cit.*, Part I, pp. 125–27; Lyser, *op. cit.*, pp. 10–12; Schütte diary, October 6, 1848, Schütte, *op. cit.*, pp. 2–3.

[43] On the evening of October 5 Parliament had adjourned until October 7.

[44] Protocol of the Executive Committee of Parliament, October 6, 1848, Dunder, *op. cit.*, p. 114 n. See also *ibid.*, pp. 112–17; *Ursache und Geschichte der Octoberereignisse*, pp. 46–47.

[45] Dunder, *op. cit.*, pp. 118–22; Füster, *op. cit.*, Vol. II, pp. 177–79; *Ursache und Geschichte der Octoberereignisse*, p. 47; Schütte diary, October 6, 1848, Schütte, *op. cit.*, p. 4.

[46] Fenner von Fenneberg, *Geschichte der Wiener Oktobertage*, Part I, p. 132; Dunder, *op. cit.*, pp. 137–40.

[47] Füster, *op. cit.*, Vol. II, p. 182.

proved a tragic mistake; the Minister was deprived of armed protection when the wild crowd poured into the building.

The various ministers who were still in the building fled and lost themselves among the crowd. Hastily disguising himself in civilian clothing, Latour hurried to his aide's room on the fourth floor, from which he hoped to escape through a small door to the loft of the adjoining church. When he discovered that the door had been bricked up, in desperation Latour then hid in an inconspicuous, dark fourth-floor room containing nothing but several chimneys.

Meanwhile, the raging mob broke into the Minister's offices and dwelling, destroyed furniture, threw books and papers into the streets, and searched room after room for him. The cry, "Latour must hang!" reverberated through the halls. At this tense moment the Parliamentary deputation arrived in the building. Borrosch and other deputies tried unsuccessfully to pacify the crowd by pleading with them not to dishonor the revolution by committing murder. Thinking that a note might appease the fury of the multitude, Smolka prevailed upon Latour's aides to lead him to the Minister. Upon Smolka's urgings, Latour wrote out his resignation, subject to the approval of the Emperor. Smolka brought the paper to the crowd, who had reached the third floor, told them that Latour had relinquished his office, and added that Parliament would impeach him.

Although some of the rioters were now satisfied, there was another burst of anger when the people learned that the Minister had made his resignation contingent upon the Emperor's approval. A new storm broke out, more frenzied than before. With crazed shouts, the demonstrators tried to force the mediator to take them to the Minister. Seeing that the crowd could no longer be restrained, Smolka declared that he would conduct them to Latour only if a sufficient number of them would vouch to protect him. At Fischhof's demand, some twenty to twenty-five armed National Guardsmen and workmen stepped forward and took an oath to defend the Minister with their own lives. Fischhof then assured the insurgents that Latour would be publicly tried for his misdeeds.

Just as the crowd reached the fourth floor, the Minister of War emerged from his hiding place, boldly declaiming that he had never feared bullets, bayonets, or daggers. The guard formed a circle around the Count. Fischhof took him by one arm and a National Guardsman by the other. Smolka and Latour's personal aides followed close behind.

As the Minister was slowly escorted from the upper stories of the building, the threats to hang him increased. On reaching the lower floors, the defenders of the Minister were pushed away from him, one by one. When Latour appeared in the courtyard, a savage cry, "Murder him! Hang him!" split the air. The crowd rushed upon the hated Minister, knocked off his hat, struck him in the face, and hit him on the head with a saber and then with a hammer and an iron bar. He was jabbed with an iron pike and pierced with a bayonet as he fell to the ground. He was beaten and stabbed with muskets, sabers, pikes, bayonets, clubs, sickles, and iron bars. The rabble then trampled upon the mangled body, and pulled it across the courtyard.

Some ruffians tried to hang him from the ledge of one of the windows in the courtyard, but the cord snapped and the corpse fell to the ground. It was dragged to the square in front of the building, and the clothes torn off. It was then hanged on a lamppost and mutilated. National Guardsmen and workers fired volleys of shots into it.[48] Until far in the night, the insane horde—men, women, and even children—intoxicated with blood and wine, danced and sang beneath the body and shrieked coarse jests about the departed Minister,[49] while girls and mothers of Vienna, as well as men, dipped their handkerchiefs and their hands in his blood and bedaubed their clothes and weapons.[50] Not until after midnight was the corpse taken down from the lamppost. The physicians who examined the body found forty-three wounds and countless abrasions and lacerations.[51]

Later in the evening the battle scene changed from Am Hof to the imperial arsenal, which the commander was defending against a large mob. The defenders managed to hold out all night, though the attackers brought up several cannon and fired them point blank into the rear of the building. Not until seven o'clock the next morning did the imperial troops leave the arsenal. Then they departed only after Parliamentary mediators had assured their commander that the the National Guard and the Academic Legion would protect it from the mob.[52]

[48] For good contemporary accounts of Latour's murder, see Kopetzky, *op. cit.*, pp. 11–45; Dunder, *op. cit.*, pp. 125–34; Unterreiter, *Die Revolution in Wien vom Oktober bis zu Ende 1848*, Vol. I, pp. 28–34; Fenner von Fenneberg, *op. cit.*, Part I, pp. 127–31; *Revolution, Belagerung und Erstürmung von Wien*, pp. 8–9; Stavenhagen, *op. cit.*, pp. 10–12.

[49] Hübner diary, Vienna, October 6, 1848, Hübner, *op. cit.*, p. 225.

[50] Kopetzky, *op. cit.*, p. 43; Dunder, *op. cit.*, p. 134.

[51] Kopetzky, *op. cit.*, pp. 43–44.

[52] Kaiser, *op. cit.*, pp. 129–37; Unterreiter, *Die Revolution in Wien vom Oktober bis zu Ende 1848*, Vol. I, pp. 39–42; *Ursache und Geschichte der Octoberereignisse*, pp. 51–52; Stavenhagen, *op. cit.*, pp. 15–16.

At this time, Parliament and the Student Committee—the only two political bodies still respected by the revolutionaries—busied themselves with measures to restore tranquillity to the unfortunate city. Parliament ordered the directors of the North[53] and South Railway[54] Companies under no circumstances to permit troops to be brought to Vienna on their trains. Also, Parliament made plans to remove all soldiers from Vienna and promised to grant a general amnesty to all persons who had participated in the riots and fighting on the 6th.[55] It issued a proclamation politely expressing the hope that the Viennese would respect the laws of the country and comply with the measures Parliament would take to restore order, security, and freedom.[56] In addition, Parliament placed the security of the city of Vienna, Parliament, and the Emperor under the protection of the National Guard.[57]

Meanwhile, the Student Committee took steps to defend the city against any possible attack by the military by erecting barricades behind the city gates and putting cannon on the city walls. Headed by Fenner von Fenneberg, a small group of radical students suggested that Parliament and the City Council be dissolved, that a provisional government be created, and that six or seven thousand armed men be dispatched to the Schönbrunn Palace to force the Emperor to return to the Hofburg, where he would be held under close surveillance.[58] After these proposals were voted down, the Student Committee decided to ask Parliament to petition the Emperor to withdraw his manifesto of October 3, dismiss his irresponsible advisers, replace the existing Ministry with a popular democratic one, send all troops away from Vienna, grant an amnesty to all persons who had participated in the rioting and fighting on the 6th, and promise that martial law would never be declared in the city of Vienna.[59]

Parliament accepted several of the propositions of the Student Committee and drafted an address to the Emperor demanding that he immediately appoint a Ministry meriting the full trust of the people, rescind the October 3 manifesto naming Jelačić imperial commissioner

[53] Smolka, "Proclamation," Vienna, October 6, 1848, Lyser, *op. cit.,* p. 14.
[54] *Ibid.,* p. 16.
[55] *Ibid.,* p. 15.
[56] *Ibid.,* pp. 15–16.
[57] Smolka, "Proclamation," Vienna, October 6, 1848, *Ursache und Geschichte der Octoberereignisse,* p. 50.
[58] Fenner von Fenneberg, *op. cit.,* Part I, pp. 156–57.
[59] Student Petition of October 6, 1848, Reschauer and Smets, *op. cit.,* Vol. II, p. 580.

The October Revolution

of Hungary, and pardon everyone who had engaged in the fighting earlier in the day.[60] Pillersdorf, Hornbostel, Borrosch, Lubomirski, and Skoda, who were commissioned to take this communication to the Emperor at Schönbrunn, were to assure Ferdinand that the recent revolt had not been directed against him personally but was merely a demonstration "against the preposterous executive measures of the Ministry."[61] In a cordial manner the Emperor received the deputation around 11:00 P.M. He assured them that he would appoint the Ministry requested by Parliament and that he would take the steps necessary to ensure the welfare and peace of the monarchy.[62]

While the Emperor was making these promises, he was hastily preparing to leave the capital again. Count Auersperg was ordered to send cannon and 3,000 troops to Schönbrunn. The Emperor's retainers quickly packed the possessions of the imperial family and readied the carriages for flight.[63] Around seven-thirty on the morning of the 7th the Emperor and his family departed from Schönbrunn under heavy military escort[64] to go by way of Krems to the loyal Moravian city of Olmütz. In a proclamation sent to Minister Krauss, with instructions to countersign it and have it posted, Ferdinand informed the Viennese that he was leaving them "to find a way to help his oppressed people," victimized by "a small number of misled people" who had brought anarchy, terror, and murder to the capital.[65] Since he felt that countersigning the proclamation would violate constitutional principles, Krauss immediately took it to Parliament, and told the deputies they should decide the matter. After commending Krauss for his integrity, Parliament then voted that he was to remain in the new Ministry being created, along with the popular Doblhoff and Hornbostel, whose appointments had already been approved by them.[66]

With the Emperor's withdrawal from the capital, there was no law-

---

[60] Smolka, "Proclamation," Vienna, October 6, 1848, Lyser, *op. cit.*, pp. 15–16; Vitzthum von Eckstädt to his mother, Vienna, October 6, 1848, Vitzthum von Eckstädt, *op. cit.*, pp. 144–45.

[61] Hans Kudlich, *Rückblicke und Erinnerungen*, Vol. III, pp. 36–37.

[62] Parliament, "Proclamation," Vienna, October 6, 1848, Unterreiter, *Die Revolution in Wien vom Oktober bis zu Ende 1848*, Vol. I, p. 61; Grüner, *op. cit.*, p. 16; *Ursache und Geschichte der Octoberereignisse*, p. 52.

[63] Fenner von Fenneberg, *op. cit.*, Part I, p. 166.

[64] Dunder, *op. cit.*, p. 173.

[65] Emperor Ferdinand, "Manifesto," n.d., Lyser, *op. cit.*, p. 21. See also the copy in Meynert, *op. cit.*, p. 564.

[66] Protocol of the 52d Sitting of Parliament, October 7, 1848, *Wiener Zeitung*, No. 278 (October 8, 1848), p. 887.

332

The Viennese Revolution of 1848

ful government in Vienna. For the next few weeks the Viennese were
to be ruled in a singularly irregular manner by such legal, semilegal, and
extralegal bodies as could win the respect of the populace: a powerless
Ministry, a slow-moving and cumbersome bureaucracy, a timid City
Council, a radical Student Committee, a demagogic and irresponsible
Central Committee of Democratic Clubs, and a rump Parliament. Each
of them gave orders to anyone who would listen and thus crippled and
delayed the work of the others.[67] All of them flooded the city with
proclamations. Indeed, from October 6 to October 31, if the Viennese
were ruled at all, they "were ruled with placards."[68]

One man constituted the Ministry, and, to make matters worse, a
man very adept at playing both ends against the middle. As we have
seen, on October 7 Parliament commissioned Doblhoff, Hornbostel,
and Krauss to take over the direction of all ministerial portfolios until a
complete government was appointed.[69] However, Doblhoff had already
fled from Vienna on the 6th, and Hornbostel insisted on handing in
his resignation even though Parliament did not want to approve it.[70]
Then a few days later he too departed from Vienna to join the Emperor
at Olmütz, and never to return.[71] This left only Minister of Finances
Krauss to assume charge of the whole Ministry.[72] He dealt with Parliament daily, approved the resolutions of the City Council, and tried to
make himself useful in every possible way. He handed out substantial
sums of money to the "defenders of Vienna" and maintained the friend-
liest relations with the democratic leaders. At the same time he was in
secret contact with the court and was sending money to Jelačić and his
Croatians. Later events showed that he had remained behind, in agreement with the court, to prevent mobs from looting the imperial
treasury.[73]

Most of the lesser officials and employees in the bureaucratic hierarchy
also stayed in Vienna. Although, at the first signs of trouble on October
6, their superiors had fled to Baden or other "safe" towns and villages

[67] Füster, *op. cit.*, Vol. II, p. 193; Schütte diary, October 12, 1848, Schütte,
op. cit., p. 12; Stavenhagen, *op. cit.*, pp. 23–24.
[68] Füster, *op. cit.*, Vol. II, p. 209.
[69] Smolka, "Proclamation," Vienna, October 7, 1848, Lyser, *op. cit.*, p. 32.
[70] Vitzthum von Eckstädt to his mother, Vienna, 10:00 P.M., October 8, 1848,
Vitzthum von Eckstädt, *op. cit.*, p. 149; Grüner, *op. cit.*, p. 29.
[71] Füster, *op. cit.*, Vol. II, p. 185; Stiles, *op. cit.*, Vol. II, p. 122.
[72] Stiles, *op. cit.*, Vol. II, pp. 122–23.
[73] Eduard Bauernfeld, *Erinnerungen aus Alt-Wien*, p. 294; Hübner diary,
Olmütz, October 24, 1848, Hübner, *op. cit.*, pp. 251–52; Hans Blum, *Die deutsche
Revolution 1848–49*, p. 328.

just outside Vienna, the underlings remained behind.[74] This large group of anonymous civil servants conducted the affairs of state during the dismal days of October.

Comprised of members who had been elected shortly before October 6, the City Council was a more conservative body than the radicals could wish. It worked hard to restore and preserve order and to foster the welfare of the people, but it was too weak and irresolute to act energetically and too timid to assume responsibility.[75] As a consequence, all too frequently it had to bend before the will of two energetic, determined extralegal governments that gradually gained tremendous power in Vienna: the Student Committee and the Central Committee of Democratic Clubs.

The first of these groups, the Student Committee, was much more moderate than the second. It was in constant touch with both Parliament and the City Council, which put considerable sums at its disposal. To the Student Committee came the most important reports, and its advice was sought on nearly all matters. It worked energetically to preserve peace, strengthen the defenses of Vienna, and give aid to the downtrodden masses.[76] Close to the hearts of the radicals and the proletariat, the Student Committee exerted an influence over the great masses of Viennese that none of the legal governing authorities could achieve.

Considerably less influential than the Student Committee was the Central Committee of Democratic Clubs, which was radical and irresponsible. It was the center for the worst demagogues and revolutionary agitators in Vienna. Through it would-be Robespierres constantly fanned the flames of hatred, stirred up the people to further violence, and spun a web of intrigue through which they hoped to gain dominant power in the state.[77]

Parliament, nominally the central authority trying to co-ordinate the activities of these various bodies, was only a rump body. Late on October 6 President Strobach and most of the other Czech deputies had fled from Vienna to Prague. There they launched an energetic protest against their radical colleagues in Vienna[78] and invited all members of

---

[74] Hübner diary, Olmütz, October 24, 1848, Hübner, *op. cit.*, p. 251.

[75] *Ibid.*; Auerbach diary, October 20, 1848, Auerbach, *op. cit.*, pp. 135–36; Meynert, *op. cit.*, p. 567.

[76] Molisch, *op. cit.*, pp. 146–52; Grüner, *op. cit.*, p. 106; Meynert, *op. cit.*, p. 568; August Silberstein, *Geschichte der Aula*, pp. 82–84.

[77] Hübner diary, Olmütz, October 24, 1848, Hübner, *op. cit.*, p. 251; Meynert, *op. cit.*, p. 568; Auerbach diary, October 12, 1848, Auerbach, *op. cit.*, pp. 77–83.

[78] Brauner, Strobach, *et al.*, "Proclamation," n.d., Dunder, *op. cit.*, pp. 381–85.

Parliament who shared their opinions to come to Brünn on October 20 to discuss measures for liberating the assembly.[79]

Although the Parliament in Vienna passed a resolution declaring that it was the only "legal, constituent, and legislative authority" in the empire,[80] it was undeniably a much weaker body after the desertion of the Czech deputies. For one thing, it no longer truly represented the Austrian part of the monarchy. Too, although a majority of the deputies remained in Vienna, that majority was so small that frequently too few deputies were present to form a quorum.[81] As a consequence, the Permanent Committee created immediately after the October 6 revolution assumed a much more important position than was usual.

Composed of energetic, resolute deputies, most of them from the extreme left, the committee was able to usurp most executive and legislative power. It issued decrees and gave orders in the name of the whole body. Even though its enactments required the sanction of the full Parliament, its decrees were often executed before Parliament had any knowledge of them.[82]

The members of this permanent committee were not radical and daring enough, however, to become heroes to the Viennese democrats. They were always careful never to sacrifice a semblance of loyalty and legality, for, above everything else, they wanted to be certain that Parliament would not be dissolved. Throughout October Parliament remained on the defensive. Its main efforts were directed toward mediating between the court and the Viennese radicals and bringing peace and harmony to the empire.[83] As a result, Parliament was hated by both sides. The court party naturally looked askance at the "revolutionary parliamentarians" in Vienna; the democrats, finding that they could not influence Parliament to do their bidding, scorned it for lack of energy and for irresolution and cowardice.[84]

Parliament's main task was to ward off the danger of attack that hovered over the city after October 6. The first threat came from the Viennese garrison, which moved to Josephstadt Glacis after fighting its way out of the city on the afternoon of the 6th and then encamped in the gardens of the Schwarzenberg Palace and the Belvedere. Enraged

[79] Palacký, Pinkas, Rieger, *et al.,* "Proclamation," Prague, October 10, 1848, Unterreiter, *Die Revolution in Wien vom Oktober zu Ende 1848,* Vol. I, pp. 70–71.
[80] Parliament, "Proclamation," n.d., Unterreiter, *op. cit.,* pp. 71–72.
[81] Auerbach diary, October 19, 1848, Auerbach, *op. cit.,* p. 131; Füster, *op. cit.,* Vol. II, p. 195; Hübner diary, Olmütz, October 24, 1848, Hübner, *op. cit.,* p. 250.
[82] Fenner von Fenneberg, *op. cit.,* Part I, p. 229.
[83] Kudlich, *op. cit.,* Vol. III, pp. 37–40; Bauernfeld, *op. cit.,* p. 297.
[84] Auerbach diary, October 18, 1848, Auerbach, *op. cit.,* pp. 121–22.

by Latour's death,[85] the troops exercised their fury by insulting and mal-treating citizens, National Guardsmen, and students who chanced to wander too close to their encampment.[86] In vain Parliament sent depu-tations to Auersperg, the commander of the troops, entreating him to quarter his troops within the city, where, incidentally, the troops would have been at the mercy of the Viennese. Asserting that his men could not return to Vienna as long as the proletariat were armed, Auersperg rejected these pleas.[87] Not until October 12 did Auersperg move his men from the Belvedere and Schwarzenberg gardens. Then he led them to Inzersdorf,[88] where the loyal Croatian troops were quartered.

On the 7th Jelačić learned of the October 6 uprising. Immediately he ordered his men to march toward Vienna so that imperial troops would be at hand in case of emergency.[89] After crossing the Austrian frontier on October 9,[90] his troops took up position the next day in the neighborhood of Schwadorf, Schwechat, and Neugebäude,[91] where they were only about two miles from the capital.[92]

The news that the Croatian army had entered Austria electrified Vienna. In spite of appeals made by both Parliament[93] and the City Council[94] for the people to remain calm, near-panic seized the inhabi-tants. The alarm was rung, and the National Guard commander ordered all defenses of the city manned. A concerted drive against spies was be-gun, barricades were strengthened, and an intense search for arms and ammunition was undertaken.[95]

A nervous Parliament tried to ascertain Jelačić's intentions and per-suade him to return to Croatia with his troops. The Ban replied that

---

[85] Vitzthum von Eckstädt to his mother, Vienna, October 7, 1848, Vitzthum von Eckstädt, *op. cit.,* p. 148.

[86] Füster, *op. cit.,* Vol. II, p. 209; Auerbach diary, October 9, 1848, Auerbach, *op. cit.,* pp. 68–69; Kaiser, *op. cit.,* pp. 138–39.

[87] Parliamentary Committee, "Proclamation," Vienna, October 10, 1848, Univ. Colo. 1848 Coll., No. II/120; City Council to Fellow Citizens, Vienna, October 10, 1848, Fenner von Fenneberg, *op. cit.,* Part I, p. 211; *ibid.,* pp. 207–208, 222; Lyser, *op. cit.,* p. 20; Grüner, *op. cit.,* pp. 44, 49–50.

[88] City Council to Fellow Citizens, Vienna, October 12, 1848, Lyser, *op. cit.,* p. 40; *Ursache und Geschichte der Octoberereignisse,* pp. 66–67.

[89] Kempen diary, October 7, 1848, Kempen, *op. cit.,* p. 110.

[90] Kempen diary, October 9, 1848, *ibid.*

[91] Kempen diary, October 10, 1848, *ibid.*

[92] Vitzthum von Eckstädt to his mother, Vienna, October 9, 1848, Vitzthum von Eckstädt, *op. cit.,* p. 152.

[93] Parliament to Inhabitants of Vienna, October 10, 1848, Fenner von Fenne-berg, *op. cit.,* Part I, pp. 202–203.

[94] City Council to Fellow Citizens, Vienna, October 10, 1848, Fenner von Fenneberg, *op. cit.,* pp. 211–12.

[95] Grüner, *op. cit.,* pp. 42–43; Pichler, *op. cit.,* p. 138.

the only orders he would obey were those of the Emperor[96] and that he had come to Vienna to restore order.[97] Still later he wrote Parliament that he had no inimical designs but wanted merely to exercise his rights as a citizen to fight anarchy and preserve the free institutions of the Fatherland.[98] Whatever Jelačić's real aims were, the Viennese soon realized that he could not be moved.[99]

Actually, Jelačić's troops were the advance guard of an army that was to surround Vienna and force the rebellious city to surrender. However, the Viennese refused to believe that the military would ever be used against them. To the very last they trusted their Emperor. Parliament continually entreated him not to abandon his subjects. On October 8 it sent him an address expressing his people's love and imploring him to return to the capital as soon as possible.[100] On October 11 Parliament drafted another memorial, in which it sought to convince Ferdinand of its fitness to advise him, asked him to appoint a popular Ministry, and besought him to stop all hostile measures against the city.[101] This deputation received a half-hearted assurance from the Emperor that he was happy to have Parliament's trust, and vague, meaningless promises that Auersperg and Jelačić would not attack Vienna.[102] On the 13th came a third letter telling the Emperor that Parliament's only aim was to prevent a bloody civil war and to fulfill its obligations to Ferdinand and the people.[103] To the bearers of this letter Ferdinand replied that he understood Parliament's attempts to quell anarchy, and he promised soon to ensure freedom for its deliberations.[104]

Still a fourth address was dispatched to the monarch on October 18, stating that the only reason peace and security had not been fully re-

---

[96] Auerbach diary, October 9, 1848, Auerbach, *op. cit.,* pp. 63–64, 67; Grüner, *op. cit.,* p. 45.

[97] Vitzthum von Eckstädt to his mother, Vienna, October 10, 1848, Vitzthum von Eckstädt, *op. cit.,* pp. 155–56; Auerbach diary, October 10, 1848, Auerbach, *op. cit.,* p. 70; Fenner von Fenneberg, *op. cit.,* Part I, pp. 205–209.

[98] Jelačić to Parliament, Hq., Roth-Neusiedel, October 13, 1848, Fenner von Fenneberg, *op. cit.,* Part I, pp. 268–69; Auerbach diary, October 13, 1848, Auerbach, *op. cit.,* p. 99.

[99] Note, for instance, Parliamentary Committee to Jelačić, Vienna, October 14, 1848, Lyser, *op. cit.,* pp. 45–46.

[100] Parliament to the Emperor, n.d., Lyser, *op. cit.,* pp. 45–46.

[101] Parliament to the Emperor, Vienna, October 11, 1848, Dunder, *op. cit.,* pp. 285–86.

[102] Grüner, *op. cit.,* pp. 100–103.

[103] Parliament to the Emperor, Vienna, October 13, 1848, Grüner, *op. cit.,* pp. 89–92.

[104] Auerbach diary, October 16, 1848, Auerbach, *op. cit.,* pp. 112–13; Vitzthum von Eckstädt to his mother, Vienna, 10:00 P.M., October 16, 1848, Vitzthum von Eckstädt, *op. cit.,* p. 166.

established in the capital was that the troops around the city were exciting the people. Only the removal of these soldiers and the immediate appointment of a popular ministry could tranquilize Vienna.[105] On the same day a deputation from the City Council begged the sovereign to send Jelačić back to Croatia, to declare a general amnesty, and to appoint a popular ministry.[106] This time the two deputations were not even received but were merely told that henceforth they were to go directly to Prince Windischgrätz with their requests.[107]

The refusal of the Emperor to appoint a new ministry and order Jelačić's troops to Croatia greatly intensified the bickering and quarreling between the "black-yellows" and the "black-red-golds." No longer was there a middle ground after October 6; either the conservatives or the radicals had to triumph.[108] On October 6 and immediately afterward, the aristocracy, higher officials, financiers, property-owners, and other wealthy bourgeoisie fled from the city, and many conservative members of the National Guard and even some lower-middle-class people departed out of terror over the proletarian uprising they believed imminent.[109] The more courageous tried to influence the City Council, the National Guard, and Parliament to restrain the activities of the radicals in the city.[110] No doubt some were also spies for the court party.

Nearly all the important people—the influential ones—sided with the Habsburgs. The democrats were the "little people": the students, the lower-middle-class artisans and shopkeepers, and the great proletarian masses.[111] The revolutionary leaders were mostly young people[112] or penniless intellectuals. There was scarcely a man of real political ability among them.[113] On the whole, they were people who had nothing to lose but their unhappy lives. Finding themselves deserted by the more affluent classes, they turned against all men of wealth. Although they made almost a cult out of the slogan "Property Is Sacred," they began to

---

[105] Parliament to Emperor Ferdinand, Vienna, October 18, 1848, Grüner, *op. cit.*, pp. 144–45.
[106] City Council, "Proclamation," Vienna, October 18, 1848, Univ. Colo. 1848 Coll., No. II/190.
[107] City Council to Fellow Citizens, October 20, 1848, Grüner, *op. cit.*, pp. 185–86.
[108] Pichler, *op. cit.*, pp. 167–68.
[109] Ernst Victor Zenker, *Die Wiener Revolution*, p. 227; Kopetzky, *op. cit.*, p. 119; [Ernst Violand], *Enthüllungen*, pp. 182–83; Bauernfeld, *op. cit.*, p. 296.
[110] Zenker, *Die Wiener Revolution*, p. 227; Grüner, *op. cit.*, p. 106.
[111] Violand, *Enthüllungen*, pp. 182–83.
[112] Auerbach diary, October 17, 1848, Auerbach, *op. cit.*, p. 117.
[113] Auerbach diary, October 18, 1848, *ibid.*, p. 122.

look upon riches as synonymous with cowardice and treason to the cause of freedom.[114] With implicit faith in the righteousness of their cause, they were determined to fight to the end.[115]

Ceaselessly goading the revolutionaries were the Central Committee of Democratic Clubs and the radical newspapers. Although the leading spirits of the committee were sadly lacking in creative ability or talent for organization, they could and did keep the masses stirred up. They proposed to arrest the Camarilla, hang all spies,[116] establish a revolutionary tribunal in place of Parliament,[117] and create a republic. They were, however, completely devoid of constructive suggestions. Also, fortunately for the Viennese, the committee, though noisy, had little influence. Of its prominent members, Becker and Jellinek were too theoretical to be readily understood. Tausenau and Schütte spoke clearly and succinctly,[118] but the rumor circulating among the proletariat that the committee was diverting into private channels the food sent to Vienna by the peasants forced Tausenau to flee to Hungary[119] and stripped Schütte of much of his influence. As a result, the notorious demagogue Chaisés became the directing force behind the committee.[120] Since he was too irresponsible for even the most radical factions,[121] the Central Committee very rapidly lost nearly all the respect of the radical Viennese.

Like the Central Committee, the radical journalists attempted to arouse the Viennese. Coarsely worded placards and pamphlets continued to appear on the streets.[122] The most radical journals, like the *Constitution,* the *Radikale,* the *Freimüthige,* the *Studenten-Courier,* and the *Nazional-Zeitung,* berated Parliament.[123] They exhorted the people to be relentless and pitiless in striking down their enemies to ensure that "the seed of freedom would bear golden fruit."[124] Above all, the papers pressed the citizens to destroy traitors to the cause of freedom—Jelačić, Wessenberg, Windischgrätz, the infamous Camarilla,

---

[114] Zenker, *Die Wiener Revolution,* p. 229.

[115] *Ibid.,* p. 230; M[athias] Koch, *Genesis der Wiener Revolution,* p. 33.

[116] Fenner von Fenneberg, *op. cit.,* Part I, pp. 169–70.

[117] Füster, *op. cit.,* Vol. II, p. 195.

[118] Kudlich, *op. cit.,* Vol. III, pp. 41–42.

[119] Dunder, *op. cit.,* pp. 430–31.

[120] Schütte diary, October 19, 1848, Schütte, *op. cit.,* p. 33.

[121] Grüner, *op. cit.,* p. 125.

[122] Unterreiter, *Die Revolution in Wien vom Oktober bis zu Ende 1848,* Vol. I, p. 96; Auerbach diary, October 20, 1848, Auerbach, *op. cit.,* p. 133.

[123] Note, for instance, *Nazional-Zeitung,* No. 69 (October 12, 1848), p. 273, Univ. Colo. 1848 Coll., No. II/148.

[124] *Kaiser Joseph auf seiner nächtlichen Wanderung um die Stadt,* Univ. Colo. 1848 Coll., No. II/104.

and the spies in their midst. Occasionally they advocated proclaiming the republic.[125]

The violent language of the democratic clubs and newspapers at least succeeded in building up tension and suspicion among the Viennese. Everyone seemed afraid. The radicals were terrified that the reactionaries might conquer Vienna. The moderates and conservatives feared the radicals and for the most part remained in their homes to avoid risking insults or attacks on the streets. In public they were wary in their speech.[126] Among intimates they remarked bitterly about Vienna's resemblance to the Paris of 1793.[127]

In spite of the unrest in the city, there was little robbery or plundering. A parliamentary proclamation placing all public and private property under the protection of the people themselves[128] and, more important, the great respect of even the most extreme radicals for property rights were enough to prevent looting by the lower classes.[129]

No one seemed to know what to do about the endless confusion and disorganization in Vienna. Everyone was issuing orders simultaneously, but nobody wanted to obey anyone else.[130] Among the democrats there were plenty with courage. "But what is courage alone without talent? It can fight and it can inflame, but it can give no character to human society."[131] Although it inspired the Viennese to heroic efforts to preserve their freedom,[132] courage was no substitute for leadership and talent. This deficiency had disastrous consequences for the military defenses of the city. Immediately after the Emperor's departure from Vienna the revolutionaries started measures to protect the capital against attack. Observation posts were established on the tower of St. Stephen's Cathedral, at the university observatory, and at the Belvedere Palace, which the Viennese took over after Auersperg's troops evacuated it. The city gates were reinforced and the barricades behind them strengthened. Other fortifications were erected at the junctions of the most important streets, as well as at strategic points in the suburbs. The university chemical laboratory was converted into a powder factory.

[125] Zenker, *Wiener Journalistik 1848*, pp. 122–25; Joseph Alexander Freiherrn von Helfert, *Die Wiener Journalistik im Jahre 1848*, pp. 234–36.

[126] Pichler, *op. cit.*, p. 141; Stavenhagen, *op. cit.*, pp. 55–56; Meynert, *op. cit.*, p. 568.

[127] Hübner diary, Olmütz, October 24, 1848, Hübner, *op. cit.*, p. 250.

[128] Grüner, *op. cit.*, pp. 75, 84.

[129] *Ibid.*, p. 125; Unterreiter, *Die Revolution in Wien vom Oktober bis zu Ende 1848*, p. 97; Bauernfeld, *op. cit.*, p. 296.

[130] Meynert, *op. cit.*, p. 568.

[131] Auerbach diary, October 20, 1848, Auerbach, *op. cit.*, p. 133.

[132] Füster, *op. cit.*, Vol. II, pp. 198–99.

Hastily improvised bullet factories were opened, and a weapon-repair shop was set up at the arsenal. At a court of summary justice the law students tried persons denounced as spies,[133] and the medical faculty of the university prepared to care for the wounded.[134]

At the heart of the defense system were the Civic Guard, the National Guard, and the Academic Legion. Composed of the more prosperous bourgeoisie, the Civic Guard was quite unreliable. The National Guard was sharply divided in sentiment. On October 6 and the days that followed, a large number of the conservative guardsmen had fled from Vienna. Of those who remained behind, many could not be relied on to fight wholeheartedly against the Habsburg troops. The membership of the Academic Legion had dropped to about one-fifth of what it had been in the spring. Many students had left Vienna;[135] by and large, those who remained were somewhat lukewarm about democracy and its defense.[136]

In order to create a larger defense force, on October 13 Parliament appropriated 200,000 florins ($96,000) for maintaining needy tradespeople, workers, and unemployed persons under arms.[137] With this money the Mobile Guard was created. In addition to daily rations of wine and tobacco, every enlisted man was to receive 25 kreutzer (20 cents) for twenty-four hours' service and 15 kreutzer (12 cents) for twelve hours' duty.[138] The noncommissioned officers were to be paid 30 kreutzer (24 cents) per day. A lieutenant was to receive 2 florins (96 cents); a captain, 4 florins[139] ($1.92); and a colonel, 8 florins[140] ($3.84)—handsome pay for soldiers. Since people were now to be compensated for soldiering, there was an immediate rush to join the Mobile Guard. By October 14 two battalions were already filled and a third was in the process of formation.[141] The Mobile Guard became the center for the unemployed, adventurers, and the most notorious rabblerousers in the city. The wages of the Mobile Guard aroused the envy of

[133] Molisch, *op. cit.*, pp. 153–54; Kiszling *et al.*, *op. cit.*, Vol. I, pp. 254–55.
[134] "Medical Faculty to the Inhabitants of Vienna," Vienna, October 20, 1848, Dunder, *op. cit.*, p. 565.
[135] Füster, *op. cit.*, Vol. II, pp. 168–69.
[136] Hübner diary, Olmütz, October 26, 1848, Hübner, *op. cit.*, p. 254.
[137] Fenner von Fenneberg, *op. cit.*, Part I, p. 267.
[138] City Council, "Proclamation," Vienna, October 12, 1848, Lyser, *op. cit.*, p. 41.
[139] General Bem to the Viennese National Guard, October 20, 1848, Univ. Colo. 1848 Coll., No. II/144.
[140] Grüner, *op. cit.*, p. 158.
[141] Wutschel, "Proclamation," Vienna, October 14, 1848, Lyser, *op. cit.*, p. 47.

the National and Civic Guardsmen and the Academic Legionnaires. As a consequence, Parliament and the City Council had to arrange to equalize pay.[142]

More than men are needed for an effective defense force. There must also be good leadership, iron discipline, and adequate training. The Viennese citizens' military forces were deficient in these qualities. After four changes in the supreme command of the National Guard between October 6 and 12, on October 13 Wenzel Cäsar Messenhauser was appointed to the post. Messenhauser proved an extremely poor choice for the position. An idealist, an honorable man with simple tastes, and a writer of some reputation, he was naïve, irresolute, hesitant, and wanting in strength and energy. He was no leader of men; he lacked organizational ability; and he understood little about military tactics. Thoroughly ignorant of the real duties of a military commander, he wasted most of his time penning bombastic proclamations.[148]

With the exception of General Bem, whom Messenhauser made commander of the Mobile Guard and chief of all military operations on October 14,[144] Messenhauser's staff members were as ill-suited for their positions as Messenhauser. Bem excelled in the qualities Messenhauser lacked and knew just when to punish, praise, or joke with his men, who served him valiantly.[145] Messenhauser's other staff officers, however, were chosen chiefly for political reasons. Fenner von Fenneberg and Haug, who secretly intrigued against their commander, were selected for the general staff mainly to appease the radicals, whereas places were reserved at headquarters for Thurn and Aigner, to please the more conservative guardsmen. The result was that neither faction was satisfied. The radicals were very angry over the "black-yellows" surrounding Messenhauser, and the moderates lifted their eyebrows over the "republicans" and "anarchists" in the high command.[146] With such a division in the top command, the headquarters of the defense forces were chaotic. Orders were issued that nobody wanted to obey,[147] and all

---

[142] Ehnl, *op. cit.,* pp. 58–59.

[143] Fenner von Fenneberg, *op. cit.,* Part I, pp. 101–104, 284; Auerbach diary, October 27, 1848, Auerbach, *op. cit.,* pp. 177–78; Grüner, *op. cit.,* p. 93; Ottocar Weber, *1848. Sechs Vorträge,* p. 47; Otto Wittner, *Moritz Hartmanns Leben und Werke,* Vol. I, pp. 270–72.

[144] Messenhauser, "Proclamation," Vienna, October 14, 1848, Grüner, *op. cit.,* p. 93.

[145] Priscilla Robertson, *Revolutions of 1848: A Social History,* pp. 242–43; Ehnl, *op. cit.,* pp. 66–67.

[146] Ehnl, *op. cit.,* p. 65.

[147] Bauernfeld, *op. cit.,* p. 297.

the staff officers were so busy drafting placards that few‚ people understood that they never had time to learn the effective strength of the different battalions and corps at their disposal.

The confusion at the top extended through the ranks. Every officer
commanded as he pleased and changed headquarters at will without
informing his superiors. As a result, reinforcements to various corps
often wasted hours aimlessly searching for the unit to which they were
assigned.[148]

The worst trouble was jn the officer corps of the Mobile Guard, where
everyone who recruited 50 men automatically became a lieutenant. To
become a captain a person had to enroll 100 men; a major, 250. Anyone
popular enough with the people to obtain 450 recruits attained the rank
of lieutenant-colonel.[149] Thus popularity, not ability, opened the road to
high command, and,‚ *ipso facto,* the Mobile Guard had to be controlled
through flattery, not orders. As a consequence, the Mobile Guard was
destined to remain an undisciplined, unorganized, untrained mass,[150]
which, through sheer weight of numbers, was able to wield inordinate
influence over the other armed bodies in Vienna.[151]

The situation might not have been hopeless if the Viennese had received assistance from elsewhere in the empire. However, the spirited
appeals of Parliament[152] and other groups to their fellow-countrymen
for aid in the battle for freedom got little response. A few radicals in
various cities and towns in the provinces wrote notes of sympathy.
Handfuls of armed forces were dispatched to the capital from Graz,
Olmütz, Brünn, and Salzburg,[153] but most of them were driven away
by Habsburg troops before they arrived. The few who actually reached
the capital were disillusioned by what they found and became anxious to
return home as soon as possible.[154]

The Viennese democrats expected the peasants in the regions around
the capital to rush to their rescue. Every day students, deputies, and
journalists traveled to the country to arouse the peasants, but their

[148] Fenner von Fenneberg, *op. cit.*, Part II, p. 78.
[149] General Bem to the Viennese National Guard, October 20, 1848, copy in
the Univ. Colo. 1848 Coll., No. II/144.
[150] Grüner, *op. cit.*, p. 174.
[151] *Ibid.*, p. 106; Bauernfeld, *op. cit.*, p. 298.
[152] See especially Parliament's "Proclamation to the Austrian People," Vienna,
October 20, 1848, Univ. Colo. 1848 Coll., No. II/214.
[153] Molisch, *op. cit.*, pp. 158–59; Auerbach diary, October 11, 1848, Auerbach,
op. cit., p. 74; Grüner, *op. cit.*, pp. 42–43, 53, 84; Fenner von Fenneberg, *op. cit.*,
Part I, p. 224; Füster, *op. cit.*, Vol. II, p. 199.
[154] Dunder, *op. cit.*, p. 592; Hübner diary, Olmütz, October 26, 1848, Hübner,
op. cit., p. 255; Kiszling, *op. cit.*, Vol. I, p. 258.

efforts were fruitless.[155] When Häfner, the editor of the *Constitution,* harangued them, he was arrested and placed in the Spielberg prison.[156] When Kudlich appealed to his peasant friends for aid, he too was apprehended. Upon his release, he hurriedly fled to Upper Austria.[157] The peasants remained wholly disinterested in the fate of the democrats.[158] Instead of helping the Viennese, they took advantage of the situation to sell their produce to the Viennese at the highest possible prices.[159]

It was on the Hungarians, however, that the Viennese democrats pinned most of their hopes. After Jelačić's soldiers evacuated Hungary to march to the environs of Vienna, the Hungarians pursued them as far as the Austrian frontier.[160] The Hungarian Parliament dispatched an address to the Parliament in Vienna praising the Viennese for their struggle for freedom and promising that the Magyar army would follow Jelačić wherever he went. If the Viennese so desired, they would even fight him on Austrian soil.[161] Fearing that they would be acting illegally by accepting this proffer of aid,[162] Parliament turned the matter over to the Vienna City Council, which, in turn, declared that such an acceptance would be unlawful without the approval of Parliament.[163] In the meantime, the Student Committee and the Central Committee of Democratic Clubs sent a deputation to Pest to seek help from the Magyars,[164] but now the Hungarians also cloaked themselves with the mantle of legality and refused to come until they received a "legal" request.

From only one source did the Viennese revolutionaries get assistance, and this was largely ineffectual moral aid. When the deputies of the extreme left at the Frankfurt Assembly learned of the desperate plight of their fellow-democrats in Vienna, they urged the German Parliament to post a note of sympathy to the Austrian capital. Although the pro-

---

[155] Grüner, *op. cit.,* p. 164; Zenker, *Die Wiener Revolution,* p. 229.

[156] Unterreiter, *Die Revolution in Wien vom Oktober bis zu Ende 1848,* Vol. I, p. 96; Vitzthum von Eckstädt to his mother, Vienna, 2:00 P.M., October 14, 1848, Vitzthum von Eckstädt, *op. cit.,* p. 163.

[157] Vitzthum von Eckstädt to his mother, Vienna, 2:00 P.M., October 14, 1848, Vitzthum von Eckstädt, *op. cit.,* p. 163; Kiszling *et al., op. cit.,* Vol. I, pp. 258–59.

[158] Grüner, *op. cit.,* p. 110.

[159] Zenker, *Die Wiener Revolution,* pp. 229–30.

[160] Stiles, *op. cit.,* Vol. II, p. 114.

[161] *Ibid.,* p. 115; Hungarian Parliament to Viennese Parliament, Pest, October 10, 1848, Fenner von Fenneberg, *op. cit.,* Part I, pp. 219–21; Bauernfeld, *op. cit.,* p. 297.

[162] Füster, *op. cit.,* Vol. II, p. 213; Auerbach diary, October 11, 1848, Auerbach, *op. cit.,* p. 75.

[163] Parliament Committee to City Council, Vienna, October 11, 1848, Lyser, *op. cit.,* pp. 36–37; Grüner, *op. cit.,* pp. 172–73.

[164] Molisch, *op. cit.,* p. 149; Fenner von Fenneberg, *op. cit.,* Part I, p. 240.

posal was rejected, upon the demand of the Viennese government Archduke John appointed Welcker and Mosle as imperial commissioners to Austria to mediate between the Habsburgs and the Viennese.[165] On October 19 the two commissioners crossed the Austrian frontier. Two days later they wrote the Austrian Parliament from Krems, announcing their intention of going directly to Olmütz to act as mediators and asking all parties to refrain from armed conflict in the meanwhile.[166] On the way they spoke to Windischgrätz, who received them courteously but coolly informed them that their intervention was futile. At Olmütz they were no more successful. In plain language Wessenberg stated that the Viennese problem was no longer one of mediation but of subjugation. After this emphatic declaration of the court's intentions, there was nothing for Welcker and Mosle to do but return to Frankfurt.[167]

In the meantime, the factions of the left at Frankfurt had sent Robert Blum and Julius Fröbel to commend the Viennese for their spirited battle for liberty and to encourage them to resist all efforts of the Habsburgs to suppress them. Two Austrians, Moritz Hartmann and Albert Trampusch, accompanied them. After leaving Frankfurt on October 13, the deputation arrived in Vienna on the 17th.[168] On reaching the capital, they issued a proclamation telling the Viennese of their Frankfurt colleagues' admiration for their courageous conduct and assuring them that their heroic deeds had encouraged fighters for freedom throughout the world.[169]

Although the Frankfurt deputies had originally intended simply to convey these sentiments to the Viennese democrats and leave the city on October 20, under the excitement of the moment they took a much more active part in the revolution. They delivered enthusiastic speeches to the Student Committee and several revolutionary assemblies, where they urged the people to resist the enemy to the end if necessary. They were elected honorary members of the Academic Legion. Both Blum

[165] Hübner diary, Olmütz, October 26, 1848, Hübner, *op. cit.*, p. 256; Paul Müller, *Windischgrätz*, pp. 141–42.

[166] Imperial Commissioners to the Presidium of Parliament, Krems, October 21, 1848, Grüner, *op. cit.*, pp. 191–92; Auerbach diary, October 21, 1848, Auerbach, *op. cit.*, pp. 140–41; *Ursache und Geschichte der Octoberereignisse*, pp. 89–92.

[167] Hübner diary, Olmütz, October 26, 1848, Hübner, *op. cit.*, p. 256; Müller, *op. cit.*, p. 142; Blum, *op. cit.*, pp. 328–29.

[168] Hübner diary, Olmütz, October 26, 1848, Hübner, *op. cit.*, pp. 256–57; Wittner, *op. cit.*, Vol. I, pp. 263, 267; Auerbach diary, October 17, 1848, Auerbach, *op. cit.*, p. 116; *Ursache und Geschichte der Octoberereignisse*, p. 93.

[169] "Proclamation, Deputies of the United Left in the German National Assembly at Frankfurt to the Heroic Inhabitants of Vienna," Vienna, October 18, 1848, Lyser, *op. cit.*, pp. 73–74.

The October Revolution

and Fröbel became corps commanders, and Hartmann served as a common soldier in the same fighting unit.[170]

Yet their efforts in behalf of the Viennese firebrands were in vain. Neither the Frankfurt delegates—nor any other radicals, for that matter—could have averted a catastrophe. The people were divided in sentiment. The government, or what was left of it, was vacillating, uncertain, and confused. The citizens' armed forces were wretchedly trained, undisciplined, and poorly led. All efforts of the Viennese to obtain effective help outside Vienna failed. In the meantime, a large army was gradually surrounding the city. The end of the revolution was rapidly approaching.

[170] Hübner diary, Olmütz, October 26, 1848, Hübner, *op. cit.*, p. 256; Grüner, *op. cit.*, pp. 150, 164; Wittner, *op. cit.*, Vol. I, pp. 274–81.

XV. The End

HEN THE IMPERIAL FAMILY reached Olmütz on October 14, they immediately readied plans to conquer the Viennese rebels. By then the only question still undecided by the Emperor was whether Parliament should be abolished at once and a state of siege declared for the whole monarchy, or whether, under the guise of constitutionality, Parliament should be transferred to some Slav city and allowed to continue. Before Prince Windischgrätz arrived at the Emperor's new temporary residence, no final decision had been made about this question.

Upon receiving news of Count Latour's murder on October 8, Windischgrätz ordered his troops to prepare themselves to march at a moment's notice.[1] The military commanders of Moravia and Galicia promised him all the men at their disposal. Windischgrätz could also reckon on the soldiers under the command of Count Auersperg and the Ban of Croatia, who were already in the environs of Vienna, and, if need be, an additional 25,000 men from Marshal Radetzky as soon as peace was restored in Upper Italy.

After making these preliminary arrangements, Windischgrätz left Prague for Olmütz, where he arrived on October 15. There he helped his brother-in-law and the future minister Prince Felix Schwarzenberg induce the Emperor to sign a strong proclamation that had been drafted by Baron von Hübner.[2] In this manifesto, published on October 16, the Emperor told his people about "the reign of terror" exercised in Vienna by a willful minority in league with a neighboring province in open rebellion, which was sending emissaries everywhere to incite the Emperor's peaceful subjects to civil war. Since one of the Emperor's most sacred

[1] Hermann Kriebel, *Feldmarschall Fürst Windisch-Grätz 1787–1862*, in *Beiträgen für die Geschichte der Jahre 1848–1849*, No. 2, p. 17.

[2] Hübner diary, Olmütz, October 16, 1848, Alexander Grafen von Hübner, *Ein Jahr meines Lebens. 1848–1849*, pp. 243–44; Rudolf Kiszling, *Schwarzenberg*, pp. 45–46.

The End

obligations was to subdue rebels who endangered the peace and security of the monarchy, he had appointed Lieutenant Field Marshal Windischgrätz commander-in-chief of all Habsburg troops except those under Field Marshal Radetzky and had granted him full powers to restore order as quickly as possible. When the rebellion was put down, the Emperor's ministers, in collaboration with Parliament, would be entrusted with curbing the licentious press, checking abuses of the right of assembly, and suppressing the anarchistic tendencies of the citizens' militia. Everyone interested in the welfare of the Emperor and the Fatherland was duty-bound to co-operate in ending the revolution in Vienna.[3]

Thus armed with dictatorial powers, on October 17 Windischgrätz ordered his troops to march to Vienna. He arrived at Stammersdorf the next day and ordered his men across the Danube. On October 21 his soldiers began occupying the areas around Vienna, and by the 23rd the city was completely encircled. On the same day Windischgrätz established headquarters at Hetzendorf, where Jelačić and Auersperg were awaiting him. Seventy thousand men now stood ready to storm the capital.[4]

Windischgrätz had just begun his march on Vienna when some of the Czech members of Parliament who had left the capital on October 6 learned of the Emperor's October 16 manifesto. Thoroughly alarmed that Windischgrätz might abuse his powers and especially that he might destroy constitutional liberties, the Czech deputies hurried to Olmütz to beseech the court to strike out some of the harsh phrases in the Emperor's proclamation. Impressed with their arguments that some of the implied threats in the Emperor's manifesto would grievously embitter loyal subjects throughout the empire, Minister-President Wessenberg and the Galician deputy Count Stadion, who had deserted Parliament for Olmütz, persuaded the Emperor to issue a milder manifesto on October 19, which was to be posted beside the first one.[5] In it Ferdinand assured the Austrians that his only aim in sending troops against the Viennese was to preserve the dignity of the constitutional throne. Pledging himself to safeguard the liberties already granted to the people, he promised

---

[3] "Emperor Ferdinand to His People," Olmütz, October 16, 1848 [Johann Peter Theodor Lyser], *Die Wiener Ereignisse*, pp. 55–56. See also "Emperor Ferdinand to Windischgrätz," Olmütz, October 16, 1848, Maximilian Ehnl, *Messenhauser*, Appendix VI, pp. 187–88.

[4] Ehnl, *op. cit.*, p. 72; Kriebel, *op. cit.*, p. 18.

[5] Hübner diary, Olmütz, October 16, and October 19, 1848, Hübner, *op. cit.*, pp. 244, 246; Paul Müller, *Windischgrätz*, pp. 145–46.

that the work of writing a constitution that had been undertaken by Parliament would be continued.[6]

The Emperor's October 19 manifesto, the only one officially sent to the capital, might have mollified the Viennese if they had not already learned of the one of the 16th.[7] Since they saw two vastly different proclamations, only the milder of which came to them through regular channels, the Viennese suspected the Emperor of perfidy.[8] While the members of Parliament hissed the October 19 manifesto,[9] the Central Committee of Democratic Clubs boldly denounced the October 16 manifesto as an act of open treason,[10] and the people changed the phrase "Ferdinand the First" at the beginning of both proclamations to "Ferdinand the Last."[11] The radical journalist Jellinek expressed the intense resentment of the democrats:[12]

The army of 60,000 men standing before the walls of Vienna is not there against the will of the "good Emperor." The good Emperor wishes to besiege the "good city of Vienna" so he can starve the citizens properly, and he wants to stop their trade so he can force them to lay down their arms—and do what the Emperor wants them to. Yes, that is how things are.

The Viennese radicals had scarcely had time to read the Emperor's hostile manifestoes when a much more threatening pronouncement confronted them. In a proclamation to "the inhabitants of Vienna" issued at Lundenburg on October 20, Windischgrätz announced that, in order to free the capital from "a small, insolent faction that shrinks from no infamous action" to subvert the legal order, he was declaring Vienna and its suburbs in a state of siege, placing all civilian officials under the authority of the military, and putting the city under martial law.[13] Windischgrätz sent one thousand copies of both this proclamation and

[6] "Imperial Manifesto," Emperor Ferdinand, Olmütz, October 19, 1848, Lyser, *op. cit.,* pp. 74–75.

[7] A copy of the October 16 manifesto was brought to the Student Committee on October 18 from Wiener Neustadt. C. Grüner, *October-Revolution,* p. 146.

[8] Lyser, *op. cit.,* p. 84.

[9] Vitzthum von Eckstädt to his mother, Vienna, 10:00 P.M., October 21, 1848, Carl Friedrich Grafen von Vitzthum von Eckstädt, *Berlin und Wien in den Jahren 1845–1852,* p. 170.

[10] Central Committee of Democratic Clubs, "Proclamation to the Sovereign People of Vienna," n.d., W. G. Dunder, *Denkschrift über die Wiener October-Revolution,* p. 567.

[11] Friedrich Unterreiter, *Die Revolution in Wien vom Oktober bis zu Ende 1848,* Vol. II, p. 73.

[12] As quoted in Grüner, *op. cit.,* p. 189.

[13] "Windischgrätz to Inhabitants of Vienna," Lundenburg, October 20, 1848, Unterreiter, *op. cit.,* Vol. I, pp. 101–102.

The End

the Emperor's October 16 manifesto to the Vienna City Council with orders to have them posted.

When the City Council submitted the Habsburg commander's latest pronouncement to it,[14] Parliament passed a resolution on the evening of October 22 that Windischgrätz' proclamation of a state of siege was unconstitutional.[15] For its part, the City Council notified Windischgrätz that it could not submit to his injunctions, since the laws of the land clearly stipulated that the council was under the direct orders of the Ministry of Interior.[16] The Viennese democrats reacted by showering the General with such epithets as "the Bombardment Prince," "the modern Tamerlane," and "the modern Alva." While some of them naïvely suggested that Parliament dispatch emissaries to the troops outside the city walls to arouse them to mutiny,[17] other hotheads talked about assassinating the Emperor.[18]

As the extremists were soon to learn to their consternation, mere words could not save the capital. On October 22, disregarding their violent protests, the Emperor ordered the immediate suspension of all sittings of Parliament in Vienna and summoned the deputies to the Moravian city of Kremsier on November 15 to resume their work of drafting a constitution.[19] Although Parliament protested that it could discharge its obligations to the Austrian people and the Emperor only by remaining in Vienna,[20] at this late stage every clear-headed observer realized that military force alone would decide the fate of the city.

On the evening of October 23, from his headquarters at Hetzendorf, Windischgrätz issued a second ultimatum to the Viennese giving them forty-eight hours to surrender. All armed bodies in the city were to be dissolved, every revolutionary club was to be abolished, and the university was to be closed. The commander of the Academic Legion, twelve students, and other persons to be designated later[21] were to be

---

[14] Grüner, *op. cit.*, p. 199; [Daniel] Fenner von Fenneberg, *Geschichte der Wiener Oktobertage*, Part II, p. 243.

[15] "Parliamentary Resolution," Vienna, October 22, 1848, Univ. Colo. 1848 Coll., Nos. II/34, II/175.

[16] "City Council to Prince Windischgrätz," Vienna, October 22, 1848, Unterreiter, *op. cit.*, Vol. I, pp. 104–105.

[17] Joseph Alexander Freiherrn von Helfert, *Die Wiener Journalistik im Jahre 1848*, pp. 230–31.

[18] Dunder, *op. cit.*, pp. 606–607.

[19] Ferdinand I, "Decree," Olmütz, October 22, 1848, Karl Schneider, *Kremsier*, pp. 58–59.

[20] "Parliamentary Committee to Emperor," Grüner, *op. cit.*, pp. 241–44.

[21] In a letter to the City Council, dated Hetzendorf, October 26, 1848, Windischgrätz announced the other persons still to be delivered up in accord with his October 23 proclamation: General Bem, Hungarian Undersecretary of State

turned over to him as hostages. All papers except the *Wiener Zeitung*, which was to print only official notices, were to be suspended for the duration of the state of siege. Anyone seeking to stir up the populace against the military and anyone bearing arms was to be tried by martial law.[22]

After a long, heated debate, Parliament declared that the above proclamation violated human rights and was a danger to the constitutional throne. It asserted that this proclamation too, like that of October 20, was unconstitutional.[23] The City Council informed Windischgrätz that it recognized Parliament as the highest authority in the land, and that the sentiments voiced by Parliament represented those of all the Viennese.[24]

Compromise appeared impossible. The democrats refused to yield on any point; Windischgrätz demanded total capitulation. Fully realizing the desperateness, if not the utter hopelessness, of their position, the radicals now devoted all their energies to preparing for the inevitable conflict. The Central Committee of Democratic Clubs exhorted the Viennese to fight to the end for their freedom, their honor, their homes, and their families.[25] The Student Committee appealed to the inhabitants to "give the world an example of patriotism similar to that of Paris, Warsaw, and Buda-Pest in the days of their greatest tribulation."[26] To inspire them to greater energy, the city offered men daily wages of 40 kreutzer (32 cents) each to work on the barricades, and women and children 30 kreutzer (24 cents) and 10 kreutzer[27] (8 cents), respectively.

Pulszky, Anton Schütte, and the murderers of Count Latour. Grüner, *op. cit.*, pp. 255–56.

[22] Prince Windischgrätz, "Proclamation," Headquarters, Hetzendorf, October 23, 1848, copy in the Univ. Colo. 1848 Coll., No. II/119. See also "Proclamation," Headquarters, Hetzendorf, November 1, 1848, Univ. Colo. 1848 Coll., No. II/55; and Vitzthum von Eckstädt to his mother, Hietzing, evening of October 24, 1848, Vitzthum von Eckstädt, *op. cit.*, pp. 172–73.

[23] "Parliamentary Resolution," Vienna, October 24, 1848, Dunder, *op. cit.*, p. 657; "Continuation of the Permanent Parliamentary Session at 5:30 P.M., October 24, 1848," *Wiener Reichstags-Blatt*, No. 92 (October 26, 1848), Univ. Colo. 1848 Coll., No. II/223. The *Wiener Reichstags-Blatt* was edited by H. Kern and published by J. Löw. Ninety-two issues appeared, the first on July 11, 1848, the last on October 26. See also Auerbach diary, October 24, 1848, Berthold Auerbach, *Tagebuch,* p. 170.

[24] "City Council to Windischgrätz," Vienna, October 25, 1848, Grüner, *op. cit.*, pp. 225–28.

[25] "Central Committee of Democratic Clubs to Inhabitants of Vienna," Vienna, October 23, 1848, Grüner, *op. cit.*, pp. 214–15.

[26] Student Committee, "Proclamation," Vienna, October, 1848, Grüner, *op. cit.*, pp. 211–13.

[27] "Student Committee to Inhabitants of Vienna," Vienna, October 26, 1848, Grüner, *op. cit.*, p. 256.

The End

Messenhauser drafted plans to assure that the barricades were always fully manned and ordered the reserve troops to remain armed at all times.[28] He empowered his corps and district commanders to sentence their men to bread-and-water arrest for periods of six hours to four days for minor infractions of discipline. He also created a military court to pass judgment on guardsmen who refused to carry out the commands of their superior officers, left their post of duty without authorization, or committed crimes against persons or property.[29] To deal with traitors, Fenner von Fenneberg was commissioned to organize and head a special security police. On October 26 he announced that all persons guilty of hiding arms, weapons, or foodstuffs were to be punished as traitors. Viennese not specifically exempted from building barricades or bearing arms were to be delivered to the nearest fortification or turned over to the security police.[30]

The Viennese moderates and conservatives were confronted with a dilemma. If they fought against Windischgrätz' army, they ran the risk of being tried by a Habsburg court-martial; if they refused to fight against Windischgrätz, the democrats would punish them.[31] Ably supported by the new espionage organization, the ultraradicals began a reign of terror against those persons labeled "black-yellows."[32] In order not to attract the attention of the proletariat and the Mobile Guard, the moderates who had not fled from the capital hid behind locked doors.[33] If they ventured out into the city, they were in danger of being maltreated or seized as potential spies. Large numbers of suspected court sympathizers were taken to the Student Committee for trial.[34] Patrols searched the streets, coffeehouses, hotels, and private homes for unarmed able-bodied men and either held them for court-martial or shoved a musket in their hands and forced them to go to the nearest barricade or the most vulnerable points in the city.[35] In the end, suspicion reigned and fear was rampant.[36]

[28] Messenhauser, "Order to All Commanders," Vienna, October 26, 1848, Grüner, *op. cit.*, pp. 249–51.
[29] Messenhauser, "Proclamation," Vienna, October 23, 1848, Univ. Colo. 1848 Coll., No. II/29.
[30] Fenner von Fenneberg, "Proclamation," Vienna, October 26, 1848, Grüner, *op. cit.*, pp. 253–55.
[31] Auerbach diary, October 25, 1848, Auerbach, *op. cit.*, pp. 171–72.
[32] Lyser, *op. cit.*, p. 86; Dunder, *op. cit.*, p. 714.
[33] Hübner diary, Florisdorf, November 1, 1848, Hübner, *op. cit.*, pp. 274–75.
[34] Grüner, *op. cit.*, p. 263.
[35] *Ibid.*, p. 248; Adolf Pichler, *Das Sturmjahr*, p. 149; Auerbach diary, October 27, 1848, Auerbach, *op. cit.*, p. 176; William H. Stiles, *Austria in 1848–49*, Vol. II, p. 140; Dunder, *op. cit.*, p. 693; Friedrich Kaiser, *Memoiren*, pp. 159–65.
[36] [Ernst Violand], *Enthüllungen*, pp. 183–84.

The frenzied efforts of the extremists to save the city were in vain. Even before Windischgrätz' troops began firing upon the capital, the food situation had become extremely grave. For a short while after October 6 the peasants had been able to bring enough food into the city to satisfy the needs of the people, but they took advantage of the disturbed conditions to charge at least 50 per cent more for their products.[37] By October 15 the imperial troops were beginning to intercept much of the produce sent to the city.[38] By the 19th they had completely cut off the milk supply and had drastically reduced the trade in foodstuffs except potatoes.[39] After a few days little food was available besides flour and cheese,[40] though there was still plenty of beer and wine. By the 24th the water supply ran out and the public wells went dry, largely because in the prevailing excitement people forgot to keep the fires lighted in the engines that pumped and filtered the water from the Danube. Three days later the street gaslighting system broke down.[41]

On October 27 Windischgrätz delivered a final ultimatum to the Viennese, warning them not to resist the Habsburg troops and to keep doors and windows locked the following day.[42]

At 11:00 A.M. on October 28 the imperial army directed an artillery barrage against the suburbs of the city. Then the infantry advanced against the rebels, and during the course of savage street-fighting systematically cleared one barricade after another. By evening, having advanced as far as the Wien River and the Danube Canal, Windischgrätz' forces were in possession of the Leopoldstadt and Landstrasse suburbs.[43] On the same day General Bem resigned as tactical commander of the

---

[37] Dunder, *op. cit.*, pp. 560–61.

[38] Grüner, *op. cit.*, p. 117; Fenner von Fenneberg, *op. cit.*, Part II, p. 8; "Continuation of the Permanent Parliamentary session at 5:30 P.M.," October 24, 1848, *Wiener Reichstags-Blatt,* No. 92 (October 26, 1848), Univ. Colo. 1848 Coll., No. II/223.

[39] Grüner, *op. cit.*, p. 157; Auerbach diary, October 20, 1848, Auerbach, *op. cit.*, p. 132.

[40] Anton Füster, *Memoiren vom März 1848 bis Juli 1849,* Vol. II, pp. 203–204.

[41] Auerbach diary, October 24, 1848, Auerbach, *op. cit.*, p. 171; Pichler, *op. cit.*, pp. 152–53; Priscilla Robertson, *Revolutions of 1848: A Social History,* p. 245.

[42] "Windischgrätz to Inhabitants of Vienna," Headquarters, Hetzendorf, October 27, 1848, Ehnl, *op. cit.*, Appendix XVII, p. 197.

[43] Schütte diary, October 28, 1848, [Anton] Schütte, *Tagebuch,* pp. 49–53; "Proclamation," Headquarters, Hetzendorf, November 1, 1848, Univ. Colo. 1848 Coll., No. II/55; Kaiser, *op. cit.*, pp. 165–68; Vitzthum von Eckstädt to his mother, Hietzing, October 28, 1848, Vitzthum von Eckstädt, *op. cit.*, pp. 175–77; Auerbach diary, October 28, 1848, Auerbach, *op. cit.*, pp. 179–85; Ehnl, *op. cit.*, p. 98; *Ursache und Geschichte der Octoberereignisse,* pp. 122–24; C. A. Ritter, *Tagebuch der letzten Oktober- und ersten November-Tage Wiens,* pp. 15–25.

defending forces and mysteriously disappeared from Vienna, not to be heard of again until he took up service with the Hungarian army.[44]

Many of the inhabitants of the conquered suburbs greeted the troops as liberators and showered them with bouquets.[45] Others remained hidden in their homes. In the suburbs the conquerors, particularly the Croatians, committed atrocities. Under the pretext of punishing the inhabitants of homes from which shots had been fired,[46] bands of soldiers broke into house after house, stealing, torturing, and killing.[47]

The reports of what was happening in the suburbs brought terror to the inner city. At National Guard headquarters it seemed obvious by afternoon that Vienna could not hold out much longer. Too few defenders were available for threatened points. Also, a serious munitions shortage developed, and strict orders had to be issued to ration supplies. Many Viennese had lost the will to fight, and certain commanding officers were becoming insubordinate. When he realized that Vienna could not be defended much longer, Messenhauser called his district commanders together at the Stallburg. There he informed them that the city could resist only a few more hours and strongly recommended that a deputation of members of the National Guard, the City Council, and Parliament try to obtain reasonable surrender terms from Windischgrätz. With the exception of the leaders of the radical Mobile Guard, those present at the meeting readily agreed to Messenhauser's proposal.[48] So did the City Council, which appointed three of its members to join a four-man deputation selected by the National Guard.[49] However, Parliament declared that all matters dealing with the protection of the city should be left to its defenders and refused to co-operate.[50]

At 8:30 on the morning of October 29 the deputation arrived at Hetzendorf. Windischgrätz had gone to the Laarberg as an observer to check on the movements of the Hungarian troops, and the Viennese

[44] Rudolph Kiszling *et al.*, *Die Revolution im Kaiserthum Österreich 1848–1849*, Vol. I, p. 277.

[45] Vitzthum von Eckstädt to his mother, Hietzing, 12:00 A.M., October 29, 1848, Vitzthum von Eckstädt, *op. cit.*, p. 176; "Proclamation," Headquarters, Hetzendorf, November 1, 1848, Univ. Colo. 1848 Coll., No. II/55.

[46] Vitzthum von Eckstädt to his mother, Hietzing, 12:00 A.M., October 29, 1848, Vitzthum von Eckstädt, *op. cit.*, p. 177.

[47] Kaiser, *op. cit.*, pp. 168–86; and Dunder, *op. cit.*, pp. 756–77, contain vivid descriptions of the looting in the suburbs on the 28th.

[48] Dunder, *op. cit.*, pp. 752–53; Ehnl, *op. cit.*, pp. 99–100; Schütte diary, October 29, 1848, Schütte, *op. cit.*, p. 54; Kiszling, *op. cit.*, Vol. I, p. 277.

[49] "City Council to Inhabitants of Vienna," Vienna, October 29, 1848, Grüner, *op. cit.*, pp. 278–79.

[50] Ehnl, *op. cit.*, p. 100.

deputies followed him there. Windischgrätz refused to modify his terms but agreed to a twelve-hour truce,[51] in the hope that the Viennese would surrender without further bloodshed.[52]

Before the deputation returned to Vienna, Messenhauser issued a proclamation stating that the struggle was hopeless and asking the defending forces to vote whether or not they wanted to continue fighting.[53] Realizing that the end was near, the moderates decided not to take up arms again. The ultraradical suburban guardsmen and the Mobile Guardsmen vowed that they preferred to go down fighting. They denounced as a traitor every citizen who uttered a cautious word in favor of surrender.[54]

In the evening, despite the efforts of the ultraradicals, representatives of all the military companies who had been summoned to National Guard headquarters voted in favor of unconditional surrender.[55] The City Council concurred in this decision.[56] On the same night a joint National Guard–City Council deputation informed Windischgrätz of the vote and asked him to enter the city and the suburbs the next day. Windischgrätz agreed and requested a commission from the City Council to arrange the last-minute details with him the next morning.[57]

On the afternoon of October 30 Windischgrätz ordered the Viennese to fly a large imperial flag from the tower of St. Stephen's Cathedral and white flags on top of the city gates to indicate that they would allow the imperial troops to enter the city peacefully. The defenders' cannon and other arms and ammunition were to be handed over within twelve hours. Until imperial troops entered the city, National Guard detachments were to protect the public buildings. Eight o'clock on the evening of the 30th was the deadline for the City Council to inform the Habsburg commander that it accepted these terms and to give adequate

---

[51] *Ibid.*, pp. 100–101.

[52] "Proclamation," Headquarters, Hetzendorf, November 1, 1848, Univ. Colo. 1848 Coll., No. II/55; Kaiser, *op. cit.*, p. 186.

[53] Messenhauser, "Proclamation," Vienna, October 29, 1848, Ehnl, *op. cit.*, pp. 101–103; Schütte diary, October 29, 1848, Schütte, *op. cit.*, p. 55.

[54] Grüner, *op. cit.*, pp. 278–79; Lyser, *op. cit.*, p. 88; Auerbach diary, October 29, 1848, Auerbach, *op. cit.*, pp. 185–86; Ritter, *op. cit.*, pp. 28–31.

[55] Auerbach diary, October 29, 1848, Auerbach, *op. cit.*, p. 186; Ehnl, *op. cit.*, pp. 104–108; "City Council to Fellow-Citizens," Vienna, October 31, 1848, Grüner, *op. cit.*, pp. 291–92.

[56] "City Council to Fellow-Citizens," Vienna, October 29, 1848, Ehnl, *op. cit.*, Appendix XX, pp. 198–99.

[57] "Messenhauser to Fellow-Citizens," Vienna, October 30, 1848, Grüner, *op. cit.*, pp. 285–86; "Proclamation," Headquarters, Hetzendorf, November 1, 1848, Univ. Colo. 1848 Coll., No. II/55; Kaiser, *op. cit.*, pp. 186–87; Schütte diary, October 29, 1848, Schütte, *op. cit.*, pp. 55–56.

The End

assurances that they would be carried out by 12:00 noon on the 31st.[58]

Either with joy or with resignation the Viennese learned that their city was to be surrendered without further bloodshed.[59] After a lengthy, bitter debate, during which the two Frankfurt deputies Blum and Fröbel advised that further resistance was senseless, the Student Committee disbanded on the evening of October 29.[60] But the extremists were still determined not to capitulate without a last, desperate struggle. In their opinion, the city was being handed over to the enemy, not because of the hopeless inadequacy of its defense, but because it had been betrayed. There was a furious outcry against the City Council and Messenhauser, who were looked upon as traitors. Mobile Guardsmen made the rounds of the city looking for turncoats and screaming for the blood of the "black-yellows."[61] By the late morning of the 30th their fury had assumed formidable proportions.[62]

Nonetheless, in spite of the threats of the ultraradicals, measures were taken during the morning of the 30th to prepare the city for the entrance of the Habsburg troops. Weapons and ammunition were delivered as ordered, and white flags were displayed in the suburbs that had not yet been occupied. To protect the city against looting, Windischgrätz promised to send soldiers there at 3:00 P.M. and appointed Major General Cordon as military commandant of the city.[63] Finally convinced that further resistance was futile, many radicals hurriedly shaved their revolutionary beards and long hair, threw away their Calabrian hats, hastily changed into civilian clothing, and lost themselves in the crowds.[64]

Then suddenly the rumor spread that the Hungarians were marching to the aid of the city. Immediately the radicals lost all thought of surrendering. Shouting enthusiastic praise of Kossuth and his men, a wild throng surged through the streets. The white flags disappeared from the city gates and the suburbs, and crowds of people feverishly began

[58] "Cordon to City Council," Headquarters, Hetzendorf, 3:00 P.M., October 30, 1848, as given in the City Council's proclamation to its fellow-citizens, Vienna, October 31, 1848, Grüner, *op. cit.*, pp. 292–95; also in Ehnl, *op. cit.*, Appendix XXI, pp. 200–201.

[59] Auerbach diary, October 29, 1848, Auerbach, *op. cit.*, p. 187.

[60] Grüner, *op. cit.*, pp. 279–82; Paul Molisch, "Die Wiener akademische Legion," *Archiv für österreichische Geschichte,* Vol. CX, Part I (1924), p. 156.

[61] Schütte diary, October 30, 1848, Schütte, *op. cit.*, p. 56; Auerbach diary, October 29, 1848, Auerbach, *op. cit.*, pp. 186–87; Grüner, *op. cit.*, p. 283; Ritter, *op. cit.*, p. 34.

[62] Ehnl, *op. cit.*, p. 110.

[63] *Ibid.*

[64] Grüner, *op. cit.*, p. 283; Auerbach diary, October 30, 1848, Auerbach, *op. cit.*, p. 189.

building barricades.[65] Many Academic Legion and Mobile Guard leaders urged Messenhauser to order the Viennese to resume the battle. At first, Messenhauser refused to believe the rumor that the Hungarians were coming, but at 10:30 A.M. he finally climbed to the observation post on top of St. Stephen's Cathedral to check whether the rumor was true. He peered through a telescope in the direction of Schwechat and clearly saw that a battle was in progress.[66]

The battle raging around Schwechat, two miles from Vienna, was between the Hungarians and the Croatian troops under Jelačić. Ever since they had followed Jelačić there late in September, the Magyar forces had remained encamped on the Austrian frontier, awaiting a "legal" request for assistance from the Viennese. Finally, on October 28, after Kossuth personally intervened, the Hungarian troops, 25,000 strong, crossed the Leitha River and moved in the direction of Vienna. The next day they arrived at Schwechat, and on the morning of October 30 a furious battle took place between them and the Croatian troops, aided by the Third Habsburg Cavalry Corps.[67]

As soon as Messenhauser appeared on the tower of St. Stephen's, he was besieged by student and Mobile Guard deputies, who demanded that he inform the people about the battle and order the Viennese to attack Windischgrätz' troops. Messenhauser muttered that he could not take the responsibility of breaking the agreement. Then, in a moment of weakness, he wrote this short notice on a sheet of paper: "Although it cannot be determined what troops are fighting or how the fight is progressing, a battle is definitely going on behind Kaiser-Ebersdorf. 11:00 A.M."[68]

The effect of Messenhauser's announcement was that whole companies of Mobile Guardsmen, some of them without leaders, hurried to the suburbs to plead with the inhabitants to resume the fight. Wild rumors spread through the city: not only were the Magyars already there, but also the Styrian militia and many Tyrolese soldiers were hurrying to beleaguered Vienna. In some suburbs nearly all the residents took up arms or hastened to strengthen the barricades, in spite of the desperate attempts of the City Council to restrain them.[69]

---

[65] Ritter, *op. cit.*, pp. 34–35; Ehnl, *op. cit.*, p. 110.
[66] Kaiser, *op. cit.*, pp. 187–89.
[67] "Proclamation," Headquarters, Hetzendorf, November 1, 1848, Univ. Colo. 1848 Coll., No. II/55; Franz Pulszky, *Mein Zeit, mein Leben*, pp. 250–55; Kiszling *et al., op. cit.*, Vol. I, pp. 284–88.
[68] Kaiser, *op. cit.*, pp. 189–90; Schütte diary, October 30, 1848, Schütte, *op. cit.*, p. 57.
[69] Schütte diary, October 30, 1848, Schütte, *op. cit.*, p. 57; Grüner, *op. cit.*, pp.

The End

At 12:45 P.M. in a second proclamation from St. Stephen's tower, Messenhauser informed the Viennese that at the moment the Hungarians seemed to be winning the battle and added: "In case a defeated army should approach the walls of the city, it will be the duty of all military forces to put themselves under arms even if they have no orders to do so."[70] This second report was a call to arms, a clear violation of the surrender agreement with Prince Windischgrätz.[71]

At 2:00 P.M. a third proclamation, also supposedly signed by Messenhauser,[72] was issued from St. Stephen's tower:[73]

A corps of troops is standing below Neugebäude. On account of the fog it cannot definitely be determined whether it is the cavalry or the Croatians. At this moment the battle is concentrated to the left of Schwechat, midway between Kaiser-Ebersdorf and Mannswörth. The thunder of cannon is so distinct that we can almost judge the number of batteries from it. For a half hour the battle has obviously been drawing closer to us.

Now the masses could no longer be held back. A horde of armed men rushed to the city walls. The surrender to Windischgrätz was completely forgotten.[74] In several suburbs, particularly Wieden, Mariahilf, and Alser, Viennese fell upon the Habsburg forces. From the inner city, too, shots were fired. Since the imperial troops were still under orders to refrain from hostilities against the Viennese, they deemed it expedient to withdraw to more protected positions.[75]

Early in the afternoon the tide of battle rapidly turned against the Hungarians, and by four o'clock they had retreated from the battlefield and were in disordered flight across the Fischa River. The next day the Croatians drove them back across the Hungarian frontier.[76]

The rout of the Hungarian army plunged the observers on the top of St. Stephen's Cathedral into despair. Gradually the people left the

---

288–89; Kaiser, *op. cit.*, pp. 190–94; Ehnl, *op. cit.*, pp. 113–14; Ritter, *op. cit.*, pp. 35–36.

[70] Kaiser, *op. cit.*, p. 194; Schütte diary, October 30, 1848, Schütte, *op. cit.*, p. 58.

[71] Ehnl, *op. cit.*, p. 114.

[72] There is good evidence to support Messenhauser's contention at his trial that he never wrote this proclamation but that his radical opponents had drafted it and forged his signature to it. See Ehnl, *op. cit.*, pp. 115–18; Dunder, *op. cit.*, p. 822.

[73] As given in Kaiser, *op. cit.*, pp. 194–95. See also Schütte diary, October 30, 1848, Schütte, *op. cit.*, p. 58.

[74] Kaiser, *op. cit.*, p. 195; Schütte diary, October 30, 1848, Schütte, *op. cit.*, p. 58; Ritter, *op. cit.*, p. 36.

[75] Kaiser, *op. cit.*, p. 196.

[76] "Proclamation," Headquarters, Hetzendorf, November 1, 1848, Univ. Colo. 1848 Coll., No. II/55; Vitzthum von Eckstädt to his mother, Hietzing, October 30, 1848, Vitzthum von Eckstädt, *op. cit.*, p. 178; Jelačić to Windischgrätz, Headquarters, Rothneusiedel, November 1, 1848, Dunder, *op. cit.*, pp. 852–53.

tower, and in a short time only Goldmark and Auerbach remained there with Messenhauser. Meanwhile, representatives of the Mobile Guard and the Central Committee of Democratic Clubs were demanding that the Student Committee, which had reconvened at the university immediately after the news of the approach of the Hungarians, replace Messenhauser with the radical Fenner von Fenneberg as commander of the defense forces. To bring pressure upon Messenhauser to resign, the crowd at the Aula passed a no-confidence vote and dispatched a student deputation to St. Stephen's with the verdict.

Messenhauser told the students that he would submit his resignation only to those who had appointed him and then calmly resumed his conversation with Auerbach about his future literary plans. The radicals then loudly denounced him as a traitor and shouted for his head. Hauk ordered his elite corps to occupy all entrances to the tower. Then, when Messenhauser repeated to a second deputation his refusal to resign, an armed worker brandished his weapon and threatened to kill him if he did not resign at once. Thereupon Messenhauser, filled with disgust, declared that he would hand in his resignation to Parliament. However, Parliament refused to be intimidated by the radicals and, knowing that many National Guard officers had already vowed to resign rather than serve under Fenner von Fenneberg, rejected Messenhauser's offer and prevailed upon him to remain in command until the surrender terms were carried out.[77]

At eight o'clock Messenhauser wrote an open letter to his fellow-Viennese asking the guard units to state as soon as possible whether or not they wanted to continue the battle.[78] Later on the same night, as a gesture of friendship to the extreme left, he appointed Fenner von Fenneberg his deputy for the Mobile Guard and Karl Redl his deputy for the Academic Legion—a fatal blunder,[79] as it proved. Supported by the Mobile Guard and the Academic Legion, Fenner von Fenneberg and Redl were then in a position to force Messenhauser to do what they demanded, while he had to accept responsibility for their actions.[80]

[77] Auerbach diary, October 30, 1848, Auerbach, *op. cit.*, pp. 191–93; Dunder, *op. cit.*, pp. 828–39; Grüner, *op. cit.*, p. 289; City Council, "Proclamation," Vienna, October 30, 1848, Grüner, *op. cit.*, p. 285; Ehnl, *op. cit.*, pp. 118–24; Molisch, *op. cit.*, pp. 156–57.

[78] Messenhauser, "Proclamation," Vienna, 8:00 P.M., October 30, 1848, Grüner, *op. cit.*, p. 290. See also Ehnl, *op. cit.*, p. 125; and Dunder, *op. cit.*, p. 841.

[79] Messenhauser, "Proclamation," Vienna, October 31, 1848, Dunder, *op. cit.*, p. 858.

[80] Ehnl, *op. cit.*, pp. 126–27.

The End

Although Messenhauser worked feverishly during the night of October 30 to save Vienna from disaster, his efforts were fruitless. When Windischgrätz learned that the Viennese had broken the terms of the surrender on the afternoon of the 30th, he angrily exclaimed: "Then Vienna must be bombarded and Messenhauser will probably be hanged."[81] Nevertheless, in spite of his bitterness over what to him was rank betrayal by the Viennese, Windischgrätz still hoped to induce them to capitulate without bloodshed. Believing that the defeat of the Hungarians would finally make them realize the hopelessness of continued resistance, on the night of October 30 Windischgrätz forwarded still another proclamation to the Viennese trying to pacify the people and warn the evildoers. The placard, however, was read by very few, for immediately after it was posted, radicals tore it down.[82]

On the same night the City Council sent a deputation to Hetzendorf, which arrived at Windischgrätz' headquarters early on the morning of the 31st. The deputation told the Habsburg commander that, although the majority of Viennese wanted to surrender unconditionally, they were unable to do so because of the reign of terror exercised by the democratic clubs, the Student Committee, and the armed proletariat. Windischgrätz was implored to order troops to the capital as soon as possible to protect the people and their property from the rabble, who seemed determined to bury themselves and their fellow-citizens in the ruins of the city.[83] So that the responsible inhabitants of the capital might make plans to receive the imperial troops, Windischgrätz extended the truce to the next day if necessary, provided that his troops were not attacked.[84]

Around noon, troops of the divisions commanded by Lieutenant Field Marshals Hartlieb and Csorich moved without opposition into the still unoccupied suburbs south and southeast of the city. By two o'clock they stood outside the Burgtor and just beyond the city walls south of the city.[85]

Meanwhile, the responsible citizens in Vienna did their best to in-

[81] Müller, *op. cit.*, p. 151. See also "Proclamation," Headquarters, Hetzendorf, November 1, 1848, Univ. Colo. 1848 Coll., No. II/55.

[82] Kiszling *et al., op. cit.*, Vol. I, pp. 289–90; Ehnl, *op. cit.*, pp. 127–28.

[83] Kaiser, *op. cit.*, p. 197; "Proclamation," Headquarters, Hetzendorf, November 1, 1848, Univ. Colo. 1848 Coll., No. II/55; Heinrich Reschauer and Moritz Smets, *Das Jahr 1848. Geschichte der Wiener Revolution*, Vol. II, p. 652.

[84] Kiszling *et al., op. cit.*, Vol. I, p. 290; Reschauer and Smets, *op. cit.*, Vol. II, p. 652; Maximilian Bach, *Geschichte der Wiener Revolution*, p. 836.

[85] Ehnl, *op. cit.*, p. 129; Kiszling, *op. cit.*, Vol. I, pp. 290–91.

fluence the people to let Windischgrätz' troops enter the city unmolested. Messenhauser issued another proclamation hoping to convince the radicals that the city could not be defended against the overpowering forces ready to attack it.[86] The City Council appealed to the citizens to lay down their arms in accord with the terms of the surrender.[87] Messenhauser's chief of staff, Haug, added his pleas to the fighting forces to yield peacefully and prevent the destruction of the capital and the horrors of a civil war.[88] Even Mobile Guard Commander Fenner von Fenneberg admonished them that further resistance could result only in the needless shedding of blood.[89]

The Mobile Guard seemed determined to sacrifice Vienna rather than submit without a struggle. Instead of turning in their arms, as required by the agreement, the guardsmen rang the tocsin and seized every available person to help man the city's defenses. They insulted and even attacked people who followed instructions and placed white flags on the city walls. Fully convinced that their commanders were traitors, a mob of maddened proletariat went to National Guard headquarters in the Stallburg with ropes and nails to take revenge on the "black-yellow" turncoats.[90] Toward noon Vienna was in a state of anarchy. There was no one in the city whose authority was respected.[91] Every semblance of law and order had disappeared.

According to the arrangements made with Windischgrätz, the imperial troops were to enter the city from the south through the Burg Gate, which was barricaded only by a large boulder. Shortly after two o'clock, ten Hofburg guards were ordered to remove the barricade. At the same time, a small detachment of National Guardsmen, who had been commanded to clear the gate of students and Mobile Guardsmen trying to tear a white flag off it, charged with fixed bayonets up the steps leading to the top of the adjacent city wall. When they arrived, they mounted a white handkerchief on a stick and waved the improvised flag in front of the military on the outside.[92]

---

[86] Messenhauser, "Proclamation," Vienna, October 31, 1848, Dunder, *op. cit.*, p. 858.

[87] City Council, "Proclamation," Vienna, October 31, 1848, Grüner, *op. cit.*, pp. 294–95; also in Dunder, *op. cit.*, p. 866.

[88] "Ernst Haug to the Viennese National Guard," n.d., Dunder, *op. cit.*, pp. 856–57.

[89] Fenner von Fenneberg, "Proclamation," Vienna, October 31, 1848, Dunder, *op. cit.*, pp. 858–59.

[90] Kaiser, *op. cit.*, p. 204; Dunder, *op. cit.*, p. 863.

[91] Pichler, *op. cit.*, p. 163.

[92] Kaiser, *op. cit.*, pp. 205–206; Dunder, *op. cit.*, p. 870.

The End

Then the Burg Gate was opened, and a couple of National Guard officers with white flags went out to speak to Lieutenant Field Marshals Csorich and Hartlieb. With a few aides, the two field marshals advanced toward the two truce negotiators. Then the gate was suddenly slammed shut, the white flag was snatched from it, and a volley of shots was fired at the imperial soldiers.[93] For as soon as the Burg Gate was opened, about two hundred Mobile Guards, with two cannon, stormed the entrance and barricaded it again. Then, shouting, "Treason! Treason! You treacherous dogs!" they rushed to the top of the gate to attack the National Guardsmen who were waving the improvised white flag. About the same time several detachments of the Mobile Guard, carting two cannon and accompanied by students and a few National Guardsmen, moved across the Augustiner bastion along the city wall toward the Burg Gate. They had scarcely placed the cannon on the walls when other Mobile Guardsmen started shooting at Windischgrätz' troops.[94]

Windischgrätz' forces quickly returned the fire and at once began to bombard the city. Grenades, six- and twelve-pound cannon balls, rockets, and grapeshot fell on the city. The defenders fought back as best they could, and noncombatants fled to cellars and other places of refuge. After desperate fighting the Burg Gate was broken down shortly after five o'clock, and the imperial troops battled their way into the Hofburg, then to St. Stephen's Square, and finally toward the university. Other soldiers poured through the Burg Gate to extinguish a fire that had started in the Hofburg and to help clear the streets of revolutionaries. Around seven o'clock the military succeeded in occupying the Kärntner Gate, thereby gaining possession of a second entrance to the city. Shortly thereafter they gained control of all the main squares in Vienna. In a little while the last embers of resistance were extinguished throughout the city.[95]

Before the fighting ended, many a fearful defender of the city slipped into a side street, threw down his musket, removed the uniform he had put on over his civilian clothes, ripped the revolutionary insignia from his hat, and casually strolled into the next thoroughfare. By evening deserted streets and alleys had become veritable military depots of dis-

[93] *Ursache und Geschichte der Octoberereignisse*, p. 127; Schütte diary, October 31, 1848, Schütte, *op. cit.*, p. 72; Reschauer and Smets, *op. cit.*, Vol. II, p. 654; Bach, *op. cit.*, p. 840.

[94] Kaiser, *op. cit.*, pp. 206–208; Dunder, *op. cit.*, pp. 870–71.

[95] Ritter, *op. cit.*, pp. 44–48; Kaiser, *op. cit.*, pp. 208–15; Dunder, *op. cit.*, pp. 871–77; Grüner, *op. cit.*, pp. 302–303; Kiszling *et al.*, *op. cit.*, Vol. I, pp. 291–92; Reschauer and Smets, *op. cit.*, Vol. II, pp. 654–55; Bach, *op. cit.*, pp. 840–43.

carded weapons. Barbers were busy cutting off the revolutionary beards and long hair of frightened democrats.[96] Other Viennese hung white flags from their windows.

The university was empty and quiet. Many of the most outspoken radicals had gone into hiding, and the curious wandered up and down the streets far into the night, expressing their astonishment over the mildness of the occupation., The hotels and coffeehouses were full. People calmly ate and drank as though nothing out of the ordinary had occurred. Weary inhabitants retired early to enjoy their first night of undisturbed sleep since October 6.[97]

By and large, the Viennese welcomed the Habsburg troops enthusiastically. The same National Guardsmen who had fired upon them earlier now embraced them as liberators.[98] When Jelačić's troops, who were still outside the city, made their formal entrance at noon on November 1, they too were welcomed by jubilant Viennese, who waved white cloths from their windows or prominently displayed the "black-yellow" colors in their buttonholes.[99] By November 1 no long-haired or bearded citizens were seen, and the Calabrian and German hats had been discarded for sedate stovepipes. For the first time in months people appeared in the streets wearing gloves. Throughout Vienna the black-yellow imperial flag had replaced the tricolored German banners.[100]

The same Viennese who just a few days before had vowed to die on the barricades before seeing Habsburg troops in Vienna now honored them. On November 1 the City Council thanked Windischgrätz for restoring law, order, and freedom to the capital. On the same day a crowd of jubilant well-wishers roundly applauded the imperial troops when they tore down the lamppost on which Count Latour's corpse had been hung.[101] When Jelačić—formerly called "robber captain" by the Viennese democrats—appeared in public, he was acclaimed as a

[96] Schütte diary, October 31, 1848, Schütte, *op. cit.,* pp. 72–73.

[97] Kaiser, *op. cit.,* pp. 211–12, 215–17; Dunder, *op. cit.,* pp. 877–78; Pichler, *op. cit.,* pp. 164–65.

[98] Vitzthum von Eckstädt to his mother, Hietzing, 10:00 P.M., November 1, 1848, Vitzthum von Eckstädt, *op. cit.,* p. 180; Grüner, *op. cit.,* p. 302.

[99] Auerbach diary, November 2, 1848, Auerbach, *op. cit.,* pp. 220–21; Vitzthum von Eckstädt to his mother, Hietzing, 10:00 P.M., November 1, 1848, Vitzthum von Eckstädt, *op. cit.,* p. 182.

[100] Hübner diary, Floris-Dorf, November 1, 1848, Hübner, *op. cit.,* p. 271; Auerbach diary, November 1 and 2, 1848, Auerbach, *op. cit.,* pp. 214, 222; Vitzthum von Eckstädt to his mother, Hietzing, 10:00 P.M., November 1, 1848, Vitzthum von Eckstädt, *op. cit.,* pp. 180–81; Robertson, *op. cit.,* p. 250.

[101] Vitzthum von Eckstädt to his mother, Hietzing, 10:00 P.M., November 1, 1848, Vitzthum von Eckstädt, *op. cit.,* pp. 182–83.

The End

savior.[102] Throughout November deputation after deputation arrived before Windischgrätz, Jelačić, and other Habsburg officials to express Vienna's gratitude.[103]

Not all the actions of the new Habsburg masters merited the compliments showered upon them. On November 1 Prince Windischgrätz declared Vienna and its environs under a state of siege and put local authorities under the control of the military. The Academic Legion and the National Guard were abolished. The Viennese were given sixty hours in which to surrender their arms and were threatened with trial by court-martial if they were found with weapons after that time. All political clubs were closed, and gatherings of more than ten people on the streets and in public places were prohibited. The press was again placed under censorship.[104]

Although on the whole the German, Bohemian, and Italian troops were well disciplined and reasonably well behaved, at first the Croatians robbed and plundered at will. Only with difficulty did Windischgrätz finally restrain Jelačić's unruly soldiers.[105] When he intervened to restore discipline among the Croatians, Windischgrätz was by no means moved by compassion for the Viennese. Since they had broken the surrender terms, he felt that the capital must be dealt with as a conquered city and that the state of siege must be harshly and strictly enforced.[106] On the night of October 31 the city gates were locked and various revolutionary leaders were arrested.[107] By the next day the city, the suburbs, and the countryside were cut off from each other by three cordons of troops and military patrols were driving revolutionaries to hastily improvised prisons.[108] Persons denounced by spies and informers as dangerous radicals were dragged from their homes, coffeehouses, and the streets to stockades in the capital or to Windischgrätz' headquarters at Hetzendorf for questioning, detainment, and military trial. All told, probably more than two thousand persons were held for questioning.[109]

---

[102] See especially Vitzthum von Eckstädt to his mother, Vienna, November 17, 1848, Vitzthum von Eckstädt, *op. cit.*, pp. 193–94.

[103] Vitzthum von Eckstädt to his mother, Vienna, November 29, 1848, Vitzthum von Eckstädt, *op. cit.*, p. 197.

[104] Windischgrätz, "Proclamation," Headquarters, Hetzendorf, November 1, 1848, Univ. Colo. 1848 Coll., No. II/167.

[105] Lyser, *op. cit.*, pp. 98–99; Grüner, *op. cit.*, pp. 312–13.

[106] Müller, *op. cit.*, p. 156.

[107] Grüner, *op. cit.*, p. 303.

[108] Pichler, *op. cit.*, pp. 168, 172.

[109] The figures vary on the total number of persons arrested. Stiles, the American *chargé d'affaires* in Vienna at the time, sets the figure at 1,600 (*op. cit.*, Vol. II, p.

According to the American *chargé d'affaires* in Vienna at the time, most of the people arrested were later released; 9 persons were executed, 9 more were sentenced to long imprisonment, 996 were acquitted, and the rest were tried by civil tribunals[110] after trial by court-martial was abolished late in November. The most prominent of those executed were Messenhauser; the radical journalists Julius Becker and Hermann Jellinek; and Robert Blum, the representative of the Frankfurt left who had worked so feverishly exhorting the Viennese to resist the Habsburg troops.

Meanwhile, Windischgrätz' brother-in-law, Prince Felix Schwarzenberg, who on October 19 had been commissioned to form a new government,[111] officially announced it on November 21. Schwarzenberg himself was minister-president and minister of foreign affairs. Prince Franz Stadion was named minister of interior; Alexander Bach, minister of justice; Bruck, minister of commerce; Krauss, minister of finances; Thinnfeld, minister of agriculture; and Cordon, minister of war. Only two of these men—Bach and Krauss—were members of the revolutionary ministry. Stadion and Bruck were reputedly liberal. The rest were conservatives.

Essentially, the new ministers were not opposed to reforms but did insist that all reforms must be granted from above. Their main objective was to re-establish the authority of the Habsburg family. To accomplish this aim, they induced Emperor Ferdinand to abdicate his throne on December 2, 1848, in favor of his eighteen-year-old nephew, Francis Joseph. For a time the new government allowed Parliament to meet at Kremsier and continue its work of drafting a constitution, but only until the Schwarzenberg ministry could prepare its own constitution, which was to be bestowed on the people by the new Emperor. When it was completed, the Parliament at Kremsier was dissolved. On March 4,

---

138). The violently anti-Habsburg Unterreiter sets the number at 2,600 (*op. cit.*, Vol. II, p. 91). Wolf says that 2,375 persons were arrested between November, 1848, and April, 1849 (*Aus der Revolutionszeit in Österreich-Ungarn 1848–49*, p. 75). Bach gives the same figure (*op. cit.*, p. 852). Endres sets the number at around 2,400 (*Revolution in Österreich 1848*, p. 158).

110 Stiles, *op. cit.*, Vol. II, p. 138.

111 On October 22, 1848, Schwarzenberg sent a letter to Radetzky from Olmütz in which he outlined the program of the new government as follows: "Suppression of the revolt everywhere and at any price, preservation of the privileges of the dynasty over against all usurpations of the revolution, recognition of the liberty granted by the Emperor to all his peoples, regulation of this liberty in the interior, and maintenance of the totality of the monarchy toward the outside world will be the program of the new ministry of which His Majesty has commissioned me to be a member." Quoted in Adolph Schwarzenberg, *Prince Felix zu Schwarzenberg, Prime Minister of Austria, 1848–1852*, p. 26.

The End

1849, the new constitution was announced, with the promise that it would go into effect as soon as the emergency was at an end. That time was never to come. Meanwhile, Habsburg and Russian troops in the summer of 1849 forced the Hungarian nationalist army to surrender.

Thus ended Austria's mid-century experiment with constitutionalism. In March the hopes and aspirations of the Viennese had centered around liberalism; by November only a small number of extremists were still convinced liberals, and most of them were desperately running for cover. The great difficulty was that liberalism meant too many things to too many people. To the Austro-Germans it meant close union with a democratic German empire and German hegemony in central Europe; to the Czechs, Italians, Hungarians, and South Slavs it signified national self-determination. In Vienna itself the radicals tried to turn the liberal idea into a democratic one, thereby arousing in the moderate liberals of the March revolution the fear of republicanism and anarchy. In other words, by the fall of 1848 the belief that the extremists had perverted the liberal idea into a republican one repelled the more affluent Viennese middle classes and made them forget their hatred of the old regime and its oppressions. Thus they joined the counterrevolution. Moreover, the Viennese alienated the non-German nationalities. In essence, the Viennese Revolution of 1848 was a liberal idea that failed.

Bibliography

CONTEMPORARY RECORDS

University of Colorado 1848 Austrian Revolution Collection

This collection consists of about 250 items, including many original pamphlets, poems, scandal sheets, newspapers, and placards and brochures posted on the streets of Vienna in 1848. The longer and more significant items in this collection (including newspaper articles of particular value) are listed below.

Abraham: "Bürger, stosst die Juden nicht zurück!" *Oesterreichische konstitutionelle deutsche Zeitung*, No. 2 (April 4, 1848), pp. 7–8. No. II/157.

"Eine alte Frage an neue Minister," *Bst! Bst! Warum? Volksfragen*, No. 22. No. II/40.

"An die Czechen," *Wahrheit*, No. 5 (June 8, 1848), pp. 17–18. No. II/217a.

"An Metternich," *Die Brieftaube*, No. 3, pp. 9–10. No. II/38.

"An die Vertreter des Volkes," *Wiener Postillon*, No. 18 (July 22, 1848), p. 70. No. 11/222.

An die Wiener Garnison. Vienna: Leop. Sommer [1848]. No. II/220.

Appel, Karl: *Loblied der Damen Wiens.* Vienna [March, 1848]. No. II/5.

An Aristocrat for Hundreds, Audiatur et altera pars! Vienna: Edlen von Ghelen'schen Erben, June 15, 1848. No. II/7.

"Der 23. und 24. August als Folge des 15. Mai," *Das Portefeuil*, No. 4 (August 26, 1848), pp. 25–28. No. II/163.

B——, Dr.: "Sturmschritt und Schneckengang," *Der Unpartheyische*, No. 7 (June 7, 1848), pp. 26–27. No. II/195.

"Bitte um gesunden Verstand und Menschlichkeit," *Gold und Larbe*, No. 3 (July 19, 1848), p. 11. No. AII/92.

Brenner, Joh. Nep.: "Aufruf an den gesammten katholischen Klerus des österr. Kaiserstaates," *Wanderer*, 35. Jahrgang, No. 115 (May 13, 1848), p. 1. No. II/215.

Die Brieftaube, various issues. No. II/38.

Brühl, National Guardsman of the Stubenviertel for Hundreds of Thousands of Like-Minded Persons: *Wer ist Schuld, dass der Kaiser fort ist?* Vienna: U. Klopf sen. und Alex. Eurich [May, 1848]. No. II/178.

Bst! Bst! Warum? Volksfragen, various issues. No. II/41.

Buchheim, Adolf: *Das waren die braven Studenten!* Vienna: U. Klopf & Alex. Eurich, March, 1848. No. II/42.

Bürger von Wien! Vienna: Jos. Stöckholzer v. Hirschfeld [March 14, 1848]. No. II/43.

Castelli, J. F.: *Offener Brief an meine lieben Mitbürger über eine unnöthige Furcht.* Vienna [1848]. No. II/45.

Commercieller Völkerbund. Zeitschrift für Politik, Industrie, Handel und Arbeit, one issue. No. II/208.

Committee of Citizens, National Guardsmen, and Students for the Preservation of Order and Security and for the Safeguarding of the Rights of the People: *Aufruf an das Landvolk!* Vienna: k. k. Hof- und Staats-Druckerei, June 4, 1848, No. II/10.

——: *Aufruf an die wackeren Städtebewohner der Provinzen.* Vienna: Hof- und Staats-Druckerei, June 4, 1848. No. II/14.

"Conzert-Anzeige," *Schwefeläther,* No. 2 (August 6, 1848), p. 6. No. II/181b.

Czapka, J., Ritter von Winstetten, Former Mayor: *Öffentliche Erklärung.* No publisher, place, or date given, but published within about two weeks after the March revolution. No. II/274.

Der deutsche Adler an die deutschen Bewohner aller Provinzen Oesterreichs. Vienna: Klopf und Eurich, Easter Monday, 1848. No. II/85.

"Die Deutschkatoliken in Wien," *Die goldene Mittelstrasse,* No. 1 (September 5, 1848), pp. 3–4. No. II/59.

Doppler: "Die Aristokratie ist nicht todt!" *Nazional-Zeitung,* No. 30 (August 23, 1848), pp. 117–18. No. II/146.

——: "Warum werden die Zwanziger so selten?" *Nazional-Zeitung,* No. 16 (August 7, 1848), p. 61. No. II/145.

Eckardt, Ludwig, National Guardsman: *Neue Volks-Himne der Wiener Studenten.* Vienna [March, 1848]. No. II/64.

Ehrlich, Heinrich: "Woher kommen die schlechten Zeiten?" *Bst! Bst! Warum? Volksfragen,* No. 25, pp. 1–2. No. II/41.

Ehrlich, W.: "Die Emancipation der Arbeiter," *Die freie Presse,* No. 2 (May 22, 1848), pp. 5–7. No. II/165a.

Endlich, J. Q.: *Zur Warnung und Belehrung für die Landwohner.* Wiener Neustadt: Heinrich Liebergesell, October 20, 1848. No. II/66.

Ereignisse in Wien am 13., 14., 15. März 1848 [Vienna, 1848]. No. II/67.

"Erzherzog Johann kommt," *Der Volksfreund,* No. 40 (June 21, 1848), p. 161. No. II/210.

F. B.: *Die weibliche Nationalgarde in Wien. Buchstäblich wahr.* Vienna: Leop. Sommer [1848]. No. II/273.

Bibliography

Ferdinand der erste constitutionelle Kaiser. Vienna, March 15, 1848. No. II/74.

Frankl, Ludwig August: *Die Universität. Erstes censurfreies Blatt aus der Josef Stöckholzer von Hirschfeld'schen Buchdruckerei.* Vienna [March 15, 1848]. No. II/83.

Die freie Presse. Ein Volksblatt, various issues. No. II/165.

Der freie Wiener. Wochenschrift für Scherz und Ernst, Novelle und Erzählung, Ironie und Satyre, Kunst und Literatur, Politik und Volks-Interessen, various issues. No. II/56.

Fremden-Blatt der k. k. Haupt- und Residenzstadt Wien, one issue.

Frieser, J.: *Bürgerkrieg in Wien.* Vienna, September, 1848. No. II/79.

Die Fuchtel. Wochen-Beilage zum Omnibus, one issue.

"Die Gemüthsseite unseres politischen Lebens," *Schwefeläther,* No. 2 (August 6, 1848), pp. 5–6. No. II/181b.

"Der geopferte Altar," *Wahrheit,* No. 5 (June 8, 1848), pp. 18–19. No. II/217a.

Der gerade Michel! Für jeden Stand, für jedes Land! Ein periodisches Flugblatt von Michel Glaub, one issue. No. II/138.

Gerhard, Friedrich: *Die Presse frei, 15. März 1848. Erstes censurfreies Gedicht.* Vienna: Carl Gerold [March 15, 1848]. No. II/89.

Glock, J. M.: "Eine Zeitfrage," *Der Unpartheyische,* No. 7 (June 7, 1848), pp. 27–28. No. II/195.

Gold und Larbe. Politisch-literarisches Tagsblatt, several issues. No. II/92.

Die goldene Mittelstrasse. Populäres Organ der gemässigten Partei, one issue. No. II/59.

Gritzner, in the Name of the Editor and All the Contributors of the *Constitution, An Wien!* Vienna, August 30, 1848. No. II/93.

"Grosser Reichstag der Schwarzgelben, Reactionäre, Liberalen, Constitutionellen, Demokraten, Republikaner," *Der gerade Michel,* No. 7, pp. 25–26. No. II/138.

"Guter Rath für die Wahlmänner in der Stadt und auf dem Lande," *Der Volksfreund,* No. 43 (June 24, 1848), p. 175. No. II/210b.

H.: "Adresse der Demokraten an den König von Preussen," *Nazional-Zeitung,* No. 16 (August 7, 1848), pp. 63–64. No. II/145.

"Die heutige Vendée," *Nazional-Zeitung,* No. 16 (August 7, 1848), pp. 61–62. No. II/145.

Hohenblum, J. G.: *Grundbedingungen des Gedeihen der Constitution in den österreichischen Staaten.* Vienna: Edlen v. Ghelen'schen Erben [1848]. No. II/98.

Höllenreich Finsterniss. Reisepass für Pater Liguorian, Teufelsohn. Vienna, 1848. No. II/100.

Jettel, T. M.: *"Ad vocem Blutigel," Wanderer,* 35. Jahrgang, No. 115 (May 13, 1848), pp. 2–3. No. II/215.

Kaiser Joseph auf seiner nächtlichen Wanderung um die Stadt [Vienna, 1848]. No. II/104.

Der Kampf um die schwarzgelben Bänder oder: Wer ist eigentlich ein Schwarzgelber? Vienna, September 6, 1848. No. II/105.

"Kein Wahlcensus!" *Oesterreichisches Volksblatt,* No. 2 (June 15, 1848), pp. 5–6. No. II/153.

"Die Klöster," *Commercieller Völkerbund,* No. 1 (April 22, 1848), p. 8. No. II/208.

K. Z.: "Die Lösung der Polenfrage," *Die freie Presse,* No. 3 (May 23, 1848), pp. 9–10. No. II/165b.

Der Landbote. Ein Wochenblatt zur Volksaufklärung, one issue. No. II/131.

Der letzte der Aristokraten. Vienna: Gedruckt bei Franz Edlen von Schmid [1848]. No. II/6.

Litolff, Henry, and Siegfried Kapper: *Chorgesang der Wiener Studenten Legion. Zur Feier der 4 Tage im März 1848! 12. 13. 14. 15. der heldenmüthigen Studirenden-Legion an der Wiener Hochschule brüderlich geweit.* 2d ed. Vienna: K. K. Hof- Buchdruckerei des L. Sommer (vormals Strauss), March 15, 1848. No. II/236.

"Die Lösung der Polenfrage," *Die freie Presse,* No. 3 (May 23, 1848), pp. 9–10. No. II/165b.

Lyser, J. P.: *Ein Frühlingstag vor dem Denkmale des Kaisers Joseph des Zweiten. Dem Volke, das Er liebte und Schätzte, am 15. März gewidmet.* First Uncensored Poem Published by Blasius Höfel's Kunst-Buchdruckerei in Vienna. March, 1848. No. II/135.

M.: "Offener Markt für politische Standreden. Freiheit und Aristokratie?" *Der freie Wiener,* No. 6 (April 17, 1848), p. 23. No. AII/56.

Das magistratisch-politische Raubnest, oder: die Wiener magistratische Beamten-Bureaukratie. Vienna: Ullmeyer, 1848. No. II/279.

"Die Maitage Wiens," *Der Landbote,* No. 1 (June 21, 1848), pp. 4–6. No. II/131.

A Man of the People: "Offenes Sendschreiben an den Kaiser von Oesterreich," *Gold und Larbe,* No. 3 (July 19, 1848), pp. 9–10. No. II/92.

Mechitaristen-Congregation: *An die Bürger und Bewohner Wiens!* Vienna, April 18, 1848. No. II/44.

Medis, Alexander: "Offenes Schreiben an die Herrn Minister des Innern und Aeussern," *Der freie Wiener,* No. 6 (April 17, 1848), pp. 21–23. No. II/56.

Nazional-Zeitung. Politisches Volksblatt für demokratische Interessen, various issues. No. II/145.

"Ein neues schreckliches Lied, wie ein frommer Kaiser für seinen eigenen Unterthanen in das Land Tyrol sich flüchten muss," *Der Postheiri,* No. 11, pp. 43–44. No. II/164.

Bibliography

Neumann, Prof. D. Jos.: *Anruf an einen sogenannten Herrn Dr. Schütte.* Vienna, April 16, 1848. No. II/149.

Der N. Oest. ständische Ausschuss an seine Mitbürger! Vienna, March 18, 1848. No. II/140.

"Noch einmal Windischgrätz und die Prager Ereignisse," *Der Volksfreund,* No. 43 (June 24, 1848), pp. 174–75. No. II/210b.

Oesterreichische konstitutionelle deutsche Zeitung. Ein Blatt für Politik, Kunst und Wissenschaft aller Völker, one issue. No. II/157.

Oesterreichischer Soldatenfreund. Zeitschrift für militärische Interessen, one issue.

Oesterreichisches Volksblatt, several issues. No. II/155.

Offene und ehrliche Bitte der getreuen Oestreicher an ihren geliebten Kaiser. Vienna, 1848. No. II/36.

P. W.: "Die Leutchen fangen an, die Masken abzuwerfen," *Die freie Presse,* No. 10 (May 31, 1848), pp. 38–39. No. II/165d.

Palme, A.: *Palmenzweig, den hochverehrten Wiener akademischen Jünglingen.* Vienna: Hirschfeld, March 15, 1848. No. II/159.

Partezettel der Camarilla. Vienna: Hirschfeld [August, 1848]. No. II/9.

A Person Interested in the First Austrian Savings Bank, *Ein Wort zur Zeit an die Interessenten der ersten österreichischen Sparkasse* [Vienna, 1848]. No. II/65.

Petition der Studierenden Wiens an den Minister des Innern. Vienna: U. Klopf sen. und A. Eurich, May 5, 1848. No. II/161.

"Das Philisterium," *Schwefeläther,* No. 2 (August 6, 1848), p. 5. No. II/181b.

"Polen," *Wahrheit,* No. 13 (June 17, 1848), pp. 50–51. No. II/217b.

"Die politische Damenwelt," *Der Stadttrompeter,* No. 1 (August 7, 1848), p. 1. No. II/15.

Der politische Esel. Tag-, Klatsch-, Schmäh- und Schimpfblatt, one issue.

"Politische Handelsverhältnisse," *Commercieller Völkerbund,* No. 1 (April 22, 1848), pp. 4–7. No. II/208.

Das Portefeuil, one issue. No. II/163.

Der Postheiri. Illustrirte Blätter für Gegenwart, Oeffentlichkeit und Gefühl, one issue. No. II/164.

Die Presse, one issue.

Die Presse an ihre Erlöser! Vienna: U. Klopf sen. und A. Eurich, March 17, 1848. No. II/60.

"Probates Mittel gegen die Reaction," *Gold und Larbe,* No. 4 (July 20, 1848), p. 13. No. II/92.

Provisional Committee of the Constitutional Club: *Programm des constitutionellen Vereines.* Vienna, September 8, 1848. No. II/169.

Rarzoni, E.: "An die Arbeiter!" *Oesterreichisches Volksblatt,* No. 7 (June 21, 1848), pp. 25–26. No. II/154.

"Rückkehr des Kaisers," *Die freie Presse*, No. 17 (June 7, 1848), pp. 65–67. No. II/165e.

Die Rückkehr des Kaisers, oder: Der Triumph der Demokratie. Vienna: Jos. Stöckholzer v. Hirschfeld [August, 1848]. No. II/76.

"Die Russen nach Wien," *Volksfreund*, No. 43 (June 24, 1848), pp. 173–74. No. II/210b.

Sandrini: "Frommer Wunsch," *Commercieller Völkerbund*, No. 1 (April 22, 1848), pp. 2–4. Nô. II/208.

Sch.: *Die Geheimnisse von Wien. Sedlnitzky, der Mädchenverführer.* Vienna: J. N. Friedrich, August, 1848. No. II/259.

Scheibe: *Eine neue Religion in Wien! und entdeckte Verruchtheit Metternichs* [Vienna, 1848]. No. II/176.

Schumacher, A.: "Die Czechenverschwörung in Prag," *Oesterreichisches Volksblatt*, No. 9 (June 24, 1848), pp. 33–34. No. II/155.

Die Schwarzgelben sollen leben! Vivat Hoch. Vienna, September 15, 1848. No. II/180.

Schwefeläther. Politisch-satyrisches Abendblatt. Mit Original-Holzschnitten, several issues. No. II/181.

"Der Slavismus im Reichstage," *Wiener Postillon*, No. 18 (July 22, 1848), pp. 69–70. No. II/222.

Sporn, Moritz: *Guter Rath an meine lieben Mitbürger wegen der Sparcasse in Folge einer höchst unnöthigen Belehrung des Herrn J. F. Castelli.* Vienna: Eigenthümer J. Sammer [1848]. No. II/278.

"Das Staatsuhrwerk," *Ankündigung der in unserem Verlage neu erscheinenden Zeitschrift: Der Volksfreund*, pp. 2–3. No. II/233.

Der Stadttrompeter. Volksthümliche Zeitschrift für Humor und Satyre, one issue. No. II/15.

"Steht es schon besser mit uns?" *Zopf und Schwert*, No. 1 [June 30, 1848], pp. 2–3. No. II/235.

Steiger, L. G.: *Am 15. März 1848.* Vienna [March, 1848]. No. 11/182.

Der Unpartheyische. Politisches Zeitblatt, one issue. No. II/195.

"Unsere Zustände," *Schwefeläther*, No. 1 (August 4, 1848), pp. 1–2. No. II/187a.

"Unser Reichstag," *Gold und Larbe*, No. 3 (July 19, 1848), p. 10. No. II/92.

A Voice in the Name of Many Seminarians: *Ein offener Brief an den Fürst-Erzbischof von Wien.* Vienna [April, 1848]. No. II/257.

Volksblatt ohne Censur. Vienna: Gerold [March, 1848]. No. II/207.

Der Volksfreund. Zeitschrift für Aufklärung und Erheiterung des Volkes, various issues. No. II/210.

Volkslied. Vienna: Carl Gerold [March, 1848]. No. II/206.

Vorwärts! Politisches Volksblatt, one issue. No. II/212.

Wahrheit! several issues. No. II/217.

Wanderer, one issue. No. II/215.

Bibliography

"Was sich in Wien ereignet hat," *Der Volksfreund*, No. 1 (March 28, 1848), pp. 1–3. No. II/209.

"Der Wiener Eckensteher," *Zopf und Schwert*, No. 1 [June 30, 1848], pp. 3–4. No. II/235.

Wiener Krakehler, one issue.

Wiener Postillon. Verbunden mit dem Anzeigeblatt des Dienstfreundes, one issue. No. II/222.

Wiener Reichstags-Blatt, one issue. No. II/223.

Wiener Tageblatt für alle Stände, various issues.

Wiener Vorstadt-Zeitung. Ein Volksblatt, one issue.

Wiener Welt-Courier. Rundschau der politischen Welt-Ereignisse, für Jene, welche das mühsame Durchlesen der Zeitungen und Journale ersparen wollen; nebst einem Anhange: zur Besprechung der wichtigsten Tagesfragen, one issue. No. II/226.

Wien's Begebenheiten in den Tagen des Aufruhrs am 13. 14. und 15. März 1848. Vienna, March, 1848. No. II/219.

Wildner-Maithstein, Ignaz: *Wackere Mitbürger des grossen herrlichen Oesterreich!* Vienna: Hirschfeld, March, 1848. No. II/227.

"Windischgrätz," *Wiener Tageblatt*, No. 15 (June 23, 1848), p. 1.

"Wir brauchen keinen Adel mehr," *Der Volksfreund*, No. 70 (July 21, 1848), p. 282. No. II/210d.

"Woher kommen die schlechten Zeiten?" *Bst! Bst! Warum? Volksfragen*, No. 25, pp. 1–2. No. II/41.

"Einige Worte über die Winkelpresse," *Gold und Larbe*, No. 4 (July 20, 1848), p. 14. No. II/92.

Zeitung für die Wiener Nationalgarde, ed. Administrative Council, one issue.

Zerboni di Sposetti, Julius: *Zuruf an alle Völker des freien Oesterreichs*. Published in the name of an association of true friends of the fatherland. Vienna, May 15, 1848. No. II/234.

"Der Zopf muss fallen," *Zopf und Schwert*, No. 1 (June 30, 1848), p. 1. No. II/235.

Zopf und Schwert. Volksblatt. Ed. Götz and Vansen, one issue. No. II/235.

Other Contemporary Records

Only the most significant newspaper articles are listed below.

"Dem Adel betreffend," *Constitution*, No. 42 (May 10, 1848), pp. 627–28.

[Andrian-Werburg, Victor von]: *Oesterreich und dessen Zukunft*. Part I, 3d ed., Hamburg: Hoffmann und Campe, 1843; Part II, 1st ed., Hamburg: Ludwig Giese, 1847.

Anonymous: *Oesterreichs innere Politik mit Beziehung auf die Verfassungsfrage.* Stuttgart: Adolph Krabbe, 1847.

"Antwort der Deutschen auf den Artikel: 'Der Slovenische Verein in Laibach, zur Verständigung an die Deutschen,'" *Beilage zur Wiener Zeitung,* No. 183 (July 4, 1848), pp. 5–6.

"Antwort der Deutschen Nation an den König von Preussen," *Wiener Zeitung,* No. 85 (March 25, 1848), p. 387.

Auerbach, Berthold: *Tagebuch aus Wien. Von Latour bis auf Windischgrätz. (September bis November 1848).* Breslau: Verlag der Schletter'schen Buchhandlung (H. Boas), 1849.

"Aufruf an den katholischen Clerus der gesammten österreichischen Provinzen!" *Constitution,* No. 10 (April 1, 1848), pp. 106–109.

Bauernfeld, Eduard: *Erinnerungen aus Alt-Wien. Mit 28 Bildern.* Ed. Josef Bindtner. Vienna: Wiener Drucke, 1923.

Bodenstedt, Friedrich Martin von: *Erinnerungen aus meinem Leben.* 2 vols. Berlin: Allgemeiner Verein für Deutsche Litteratur, 1888–90.

Brandstetter, B.: "Wer ist denn Alles Arbeiter?" *Das Wiener allgemeine Arbeiter-Blatt,* No. 5 (May 29, 1848), p. 10.

Brezina, Dr. Severin, Leopold Mayer, Baron Johann Dercsényi, and Dr. Joseph Neumann: "Was haben wir errungen? Was haben wir zu hoffen?" *Constitution,* No. 22 (April 15, 1848), pp. 330–36.

Buschmann, Dr. Gotthard Freiherrn von: "Aufruf an alle wahren Oesterreicher in der Frankfurter Sache," *Wiener Zeitung,* No. 111 (April 20, 1848), p. 530.

[————, and Ritter Anton von Schmerling]: *Die niederösterreichischen Landstände und die Genesis der Revolution in Oesterreich im Jahre 1848.* Vienna: P. Rohrmann'sche Hofbuchhandlung, 1850.

Callot, Eduard Freiherr von: "Mitbürger!" *Constitution,* No. 5 (March 27, 1848), pp. 35–37.

Cohn, Hermann: "Ein- oder Zwei- Kammer-System; Bundesstaat oder Staaten-Bund!" *Constitution,* No. 29 (April 25, 1848), pp. 447–49.

Die Constitution. Tagblatt für constitutionelles Volksleben und Belehrung, all issues from March 20 to July 30, 1848.

A Constitutional Christian: "Constitution! Ich lieb Dich von Herzen, mit Schmerzen, ein wenig oder gar nicht! ! !" *Constitution,* No. 24 (April 18, 1848), pp. 367–72.

Die Constitution und der Adel. By the author of the pamphlet *Die österreichische Aristokratie.* Vienna: Jasper, Hügel und Manz, 1848.

"Die Czechen und ihre Sprache," *Constitution,* No. 5 (March 27, 1848), pp. 43–45.

"Czechen und ihre Sprache," *Constitution,* No. 22 (April 15, 1848), pp. 318–21.

Dolde, Carl: "Ein freies Polen," *Constitution,* No. 21 (April 14, 1848), p. 308–309.

Bibliography

Dunder, W. G.: *Denkschrift über die Wiener October-Revolution. Ausführliche Darstellung aller Ereignisse aus ämtlichen Quellen geschöpft, mit zahlreichen Urkunden begleitet, dann nach eigenen Erlebnissen und nach authentischen Berichten von Augenzeugen und Autoritäten, nebst einem Rückblick auf die vorausgegangenen Zustände vom 13. März bis 5. October 1848, dem Namen-Verzeichnisse der Minister, der Reichstags-Abgeordneten, der Gemeinderäthe, der Nationalgarde-Verwaltungsräthe, dem Stande des Ober-Commando-Offizier-Corps, der Nationalgarde- und der k. k. Militär-Macht.* Vienna: Verlags-Eigenthum des Verfassers, 1849.

Ehrlich, Jakob: "Die Universität geschlossen, oder die Verschwörung der 105 schwarzgelben Manichäer gegen die Studenten," *Constitution*, No. 44 (May 12, 1848), pp. 640–41.

Elmar, Carl: "Schwärmer-oder— —?!" *Constitution*, No. 11 (April 3, 1848), pp. 132–34.

Engels, Frederick [and Karl Marx]: *Germany: Revolution and Counter-Revolution* (Vol. XIII of *Marxist Library: Works of Marxism-Leninism*). New York: International Publishers, 1933.

"Erzherzog Johann als Stellvertreter Sr. Majestät," *Wiener Zeitung*, No. 182 (July 3, 1848), p. 25.

Eyring, Eduard: "Das schnellste Mittel dem Staate, ohne Bedrückung der Unterthanen, von Schulden zu befreien, wie auch die grossartigsten Unternehmungen, welche dem Lande nothwendig sind, bewerkstelligen zu können," *Constitution*, No. 46 (May 15, 1848), pp. 660–61.

F. S. v. M.: "Warum noch immer kein Programm?" *Constitution*, No. 17 (April 10, 1848), pp. 230–33.

Fenner von Fenneberg, [Daniel]: *Geschichte der Wiener Oktobertage. Geschildert und mit allen Aktenstücken belegt.* 2 parts in 1 vol. Leipzig: Verlagsbureau, 1849.

Ficquelmont, [Karl] L[udwig] Grafen: *Aufklärungen über die Zeit vom 20. März bis zum 4. Mai 1848.* Leipzig: Johann Ambrosius Barth, 1850.

Franck, Dr.: "Panslavismus vor der Thür," *Constitution*, No. 41 (May 8, 1848), pp. 616–17.

———: "Wien verurtheilt!" *Constitution*, No. 57 (May 30, 1848), pp. 733–34.

Frankl, Ludwig August: *Erinnerungen.* Ed. Stefan Hock. Prague: J. E. Calve'sche k. u. k. Hof- u. Universitäts- Buchhandlung, 1910.

Freund, "Der Slavismus," *Constitution*, No. 69 (June 15, 1848), p. 832.

"Die Friedensunterhandlung in Italien," *Wiener Zeitung*, No. 180 (July 1, 1848), p. 1.

Friedländer, Emanuel: "Das Haus Rothschild," *Constitution*, No. 51 (May 23, 1848), p. 698.

Füster, Anton: *Memoiren vom März 1848 bis Juli 1849. Beitrag zur*

Geschichte der Wiener Revolution. 2 vols. Frankfurt am Main: Literarische Anstalt (J. Rütten), 1850.

Gräffer, Franz: *Kleine Wiener Memoiren und Wiener Dosenstücke.* Ed. with introduction, notes, and alphabetical register by Anton Schlossar in collaboration with Gustav Gugitz. 2 vols. Munich: Georg Müller, 1918, 1922.

Grillparzer, [Franz]: "Erinnerungen aus dem Jahre 1848," Vol XX, pp. 185–202, in *Grillparzers sämtliche Werke.* Ed. with introduction by August Sauer. 5th ed., 20 vols. Stuttgart: J. G. Cotta'schen Buchhandlung Nachfolger, n.d.

———, [Franz]: "Historische und politische Studien," Vol. XIV, pp. 51–188, in *Grillparzers sämtliche Werke.* Ed. with introduction by August Sauer. 5th ed., 20 vols. Stuttgart: J. G. Cotta'schen Buchhandlung Nachfolger, n.d.

Grüner, C.: *Die Geschichte der October-Revolution in Wien, ihre Ursachen und nächsten Folgen.* Leipzig: K. F. Köhler, 1849.

Hadamowsky, Franz (ed.): *1848. Ein Wiener Volksdichter erlebt die Revolution. Die Memoiren Friedrich Kaisers.* Vienna: Bellaria-Verlag, 1848.

Hammerschmid, Dr.: "Die Emancipation der Juden betreffend," *Wiener Zeitung,* No. 90 (March 30, 1848), p. 418.

[Hartig, Franz Graf von]: *Genesis der Revolution in Oesterreich im Jahre 1848.* 2d ed. Leipzig: Friedrich Fleischer, 1850. (See also William Coxe: *History of the House of Austria,* for translation of this work.)

Hartmann, Moritz: *Reimchronik des Pfaffen Maurizius.* Stuttgart: Verlag der J. G. Cotta'schen Buchhandlung, 1874.

Hauk, L.: "Die Camarilla," *Constitution,* No. 68 (June 14, 1848), p. 826.

Hebbel, Friedrich: *Tagebücher.* With a foreword, ed. Felix Bamberg. 2 vols. Berlin: G. Grote'sche Verlagsbuchhandlung, 1885–87.

Helfert, Joseph Alexander Freiherrn von: "Radetzky in den Tagen seiner ärgsten Bedrängniss. Amtlicher Bericht des Feldmarschalls vom 18. bis zum 30. März 1848," *Archiv für österreichische Geschichte.* Ed. Historical Commission of the Imperial Academy of Sciences, Vol. XCV (1906), pp. 145–62.

———: *Der Wiener Parnass im Jahre 1848.* Vienna: Manz'sche k. k. Hof-Verlags- und Universitäts-Buchhandlung, 1882.

Herzog, J.: "Lied eines Deserteurs aus dem Corps der Freiwilligen nach Italien," *Constitution,* No. 27 (April 21, 1848), pp. 422–23.

Hillisch, Jos. Herm., in the Name of Several Typographers: "Arbeiter-Angelegenheiten. An den Herrn Direktor der k. k. Staatsdruckerei," *Constitution,* No. 23 (April 17, 1848), pp. 355–56.

[Hormayr, Joseph Freiherrn von]: *Kaiser Franz und Metternich. Ein nachgelassenes Fragment.* Leipzig: Wiedmann'sche Buchhandlung, 1848.

Bibliography

Hrczka, Josef: "Der 15. Mai," *Constitution*, No. 49 (May 18, 1848), pp. 680–82.

———: "Seit acht Tagen," *Constitution*, No. 32 (April 28, 1848), pp. 487–91.

———: "Unsere Girondisten," *Constitution*, No. 61 (June 5, 1848), pp. 766–67.

Hübner, Alexander Grafen von: *Ein Jahr meines Lebens. 1848–1849.* Leipzig: F. A. Brockhaus, 1891.

"Ideen über Finanzen," *Constitution*, No. 13 (April 5, 1848), pp. 157–59.

"Die Italienische Frage," *Wiener Zeitung*, No. 165 (June 15, 1848), pp. 781–82.

K.: "Reaction und Jesuitismus," *Constitution*, No. 54 (May 26, 1848), p. 720; No. 57 (May 30, 1848), pp. 736–37; No. 60 (June 3, 1848), pp. 760–61; and No. 63 (June 7, 1848), p. 785.

Kaiser, Friedrich: *Memoiren*. See Franz Hadamowsky.

"Eine Katzenmusik sammt daran geknüpften Reflexionen," *Constitution*, No. 16 (April 8, 1848), pp. 212–14.

Klein, Tim (ed.): *1848. Der Vorkampf deutscher Einheit und Freiheit. Erinnerungen, Urkunden, Berichte, Briefe.* Munich: Wilhelm Lange-wiesche-Brandt Ebenhausen, 1914.

K——l——u——t, a German in Vienna, "Schwarz, Roth, Gold!" *Constitution*, No. 37 (May 4, 1848), p. 583.

Koch, M[athias]: *Genesis der Wiener Revolution*. Vienna: J. B. Wallishausser [1850].

[Kopetzky, Emanuel]: *Ergebnisse der von dem kaiserlich-königlichen Militär-Gerichte geführten Untersuchung wider die Mörder des k. k. Kriegsministers, General-Feldzeugmeisters Theodor Grafen Baillet von Latour.* Vienna: Aus der kaiserlich-königlichen Hof- und Staats-Druckerei, 1850. (See also William Coxe: *History of the House of Austria*, for translation of this work.)

Kudlich, Hans: *Rückblicke und Erinnerungen*. 3 vols. Vienna: A. Hartleben's Verlag, 1873.

Kürnberger, Ferdinand: *Briefe eines politischen Flüchtlings*. Ed. Otto Erich Deutsch. Leipzig: E. P. Tal & Co., 1920.

Kürnberger, F.: "Erzherzog Johann, Oesterreich und Deutschland," *Beilage zur Wiener Zeitung*, No. 195 (July 16, 1848), pp. 24–25.

L. H. K.: "Bericht des Abend-Concertes vom 2. Mai 1848," *Constitution*, No. 37 (May 4, 1848), pp. 587–88.

Laube, Heinrich: *Das erste deutsche Parlament*. 3 vols. Leipzig: Weidmann'sche Buchhandlung, 1849.

"Letter sent by František Palacký to Frankfurt," *The Slavonic and East European Review*, Vol. XXVI (April, 1948), pp. 303–308.

Lugano, Adolph: *Der Fortbestand Oesterreichs bedingt durch einen in-*

nigen Anschluss an Deutschland als Herz eines centraleuropäischen Völkerbundes. Vienna: Carl Gerold, 1848.

[Lyser, Johann Peter Theodor]: Die Wiener-Ereignisse vom 6. Oktober bis 12. November 1848. Geschildert von einem Augenzeugen. Mit allen während dieses Zeitraums erschienenen Kundmachungen und Proclamationen. Vienna: Druck und Verlag von Jos. Keck & Sohn, 1849.

M. N——c: "Offenes Sendschreiben an die Pseudo-Christen und Philister in Bezug der Emancipation der Juden," Constitution, No. 49 (May 18, 1848), pp. 685–86.

"Manifesto of the First Slavonic Congress to the Nations of Europe," The Slavonic and East European Review, Vol. XXVI (April, 1948), pp. 309–13.

Aus Metternich's nachgelassenen Papieren. Published by Prince Richard Metternich-Winneburg, ed. and arr. Alfons von Klinkowström. Authorized German original edition. 8 vols. Vienna: Wilhelm Braumüller, 1880–84.

Mild, Bonifacius, Herzog von Angoulême: Episteln an die Aristokratie, zu ihrem Troste und zu ihrer Erbauung. Vienna: Sallmayer & Comp., 1848.

[Moering, Karl]: Sibyllinischen Bücher aus Oesterreich. 2 vols. Hamburg: Hoffmann und Campe, 1848.

N. F. P.: "Ausserordentlicher Geldweg für die Arbeiter Wiens," Constitution, No. 63 (June 7, 1848), p. 786.

"Nationalität," Wiener Zeitung, No. 160 (June 9, 1848), p. 758.

"Nationalität und Sprache," Constitution, No. 97 (July 20, 1848), pp. 1058–59.

"Die neuen Minister," Constitution, No. 3 (March 23, 1848), pp. 17–18.

"Das neue Slavenreich," Wiener Zeitung, No. 155 (June 4, 1848), pp. 735–36.

Niederhuber, [A.]: "Das Frankfurter Parlament," Constitution, No. 73 (June 20, 1848), pp. 863–64.

——: "Kein Traum," Constitution, No. 50 (May 22, 1848), pp. 688–89.

——: "Das Ministerium muss in Anklagestand versetzt werden," Constitution, No. 56 (May 29, 1848), pp. 729–30.

——: "Polen und seine Wiederherstellung," Constitution, No. 64 (June 8, 1848), pp. 792–93.

——: "Wohlfeiles Brot! wohlfeile Presse!" Constitution, No. 37 (May 4, 1848), pp. 585–86.

Oesterreichisch-kaiserlich-privilegirte Wiener-Zeitung, all issues for 1848.

Oestreich's Befreiungstage! oder der 13. 14. und 15. März 1848 in Wien. Geschildert von Augenzeugen. Mit allen bezüglichen Proklamationen und den wichtigsten Flugschriften. Erste censurfreie Broschüre. Vienna: M. F. Jasper's Verlag, March 17, 1848.

Bibliography

Pertteseilheim, E. W., Citizen and Merchant: "Vorschlag zur momentanen Abhilfe der nahenden und mit Grund zu befürchtenden Zinsnoth," *Constitution*, No. 24 (April 18, 1848), pp. 372–73.

Pichler, Adolf: *Das Sturmjahr. Erinnerungen aus den März- und Oktobertagen 1848*. Berlin: Meyer und Wunder, 1903.

Pillersdorf, Baron [Franz Xaver]: *Austria in 1848 and 1849. The Political Movement in Austria. During the Years 1848 & 1849*. Trans. George Gaskell. London: Richard Bentley, 1850.

Pulszky, Franz: *Mein Zeit, mein Leben*. 4 vols. Pressburg: Carl Stampfel, 1880–83.

R.: "Zanini's Abdankung," *Constitution*, No. 36 (May 3, 1848), pp. 551–52.

R. E. v. E.: "Das Journal des Debats über die Oesterreichische Lebensfrage," *Wiener Zeitung*, No. 152 (June 1, 1848), p. 723.

"Radikale und antiministerielle Presse," *Wiener Zeitung*, No. 240 (September 3, 1848), pp. 562–63.

Revolution, Belagerung und Erstürmung von Wien im October 1848. Mit Portrait des Windisch-Grätz, Jellachich, Bem, Messenhauser, Kossuth, und drei Scenenbildern, nebst Plan des Kampfplatzes in Wien und der Umgegend, mit Angabe der ausgezeichnetsten öffentlichen und Privat-Gebäude, Strassen, Plätze, Vertheidigungspunkte in und um Wien. Ed. O. Fr. Leipzig: Verlag von F. W. Goedsche [1848].

Ritter, C. A.: *Tagebuch der letzten Oktober- und ersten November- Tage Wiens*. Ed. by editor of the *Wiener-Postillon*. No publisher or place given; preface dated Linz, November 10, 1848.

"Rückblicke," *Beilage zur Wiener Zeitung*, No. 236 (August 30, 1848), p. 75.

S.: "Die Reaction," *Das Wiener allgemeine Arbeiter-Blatt*, No. 4 (May 25, 1848), pp. 7–8.

———: "Die Republikaner," *Das Wiener allgemeine Arbeiter-Blatt*, No. 6 (May 30, 1848), p. 12.

S———, Dr.: "Offenes Schreiben. Hochwürdige, Ehrwürdige, und löbliche Stifter, Klöster und Konvente der österreichischen Monarchie!" *Constitution*, No. 30 (April 26, 1848), pp. 464–65.

Sander, Friedrich: "Arbeiter-Verein," *Constitution*, No. 39 (May 6, 1848), p. 602.

———: "Das Wahlgesetz. Stimme eines Arbeiters," *Constitution*, No. 46 (May 15, 1848), pp. 655–56.

Sch———r, Dr. E. E.: "Frankreich's Einrücken in Oesterreichisch-Italien sei ein *causus belli* für Deutschland," *Beilage zur Wiener Zeitung*, No. 221 (August 12, 1848), pp. 55–56.

Schlesinger, Wilhelm: "Um's Himmelswillen gebt uns Vertrauen, um's Himmelswillen seid liberal!" *Wiener Zeitung*, No. 151 (May 31, 1848), p. 719.

Schuselka, Franz: *Beleuchtung der Aufklärungen des Herrn L. Grafen Ficquelmont*. Vienna: Jasper, Hügel & Manz, 1850.

———: *Deutsche Worte eines Oesterreichers*. Hamburg: Hoffmann und Campe, 1843.

———: *Oesterreich über Alles wenn es nur will*. Hamburg: Hoffmann und Campe, 1848.

———: *Oesterreichische Vor- und Rückschritte*. Hamburg: Hoffmann und Campe, 1847.

———: "Das Vaterland in Gefahr," *Wiener Zeitung*, No. 93 (April 2, 1848), pp. 437–38.

Schütte, Dr. [Anton]: *Die Wiener Oktober-Revolution. Aus dem Tagebuch des Dr. Schütte*. Prague: Friedrich Ehrlich, November, 1848.

"Seit acht Tagen," *Constitution*, No. 32 (April 28, 1848), pp. 487–91.

Several Viennese Typographers: "Ein freies Wort für gedrückte Arbeiter an den Herrn Direktor der k. k. Staatsdruckerei," *Constitution*, No. 13 (April 5, 1848), pp. 153–57.

Silberstein, August: *Geschichte der Aula. Die Wiener Universität und die akademische Legion vom März bis Ende October 1848*. Mannheim: J. P. Grohe, 1848.

"Sprachwirren auf dem constituirenden Reichstage und ihre Lösung," *Beilage zur Wiener Zeitung*, No. 199 (July 20, 1848), pp. 24–25.

Springer, Anton (ed.): *Protokolle des Verfassungs-Ausschusses im Oesterreichischen Reichstage 1848–1849*. Leipzig: S. Hirzel, 1885.

St., Dr.: "Aristokratie, Bureaukratie und Constitution," *Constitution*, No. 8 (March 30, 1848), pp. 79–83.

Stavenhagen, Carl: *Wiens furchtbarer Oktober 1848. Die Belagerung, Vertheidigung und Einnahme der österreichischen Kaiserstadt, nach zuverlässigen Beobachtungen und Quellen. Mit vielen bildlichen Darstellungen nach der Natur*. Prague: C. Hennig's Verlag, 1848.

Stiles, William H.: *Austria in 1848–49: Being a History of the Late Political Movements in Vienna, Milan, Venice, and Prague; with Details of the Campaigns of Lombardy and Novara; a Full Account of the Revolution in Hungary; and Historical Sketches of the Austrian Government and the Provinces of the Empire*. 2 vols. New York: Harper, 1852.

Das Tagebuch des Polizeiministers Kempen von Fichtenstamm, 1848 bis 1859. Ed. Josef Karl Mayr. Vienna: Österreichischer Bundesverlag für Unterricht, Wissenschaft und Kunst, 1931.

Tebeldi, Albrecht [pseud. Dr. Karl Beidtel], *Die Geldangelegenheiten Oestreichs*. Leipzig: Barth, 1847.

Ein Tiroler: "Die Italienische Frage," *Wiener Zeitung*, No. 165 (June 15, 1848), pp. 781–82.

"Tirol mit Vorarlberg in seinen socialen und politischen Zuständen," *Die Gegenwart. Ein encyklopädische Darstellung der neuesten Zeit-*

Bibliography

geschichte für alle Stände. Leipzig: F. A. Brockhaus, 1850, Vol. IV, pp. 52–123.

Töletényi, M.: "Ungarn," *Constitution,* No. 36 (May 3, 1848), pp. 567–68.

Turnbull, P. E.: *Oesterreichs sociale und politische Zustände.* Trans. E. A. Moriarty. Leipzig: J. J. Weber, 1840.

"Die Ungarischen Fragen," *Wiener Zeitung,* No. 179 (June 30, 1848), p. 856.

"Ungarns Stellung im Oesterreichischen Staatsverbande," *Wiener Zeitung,* No. 100 (April 9, 1848), p. 476.

Unterreiter, Friedrich: *Die Revolution in Wien vom Juni bis September 1848. Mit allen ihren Ursachen und Wirkungen fortlaufend bis auf die nächsten Tage auf das freisinnigste nach eigener Anschauung und den besten Quellen dargestellt.* 2 vols. in 1. Vienna: M. Lell, 1848.

————: *Die Revolution in Wien vom März und Mai 1848. Mit allen ihren Ursachen und Wirkungen fortlaufend bis auf die nächsten Tage, auf das freisinnigste nach eigener Anschauung und den besten Quellen dargestellt.* 3 vols. in 1. Vienna: Carl Ueberreuter, 1848.

————: *Die Revolution in Wien vom Oktober bis zu Ende 1848. Mit allen ihren Ursachen und Wirkungen fortlaufend bis auf die nächsten Tage, auf das freisinnigste nach eigener Anschauung und den besten Quellen dargestellt.* 3 vols. in 1. Vienna: M. Lell, 1848–49.

Ursache und Geschichte der Octoberereignisse zu Wien. By an eyewitness. Leipzig: Vereins-Verlagsbuchhandlung, 1848.

[Usedom, Ludwig Guido von]: *Politische Briefe und Charakteristiken aus der deutschen Gegenwart.* Berlin: Wilhelm Hertz, 1849.

"Verhältniss zwischen Oesterreich und Ungarn," *Beilage zur Wiener Zeitung,* No. 193 (July 14, 1848), p. 19.

[Violand, Ernst]: *Enthüllungen aus Oesterreichs jüngster Vergangenheit.* By a Member of the Left of the Dissolved Parliament. Hamburg: Hoffmann und Campe, 1849.

————: *Die sociale Geschichte der Revolution in Oesterreich.* Leipzig: Otto Wigand, 1850.

Vitzthum von Eckstädt, Carl Friedrich Grafen von: *Berlin und Wien in den Jahren 1845–1852. Politische Privatbriefe.* 2d ed., Stuttgart: J. G. Cotta'schen Buchhandlung, 1886.

"Vorläufige Beurtheilung der neuen Constitution," *Constitution,* No. 31 (April 27, 1848), pp. 471–74.

"Wachsamkeit und Ausdauer," *Constitution,* No. 1 (March 20, 1848), pp. 1–3.

"Das Wahlgesetz," *Constitution,* No. 63 (June 7, 1848), p. 784.

"Das Wahlgesetz," *Wiener Zeitung,* No. 127 (May 7, 1848), p. 611.

"Was uns Noth thut," *Wiener Zeitung,* No. 89 (March 29, 1848), p. 411.

"Welchen Einfluss werden die Ergebnisse der grossen Märzwoche auf die österreichische Bureaukratie üben?" *Constitution,* No. 7 (March 29, 1848), pp. 64–66.

Das Wiener allgemeine Arbeiter-Blatt, all issues, May 22–June 2, 1848.

Wiener Zeitung. See *Oesterreichisch-kaiserlich-privilegirte Wiener Zeitung.*

Wild: "Vorschlag in der Arbeiter-Angelegenheit," *Constitution,* No. 67 (June 13, 1848), pp. 818–19.

Wintersberg: "Was noch geschehen muss," *Constitution,* No. 48 (May 17, 1848), p. 672.

Wirkner, Ludwig von: *Meine Erlebnisse. Blätter aus dem Tagebuche meines öffentlichen Wirkens vom Jahre 1825–1852.* Pressburg: Commissionssager von C. Stampfel's k. k. Buchhandlung, 1879.

"Wollen wir Preussen werden?" *Constitution,* No. 5 (March 27, 1848), pp. 33–34.

Zang, August: *Flugschrift 1848 für das allgemeine gleiche Wahlrecht: Lebensfrage für die österreichische Monarchie.* Graz: Deutschen Vereins-Druckerei, 1907.

Zedlitz, [Joseph Christian Freiherr von]: *Soldaten-Büchlein.* Stuttgart: J. G. Cotta'scher Verlag, 1860.

"Zur Arbeiterfrage," *Wiener Zeitung,* No. 155 (June 4, 1848), p. 726.

"Zur Verständigung," *Wiener Zeitung,* No. 125 (May 5, 1848), p. 602.

SPECIAL ARTICLES

Black, C. E.: "Poznań and Europe in 1848," *Journal of Central European Affairs,* Vol. VIII, No. 2 (July, 1948), pp. 191–206.

Blum, Jerome: "Transportation and Industry in Austria, 1815–1848," *The Journal of Modern History,* Vol. XV, No. 1 (March, 1943), pp. 24–38.

Brunner, Otto: "The Political Ideas of the Hapsburg Monarchy," International Studies Conference, 10th Session, Paris, June 28–July 3, 1937.

Doblinger, Max: "Der burschenschaftliche Gedanke auf Österreichs Hochschulen vor 1859," *Quellen und Darstellungen zur Geschichte der Burschenschaft und der deutschen Einheitsbewegung.* Commissioned by the Historical Commission of the Burschenschaften, ed. Herman Haupt. Heidelberg: Carl Winters Universitätsbuchhandlung, 1925, Vol. VIII, pp. 31–150.

Engel-Jánosi, Friedrich: "Der Wiener juridisch-politische Leseverein. Seine Geschichte bis zur Märzrevolution," *Mitteilungen des Vereines für Geschichte der Stadt Wien (früher Altertums-Verein zu Wien).* Secretary, Dr. Josef Kallbrunner, Vol. IV (1923), pp. 58–66.

Bibliography

————: "Zur Genesis der Revolution von 1848. Die Verfassungsfrage im deutschen Österreich 1815–48," *Zeitschrift für öffentliches Recht,* ed. in association with Max Hussarek, Max Layer, and Adolf Menzel by Hans Kelsen, Vol. III (1922–23), pp. 571–82.

Falk, Minna R.: "Alexander Bach and the *Leseverein* in the Viennese Revolution of 1848," *Journal of Central European Affairs,* Vol. VIII, No. 2 (July, 1948), pp. 139–59.

Macůrek, Josef: "The Achievements of the Slavonic Congress," *The Slavonic and East European Review,* Vol. XXVI, No. 67 (April, 1948), pp. 329–40.

Mehring, Franz: "Deutsche Zustande," and "Die Klassen Kämpfe der deutschen Revolution," in *Historische Aufsätze zur Preussisch-Deutschen Geschichte. Sammelband zusammengestellt und herausgegeben anlässlich des 100. Geburtstags Franz Mehrings am 27. Februar 1946.* 2d ed. Berlin: J. H. W. Dietz Nachf., 1946, pp. 144–255.

Odložilík, Otakar: "Storm over the Danube," *Journal of Central European Affairs,* Vol. VIII, No. 2 (July, 1948), pp. 129–38.

Rath, R. John: "The Failure of an Ideal: The Viennese Revolution of 1848," *The Southwestern Social Science Quarterly,* Vol. XXXIV, No. 2 (September, 1953), pp. 3–20.

————: "Public Opinion During the Viennese Revolution of 1848," *Journal of Central European Affairs,* Vol. VIII, No. 2 (July, 1948), pp. 160–80.

————: "Training for Citizenship in the Austrian Elementary Schools During the Reign of Francis I," *Journal of Central European Affairs,* Vol. IV, No. 2 (July, 1944), pp. 147-64.

————: "The Viennese Liberals of 1848 and the Nationality Problem," *Journal of Central European Affairs,* Vol. XV, No. 3 (October, 1955), pp. 227–29.

"Vor hundert Jahren. Vorboten der Zweiten Revolution," *Wiener Zeitung,* 241. Jahrgang, No. 106 (May 6, 1948), p. 2.

SPECIAL WORKS

Arneth, Alfred Ritter von: *Johann Freiherr von Wessenberg. Ein österreichischer Staatsmann des neunzehnten Jahrhunderts.* 2 vols. in 1. Vienna: Wilhelm Braumüller, 1898.

Bach, Maximilian: *Geschichte der Wiener Revolution im Jahre 1848.* Vienna: Erste Wiener Volksbuchhandlung (Ignaz Brand), 1898.

Beidtel, Ignaz: *Geschichte der österreichischen Staatsverwaltung 1740–*

1848. 2 vols. Innsbruck: Wagner'schen Universitäts-Buchhandlung, 1896–98.

Berger, Adolph Franz: *Felix Fürst zu Schwarzenberg, K. K. Ministerpräsident uc. Ein biographisches Denkmal.* 2 vols. Leipzig: Otto Spamer, 1853.

Bibl, Viktor: *Die Niederösterreichischen Stände im Vormärz. Ein Beitrag zur Vorgeschichte der Revolution des Jahres 1848.* Ed. the Society for Modern Austrian History. Vienna: Gerlach & Wiedling, 1911.

Blum, Hans: *Die deutsche Revolution 1848–49. Eine Jubiläumsgabe für das deutsche Volk.* Florence: Eugen Diederich, 1898.

Blum, Jerome: *Noble Landowners and Agriculture in Austria, 1815–1848: A Study in the Origins of the Peasant Emancipation of 1848.* In the Johns Hopkins University *Studies in Historical and Political Science,* Ser. LXV, No. 2, 1948.

Ehnl, Maximilian: *Wenzel Cäsar Messenhauser, Nationalgarde-Oberkommandant von Wien 1848.* Vienna: Verlag Ing. Emil Ratzenhofer, 1948.

Elbinger, Carl: *Witz und Satire Anno 1848. Mit 16 Bildseiten.* Vienna: Wiener-Verlag, 1948.

Endres, Robert: *Revolution in Österreich 1848.* Vienna: Danubia-Verlag, 1947.

Fejtö, François (ed.): *1848 dans le monde: le printemps des peuples.* 2 vols. Paris: Éditions de minuit, 1948.

Fischer, Ernst: *Österreich 1848. Probleme der demokratischen Revolution in Oesterreich.* Vienna: Stern-Verlag, 1946.

Goldmark, Josephine: *Pilgrims of '48: One Man's Part in the Austrian Revolution of 1848 and a Family Migration to America.* New Haven, Conn.: Yale University Press, 1930.

Hartmann, Otto: *Die Volkserhebung der Jahre 1848 und 1849 in Deutschland.* Berlin: Hugo Bermühler, 1900.

Helfert, Joseph Alexander Freiherrn von: *Geschichte der österreichischen Revolution im Zusammenhange mit der mitteleuropäischen Bewegung der Jahre 1848–1849,* Vol. I: *Bis zur österreichischen Verfassung vom 25. April 1848.* Freiburg: Herdersche Verlagshandlung, 1907.

———: *Die Wiener Journalistik im Jahre 1848.* Vienna: Manz'sche k. k. Hof- Verlags- und Universitäts- Buchhandlung, 1877.

Heuss, Theodor: *1848. Werk und Erbe.* Stuttgart: Curt E. Schwab, 1948.

Hugelmann, Karl: "Die österreichischen Landtage im Jahre 1848," *Archiv für österreichische Geschichte,* published under the auspices of the Vienna Academy of Sciences, Philosophical-Historical Section, Historical Commission, Vol. CXI (1930), pp. 1–495.

Kann, Robert A.: *The Multinational Empire: Nationalism and National Reform in the Habsburg Monarchy, 1848–1918.* 2 vols. New York: Columbia University Press, 1950.

Bibliography

Kasamas, Alfred: *Das Jahr 1848.* In *Politische Zeitprobleme,* No. 25. Vienna: Österreichischer Verlag, 1948.

Kiszling, Rudolf: *Fürst Felix zu Schwarzenberg. Der politische Lehrmeister Kaiser Franz Josephs.* Graz: Hermann Böhlaus Nachf., 1952.

———, J. Diakow, M. Ehnl, G. Hubka, and E. Steinitz: *Die Revolution im Kaisertum Österreich 1848–1849.* 2 vols. Vienna: Universum Verlag, 1948.

Kohn, Hans: *Pan-Slavism, Its History and Ideology.* Notre Dame, Ind.: University of Notre Dame Press, 1953.

Kriebel, Hermann: *Feldmarschall Fürst Windisch-Grätz 1787–1862* (lecture at the Bavarian Imperial War Academy in 1906). In *Beiträgen für die Geschichte der Jahre 1848–1849,* No. 2. Innsbruck: Universitäts-Verlag Wagner, 1929.

———: *Ueber die Bezwingung innerer Unruhen, nach den Erfahrungen der Geschichte in der ersten Hälfte des XIX. Jahrhunderts.* In *Beiträgen für die Geschichte der Jahre 1848–49.* Ed. Prince Franz zu Windisch-Grätz. Innsbruck: Universitäts-Verlag Wagner, 1929.

Krones, Dr. F. von: *Moritz von Kaiserfeld. Sein Leben und Wirken als Beitrag zur Staatsgeschichte Oesterreichs in den Jahren 1848 bis 1884.* Leipzig: Duncker & Humbolt, 1888.

Legge, J. G.: *Rhyme and Revolution in Germany: A Study in German History, Life, Literature and Character 1813–1850.* London: Constable and Co., 1918.

Mehring, Franz: *Karl Marx: The Story of His Life.* New York: Covici-Friede Publishers, 1935.

Meynert, Hermann: *Geschichte der Ereignisse in der österreichischen Monarchie während der Jahre 1848 und 1849 in ihren Ursachen und Folgen.* Vienna: Carl Gerold und Sohn, 1853.

———: *Kaiser Franz I. Zur Geschichte seiner Regierung und seiner Zeit. Nach Originalmittheilungen und ungedruckten Quellen.* Vienna: Hoelder, 1872.

Molisch, Paul: "Die Wiener akademische Legion und ihr Anteil an den Verfassungskämpfen des Jahres 1848. Nebst einer Besprechung der übrigen 1848er Studentenlegionen," *Archiv für österreichische Geschichte,* Vol. CX, Part 1 (1924), pp. 1–208.

Müller, Paul: *Feldmarschall Fürst Windischgrätz. Revolution und Gegenrevolution in Österreich.* Vienna: Wilhelm Braumüller, 1934.

Namier, L. B.: *1848: The Revolution of the Intellectuals.* London: Geoffrey Cumberlege, 1944.

Novotny, Alexander: *1848: Österreichs Ringen um Freiheit und Völkerfrieden vor hundert Jahren.* Vienna: "Styria" Steirische Verlagsanstalt, 1948.

Ravelsberg, Ferdinand Strobl von: *Feldmarschall Radetzky. Sein Leben und Wirken.* Vienna: C. W. Stern Verlag, 1907.

386

The Viennese Revolution of 1848

Reschauer, Heinrich, and Moritz Smets: *Das Jahr 1848. Geschichte der Wiener Revolution.* 2 vols. Vienna: Waldheim, 1872.

Robertson, Priscilla: *Revolutions of 1848: A Social History.* Princeton, N.J.: Princeton University Press, 1952.

Schlitter, Hanns: *Aus Österreichs Vormärz,* Vol. I: *Galizien und Krakow.* Zürich: Amalthea-Verlag, 1920.

———: *Aus Österreichs Vormärz,* Vol. II: *Böhmen.* Zürich: Amalthea-Verlag, 1920.

———: *Aus Österreichs Vormärz,* Vol. III: *Ungarn.* Zürich: Amalthea-Verlag, 1920.

———: *Aus Österreichs Vormärz,* Vol. IV: *Niederösterreich.* Zürich: Amalthea-Verlag, 1920.

Schneider, Karl: *Der Reichstag von Kremsier.* In Karl Schneider (ed.), *Aus Österreichs Vergangenheit. Quellenbücher zur österreichischen Geschichte,* No. 2. Leipzig: Schulwissenschaftlicher Verlag A. Haase, 1917.

Schwarzenberg, Adolph: *Prince Felix zu Schwarzenberg, Prime Minister of Austria, 1848–1852.* New York: Columbia University Press, 1946.

Srbik, Heinrich Ritter von: *Metternich, der Staatsmann und der Mensch.* 2 vols. Munich: F. Bruckmann, 1925.

Stadelmann, Rudolf: *Soziale und politische Geschichte der Revolution von 1848.* Munich: Münchner Verlag (bisher F. Bruckmann Verlag), 1948.

Valentin, Veit: *1848: Chapters of German History.* London: George Allen and Unwin, Ltd., 1940.

Valjavic, Fritz: *Der Josephinismus. Zur geistigen Entwicklung Österreichs im 18. und 19. Jahrhundert.* Brünn: Rohrer Verlag, 1944.

Verzeichniss der im Jahre 1848 in Wien erschienenen Zeitungen und periodischen Schriften. (Als Manuscript gedruckt.) No publisher, place, or date given.

Wanderer, Maria Theresia: *Revolutionsstürme Achtundvierzig. Ereignisse, Urkunden, Briefe, Dichtungen.* Vienna: Bellaria-Verlag, 1948.

Weber, Ottocar: *1848. Sechs Vorträge.* Leipzig: Teubner, 1904.

Wentzcke, Paul: *Kritische Bibliographie der Flugschriften zur deutschen Verfassungsfrage 1848–1851.* Halle: Max Niemeyer, 1911.

Wittner, Otto: *Moritz Hartmanns Leben und Werke. Ein Beitrag zur politischen und literarischen Geschichte Deutschlands im XIX. Jahrhundert.* Vols. XVII and XIX in *Bibliothek Deutscher Schriftsteller aus Böhmen.* Ed. under the auspices of the Society for Furthering German Science, Art and Literature in Bohemia. Prague: J. G. Calvesche k. u. k. Hof- und Universitäts-Buchhandlung (Josef Koch), 1906–1907.

Wolf, G.: *Aus der Revolutionszeit in Österreich-Ungarn (1848–49).* Vienna: Alfred Hölder, 1885.

Bibliography

Zenker, E[rnst] V[ictor]: *Geschichte der Wiener Journalistik von den Anfängen bis zum Jahre 1848. Ein Beitrag zur deutschen Culturgeschichte.* Vienna: Wilhelm Braumüller, 1892.

————: *Geschichte der Wiener Journalistik während des Jahres 1848.* Vienna: Wilhelm Braumüller, 1893.

————: *Die Wiener Revolution 1848 in ihren socialen Voraussetzungen und Beziehungen.* Vienna: A. Hartleben's Verlag, 1897.

GENERAL HISTORIES AND REFERENCES

Allgemeine Deutsche Biographie. 56 vols. Leipzig: Duncker & Humblot, 1875–1912.

Bibl, Viktor: *Der Zerfall Österreichs*, Vol. II: *Von Revolution zu Revolution.* Vienna: Rikola Verlag, 1924.

Charmatz, Richard: *Vom Kaiserreich zur Republik. Österreichs Kampf um die Demokratie 1747–1947.* Vienna: Jedermann-Verlag, 1947.

Coxe, William: *History of the House of Austria, from the Foundation of the Monarchy by Rhodolph of Hapsburgh to the Death of Leopold the Second: 1218 to 1792. With a Continuation by W. K. Kelly and Bound with Genesis; or, Details of the Late Austrian Revolution by Graf Franz von Hartig.* 4th ed. 4 vols. London: George Bell and Sons, 1882.

Friedjung, Heinrich: *Österreich von 1848 bis 1860.* 3d ed. 2 vols. Stuttgart: J. G. Cotta'sche Buchhandlung Nachfolger, 1908, 1912.

Der Grosse Brockhaus: Handbuch des Wissens in zwanzig Bänder. 15th ed. 20 vols. Leipzig: F. A. Brockhaus, 1928–35.

Hantsch, Hugo: *Die Geschichte Österreichs.* 2 vols. Graz: "Styria" steirische Verlagsanstalt [1937, 1950].

Kosáry, Dominic G.: *A History of Hungary.* Cleveland, Ohio: The Benjamin Franklin Bibliophile Society, 1941.

May, Arthur J.: *The Hapsburg Monarchy 1867–1914.* Cambridge, Mass.: Harvard University Press, 1951.

Mendenhall, Thomas C., Basil D. Henning, Archibald S. Foord, *et al.* (eds.): *The Quest for a Principle of Authority in Europe 1715–Present: Select Problems in Historical Interpretation.* New York: Henry Holt and Company, Inc., 1948.

Meyer, Werner: *Vormärz. Die Ära Metternich 1815 bis 1848.* Potsdam: Potsdamer Verlagsgesellschaft, 1948.

Schnabel, Franz: *Deutsche Geschichte im neunzehnten Jahrhundert.* 2d ed. 4 vols. Freiburg: Herder & Co., 1948–51.

Springer, Anton: *Geschichte Oesterreichs seit dem Wiener Frieden 1809.* 2 vols. Leipzig: S. Hirzel, 1863–65.

Taylor, A. J. P.: *The Habsburg Monarchy 1815–1918.* London: Macmillan and Company, Ltd., 1941.

Weill, Georges: *L'éveil des nationalités et le mouvement libéral (1815–1848).* Vol. XV of *Peuples et civilisations,* ed. Louis Halphen and Philippe Sagnac. Paris: Presses universitaires de France, 1930.

Wurzbach, Constant von: *Biographisches Lexikon des Kaiserthums Oesterreich, enthaltend die Lebensskizzen derjenigen Personen, welche seit 1750 in den österreichischen Kronländern gelebt und gewirkt haben.* 60 vols. Vienna: Universitäts-Buchdruckerei von Zamarski, 1856–91.

Dramatis Personae of the Revolution

Aigner, Joseph Matthäus
Born in 1818 in Vienna, the son of a jeweler who was also a goldsmith and portrait-painter; appointed commander of the Academic Legion on September 13, 1848, and made one of Messenhauser's staff officers in October; condemned to death on November 23 by Habsburg military court but given unconditional pardon by Windischgrätz.

Albert Friedrich Rudolph von Habsburg, Archduke of Austria (1817–95)
Oldest son of Archduke Charles (hero of Aspern); devoted lifetime to the Habsburg army; promoted to lieutenant field marshal in 1843; in 1845 appointed commanding general of Austria above and below Enns River; in this capacity supreme commander of military forces in Vienna on March 13; on March 14 resigned command and retired to landholdings, then joined Radetzky's army in Italy; in 1851 made commander of the third army and military governor of Hungary; 1866–1895 inspector general of the Habsburg army.

Andrian-Werburg, Baron Victor von (1813–58)
Born in Görz; studied in Vienna; entered the Austrian civil service at Venice; in 1842 his book *Oesterreich und dessen Zukunft*, published anonymously, aroused great interest in Austria and in Germany; in 1846 left civil service to champion the cause of the Austrian Estates; in 1848 sent to the Frankfurt Preliminary Parliament by the Lower Austrian Estates, later appointed to Committee of Fifty; elected to the Frankfurt Assembly from Wiener Neustadt, and later made vice-president of the Frankfurt Assembly and a member of the constitutional committee.

Apponyi, Count György (1808–99)
Outstanding leader of the aristocratic conservative party in Hungary; in 1844 Landtag opposed attempts of radical party headed by Kossuth to gain more autonomy for Hungary; in 1846 appointed court chancellor; bitterly hated by the liberals because of his strong conservative stand, particularly in the 1847 Landtag; resigned in March, 1848, and temporarily withdrew from public affairs; later led the Hungarian nationalist party and supported Deák in the negotiations that led to the Austro-Hungarian Compromise of 1867.

Arthaber, Rudolph Edler von (1795–1867)
Weathy Viennese manufacturer and art patron; owned among the largest textile factories in Austria (in 1832 they contained 4,000 spindles in them and employed 8,000 workers); established a concern in Leipzig devoted exclusively to promoting the export of Austrian wares to Germany; helped create the Lower Austrian Manufacturers' Association; in 1836 made an honorary member of the Imperial Art Academy; in 1841 knighted for his services to Austrian industry.

Auerbach, Bertold (1812–82)
Liberal German novelist and writer of short stories, especially about life

390

in the Black Forest; among his best works are his edition of Spinoza's collected works, *Schwarzwälder Dorfgeschichte, Barfüssele, Edelweiss,* and *Wolfried.*

Auersperg, Count Anton Alexander von (pseud. Anastasius Grün), (1806–76)
Austrian poet and liberal, born in Carniola and lived much of his life in Graz; gained fame in Germany for poetry; published two collections of poems, *Blätter der Liebe* and *Der letzte Ritter* (Munich, 1830); published influential *Spaziergänge eines Wiener Poeten* in Hamburg in 1831, which made him famous among German liberals; later wrote epics, lyrics, and political poems.

Auersperg, Count Maximilian (1771–1850)
Joined Habsburg army as a cadet in 1787; fought in the Napoleonic Wars; in 1810 promoted to colonel; in 1815 made commander of a cavalry brigade in Galicia, and in 1829 a lieutenant field marshal; in 1836 appointed commanding general in the Banat; resigned from the army late in 1848.

Bach, Baron Alexander von (1813–93)
Studied law and languages at the University of Vienna and entered the Austrian civil service as a young man; promoted rapidly because of experience, ability, connections, and knowledge of the administration; in the 1840's traveled through most of Europe and in the Orient; in the years before the revolution he gained a reputation as a liberal; entered the Wessenberg-Doblhoff ministry as minister of justice in July, 1848; lost support of liberals and democrats because of his stand for law and order; after the murder of Count Latour on October 6, 1848, withdrew from the ministry; again became minister of justice on November 21, 1848, in a cabinet of "strong men" under Premier Schwarzenberg; from July, 1849, to

1859 minister of interior; in 1852 succeeded Schwarzenberg as head of the Ministry; Austrian ambassador to the Vatican 1859–1867.

Bassermann, Friedrich Daniel (1811–55)
Founder with Karl Mathy of the Bassermannsche Verlagsbuchhandlung in Mannhein; after 1841 member of the Baden Diet, in which he was a leader of the liberal opposition; his February 12, 1848, proposal to call a national assembly made him famous all over Germany; later a member of both the Preliminary Parliament and the Frankfurt Assembly.

Batthyány, Count Lajos (1809–49)
Born at Pressburg; spent his early life in the army; studied German and French literature and then history and political science; later learned the Magyar language; married Countess Antonie Zichy; he toured Europe extensively; became interested in Hungarian politics; in 1838 elected to the Hungarian Diet; at first a partisan of Count Széchenyi and opponent of Lajos Kossuth; became president of the Industrial Union and later allied himself with Kossuth; on April 3, 1848, made premier of Hungary; on September 15 resigned with rest of Ministry in protest over the favor the Habsburgs were showing the Ban of Croatia; retired to his estates; arrested on January 8, 1849, and executed on October 6 of the same year for high treason against the Habsburg monarchy.

Bäuerle, Adolf (1786–1859)
Born in Vienna; early showed signs of great talent as a playwright; first play, *Sigmund der Stahlerne,* published when he was sixteen years old; in the next 50 years wrote more than a score of popular plays; secretary of the Leopoldstädter Theater 1809–28; also editor of the *Wiener allgemeine Theater-Zeitung,* the most widely circulated paper in the monarchy 1820–

Dramatis Personae of the Revolution

1847; in 1848 founded and edited the *Geissel* to counteract the influence of the radicals; in December of the same year founded the *Volksboten,* which later became the popular *Wiener Telegraph.*

Bauernfeld, Eduard von (1802–90)

Born in Vienna, orphaned at an early age and extremely poor during his youth; in 1826 became a state employee and began to devote himself to literature, turning out a large number of comedies, poems, dialogues, satires, etc. A liberal and at times a rather caustic opponent of the government during the prerevolutionary period but was protected by his friendship with Kolowrat.

Baumgartner, Count Andreas von (1793–1865)

Professor of physics at the University of Vienna; his *Naturlehre,* first published in 1823, became an outstanding physics textbook in Austrian and German schools; in 1845 resigned from teaching position to become director of the Austrian tobacco factories; superintended the building of the electric telegraph system in Austria 1846–48; in 1847 made director of the Austrian railway system; minister of public works in the Pillersdorf government during the 1848 Revolution; in July, when the Wessenberg-Doblhoff ministry was formed, made a section chief in the Ministry of Finances; in 1851 appointed minister of commerce and later in the same year minister of finances.

Becker, Alfred Julius (1803–48)

Obscure revolutionary figure; for a time tried to practice law but was unsuccessful; became a musician and music critic of doubtful ability; edited *Der Radikale,* an extreme leftist revolutionary newspaper; one of the fourteen persons Windischgrätz demanded must be delivered up to him late in October, 1848; shot by the Habsburgs for activities during the revolution.

Beidtel, Karl

Son of Ignaz Beidtel, well-known Austrian political writer and jurist.

Bem, Jósef (1795–1850)

Polish revolutionary leader; distinguished himself in the Polish revolution of 1830–31; fled to Paris, and in February, 1848, went to Lemberg; in the fall of the same year offered his services to Kossuth; came through Vienna on October 14 on his way to the Hungarian capital; Messenhauser prevailed upon him to help defend the city; on October 28 secretly left Vienna to join the Hungarian army and fought against the Austrians and Russians in 1849; when the Hungarians were defeated, escaped to Turkey, embraced Mohammedanism and became a pasha.

Bernolák, Antonín

Born in 1813 in Érsek-Ujvár, Hungary; Catholic clergyman and philologist; almost singlehandedly laid basis for Slovak as a literary language.

Blum, Hans

Son of Robert Blum; jurist and writer.

Blum, Robert (1807–48)

Leipzig theater cashier, poet, and radical agitator of Saxony; became leader of the extreme left in the Frankfurt Assembly; sentenced to death and shot on November 9, 1848, for his activities in the defense of Vienna in October.

Bombelles, Count Henry (1789–1850)

Born in Versailles; entered the Austrian military service in 1805; in 1815 made Archduke Ferdinand's adjutant; thereafter served in diplomatic posts in London, Lisbon, Saint Petersburg, and Turin; in 1836 appointed teacher of Archduke Francis Charles's sons and specially entrusted with the education of the future Emperor Francis Joseph; accompanied the royal family to Innsbruck in May, 1848; shortly thereafter retired to private life.

Brunner, Sebastian (1814–93)

Studied theology at the University of Vienna and then became a priest; chaplain and curate in various parishes in the Vienna diocese and finally in Vienna; preacher in the university church and later superintendent of endowments of the University of Vienna; on April 15, 1848, founded the *Wiener Kirchenzeitung* to defend the Catholic church against the attacks of the radicals; wrote many religious articles, pamphlets, books, humorous tales, and attacks on the Hegelians, Schopenhauer, Goethe, and Heine, among others.

Buchheim, Adolf

Student from Raab, member of the juridical corps of the Academic Legion, and coeditor of the *Politischer Studenten-Courier* (radical student newspaper); when Windischgrätz attacked Vienna, fled to Prague, then to Germany.

Castelli, Ignaz Franz (1781–1862)

Austrian journalist, poet, and dramatist; wrote over two hundred plays, most of which were adapted from French originals and satirized the Viennese.

Charles Louis von Habsburg, Archduke of Austria (1771–1847)

Son of Emperor Leopold II and the outstanding Austrian general of the Napoleonic Wars; retired from active military duty in 1809 to write books on the theory and art of warfare; one of the most liberal of the early-nineteenth-century Austrian archdukes.

Colloredo-Mannsfeld, Count Ferdinand (1777–1848)

Spent early adulthood in the Austrian diplomatic service; returned to private life in 1808; in 1822 re-entered public life as a member of the Lower Austrian Estates, where he tried to influence the government to institute reforms; in 1826 became president of the First Austrian Savings Bank; in 1835 made a director of a fire insurance company; a member of the directing committee of the Agricultural Society of Vienna; first president of the Lower Austrian Manufacturers' Association; when the 1848 Revolution broke out, took over command of the Viennese Academic Legion but resigned after various unpleasant experiences; thereafter withdrew completely from public life.

Cotta von Cottendorf, Baron Johann Friedrich (1764–1832)

In 1787 became manager of the J. G. Cottasche Buchhandlung of Tübingen; in 1795 founded with Schiller the literary journal *Horen;* in 1798 founded the *Allgemeine Zeitung;* in 1811 opened branch office in Stuttgart.

Cotta von Cottendorf, Baron Johann Georg (1796–1863)

Son of Baron Johann Friedrich; assumed control of the Cottasche Buchhandlung upon his father's death; bought out G. J. Göschen in Leipzig in 1839 and. Vogel in Landshut in 1845.

Czapka, Ignaz, Knight of Winstetten

Born in 1792; entered the Viennese magistracy in a minor position in 1815; in 1823 became a magisterial counselor; in 1835 appointed vice-mayor of Vienna; mayor of Vienna 1838–48; instituted many reforms and city improvements; fled from Vienna in March, 1848; in 1856 became director of the Vienna police.

Dahlmann, Friedrich Christoph (1785–1860)

German historian and political leader; taught at the universities of Kiel, Göttingen, and Bonn; in 1837 with six other professors discharged from the University of Göttingen after protesting when the Hanoverian Duke Ernest Augustus rescinded the constitution granted four years earlier; later moderate constitutional liberal in the Frankfurt Assembly.

Deym von Stritetz, Count Friedrich (1801–53)

Well-known authority on finance and political economy; best writings: *Drei Denkschriften* (1848), *Das Bank- und Notenwesen mit Bezug auf die Geld- und Finanzverhältnisse in Oesterreich* (1850), and *Vorschläge und Entwürfe zur Vertretung und Förderung der Ackerbau-Interessen in Oesterreich* (1851).

Dietrichstein-Proskau-Lestic, Count Moritz von (1775–1864)

Wealthy landowner and court official; served as an officer in the imperial army; he was appointed teacher of Napoleon's son, the Duke of Reichstadt; made, in turn, count of imperial music, director of the Imperial Theater, director of the imperial coin and antique collection, chief of the Imperial Exchequer, and deputy of the chief master of the court; in 1852 retired to his family estates.

Doblhoff-Dier, Baron Anton von (1800–72)

One of the most liberal members of the Lower Austrian Estates; especially popular with the opponents of the Habsburgs; in May, 1848, appointed minister of trade, agriculture, and industry; in July became minister of interior and the leading member of the Wessenberg-Doblhoff government; member of the revolutionary parliament not only as a minister but also as a representative of the city of Vienna; in October, 1848, withdrew from public affairs. In March, 1849, plenipotentiary extraordinary and Austrian minister at The Hague.

Ebersberg, Joseph Sigmund (1799–1854)

Studied philosophy and law at the University of Vienna; for a time private secretary to Hofrat Hartel Edler von Luchsenstein; wrote a number of books for boys and girls, 1820–40, which were translated into various European languages; in 1824 founded a youth magazine, *Die Feierstunden*, renamed *Oesterreichischer Zuschauer* in 1831; in 1848 changed his paper into a political journal, *Wiener Zuschauer*, championing conservative interests.

Ehrlich, A. H.

Born in 1820; son of Viennese merchant; talented in music and languages; in 1848 edited *Bst! Bst! Warum? Volksfragen* and wrote pamphlets; after the October outbreak went to Olmütz and Kremsier, where he worked as a journalist; in 1850 went to Paris to teach piano and languages.

Endlicher, Stephan Ladislaus (1804–49)

Well-known authority on Asiatic languages and botany; in 1840 made professor of botany at the University of Vienna and director of the botanical garden; wrote many articles and other works on philological and botanical subjects; during the 1848 Revolution attempted to curb the students and counteract the influence of radical agitators on them.

Falke, Oskar

See Georg Peter.

Fenner von Fenneberg, Daniel (1820–63)

Born in Trient, in the Tyrol; son of a lieutenant field marshal in the Habsburg army; trained in the Wiener Neustadt Military Academy and commissioned an officer in the imperial army; dismissed from army in 1843; in 1847, after attacking Austrian army organization in his book *Oesterreich und seine Armee*, went to south Germany; returned to Vienna after the March uprising and took a prominent part in left-wing politics during the revolution; late in October, 1848, when Vienna was bombarded by

Windischgrätz' troops, became Messenhauer's adjutant; after the surrender of Vienna, fled to Germany, where for a short time he was commander-in-chief of the insurgent forces in the Palatinate in 1849; fled to Baden and then to Switzerland; later moved to the United States, where he founded a German paper, *Atlantis,* in New York City.

Ferdinand I (1793–1875)
Emperor of Austria (1835–48). Son of Emperor Francis I; a weak-minded epileptic whose government was controlled by Council of State headed by Archduke Louis but dominated by Metternich and Kolowrat; abdicated on December 2, 1848, and retired to Prague.

Ficquelmont, Count Karl Ludwig (1777–1857)
Military man and diplomat; born in Lorraine but came to Austria with his family during the early years of the French Revolution; in 1793 began service in the Habsburg army; in 1805 promoted to the rank of major; in 1809 became a colonel; in 1814 a major general; diplomatic career began in 1815, when he was sent to Sweden as plenipotentiary extraordinary; in 1820 sent to Tuscany and in 1821 to Naples as the Austrian diplomatic representative; in 1840 appointed chief of the military section in the Foreign Office; on March 21, 1848, he became minister of foreign affairs in the first Austrian constitutional ministry; a few weeks later provisionally replaced Kolowrat as minister-president; on May 4 resigned after a noisy demonstration against him, and retired to private life; later wrote several books on European political and diplomatic affairs.

Fischhof, Adolph (1816–93)
Born at Pest and studied medicine at Vienna; in 1846 became an assistant doctor at the Vienna General Hospital and took up residence there; first became active in politics on March 13, 1848; later became prominent member of the Viennese Security Committee and the "leftist" group in the Austrian Parliament; when Parliament dissolved in 1849, arrested and investigated for his political activities but finally freed; thereafter retired to private life.

Francis I (II) (1768–1835)
Holy Roman Emperor (1792–1806) and Emperor of Austria (1804–35). Son of Leopold II; joined all coalitions against France except one; proclaimed himself emperor of Austria in 1804 and abdicated as ruler of Holy Roman Empire in 1806; after overthrow of Napoleon in 1814–15 became leader of the conservative forces of central Europe.

Francis Charles Joseph von Habsburg, Archduke of Austria (1802–75)
Brother of Emperor Ferdinand; married Archduchess Sophie, a princess of the Wittelsbach house of Bavaria; father of future Emperor Francis Joseph; took no active part in politics.

Francis Joseph (1830–1916)
Emperor of Austria (1848–1916) and King of Hungary (1867–1916). Son of Archduke Francis Charles and Archduchess Sophie and nephew of Emperor Ferdinand I; became emperor on December 2, 1848, after Ferdinand's abdication; during his reign Austria was expelled from Germany and Italy, the Austrian Empire was divided into a dual monarchy (1867) and national tensions that finally resulted in the overthrow of the Habsburg monarchy reached their peak.

Frankl, Ludwig August (1810–94)
Austrian poet born in Bohemia, author of satirical poems, travel books, epics and ballads, biographies, and works on Jewish subjects; in 1848 he became editor and publisher of the *Sonntagsblätter;* prominent democratic spokesman of the Viennese Revolution; later professor of aesthetics at the Conservatory of the Vienna Music Society;

Dramatis Personae of the Revolution

founded the first Jewish school in Jerusalem.

Freund, Karl

Born in 1818 in Zsidovár, Hungary, son of an Austrian civil servant; entered the Habsburg service in 1837; assigned to Temesvár, later transferred to the Imperial Exchequer in Vienna; in April, 1848, elected to the Central Committee of Citizens, Students, and National Guardsmen; on June 1 became deputy chairman of the Security Committee; later elected to the Vienna City Council; in 1850 appointed general secretary and in 1852 a reviewer of the Communications Directory; later dismissed because of his revolutionary activities in 1848 and became secretary of the Theiss Railway Company.

Fröbel, Julius (1805–93)

Professor of mineralogy at the University of Zürich; in 1842 established a radical press devoted to spreading revolutionary doctrines; elected to the Frankfurt Assembly, where he was one of the leaders of the extreme left; condemned to death by the Habsburg military court for his actions in Vienna in October, 1848, but sentence countermanded by Windischgrätz; lived in the United States 1849–57; returned to Vienna in 1862 and championed Austrian program for reforming the German Confederation; in 1867 he became editor of the moderate liberal *Süddeutsche Presse* in Munich.

Füster, Anton

Born in 1808 in Carniola; received doctorate in theology at the University of Vienna; returned to Carniola to become a preacher at Laibach and then at Trieste; in 1839 appointed professor of theology and general pedagogy at Görz; in 1847 appointed to same position at the University of Vienna; during the revolution was one of the most radical leaders of the Academic Legion; elected to the Austrian Parliament, where he joined the extreme left; fled from Austria when

Parliament was dissolved in March, 1849; lived for a time in London and then went to the United States.

Gagern, Heinrich von (1799–1880)

Born at Bayreuth; fought at Waterloo and was an active Burschenschaft member in his student days; later entered the civil service of the Grand Duchy of Hesse; in 1832 elected to the Hessian Second Chamber, but was dismissed the next year because of his ardent liberalism; in 1848 he was at the head of the Hessian ministry for a short time; he participated in both the March 5 Heidelberg assembly and in the Preliminary Parliament; on May 19 elected president of the Frankfurt Assembly; on December 15 succeeded Schmerling as chairman of the German Ministry; left the assembly on May 20, 1849; after 1852 lived in Heidelberg.

Gaj, Ljudevit (1809–72)

Croatian national writer; spent much of his life urging the Croatians and Serbs to join in opposing the rule of the Hungarians.

Goldmark, Joseph

Born in 1818 in Hungary; studied philosophy and medicine in Vienna; received doctorate in medicine in 1847 and joined staff of the Vienna General Hospital; on March 13, 1848, earned wide fame for his speech before the Landhaus; became captain of a medical company in the Academic Legion, president of the Student Committee, and a prominent member of the Security Committee; elected to the Austrian Parliament, a member of the extreme left; when Parliament dissolved, fled to the United States and opened a percussion-cap factory.

Grillparzer, Franz (1791–1872)

Austria's most outstanding nineteenth-century dramatist and poet and a government employee; wrote some excellent verse and a well-known short story, "Der arme Spielmann," but was best known for his dramas, which were especially noted for their power and poetic beauty.

Grünn, Anastasius
See Count Anton Alexander von Auersperg.

Häfner, Leopold
Born in 1820 in Vienna; practiced law unsuccessfully; wrote anonymous attacks on Austria for the Leipzig book market and theater criticisms and belletristic articles for Viennese papers; founded the *Constitution* on March 20, 1848, and built the newspaper into the most powerful organ of the extreme left in Vienna; in October, 1848, secretly left Vienna on a steamboat, but was recognized, arrested, and held in prison for seven months; after his release, went to Dresden, where he obtained an emigration visa; arrested for his participation in the May 3, 1849, revolt in Dresden, but his passport protected him from being returned to Austria; sent to Hamburg on the understanding that he would sail for America, but did not do so; thereafter lived in various places in Europe.

Hammer-Purgstall, Baron Joseph von (1774–1856)
Writer, translator, scholar, orientalist, and prominent state employee; became first president of the Royal Academy of Sciences, founded in 1847.

Hartig, Count Franz (1789–1865)
Habsburg state official during the pre-revolutionary period; in 1819 became an aulic councilor and reviewer in the court chancellery; governor of Inner Austria, 1819–25; head of the government of Milan 1836–40; in 1840 called to Vienna, where he was made a state and conference minister and chief of internal affairs; considered to be Kolowrat's possible successor.

Hartmann, Moritz (1821–72)
Bohemian-born German writer; studied at the University of Prague; went to Vienna, where he became a good friend of Heinrich Landesmann; collection of poetic verses, *Kelch und Schwert* (1845), brought difficulties with the Austrian censor; until 1848 spent much of his time in Brussels, Paris, and Leipzig; in 1848 elected to the Frankfurt Assembly, where he belonged to the extreme left; after 1848 lived abroad for many years; returned to Vienna in 1868 to serve on the staff of the *Neue freie Presse*.

Hebbel, Christian Friedrich (1813–63)
Well-known German poet and playwright, the son of a mason; studied at Heidelberg and Munich universities; in 1839 went to Hamburg, where he completed his first drama, *Judith,* in 1841; in 1843 he went to Paris and then to Italy; in 1846 came to Vienna practically penniless; married the well-known actress Christine Enghaus; was especially noted for his dramas, some of the outstanding being *Maria Magdalena* (1844), *Herodes und Marianne* (1850), *Julia* (1851), *Michelangelo* (1851), and *Die Nibelungen* (1862).

Hecker, Friedrich (1811–81)
Mannheim lawyer; with Gustav Struve led the radical party in the Baden Second Chamber; with the outbreak of the Revolution of 1848 advocated a socialized German republic; after failure to win support of the Preliminary Parliament at Frankfurt, started a republican revolution at Constance on April 12, hoping that it would spread through southwestern Germany; after the revolt was suppressed, fled from Switzerland; in the fall of 1848 went to the United States, where he became a farmer in Illinois and a colonel in the Union Army.

Helfert, Baron Joseph Alexander von (1820–1910)
Outstanding nineteenth-century Austrian historian; before the revolution, was a jurist and a government employee in Prague and Vienna; in 1847 employed by the University of Cracow to teach canon law; in the summer

Dramatis Personae of the Revolution

of 1848 returned to his native Prague, where he was elected a conservative representative to Parliament; chief of the education and culture section of the Austrian Ministry, 1861–65; later re-elected to Parliament.

Hock, Baron Karl Ferdinand von
Born in 1808 in Prague; received doctor's degrees in philosophy and in jurisprudence at the University of Vienna; entered the Austrian civil service and served several years in Trieste and Salzburg; called to Vienna to be director of the Central Customs Office; in 1847 assigned to the General Railway Directory, and the next year appointed second director; wrote a number of articles and books on various subjects; his first major work, *Der Handel Oesterreichs,* published in 1844 in Vienna; on April 1, 1848, became editor of the *Constitutionelle Donau Zeitung,* an organ of the conservative groups in Vienna; in 1849 assigned to the Ministry of Commerce, of which he became vice-president in 1854.

Horn, Uffo Daniel (1817–60)
Austrian poet born at Trautenau, Bohemia; in 1838 moved to Vienna and joined theatrical circle; after a bitter quarrel with the journalist Moritz Saphir in 1839, left Vienna for Hamburg, where he wrote articles for various German newspapers and satirical pamphlets for Hoffman und Campe; in 1840 returned to Prague, where he helped with the *Almanach Libussa* and wrote several plays; lived in Dresden, 1846–48; in the spring of 1848 returned to Prague and for a short time played an active role in the revolution there; went to Gräfenberg and then to Leipzig; fought with revolutionary forces in Schleswig in 1849, then returned to his native Trautenau, where he spent the rest of his life.

Hornbostel, Friedrich Theodor von (1815–88)
Wealthy Viennese industrialist and director of many business enterprises; from July to October, 1848, minister of commerce in the Wessenberg-Doblhoff cabinet; head of the Austrian Manufacturers' Association, 1848–49.

Hoyos-Sprinzenstein, Count Johann (1779–1849)
Entered the Austrian military service by way of the Landwehr in 1809; soon made commander of a Landwehr battalion; fought in the military campaigns of 1813–15; joined the regular army as a colonel without pay in 1815; in 1821 became a secret counselor in the Habsburg government service; later made lord high steward and finally grand master of the hunt; in 1836 promoted to the rank of lieutenant field marshal; for a time commander-in-chief of the Viennese National Guard; on May 22, 1848, retired to private life.

Hradschiner, B.
See Adolph Maria Pinkas.

Hübner, Count Joseph Alexander von (1811–92)
Prominent Austrian diplomat and statesman; in 1844 sent to Leipzig as consul-general; with the first revolutionary stirrings in Italy, went to Milan to join Archduke Rainer's government; when the revolt broke out in Milan in March, 1848, held there for a time as a hostage; after his release returned to Vienna as a private citizen; re-entered government service in October, 1848; acting under Schwarzenberg's orders, supervised the Emperor's flight from Vienna to Olmütz in October, 1848; became a prominent member of the Schwarzenberg-Stadion ministry; Austrian minister to France, 1849–60; later served in Austrian ministries.

Hye von Glunek, Baron Anton (1807–94)
Teacher of law; in 1833 became professor of law at the Theresian Knights' Academy; in 1842 appointed to the legal faculty of the University of Vienna; before the revolution was especially well liked by liberal students, and considered one of the most

advanced liberals on the faculty; on March 12 and 13, 1848, tried to pre-; vent the students from taking revolutionary steps and thereby lost much of the popularity with the more radical students; helped draft the unpopular press law decreed on April 1, after which the students turned against him; in May, 1848, recommended that the government dissolve the Academic Legion and send the non-Viennese students home; arrested by the Security Committee, tried and convicted of high treason against the people, and turned over to the criminal court for conviction; released by the court; weary of the revolution, left Vienna and went into retirement in Upper Austria; after the revolution, returned to Vienna to become an official in the Ministry of Justice; became minister of justice in 1867 and a member of the House of Lords in 1869.

Inzaghi, Count Karl Borromäus (1777–1856)

One of Emperor Ferdinand's most trusted officials; entered government service at Graz and went from there to Galicia; became chamberlain, then cabinet secretary, then chief steward of Archduke Rainer, the Habsburg viceroy in Italy; in 1818 made governor in Laibach; sent to Venice in the same capacity; later made first court chancellor and then chief chancellor of the United Aulic Chancellery, president of the Aulic Education Commission, and royal chamberlain; dismissed from the government after the March, 1848, revolt; spent the rest of his life in retirement in Graz.

Jelačić od Bužima, Count Josip (1801–59)

Born at Peterwardein, the son of Field Marshal Franz von Jelačić; attended the Theresian Academy; joined the Habsburg army in 1819; promoted to colonel in 1841; in March, 1848, promoted to major general and appointed Ban of Croatia; on April 7 promoted

to lieutenant field marshal; refused to recognize the Hungarian Ministry at Pest and convened a Croatian-Illyrian diet to meet at Agram; aroused the anger of the Hungarians, who forced Emperor Ferdinand to dismiss him on June 10; supported by the South Slavs, continued to act as governor and began to arm the Croats and Slovenes against the Hungarians; on September 11 led his troops across the Drau River into Hungary; after fighting the Magyar troops for several weeks, sent his forces to help Windischgrätz capture Vienna; later helped conquer Hungary; returned to Agram as governor and commanding general of Croatia, Slavonia, and Dalmatia; made a count in 1855.

Jellinek, Hermann (1822–48) ̄

Born at Drslowitz, in Moravia, and educated at Ungarisch-Brod and the universities of Prague, Leipzig (where he became acquainted with Robert Blum), and Berlin; studied languages and philosophy, composed hundreds of poems, and wrote such violent political polemics that he was expelled from both Leipzig and Berlin; came to Vienna in March, 1848, and devoted himself wholly to journalism; wrote unrestrained and radical articles for the *Allgemeine Oesterreichische Zeitung* and later for the *Radikale;* arrested on November 5 and condemned to death for his treasonable agitation during the revolution; executed on November 23 with A. J. Becker.

John Baptist Joseph Fabian Sebastian von Habsburg, Archduke of Austria (1782–1859)

Youngest brother of Emperor Francis; commander-in-chief of the Austrian army in Bavaria in 1800 and of the Austrian army in Italy in 1809, did not participate in the War of Liberation (1813–14); in 1815–16 traveled in England; went into retirement in Styria; in 1823 he married a commoner; largely because of his mar-

Dramatis Personae of the Revolution

riage, was looked upon as the most liberal of the archdukes; in June, 1848, after Emperor Ferdinand fled from Vienna to Innsbruck, was sent to Vienna as the Emperor's regent with full powers to act in his name; elected regent of Germany and left Vienna to go to Frankfurt in that capacity; resigned in December, 1849, and retired to private life in Styria.

Kaiser, Friedrich (1814–74)

Son of an Austrian army officer; was a talented poet, playwright, and actor; in the 1840's took an active part in the Concordia Society; played a prominent role in the 1848 Revolution and was one of the leading figures in the Academic Legion; after the revolution, arrested because of his legion activities, but soon freed; thereafter resumed his career as a playwright.

Kleyle, Cavalier Karl von (1812–59)

Administrator of the archducal properties in Teschen; introduced reforms and increased income from the properties; in 1846 called to Vienna as administrator of all archducal properties; secretly opposed the Habsburg regime; in 1848 resigned to enter the civil service in the Ministry of Interior, first under Pillersdorf, and then under Doblhoff and Stadion; later was made chief of the Division of Agriculture in the newly created Ministry of Agriculture and Mining; after the abolition of this ministry, transferred to the Ministry of Finances.

Koch, Mathias

Writer of various minor works, mostly travel books, in the 1830's and 1840's; in the summer and early fall of 1848, wrote several placards and pamphlets attacking the radical revolutionaries and demanding the suppression of the revolt.

Kolowrat-Liebsteinsky, Count Franz Anton (1778–1861)

Born and educated in Prague; in 1799 received first administrative appointment as a minor district official in Bohemia; a few years later he became captain of the city of Prague; burgrave-in-chief of Bohemia, 1810–25; called to Vienna as state and conference minister in charge of the internal administration; conservative by nature but did not oppose reform, and was considered a progressive by the people; a bitter enemy of Metternich.

Kossuth, Lajos (1802–84)

Hungarian lawyer and one of the most radical members of the Hungarian Diet; imprisoned, 1837–40, for opposition activities; released by government because of pressure of public opinion; became editor of the *Pesti hirlap* and used the paper to advocate a broad program of liberal reforms; upon re-election to the diet in 1847, became a fiery orator against the Habsburg government; after the Viennese Revolution of March, 1848, when the Batthyány government was formed in Hungary, became finance minister in the cabinet, representing the extreme left wing; when the Batthyány ministry collapsed, became head of the government and virtual dictator; with the defeat of the Hungarian army by the Habsburgs in 1849, fled to Turkey, made a highly successful speaking tour in the United States and England, and finally settled down in exile in England.

Krauss, Baron Philipp von (1792–1861)

Austrian civil servant with the Galician government at Lemberg; became a government secretary in 1817 and a government counselor in 1823; in 1826 called to Vienna to serve in the Royal Exchequer; in 1840 transferred to the State Council; in July, 1847, became second vice-president of the Galician government; from early in April, 1848, until December, 1851, was minister of finances in the revolutionary government; member of the imperial council until 1860; in 1861 appointed to the House of Lords and was made vice-president of that body.

Kübeck von Kübau, Baron Karl Friedrich von (1780–1855)

Entered Austrian civil service in Olmütz in 1800; in 1803 transferred to the presidial bureau of the Moravian-Silesian government; in 1809 became imperial secretary in the United Aulic Chancellery, and in 1814 a member of the financial section of the State Council; in 1840 appointed president of the Imperial Exchequer, where he supervised the building of the first national railway in 1841 and the establishment of the telegraph network in 1846; in March, 1848, appointed minister of finances but resigned shortly afterwards because of ill health and retired to his estates in Moravia; in the fall of 1849 made chief of the provisional central committee in Frankfurt; in 1850 became president of the Austrian Imperial Council.

Kudlich, Hans (1823–1917)

Born in Austrian Silesia; a student of jurisprudence at the University of Vienna when the 1848 Revolution broke out; elected to the Austrian Parliament as a Silesian deputy; in Parliament became popular for first proposing the abolition of the *Robot* and other peasant services; after Parliament was dissolved, went to Germany and then to Switzerland, where he tried to stir up revolts; tried and convicted in absentia for his activities in the Austrian revolution; left Switzerland for the United States and settled down in Hoboken, New Jersey, to practice medicine.

Kuranda, Ignaz (1811–84)

Born in Prague, son of a book-dealer; in 1834 went to Vienna and wrote theatrical reviews and short sketches on Viennese life for the *Telegraph;* also wrote several plays; in 1838 went to Stuttgart to attend the opening performance of his play *The Last White Rose;* journeyed to Paris, Brussels, and Leipzig; editor of the anti-Habsburg paper the *Grenzboten,* 1841–48; in March, 1848, returned to Austria and was elected to the Frankfurt Assembly; he left Frankfurt in September, 1848, to become the founder and editor of the *Ostdeutsche Post* in Vienna.

Lamberg, Count Francis Philipp (1791–1848)

Born in Moor, Hungary; began service in the Habsburg army in 1810 and in 1823 advanced to the rank of major; in 1829 made a colonel, in 1832 a major general, and in 1842 a lieutenant field marshal; inherited a position in the Hungarian Table of Magnates and supported the Magyars; chosen imperial commissioner to Hungary in September, 1848; murdered in Pest on September 28, 1848, by Hungarian extremists.

Landesmann, Heinrich (pseud. Hieronymus Lorm), (1821–1902)

Austrian poet and journalist; born at Nikolsburg, Moravia; early showed poetic talents; first verses published when he was sixteen years old; many of his poems were printed in the *Österreichischen Morganblatt;* also wrote many criticisms of conditions in Austria, which were printed in various German papers; attacked Metternich regime in *Wiens poetische Schwingen und Federn,* published in Leipzig in 1846; in 1848 wrote articles for revolutionary journals, especially Zang's *Presse,* criticizing Viennese radicals; in 1850 became literary critic for the *Wiener Zeitung.*

Latour, Count Theodor Baillet von (1780–1848)

Son of an Austrian field marshal; attended the Wiener Neustadt Military Academy, then joined the army; by 1813 had advanced to the rank of colonel; in 1822 became a brigadier general; in 1831 appointed lieutenant field marshal, and in 1841 field marshal; minister of war from April 30 to October 6, 1848, when he was murdered by the Viennese.

Löhner, Ludwig von (pseud. Ludwig Rehland and Ludwig von Morajn), (1812–52)

Physician, politician, and writer; born in Prague, studied in Prague and in Italy, then came to Vienna to practice medicine; joined the staff of the Vienna General Hospital, and was a leader of a group opposing the outmoded teaching methods of the Vienna medical faculty; became known for radical political views and played a prominent role in the March, 1848, revolt; in April helped organize a club of Germans from Bohemia, Moravia, and Silesia to protect German nationality against Czech aggression; elected to the Austrian Parliament, where he became the leader of the left-wing German-Bohemian representatives.

Lorm, Hieronymus
See Heinrich Landesmann.

Louis Joseph Anton von Habsburg, Archduke of Austria

Born in 1784; brother of Emperor Francis I; in 1816 appointed state councilor, and in 1822 general director of the artillery; a particularly close associate of his brother, and during Francis' absence from Vienna signed letters and decrees in his name.

Löwe, Ludwig (1795–1855)
Popular actor in Vienna, Prague, and Germany, especially noted for comic roles.

Mahler, Moriz
Born in 1820 in Vienna; began journalistic career at early age by writing humorous articles for *Der Ungar,* in Pest; returned to Vienna in the late 1840's and wrote for Saphir's *Humoristen* and Bäuerle's *Theater-Zeitung;*

in 1848 founded the *Freimüthige;* escaped from Vienna during the October revolution; during the next twelve years lived in France, Belgium, Germany, and Switzerland; later obtained an entry permit to visit Austria for six months; interned in Graz for a few months, where he wrote violent attacks on the monarchy for the *Volksstimme,* for which the editor and chief personnel of the paper were tried in the criminal courts; Mahler escaped punishment by fleeing to Paris.

Messenhauser, Wenzel Cäsar (1813–48)

Son of a regimental musician; entered the Habsburg army as a private in 1829 and slowly advanced through the ranks; became a lieutenant in 1840; spent all his free time reading and soon developed talents as a writer; wrote poetry, then a ten-volume history of the ancient world, for which he could find no publisher; began writing dramas, and in 1841 his play *Demosthenes. Ein Trauerspiel in vier Acten* published in Vienna; in 1840 transferred to the Hoch- und Deutschmeister Regiment in Vienna; met Saphir and wrote many poems, anecdotes, and other short pieces for his *Humorist;* sent to Galicia with his regiment in 1846; wrote *Wildnis und Parquet,* published in Vienna in 1847, and two works on the loneliness of garrison life, *Die Polengräber* and the *Ernsten Geschichte,* both published in Leipzig in 1848; was at work on a novel, *Der Ratsherr,* when the 1848 Revolution broke out; decided to make a career for himself as a writer and left the army in March, 1848; started a journal in Vienna, *Die Volkstribune,* which failed because of its unpopular moderate tone; at the instigation of his friend Ludwig Frankl, joined the Academic Legion; spent most of the summer of 1848 working on *Der Ratsherr* and other works and took little interest in revolutionary politics until he was appointed commander-in-chief of the

National Guard in October; shot on November 16, 1848, for his actions in the October revolution.

Metternich, Prince Klemens Wenzel Nepomuk Lothar von (1773–1859)

Born in the Rhineland in 1773; in 1795 married the granddaughter of the Austrian chancellor and foreign minister Count Wenzel von Kaunitz; marriage brought him not only great estates but admission to the highest court circles; in 1801 became Austrian envoy to Saxony; in 1803 was made Austrian ambassador to Berlin; in 1806 transferred to Paris and returned in 1809 to become the Austrian minister of foreign affairs; in 1821 became imperial chancellor and in 1826 president of the Ministerial Conference; in 1848 fled to England; returned to Vienna in 1851.

Milde, Vincenz Eduard (1777–1853)

Catholic clergyman; honorary canon of St. Stephen's, Bishop of Leitmeritz, and professor of pedagogy at the University of Vienna; made archbishop of Vienna in 1832.

Moering, Karl (1810–70)

Born in Vienna; in 1829 commissioned a lieutenant in the Habsburg army; in 1841 accompanied an expedition to Syria to protect the Sultan against possible attack by Mehemet Ali; afterward went to England and North America; after returning to Austria became the teacher of mathematics and military tactics for the four sons of Archduke Rainer, the Habsburg viceroy of Lombardy; in 1849 promoted to the rank of major; in 1856 became a colonel, in 1862 a brigadier general, in 1863 a major general, and in 1867 a lieutenant field marshal; during the period immediately preceding the 1848 Revolution, wrote treatises attacking the Habsburg regime, the most significant of which was *Sibyllinischer Bücher aus Oesterreich,* published in Hamburg in early

1848; the manuscript was sent to the publisher by Baron von Doblhoff, and Franz Schuselka persuaded Hoffman und Campe to publish it; the identity of the author was not discovered until March, 1848.

Montecuccoli, Count Albert Raimund (1802–52)

Descendant of a well-known family of north Italian nobility; devoted his adult life to the Austrian civil service; in 1830 became a secretary in the provincial government of Upper Austria; in 1833 appointed *Kreishauptmann* at Ried; in 1833 sent to Salzburg in the same capacity; in 1838 appointed aulic councilor in the provisional government of Upper Austria; in 1844 went to Lombardy as vice-president of the government; in 1847 sent to Vienna as marshal of the Lower Austrian Estates; on March 13, 1848, led the Lower Austrian Estates' delegation to the Emperor to try to persuade him to make timely reforms; after the revolution in Italy, sent to Milan again, this time as chief of the first section of the general government; later transferred back to Vienna to become chief of the first section of the Ministry of Interior.

Morajn, Ludwig von

See Ludwig von Löhner.

Mühlfeld, Karl Eugen Megerle von (1810–68)

Viennese liberal lawyer; in 1848 elected by the city of Vienna to the Frankfurt Assembly; after its failure, returned to Vienna to resume law practice; wrote many articles on legal subjects, and in 1854 became president of the Viennese lawyers' chamber; later a prominent member of the Austrian Parliament and one of the leaders of the Greater Austrian party.

Nestroy, Johann (1802–62)

One of the most popular Viennese actors and opera stars of the 1840's; also wrote large number of librettos and plays.

Dramatis Personae of the Revolution

Neustadt, Adolph (pseud. Stephan Thurm)

Born in 1812 in Prague; in 1837 went to Vienna; employed as journalist by Bäuerle and Saphir; became a close friend of Kuranda and Frankl; wrote articles for many German newspapers, most of them under his pseudonym, and helped edit the *Oesterreichischen National-Encyklopädie;* in 1839 an order was given for his arrest, but he escaped across the border to Hungary; obtained a position on the *Pest Tagblatt* through Saphir; later became a citizen of Pressburg and editor of the *Pressburger Zeitung;* fled from Pressburg to Prague during an anti-Semitic riot in the spring of 1848; after the miscarriage of the revolution, was expelled from Prague and went to Trieste; later returned to Vienna to become editor of the *Oesterreichische Zeitung.*

Palacký, František (1798–1876)

Bohemian historian and politician and champion of Czech nationalism; in 1839 named historiographer of Bohemia and in that capacity wrote, despite many altercations with Austrian censors, five-volume *History of the Bohemian People* (1836–67), which was very influential in creating a Bohemian national consciousness; in June, 1848, was one of the most prominent members of the Slav Congress at Prague; after 1861 was a member of the upper house of the Austrian Reichsrat, as well as of the Bohemian Landtag; led the Old Czech party and sought to create an autonomous Czech nation within the Habsburg monarchy.

Pannasch, Anton (1789–1855)

Born in Brussels; parents emigrated to Vienna shortly after his birth; educated at the Wiener Neustadt Military Academy and became an officer in the imperial army in 1809; in school showed considerable talents as a poet and playwright and continued to develop these abilities in the army; between 1817 and 1849 wrote ten dramas, most of which were produced

in the Vienna Burgtheater and in Germany; gradually advanced through the army ranks and became lieutenant colonel in 1841; dismissed from the service in 1844; appointed National Guard commander but soon resigned and secured a post in the Ministry of War archives, which he held until his death.

Pereira-Arnstein, Baron Louis von (1803–58)

Prominent Viennese banker; subsidized many artistic endeavors and was himself a painter and sculptor of some note.

Peter, Georg (pseud. Oskar Falke)

Philosophy student at the University of Vienna; in 1848 coeditor of the *Politischer Studenten-Courier;* fled from Vienna in October and later went to the United States, where he eventually amassed a large fortune in the rubber industry.

Pichler, Adolf

Born in 1819; well-known Tyrolese poet and authority on natural science; went to Innsbruck and then to Vienna to study; lived chiefly upon the money he could earn from writing and lecturing; in 1846 a collection of his poems on the Tyrol was published under the title *Frühlieder aus Tirol;* in April, 1848, received his doctorate and left Vienna as captain of an academic volunteer company for the defense of the Tyrol; fought in several battles in Italy and was decorated with the Iron Cross for bravery; in the fall of 1848 returned to Vienna and lived there during the turbulent October days; in November returned to Innsbruck to resume his career; in 1859 became an assistant at the University of Innsbruck, and in 1867 was appointed professor of mineralogy and geology at the same university.

Pillersdorf, Baron Franz Xaver (1786–1862)

Born in Brünn. In 1808 joined the civil service as a government secretary; in 1811 appointed imperial secretary in the Royal Exchequer and in 1815 promoted to the rank of imperial counselor; in 1824 became fourth vice-president and in 1831 first vice-president of the Royal Exchequer; in 1832 appointed chancellor in the United Aulic Chancellery; in 1843 became a member of both the Lower Austrian and the Galician Estates; in 1844 the title Aulic Chancellor was given to him; in 1845 made an honorary citizen of Vienna, in 1846 an honorary member of the Academy of Arts, and somewhat later an honorary member of the Academy of Sciences; on March 17, 1848, appointed minister of interior in the first Austrian constitutional Ministry, and early in May became minister-president; in July forced to resign by the Security Committee; in the meantime had been elected to Parliament, and in October was elected second vice-president of that body; in 1849 was investigated for his revolutionary activities; was not imprisoned but spent the next eleven years in retirement answering the many bitter attacks made upon him; in 1861 elected to the Austrian House of Representatives.

Pinkas, Adolph Maria (pseud. B. Hradschiner), (1800–65)
Bohemian publicist and lawyer and was well known for his progressive ideas and the courage with which he expressed them; in 1848 elected to the Austrian Parliament and became a leader of the liberal party opposing both the radicals and the feudal-clerical group; an industrious correspondent for the *Grenzboten* and wrote for it under various names.

Pulszky, Franz (1814–97)
Hungarian archaeologist, publicist, and politician; traveled widely in Europe and wrote several articles; chosen as a representative to the Hungarian Diet at Pressburg in 1839; an active champion of reform, but was not re-elected to the diets of 1843 and 1847; busied himself as a journalist during these years; when the revolution broke out in Pest on March 15,

1848, was appointed by Archduke Stephen, the palatine of Hungary, as imperial commissioner with extraordinary powers to preserve peace and order; in this capacity chiefly responsible for putting down a Jewish pogrom that broke out in Stuhlweissenburg; in April was appointed undersecretary in the Hungarian Ministry of Finances; in May became undersecretary of foreign affairs and went to Vienna to take over the functions of the Foreign Office when his superior, Prince Paul Esterházy, accompanied the Emperor to Innsbruck; in this position had considerable influence on public opinion and on the Viennese press; on October 5, 1848, dismissed from his post by Emperor Ferdinand and left Vienna for Pest; the Hungarian Ministry, disobeying the Emperor's orders, immediately sent him back to his post in Vienna, where he remained until the end of October; later became minister of commerce in the Hungarian cabinet; when the Russians indicated that they would send help to the Habsburgs in Hungary, was sent abroad to enlist sympathies for the Hungarian cause; while in London, sentenced to death by the Habsburg government for complicity in the Hungarian rebellion; thereafter made his living as a journalist for various English papers; *London Daily News* correspondent in Turin 1860–1866; pardoned by the Habsburgs and returned to Hungary.

Purtscher, Adolf (1815–51)
Born in the Tyrol and educated in a Jesuit college; went to Vienna to study medicine but retained a great interest in poetry and philosophy; in 1848 took part in student politics and was elected to the Austrian Parliament; withdrew from political life after the revolution.

Radetzky von Radetz, Count Joseph Wenzel (1766–1858)
Served in the Habsburg army in the Napoleonic Wars; Schwarzenberg's chief of staff in 1813–14 and again in 1815; promoted to field marshal in 1836; commanded Austrian troops in

Dramatis Personae of the Revolution

Italy in 1848–49; governor-general of Lombardy-Venetia, 1849–57.

Radowitz, Joseph Maria von (1797–1853)

General in the Prussian army; member of the romanticist conservative circle around Crown Prince Frederick William and closely associated with the editors of the ultraconservative *Politisches Wochenblatt;* in 1836 appointed Prussian military representative at Frankfurt; in 1847–48 helped King Frederick William IV draw up a plan for the reform of the German Confederation; in 1848 a conservative leader in the Frankfurt Assembly; after the assembly was dissolved, became the Prussian King's chief diplomatic adviser; in 1850 appointed foreign minister; resigned in December of the same year because of Prussia's humiliating diplomatic defeat by Austria at the Erfurt Parliament.

Rainer Joseph Johann von Habsburg, Archduke of Austria (1783–1853)

Son of Leopold II and brother of Emperor Francis; viceroy of Lombardo-Venetian kingdom from 1818 to March, 1848; thereafter retired to private life.

Rehland, Ludwig

See Ludwig von Löhner.

Rimmer, Albert (1818–55)

Born in Olmütz; served a short time as an infantry officer; left the army to enter the Austrian civil service; wrote several articles for such papers as Frankl's *Sonntagsblätter,* Biedermann's *Deutsche Wochenschrift,* the *Kölnische Zeitung,* and the *Breslauer Zeitung;* was especially active in behalf of the *Grenzboten,* for which he wrote articles on politics and political economy; suffered from insanity during the last years of his life.

Ronge, Johannes (1813–87)

Born in Silesia; in 1840 became curate at Grottkau but was dismissed three years later because of the furor over an essay he had written, "Rome and the Breslau Cathedral"; became a teacher in Laurahütte, in Upper Silesia; there laid the foundations for his German-Catholic movement, which led to his excommunication from the Catholic church; thereafter wrote tracts expounding the bases of the new religion and traveled all over Germany establishing German-Catholic congregations; in 1845 became the preacher of the German-Catholic congregation in Breslau; movement became quite popular in south Germany; in 1849 left Germany for London; in 1861 returned to Breslau; later moved to Frankfurt and finally (in 1873) to Darmstadt.

Sander, Friedrich

Revolutionary journalist and ardent champion of the Viennese workers; contributed to the *Constitution* and assistant editor of M. Gritzner's *Das Wiener allgemeine Arbeiter-Blatt;* founder of the First General Workers' Union.

Saphir, Moritz Gottlieb (1795–1858)

Austrian journalist, humorist, and editor of *Der Humorist* 1837–1858.

Schindler, Julius Alexander (pseud. Julius von der Traun)

Born in 1819 in Vienna; wrote poems, articles, and brochures attacking the Austrian government that were smuggled abroad for publication; lived in Steyr during most of this period and was able to keep his identity secret from the police for a long time; became especially interested in the estates movement and in 1846–47 wrote *Beiträge zur Verständnisse der ständischen Bewegung in den deutsch-österreichischen Provinzen,* championing their struggle for greater political influence.

Schmerling, Cavalier Anton von (1805–93)

Entered Austrian state service in 1829; advanced rapidly, and by 1846 had become a counselor of the Court of Appeals; belonged to the Lower Austrian Estates, where he became known as an ardent liberal and opponent of the Habsburg regime; after the 1848 Revolution broke out became the first adjutant to Count Hoyos, the commander of the Viennese National Guard; was sent to Frankfurt, and, after Archduke John became imperial regent, became minister of interior and minister of foreign affairs in the provisional German government; at Frankfurt became an ardent champion of Austrian interests and was attacked by the radicals in the assembly for his efforts in behalf of the Habsburgs; in April, 1849, left Frankfurt to return to Vienna; in July, 1849, became minister of justice in the reactionary Schwarzenberg government; premier of Austria, 1860–65; first president of the Austrian Supreme Court, 1865–91.

Schrötter, Anton, Knight of Kristelli (1802–75)

Viennese scientist; named an assistant in chemistry at the Viennese Polytechnical Institute; in 1830 sent to the University of Graz to teach chemistry; in 1843 returned to the Viennese Polytechnical Institute as professor of technical chemistry, in which position he remained the rest of his life.

Schuselka, Franz (1811–89)

Born in Bohemia and educated in law at the University of Vienna; after graduation became a private tutor and a writer on legal and popular subjects; soon came into conflict with the censors and decided to live in Germany; spent much of his time at Jena, writing political pamphlets criticizing Austrian and German affairs; a bitter critic of the Catholic church and was converted to Ronge's new German-Catholic movement; forced to leave Jena and moved to Hamburg in 1846; continued writing articles for liberal German newspapers as well as political pamphlets; when the Revolution of 1848 broke out, hurried back to Vienna; the students at the University of Vienna elected him to the preliminary parliament at Frankfurt; elected

to the Frankfurt Assembly; soon resigned from this position and was elected to the Austrian Parliament, where he was one of the prominent leaders of the left; after the revolution resumed literary activities, and in the 1860's again became a member of the Austrian Parliament.

Schütte, Anton

Revolutionary figure of obscure origins; suspected of being an agent of the Russian Czar, a Jesuit, or an agent of the two Baden radicals Hecker and Struve; most Viennese seem to have thought he was a foreign emissary trying to take over leadership of the workers' movement in order to proclaim a German republic; claimed to have come from Westphalia and to have studied at Bonn, Heidelberg, and Berlin; said he had lived a long time in France and had studied parliamentary procedures; also claimed to be an authority on the Orient.

Schwarzenberg, Prince Felix (1800–52)

Born in Krumau, Bohemia; entered the Austrian army in 1819; in 1831 he became a major, in 1834 a lieutenant colonel, in 1835 a colonel, in 1842 a major general, and in 1848 a lieutenant field marshal; also served Emperor Ferdinand in various diplomatic capacities; in 1824 appointed naval attaché in St. Petersburg; dismissed from this post two years later; served on special diplomatic missions in Rio de Janeiro and Lisbon, then was attached to the London and Paris embassies; legation counselor in Berlin, 1831–38; in 1838 sent to Turin as Austrian minister to the courts of Sardinia and Parma; from 1844 to March, 1848, Austrian minister at Naples; served in Marshal Radetzky's army, and, after the Marshal reconquered Lombardy, was for a short time military and civil governor of Milan; went to Vienna in September, and, after October 6, to Olmütz; on November 24 the Emperor appointed him minister-president and minister of foreign affairs in the new ministry of "strong men"; remained in this office until his death.

Schwarzer, Ernst von (1808–60)

Son of an Austrian soldier; spent ten years of his early life as an enlisted man in the Habsburg army; after release from military service, worked in a number of trades, as painter, secretary, language and mathematics teacher, brewer, peat-miner, and farm-manager; in 1842 took a job with the Prague Manufacturers' Association and the next year became manager of the Mittrowsky Iron Works in Moravia; in 1844 appointed editor-in-chief of the *Oesterreichischen Lloyd,* in Trieste; when on March 31, 1848, the *Oesterreichische Beobachter,* of Vienna, altered its editorial policy and changed its name to *Oesterreichische Zeitung,* Schwarzer was made its editor; in April appointed to the Frankfurt Committee of Fifty; in June was elected to the Austrian Parliament; on July 17 was made minister of public works in the Doblhoff-Wessenberg ministry; resigned on September 19 to resume editorship of the *Allgemeine österreichischen Zeitung;* also resigned from Parliament shortly before it was dissolved; after his newspaper was abolished by police order, became editor of the *Wanderer* and, in 1854, editor and publisher of the *Donau.*

Sedlnitzky, Count Josef (1778–1855)

Born in Silesia; after leaving the University of Vienna, served the Austrian government in minor capacities in Galicia and Bohemia and rapidly rose to become vice-president of the Galician government; in 1815 called to Vienna to become vice-president of the Supreme Police and Censorship Office; in 1817 became president of the office and served in that capacity until March, 1848.

Silberstein, August

Born in 1827 in Ofen; left for Vienna at an early age and worked his way through the University of Vienna chiefly by teaching and writing newspaper articles; in 1848 became a member of the Academic Legion Committee; after the revolution was put down in Vienna, fled to Germany, where he worked for various newspapers; after a time returned to Austria; tried and sentenced to several years' imprisonment at Spielberg for his revolutionary activities; after his release from prison resumed his career as a writer.

Smolka, Franz (1810–99)

Lemberg lawyer and Polish nationalist leader; elected vice-president of Parliament shortly before October 6; president from October 12 to December 20, 1848, and again after January 20, 1849; from 1849 to 1859 lived in political retirement; elected to both the Galician Diet and the Austrian Parliament in 1859, where he was one of the leaders of the Polish party.

Sommaruga, Baron Franz Vincenz Emmanual von (1780–1860)

Trained in law at the University of Vienna; in 1807 appointed teacher of Emperor Francis' three sons; in 1818 became a member of the Austrian judiciary; in 1831 became an aulic judicial councilor, and in 1832 appointed *rector magnificus* of the University of Vienna; in 1847 became second president of the Lower Austrian Court of Appeals; on March 26, 1848, made minister of education and a month later minister of justice in the provisional government; resigned from the cabinet in July, 1848, and again became second president, and later president, of the Austrian Court of Appeals; in 1857 made vice-president of the Supreme Court of Justice.

Sophie, Archduchess of Austria (1805–72)

Daughter of King Maximilian Joseph of Bavaria; in 1824 married Emperor Ferdinand's younger brother, Archduke Francis Charles; a spirited, domineering woman who took an active part in placing her son Francis

Joseph on the throne in December, 1848.

Stadion-Warthausen, Count Franz Seraph (1806–53)

Son of Count Johann Philipp Stadion (Austrian minister of foreign affairs, 1805–1809, and minister of finance after 1815); at twenty-one entered the Austrian civil service as a minor employee in the Lower Austrian government; in 1828 transferred to the Galician government; in 1832 made government secretary at Innsbruck, and in 1834 appointed secretary of the Imperial Exchequer; in 1841 was made governor of the Küstenland, and in 1847 governor of Galicia; after the outbreak of the 1848 Revolution, granted several reforms to the Poles on his own initiative, but by harsh repression of all disorders incurred the hatred of the radicals; in May asked by the Habsburg court to form a new ministry but he refused to do so; in the summer of 1848 elected to the Austrian Parliament and resigned as governor of Galicia; in Parliament led the Ruthenian deputies and sat on the right; after the October 6 revolution, left Vienna for Prague and then Olmütz; on November 22, 1848, appointed minister of interior in the Schwarzenberg cabinet.

Staudigl, Joseph (1807–61)

Extremely popular basso of the Viennese operatic stage in the 1840's.

Stephen Viktor von Habsburg, Archduke of Austria (1817–67)

Son of Archduke Joseph (palatine of Hungary and brother of Emperor Francis); in 1844 appointed *Statthalter* of Bohemia; after the death of his father in 1847, succeeded him as palatine of Hungary; very popular in Hungary at the time of the revolution; as tension developed in Hungary, unsuccessfully tried to mediate between the Batthyány government and Jelačić, the Ban of Croatia; resigned as palatine in September, 1848, and returned to Vienna.

Stifft, Baron Andreas von (1787–1861)

Leading Austrian agriculturalist, economist, and financial expert; in 1833 became an active member of the Royal Agricultural Society of Vienna; published articles on economic matters in the journal of the society; *Allgemeine land- und forstwirthschaftlichen Zeitung;* a prominent member of the liberal party in the Lower Austrian Estates in the 1840's; during the revolution, became undersecretary in the Ministry of Finances in the Wessenberg-Doblhoff ministry; in 1850 severed connections with the government and retired to private life.

Storch, A. M.

Popular Viennese composer and violinist; concertmaster at the Carl Theater and later at the Josephstadt Theater; composed the music for many operas, operettas, ballets, etc.; in 1842 joined the famous Viennese Men's Glee Club and was its choirmaster for eight years.

Strobach, Anton (1814–56)

Attorney attached to the Bohemian provincial court, 1842–48; mayor of Prague, April 9–May 10, 1848; elected to the Austrian Parliament, and on July 20 named first vice-president of that body; president from August 17 to October 12, 1848, and again from December 20, 1848, to January 20, 1849; appointed judicial counselor with the Bohemian government in July, 1849, but dismissed from this post in 1853.

Stubenrauch, Moriz von (1811–65)

Viennese lawyer and professor of law; in 1836 became an adjunct at the University of Vienna; in 1838 appointed to the faculty of the University of Lemberg; in 1839 became professor of law at the Theresian Knights' Academy in Vienna; in 1850 made professor of law at the University of Vienna; served on numerous commissions and was consulted on

Dramatis Personae of the Revolution

nearly all important legal, political, or economic questions by the government and other interested parties; on March 19, 1848, became coeditor with Heyssler of the *Wiener Zeitung;* attacked by the democrats because the *Wiener Zeitung* was not radical enough; toward the end of June, 1848, resigned from the paper, then devoted himself again to teaching; committed suicide in 1865 because of financial difficulties.

Széchenyi, Count István (1791–1860)

Best-known Hungarian reformer of the generation preceding the 1848 Revolution; in 1825 resigned from the imperial service and took his place in the Hungarian Diet at Pressburg; supported a large number of reforms; donated an enormous sum of money to establish a Hungarian academy to foster the Hungarian languages; directed many of the academy's activities; worked for improvements in the commercial, economic, and cultural life of the country; in the 1840's his moderate policies were violently attacked by Kossuth and the radical party; attempted, in turn, to restrain the extremists; his mind gave way under the strain of his political activities, and in 1860 he committed suicide.

Taaffe, Count Ludwig Patrick (1791–1855)

Member of the Austrian judicial service; served the government for some years in minor offices; in 1814 appointed to the Court of Appeals in Venice; in 1815 transferred to Milan in the same capacity; in 1818 made president of the Mercantile and Commercial Court in Milan and vice-president of the Milanese Civil Tribunal; in 1819 appointed vice-president and in 1822 governor of Styria and Carinthia; in 1823 made governor of Galicia; in 1834 appointed president of the Supreme Austrian Judicial Administration; in 1836 the law faculty of the University of Vienna chose him as *rector magnificus;* in March, 1848,

became minister of justice but left this post on April 22 to return to his position as president of the Judicial Administration, where he remained until his death.

Talatzko von Gestieticz, Baron John

President of the Lower Austrian government; a protégé of Count Kolowrat.

Tausenau, Karl (1808–73)

Born in Prague and went to Vienna some years before the revolution to become a language teacher; in Vienna openly expressed extreme leftist views, which were not only strongly liberal but also tinged with the theories of the French Utopian Socialists; during the 1848 Revolution, became one of the most powerful and influential of the Viennese revolutionary agitators; spoke in public repeatedly, criticizing the men in power and inciting the crowd to carry the revolution further to the left; wrote many articles for leftist journals; one of the prominent members of the Democratic Club, and became its leader in September, 1848; in October made chairman of the Central Committee of Radical Clubs, formed to co-ordinate the work of the radical associations; late in October fled from Austria; in 1850 settled permanently in London and resumed his former profession as language teacher, adopted English views, and had little to do with the other German refugees in London.

Thun-Hohenstein, Count Franz Anton, II (1809–70)

Son of a Bohemian landowner well known for the many reforms he instituted on his estates and for his work in spreading the industrial revolution to Bohemia. Franz Anton Thun II was noted for his efforts in fostering the artistic and cultural life of Bohemia; before 1848 a member of the Bohemian Estates and a leader in the movement to obtain more rights and privileges for the estates; in 1848 participated in revolutionary activities in

Prague and became a major in the National Guard; however, opposed the Prague rebellion of June, 1848, and led his battalion to help the military suppress it; thereby angered the radicals and was forced to flee to Saxony; returned to Bohemia in October, 1848, after the revolution was over.

Thun-Hohenstein, Count Leopold Leo (1811–88)

Born at Tetschen in 1811, the third son of Count Franz Anton Thun-Hohenstein; studied law at the University of Prague and traveled through Europe; entered the Austrian civil service; in 1847 became a counselor in the Galician government, and in April, 1848, was appointed president of the Bohemian government; in Prague incurred the hatred of both the Czech and the German extremists because of his attempt to maintain a neutral position between them; dismissed by Vienna cabinet shortly after Windischgrätz bombarded Prague; Austrian minister of education, 1849–60; in 1861 given a life appointment to the House of Lords.

Traun, Julius von der

See Julius Alexander Schindler.

Tuvora, Joseph (1811–71)

Born in Neustria, Hungary; for a time wrote theater criticisms for Bäuerle's *Theater-Zeitung;* after difficulties with Austrian censors, wrote reports about Austrian conditions for liberal German papers; although a state employee, furnished the French and Russian embassies with secret information about political conditions in Austria; in 1848 wrote articles for Häfner's *Constitution,* then joined staff of the *Freimüthige* and later the *Radikale;* although one of the most radical of the revolutionary journalists, in October, 1848, became supporter of Jelačić and a paid Habsburg propagandist; after 1848 gambled on the stock market and led life of luxury until his death.

Ungár, Adolph

Hungarian student working on his doctorate at the University of Vienna when the Viennese Revolution broke out; a violent and bitter polemicist.

Usedom, Ludwig Guido von (1804–84)

Prussian diplomat; from 1845 to 1848 and again from 1849 to 1854, plenipotentiary extraordinary and minister with full powers to the papal court at Rome.

Vincke, Baron Georg von (1811–75)

Liberal member of the Prussian United Diet of 1847; at the Frankfurt Assembly led the conservative faction; member of the Prussian House of Representatives, 1849–67, where he led the moderate liberals; member of the Diet of the North German Confederation, 1867–70.

Violand, Ernst (1821–75)

Born in Lower Austria and studied law at the University of Vienna; after leaving the university, took up state employment; during the 1848 Revolution, one of the most outspoken of the left-wing democratic leaders; frequent contributor to the leftist newspapers, such as the *Radikale;* somewhat later became a leader of the extreme left in Parliament; emigrated to the United States after the revolution.

Vitzthum von Eckstädt, Carl Grafen von (1819–95)

Saxon legation secretary in Vienna in 1848; Saxon envoy in London and Brussels, 1853–66; Austrian envoy in Brussels, 1863–73; wrote several books of observations at the various posts where he served.

Waldmüller, Ferdinand Georg (1782–1865)

Famous Viennese portrait-painter and professor at the Viennese Art Academy.

Weis, John Baptist (1801–62)

Born in Bohemia; studied philosophy at the University of Vienna; entered the Austrian civil service and eventually became a member of the Board of Accounts of the Imperial War Office; after ten years left government service to devote all his time to writing; in 1830 published the popular *Oesterreichischen Volksfreund;* in 1837 published a continuation of Joseph Richter's humor sheet *Eipeldauer Briefe* under the title *Briefe des Hans Jörgel aus Gumpoldskirchen an seinen Schwager in Feselau,* the name of which was changed to *Der Constitutionelle Hansjörgel;* bitterly attacked by the radicals; in 1849 founded the *Oesterreichische Volkszeitung.*

Welcker, Karl Theodor (1790–1869)

Born in Hesse; in 1814 became professor of law at the University of Kiel, where he and Dahlmann edited the *Kieler Blätter;* in 1816 went to the University of Heidelberg, in 1819 to Bonn, and in 1823 to the University of Freiburg; after 1831 with his colleague Karl Rotteck led the liberal opposition in the Baden Second Chamber; with Rotteck edited the *Staatslexikon. Enzyklopädie der Staatswissenschaft,* which had a tremendous influence on the pre-1848 German liberals; dismissed from the University of Freiburg in 1841 on account of his radicalism; a member of the Greater German Left in the Frankfurt Assembly.

Wessenberg-Ampringen, Baron Johann Philipp von (1773–1858)

Born in Dresden; son of an Austrian diplomat; studied law at Strassburg and Freiburg; entered the Austrian civil service at the age of twenty-one; in 1801 became legation secretary in the Austrian embassy at Berlin; in 1805 was sent to Kassel as resident minister; and in 1809 went on a special mission to Berlin to try to persuade the Prussians to join the war against Napoleon; in 1811 became Austrian minister at Munich; in 1814–15 was one of the Austrian plenipotentiaries at the Congress of Vienna;

in 1819 resigned his post as minister to Bavaria and retired to private life; in 1830, was one of the Austrian plenipotentiaries at the London Conference; was minister of foreign affairs from May to November, 1848, when he was replaced by Prince Felix Schwarzenberg; then returned to private life.

Wildner von Maithstein, Ignaz (1802–54)

Son of a penniless captain in the imperial army; worked his way through the Gymnasium and later through the University of Vienna; received doctorate in jurisprudence in 1832; entered the government service and wrote several legal works and taught law; in 1839 founded the legal journal the *Jurist,* of which he was editor the rest of his life; because of his vast knowledge of jurisprudence, sent by Metternich to Hungary in 1839 to work out several projects for the Hungarian Diet; knighted as a result of his work there; on March 15, 1848, founded a political paper, *Das Panier des Fortschritts,* which ceased publication on June 24 of the same year; elected to the revolutionary Austrian Parliament; after 1848 he continued writing treatises on legal topics.

Windischgrätz, Prince Alfred Candid Ferdinand zu (1787–1862)

Wealthy Austrian landowner and military man; in 1804 commissioned lieutenant in the Habsburg army, in 1809 promoted to major, and in 1813 to colonel; in 1826 achieved the rank of major general, and in 1833 that of lieutenant field marshal; in 1826 was given command of the grenadier brigade in Prague; remained in Prague in various military capacities until 1840, when he was named commanding general of Bohemia, a position he held until the fall of 1848; happened to be in Vienna at the time the March revolution broke out; returned to Prague shortly thereafter and put down a revolt of the Czech nationalists in June, 1848; in October commanded the army that captured Vienna from the revolutionaries; was sent against the Hungarians but was dismissed after the Hungarians inflicted severe defeats on his army; later held various government positions.

Wirkner, Baron Ludwig von (1802–82)

Hungarian official who entered the state service in 1825 as a minor employee in the Aulic Chancellery; came into contact with Metternich, who took a special liking to him; gradually became one of Metternich's trusted advisers on Hungarian affairs; his official and secret activities aroused the suspicion of the Hungarian radicals; Kossuth exiled him from the country during the March revolution in Hungary, and his life was also in danger in Vienna; during the May revolution in Vienna, Pulszky warned him that his life was in danger and he fled from the capital to Aussig to live in retirement.

Würth, Joseph von (1817–55)

Lawyer and Austrian civil servant; in the 1840's became known for his articles on various legal subjects and for his book *Die neuesten Fortschritte des Gefangnisswesens in Frankreich, England, Schottland, Belgien, und der Schweiz*, published in 1844; in 1847 became protocol adjunct with the royal Supreme Court of Justice; in 1848 elected to the Frankfurt Assembly; in July, 1848, became undersecretary when Schmerling was made provisional German minister of interior; at Frankfurt had the reputation of being an ardent defender of the Austrian cause; withdrew from Frankfurt after the National Assembly offered the crown of Germany to the Prussian King; on his return to Vienna became a counselor in the Supreme Court and held this office until his death.

Zang, August (1807–88)

Son of a Viennese physician; joined the Habsburg army at an early age but resigned in 1836; shortly afterward went to Paris to establish a Viennese pastry shop; after making a success of this enterprise, became interested in Parisian journalism and soon made the acquaintance of several French journalists; learned about the March revolution in Vienna and returned to found the *Presse* on July 3.

Zanini, Peter (1786–1855)

Commoner who began service with the Habsburg army in 1808; in 1815 promoted to captain and in 1820 to major; in 1830 assigned to the Imperial War Council and promoted to lieutenant colonel; in 1836 promoted to major-general, and later to field marshal; on April 2, 1848, appointed minister of war but resigned less than a month later to return to the Central Military Administration Board; retired to private life late in 1848.

Zerboni di Sposetti, Julius von (1805–84)

Son of a Prussian who emigrated to Austria in 1816; spent a short time in the Austrian civil service, then became an agricultural administrator in Moravia and Silesia; eventually settled in Vienna to write poetry; in 1848 he courageously fought the extremists and, with Rudolf von Vivenot, formed the Constitutional Monarchical Club to oppose the radicals; after the revolution, withdrew from all political and literary activities.

Index

Academic Legion: creation of, 69; role of, 72; praised during March revolution, 100–101; organization of, 122–23; influence of radicals on, 123, 173; views of, 175–76, 181; attacks on, 198–99, 206, 288; morale of, 206, 312; attempts to abolish, 207, 208, 210–11; insults Emperor, 286–87; role of, in August riots, 293, 296; role of, in September riots, 310; role of, in October 6 revolution, 325–26; weakness of, in October, 340; abolition of, 363

Administrative reforms, demands for: 21, 23, 25, 39, 41, 43–44, 61, 74

Aigner, Joseph: 312, 324, 325, 341, 389

Albert Friedrich Rudolph von Habsburg, Archduke of Austria: role of, in March revolution, 65; opposes ouster of Metternich, 69; is dismissed, 74, 79–80, 126; denounced, 95; vita, 389

Allgemeine deutsche Zeitung: 20

Allgemeine Oesterreichische Zeitung: 157, 162, 181, 321

Allgemeine Zeitung: 21

Andrian-Werburg, Baron Victor von: 21–23, 389

Anschluss with Germany: desired by revolutionaries, 133, 134, 191, 214, 251; envisioned by Viennese, 137–40; feared by conservatives, 253

Anti-Semitism: evidences of, 102–105, 298, 303; arguments against, 103–105

Apponyi, Count György: 79–80, 389

Aristocracy: defined, 158–59; members of, leave Vienna, 194, 281, 337;

denounced by radical writers, 227–31, 239, 249, 259–60

Arthaber, Rudolph Edler von: 42, 73, 389

Association for the Preservation of the Rights of the People: 322

Association of the Friends of the People: 173–74, 181

Auersperg, Count Anton Alexander von: 19, 390

Auersperg, Count Maximilian: 121, 202, 335, 346, 347, 390

August 21–23 workers' riots: causes of, 290–91; demonstrations during, 291–94; casualties during, 293–94; significance of, 296–97

Austria and Its Future: 21–23

Austria's Internal Policies: 25–26

Bach, Baron Alexander von: joins Legal-Political Reading Club, 30; helps draft petitions, 37, 43, 73; quarrels with Mayor of Vienna, 82–83; assists with March 31 press law, 131; positions held by, 136, 270, 278, 364; hated by democrats, 289; favors measures against workers, 292; urges Emperor's approval of bills passed by Parliament, 316; vita, 390

Banks, run on: 35, 202–204

Batthyány, Count Lajos: 318, 390

Bäuerle, Adolf: 223, 245, 390–91

Bauernfeld, Eduard von: observations on government by, 19, 20, 33, 83; joins Legal-Political Reading Club, 30; is host to liberals, 32; drafts and signs petitions, 42–43, 73; vita, 391

414

Index

Index

Index

Index